计量经济分析及Stata应用

王周伟　崔百胜　李小平　编著

北京大学出版社
PEKING UNIVERSITY PRESS

图书在版编目(CIP)数据

计量经济分析及 Stata 应用/王周伟,崔百胜,李小平编著. —北京:北京大学出版社,2023.7
ISBN 978-7-301-34207-7

Ⅰ. ①计… Ⅱ. ①王… ②崔… ③李… Ⅲ. ①计量经济学—统计分析—应用软件—教材
Ⅳ. ①F224.0-39

中国国家版本馆 CIP 数据核字(2023)第 124000 号

书　　名	计量经济分析及 Stata 应用 JILIANG JINGJI FENXI JI Stata YINGYONG
著作责任者	王周伟　崔百胜　李小平　编著
责 任 编 辑	杨丽明
标 准 书 号	ISBN 978-7-301-34207-7
出 版 发 行	北京大学出版社
地　　址	北京市海淀区成府路 205 号　100871
网　　址	http://www.pup.cn　新浪微博:@北京大学出版社
电 子 信 箱	zpup@pup.cn
电　　话	邮购部 010-62752015　发行部 010-62750672　编辑部 021-62071998
印 刷 者	河北滦县鑫华书刊印刷厂
经 销 者	新华书店
	787 毫米×1092 毫米　16 开本　26.5 印张　661 千字
	2023 年 7 月第 1 版　2023 年 7 月第 1 次印刷
定　　价	98.00 元

前 言

计量经济分析方法是经济管理研究乃至整个社会科学中最为核心的数据分析方法，新时代经济社会发展的数字化、智能化与智慧化大趋势，使得计量经济分析方法的综合应用成为基本职业技能。

综合应用计量经济分析方法需要利用软件实现。Stata 软件的数据分析方法体系较为系统，有菜单操作，有程序代码实现，简单易用且灵活高效，配有便利的帮助系统，资源更新便捷，Stata 软件已成为当今最为流行的计量分析软件。本书旨在为计量经济分析方法及其实现提供最为翔实的计量经济分析知识和 Stata 软件综合应用教程，读者即使只是初步接触，也能仿照书中代码与实例，利用 Stata 软件进行一定的数据处理、计量经济建模分析与应用。

本书的特色如下：

第一，内容全面。本书介绍了初级计量经济分析中的常见专题与模型，如序数结果模型、分类结果模型、计数结果模型等，包括各种“由小到大、由简单到复杂”的模型族，并针对每一类模型在知识与方法方面进行了丰富拓展。这些拓展有利于模型优化，也为选择更为贴近实际的模型提供了可选项。

第二，代码详细。本书代码语法翔实，给出了每一种模型的 Stata 估计与检验代码，也给出了代码语法的所有选项及其说明，是一本非常翔实具体的计量分析 Stata 手册，这对于初学者快速掌握 Stata 计量分析非常有用。

第三，示例丰富。本书针对所介绍的每一种模型与方法，均配备了相应的 Stata 应用实例，读者结合应用实例以及 Stata 代码语法，即可明确模型的主要设置，不仅可以对实例的结果进行“复现”，也可以利用自己的数据通过替换变量与参数设置，完成“临摹复刻”。

本书综合了本课程领域知识体系的发展趋势和 Stata 软件资源优势，设置了 11 个章节①以及一个附录。附录对 Stata 计量分析过程中常用的命令代码作了汇总与介绍，使读者能够快速掌握 Stata 分析的主要基本操作。11 个章节主要包括线性回归模型、非线性回归模型以及时间序列分析三个主要模块。其中，线性回归分析模块主要包括基础回归分析、线性回归拓展以及复杂线性回归分析；非线性回归分析模块主要

① 目录中带有“*”的章节表示难度较大，本科阶段可选读。

包括二值选择、分类结果变量、序数结果变量、计数结果变量分析等;时间序列分析模块主要包括均值趋势建模、波动率建模、成分分解建模以及结构转换建模等。计量经济分析技术学习最为有效的方法就是“做中学”,边学知识,边练习软件实现。为便于学习,我们制作了相关 PPT,也配套制作了数据集以及配有注释说明程序代码的 do 文件与日志文件。

多年来,我们一直在为本科生、研究生讲授“计量经济学”课程,熟悉本学科知识体系,能够娴熟操作 Stata 软件,实现数据分析任务。知识体系编写部分,我们综合参考了主流教材及文献资料和 Stata 软件帮助文档;Stata 应用实例的数据借用 Stata 软件自带数据,数据处理实现的程序代码主要汇编自 Stata 软件技术文档、Stata 期刊和社区资源。为简明扼要,在前言部分予以统一说明,书中只作了个别引用注释。为此,对所有在本书编写过程中提供过帮助的学者和 Stata 公司及其全体员工,我们表示最诚挚的谢意。

当然,由于自身水平有限,计量经济学又处于蓬勃发展之中,编写过程中难免存在不足、遗漏与错误,恳请同行专家和读者对本书提出宝贵意见和建议,以使我们今后能够不断对之加以完善修正。联系方式为:wangzhouw@163.com。

编　者

2023 年 6 月

目　录

第1章 线性回归

1.1 线性回归

1.1.1 多元线性回归模型及其矩阵表示

在计量经济学中，如果总体函数描述了一个被解释变量与多个解释变量之间的线性关系，由此设定的总体回归函数就是多元线性回归模型。与一元线性回归模型类似，所谓多元线性回归模型是指对各个回归参数而言是线性的，而对于变量则可以是线性的，也可以是非线性的。

多元线性回归模型的矩阵形式可表示为：①

$$\boldsymbol{Y} = \boldsymbol{X\beta} + \boldsymbol{U} \tag{1.1}$$

$$E(\boldsymbol{Y} \mid \boldsymbol{X}) = \boldsymbol{X\beta} \tag{1.2}$$

其中，被解释变量列向量 $\boldsymbol{Y} = \begin{bmatrix} Y_1 \\ Y_2 \\ \vdots \\ Y_n \end{bmatrix}$；解释变量参数列向量 $\boldsymbol{\beta} = \begin{bmatrix} \beta_0 \\ \beta_1 \\ \vdots \\ \beta_n \end{bmatrix}$；解释变量向量 $\boldsymbol{X} = \begin{bmatrix} 1 & X_{11} & X_{21} & \cdots & X_{k1} \\ 1 & X_{12} & X_{22} & \cdots & X_{k2} \\ \vdots & \vdots & \vdots & & \vdots \\ 1 & X_{1n} & X_{2n} & \cdots & X_{kn} \end{bmatrix}$；随机误差项 $\boldsymbol{U} = \begin{bmatrix} u_1 \\ u_2 \\ \vdots \\ u_n \end{bmatrix}$。

这里的 $\boldsymbol{X}$ 是由解释变量 X_{ij} 的数据构成的矩阵，其中截距项可视为解释变量，总是取值为1。$\boldsymbol{X}$ 有时也称为数据矩阵或设计矩阵。随机误差项代表在回归模型中没有列出来的所有其他影响因素相关作用之和。

1.1.2 多元线性回归模型参数的 OLS 估计

现代多元线性回归模型参数估计的方法有很多种，如最小二乘估计、最大似然估

① 书写说明：小写和斜体（如 x）显示的符号是标量；小写和黑体（如 $\boldsymbol{x}$）显示的符号是矢量；大写和黑体（如 $\boldsymbol{X}$）显示的符号是矩阵。

计、矩估计、广义矩估计等方法。经典的线性回归理论是对模型作出经典假设，然后对多元线性回归模型的参数，利用最小二乘法进行有效估计，并分析参数估计量的统计性质。

对于模型，这些经典假设包括：

(1) 随机误差项服从均值为 0、同方差的正态分布，即

$$u_i \sim N(0, \sigma^2)$$

(2) 随机误差项之间不相关，即随机误差项之间的协方差等于 0，表达式为：

$$\text{cov}(u_i, u_j) = 0, \quad i \neq j$$

(3) 解释变量与随机误差项之间不相关，即协方差等于 0，表达式为：

$$\text{cov}(x_i, u_i) = 0$$

(4) 解释变量 x 是非随机的，这说明 y_i 的概率分布均值为：

$$E(y_i \mid x_i) = E(\boldsymbol{X\beta} + \boldsymbol{U}) = \boldsymbol{X\beta}$$

多元线性回归模型需要用样本信息建立的样本回归函数尽可能“接近”地去估计总体回归函数。普通最小二乘法(OLS)就是通过使残差平方和(RSS)最小化求解出回归模型中的变量参数估计值。按 OLS 准则，参数估计值应该使模型残差平方和最小化，由此确定样本回归函数。

设$(Y_i, X_{1i}, X_{2i}, \cdots, X_{ki})$为第 i 次观测样本$(i=1,2,3,\cdots,n)$，由式(1.2)可知，残差为：

$$e_i = Y_i - (\hat{\beta}_0 + \hat{\beta}_1 X_{1i} + \hat{\beta}_2 X_{2i} + \cdots + \hat{\beta}_k X_{ki}) \tag{1.3}$$

要使残差平方和

$$\sum e_i^2 = \sum [Y_i - (\hat{\beta}_0 + \hat{\beta}_1 X_{1i} + \hat{\beta}_2 X_{2i} + \cdots + \hat{\beta}_k X_{ki})]^2 \tag{1.4}$$

达到最小，其必要条件是：

$$\frac{\partial(\sum e_i^2)}{\partial \hat{\beta}_j} = 0 \quad (j = 0, 1, 2, \cdots, k) \tag{1.5}$$

即

$$\begin{gathered} -2\sum [Y_i - (\hat{\beta}_0 + \hat{\beta}_1 X_{1i} + \hat{\beta}_2 X_{2i} + \cdots + \hat{\beta}_k X_{ki})] = 0 \\ -2\sum X_{1i}[Y_i - (\hat{\beta}_0 + \hat{\beta}_1 X_{1i} + \hat{\beta}_2 X_{2i} + \cdots + \hat{\beta}_k X_{ki})] = 0 \\ \vdots \\ -2\sum X_{ki}[Y_i - (\hat{\beta}_0 + \hat{\beta}_1 X_{1i} + \hat{\beta}_2 X_{2i} + \cdots + \hat{\beta}_k X_{ki})] = 0 \end{gathered} \tag{1.6}$$

注意上述各式中方括号内的各项恰好为残差 e_i，从而上述 $k+1$ 个方程可写成如下形式：

$$\begin{bmatrix} \sum e_i \\ \sum X_{1i} e_i \\ \vdots \\ \sum X_{ki} e_i \end{bmatrix} = \begin{bmatrix} 1 & 1 & \cdots & 1 \\ X_{11} & X_{12} & \cdots & X_{1n} \\ \vdots & \vdots & & \vdots \\ X_{k1} & X_{k2} & \cdots & X_{kn} \end{bmatrix} \begin{bmatrix} e_0 \\ e_1 \\ \vdots \\ e_n \end{bmatrix} = \boldsymbol{X}'\boldsymbol{e} = \begin{bmatrix} 0 \\ 0 \\ \vdots \\ 0 \end{bmatrix} \tag{1.7}$$

对样本回归模型两边同乘以样本观测值矩阵 $\boldsymbol{X}$ 的转置矩阵 $\boldsymbol{X}'$，有

$$\boldsymbol{X}'\boldsymbol{Y}=\boldsymbol{X}'\boldsymbol{X}\hat{\boldsymbol{\beta}}+\boldsymbol{X}'\boldsymbol{e} \tag{1.8}$$

由极值条件式(1.7)，可得正规方程组

$$\boldsymbol{X}'\boldsymbol{Y}=\boldsymbol{X}'\boldsymbol{X}\hat{\boldsymbol{\beta}} \tag{1.9}$$

由古典假定条件中的无多重共线性假定，可知$(\boldsymbol{X}'\boldsymbol{X})^{-1}$存在，用$(\boldsymbol{X}'\boldsymbol{X})^{-1}$左乘方程(1.9)两端，得到多元线性回归模型参数向量 $\boldsymbol{\beta}$ 最小二乘估计式的矩阵表达式：

$$\hat{\boldsymbol{\beta}}_{OLS}=(\boldsymbol{X}'\boldsymbol{X})^{-1}\boldsymbol{X}'\boldsymbol{Y} \tag{1.10}$$

在满足经典线性回归模型的基本假设条件下，利用 OLS 估计得到的系数估计量，就是所有线性、无偏估计量中方差最小的，即 OLS 估计量是最优线性无偏估计量(best linear unbiased estimator，BLUE)。

1.1.3 随机扰动项方差的估计

参数估计量的方差或标准差是衡量参数估计量接近真实参数的重要指标，据此可以判断参数估计量的可靠性。但在参数估计量方差的表达式中，随机扰动项的方差 σ^2 是未知的，参数估计量方差实际上无法直接计算。为此，需要对 σ^2 进行估计。

根据式(1.1)和(1.2)得到参数估计值以后，即可计算残差向量：

$$\boldsymbol{e}=\boldsymbol{Y}-\hat{\boldsymbol{Y}}=\boldsymbol{Y}-\boldsymbol{X}\hat{\boldsymbol{\beta}} \tag{1.11}$$

据此可得残差平方和：

$$\sum e_i^2=\boldsymbol{e}'\boldsymbol{e} \tag{1.12}$$

因为残差平方和具有如下性质：

$$E\left(\sum e_i^2\right)=E(\boldsymbol{e}'\boldsymbol{e})=(n-k-1)\sigma^2 \tag{1.13}$$

即

$$E\left(\frac{\sum e_i^2}{n-k-1}\right)=\sigma^2 \tag{1.14}$$

若记

$$\hat{\sigma}^2=\frac{\sum e_i^2}{n-k-1} \tag{1.15}$$

则 $\hat{\sigma}^2$ 就是随机扰动项方差 σ^2 的无偏估计。一般地，称 $\hat{\sigma}^2$ 为估计的方差，$\hat{\sigma}$ 为估计的标准误差。于是，参数估计量 $\hat{\beta}_j(j=0,1,2,\cdots,k)$的方差 $\mathrm{var}(\hat{\beta}_j)$就可借助 $\hat{\sigma}$ 来估计，因为随机扰动项同方差和无序列相关，从而有参数估计量方差的默认估计式：

$$\begin{aligned}\mathrm{var}(\hat{\beta}_j)&=E\{[\beta_j-E(\beta_j)][\beta_j-E(\beta_j)]'\}\\&=(\boldsymbol{X}'\boldsymbol{X})^{-1}\boldsymbol{X}'E(\boldsymbol{e}\boldsymbol{e}')\boldsymbol{X}(\boldsymbol{X}'\boldsymbol{X})^{-1}\\&=(\boldsymbol{X}'\boldsymbol{X})^{-1}\sigma^2=\hat{\sigma}^2c_{ij}=\left(\frac{\sum e_i^2}{n-k-1}\right)c_{ij}\end{aligned} \tag{1.16}$$

式中，c_{ij} 为矩阵$(\boldsymbol{X}'\boldsymbol{X})^{-1}$的第 i 行第 j 列的元素。

如果随机误差项服从正态分布，由于系数的 OLS 估计量是正态分布随机变量的线性函数，因此系数估计值也服从正态分布：

$$\hat{\beta}_j \sim N(\beta_j, \mathrm{var}(\hat{\beta}_j))$$

1.1.4 多元线性回归模型参数的区间估计

为了说明参数真实值的可能范围和可靠性，还需要在对参数点估计的基础上对多元线性回归模型参数作区间估计。

当用式(1.15)对随机扰动项方差 σ^2 作出估计后，用 $\hat{\sigma}^2$ 代替 σ^2，可以证明：

$$t^* = \frac{\hat{\beta}_j - \beta_j}{\mathrm{SE}(\hat{\beta}_j)} \sim t(n-k-1) \tag{1.17}$$

式中，$\mathrm{SE}(\hat{\beta}_j)$ 为参数估计值的估计标准差，由式(1.16)的参数估计值的方差开平方运算可得。给定 α，查 t 分布表的自由度为 $n-k$ 的临界值 t，则有

$$P\left[-t_{\alpha/2}(n-k-1) \leqslant t^* = \frac{\hat{\beta}_j - \beta_j}{\mathrm{SE}(\hat{\beta}_j)} \leqslant t_{\alpha/2}(n-k-1)\right] = 1-\alpha \quad (j=1,2,\cdots,k) \tag{1.18}$$

即

$$P[\hat{\beta}_j - t_{\alpha/2}\mathrm{SE}(\hat{\beta}_j) \leqslant \beta_j \leqslant \hat{\beta}_j + t_{\alpha/2}\mathrm{SE}(\hat{\beta}_j)] = 1-\alpha \tag{1.19}$$

这就是多元线性回归模型参数估计的置信度为 $1-\alpha$ 的置信区间。

1.1.5 多元线性回归模型的检验

对已经估计出参数的多元线性回归模型的有效性检验，首先是所估计出的模型的拟合优度检验、回归方程的显著性检验和回归参数的显著性检验，其次是假定条件是否满足的检验。

1.1.5.1 拟合优度检验

在多元线性回归模型中，拟合优度是指样本回归直线与观测值之间的拟合程度，我们用可决系数 R^2 来衡量估计出的模型对观测值的拟合程度，即拟合优度。

(1) 多重可决系数

在多元线性回归模型中，“回归平方和”与“总离差平方和”的比值称为多重可决系数，用 R^2 表示。Y 的变差分解式为

$$\begin{gathered}\sum(Y_i - \bar{Y})^2 = \sum(Y_i - \hat{Y}_i)^2 + \sum(\hat{Y}_i - \bar{Y})^2 \\ \mathrm{TSS} = \mathrm{RSS} + \mathrm{ESS}\end{gathered} \tag{1.20}$$

其中，自由度为$(n-1)=(n-k-1)+k$。总离差平方和 TSS 反映了被解释变量观测值总变差的大小；回归平方和 ESS 反映了被解释变量中回归估计值总变差的大小，它是被解释变量观测值总变差中由多个解释变量作出解释的那部分变差；残差平方和 RSS 反映了被解释变量观测值与估计值之间的变差。显然回归平方和 ESS 越大，残差平方和 RSS 就越小，从而被解释变量观测值总变差中能由解释变量

解释的那部分变差就越大，模型对观测数据的拟合程度就越高。因此，我们定义多重可决系数为：

$$R^2 = \frac{\text{ESS}}{\text{TSS}} \tag{1.21}$$

或者表示为：

$$R^2 = \frac{\text{TSS} - \text{RSS}}{\text{TSS}} = 1 - \frac{\text{RSS}}{\text{TSS}} = 1 - \frac{\sum e_i^2}{\sum (Y_i - \bar{Y})^2} \tag{1.22}$$

多重可决系数是介于0和1之间的一个数，R^2 越接近1，模型对数据的拟合程度就越好。

多重可决系数可用矩阵表示，因为

$$\text{TSS} = \boldsymbol{Y}'\boldsymbol{Y} - n\bar{Y}^2 \tag{1.23}$$

$$\text{ESS} = \hat{\beta}'\boldsymbol{X}'\boldsymbol{Y} - n\bar{Y}^2 \tag{1.24}$$

所以

$$R^2 = \frac{\text{ESS}}{\text{TSS}} = \frac{\hat{\beta}'\boldsymbol{X}'\boldsymbol{Y} - n\bar{Y}^2}{\boldsymbol{Y}'\boldsymbol{Y} - n\bar{Y}^2} \tag{1.25}$$

(2) 修正的可决系数

由式(1.25)容易证明，多重可决系数还可以表示为：

$$R^2 = \frac{\hat{\beta}_1 \sum x_{1i} y_i + \hat{\beta}_2 \sum x_{2i} y_i + \cdots + \hat{\beta}_k \sum x_{ki} y_i}{\sum y_i^2} \tag{1.26}$$

式(1.26)表明，多重可决系数是模型中解释变量个数的不减函数，也就是说，当模型中解释变量个数增加时，R^2 的值会变大。因此，不同的模型之间不能简单地通过对比 R^2 来判断优劣，这样不利于比较判别。同时，可决系数只涉及变差，没有考虑自由度。显然，如果用自由度去校正所计算的变差，可以纠正解释变量个数不同引起的对比困难。因为在样本容量一定的情况下，增加解释变量必定使得待估参数的个数增加，从而会损失自由度。为此，可以用自由度去修正 R^2 的残差平方和与回归平方和，从而引入修正的可决系数 R_a^2，即调整拟合优度，其计算公式为：

$$R_a^2 = 1 - \frac{\dfrac{\sum e_i^2}{n-k}}{\dfrac{\sum (Y_i - \bar{Y})^2}{n-1}} = 1 - \frac{n-1}{n-k} \frac{\sum e_i^2}{\sum (Y_i - \bar{Y})^2} \tag{1.27}$$

R^2 与 R_a^2 之间有如下关系：

$$R_a^2 = 1 - (1 - R^2) \frac{n-1}{n-k} \tag{1.28}$$

由式(1.28)可以看出，当 $k > 1$ 时，$R_a^2 < R^2$，这意味着随着解释变量的增加，R_a^2 将小于 R^2。需要注意，R^2 为非负，但按式(1.28)计算的修正的可决系数 R_a^2 可能为负，这时规定 $R_a^2 = 0$。

这里需指出，对样本估计的回归模型计算的可决系数和修正的可决系数也是随着抽样而变动的随机变量，这样度量的拟合优度的显著性还需要进行检验。

在实际的计量经济分析中，往往希望 R^2 和 R_a^2 越大越好。但是我们应该明确，可决系数只是对模型拟合优度的度量，R^2 和 R_a^2 越大，只是说明列入模型中的解释变量对被解释变量的联合影响程度越大，并非说明模型中各个解释变量对被解释变量的影响程度也越大。在回归分析中，不仅需要模型的拟合优度高，还要得到总体回归系数的可靠估计量。因此在选择模型时，不能单纯地凭可决系数的高低断定模型的优劣，在某些时候，为了通盘考虑模型的可靠度及其经济意义，可以适当降低对可决系数的要求。

1.1.5.2　回归方程的显著性检验

假设检验的基本任务是根据样本所提供的信息，对未知总体分布的某些方面的假设作出合理的判断。其基本思想是：在某种原假设成立的条件下，利用适当的统计量和给定的显著性水平，构造一个小概率事件，可以认为小概率事件在一次观察中基本不会发生，如果该事件发生了，就认为原假设不真，从而拒绝原假设，接受备择假设。

回归模型的总体显著性检验，旨在对模型中被解释变量与解释变量之间的线性关系在总体上是否显著成立作出判断。检验假设的形式为：

$$H_0: \beta_1 = \beta_2 = \cdots = \beta_k$$

$$H_1: \beta_j\ (j = 1, 2, \cdots, k)\ \text{不全为零}$$

这种假设检验是在方差分析基础上利用 F 检验进行的。如前所述，被解释变量 $\mathbf{Y}$ 观测值的总变差有式(1.22)的分解形式，将自由度考虑进去进行方差分析，可得方差分析表，如表1.1所示。

表1.1　方差分析表

变差来源	平方和	自由度	方差
回归	$\mathrm{ESS} = \sum(\hat{Y}_i - \bar{Y})^2$	k	ESS/k
残差	$\mathrm{RSS} = \sum(Y_i - \hat{Y}_i)^2$	$n-k-1$	RSS/$(n-k-1)$
总变差	$\mathrm{TSS} = \sum(Y_i - \bar{Y})^2$	$n-1$	

可以证明，在 H_0 成立的条件下，统计量

$$F = \frac{\mathrm{ESS}/(k-1)}{\mathrm{RSS}/(n-k)} \sim F(k, n-k-1) \tag{1.29}$$

即统计量 F 服从自由度为 k 和 $n-k-1$ 的 F 分布。

给定显著性水平 α，在 F 分布表中查出自由度为 k 和 $n-k-1$ 的临界值 $F_\alpha(k, n-k-1)$，将样本观测值代入式(1.29)计算 F 值，然后对 F 值与临界值 $F_\alpha(k, n-$

$k-1$)进行比较。若 $F>F_{\alpha}(k,n-k-1)$，则拒绝原假设 H_0，说明回归方程显著，即列入模型的各个解释变量联合起来对被解释变量有显著影响；若 $F<F_{\alpha}(k,n-k-1)$，则不能拒绝原假设 H_0，说明回归方程不显著，即列入模型的各个解释变量联合起来对被解释变量影响不显著。

1.1.5.3 回归参数的显著性检验

多元回归分析的目的，不仅是获得较高拟合优度的模型，也不仅是要寻找方程整体的显著性，而是要对各个总体回归参数作出有意义的估计。因为方程的整体线性关系显著并不一定表示每个解释变量对被解释变量的影响都是显著的。因此，还需要分别对每个解释变量进行显著性检验。多元回归分析中对各个回归系数的显著性检验，目的在于分别检验当其他解释变量不变时，该回归系数对应的解释变量是否对被解释变量有显著影响。

如果回归系数的估计量服从正态分布：

$$\hat{\beta} \sim N[\beta,\sigma^2(\boldsymbol{X}'\boldsymbol{X}^{-1})] \tag{1.30}$$

其标准化随机变量服从标准正态分布：

$$Z=\frac{\hat{\beta}_j-\beta_j}{\sqrt{\operatorname{var}(\hat{\beta}_j)}} \sim N(0,1) \tag{1.31}$$

已知 $\operatorname{var}(\hat{\beta}_j)=\sigma^2 c_{jj}$，而 σ^2 未知，故 $\operatorname{var}(\hat{\beta}_j)$ 也未知。但正如前面已经讨论过的，可以用 $\hat{\sigma}^2$ 代替 σ^2 对 $\hat{\beta}_j$ 作变换，而且可以证明所构造的统计量服从自由度为 $n-k-1$ 的 t 分布，即

$$t=\frac{\hat{\beta}_j-\beta_j}{\sqrt{\hat{\sigma}^2 c_{jj}}}=\frac{\hat{\beta}_j-\beta_j}{\hat{\sigma}\sqrt{c_{jj}}} \sim t(n-k-1) \tag{1.32}$$

这样，就可以用 t 统计量对各个参数作显著性检验。具体步骤如下：

(1) 提出假设检验

$$H_0:\beta_j=0(j=1,2,\cdots,k)$$
$$H_1:\beta_j\neq 0(j=1,2,\cdots,k)$$

(2) 计算统计量

在 H_0 成立的条件下，式(1.32)变为：

$$t=\frac{\hat{\beta}_j-0}{\hat{\sigma}\sqrt{c_{jj}}}=\frac{\hat{\beta}_j}{\hat{\sigma}\sqrt{c_{jj}}} \sim t(n-k-1) \tag{1.33}$$

根据样本观测值计算 t 统计量的值：

$$t^*=\frac{\hat{\beta}_j}{\hat{\sigma}\sqrt{c_{jj}}} \tag{1.34}$$

(3) 检验

给定显著性水平 α，查自由度为 $n-k-1$ 的 t 分布表，得临界值 $t_{\alpha/2}(n-k-1)$。

若 $|t^*|\geqslant t_{\alpha/2}(n-k-1)$，就拒绝 H_0，但不拒绝 H_1，说明在其他解释变量不变的情况下，解释变量 X_j 对被解释变量 $\boldsymbol{Y}$ 的影响是显著的。

若 $|t^*|<t_{\alpha/2}(n-k-1)$，就不拒绝 H_0，也不拒绝 H_1，说明在其他解释变量不变

的情况下，解释变量 X_j 对被解释变量 $\boldsymbol{Y}$ 的影响不显著。

从 t 分布表可以看出，在给定显著性水平 $\alpha=0.05$ 的情况下，当自由度大于 10 时，临界值 $t_{\alpha/2}$ 基本上都接近 2。因此，当系数估计的 t 统计量的绝对值超过 2 时，我们可以粗略作出判断，在显著性水平 0.05 下可以拒绝原假设 H_0，认为相应解释变量对被解释变量的影响是显著的，此时犯错误的概率不超过 0.05。系数估计的 t 统计量的绝对值越大于 2，则犯错误的概率越小。

一般来说，多元线性回归模型在经过参数估计和模型检验后，应对回归分析结果作出分析判断。倘若某个解释变量对被解释变量的影响不显著，则应在模型中剔除该解释变量，此时多元线性回归模型应重新建立，并且寻求新模型参数的估计及对新模型进行假设检验，直到获得较为满意的模型为止。

1.1.6 加权回归估计

前述 OLS 估计及其检验过程适用于简单随机抽样测到的数据的分析。而对于非简单随机抽样得到的数据，特别是非均衡抽样问题，若样本存在过度抽样和抽样不足，则需要通过对不同抽样量的样本数据赋予权重进行加权回归估计。Stata 软件中多数估计命令都可以增加选项“weight”，实现加权数据的概率加权估计，得到参数的加权估计量。

Stata 软件允许四种权重：

(1) fweights：频率权重，是指重复观测的数量的权重。

(2) pweights：抽样权重，表示由于采样设计而包括观测的概率的倒数的权重。

(3) aweights：分析权重，是与观察结果的方差成反比的权重。也就是说，假设第 j 个观测值的方差为 σ^2/w_j，其中 w_j 是权重。通常，观察结果表示平均值，而权重是产生平均值的元素的数量。对于大多数 Stata 命令来说，记录的分析权重的量纲是无关紧要的，Stata 内部将它们重新缩放为 N，即数据观测数量。

(4) iweights：重要性权重，是在某种模糊意义上表示观察的“重要性”的权重。iweights 没有正式的统计定义；任何支持 iweights 的命令都将准确地定义如何处理它们。通常，它们是为那些想要生成特定计算的程序员准备的。

设 $\boldsymbol{v}$ 是用户指定的权重列向量，设 $\boldsymbol{w}$ 是归一化权重的列向量，则有 $\boldsymbol{w}=\{\boldsymbol{v}/(\boldsymbol{1}'\boldsymbol{v})\}(\boldsymbol{1}'\boldsymbol{1})$。对于重复的观测值，fweights 设定提供了重复观测值的个数，$\boldsymbol{w}=\boldsymbol{v}$。当未规定稳健标准误差时，iweights 被视为 fweights。相反，当指定了 vce(robust)、vce(cluster clustvar)、vce(hc2)或者 vce(hc3)时，iweights 被视为 aweights 它常用于不同的加权补偿需要，对具有不同方差的不同观测值按照已知方差的大小进行赋权加权。

如果用户指定了权重，则上述公式中的观测数 N 定义为 $\boldsymbol{1}'\boldsymbol{w}$，iweights 被圆整为整数。权重之和为 $\boldsymbol{1}'\boldsymbol{w}$。将上述公式中的 $\boldsymbol{X}'\boldsymbol{X}$，$\boldsymbol{X}'\boldsymbol{Y}$ 和 $\boldsymbol{Y}'\boldsymbol{Y}$ 分别替换为 $\boldsymbol{X}'\boldsymbol{D}\boldsymbol{X}$，$\boldsymbol{X}'\boldsymbol{D}\boldsymbol{Y}$ 和 $\boldsymbol{Y}'\boldsymbol{D}\boldsymbol{Y}$，其中 $\boldsymbol{D}$ 是对角矩阵，其对角线元素是 w 的元素，则可以得到加权回归的加权最小二乘估计量和模型检验统计量计算式。比如，给定权重 w_i，y_i 对 X_i 的加权最小二乘估计量为：

$$\hat{\beta}_{WLS} = \left(\sum_{i=1}^{N} w_i \boldsymbol{x}_i \boldsymbol{x}_i'\right)^{-1} \sum_{i=1}^{N} w_i \boldsymbol{x}_i \boldsymbol{y}_i \tag{1.35}$$

模型参数的 OLS 估计量$\hat{\beta}_{OLS}$ 是权重相等时的加权最小二乘估计量$\hat{\beta}_{WLS}$。

1.1.7 稳健标准误估计

如果解释变量外生性、同方差和观测值不相关的三个经典假设条件同时成立，$\hat{\beta}$ 服从渐进正态分布，其默认的（渐近）方差—协方差矩阵（VCE）估计量为：

$$\hat{V}_{default}(\hat{\beta}) = s^2(\boldsymbol{X}'\boldsymbol{X})^{-1} \tag{1.36}$$

其中，$s^2=(N-k)^{-1}\sum_i \hat{\boldsymbol{e}}_i^2=(N-k)^{-1}\sum^i(y_i-\boldsymbol{X}_i'\hat{\beta})^2$。

如果误差项是异方差、不相关的，则 OLS 估计量的 VCE 需要选用异方差—稳健估计量。

（1）稳健方差计算。稳健方差的计算公式为：

$$\hat{V}_{robust} = q_c \hat{\boldsymbol{V}} \left(\sum_{k=1}^{M} \boldsymbol{u}_k^{(G)'} \boldsymbol{u}_k^{(G)}\right) \hat{\boldsymbol{V}} \tag{1.37}$$

式中，$\boldsymbol{u}_k^{(G)}=\sum_{j\in G_k} w_j \boldsymbol{u}_j$，$G_1,G_2,\cdots,G_M$ 是 vce 指定的簇（cluster clustvar），w_j 是用户指定的权重，如果指定了权重或 pweights，则进行归一化；如果未指定权重，则等于 1。

当不同观测值的误差项在同一聚类内部或组内相关，但不同聚类之间的误差项不相关时，OLS 估计量的 VCE 需要选用聚类—稳健估计量。

对于无聚类的 fweights，稳健方差计算公式为：

$$\hat{V}_{cluster} = q_c \hat{\boldsymbol{V}} \left(\sum_{j=1}^{N} w_j \boldsymbol{u}_j' \boldsymbol{u}_j\right) \hat{\boldsymbol{V}} \tag{1.38}$$

如果未指定 vce(cluster clustvar)，则 $M=N$，并且每个集群包含 1 个观测值。此计算的输入变量为：$\hat{\boldsymbol{V}}$ 是式(1.36)计算的方差矩阵；$\boldsymbol{u}_j$，$j=1,\cdots,N$ 是分数（scores）的行向量；q_c 是一个恒定的有限样本调整。因此，我们现在可以通过定义这三个变量来描述估计法如何应用稳健计算公式。

对于 q_c，回归类公式为 $q_c=\frac{N-1}{N-k}\frac{M}{M-1}$；渐进类公式为 $q_c=\frac{M}{M-1}$。式中，M 是聚类数量，N 是观测值数量。对于权重，如果权重是频率权重，则 N 表示权重之和，在所有其他情况下，N 表示数据集中的观测数（忽略权重）。另外，无论是否加权，当没有设定 vce(clustvar)时，都有 $q_c=N/(N-k)$。

（2）稳健回归计算。对于回归模型 $\boldsymbol{y}=\boldsymbol{a}+\boldsymbol{Xb}+\boldsymbol{\varepsilon}$，$\hat{V}=\boldsymbol{A}^{-1}$，$\boldsymbol{A}=\boldsymbol{X}'\boldsymbol{X}$，$\boldsymbol{a}=\boldsymbol{X}'\boldsymbol{y}$。

设定 vce(robust)时，$\boldsymbol{u}_j=(y_j-\boldsymbol{x}_j\boldsymbol{b})\boldsymbol{x}_j$，式中，$q_c=\frac{N-1}{N-k}\frac{M}{M-1}$。

设定 vce(hc2)时，$\boldsymbol{u}_j=\frac{1}{\sqrt{1-h_{jj}}}(y_j-\boldsymbol{x}_j\boldsymbol{b})\boldsymbol{x}_j$，式中，$q_c=1$，$h_{jj}=\boldsymbol{x}_j(\boldsymbol{X}'\boldsymbol{X})^{-1}\boldsymbol{x}_j'$。

设定 vce(hc3)时，$\boldsymbol{u}_j=\frac{1}{1-h_{jj}}(y_j-\boldsymbol{x}_j\boldsymbol{b})\boldsymbol{x}_j$，式中，$q_c=1$，$h_{jj}=\boldsymbol{x}_j(\boldsymbol{X}'\boldsymbol{X})^{-1}\boldsymbol{x}_j'$。

Stata 命令中的选项"options"可以设置 SE/Robust 为 vce(vcetype)，进行稳健标准误估计。vce(vcetype)指定了报告的标准误差的类型，其中包括从渐近理论(ols)导出的标准误差，对某些类型的错误指定是稳健的(robust)，允许组内相关性(cluster clustvarlist)，以及使用 bootstrap 或 jackknife 方法(bootstrap，jackknife)。vcetype 可以是 ols、robust、cluster clustvar、bootstrap、jackknife、hc2 或 hc3。其中，默认情况下，vce(ols)使用普通最小二乘回归的标准方差估计量。vce(cluster-clustvarlist)规定，标准误差允许由 cluster-varlist 中的一个或多个变量定义的组内相关性，从而放宽了观测独立的通常要求。例如，vce(cluster-clustvar1)产生聚类稳健标准误差，该误差允许在由 clustervar1 定义的组之间独立但不一定在组内独立的观测。读者也可以键入 vce(cluster-clustvar1，clustervar2... clusterp)来说明由 p 个变量形成的组内的相关性(多向聚类)。

1.1.8 线性回归的 Stata 实现

线性回归分析的 Stata 命令为 regress。regress 执行普通最小二乘线性回归。regress 还可以进行加权估计，计算稳健和聚类稳健的标准误差，并可以调整复杂调查设计的结果。

regress 的语法格式为：

regress depvar [indepvars] [if] [in] [weight] [, options]

其中，indepvars 可以包含因子变量。depvar 和 indepvars 可以包含时间序列操作符。regress 允许使用 bayes、bootstrap、by、collect、fmm、fp、jackknife、mfp、mi estimate、nestreg、rolling、statsby、stepwise 和 svy 前缀。

weight(权重)允许使用 aweights、fweights、iweights、pweights。

模型的选项及含义为：

(1) noconstant：抑制常数项；

(2) hascons：用户提供的常量；

(3) tsscons：用常数计算平方和(很少使用)。

SE/Robust 的选项(options)为 vce(vcetype)，vcetype 可以是 ols、robust、cluster clustvar、bootstrap、jackknife、hc2 或 hc3。

报告的选项及含义为：

(1) level(#)：设置置信度水平，默认值为水平(95)；

(2) beta：报告标准化贝塔系数；

(3) eform(string)：报告指数系数并标记为字符串；

(4) depname(varname)：替换因变量名称，为程序员选项；

(5) display_options：选项控制列和列格式、行间距、线宽、省略变量的显示、基单元格和空单元格以及因子变量标签；

(6) noheader：抑制输出标题；

(7) notable:抑制系数表;

(8) plus:使表格可扩展;

(9) msel:强制均方误差为1;

(10) coeflegend:显示图例而不是统计信息。

菜单操作路径为:

Statistics>Linear models and related>Linear regression

例 1.1　多元线性回归

假设我们有74辆汽车的里程等级(mileage rating)和重量(weight)数据。数据中的变量是mpg、weight和foreign等。还有一个变量为汽车产地,假设国外汽车的值为1,国内汽车的值为0。我们希望拟合模型:

$$\text{mpg} = \beta_0 + \beta_1 \text{weight} + \beta_2 \text{foreign} + \boldsymbol{\varepsilon}$$

```
* 导入数据
. use https://www.stata-press.com/data/r17/auto
* 查看数据集变量特征
. describe
```

运行结果如图1.1所示。

```
Contains data from https://www.stata-press.com/data/r17/auto.dta
 Observations:            74                  1978 automobile data
    Variables:            12                  13 Apr 2020 17:45
                                              (_dta has notes)
-----------------------------------------------------------------------
Variable      Storage   Display    Value
    name         type    format    label      Variable label
-----------------------------------------------------------------------
make            str18   %-18s                 Make and model
price           int     %8.0gc                Price
mpg             int     %8.0g                 Mileage (mpg)
rep78           int     %8.0g                 Repair record 1978
headroom        float   %6.1f                 Headroom (in.)
trunk           int     %8.0g                 Trunk space (cu. ft.)
weight          int     %8.0gc                Weight (lbs.)
length          int     %8.0g                 Length (in.)
turn            int     %8.0g                 Turn circle (ft.)
displacement    int     %8.0g                 Displacement (cu. in.)
gear_ratio      float   %6.2f                 Gear ratio
foreign         byte    %8.0g      origin     Car origin
-----------------------------------------------------------------------
Sorted by: foreign
```

图 1.1

```
* 查看变量 price 与 mpg 的前 5 条数据
. list price mpg in 1/5
```

运行结果如图1.2所示。

	price	mpg
1.	4,099	22
2.	4,749	17
3.	3,799	22
4.	4,816	20
5.	7,827	15

图 1.2

*变量数据描述统计

```
. summarize
```

运行结果如图 1.3 所示。

Variable	Obs	Mean	Std. dev.	Min	Max
make	0				
price	74	6165.257	2949.496	3291	15906
mpg	74	21.2973	5.785503	12	41
rep78	69	3.405797	.9899323	1	5
headroom	74	2.993243	.8459948	1.5	5
trunk	74	13.75676	4.277404	5	23
weight	74	3019.459	777.1936	1760	4840
length	74	187.9324	22.26634	142	233
turn	74	39.64865	4.399354	31	51
displacement	74	197.2973	91.83722	79	425
gear_ratio	74	3.014865	.4562871	2.19	3.89
foreign	74	.2972973	.4601885	0	1

图 1.3

*拟合线性回归

```
. regress mpg weight foreign
```

运行结果如图 1.4 所示。

*生成新变量,拟合一个更好的线性回归

```
. gen gp100m = 100/ mpg
. regress gp100m weight foreign
```

运行结果如图 1.5 所示。

Source	SS	df	MS		Number of obs	=	74
					F(2, 71)	=	69.75
Model	1619.2877	2	809.643849		Prob > F	=	0.0000
Residual	824.171761	71	11.608053		R-squared	=	0.6627
					Adj R-squared	=	0.6532
Total	2443.45946	73	33.4720474		Root MSE	=	3.4071

mpg	Coefficient	Std. err.	t	P>|t|	[95% conf. interval]	
weight	-.0065879	.0006371	-10.34	0.000	-.0078583	-.0053175
foreign	-1.650029	1.075994	-1.53	0.130	-3.7955	.4954422
_cons	41.6797	2.165547	19.25	0.000	37.36172	45.99768

图 1.4

Source	SS	df	MS		Number of obs	=	74
					F(2, 71)	=	113.97
Model	91.1761694	2	45.5880847		Prob > F	=	0.0000
Residual	28.4000913	71	.400001287		R-squared	=	0.7625
					Adj R-squared	=	0.7558
Total	119.576261	73	1.63803097		Root MSE	=	.63246

gp100m	Coefficient	Std. err.	t	P>|t|	[95% conf. interval]	
weight	.0016254	.0001183	13.74	0.000	.0013896	.0018612
foreign	.6220535	.1997381	3.11	0.003	.2237871	1.02032
_cons	-.0734839	.4019932	-0.18	0.855	-.8750354	.7280677

图 1.5

* 不拟合模型，只获得 β 系数

.regress, beta

运行结果如图 1.6 所示。

Source	SS	df	MS		Number of obs	=	74
					F(2, 71)	=	113.97
Model	91.1761694	2	45.5880847		Prob > F	=	0.0000
Residual	28.4000913	71	.400001287		R-squared	=	0.7625
					Adj R-squared	=	0.7558
Total	119.576261	73	1.63803097		Root MSE	=	.63246

gp100m	Coefficient	Std. err.	t	P>|t|	Beta
weight	.0016254	.0001183	13.74	0.000	.9870255
foreign	.6220535	.1997381	3.11	0.003	.2236673
_cons	-.0734839	.4019932	-0.18	0.855	.

图 1.6

＊不要截距项

```
.regress weight length, noconstant
```

运行结果如图 1.7 所示。

Source	SS	df	MS			
Model	703869302	1	703869302	Number of obs	=	74
Residual	14892897.8	73	204012.299	F(1, 73)	=	3450.13
				Prob > F	=	0.0000
				R-squared	=	0.9793
				Adj R-squared	=	0.9790
Total	718762200	74	9713002.7	Root MSE	=	451.68

weight	Coefficient	Std. err.	t	P>|t|	[95% conf.	interval]
length	16.29829	.2774752	58.74	0.000	15.74528	16.8513

图 1.7

＊包含常数项

```
.regress weight length bn.foreign, hascons
```

运行结果如图 1.8 所示。

Source	SS	df	MS			
Model	39647744.7	2	19823872.3	Number of obs	=	74
Residual	4446433.7	71	62625.8268	F(2, 71)	=	316.54
				Prob > F	=	0.0000
				R-squared	=	0.8992
				Adj R-squared	=	0.8963
Total	44094178.4	73	604029.841	Root MSE	=	250.25

weight	Coefficient	Std. err.	t	P>|t|	[95% conf.	interval]
length	31.44455	1.601234	19.64	0.000	28.25178	34.63732
foreign						
Domestic	-2850.25	315.9691	-9.02	0.000	-3480.274	-2220.225
Foreign	-2983.927	275.1041	-10.85	0.000	-3532.469	-2435.385

图 1.8

＊子样本回归

```
.regress mpg weight foreign if headroom>3
```

运行结果如图 1.9 所示。

＊定义约束条件

```
.constraint def 1 weight + foreign = 1
```

＊有约束的 OLS 回归

```
.cnsreg mpg weight foreign, c(1)
```

运行结果如图 1.10 所示。

Source	SS	df	MS			
Model	281.543978	2	140.771989	Number of obs	=	30
Residual	100.622689	27	3.72676625	F(2, 27)	=	37.77
				Prob > F	=	0.0000
Total	382.166667	29	13.1781609	R-squared	=	0.7367
				Adj R-squared	=	0.7172
				Root MSE	=	1.9305

mpg	Coefficient	Std. err.	t	P>|t|	[95% conf.	interval]
weight	-.0056885	.0007025	-8.10	0.000	-.0071299	-.004247
foreign	-.7630004	1.553462	-0.49	0.627	-3.95044	2.42444
_cons	38.12184	2.568431	14.84	0.000	32.85185	43.39182

图 1.9

```
Constrained linear regression                     Number of obs =     74
                                                  Root MSE      = 3.5255

 ( 1)  weight + foreign = 1
```

mpg	Coefficient	Std. err.	t	P>|t|	[95% conf.	interval]
weight	-.0056551	.0005307	-10.66	0.000	-.0067131	-.0045971
foreign	1.005655	.0005307	1894.85	0.000	1.004597	1.006713
_cons	38.07359	1.653941	23.02	0.000	34.77652	41.37066

图 1.10

```
* 检验单位边际效应显著性
.test weight = 1
```

运行结果如图 1.11 所示。

```
 ( 1)  weight = 1

       F(  1,    72) = 3.6e+06
            Prob > F =    0.0000
```

图 1.11

```
* 联合检验
.test weight foreign
```

运行结果如图 1.12 所示。

```
( 1)  weight = 0
( 2)  foreign = 0
      Constraint 1 dropped

      F(  1,    72) = 3.6e+06
           Prob > F =    0.0000
```

图 1.12

* 非线性假设检验

.testnl _b[weight] = _b[foreign]^2

运行结果如图 1.13 所示。

```
(1)  _b[weight] = _b[foreign]^2

           chi2(1) =   404930.65
       Prob > chi2 =       0.0000
```

图 1.13

* 稳健标准误差回归

.sysuse auto, clear

.generate gpmw = ((1/ mpg)/ weight) * 100 * 1000

.regress gpmw foreign

运行结果如图 1.14 所示。

```
      Source |       SS           df       MS      Number of obs   =        74
-------------+----------------------------------   F(1, 72)        =     20.07
       Model |  .936705572         1  .936705572   Prob > F        =    0.0000
    Residual |  3.36079459        72  .046677703   R-squared       =    0.2180
-------------+----------------------------------   Adj R-squared   =    0.2071
       Total |  4.29750017        73  .058869865   Root MSE        =    .21605

------------------------------------------------------------------------------
        gpmw | Coefficient  Std. err.      t    P>|t|     [95% conf. interval]
-------------+----------------------------------------------------------------
     foreign |   .2461526   .0549487     4.48   0.000     .1366143    .3556909
       _cons |   1.609004   .0299608    53.70   0.000     1.549278     1.66873
------------------------------------------------------------------------------
```

图 1.14

.regress gpmw foreign, vce(robust)

运行结果如图 1.15 所示。

.regress gpmw foreign, vce(hc2)

运行结果如图 1.16 所示。

```
Linear regression                               Number of obs     =         74
                                                F(1, 72)          =      13.13
                                                Prob > F          =     0.0005
                                                R-squared         =     0.2180
                                                Root MSE          =     .21605

------------------------------------------------------------------------------
             |               Robust
        gpmw | Coefficient  std. err.      t    P>|t|     [95% conf. interval]
-------------+----------------------------------------------------------------
     foreign |   .2461526   .0679238     3.62   0.001     .1107489    .3815563
       _cons |   1.609004   .0234535    68.60   0.000      1.56225    1.655758
------------------------------------------------------------------------------
```

图 1.15

```
Linear regression                               Number of obs     =         74
                                                F(1, 72)          =      12.93
                                                Prob > F          =     0.0006
                                                R-squared         =     0.2180
                                                Root MSE          =     .21605

------------------------------------------------------------------------------
             |             Robust HC2
        gpmw | Coefficient  std. err.      t    P>|t|     [95% conf. interval]
-------------+----------------------------------------------------------------
     foreign |   .2461526   .0684669     3.60   0.001     .1096662    .3826389
       _cons |   1.609004   .0233601    68.88   0.000     1.562437    1.655571
------------------------------------------------------------------------------
```

图 1.16

. regress gpmw foreign, vce(hc3)

运行结果如图 1.17 所示。

```
Linear regression                               Number of obs     =         74
                                                F(1, 72)          =      12.38
                                                Prob > F          =     0.0008
                                                R-squared         =     0.2180
                                                Root MSE          =     .21605

------------------------------------------------------------------------------
             |             Robust HC3
        gpmw | Coefficient  std. err.      t    P>|t|     [95% conf. interval]
-------------+----------------------------------------------------------------
     foreign |   .2461526    .069969     3.52   0.001     .1066719    .3856332
       _cons |   1.609004    .023588    68.21   0.000     1.561982    1.656026
------------------------------------------------------------------------------
```

图 1.17

. webuse regsmpl, clear

. regress ln_wage age c.age#c.age tenure,vce(cluster id)

运行结果如图 1.18 所示。

```
Linear regression                               Number of obs     =     28,101
                                                F(3, 4698)        =     748.82
                                                Prob > F          =     0.0000
                                                R-squared         =     0.1644
                                                Root MSE          =     .43679

                          (Std. err. adjusted for 4,699 clusters in idcode)
------------------------------------------------------------------------------
             |               Robust
     ln_wage | Coefficient  std. err.      t    P>|t|     [95% conf. interval]
-------------+----------------------------------------------------------------
         age |   .0752172   .0045711    16.45   0.000     .0662557    .0841788
             |
 c.age#c.age |  -.0010851   .0000778   -13.94   0.000    -.0012377   -.0009325
             |
      tenure |   .0390877   .0014425    27.10   0.000     .0362596    .0419157
       _cons |   .3339821   .0641918     5.20   0.000      .208136    .4598282
------------------------------------------------------------------------------
```

图 1.18

* 加权回归

. sysuse census

. regress death medage i.region [aw = pop]

运行结果如图 1.19 所示。

```
(sum of wgt is 225,907,472)

      Source |       SS           df       MS      Number of obs   =        50
-------------+----------------------------------   F(4, 45)        =      3.74
       Model |  4.0537e+10         4  1.0134e+10   Prob > F        =    0.0104
    Residual |  1.2191e+11        45  2.7091e+09   R-squared       =    0.2495
-------------+----------------------------------   Adj R-squared   =    0.1828
       Total |  1.6245e+11        49  3.3153e+09   Root MSE        =     52049

------------------------------------------------------------------------------
       death | Coefficient  Std. err.      t    P>|t|     [95% conf. interval]
-------------+----------------------------------------------------------------
      medage |   11210.38   5351.147     2.09   0.042     432.6187    21988.14
             |
      region |
     N Cntrl |  -19227.42   24372.19    -0.79   0.434    -68315.53    29860.69
       South |  -29079.48   23020.97    -1.26   0.213    -75446.09    17287.12
        West |   27881.38   26603.78     1.05   0.300    -25701.39    81464.14
             |
       _cons |  -246613.5   171013.2    -1.44   0.156    -591051.9    97824.84
------------------------------------------------------------------------------
```

图 1.19

* 计算被解释变量的预测值

. predict fdeath

* 计算残差

```
.predict e1,residual
```

运行结果略。

1.1.9 工具变量与两阶段最小二乘法

OLS的经典假设之一就是解释变量与随机项不相关，如果二者相关，即存在随机解释变量问题，OLS估计量就是不一致的。实践中，随机解释变量问题是普遍存在的，为此计量经济分析应选用合适的工具变量，利用两阶段最小二乘法（2SLS或TSLS）与广义矩估计法（GMM）等进行估计。

一个有效的工具变量应该满足两个条件：

（1）相关性：工具变量与解释变量相关，即 $\mathrm{Cov}(x_t, p_t) \neq 0$；

（2）外生性：工具变量与扰动项不相关，即 $\mathrm{Cov}(x_t, u_t) = 0$。

两阶段最小二乘法就是利用有效工具变量，分两步估计有随机解释变量问题的计量模型的有效方法。

第一步，使每个内生解释变量 $\boldsymbol{x}$ 对所有工具变量 $\boldsymbol{z}$ 回归，得到拟合值 $\hat{x}_i$，分离出内生解释变量的外生部分，即

$$\hat{\boldsymbol{X}} \equiv (\hat{\boldsymbol{x}}_1 \hat{\boldsymbol{x}}_2 \cdots \hat{\boldsymbol{x}}_K) = \boldsymbol{P}(\boldsymbol{x}_1 \boldsymbol{x}_2 \cdots \boldsymbol{x}_K) = \boldsymbol{PX} = \boldsymbol{Z}[(\boldsymbol{Z}'\boldsymbol{Z})^{-1}\boldsymbol{Z}'\boldsymbol{X}] \tag{1.39}$$

第二步，用第一步回归得到的拟合值 $\hat{x}_i$ 替换内生解释变量，再用原模型 $\boldsymbol{y} = \boldsymbol{x\beta} + \boldsymbol{\varepsilon}$ 对被解释变量作回归估计，得到参数的2SLS估计值，即使用内生解释变量的外生部分作回归。

$$\hat{\boldsymbol{\beta}}_{\mathrm{IV}} = (\hat{\boldsymbol{\beta}}'\boldsymbol{X})^{-1}\hat{\boldsymbol{\beta}}'\boldsymbol{y} = (\hat{\boldsymbol{\beta}}'\hat{\boldsymbol{\beta}})^{-1}\hat{\boldsymbol{\beta}}'\boldsymbol{y} \tag{1.40}$$

在球形扰动项假设下，由2SLS估计得到参数估计值是最为渐进有效的。把式(1.39)代入式(1.40)，可得2SLS参数估计值的表达式为：

$$\hat{\boldsymbol{\beta}}_{\mathrm{2SLS}} = (\boldsymbol{X}'\boldsymbol{PX})^{-1}\boldsymbol{X}'\boldsymbol{Py} = [\boldsymbol{X}'\boldsymbol{Z}(\boldsymbol{Z}'\boldsymbol{Z})^{-1}\boldsymbol{Z}'\boldsymbol{X}]^{-1}\boldsymbol{X}'\boldsymbol{Z}(\boldsymbol{Z}'\boldsymbol{Z})^{-1}\boldsymbol{Z}'\boldsymbol{y} \tag{1.41}$$

2SLS实现的语法格式为：

```
ivregress estimator depvar [varlist1] (varlist2 = varlist_iv) [if] [in]
[weight] [, options]
```

其中，varlist1是外部变量列表。varlist2是内生变量列表。varlist_iv是与varlist1一起使用的外部变量列表，作为varlist2的工具。

估计方法（estimator）选项及其含义为：

（1）2sls：两阶段最小二乘法（2SLS）；

（2）liml：有限信息最大似然法（LIML）；

（3）gmm：广义矩估计法（GMM）。

其他选项查阅ivregress命令帮助文件。

菜单操作路径为：

Statistics>Endogenous covariates>Linear regression with endogenous covariates

ivregress为拟合线性模型，其中一个或多个回归系数是内生确定的。ivregress支持通过2SLS、LIML和GMM进行估计。

(1) 解释变量内生性检验。把变量矩阵 Y 分区为 $Y=[Y_1\ Y_2]$，其中 Y_1 表示内生性正在测试的 p_1 个内生回归系数，Y_2 表示内生性未测试的 p_2 个内生回归系数。如果正在测试所有内生回归系数的内生性，则 $Y=Y_1,p_2=0$。GMM 估计后，estat endogenous 命令使用估计时要求的同一类型的权重矩阵（使用 wmatrix()选项）将 Y_1 视为外生的模型进行重新调整；用 J_e 表示来自该模型的萨根(Sargan)统计；用 $\boldsymbol{W}_e$ 表示估计权重矩阵，设 $S_e=\boldsymbol{W}_e^{-1}$，estat innovative 从 S_e 中删除与 Y_1 表示的变量相对应的行和列；用 $\boldsymbol{W}_e'$ 表示所得矩阵的逆矩阵。接下来，estat endogenous 把 Y_1 和 Y_2 用权重矩阵 $\boldsymbol{W}_e'$ 处理为内生变量后，拟合模型。用 J_c 表示该模型中的萨根统计量。那么，有

$$C=(J_e-J_c)\sim\chi^2(p_1) \tag{1.42}$$

如果简单地使用原始模型中的 J 统计量，通过 ivregress 拟合来代替 J_c，那么在有限样本中，J_e-J 可能是负数。estat endogenous 使用的程序保证产生 $C\geqslant 0$。

令 $\hat{\boldsymbol{u}}_c$ 表示将 Y_1 和 Y_2 都视为内生的模型的残差，$\hat{\boldsymbol{u}}_e$ 表示仅将 Y_2 视为内生的模型的残差。Durbin(1954)①的统计量为：

$$D=\frac{\hat{\boldsymbol{u}}_e'\boldsymbol{P}_{ZY_1}\hat{\boldsymbol{u}}_e-\hat{\boldsymbol{u}}_c'\boldsymbol{P}_Z\hat{\boldsymbol{u}}_c}{\hat{\boldsymbol{u}}_e'\hat{\boldsymbol{u}}_e/N} \tag{1.43}$$

式中，$\boldsymbol{P}_Z=\boldsymbol{Z}(\boldsymbol{Z}'\boldsymbol{Z})^{-1}\boldsymbol{Z}'$，$\boldsymbol{P}_{ZY_1}=[\boldsymbol{Z}\quad \boldsymbol{Y}_1]([\boldsymbol{Z}\quad \boldsymbol{Y}_1]'[\boldsymbol{Z}\quad \boldsymbol{Y}_1])^{-1}[\boldsymbol{Z}\quad \boldsymbol{Y}_1]'$，$D\sim\chi^2(p_1)$。

Wu-Hausman (Wu，1974②；Hausman，1978③)检验统计量为：

$$\mathrm{WH}=\frac{(\hat{\boldsymbol{u}}_e'\boldsymbol{P}_{ZY_1}\hat{\boldsymbol{u}}_e-\hat{\boldsymbol{u}}_c'\boldsymbol{P}_Z\hat{\boldsymbol{u}}_c)/p_1}{\{\hat{\boldsymbol{u}}_e'\hat{\boldsymbol{u}}_e-(\hat{\boldsymbol{u}}_e'\boldsymbol{P}_{ZY_1}\hat{\boldsymbol{u}}_e-\hat{\boldsymbol{u}}_c'\boldsymbol{P}_Z\hat{\boldsymbol{u}}_c)\}/(N-k_1-p-p_1)}\sim F(p_1,N-k_1-p-p_1) \tag{1.44}$$

解释变量内生性检验的语法格式为：

```
estat endogenous [varlist] [, lags(#) forceweights forcenonrobust]
```

(2) 过度识别限制检验。设 χ^2 统计量是运行辅助回归 $\hat{\boldsymbol{u}}=\boldsymbol{Z}\delta+\boldsymbol{e}$ 获得的，其中，$\hat{\boldsymbol{u}}$ 是样本残差，$\boldsymbol{e}$ 是随机误差项。萨根统计量为：

$$S=N\left(1-\frac{\hat{\boldsymbol{e}}'\hat{\boldsymbol{e}}}{\hat{\boldsymbol{u}}'\hat{\boldsymbol{u}}}\right)\sim\chi^2(m) \tag{1.45}$$

式中，$\hat{\boldsymbol{e}}$ 为辅助回归的残差，m 为过度识别限制的数量，等于 k_z-k，k 是内生回归数。

巴斯曼(Basmann)统计量为：

$$B=S\,\frac{N-k_z}{N-S}\sim\chi^2(m) \tag{1.46}$$

① Durbin, J. Errors in Variables. *Review of the International Statistical Institute*, 1954. 22.

② Wu, D. M. Alternative Tests of Independence between Stochastic Regressors and Disturbances: Finite Sample Results. *Econometrica*, 1974, 42.

③ Hausman, J. A. Specification Tests in Econometrics. *Econometrica*, 1978, 46.

Wooldridge(1995)①的过度识别限制分数测试与 Sargan(1958)②在独立同分布(i. i. d.)假设下的统计数据相同，因此，除非在估计时使用稳健的 VCE，否则不会重新计算。其检验统计量为：

$$W = N - \mathrm{RSS} \sim \chi^2(m) \tag{1.47}$$

LIML 估计后，Anderson-Rubin 过度识别限制检验(Anderson and Rubin，1950)③的统计量为：

$$\mathrm{AR} = N(\kappa - 1) \sim \chi^2(m) \tag{1.48}$$

其中，κ 是给定矩阵的最小特征值。

LIML 估计后的 Basmann 统计量为：

$$B_F = (\kappa - 1)(N - k_Z)/m \sim F(m, N - k_Z) \tag{1.49}$$

Hansen 过度识别限制检验的 J 统计量就是样本量乘以 GMM 目标函数的值，在过度识别限制检验原假设下 $J \sim \chi^2(m)$。

过度识别限制检验的语法格式为：

estat overid [, lags(#) forceweights forcenonrobust]

1.1.10 广义矩估计法

这里，小写和斜体(如 x)显示的符号是标量；小写和黑体(如 $\boldsymbol{x}$)显示的符号是矢量；大写和黑体(如 $\boldsymbol{X}$)显示的符号是矩阵。

随机解释变量问题模型为：

$$\begin{aligned} \boldsymbol{y} &= \boldsymbol{Y\beta}_1 + \boldsymbol{X}_1\boldsymbol{\beta}_2 + \boldsymbol{u} = \boldsymbol{X\beta} + \boldsymbol{u} \\ \boldsymbol{Y} &= \boldsymbol{X}_1\boldsymbol{\Pi}_1 + \boldsymbol{X}_2\boldsymbol{\Pi}_2 + \boldsymbol{v} = \boldsymbol{Z\Pi} + \boldsymbol{V} \end{aligned} \tag{1.50}$$

其中，$\boldsymbol{y}$ 是 $N\times 1$ 维的左边变量向量，N 是样本规模，$\boldsymbol{Y}$ 是 p 个内生回归的 $N\times p$ 维变量矩阵，$\boldsymbol{X}_1$ 是 k_1 个外生回归的 $N\times k_1$ 维变量矩阵，$\boldsymbol{X}_2$ 是 k_2 个外生回归的 $N\times k_2$ 维变量矩阵，$\boldsymbol{X}=[\boldsymbol{Y} \quad \boldsymbol{X}_1]$，$\boldsymbol{Z}=[\boldsymbol{X}_1 \quad \boldsymbol{X}_2]$，$\boldsymbol{u}$ 和 $\boldsymbol{v}$ 是随机误差项矩阵。

单方程工具变量回归的广义矩估计法，先利用 2SLS 估计获得初始的一致估计 $\boldsymbol{\beta}=[\boldsymbol{\beta}_1, \boldsymbol{\beta}_2]$，再利用该一致估计，计算权重矩阵和 GMM 估计值。

$$\boldsymbol{b}_{\mathrm{GMM}} = \{\boldsymbol{X}'\boldsymbol{ZWZ}'\boldsymbol{X}\}^{-1}\boldsymbol{X}'\boldsymbol{ZWZ}'\boldsymbol{y} \tag{1.51}$$

GMM 估计值的方差为：

$$\mathrm{Var}(\boldsymbol{b}_{\mathrm{GMM}}) = n\{\boldsymbol{X}'\boldsymbol{ZWZ}'\boldsymbol{X}\}^{-1}\boldsymbol{X}'\boldsymbol{ZW}\hat{\boldsymbol{S}}\boldsymbol{WZ}'\boldsymbol{X}\{\boldsymbol{X}'\boldsymbol{ZWZ}'\boldsymbol{X}\}^{-1}$$

如果设定 vce(unadjusted)，则 $\mathrm{Var}(\boldsymbol{b}_{\mathrm{GMM}}) = n\{\boldsymbol{X}'\boldsymbol{ZWZ}'\boldsymbol{X}\}^{-1}$。

权重矩阵 $\boldsymbol{W}$ 使用初始 2SLS 估计的残差计算，而 S 使用基于 $\boldsymbol{b}_{\mathrm{GMM}}$ 的残差估计。

---

① Wooldridge, J. M. Score Diagnostics for Linear Models Estimated by Two Stage Least Squares. in G. S. Maddala, P. C. B. Phillips, and T. N. Srinivasan. *Advances in Econometrics and Quantitative Economics: Essays in Honor of Professor C. R. Rao*. Oxford: Blackwell, 1995.

② Sargan, J. D. The Estimation of Economic Relationships Using Instrumental Variables, *Econometrica*, 1958, 26.

③ Anderson, T. W., and H. Rubin. The Asymptotic Properties of Estimates of the Parameters of a Single Equation in a Complete System of Stochastic Equations. *Annals of Mathematical Statistics*, 1950, 21.

wmatrix()选项影响 $\boldsymbol{W}$ 的形式，而 vce()选项影响 $\boldsymbol{S}$ 的形式。除了使用不同的残差外，$\boldsymbol{W}^{-1}$ 和 $\boldsymbol{S}$ 的公式是相同的，所以我们重点估计 $\boldsymbol{W}^{-1}$。

如果设定 wmatrix(unadjusted)，则 $\boldsymbol{W}^{-1}=\frac{s^2}{n}\sum_i \boldsymbol{z}_i\boldsymbol{z}_i'$。式中，$s^2=\sum_i u_i^2/n$。如果误差是同向的，则该权重矩阵是合适的。如果设定 wmatrix(robust)，则 $\boldsymbol{W}^{-1}=\frac{1}{n}\sum_i u_i^2\boldsymbol{z}_i\boldsymbol{z}_i'$。如果误差是异方差的，则这个权重是合适的。如果设定 wmatrix(cluster clustvar)，则 $\boldsymbol{W}^{-1}=\frac{1}{n}\sum_c \boldsymbol{q}_c\boldsymbol{q}_c'$。式中，$c$ 是聚类数，$\boldsymbol{q}_c=\sum_{i\in c_j} u_i\boldsymbol{Z}_i$，$c_j$ 表示第 j 类。如果设定 wmatrix(hac kernel[#])，则 $\boldsymbol{W}^{-1}=\frac{1}{n}\sum_i u_i^2\boldsymbol{z}_i\boldsymbol{z}'_i+\frac{1}{n}\sum_{l=1}^{l=n-1}\sum_{i=l+1}^{i=n}K(l,m)u_iu_{i-l}(\boldsymbol{z}_i\boldsymbol{z}_{i-l}'+\boldsymbol{z}_{i-l}\boldsymbol{z}_i')$。式中，$K(l,m)$ 为核函数。

例 1.2　单方程模型的工具变量回归

```
* 下载数据
.clear
.webuse hsng2
(1980 Census housing data)
* 通过 2SLS 拟合回归，请求小样本统计
.ivregress 2sls rent pcturban (hsngval = faminc i.region), small
```

运行结果如图 1.20 所示。

```
Instrumental variables 2SLS regression

      Source |       SS           df       MS      Number of obs   =        50
-------------+----------------------------------   F(  2,     47)  =     42.66
       Model |  36677.4033         2  18338.7017   Prob > F        =    0.0000
    Residual |  24565.7167        47  522.674823   R-squared       =    0.5989
-------------+----------------------------------   Adj R-squared   =    0.5818
       Total |    61243.12        49  1249.85959   Root MSE        =    22.862

------------------------------------------------------------------------------
        rent | Coefficient  Std. err.      t    P>|t|     [95% conf. interval]
-------------+----------------------------------------------------------------
     hsngval |   .0022398   .0003388     6.61   0.000     .0015583    .0029213
    pcturban |    .081516   .3081528     0.26   0.793    -.5384074    .7014394
       _cons |   120.7065   15.70688     7.68   0.000     89.10834    152.3047
------------------------------------------------------------------------------
Instrumented: hsngval
 Instruments: pcturban faminc 2.region 3.region 4.region
```

图　1.20

```
.estat firststage
```

运行结果如图 1.21 所示。

```
* 获得过度识别限制的 Sargan 和 Basmann 测试
.estat overid
```

运行结果如图 1.22 所示。

```
First-stage regression summary statistics

                        Adjusted      Partial
    Variable    R-sq.      R-sq.        R-sq.      F(4,44)   Prob > F

     hsngval   0.6908     0.6557       0.5473      13.2978     0.0000


Minimum eigenvalue statistic = 13.2978

Critical Values                      # of endogenous regressors:    1
H0: Instruments are weak             # of excluded instruments:     4

                                         5%      10%      20%      30%
2SLS relative bias                     16.85    10.27     6.71     5.34

                                        10%      15%      20%      25%
2SLS size of nominal 5% Wald test      24.58    13.96    10.26     8.31
LIML size of nominal 5% Wald test       5.44     3.87     3.30     2.98
```

图 1.21

```
Tests of overidentifying restrictions:

Sargan (score) chi2(3) =  11.2877  (p = 0.0103)
Basmann chi2(3)        =  12.8294  (p = 0.0050)
```

图 1.22

* 测试 hsngval 是否可以被视为外源性

.estat endogenous

运行结果如图 1.23 所示。

```
Tests of endogeneity
H0: Variables are exogenous

Durbin (score) chi2(1)          =  12.8473  (p = 0.0003)
Wu-Hausman F(1,46)              =  15.9067  (p = 0.0002)
```

图 1.23

* 使用 LIML 估计器拟合回归

.ivregress liml rent pcturban (hsngval = faminc i.region)

运行结果如图 1.24 所示。

* 使用默认的异方差稳健权重矩阵通过 GMM 拟合回归

.ivregress gmm rent pcturban (hsngval = faminc i.region)

运行结果如图 1.25 所示。

Instrumental variables LIML regression

Number of obs	=	50
Wald chi2(2)	=	75.71
Prob > chi2	=	0.0000
R-squared	=	0.4901
Root MSE	=	24.992

rent	Coefficient	Std. err.	z	P>|z|	[95% conf.	interval]
hsngval	.0026686	.0004173	6.39	0.000	.0018507	.0034865
pcturban	-.1827391	.3571132	-0.51	0.609	-.8826681	.5171899
_cons	117.6087	17.22625	6.83	0.000	83.84587	151.3715

Instrumented: hsngval
Instruments: pcturban faminc 2.region 3.region 4.region

图 1.24

Instrumental variables GMM regression

GMM weight matrix: Robust

Number of obs	=	50
Wald chi2(2)	=	112.09
Prob > chi2	=	0.0000
R-squared	=	0.6616
Root MSE	=	20.358

rent	Coefficient	Robust std. err.	z	P>|z|	[95% conf.	interval]
hsngval	.0014643	.0004473	3.27	0.001	.0005877	.002341
pcturban	.7615482	.2895105	2.63	0.009	.1941181	1.328978
_cons	112.1227	10.80234	10.38	0.000	90.95052	133.2949

Instrumented: hsngval
Instruments: pcturban faminc 2.region 3.region 4.region

图 1.25

* 获取所有第一阶段回归诊断

```
.estat firststage, all
```

运行结果如图 1.26 所示。

First-stage regression summary statistics

Variable	R-sq.	Adjusted R-sq.	Partial R-sq.	Robust F(4,44)	Prob > F
hsngval	0.6908	0.6557	0.5473	11.4178	0.0000

Shea's partial R-squared

Variable	Shea's partial R-sq.	Shea's adj. partial R-sq.
hsngval	0.5473	0.4958

图 1.26

* 获得 Hansen 的 J 统计量

```
. estat overid
```

运行结果如图 1.27 所示。

```
Test of overidentifying restriction:

Hansen's J chi2(3) =  6.8364 (p = 0.0773)
```

图 1.27

* 测试 hsngval 是否可以被视为外源性

```
. estat endogenous hsngval
```

运行结果如图 1.28 所示。

```
Test of endogeneity (orthogonality conditions)
H0: Variables are exogenous

GMM C statistic chi2(1) =  .020293  (p = 0.8867)
```

图 1.28

* 使用异方差稳健权重矩阵通过 GMM 拟合回归,要求非稳健标准误差

```
. ivregress gmm rent pcturban (hsngval = faminc i.region), vce(unadjusted)
```

运行结果如图 1.29 所示。

```
Instrumental variables GMM regression          Number of obs   =        50
                                               Wald chi2(2)    =     64.47
                                               Prob > chi2     =    0.0000
                                               R-squared       =    0.6616
GMM weight matrix: Robust                      Root MSE        =    20.358
```

rent	Coefficient	Std. err.	z	P>|z|	[95% conf. interval]	
hsngval	.0014643	.0004766	3.07	0.002	.0005302	.0023984
pcturban	.7615482	.2989475	2.55	0.011	.1756218	1.347474
_cons	112.1227	13.86695	8.09	0.000	84.94399	139.3014

```
Instrumented: hsngval
 Instruments: pcturban faminc 2.region 3.region 4.region
```

图 1.29

* 通过 2SLS 拟合具有内生因子相互作用的回归

```
. ivregress 2sls rent pcturban (c.popgrow##c.popgrow = c.faminc##c.faminc i.region)
```

运行结果如图 1.30 所示。

```
Instrumental variables 2SLS regression          Number of obs     =         50
                                                Wald chi2(3)      =      29.35
                                                Prob > chi2       =     0.0000
                                                R-squared         =     0.3313
                                                Root MSE          =     28.619

------------------------------------------------------------------------------------
               rent | Coefficient  Std. err.      z    P>|z|     [95% conf. interval]
--------------------+---------------------------------------------------------------
            popgrow |   2.052514   2.136701     0.96   0.337    -2.135344    6.240371
                    |
c.popgrow#c.popgrow |  -.0364216   .0515496    -0.71   0.480    -.1374569    .0646138
                    |
           pcturban |   1.707642   .5499254     3.11   0.002     .6298081    2.785476
              _cons |   104.0526   45.83757     2.27   0.023     14.21265    193.8926
------------------------------------------------------------------------------------
Instrumented: popgrow c.popgrow#c.popgrow
 Instruments: pcturban faminc c.faminc#c.faminc 2.region 3.region 4.region
```

图 1.30

1.2 模型经典假设检验

多元线性回归模型的统计检验通过之后，就需要对其模型估计方法(即 OLS)有效性的前提假设(即经典假设)是否成立及其合理性，逐条进行假设检验了。具体包括随机误差项的零均值假设检验、正态性检验、异方差检验、序列相关性检验、截面相关性检验、随机项与解释变量不相关(即随机解释变量问题)的假设检验以及解释变量间不相关(即无多重共线性)的假设检验。其中，序列相关性检验见 8.1 节；截面相关性检验见 1.3.4 节；随机解释变量问题见 1.1.9 节和 1.1.10 节。解释变量间相关即某一解释变量可以由其他解释变量线性组合表示，也即多重共线性，其严重程度判断方法见 1.3.2 节。

1.2.1 随机误差项的零均值和正态性假设检验

随机误差项的零均值和正态性假设检验主要利用统计检验方法。

随机误差项的零均值检验可以利用均值比较的 t 检验法，其 Stata 实现命令为 ttest，该命令对均值相等性进行 t 检验。该测试可针对一个假设总体平均值对一个样本进行。配对和非配对数据可进行两次样本测试。在两样本未配对情况下，可以选择放宽方差相等的假设。语法格式为：

ttest varname = = # [if] [in] [, level(#)]

随机误差项的正态性检验可以利用图形分析作初步判断，也可以对其作正态性检验。图形分析主要利用标准正态分布诊断的概率图(命令 pnorm)和正态分布分位数图(命令 qnorm)，正态性检验方法及其命令有偏度和峰度正态性检验(命令 sktest)、Shapiro-Wilk 正态性检验(命令 swilk)和 Shapiro-Francia 正态性检验(命令 sfrancia)。

多个随机误差项和随机项与解释变量不相关的检验可以利用 Stata 的多变量检验命令 mvtest。mvtest 命令对多元变量的均值、协方差和相关性进行多元检验,并对单变量、双变量和多元变量的正态性进行检验。可以提供一个样本和多个样本进行检验。mvtest 提供的所有多样本测试均假设为独立样本。结构方程建模为估计均值、协方差和相关性以及测试各组间的差异提供了更通用的框架。语法格式为:

```
mvtest subcommand ... [, ...]
```

其中,子命令(subcommand)的选项及其含义为:

(1) means:测试平均值;

(2) covariances:检验协方差;

(3) correlations:测试相关性;

(4) normality:检验多元正态性。

1.2.2 异方差检验

对于随机误差项的同方差假设检验,可以先计算出误差及其方差序列,再利用变量与残差图形作初步判断,也可以利用统计检验中的方差比较检验法检验方差齐性,命令为 sdtest,或者用方差齐性的稳健检验法,命令为 robvar。

异方差检验(test for heteroskedasticity)主要包括 Breusch 和 Pagan(1979)①、Cook 和 Weisberg(1983)②异方差检验以及 Szroeter 秩检验三个版本。

estat hettest 实现 Breusch 和 Pagan(1979)、Cook 和 Weisberg(1983)版本的异方差检验。三个版本的检验都提出了验证 $\text{Var}(e_i)=\sigma^2\exp(\boldsymbol{zt})$ 中的 $\boldsymbol{t}=0$ 这一原假设。在默认执行的正态版本中,原假设还包括回归扰动是方差为 σ^2 的独立正态抽样的假设。如果没有指定 varlist,则对 z 使用拟合值 $\boldsymbol{x}\hat{\boldsymbol{\beta}}$。如果 varlist 或 rhs 选项被指定,则对 z 使用指定的变量。其增广回归(augmented regression)模型为:

$$\hat{e}_i^2/\hat{\sigma}^2=a+\boldsymbol{z}_i\boldsymbol{t}+v_i$$

最初的 Breusch 和 Pagan(1979)、Cook 和 Weisberg(1983)版本的异方差检验认为,假设 e_i 为正态分布,在原假设成立的情况下,分数检验统计量 S 等于增广回归模型的残差平方和除以 2,且服从自由度为遗漏变量数量(m)的卡方分布。

Koenker(1981)③提出,假设 e_i 为 i. i. d,则检验统计量 $S=N\times R^2$,服从自由度为 m 的大样本卡方分布,其中 N 为观测数,R^2 为增广回归模型的拟合优度。

Wooldridge(2020)④认为,假设 e_i 为 i. i. d,则可以利用遗漏变量参数等于 0(即 $\boldsymbol{t}=0$)的 F 检验。

---

① Breusch, T. S., and A. R. Pagan. A Simple Test for Heteroscedasticity and Random Coefficient Variation. *Econometrica*, 1979, 47.

② Cook, R. D., and S. Weisberg. Diagnostics for Heteroscedasticity in Regression. *Biometrika*, 1983, 70.

③ Koenker, R. A Note on Studentizing a Test for Heteroskedasticity. *Journal of Econometrics*, 1981, 172.

④ Wooldridge, J. M. *Introductory Econometrics: A Modern Approach* (7th ed.). Boston: Cengage Learning, 2020.

estat hettest 的语法格式为：

```
estat hettest [varlist] [, rhs [normal | iid | fstat] mtest[(spec)]]
```

各选项及含义如下：

(1) rhs：规定对拟合回归模型的右侧(解释性)变量进行异方差检验。rhs 选项可以与 varlist 结合使用，在这种情况下，varlist 中的变量包括在含解释变量的方差模型中。

(2) normal：默认情况下，会让 estat hettest 计算进行原始的 Breusch 和 Pagan (1979)、Cook 和 Weisberg(1983)版本的异方差检验，该检验假设回归扰动为正态分布。

(3) iid：导致 estat hettest 计算放弃正态性假设的分数检验。

(4) fstat：使 estat hettest 计算放弃正态性假设的 F 检验。

(5) mtest[(spec)]：规定要进行多次测试，以调整 p 值。该选项支持以下规范(spec)：

① bonferroni：bonferroni 的多重检验调整；

② holm：holm 的多重检验调整；

③ sidak：sidak 的多重检验调整；

④ noadjust：多次检验无调整。

可以在没有参数的情况下指定 mtest，这相当于指定 mtest(noadjust)，也就是说，应使用未经调整的 p 值对各个变量进行测试。默认情况下，estat hettest 不会执行多个测试。mtest 不能与 iid 或 fstat 一起指定。

菜单操作路径为：

Statistics>Postestimation

针对某个变量 x 的残差方差增加的备选方案的同方差性 Szroeter 检验的检验统计量定义为：

$$H=\frac{\sum_{i=1}^{n}h(x_i)e_i^2}{\sum_{i=1}^{n}e_i^2} \tag{1.52}$$

其中，$h(x_i)$是变量 x_i 的权重函数；H 是 $h(x_i)$以平方残差作为权重的加权平均。

estat szroeter 对 varlist 中的每个变量的异方差进行 Szroeter 秩检验，如果指定 rhs，则对回归的解释变量进行检验。

estat szroeter 的语法格式为：

```
estat szroeter [varlist] [, rhs mtest(spec)]
```

各选项含义同 estat hettest 命令。

菜单操作路径为：

Statistics>Postestimation

estat szroeter 对 varlist 中的每个变量的异方差进行 Szroeter 秩检验，如果指定 rhs，则对回归的解释变量进行检验。

1.2.3 信息矩阵检验

estat imtest 对回归模型进行信息矩阵检验，并根据 Cameron 和 Trivedi(1990)① 的观点，将正交分解为异方差 δ_1、非正态偏度 δ_2 和非正态峰度 δ_3 的联合检验。该分解通过三个辅助回归进行。设 e 为回归残差，$\hat{\sigma}^2$ 是回归中 σ^2 的最大似然估计，n 是观测数量，X 是 k 个变量集，R_{un}^2 是来自回归的去中心化 R^2。这里，δ_1 等于 $e^2-\hat{\sigma}^2$ 关于变量集 X 的变量叉乘的回归中的 nR_{un}^2，δ_2 等于 $e^3-3\hat{\sigma}^2e$ 关于变量集 X 的回归中的 nR_{un}^2，δ_3 等于 $e^4-6\hat{\sigma}^2e^2-3\hat{\sigma}^4$ 关于变量集 X 的回归中的 nR_{un}^2，δ_1、δ_2 和 δ_3 渐进地服从卡方分布。信息检验统计量 $\delta=\delta_1+\delta_2+\delta_3$，渐进服从自由度为 $1/2k(k+3)$的卡方分布。

white 对非限制形式的异方差的同方差检验可以作为一个选项。white 异方差检验通常类似于 Cameron 和 Trivedi(1990)②的分解。其检验统计量为利用 $\hat{u}^2$ 关于变量集 X 的变量叉乘的回归得到的 nR^2，近似于 δ_1。

estat imtest 的语法格式为：

```
estat imtest [, preserve white]
```

各选项含义如下：

(1) preserve：指定保留内存中的数据，删除计算中不需要的所有变量和案例，并在结束时恢复原始数据。对于大型数据集，此选项的成本很高。estat imtest 必须对 $k(k+1)/2$ 个临时变量执行辅助回归，其中 k 是回归数，否则可能无法执行测试。

(2) white：指定也要执行 white 的原始异方差测试。

菜单操作路径为：

```
Statistics>Postestimation
```

1.3 模型设定检验

1.3.1 Ramsey 遗漏变量检验

Ramsey 遗漏变量检验的辅助回归模型为：

$$y_i=\boldsymbol{x}_i\boldsymbol{b}+\boldsymbol{Z}_i\boldsymbol{t}+\boldsymbol{u}_i$$

该检验对 $t=0$ 的原假设做 F 检验。检验默认如果没有指定 rhs 选项，则对 $\boldsymbol{z}$ 使用拟合值的幂，即 $\boldsymbol{z}_i=(\hat{y}_i^2,\hat{y}_i^3,\hat{y}_i^4)$。如果指定 rhs 选项，则 $\boldsymbol{z}_i=(x_{1i}^2,x_{1i}^3,x_{1i}^4,x_{2i}^2,\cdots,x_{mi}^4)$。

estat ovtest 对遗漏变量进行两个版本的 Ramsey(1969)③回归误差设定检验

---

① Cameron, A. C., and P. K. Trivedi. The Information Matrix Test and Its Applied Alternative Hypotheses. University of California-Davis. Institute of Governmental Affairs. Working paper, 1990.

② Ibid.

③ Ramsey, J. B. Tests for Specification Errors in Classical Linear Least-squares Regression Analysis. *Journal of the Royal Statistical Society Series B*, 1969, 31.

(RESET)。这个检验相当于拟合 $y = \boldsymbol{xb} + \boldsymbol{zt} + \boldsymbol{\mu}$，然后检验 $t=0$。

estat ovtest 的语法格式为：

```
estat ovtest [, rhs]
```

其中，rhs 规定在检验中使用右侧(解释性)变量的幂，而不是拟合值的幂。

菜单操作路径为：

```
Statistics>Postestimation
```

1.3.2 自变量的方差膨胀因子

estat vif 计算线性回归模型中指定的自变量是否中心化的方差膨胀因子(variance inflation factor，VIF)。x_j 的中心化的方差膨胀因子(VIF_c)为：

$$\mathrm{VIF}_c(x_j) = \frac{1}{1-\hat{R}_j^2}$$

式中，$\hat{R}_j^2$ 为 x_j 与所有其他解释变量的含截距回归的中心多重相关系数的平方。

x_j 的非中心化的方差膨胀因子(VIF_{uc})为：

$$\mathrm{VIF}_{uc}(x_j) = \frac{1}{1-\widetilde{R}_j^2}$$

式中，$\hat{R}_j^2$ 为 x_j 与包括常数项在内的所有其他解释变量的无截距回归的非中心多重相关系数的平方。VIF 越大，说明多重共线性问题越严重。一个经验规则是，VIF 最大不能超过 10。

estat vif 的语法格式为：

```
estat vif [, uncentered]
```

1.3.3 效应度量

estat esize 计算 regress 或 anova 之后的线性模型的效应大小。默认情况下，estat esize 报告 η^2 估计值，这相当于 R^2 估计值。计算公式为：

$$\hat{\eta}^2 = \frac{F}{F + \mathrm{d}f_{\mathrm{den}}/\mathrm{d}f_{\mathrm{num}}} \tag{1.53}$$

式中，F 为方程显著性联合检验统计量 F 值，$\mathrm{d}f_{\mathrm{num}}$ 为分子自由度，$\mathrm{d}f_{\mathrm{den}}$ 为分母自由度。

与等效估计量 R^2 一样，η^2 也有向上的偏差。效应大小的较小偏差估计值为 ε^2 和 ω^2：

$$\hat{\varepsilon}^2 = \frac{F-1}{F + \mathrm{d}f_{\mathrm{den}}/\mathrm{d}f_{\mathrm{num}}} = \hat{\eta}^2 - \frac{\mathrm{d}f_{\mathrm{num}}}{\mathrm{d}f_{\mathrm{den}}}(1-\hat{\eta}^2) \tag{1.54}$$

$$\hat{\omega}^2 = \frac{F-1}{F + (\mathrm{d}f_{\mathrm{den}}+1)/\mathrm{d}f_{\mathrm{num}}} \tag{1.55}$$

η^2 估计值的置信区间是通过使用非中心 F 分布估计的。如果指定选项 epsilon，则 estat esizeb 报告 ε^2 估计值。如果指定选项 omega，则 estat esize 报告 ω^2 估计值。

estat esize 的语法格式为：

estat esize [, epsilon omega level(#)]

各选项含义如下：

(1) epsilon：指定报告效应大小的 epsilon 平方估计值，默认值为 eta 平方估计值。

(2) omega：指定报告效应大小的 ω(omega)平方估计值，默认值为 eta 平方估计值。

(3) level(#)：指定置信区间的置信水平(以百分比表示)，默认值为 level(95)或按“设置级别”设置。

例 1.3 模型设定检验

* 加载数据 auto.dta 并回归

. sysuse auto, clear

. regress price weight foreign##c.mpg

运行结果如图 1.31 所示。

Source	SS	df	MS			
Model	350319665	4	87579916.3	Number of obs	=	74
Residual	284745731	69	4126749.72	F(4, 69)	=	21.22
				Prob > F	=	0.0000
Total	635065396	73	8699525.97	R-squared	=	0.5516
				Adj R-squared	=	0.5256
				Root MSE	=	2031.4

price	Coefficient	Std. err.	t	P>|t|	[95% conf.	interval]
weight	4.613589	.7254961	6.36	0.000	3.166263	6.060914
foreign						
Foreign	11240.33	2751.681	4.08	0.000	5750.878	16729.78
mpg	263.1875	110.7961	2.38	0.020	42.15527	484.2197
foreign#c.mpg						
Foreign	-307.2166	108.5307	-2.83	0.006	-523.7294	-90.70368
_cons	-14449.58	4425.72	-3.26	0.002	-23278.65	-5620.51

图 1.31

* 遗漏变量的 Ramsey 检验

. estat ovtest

运行结果如图 1.32 所示。

```
Ramsey RESET test for omitted variables
Omitted: Powers of fitted values of price

H0: Model has no omitted variables

F(3, 66) =   7.77
Prob > F = 0.0002
```

图 1.32

* 异方差检验

.estat hottest

运行结果如图 1.33 所示。

```
Breusch-Pagan/Cook-Weisberg test for heteroskedasticity
Assumption: Normal error terms
Variable: Fitted values of price

H0: Constant variance

    chi2(1) =   6.50
Prob > chi2 = 0.0108
```

图 1.33

* 三个版本的异方差检验

.estat hettest weight foreign# #c.mpg, mtest(b)

运行结果如图 1.34 所示。

```
Breusch-Pagan/Cook-Weisberg test for heteroskedasticity
Assumption: Normal error terms
H0: Constant variance

    Variable        chi2   df        p

      weight       15.24    1   0.0004*
     foreign
    Foreign         6.15    1   0.0525*
         mpg        9.04    1   0.0106*
    foreign#
       c.mpg
    Foreign         6.02    1   0.0566*

Simultaneous       15.60    4   0.0036

* Bonferroni-adjusted p-values
```

图 1.34

* 异方差的秩检验

.estat szroeter, rhs mtest(holm)

运行结果如图 1.35 所示。

* 异方差、偏度和峰度检验

.estat imtest

运行结果如图 1.36 所示。

Szroeter's test for homoskedasticity

H0: Variance constant
Ha: Variance monotonic in variables

Variable	chi2	df	p
weight	17.07	1	0.0001*
foreign			
Foreign	6.15	1	0.0131*
mpg	11.45	1	0.0021*
foreign#c.mpg			
Foreign	6.17	1	0.0260*

* Holm-adjusted *p*-values

图 1.35

Cameron & Trivedi's decomposition of IM-test

Source	chi2	df	p
Heteroskedasticity	18.86	10	0.0420
Skewness	11.69	4	0.0198
Kurtosis	2.33	1	0.1273
Total	32.87	15	0.0049

图 1.36

```
* 估算 eta 平方、ε 平方和 ω 平方效应大小
.estat esize, level(90)
```

运行结果如图 1.37 所示。

Effect sizes for linear models

Source	Eta-squared	df	[90% conf.	interval]
Model	.5516277	4	.3915662	.6261954
weight	.3695156	1	.2195846	.4869379
foreign	.1947378	1	.0710273	.322397
mpg	.0283351	1	.	.1171974
foreign#c.mpg	.1040449	1	.0176176	.2228799

Note: Eta-squared values for individual model terms are partial.

图 1.37

```
.estat esize, omega
```

运行结果如图 1.38 所示。

Effect sizes for linear models

Source	Omega-squared	df
Model	.5222415	4
weight	.357115	1
foreign	.1809555	1
mpg	.0140551	1
foreign#c.mpg	.0898928	1

Note: Omega-squared values for individual model terms are partial.

图 1.38

1.3.4 随机误差项截面相关的莫兰检验

标准的多元线性模型为：

$$\boldsymbol{y} = \boldsymbol{X}\beta + \boldsymbol{u} \tag{1.56}$$

式中，$\boldsymbol{y}$ 为 $n\times 1$ 维的被解释变量向量，$\boldsymbol{X}$ 为 $n\times k$ 维的协变量矩阵，$\boldsymbol{\beta}$ 为 $k\times l$ 维的回归参数向量，$\boldsymbol{u}$ 为均值为 0、方差为 σ^2 的 $n\times 1$ 维的正态分布随机误差项向量。

Moran 检验的原假设为 $H_0:E(\boldsymbol{uu}')=\sigma^2\boldsymbol{I}$。假设随机项的截面空间相关矩阵为 $\boldsymbol{W}_1$，则 Moran 检验的检验统计量为：

$$I = \frac{\hat{\boldsymbol{u}}'\boldsymbol{W}_1\hat{\boldsymbol{u}}}{\hat{\sigma}^2[tr\{(\boldsymbol{W}_1'+\boldsymbol{W}_1)\boldsymbol{W}_1\}]^{1/2}} \tag{1.57}$$

式中，$\hat{\boldsymbol{u}}=\boldsymbol{y}-\boldsymbol{X}\hat{\boldsymbol{\beta}}$，$\hat{\sigma}^2=\hat{u}'\hat{u}/2$。在适当的假设下，$I\sim N(0,1)$，$I^2\sim\chi^2(1)$。

如果不知道任何相关矩阵的信息，就需要利用经验统计量：

$$I(q)^2 = \begin{bmatrix}\hat{\boldsymbol{u}}'\boldsymbol{W}_1\hat{\boldsymbol{u}}/\hat{\sigma}^2\\ \vdots \\ \hat{\boldsymbol{u}}'\boldsymbol{W}_q\hat{\boldsymbol{u}}/\hat{\sigma}^2\end{bmatrix}'\Phi^{-1}\begin{bmatrix}\hat{\boldsymbol{u}}'\boldsymbol{W}_1\hat{\boldsymbol{u}}/\hat{\sigma}^2\\ \vdots \\ \hat{\boldsymbol{u}}'\boldsymbol{W}_q\hat{\boldsymbol{u}}/\hat{\sigma}^2\end{bmatrix} \tag{1.58}$$

式中，$\Phi=(\phi_{rs})$，当 $r,s=1,\cdots,q$ 时，$\phi_{rs}=\frac{1}{2}\mathrm{tr}\{(\boldsymbol{W}_r+\boldsymbol{W}_r')(\boldsymbol{W}_s+\boldsymbol{W}_s')\}$。在原假设成立时，$I(q)^2\sim\chi^2(q)$。

随机项截面相关的 Moran 检验的语法格式为：

```
estat moran, errorlag(spmatname) [errorlag(spmatname)…]
```

快速启动 y 在 x_1 和 x_2 上的线性回归，然后使用空间加权矩阵 $\boldsymbol{W}$ 测试残差之间的空间相关性：

```
regress y x1 x2
estat moran, errorlag(W)
```

在输入相同的回归命令后，添加另一个空间权重矩阵：

```
estat moran, errorlag(W) errorlag(M)
```

再进行无自变量回归：

```
regress y
estat moran, errorlag(W)
```

菜单操作路径为：

Statistics>Postestimation

1.3.5 信息准则

AIC(Akaike information criterion)的计算公式为：

$$AIC = -2\ln L + 2k \tag{1.59}$$

式中，$\ln L$ 是模型的最大对数似然值，k 是估计的参数个数。

BIC Bayesian information criterion)的计算公式为：

$$BIC = -2\ln L + k\ln N \tag{1.60}$$

AIC 和 BIC 两个信息准则估算的语法格式均为：

```
estat ic [, n(#)]
```

菜单操作路径为：

Statistics>Postestimation

1.3.6 参数估计值一致有效性的 Hausman 设定检验

hausman 命令是 Hausman 设定检验的一般实现，它比较了已知的一致估计量 $\hat{\theta}_1$ 与检验假设下的有效估计量 $\hat{\theta}_2$。零假设是估计量 $\hat{\theta}_2$ 确实是有效的(且一致的)真参数的估计量。如果是这种情况，则两个估计值之间不应存在系统性差异。如果估计值存在系统性差异，就有理由怀疑有效估计值所依据的假设。

如果估计量被加权或数据被聚类，则违反了效率假设，因此不能使用 hausman 命令，但可以通过使用 hausman 命令指定 force 选项来强制测试。

Hausman 设定检验的检验统计量为：

$$H = (\beta_c - \beta_e)'(V_c - V_e)^{-1}(\beta_c - \beta_e) \tag{1.61}$$

式中，β_c 是一致估计的系数向量；β_e 是有效估计的系数向量；V_c 是一致估计量的协方差矩阵；V_e 是有效估计量的协方差矩阵

该检验统计量服从卡方分布，自由度为方差矩阵中差值的秩。当差值为正定值时，所比较的是模型中的公共参数数量。

Hausman 设定检验的语法格式为：

```
hausman name-consistent [name-efficient] [, options]
```

菜单操作路径为：

Statistics>Postestimation

例 1.4 Hausman 设定检验

```
* 下载数据
.clear
.sysuse auto
```

(1978 automobile data)

. regress mpg price

运行结果如图 1.39 所示。

```
      Source |       SS           df       MS      Number of obs   =        74
-------------+----------------------------------   F(1, 72)        =     20.26
       Model |  536.541807         1  536.541807   Prob > F        =    0.0000
    Residual |  1906.91765        72  26.4849674   R-squared       =    0.2196
-------------+----------------------------------   Adj R-squared   =    0.2087
       Total |  2443.45946        73  33.4720474   Root MSE        =    5.1464

------------------------------------------------------------------------------
         mpg | Coefficient  Std. err.      t    P>|t|     [95% conf. interval]
-------------+----------------------------------------------------------------
       price |  -.0009192   .0002042    -4.50   0.000    -.0013263   -.0005121
       _cons |   26.96417   1.393952    19.34   0.000     24.18538    29.74297
------------------------------------------------------------------------------
```

图 1.39

. estimates store reg

. heckman mpg price, select(foreign = weight)

运行结果如图 1.40 所示。

```
Heckman selection model                         Number of obs     =         74
(regression model with sample selection)              Selected    =         22
                                                      Nonselected =         52

                                                Wald chi2(1)      =       3.33
Log likelihood = -94.94709                      Prob > chi2       =     0.0679

------------------------------------------------------------------------------
             | Coefficient  Std. err.      z    P>|z|     [95% conf. interval]
-------------+----------------------------------------------------------------
mpg          |
       price |   -.001053   .0005769    -1.83   0.068    -.0021837    .0000776
       _cons |   34.05654   3.015942    11.29   0.000      28.1454    39.96768
-------------+----------------------------------------------------------------
foreign      |
      weight |   -.001544   .0003295    -4.69   0.000    -.0021898   -.0008983
       _cons |   3.747496   .8814804     4.25   0.000     2.019826    5.475166
-------------+----------------------------------------------------------------
     /athrho |  -.7340315   .5612249    -1.31   0.191    -1.834012    .3659491
    /lnsigma |   1.733092   .2358148     7.35   0.000     1.270904    2.195281
-------------+----------------------------------------------------------------
         rho |  -.6255256   .3416276                     -.9502171    .3504433
       sigma |   5.658124   1.334269                      3.564072    8.982524
      lambda |  -3.539301   2.633223                     -8.700324    1.621722
------------------------------------------------------------------------------
LR test of indep. eqns. (rho = 0): chi2(1) = 1.25         Prob > chi2 = 0.2629
```

图 1.40

* 指定公式()选项,当一个估计器使用公式名称而另一个不使用时,强制进行比较

. hausman reg. , equation(1:1)

运行结果如图 1.41 所示。

```
                 ---- Coefficients ----
             |      (b)          (B)            (b-B)     sqrt(diag(V_b-V_B))
             |      reg           .          Difference          Std. err.
-------------+----------------------------------------------------------------
       price |   -.0009192    -.001053        .0001339                .
------------------------------------------------------------------------------
                          b = Consistent under H0 and Ha; obtained from regress.
           B = Inconsistent under Ha, efficient under H0; obtained from heckman.

Test of H0: Difference in coefficients not systematic

chi2(1) = (b-B)'[(V_b-V_B)^(-1)](b-B)
        = -0.06

Warning: chi2 < 0 ==> model fitted on these data
         fails to meet the asymptotic assumptions
         of the Hausman test; see suest for a
         generalized test.
```

图 1.41

* 设置 probit

. probit foreign weight

运行结果如图 1.42 所示。

```
Probit regression                                       Number of obs =     74
                                                        LR chi2(1)    =  32.25
                                                        Prob > chi2   = 0.0000
Log likelihood = -28.908406                             Pseudo R2     = 0.3581

------------------------------------------------------------------------------
     foreign | Coefficient  Std. err.      z    P>|z|     [95% conf. interval]
-------------+----------------------------------------------------------------
      weight |  -.0015049   .0003265    -4.61   0.000    -.0021447   -.0008651
       _cons |   3.655625   .8775791     4.17   0.000     1.935601    5.375648
------------------------------------------------------------------------------
```

图 1.42

. estimates store probit_for

. heckman mpg price, select(foreign = weight)

运行结果如图 1.43 所示。

* 比较 Probit 模型和 Heckman 模型的选择方程

. hausman probit_for. , equation(1:2)

运行结果如图 1.44 所示。

```
Heckman selection model                         Number of obs     =         74
(regression model with sample selection)              Selected    =         22
                                                      Nonselected =         52

                                                Wald chi2(1)      =       3.33
Log likelihood = -94.94709                      Prob > chi2       =     0.0679

------------------------------------------------------------------------------
             | Coefficient  Std. err.      z    P>|z|     [95% conf. interval]
-------------+----------------------------------------------------------------
mpg          |
       price |   -.001053   .0005769    -1.83   0.068    -.0021837    .0000776
       _cons |   34.05654   3.015942    11.29   0.000      28.1454    39.96768
-------------+----------------------------------------------------------------
foreign      |
      weight |   -.001544   .0003295    -4.69   0.000    -.0021898   -.0008983
       _cons |   3.747496   .8814804     4.25   0.000     2.019826    5.475166
-------------+----------------------------------------------------------------
     /athrho |  -.7340315   .5612249    -1.31   0.191    -1.834012    .3659491
    /lnsigma |   1.733092   .2358148     7.35   0.000     1.270904    2.195281
-------------+----------------------------------------------------------------
         rho |  -.6255256   .3416276                     -.9502171    .3504433
       sigma |   5.658124   1.334269                      3.564072    8.982524
      lambda |  -3.539301   2.633223                     -8.700324    1.621722
------------------------------------------------------------------------------
LR test of indep. eqns. (rho = 0): chi2(1) = 1.25          Prob > chi2 = 0.2629
```

图 1.43

```
                 ---- Coefficients ----
             |      (b)          (B)            (b-B)     sqrt(diag(V_b-V_B))
             |   probit_for       .          Difference       Std. err.
-------------+----------------------------------------------------------------
      weight |   -.0015049     -.001544        .0000391              .
------------------------------------------------------------------------------
                          b = Consistent under H0 and Ha; obtained from probit.
           B = Inconsistent under Ha, efficient under H0; obtained from heckman.

Test of H0: Difference in coefficients not systematic

chi2(1) = (b-B)'[(V_b-V_B)^(-1)](b-B)
        = -0.78

Warning: chi2 < 0 ==> model fitted on these data
         fails to meet the asymptotic assumptions
         of the Hausman test; see suest for a
         generalized test.
```

图 1.44

1.4 模型设定形式检验

1.4.1 参数线性组合检验分析

参数线性组合检验分析的语法格式为：

lincom exp [, options]

其中，exp 是系数的任何线性组合，是检验的有效语法。

各选项含义为：

(1) eform:通用标签;

(2) or:比值比(odds ratio);

(3) hr:风险比(hazard ratio);

(4) shr:次危险比;

(5) irr:发生率比率;

(6) rrr:相对风险比率;

(7) level(#):设置置信度级别,默认值为级别(95);

(8) display_options:控制列格式;

(9) df(#):使用具有#自由度的 t 分布计算 p 值和置信区间。

菜单操作路径为:

Statistics>Postestimation

例 1.5 参数线性组合检验分析

```
* 下载数据
.clear
.webuse regress
.regress y x1 x2 x3
```

运行结果如图 1.45 所示。

Source	SS	df	MS			
				Number of obs	=	148
				F(3, 144)	=	96.12
Model	3259.3561	3	1086.45203	Prob > F	=	0.0000
Residual	1627.56282	144	11.3025196	R-squared	=	0.6670
				Adj R-squared	=	0.6600
Total	4886.91892	147	33.2443464	Root MSE	=	3.3619

y	Coefficient	Std. err.	t	P>|t|	[95% conf.	interval]
x1	1.457113	1.07461	1.36	0.177	-.666934	3.581161
x2	2.221682	.8610358	2.58	0.011	.5197797	3.923583
x3	-.006139	.0005543	-11.08	0.000	-.0072345	-.0050435
_cons	36.10135	4.382693	8.24	0.000	27.43863	44.76407

图 1.45

```
* 估计系数的线性组合
.lincom x2 - x1
```

运行结果如图 1.46 所示。

(1) - x1 + x2 = 0

y	Coefficient	Std. err.	t	P>|t|	[95% conf.	interval]
(1)	.7645682	.9950282	0.77	0.444	-1.20218	2.731316

图 1.46

```
. lincom 3 * x1 + 500 * x3
```

运行结果如图 1.47 所示。

(1) 3*x1 + 500*x3 = 0

y	Coefficient	Std. err.	t	P>|t|	[95% conf.	interval]
(1)	1.301825	3.396624	0.38	0.702	-5.411858	8.015507

图　1.47

```
. lincom 3 * x1 + 500 * x3 - 12
```

运行结果如图 1.48 所示。

(1) 3*x1 + 500*x3 = 12

y	Coefficient	Std. err.	t	P>|t|	[95% conf.	interval]
(1)	-10.69818	3.396624	-3.15	0.002	-17.41186	-3.984493

图　1.48

1.4.2　参数非线性组合检验分析

对于 $1\times k$ 维的参数估计值 $\hat{\theta}=(\hat{\theta}_1,\cdots,\hat{\theta}_k)$ 考虑 p 维的转换 $g(\hat{\boldsymbol{\theta}})=[g_1(\hat{\boldsymbol{\theta}}),g_2(\hat{\boldsymbol{\theta}}),\cdots,g_p(\hat{\boldsymbol{\theta}})]$，该转换的估计方差—协方差为 $\widehat{\mathrm{Var}}\{g(\hat{\boldsymbol{\theta}})\}=\boldsymbol{GVG}'$，其中，$\boldsymbol{G}$ 是 $p\times k$ 维的导数矩阵，$\boldsymbol{V}$ 是 $\hat{\theta}$ 的估计的方差—协方差矩阵。

$$\boldsymbol{G}_{ij}=\left.\frac{\partial g_i(\boldsymbol{\theta})}{\partial \theta_j}\right|_{\boldsymbol{\theta}=\hat{\boldsymbol{\theta}}}\quad i=1,\cdots,p\quad j=1,\cdots,k$$

Wald 检验的原假设为：

$$H_0:g_i(\hat{\boldsymbol{\theta}})=0$$

检验统计量为：

$$Z_i=\frac{g_i(\hat{\boldsymbol{\theta}})}{[\widehat{\mathrm{Var}}_{ii}\{g(\hat{\boldsymbol{\theta}})\}]^{1/2}}\tag{1.62}$$

式中，$\hat{\theta}$ 的方差—协方差矩阵为渐进协方差矩阵，Z_i 近似服从高斯分布。$g_i(\boldsymbol{\theta})$ 的 $1-\alpha$ 置信区间为：$g_i(\hat{\boldsymbol{\theta}})\pm z_{\alpha/2}[\widehat{\mathrm{Var}}_{ii}\{g(\hat{\boldsymbol{\theta}})\}]^{1/2}$。

对于线性回归，Z_i 近似服从 $t_1(r)$ 分布，r 为原始拟合模型的剩余自由度。$g_i(\boldsymbol{\theta})$ 的 $1-\alpha$ 置信区间为：$g_i(\hat{\boldsymbol{\theta}})\pm t_{\alpha/2,r}[\widehat{\mathrm{Var}}_{ii}\{g(\hat{\boldsymbol{\theta}})\}]^{1/2}$。

参数非线性组合检验分析的语法格式为：

(1) 一个表达式参数的非线性组合：

```
nlcom [name:]exp [, options]
```

(2) 多个表达式参数的非线性组合：

nlcom ([name:]exp) [([name:]exp) ...] [, options]

nlcom 命令可以在任何 Stata 估计命令(包括测量估计)后，计算参数估计非线性组合的点估计、标准误差、测试统计、显著性水平和置信区间。结果以用于显示估算结果的常用表格形式显示。计算基于 delta 方法，这是一种适用于大样本的近似方法。

nlcom 和 predictnl 都使用 delta 方法。它们对拟合模型的估计参数向量进行非线性变换，并应用 delta 方法计算变换的方差、标准误差、Wald 检验统计量等。nlcom 是为参数函数设计的，predictnl 是为参数和数据的功能设计的，即用于预测。

nlcom 以两种方式概括了 lincom。首先，nlcom 允许变换是非线性的。其次，nlcom 可用于同时估计许多变换(线性或非线性)，并获得这些变换的估计方差—协方差矩阵。

例 1.6　参数非线性组合检验分析

* 下载数据

.clear

.webuse regress

* 拟合线性回归模型

.regress y x1 x2 x3

运行结果略。

* 估计 x_2 和 x_3 乘积的系数

.nlcom _b[x2] * _b[x3]

运行结果如图 1.49 所示。

_nl_1: _b[x2]*_b[x3]

y	Coefficient	Std. err.	z	P>|z|	[95% conf.	interval]
_nl_1	-.013639	.005572	-2.45	0.014	-.0245599	-.002718

图 1.49

* 联合估计 x_1 和 x_2 以及 x_2 和 x_3 上系数的比率，并将结果发布到 e()

.nlcom (ratio1: _b[x1]/_b[x2]) (ratio2: _b[x2]/_b[x3]), post

运行结果如图 1.50 所示。

ratio1: _b[x1]/_b[x2]
ratio2: _b[x2]/_b[x3]

y	Coefficient	Std. err.	z	P>|z|	[95% conf.	interval]
ratio1	.6558606	.4221027	1.55	0.120	-.1714455	1.483167
ratio2	-361.8945	140.0704	-2.58	0.010	-636.4273	-87.36165

图 1.50

```
* 测试上述两个比率是否相等
.test _b[ratio1] = _b[ratio2]
```

运行结果如图 1.51 所示。

```
( 1)  ratio1 - ratio2 = 0

           chi2(  1) =    6.69
         Prob > chi2 =    0.0097
```

图 1.51

1.4.3 单方程模型设定的链接测试

链接测试(link test)基于这样一个想法，即如果正确指定了回归或类似回归的方程，则除了偶然性之外，应该不再能够找到其他显著的自变量。一种设定错误称为链路错误。在回归中，这意味着因变量需要一个转换或"链接"函数才能与自变量正确关联。链接测试的想法是在方程中添加一个自变量，如果存在链接错误，该自变量可能就会特别重要。

设模型为 $\boldsymbol{y}=f(\boldsymbol{X}\hat{\boldsymbol{\beta}})$，$\hat{\boldsymbol{\beta}}$ 为参数估计值。链接检验计算 _hat $=\boldsymbol{X}\hat{\boldsymbol{\beta}}$ 和 _hatsq $=$ _hat^2。然后模型中加进这两个变量，再次拟合模型，用这两个变量的显著性检验判断模型设定的偏误。

单方程模型设定的关联检验的语法格式为：

```
linktest [if] [in] [, cmd_options]
```

1.4.4 模型约束的估计后似然比检验

设 L_0 和 L_1 分别为与全模型和受约束模型相关联的对数似然值。似然比检验的检验统计量为：$LR=-2(L_1-L_0)$。

如果受约束模型为真，则 LR 近似为 $\chi^2(d_0,d_1)$，其中 d_0 和 d_1 分别是与完整模型和约束模型相关的模型自由度。

lrtest 将模型的自由度确定为 $e(V)$ 的秩，计算为 invsym($e(V)$) 的非零对角元素数。

估计后似然比检验的语法格式为：

```
lrtest modelspec1 [modelspec2] [, options]
```

lrtest 命令对统计模型的参数向量满足某种平滑约束的零假设进行似然比检验。要进行检验，必须使用最大似然法（或某些等效方法）拟合非限制模型和限制模型，并且必须使用 estimates store 存储至少一个模型的结果。

例 1.7　嵌套模型的似然比检验

```
* 下载数据
.clear
.webuse lbw
(Hosmer & Lemeshow data)
```

.logit low age lwt i.race smoke ptl ht ui

运行结果如图 1.52 所示。

```
Logistic regression                                     Number of obs =    189
                                                        LR chi2(8)    =  33.22
                                                        Prob > chi2   = 0.0001
Log likelihood = -100.724                               Pseudo R2     = 0.1416

         low | Coefficient  Std. err.      z    P>|z|     [95% conf. interval]
-------------+----------------------------------------------------------------
         age |  -.0271003   .0364504    -0.74   0.457    -.0985418    .0443412
         lwt |  -.0151508   .0069259    -2.19   0.029    -.0287253   -.0015763
             |
        race |
       Black |   1.262647   .5264101     2.40   0.016     .2309024    2.294392
       Other |   .8620792   .4391532     1.96   0.050     .0013548    1.722804
             |
       smoke |   .9233448   .4008266     2.30   0.021      .137739    1.708951
         ptl |   .5418366    .346249     1.56   0.118     -.136799    1.220472
          ht |   1.832518   .6916292     2.65   0.008     .4769494    3.188086
          ui |   .7585135   .4593768     1.65   0.099    -.1418484    1.658875
       _cons |   .4612239    1.20459     0.38   0.702    -1.899729    2.822176
```

图 1.52

.estimates store A

* 减少一个变量,再估计模型

.logit low lwt i.race smoke ht ui

运行结果如图 1.53 所示。

```
Logistic regression                                     Number of obs =    189
                                                        LR chi2(6)    =  30.43
                                                        Prob > chi2   = 0.0000
Log likelihood = -102.11978                             Pseudo R2     = 0.1297

         low | Coefficient  Std. err.      z    P>|z|     [95% conf. interval]
-------------+----------------------------------------------------------------
         lwt |  -.0167026   .0068014    -2.46   0.014    -.0300331   -.0033721
             |
        race |
       Black |   1.324055   .5214119     2.54   0.011     .3021063    2.346004
       Other |   .9266461    .430342     2.15   0.031     .0831913    1.770101
             |
       smoke |   1.035816   .3925275     2.64   0.008      .266476    1.805155
          ht |   1.870299   .6907696     2.71   0.007     .5164154    3.224183
          ui |   .9049472    .447533     2.02   0.043     .0277987    1.782096
       _cons |   .0526554   .9377226     0.06   0.955    -1.785247    1.890558
```

图 1.53

.estimates store B

* 似然比检验

.lrtest A.

运行结果如图 1.54 所示。

```
Likelihood-ratio test
Assumption: B nested within A

 LR chi2(2) =   2.79
Prob > chi2 = 0.2476
```

图 1.54

＊用五个变量再估计模型

.logit low lwt smoke ht ui

运行结果如图 1.55 所示。

```
Logistic regression                          Number of obs =    189
                                             LR chi2(4)    =  21.82
                                             Prob > chi2   = 0.0002
Log likelihood = -106.42478                  Pseudo R2     = 0.0930
```

low	Coefficient	Std. err.	z	P>|z|	[95% conf.	interval]
lwt	-.0162771	.0065445	-2.49	0.013	-.0291041	-.0034501
smoke	.6528692	.3356573	1.95	0.052	-.005007	1.310745
ht	1.921019	.6825224	2.81	0.005	.5833	3.258739
ui	.8963519	.442908	2.02	0.043	.0282682	1.764436
_cons	.7184771	.8490134	0.85	0.397	-.9455586	2.382513

图 1.55

.estimates store C

＊似然比检验

.lrtest B

Likelihood-ratio test

Assumption：C nested within B

LR chi2(2) = 8.61

Prob>chi2 = 0.0135

.lrtest C A，stats

运行结果如图 1.56 所示。

```
Likelihood-ratio test
Assumption: C nested within A

 LR chi2(4) =  11.40
Prob > chi2 = 0.0224

Akaike's information criterion and Bayesian information criterion
```

Model	N	ll(null)	ll(model)	df	AIC	BIC
C	189	-117.336	-106.4248	5	222.8496	239.0583
A	189	-117.336	-100.724	9	219.448	248.6237

Note: BIC uses N = number of observations. See [R] BIC note.

图 1.56

例 1.8 组合模型的似然比检验

我们想在 Heckman 模型框架中检验参与决策是否随机独立于结果(工资率)。如果该相关性为 0,则 Heckman 模型相当于结果回归和参与概率模型的组合。

```
* 下载数据
.clear
.webuse womenwk
.heckman wage educ age, select(married children educ age)
```

运行结果如图 1.57 所示。

```
Heckman selection model                         Number of obs     =      2,000
(regression model with sample selection)              Selected    =      1,343
                                                      Nonselected =        657

                                                Wald chi2(2)      =     508.44
Log likelihood = -5178.304                      Prob > chi2       =     0.0000
```

wage	Coefficient	Std. err.	z	P>|z|	[95% conf.	interval]
wage						
education	.9899537	.0532565	18.59	0.000	.8855729	1.094334
age	.2131294	.0206031	10.34	0.000	.1727481	.2535108
_cons	.4857752	1.077037	0.45	0.652	-1.625179	2.59673
select						
married	.4451721	.0673954	6.61	0.000	.3130794	.5772647
children	.4387068	.0277828	15.79	0.000	.3842534	.4931601
education	.0557318	.0107349	5.19	0.000	.0346917	.0767718
age	.0365098	.0041533	8.79	0.000	.0283694	.0446502
_cons	-2.491015	.1893402	-13.16	0.000	-2.862115	-2.119915
/athrho	.8742086	.1014225	8.62	0.000	.6754241	1.072993
/lnsigma	1.792559	.027598	64.95	0.000	1.738468	1.84665
rho	.7035061	.0512264			.5885365	.7905862
sigma	6.004797	.1657202			5.68862	6.338548
lambda	4.224412	.3992265			3.441942	5.006881

LR test of indep. eqns. (rho = 0): chi2(1) = 61.20   Prob > chi2 = 0.0000

图 1.57

```
. estimates store H
. regress wage educ age
```

运行结果如图 1.58 所示。

Source	SS	df	MS			
				Number of obs	=	1,343
				F(2, 1340)	=	227.49
Model	13524.0337	2	6762.01687	Prob > F	=	0.0000
Residual	39830.8609	1,340	29.7245231	R-squared	=	0.2535
				Adj R-squared	=	0.2524
Total	53354.8946	1,342	39.7577456	Root MSE	=	5.452

wage	Coefficient	Std. err.	t	P>|t|	[95% conf.	interval]
education	.8965829	.0498061	18.00	0.000	.7988765	.9942893
age	.1465739	.0187135	7.83	0.000	.109863	.1832848
_cons	6.084875	.8896182	6.84	0.000	4.339679	7.830071

图 1.58

```
. estimates store R
. generate dinc = ! missing(wage)
. probit dinc married children educ age
```

运行结果如图 1.59 所示。

Probit regression　　Number of obs = 2,000

LR chi2(4) = 478.32

Prob > chi2 = 0.0000

Log likelihood = -1027.0616　　Pseudo R2 = 0.1889

dinc	Coefficient	Std. err.	z	P>|z|	[95% conf.	interval]
married	.4308575	.074208	5.81	0.000	.2854125	.5763025
children	.4473249	.0287417	15.56	0.000	.3909922	.5036576
education	.0583645	.0109742	5.32	0.000	.0368555	.0798735
age	.0347211	.0042293	8.21	0.000	.0264318	.0430105
_cons	-2.467365	.1925635	-12.81	0.000	-2.844782	-2.089948

图 1.59

```
. estimates store P
* 似然比检验
. lrtest H (R P), df(1)
```

运行结果如图 1.60 所示。

```
Likelihood-ratio test
Assumption: (R, P) nested within H

 LR chi2(1) =   61.20
Prob > chi2 = 0.0000
```

图 1.60

例 1.9 邹氏似然比检验

邹氏(Chow)似然比检验适用于规定模型的所有系数在数据不相连的子集之间不变化的假设。

```
* 下载数据
.clear
.webuse vote, clear
(voting data example)
.logit vote age moinc dependents
```

运行结果略。

```
.estimates store All
.logit vote age moinc dependents if county==1
```

运行结果略。

```
.estimates store A1
.logit vote age moinc dependents if county==2
```

运行结果略。

```
.estimates store A2
.logit vote age moinc dependents if county==3
```

运行结果略。

```
.estimates store A3
* 邹氏似然比检验
.lrtest (All) (A1 A2 A3), df(7)
```

运行结果如图 1.61 所示。

```
Likelihood-ratio test
Assumption: All nested within (A1, A2, A3)

 LR chi2(7) =   19.16
Prob > chi2 = 0.0077
```

图 1.61

1.4.5 估计后线性假设 Wald 检验

令参数估计值向量为 $\boldsymbol{b}$,估计的方差—协方差矩阵为 $\mathbf{V}$,令 $\boldsymbol{Rb}=\boldsymbol{r}$ 表示 q 个联合检验的 q 个线性假设集合。Wald 检验的检验统计量为:

$$W=(Rb-r)'(\mathrm{RVR}')^{-1}(Rb-r) \tag{1.63}$$

如果估算命令使用 Z 统计数据报告其显著性水平,则为具有 q 自由度的 χ^2 分布:$W\sim\chi^2_q$。如果估算命令使用具有 d 自由度的 t 统计量报告其显著性水平,则统计量 $F=\frac{1}{q}W\sim F(q,d)$。

估计后线性假设 Wald 检验的语法格式为:

(1) 基本语法

① 检验参数等于 0:

```
test coeflist
```

② 检验线性表达式相等:

```
test exp = exp [= ...]
```

③ 检验方程中的参数等于 0:

```
test [eqno] [: coeflist]
```

④ 检验方程之间的参数相等:

```
test [eqno = eqno [= ...]] [: coeflist]
testparm varlist [, testparm_options]
```

(2) 完全语法

```
test (spec) [(spec) ...] [, test_options]
```

其中,testparm_options 选项及含义为:

(1) equal:假设系数彼此相等;

(2) equation(eqno):指定用于检验假设的公式名称或编号;

(3) nosvyadjust:计算调查结果的未调整 Wald 测试;

(4) df(#):使用分母自由度为#的 F 分布作为检验统计量的参考分布,对于测量数据,#指定设计自由度,除非指定了 nosvyadjust。

test_options 选项及含义为:

(1) mtest[(opt)]:分别测试每个条件;

(2) coef:报告估计的约束系数;

(3) accumulate:将测试假设与先前测试的假设联合检验;

(4) notest:抑制输出;

(5) common:检验所有方程式通用的变量;

(6) constant:包括待测系数中的常数;

(7) nosvyadjust:含义同前述 nosvyadjust 选项。

(8) minimum:使用常数进行测试,下降项直到测试变得非奇异,剩余项不使用常数进行测试;

(9) matvlc(matname):保存方差—协方差矩阵,为程序员选项;

(10) df(#):含义同前述 df(#)选项。

test 命令对最近拟合模型的参数进行简单和复合线性假设的 Wald 检验。

例 1.10 单方程估计后线性假设 Wald 检验

```
* 下载数据
.clear
.webuse census3
(1980 Census data by state)
.regress brate medage medagesq i.region
```

运行结果略。

```
* 检验 3.region 的系数为 0
.test 3.region = 0
```

运行结果如图 1.62 所示。

```
( 1)  3.region = 0

      F(  1,    44) =    3.47
           Prob > F =    0.0691
```

图 1.62

```
* 上一个测试命令的简写
.test 3.region
```

运行结果略。

```
* 检验 2.region 的系数=4.region 的系数
.test 2.region = 4.region
```

运行结果如图 1.63 所示。

```
( 1)  2.region - 4.region = 0

      F(  1,    44) =    2.84
           Prob > F =    0.0989
```

图 1.63

```
* 将完成代数运算,然后进行测试
.test 2 * (2.region - 3 * (3.region - 4.region)) = 3.region + 2.region + 6 *
(4.region - 3.region)
```

运行结果如图 1.64 所示。

```
( 1)  2.region - 3.region = 0

      F(  1,    44) =    5.06
          Prob > F =    0.0295
```

图 1.64

＊测试 2.region 的系数和 3.region 的系数共同等于 0

.test (2.region = 0) (3.region = 0)

运行结果如图 1.65 所示。

```
( 1)  2.region = 0
( 2)  3.region = 0

      F(  2,    44) =    6.42
          Prob > F =    0.0036
```

图 1.65

＊以下两个命令等效于前一个测试命令

.test 2.region = 0

运行结果略。

.test 3.region = 0, accumulate

运行结果略。

＊测试 2. region、3. region 和 4. region 的系数均为 0;testparm 可理解 varlist

.testparm i(2/4).region

运行结果如图 1.66 所示。

```
( 1)  2.region = 0
( 2)  3.region = 0
( 3)  4.region = 0

      F(  3,    44) =    8.85
          Prob > F =    0.0001
```

图 1.66

在上面的示例中,可以用任何单个公式估计命令(如 clogit、logistic、logit 和 logit)替换回归。

例 1.11　多方程估计后线性假设 Wald 检验

＊下载数据

.clear

.sysuse auto

(1978 automobile data)

```
.sureg (price foreign mpg displ) (weight foreign length)
```

运行结果如图 1.67 所示。

Seemingly unrelated regression

Equation	Obs	Params	RMSE	"R-squared"	chi2	P>chi2
price	74	3	2165.321	0.4537	49.64	0.0000
weight	74	2	245.2916	0.8990	661.84	0.0000

	Coefficient	Std. err.	z	P>|z|	[95% conf.	interval]
price						
foreign	3058.25	685.7357	4.46	0.000	1714.233	4402.267
mpg	-104.9591	58.47209	-1.80	0.073	-219.5623	9.644042
displacement	18.18098	4.286372	4.24	0.000	9.779842	26.58211
_cons	3904.336	1966.521	1.99	0.047	50.0263	7758.645
weight						
foreign	-147.3481	75.44314	-1.95	0.051	-295.2139	.517755
length	30.94905	1.539895	20.10	0.000	27.93091	33.96718
_cons	-2753.064	303.9336	-9.06	0.000	-3348.763	-2157.365

图 1.67

```
*检验 foreign 在价格方程中的显著性
.test [price]foreign
```

运行结果如图 1.68 所示。

```
( 1)  [price]foreign = 0

           chi2(  1) =   19.89
         Prob > chi2 =    0.0000
```

图 1.68

```
*测试两个方程式中的"foreign"联合为 0
.test [price]foreign [weight]foreign
```

运行结果如图 1.69 所示。

```
( 1)  [price]foreign = 0
( 2)  [weight]foreign = 0

           chi2(  2) =   31.61
         Prob > chi2 =    0.0000
```

图 1.69

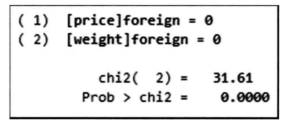

1.4.6 估计后非线性假设 Wald 检验

令参数估计值的 $1\times k$ 维向量为 $\boldsymbol{b}$，估计的 $k\times k$ 维方差—协方差矩阵为 $\mathbf{V}$，令 $\boldsymbol{R}(\boldsymbol{b})=\boldsymbol{q}$ 表示 $\boldsymbol{q}$ 个联合检验的 $\boldsymbol{q}$ 个线性或非线性的假设集合，$\boldsymbol{R}$ 为 $j\times 1$ 维的函数矩阵。Wald 检验的检验统计量为：

$$W=\{\boldsymbol{R}(\boldsymbol{b})-\boldsymbol{q}\}'(\mathbf{GVG}')^{-1}\{\boldsymbol{R}(\boldsymbol{b})-\boldsymbol{q}\} \tag{1.64}$$

式中，$\boldsymbol{G}$ 是 $\boldsymbol{R}(\boldsymbol{b})$ 相对于 $\boldsymbol{b}$ 的导数矩阵。如果 $\mathbf{V}$ 是渐近协方差矩阵，则 W 分布为 χ^2 分布。对于线性回归，$F=W/j$ 分布为 F 分布。

估计后非线性假设 Wald 检验的语法格式为：

testnl exp = exp [= exp ...] [, options]

testnl (exp = exp [= exp...]) [(exp = exp [= exp ...]) ...] [, options]

各选项含义同 test 选项。

testnl 检验(线性或非线性)关于最近拟合模型估计参数的假设。testnl 对最近拟合模型的估计参数进行平滑非线性(或线性)假设的 Wald 检验。p 值基于 delta 方法，这是一种适用于大样本的近似值。

例 1.12 估计后非线性假设 Wald 检验

```
* 下载数据
.clear
.sysuse auto
(1978 automobile data)
.generate weightsq = weight^2
.regress price mpg trunk length weight weightsq foreign
```

运行结果如图 1.70 所示。

Source	SS	df	MS
Model	375474688	6	62579114.7
Residual	259590708	67	3874488.18
Total	635065396	73	8699525.97

Number of obs	=	74
F(6, 67)	=	16.15
Prob > F	=	0.0000
R-squared	=	0.5912
Adj R-squared	=	0.5546
Root MSE	=	1968.4

price	Coefficient	Std. err.	t	P>|t|	[95% conf.	interval]
mpg	-64.62704	72.34631	-0.89	0.375	-209.0309	79.7768
trunk	-53.39166	80.54524	-0.66	0.510	-214.1606	107.3773
length	-67.08006	36.144	-1.86	0.068	-139.2238	5.063663
weight	-1.802345	3.025814	-0.60	0.553	-7.841894	4.237204
weightsq	.0010688	.0004072	2.62	0.011	.0002561	.0018815
foreign	3141.576	654.8604	4.80	0.000	1834.469	4448.683
_cons	15009.77	6378.199	2.35	0.022	2278.831	27740.71

图 1.70

```
* 检验一个非线性约束
.testnl _b[mpg] = 1/_b[weight]
```

运行结果如图 1.71 所示。

```
(1)  _b[mpg] = 1/_b[weight]

           chi2(1) =        0.78
       Prob > chi2 =        0.3780
```

图 1.71

```
* 测试多个非线性约束
.testnl (_b[mpg] = 1/_b[weight]) (_b[trunk] = 1/_b[length])
```

运行结果如图 1.72 所示。

```
(1)  _b[mpg] = 1/_b[weight]
(2)  _b[trunk] = 1/_b[length]

           chi2(2) =        1.14
       Prob > chi2 =        0.5651
```

图 1.72

```
* 分别测试多个非线性约束,并使用 Holm 方法调整 p 值
.testnl (_b[mpg] = 1/_b[weight]) (_b[trunk] = 1/_b[length]), mtest(holm)
```

运行结果如图 1.73 所示。

```
(1)  _b[mpg] = 1/_b[weight]
(2)  _b[trunk] = 1/_b[length]

        |      chi2     df    p > chi2
--------+------------------------------
  (1)   |      0.78      1     0.7560*
  (2)   |      0.44      1     0.5075*
--------+------------------------------
  All   |      1.14      2     0.5651

Holm-adjusted p-values
```

图 1.73

1.5 回归图形分析

1.5.1 添加变量图

1. 添加变量图

avplot 在回归之后，绘制了一个添加变量图(又称部分回归杠杆图、部分回归图或调整的部分残差图)。indepvar 可以是一个独立的变量(又称预测者、载体或协变量),该变量目前或许在模型中。

avplot 的语法格式为:

avplot indepvar [, avplot_options]

菜单操作路径为:

Statistics>Linear models and related>Regression diagnostics>Added-variable plot

2. 在一个图像中添加所有变量图

avplots 将所有添加变量的图绘制在一张图片上。

avplots 的语法格式为:

avplots [, avplots_options]

菜单操作路径为:

Statistics>Linear models and related>Regression diagnostics>Added-variable plot

例 1.13 绘制添加变量图

```
* 加载数据 auto.dta 并回归
. sysuse auto
. regress price weight foreign##c.mpg
```

运行结果如图 1.74 所示。

Source	SS	df	MS			
				Number of obs	=	74
				F(4, 69)	=	21.22
Model	350319665	4	87579916.3	Prob > F	=	0.0000
Residual	284745731	69	4126749.72	R-squared	=	0.5516
				Adj R-squared	=	0.5256
Total	635065396	73	8699525.97	Root MSE	=	2031.4

price	Coefficient	Std. err.	t	P>|t|	[95% conf.	interval]
weight	4.613589	.7254961	6.36	0.000	3.166263	6.060914
foreign						
Foreign	11240.33	2751.681	4.08	0.000	5750.878	16729.78
mpg	263.1875	110.7961	2.38	0.020	42.15527	484.2197
foreign#c.mpg						
Foreign	-307.2166	108.5307	-2.83	0.006	-523.7294	-90.70368
_cons	-14449.58	4425.72	-3.26	0.002	-23278.65	-5620.51

图 1.74

* 添加变量图

```
.avplot mpg
```

运行结果如图 1.75 所示。

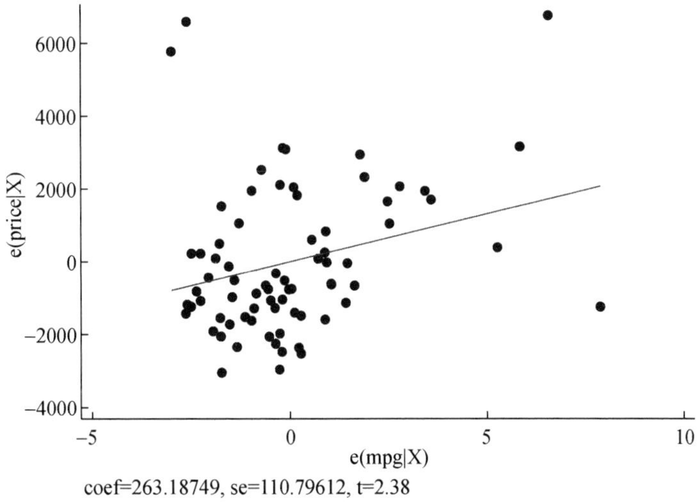

图 1.75

* 将所有添加变量的图绘制在一张图片上

```
.avplots
```

运行结果如图 1.76 所示。

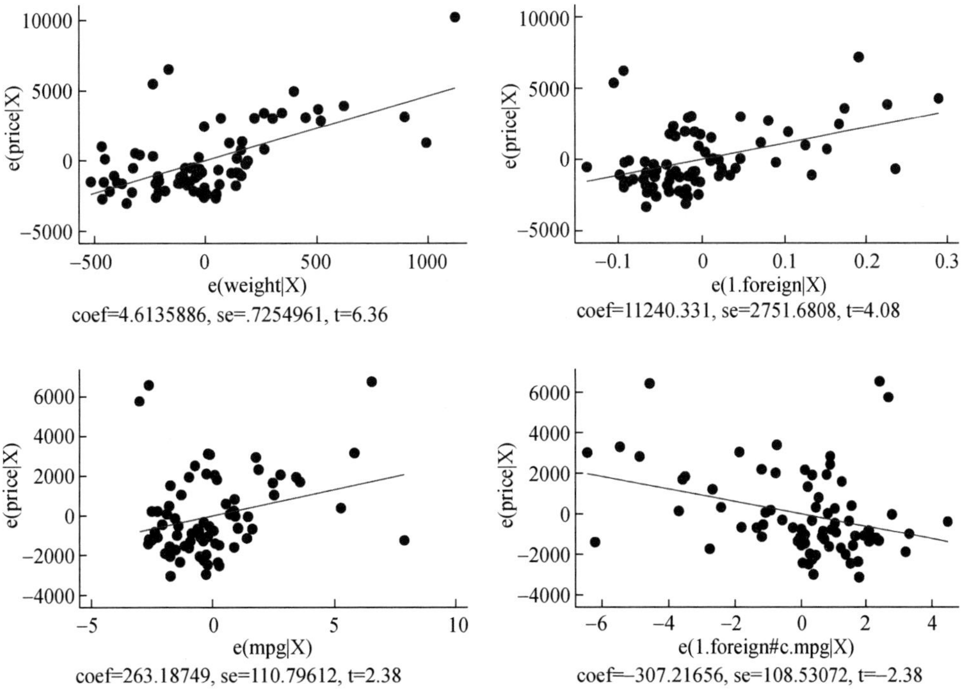

图 1.76

1.5.2 分量和残差图

cprplot 在回归后绘制分量和残差图(又称部分残差图)。indepvar 必须是当前模型中的一个自变量。

cprplot 的语法格式为:

cprplot indepvar [, cprplot_options]

菜单操作路径为:

Statistics > Linear models and related > Regression diagnostics > Component - plus - residual plot

例 1.14 绘制分量和残差图

* 加载数据 auto1.dta 并回归

```
.webuse auto1
.regress price mpg weight
```

运行结果如图 1.77 所示。

Source	SS	df	MS		
				Number of obs =	74
				F(2, 71) =	14.90
Model	187716578	2	93858289	Prob > F =	0.0000
Residual	447348818	71	6300687.58	R-squared =	0.2956
				Adj R-squared =	0.2757
Total	635065396	73	8699525.97	Root MSE =	2510.1

price	Coefficient	Std. err.	t	P>|t|	[95% conf.	interval]
mpg	-55.9393	75.24136	-0.74	0.460	-205.9663	94.08771
weight	1.710992	.5861682	2.92	0.005	.5422063	2.879779
_cons	2197.9	3190.768	0.69	0.493	-4164.311	8560.11

图 1.77

* 绘制分量和残差图

```
.cprplot mpg, mspline msopts(bands(13))
```

运行结果如图 1.78 所示。

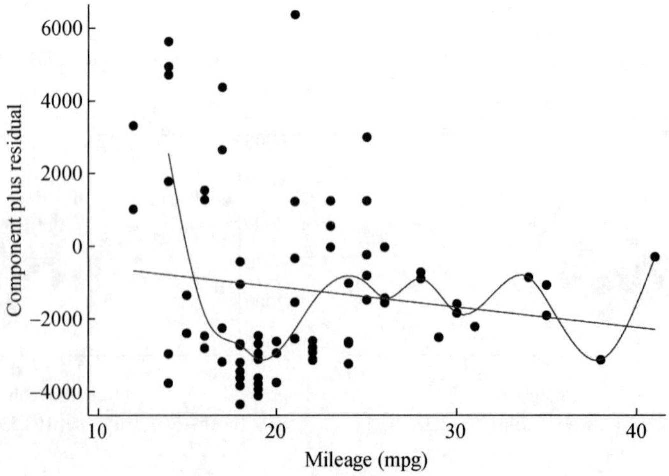

图 1.78

1.5.3 残差拟合图

rvfplot 绘制了一个残差拟合图，即残差与拟合值的对比图。

rvfplot 的语法格式为：

rvfplot [, rvfplot_options]

菜单操作路径为：

Statistics>Linear models and related>Regression diagnostics>Residual-versus-fitted plot

例 1.15 绘制残差拟合图

```
* 加载数据并回归
. sysuse auto
. regress price weight foreign##c.mpg
```

运行结果如图 1.79 所示。

Source	SS	df	MS
Model	350319665	4	87579916.3
Residual	284745731	69	4126749.72
Total	635065396	73	8699525.97

Number of obs	=	74
F(4, 69)	=	21.22
Prob > F	=	0.0000
R-squared	=	0.5516
Adj R-squared	=	0.5256
Root MSE	=	2031.4

price	Coefficient	Std. err.	t	P>|t|	[95% conf.	interval]
weight	4.613589	.7254961	6.36	0.000	3.166263	6.060914
foreign						
Foreign	11240.33	2751.681	4.08	0.000	5750.878	16729.78
mpg	263.1875	110.7961	2.38	0.020	42.15527	484.2197
foreign#c.mpg						
Foreign	-307.2166	108.5307	-2.83	0.006	-523.7294	-90.70368
_cons	-14449.58	4425.72	-3.26	0.002	-23278.65	-5620.51

图 1.79

```
* 绘制残差拟合图
. rvfplot, yline(10)
```

运行结果如图 1.80 所示。

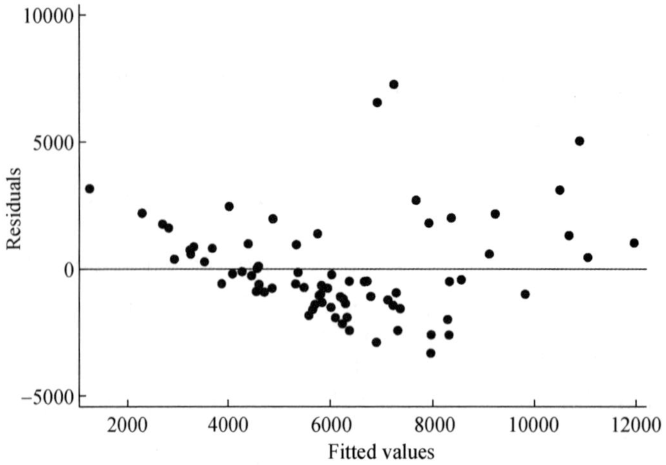

图 1.80

1.5.4 残差及预测值图

rvpplot 绘制残差与预测值的关系图(又称独立变量图或载体图)。

rvpplot 的语法格式为:

rvpplot indepvar [, rvpplot_options]

菜单操作路径为:

Statistics>Linear models and related>Regression diagnostics>Residual-versus-predictor plot

例 1.16 残差及预测值图

* 加载数据并回归

. webuse auto1

. regress price mpg weight

运行结果如图 1.81 所示。

Source	SS	df	MS		Number of obs	=	74
					F(2, 71)	=	14.90
Model	187716578	2	93858289		Prob > F	=	0.0000
Residual	447348818	71	6300687.58		R-squared	=	0.2956
					Adj R-squared	=	0.2757
Total	635065396	73	8699525.97		Root MSE	=	2510.1

price	Coefficient	Std. err.	t	P>|t|	[95% conf.	interval]
mpg	-55.9393	75.24136	-0.74	0.460	-205.9663	94.08771
weight	1.710992	.5861682	2.92	0.005	.5422063	2.879779
_cons	2197.9	3190.768	0.69	0.493	-4164.311	8560.11

图 1.81

```
* 绘制残差及预测值图
.rvpplot mpg, yline(0)
```

运行结果如图 1.82 所示。

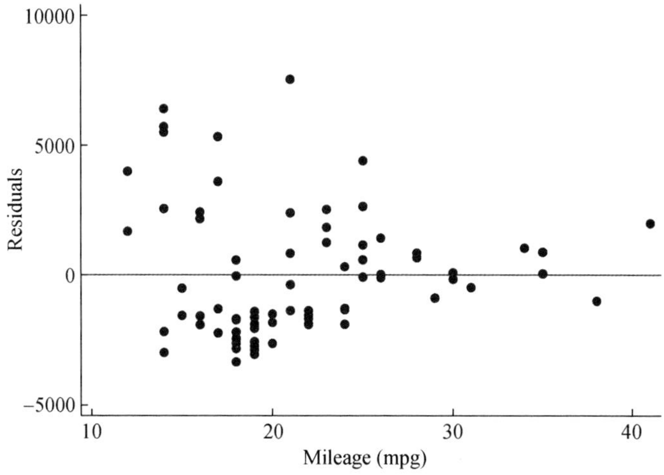

图 1.82

1.6 模型预测分析

所谓预测，是指在对各个解释变量给定样本以外数值 $\boldsymbol{X}_f=(1,X_{1f},X_{2f},\cdots,X_{kf})$ 的条件下，对预测期被解释变量 $\boldsymbol{Y}$ 的平均值 $E(\boldsymbol{Y}_f)$ 及个别值 Y_f 进行估计，所进行的估计分为点估计和区间估计，从而预测有点预测和区间预测两种。

1.6.1 点预测

点预测就是根据给定解释变量的值，预测相应的被解释变量的一个可能值。设多元线性回归模型为：

$$\boldsymbol{Y}=\boldsymbol{X\beta}+\boldsymbol{U} \tag{1.65}$$

若根据观测样本已经估计出参数 $\boldsymbol{\beta}$，得到样本回归方程且模型通过检验，即

$$\hat{\boldsymbol{Y}}=\boldsymbol{X}\hat{\boldsymbol{\beta}} \tag{1.66}$$

把样本以外各个解释变量的值表示为行向量 $\boldsymbol{X}_f=(1,X_{1f},X_{2f},\cdots,X_{kf})$，直接代入所估计的多元样本回归函数，就可以计算出被解释变量的点预测值 $\hat{\boldsymbol{Y}}_f$。

$$\hat{\boldsymbol{Y}}_f=\boldsymbol{X}_f\hat{\boldsymbol{\beta}}=\hat{\beta}_0+\hat{\beta}_1X_{1f}+\hat{\beta}_2X_{2f}+\cdots+\hat{\beta}_kX_{kf} \tag{1.67}$$

对式(1.65)两边取期望，得

$$\begin{aligned}E(\hat{\boldsymbol{Y}}_f)&=E(\hat{\beta}_0+\hat{\beta}_1X_{1f}+\hat{\beta}_2X_{2f}+\cdots+\hat{\beta}_kX_{kf})\\&=\beta_0+\beta_1X_{1f}+\beta_2X_{2f}+\ldots+\beta_kX_{kf}=E(\boldsymbol{Y}_f)\end{aligned} \tag{1.68}$$

这说明 $\hat{\boldsymbol{Y}}_f$ 是 $E(\boldsymbol{Y}_f)$ 的无偏估计量，从而可以用 $\hat{\boldsymbol{Y}}_f$ 作为 $E(\boldsymbol{Y}_f)$ 和 $\boldsymbol{Y}_f$ 的点预测值。

1.6.2 平均值 $E(\boldsymbol{Y}_f)$ 的区间预测

为了对预测期平均值 $E(\boldsymbol{Y}_f)$ 作区间预测，必须明确得到点预测值 $\hat{\boldsymbol{Y}}_f$ 与预测期平均值 $E(\boldsymbol{Y}_f)$ 的关系，并分析其概率分布性质。如果记 $\hat{\boldsymbol{Y}}_f$ 和 $E(\boldsymbol{Y}_f)$ 的偏差为 $\boldsymbol{w}_f$，即

$$\boldsymbol{w}_f = \hat{\boldsymbol{Y}}_f - E(\boldsymbol{Y}_f) \tag{1.69}$$

因为 $\hat{\boldsymbol{Y}}_f$ 服从正态分布，$\boldsymbol{w}_f$ 也服从正态分布，而且

$$E(\boldsymbol{w}_f) = E[\hat{\boldsymbol{Y}}_f - E(\boldsymbol{Y}_f)] = E(\hat{\boldsymbol{Y}}_f) - E(\boldsymbol{Y}_f) = \boldsymbol{0} \tag{1.70}$$

可以证明，$\boldsymbol{w}_f$ 的方差为 $\sigma^2 X_f(\boldsymbol{X}'\boldsymbol{X})^{-1}\boldsymbol{X}'_f$，即

$$\boldsymbol{w}_f \sim N[0, \sigma^2 \boldsymbol{X}_f(\boldsymbol{X}'\boldsymbol{X})^{-1}\boldsymbol{X}'_f] \tag{1.71}$$

若用 $\hat{\sigma}^2$ 代替未知的 σ^2，构造如下统计量：

$$t = \frac{\hat{\boldsymbol{w}}_f - E(\boldsymbol{w}_f)}{SE(\hat{\boldsymbol{w}}_f)} = \frac{\hat{Y} - E(\boldsymbol{Y}_f)}{\hat{\sigma}\sqrt{\boldsymbol{X}_f(\boldsymbol{X}'\boldsymbol{X})^{-1}\boldsymbol{X}'_f}} \tag{1.72}$$

该统计量 t 服从自由度为 $n-k$ 的 t 分布。

给定显著性水平 α，查自由度为 $n-k$ 的 t 分布表，可得临界值 $t_{\alpha/2}(n-k)$，则 $\boldsymbol{Y}_f$ 的平均值 $E(\boldsymbol{Y}_f)$ 的置信度为 $1-\alpha$ 的预测区间为：

$$\hat{\boldsymbol{Y}}_f - t_{\alpha/2}\hat{\sigma}\sqrt{\boldsymbol{X}_f(\boldsymbol{X}'\boldsymbol{X})^{-1}\boldsymbol{X}'_f} \leqslant E(\boldsymbol{Y}_f) \leqslant \hat{\boldsymbol{Y}}_f + t_{\alpha/2}\hat{\sigma}\sqrt{\boldsymbol{X}_f(\boldsymbol{X}'\boldsymbol{X})^{-1}\boldsymbol{X}'_f} \tag{1.73}$$

1.6.3 个别值 $\boldsymbol{Y}_f$ 的区间预测

要对预期个别值 $\boldsymbol{Y}_f$ 作区间预测，除了已经得到的点预测值 $\hat{\boldsymbol{Y}}_f$ 以外，还要分析 $\hat{\boldsymbol{Y}}_f$ 和 $\boldsymbol{Y}_f$ 的联系，并明确其概率分布性质。显然，与 $\hat{\boldsymbol{Y}}_f$ 和 $\boldsymbol{Y}_f$ 有关的是残差 $\boldsymbol{e}_f$。

$$\boldsymbol{e}_f = \boldsymbol{Y}_f - \hat{\boldsymbol{Y}}_f \tag{1.74}$$

因为 $\boldsymbol{Y}_f$ 与 $\hat{\boldsymbol{Y}}_f$ 均服从正态分布，$\boldsymbol{e}_f$ 也服从正态分布，而且

$$\begin{aligned} E(\boldsymbol{e}_f) &= E(\boldsymbol{Y}_f - \hat{\boldsymbol{Y}}_f) = E(\boldsymbol{X}_f\boldsymbol{\beta} + \boldsymbol{u}_f + \boldsymbol{X}_f\hat{\boldsymbol{\beta}}) \\ &= \boldsymbol{X}_f E(\boldsymbol{\beta}) + E(\boldsymbol{u}_f) + \boldsymbol{X}_f E(\hat{\boldsymbol{\beta}}) = \boldsymbol{0} \end{aligned} \tag{1.75}$$

还可以证明，$\boldsymbol{e}_f$ 的方差为 $\sigma^2[1+\boldsymbol{X}_f(\boldsymbol{X}'\boldsymbol{X})^{-1}\boldsymbol{X}'_f]$，即

$$e_f \sim N\{0, \sigma^2[1 + \boldsymbol{X}_f(\boldsymbol{X}'\boldsymbol{X})^{-1}\boldsymbol{X}'_f]\} \tag{1.76}$$

若用 $\hat{\sigma}^2$ 代替未知的 σ^2，构造如下统计量：

$$t = \frac{e_f - E(e_f)}{SE(e_f)} = \frac{\boldsymbol{Y}_f - \hat{\boldsymbol{Y}}_f}{\hat{\sigma}\sqrt{1 + \boldsymbol{X}_f(\boldsymbol{X}'\boldsymbol{X})^{-1}\boldsymbol{X}'_f}} \tag{1.77}$$

则该统计量 t 服从自由度为 $n-k$ 的 t 分布。

给定显著性水平 α，查自由度为 $n-k$ 的 t 分布表，可得临界值 $t_{\alpha/2}(n-k)$。则 $\boldsymbol{Y}_f$ 的置信度为 $1-\alpha$ 的预测区间为：

$$\hat{Y}_f - t_{\alpha/2}\hat{\sigma}\sqrt{\boldsymbol{X}_f(\boldsymbol{X}'\boldsymbol{X})^{-1}\boldsymbol{X}'_f} \leqslant \boldsymbol{Y}_f \leqslant \hat{\boldsymbol{Y}}_f + t_{\alpha/2}\hat{\sigma}\sqrt{\boldsymbol{X}_f(\boldsymbol{X}'\boldsymbol{X})^{-1}\boldsymbol{X}'_f} \tag{1.78}$$

1.6.4 预测效果评价分析

定义投影矩阵(projection matrix)的对角线元素为 $h_j = \boldsymbol{x}_j(\boldsymbol{X}'\boldsymbol{X})^{-1}\boldsymbol{x}'_j$，则预测标

准差为：

$$s_{p_j}=\sqrt{\boldsymbol{x}_j\mathbf{V}\boldsymbol{x}_j'}=s\sqrt{h_j} \tag{1.79}$$

预测均方根误差为：

$$s_{f_j}=s\sqrt{1+h_j} \tag{1.80}$$

定义残差为 $\hat{e}_j=y_j-\hat{y}_j$；残差的标准差为 $s_{r_j}=s\sqrt{1-h_j}$；标准化残差为 $\hat{e}_{s_j}=\hat{e}_j/s_{r_j}$；学生化残差(rstudent)为 $r_j=\dfrac{\hat{e}_j}{s_{(j)}\sqrt{1-h_j}}$；删除第 j 个观测值后的均方根误差为 $s_{(j)}^2=\dfrac{s^2(n-k)}{n-k-1}-\dfrac{\hat{e}_j^2}{(n-k-1)(1-h_j)}$。则有以下公式：

库克距离(cooksd)为：

$$D_j=\frac{\hat{e}_{s_j}^2(s_{p_j}/s_{r_j})^2}{k}=\frac{h_j\hat{e}_j^2}{ks^2(1-h_j)^2} \tag{1.81}$$

DFITS(dfits)为：

$$\mathrm{DFITS}_j=r_j\sqrt{\frac{h_j}{1-h_j}} \tag{1.82}$$

Welsch 距离(welsch)为：

$$W_j=\frac{r_j\sqrt{h_j(n-1)}}{1-h_j} \tag{1.83}$$

COVRATIO (covratio)为：

$$\mathrm{COVRATIO}_j=\frac{1}{1-h_j}\left(\frac{n-k-\hat{e}_{s_j}^2}{n-k-1}\right)^k \tag{1.84}$$

参数成分分析(DFBETAs)度量的是变量的最直接影响。DFBETAs 关注一个系数，并在包含和排除第 i 个观测值时，测量回归系数之间的差异，该差异即为系数的估计标准差规范化，即观测值至少改变了一个标准误差。对于模型(1.1)，回归变量 x_i 的参数成分分析计算公式为：

$$\mathrm{DFBETA}_j=\frac{r_ju_j}{\sqrt{U^2(1-h_j)}} \tag{1.85}$$

式中，u_j 是从 $\boldsymbol{x}_i$ 关于剩余 $\boldsymbol{x}$ 回归中得到的残差；$U^2=\sum_j u_j^2$。

1.6.5 线性模型预测分析的实现

模型预测分析实现的 predict 命令语法格式为：

```
predict [type] newvar [if] [in] [, statistic]
```

其中，statistic 的选项及含义为：

(1) xb：线性预测，为默认值；

(2) residuals：残差；

(3) score：得分，相当于残差；

(4) rstandard：标准化残差；

(5) rstudent:学生化(jackknifed)残差;

(6) cooksd:库克距离;

(7) leverage | hat:杠杆|帽子杠杆(帽子矩阵的对角线元素);

(8) pr(a,b):pr(y | a<y<b);

(9) e(a,b):e(y | a<y<b);

(10) ystar(a,b): E(y*),y*=max(a,min(y,b));

(11) *dfbeta(varname):varname 的 dfbeta;

(12) stdp:线性预测的 stdp 标准误差;

(13) stdf:预测的标准误差;

(14) stdr:残差的标准误差;

(15) *covratio: covratio;

(16) *dfits: DFITS;

(17) *welsch:Welsch 距离。

菜单操作路径为:

```
Statistics>Postestimation
```

predict 命令创建一个新变量,其中包含预测,如线性预测、残差、标准化残差、学生化残差、库克距离、杠杆、概率、期望值、varname 的 DFBETAs、标准误差、COVRATIO、DFITS 和 Welsch 距离。

例 1.17 模型预测分析

```
* 下载数据
.clear
.sysuse auto
(1978 automobile data)
.regress mpg weight foreign
```

运行结果如图 1.83 所示。

Source	SS	df	MS		
				Number of obs =	74
				F(2, 71) =	69.75
Model	1619.2877	2	809.643849	Prob > F =	0.0000
Residual	824.171761	71	11.608053	R-squared =	0.6627
				Adj R-squared =	0.6532
Total	2443.45946	73	33.4720474	Root MSE =	3.4071

mpg	Coefficient	Std. err.	t	P>|t|	[95% conf.	interval]
weight	-.0065879	.0006371	-10.34	0.000	-.0078583	-.0053175
foreign	-1.650029	1.075994	-1.53	0.130	-3.7955	.4954422
_cons	41.6797	2.165547	19.25	0.000	37.36172	45.99768

图 1.83

```
* 获取预测值
```

```
.predict pmpg
(option xb assumed; fitted values)
.summarize pmpg mpg
```

运行结果如图 1.84 所示。

Variable	Obs	Mean	Std. dev.	Min	Max
pmpg	74	21.2973	4.709779	9.794333	29.82151
mpg	74	21.2973	5.785503	12	41

图 1.84

```
*样本外预测
*下载数据
.clear
.webuse newautos, clear
(New automobile models)
*获得样本外预测
.predict mpg
(option xb assumed; fitted values)
.list, divider
```

运行结果如图 1.85 所示。

	make	weight	foreign	mpg
1.	Pont. Sunbird	2690	Domestic	23.95829
2.	Volvo 260	3170	Foreign	19.14607

图 1.85

```
*数据加权预测
.use https://www.stata-press.com/data/r17/auto, clear
(1978 automobile data)
.regress mpg weight foreign
```

运行结果如图 1.86 所示。

Source	SS	df	MS			
				Number of obs	=	74
				F(2, 71)	=	69.75
Model	1619.2877	2	809.643849	Prob > F	=	0.0000
Residual	824.171761	71	11.608053	R-squared	=	0.6627
				Adj R-squared	=	0.6532
Total	2443.45946	73	33.4720474	Root MSE	=	3.4071

mpg	Coefficient	Std. err.	t	P>|t|	[95% conf.	interval]
weight	-.0065879	.0006371	-10.34	0.000	-.0078583	-.0053175
foreign	-1.650029	1.075994	-1.53	0.130	-3.7955	.4954422
_cons	41.6797	2.165547	19.25	0.000	37.36172	45.99768

图 1.86

.predict xdist, hat

.summarize xdist, detail

运行结果如图 1.87 所示。

Leverage

	Percentiles	Smallest		
1%	.0192325	.0192325		
5%	.0192686	.0192366		
10%	.0193448	.019241	Obs	74
25%	.0220291	.0192686	Sum of wgt.	74
50%	.0383797		Mean	.0405405
		Largest	Std. dev.	.0207624
75%	.0494002	.0880814		
90%	.0693432	.099715	Variance	.0004311
95%	.0880814	.099715	Skewness	1.159745
99%	.1003283	.1003283	Kurtosis	4.083313

图 1.87

.list foreign make mpg if xdist>.08, divider

* 标准化和学生化残差

运行结果如图 1.88 所示。

* 下载数据

.clear

.sysuse auto, clear

(1978 automobile data)

.regress price weight foreign##c.mpg

运行结果如图 1.89 所示。

	foreign	make	mpg
24.	Domestic	Ford Fiesta	28
26.	Domestic	Linc. Continental	12
27.	Domestic	Linc. Mark V	12
43.	Domestic	Plym. Champ	34
64.	Foreign	Peugeot 604	14

图 1.88

Source	SS	df	MS			
				Number of obs	=	74
				F(4, 69)	=	21.22
Model	350319665	4	87579916.3	Prob > F	=	0.0000
Residual	284745731	69	4126749.72	R-squared	=	0.5516
				Adj R-squared	=	0.5256
Total	635065396	73	8699525.97	Root MSE	=	2031.4

price	Coefficient	Std. err.	t	P>|t|	[95% conf.	interval]
weight	4.613589	.7254961	6.36	0.000	3.166263	6.060914
foreign						
Foreign	11240.33	2751.681	4.08	0.000	5750.878	16729.78
mpg	263.1875	110.7961	2.38	0.020	42.15527	484.2197
foreign#c.mpg						
Foreign	-307.2166	108.5307	-2.83	0.006	-523.7294	-90.70368
_cons	-14449.58	4425.72	-3.26	0.002	-23278.65	-5620.51

图 1.89

```
* 杠杆与残差平方图
.lvr2plot
* 标准化残差
.predict esta if e(sample), rstandard
* 学生化残差
.predict estu if e(sample), rstudent
.list make price esta estu if make = = "VW Diesel"
```

运行结果如图 1.90 所示。

```
.DFITS influence measure
* 下载数据
.clear
```

	make	price	esta	estu
71.	VW Diesel	5,397	.6142691	.6114758

图 1.90

```
.sysuse auto, clear
(1978 automobile data)
.regress price weight foreign##c.mpg
```

运行结果略。

```
* DFITS 影响度量
.predict dfits, dfits
.list make price dfits if abs(dfits)>2*sqrt(5/74), divider
```

运行结果如图 1.91 所示。

	make	price	dfits
12.	Cad. Eldorado	14,500	.9564455
13.	Cad. Seville	15,906	1.356619
24.	Ford Fiesta	4,389	.5724172
27.	Linc. Mark V	13,594	.5200413
28.	Linc. Versailles	13,466	.8760136
42.	Plym. Arrow	4,647	-.9384231

图 1.91

```
* 库克距离
.predict cooksd if e(sample), cooksd
.list make price cooksd if cooksd>4/74, divider
```

运行结果如图 1.92 所示。

	make	price	cooksd
12.	Cad. Eldorado	14,500	.1492676
13.	Cad. Seville	15,906	.3328515
24.	Ford Fiesta	4,389	.0638815
28.	Linc. Versailles	13,466	.1308004
42.	Plym. Arrow	4,647	.1700736

图 1.92

```
* 威尔士距离
. predict wd, welsch
. list make price wd if abs(wd)>3 * sqrt(5), divider
```

运行结果如图 1.93 所示。

	make	price	wd
12.	Cad. Eldorado	14,500	8.394372
13.	Cad. Seville	15,906	12.81125
28.	Linc. Versailles	13,466	7.703005
42.	Plym. Arrow	4,647	-8.981481

图 1.93

```
* COVRATIO 影响度量
. predict covr, covratio
. list make price covr if abs(covr - 1) >= 3 * 5/74, divider
```

运行结果如图 1.94 所示。

	make	price	covr
12.	Cad. Eldorado	14,500	.3814242
13.	Cad. Seville	15,906	.7386969
28.	Linc. Versailles	13,466	.4761695
43.	Plym. Champ	4,425	1.27782
53.	Audi 5000	9,690	1.206842
57.	Datsun 210	4,589	1.284801
64.	Peugeot 604	12,990	1.348219
66.	Subaru	3,798	1.264677
71.	VW Diesel	5,397	1.630653
74.	Volvo 260	11,995	1.211888

图 1.94

```
* DFBETAs 影响度量
. sort foreign make
. predict dfor, dfbeta(1.foreign)
. list make price foreign dfor if abs(dfor)>2/sqrt(74), divider
```

运行结果如图 1.95 所示。

	make	price	foreign	dfor
12.	Cad. Eldorado	14,500	Domestic	-.5290519
13.	Cad. Seville	15,906	Domestic	.8243419
28.	Linc. Versailles	13,466	Domestic	-.5283729
42.	Plym. Arrow	4,647	Domestic	-.6622424
43.	Plym. Champ	4,425	Domestic	.2371104
64.	Peugeot 604	12,990	Foreign	.2552032
69.	Toyota Corona	5,719	Foreign	-.256431

图 1.95

```
* 回归中所有变量的 DFBETAs
.dfbeta
Generating DFBETA variables ...
    _dfbeta_1: DFBETA weight
    _dfbeta_2: DFBETA 1.foreign
    _dfbeta_3: DFBETA mpg
    _dfbeta_4: DFBETA 1.foreign#c.mpg
.dfbeta mpg weight
Generating DFBETA variables...

    _dfbeta_5: DFBETA weight
    _dfbeta_6: DFBETA mpg
```

1.6.6 一般预测分析

估计后获得非线性预测、标准误差等的命令语法格式为：

predictnl [type] newvar = pnl_exp [if] [in] [, options]

各选项及含义为：

(1) se(newvar)：创建包含标准误差的新变量 newvar；

(2) 方差(newvar)：创建包含方差的新变量 newvar；

(3) wald(newvar)：创建包含 Wald 测试统计信息的新变量 newvar；

(4) p(newvar)：创建包含 Wald 测试的 p 值的新变量 newvar；

(5) ci(newvars)：创建包含置信区间下限和上限的新变量 newvars；

(6) level(#)：设置置信度级别，默认值为置信水平(95)；

(7) g(stub)：创建包含观测特定导数的 stub 1、stub 2、stubk。

predictnl 命令在任何 Stata 估计命令后都会计算(可能的)非线性预测，并可选地计算这些预测的方差、标准误差、Wald 检验统计、p 值和置信区间等。与 testnl 和 nlcom 命令不同，predictnl 生成数据函数(即预测)，而不是标量。因此，predictnl 生成的量在数据中的观测值上矢量化。

例 1.18 非线性预测 predictnl

* probit 模型的非线性预测

* 下载数据

.clear

.webuse lbw

(Hosmer & Lemeshow data)

* 拟合最大似然 probit 模型

.probit low lwt smoke ptl ht

运行结果如图 1.96 所示。

```
Probit regression                                    Number of obs =    189
                                                     LR chi2(4)    =  21.31
                                                     Prob > chi2   = 0.0003
Log likelihood = -106.67851                          Pseudo R2     = 0.0908
```

low	Coefficient	Std. err.	z	P>|z|	[95% conf. interval]	
lwt	-.0095164	.0036875	-2.58	0.010	-.0167438	-.0022891
smoke	.3487004	.2041772	1.71	0.088	-.0514794	.7488803
ptl	.365667	.1921201	1.90	0.057	-.0108815	.7422154
ht	1.082355	.410673	2.64	0.008	.2774503	1.887259
_cons	.4238985	.4823224	0.88	0.379	-.5214361	1.369233

图 1.96

* 计算预测及其标准误差

.predictnl phat = normal(_b[_cons] + _b[ht] * ht + _b[ptl] * ptl + _b[smoke] * smoke + _b[lwt] * lwt), se(phat_se)

.summarize phat

运行结果如图 1.97 所示。

Variable	Obs	Mean	Std. dev.	Min	Max
phat	189	.3113855	.15338	.0395983	.8328622

图 1.97

* 参数生存模型的非线性预测

* 下载数据

.clear

.webuse drugtr, clear

(Patient survival in drug trial)

* 拟合参数生存模型

.streg drug age, dist(weibull)

运行结果如图 1.98 所示。

Weibull PH regression

No. of subjects = 48　　Number of obs = 48
No. of failures = 31
Time at risk = 744
LR chi2(2) = 35.39
Log likelihood = -42.931335　　Prob > chi2 = 0.0000

_t	Haz. ratio	Std. err.	z	P>|z|	[95% conf.	interval]
drug	.1111431	.045433	-5.37	0.000	.0498803	.2476487
age	1.127725	.0419062	3.23	0.001	1.048511	1.212925
_cons	.0000253	.0000589	-4.55	0.000	2.65e-07	.0024186
/ln_p	.5204297	.1389037	3.75	0.000	.2481834	.792676
p	1.682751	.2337403			1.281695	2.209301
1/p	.5942651	.0825456			.452632	.7802168

Note: _cons estimates baseline hazard.

图　1.98

```
* 计算预测平均生存时间及其标准误差
.predictnl t_hat = predict(mean time), se(t_hat_se)
.summarize t_hat
```

运行结果如图 1.99 所示。

Variable	Obs	Mean	Std. dev.	Min	Max
t_hat	48	24.83049	17.04453	4.016516	61.84451

图　1.99

```
.list t_hat
```

运行结果略。

1.6.7　模型系统预测

forecast 命令是一组命令,用于通过求解模型获得预测,这些模型是共同确定一个或多个变量结果的方程集合。方程可以是使用诸如 regrese、ivregrese、var 或 reg3 等估计命令拟合的随机关系,也可以是称为恒等式的非随机关系,将一个变量表示为其他变量的确定性函数。预测模型还可能包括外部变量,这些变量的值是已知的,或者是由被检查系统范围之外的因素决定的。forecast 命令还可用于在单方程模型中获取动态预测。

forecast 命令集合允许通过使用 add factors 和类似设置将外部信息合并到预测中,同时可以指定某些模型变量的未来路径,并获取基于该路径的其他变量的预测。每组预测变量都有自己的名称前缀或后缀,因此可以根据其他方案比较预测。预测的置信区间可以通过随机模拟获得,并且可以包含参数不确定性和加性误差项。

forecast 命令可适用于时间序列和面板数据集。其中,时间序列数据集可能不包含任何间隙,面板数据集必须是强平衡的。

forecast 命令的语法格式为：

```
forecast subcommand... [, options]
```

其子命令选项(subcommand)及定义为：

(1) create:创建新模型；

(2) estimates:将估算结果添加到当前模型；

(3) identity:指定恒等式(非随机方程)；

(4) coefvector:通过系数向量指定方程；

(5) exogenous:声明外生变量；

(6) solve:提前一步或动态预测；

(7) adjust:通过添加因子分解、替换等方式调整变量；

(8) describe:描述模型；

(9) list:列出构成当前模型的所有预测命令；

(10) clear:从内存中清除当前模型；

(11) drop:删除预测变量；

(12) query:检查预测模型是否已启动。

快速启动以下程序：

(1) 估计线性回归和 ARIMA 回归，并将其结果分别存储为 myreg 和 myarima

```
regress y1 x1 x2
estimates store myreg
arima y2 x3 y1, ar(1) ma(1)
estimates store myarima
```

(2) 创建名为 mymodel 的预测模型

```
forecast create mymodel
```

(3) 将存储的估计值 myreg 和 myarima 添加到预测模型 mymodel

```
forecast estimates myreg
forecast estimates myarima
```

(4) 使用 mymodel 模型计算 2012 年至 2020 年 y_1 和 y_2 的动态预测，整个预测期的非缺失值为 x_1、x_2 和 x_3：

```
forecast solve, begin(2012) end(2020)
```

例 1.19　forecast 预测

reg3 的示例 3 显示了如何使用三阶段最小二乘估计(3SLS)拟合 Klein(1950)[1]的美国经济模型。在这里，我们关注的是，一旦参数得到估计，如何通过该模型进行预测。在克莱因模型中，有 7 个方程描述 7 个内生变量。其中 3 个方程是随机关系，其余方程是恒等式。

$$c_t = \beta_0 + \beta_1 p_t + \beta_2 p_{t-1} + \beta_3 w_t + \varepsilon_{1t}$$
$$i_t = \beta_4 + \beta_5 p_t + \beta_6 p_{t-1} + \beta_7 k_{t-1} + \varepsilon_{2t}$$
$$wp_t = \beta_8 + \beta_9 y_t + \beta_{10} y_{t-1} + \beta_{11} yr_t + \varepsilon_{3t}$$

① Klein, L. R. *Economic Fluctuations in the United States 1921—1941*. New York: Wiley, 1950.

$$y_t = c_t + i_t + g_t$$
$$p_t = y_t - t_t - wp_t$$
$$k_t = k_{t-1} + i_t$$
$$w_t = wg_t + wp_t$$

其中,c 为消费(内生变量);p 为私营部门利润(内生变量);wp 为私营部门工资(内生变量);wg 为政府部门工资(外生变量);w 为工资总额(内生变量);i 为投资(内生变量);k 为股本(内生变量);y 为国民收入(内生变量);g 为政府支出(外生变量);t 为间接税收+净出口(外生变量);yr 为时间趋势(=年-1931 年)(外生变量)。

```
* 下载数据
. clear
. webuse klein2
. reg3 (c p L.p w) (i p L.p L.k) (wp y L.y yr) if year < 1939, endog(w p y) exog(t wg g)
```

运行结果如图 1.100 所示。

Three-stage least-squares regression

Equation	Obs	Params	RMSE	"R-squared"	chi2	P>chi2
c	18	3	.7413768	0.9780	797.59	0.0000
i	18	3	.9189338	0.9348	262.75	0.0000
wp	18	3	.6816093	0.9763	766.38	0.0000

	Coefficient	Std. err.	z	P>|z|	[95% conf.	interval]
c						
p						
--.	.2204318	.0653683	3.37	0.001	.0923123	.3485514
L1.	.0165582	.0676045	0.24	0.807	-.1159442	.1490607
w	.8973778	.045007	19.94	0.000	.8091657	.98559
_cons	13.0166	1.436887	9.06	0.000	10.20036	15.83285
i						
p						
--.	.5163513	.1126656	4.58	0.000	.2955308	.7371719
L1.	.3261585	.1039031	3.14	0.002	.1225121	.5298048
k						
L1.	-.1145147	.0258856	-4.42	0.000	-.1652497	-.0637798
_cons	10.30534	5.420729	1.90	0.057	-.3190919	20.92977
wp						
y						
--.	.4276193	.034903	12.25	0.000	.3592107	.496028
L1.	.1673702	.0313475	5.34	0.000	.1059302	.2288102
yr	.141803	.030548	4.64	0.000	.08193	.2016761
_cons	1.044186	1.298511	0.80	0.421	-1.500848	3.589221

Endogenous variables: c i wp w p y
Exogenous variables: L.p L.k L.y yr t wg g

图 1.100

```
. estimates store klein
* 创建一个新预测模型
. forecast create kleinmodel
  Forecast model kleinmodel started.
* 将使用 reg3 拟合的随机方程添加到 klein 模型中
. forecast estimates klein
  Added estimation results from reg3.
  Forecast model kleinmodel now contains 3 endogenous variables.
* 指定确定模型中其他四个内生变量的四个恒等式
. forecast identity y = c + i + g
  Forecast model kleinmodel now contains 4 endogenous variables.
. forecast identity p = y - t - wp
  Forecast model kleinmodel now contains 5 endogenous variables.
. forecast identity k = L.k + i
  Forecast model kleinmodel now contains 6 endogenous variables.
. forecast identity w = wg + wp
  Forecast model kleinmodel now contains 7 endogenous variables.
* 确定四个外部变量
. forecast exogenous wg
  Forecast model kleinmodel now contains 1 declared exogenous variable.
. forecast exogenous g
  Forecast model kleinmodel now contains 2 declared exogenous variables.
. forecast exogenous t
  Forecast model kleinmodel now contains 3 declared exogenous variables.
. forecast exogenous yr
  Forecast model kleinmodel now contains 4 declared exogenous variables.
* 获取动态预测
. forecast solve, prefix(bl_) begin(1939)
```

运行结果如图 1.101 所示。

```
Computing dynamic forecasts for model kleinmodel.

Starting period:  1939
Ending period:    1941
Forecast prefix:  bl_

1939:  ............................................................
       ............................................................
1940:  ............................................................
       ........................................................
1941:  ............................................................
       .........................................................

Forecast 7 variables spanning 3 periods.
```

图 1.101

通过画图可得如图 1.102 所示的结果。

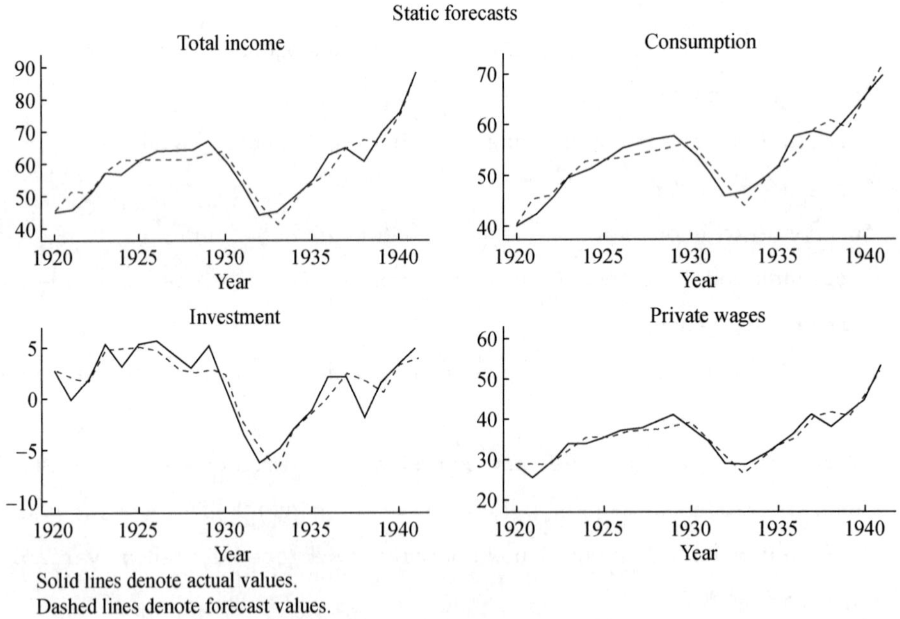

图 1.102

1.7 模型变量的边际效应分析

令 $\boldsymbol{\theta}$ 为模型的参数向量，z 是协方差向量，$f(z,\boldsymbol{\theta})$ 为返回预测变量值的标量值函数。边际效应分析可用 margins 命令估计：

$$p(\boldsymbol{\theta})=\frac{1}{M_{S_p}}\sum_{j=1}^{M}\delta_j(S_p)f(\boldsymbol{z}_j,\boldsymbol{\theta}) \tag{1.86}$$

式中，$\delta_j(S_p)$用来标示子样本集 S_p 中的元素：

$$\delta_j(S_p)=\begin{cases}1, & j\in S_p\\ 0, & j\notin S_p\end{cases}$$

M_{S_p} 是子样本量：

$$M_{S_p}=\sum_{j=1}^{M}\delta_j(S_p)$$

其中，M 是总样本量。

令 $\hat{\theta}$ 为参数估计值向量，则 margins 命令估计：

$$\hat{p}=\frac{1}{w}\sum_{j=1}^{N}\delta_j(S_p)w_jf(\boldsymbol{z}_j,\hat{\boldsymbol{\theta}}) \tag{1.87}$$

式中，$w=\sum_{j=1}^{N}\delta_j(S_p)w_j$，$\delta_j(S_p)$表示观察值 j 是否在亚群 S_p 中，w_j 是第 j 次观察的权重，N 是样本量。

margins 命令可用于估计边际效应和偏边际效应。对于连续协变量 x 的边际效应，margins 命令估计公式为：

$$\hat{p}=\frac{1}{w}\sum_{j=1}^{N}\delta_j(S_p)w_jh(\boldsymbol{z}_j,\hat{\boldsymbol{\theta}}) \tag{1.88}$$

式中，$h(\boldsymbol{z},\boldsymbol{\theta})=\dfrac{\partial f(\boldsymbol{z},\boldsymbol{\theta})}{\partial x}$。

因子变量 A 水平 k 的边际效应是将其边际与基准水平的边际进行比较的简单对比（也称为差异）。即

$$h(\boldsymbol{z},\boldsymbol{\theta})=f(\boldsymbol{z},\boldsymbol{\theta}\mid A=k)-f(\boldsymbol{z},\boldsymbol{\theta}\mid A=\text{base})$$

（1）margins 命令估计线性预测的响应边际的语法格式为：

```
margins [marginlist] [, options]
margins [marginlist], predict(statistic ...) [options]
```

其中，statistic 选项及含义默认为 xb 即线性预测值。

菜单操作路径为：

```
Statistics>Postestimation
```

（2）边际效应绘图的语法格式为：

```
marginsplot [, options]
```

其主要选项及含义为：

① xdimension(dimlist[,dimopts])：使用 dimlist 定义 x 轴；

② plotdimension(dimlist[,dimopts])：为 dimlist 中的组创建打印；

③ bydimension(dimlist[,dimopts])：为 dimlist 中的组创建子图；

④ graphdimension(dimlist[,dimopts])：为 dimlist 中的组创建图形；

⑤ horizontal：交换 x 轴和 y 轴；

⑥ noci:不绘制置信区间;

⑦ derivlabel:使用附加在边际效应变量上的标签;

⑧ name(name | stub[,replace]):图形的名称,如果有多个图形,则为 stub。

标签类选项及其含义为:

① allxlabel:在 x 轴上为每个值放置记号和标签;

② nolabels:标签组及其值,而不是其标签;

③ allsimplelabels:在所有标签中放弃变量名和等号;

④ nosimplelabels:在所有标签中包括变量名和等号;

⑤ separator(string):在标注中指定多个变量时标签的分隔符;

⑥ separator:不使用分离器。

画图类选项及其含义为:

① plotopts(plot_options):影响所有边距打印的格式副本;

② plot#opts(plot_options):影响第#页边距打印的格式副本;

③ recast(plottype):使用 plottype 打印边距。

CI 图类选项及其含义为:

① ciopts(rcap_options):影响所有置信区间图的格式副本;

② ci#opts(rcap_options):影响第#个置信区间图的格式副本;

③ recastci(plottype):使用 plottype 绘制置信区间;

④ mcompare(method):针对多重比较进行调整;

⑤ level(#):设置置信级别。

成对类选项及其含义为:

① unique:仅打印唯一成对比较;

② csort:先排序比较类别。

添加绘图类选项及其含义为:

① addplot(绘图):将其他绘图添加到图形中;

② twoway_options:表示 twoway_options 选项中记录的任何选项;

③ byopts(byopts):指定子图如何组合、标记等。

例 1.20　模型边际分析

```
* 下载数据
.clear
.webuse nhanes2
* 回归收缩压对年龄组、性别及其相互作用的影响
.regress bpsystol agegrp##sex
```

运行结果如图 1.103 所示。

Source	SS	df	MS			
				Number of obs	=	10,351
				F(11, 10339)	=	312.88
Model	1407229.28	11	127929.935	Prob > F	=	0.0000
Residual	4227440.75	10,339	408.882943	R-squared	=	0.2497
				Adj R-squared	=	0.2489
Total	5634670.03	10,350	544.412563	Root MSE	=	20.221

bpsystol	Coefficient	Std. err.	t	P>|t|	[95% conf.	interval]
agegrp						
30-39	.7956175	.9473117	0.84	0.401	-1.061297	2.652532
40-49	5.117078	1.018176	5.03	0.000	3.121256	7.1129
50-59	12.20018	1.022541	11.93	0.000	10.1958	14.20456
60-69	16.85887	.8155092	20.67	0.000	15.26031	18.45742
70+	22.50889	1.130959	19.90	0.000	20.29199	24.72579
sex						
Female	-12.60132	.8402299	-15.00	0.000	-14.24833	-10.9543
agegrp#sex						
30-39#Female	4.140156	1.31031	3.16	0.002	1.571695	6.708617
40-49#Female	8.644866	1.412067	6.12	0.000	5.876941	11.41279
50-59#Female	11.83134	1.406641	8.41	0.000	9.074051	14.58863
60-69#Female	14.093	1.130882	12.46	0.000	11.87625	16.30975
70+#Female	15.86608	1.542296	10.29	0.000	12.84288	18.88928
_cons	123.8862	.6052954	204.67	0.000	122.6997	125.0727

图 1.103

* 各年龄组血压预测范围

.margins agegrp

运行结果如图 1.104 所示。

Predictive margins　　　　Number of obs = 10,351
Model VCE: OLS

Expression: Linear prediction, predict()

	Margin	Delta-method std. err.	t	P>|t|	[95% conf.	interval]
agegrp						
20-29	117.2684	.419845	279.31	0.000	116.4454	118.0914
30-39	120.2383	.5020813	239.48	0.000	119.2541	121.2225
40-49	126.9255	.56699	223.86	0.000	125.8141	128.0369
50-59	135.682	.5628593	241.06	0.000	134.5787	136.7853
60-69	141.5285	.3781197	374.30	0.000	140.7873	142.2696
70+	148.1096	.6445073	229.80	0.000	146.8463	149.373

图 1.104

* 边际效应剖面图

.marginsplot

运行结果如图 1.105 所示。

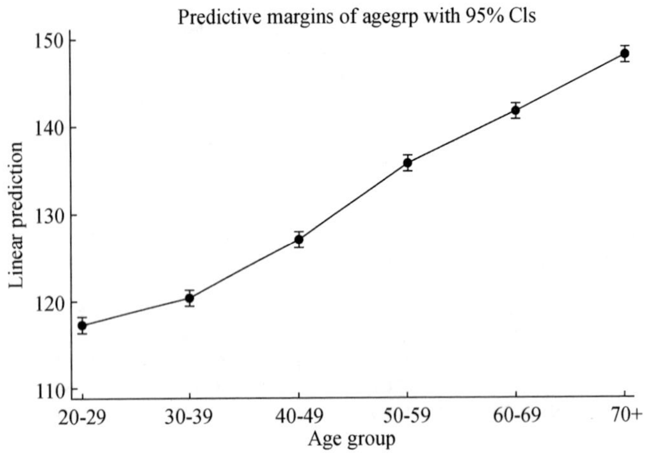

图 1.105

＊年龄组和性别之间互动的边际效应

.margins agegrp＃sex

运行结果如图 1.106 所示。

Adjusted predictions　　Number of obs = 10,351
Model VCE: OLS

Expression: Linear prediction, predict()

	Margin	Delta-method std. err.	t	P>|t|	[95% conf.	interval]
agegrp#sex						
20-29#Male	123.8862	.6052954	204.67	0.000	122.6997	125.0727
20-29#Female	111.2849	.5827553	190.96	0.000	110.1426	112.4272
30-39#Male	124.6818	.728709	171.10	0.000	123.2534	126.1102
30-39#Female	116.2207	.692755	167.77	0.000	114.8627	117.5786
40-49#Male	129.0033	.8187185	157.57	0.000	127.3984	130.6081
40-49#Female	125.0468	.7859058	159.11	0.000	123.5063	126.5874
50-59#Male	136.0864	.8241405	165.13	0.000	134.4709	137.7019
50-59#Female	135.3164	.7703532	175.66	0.000	133.8064	136.8264
60-69#Male	140.7451	.5465096	257.53	0.000	139.6738	141.8163
60-69#Female	142.2368	.5236736	271.61	0.000	141.2103	143.2633
70+#Male	146.3951	.9553456	153.24	0.000	144.5224	148.2678
70+#Female	149.6599	.8717829	171.67	0.000	147.951	151.3687

图 1.106

＊交互边际效应图

.marginsplot

运行结果如图 1.107 所示。

＊男性和女性对比，每个年龄组的边际估计

.margins r.sex@agegrp

运行结果如图 1.108 所示。

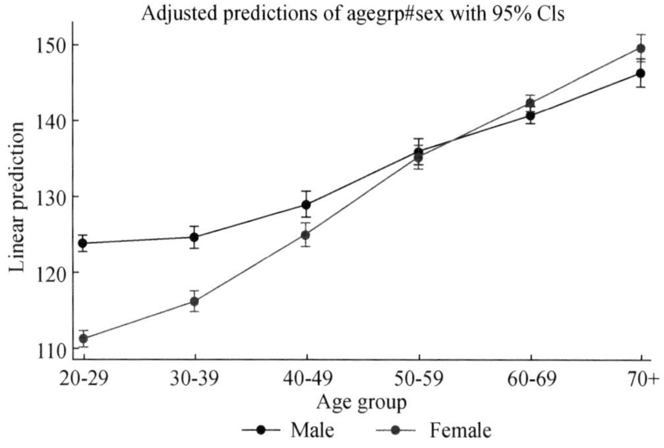

图 1.107

Contrasts of adjusted predictions　　Number of obs = **10,351**
Model VCE: **OLS**

Expression: **Linear prediction, predict()**

	df	F	P>F
sex@agegrp			
(Female vs Male) 20-29	1	224.92	0.0000
(Female vs Male) 30-39	1	70.82	0.0000
(Female vs Male) 40-49	1	12.15	0.0005
(Female vs Male) 50-59	1	0.47	0.4949
(Female vs Male) 60-69	1	3.88	0.0488
(Female vs Male) 70+	1	6.37	0.0116
Joint	6	53.10	0.0000
Denominator	10339		

	Contrast	Delta-method std. err.	[95% conf.	interval]
sex@agegrp				
(Female vs Male) 20-29	-12.60132	.8402299	-14.24833	-10.9543
(Female vs Male) 30-39	-8.461161	1.005448	-10.43203	-6.490288
(Female vs Male) 40-49	-3.956451	1.134878	-6.181031	-1.731871
(Female vs Male) 50-59	-.7699782	1.128119	-2.981309	1.441353
(Female vs Male) 60-69	1.491684	.756906	.0080022	2.975367
(Female vs Male) 70+	3.264762	1.293325	.729594	5.79993

图 1.108

* 男女年龄组边际效应的绘图对比和置信区间

```
.marginsplot
```

运行结果如图 1.109 所示。

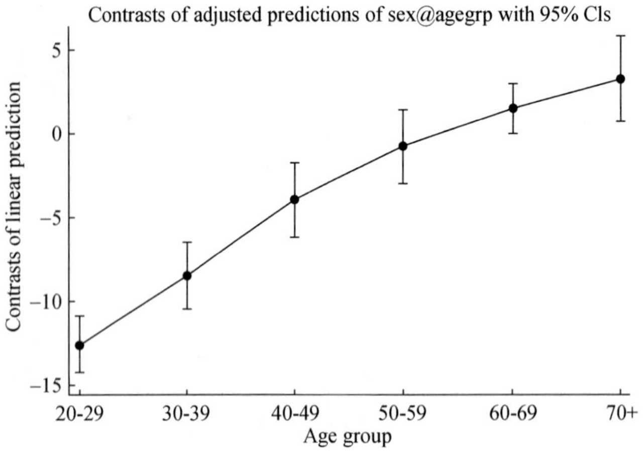

图 1.109

1.8 约束线性回归

对于参数约束回归,我们可以通过修改自变量列表来获得约束线性回归估计。例如,在存在一个约束条件的情况下,我们想拟合模型:mpg=$\beta_0+\beta_1$ price $+\beta_2$ weight $+u$,拟合约束条件为 $\beta_1=\beta_2$,则模型可改写为:

$$\text{mpg}=\beta_0+\beta_1(\text{ price }+\text{ weight })+u$$

并根据 price+weight 对 mpg 进行回归。总和上的估计系数就是 $\beta_1=\beta_2$ 约束回归参数估计值。

对于多个约束条件,模型可以根据多个同时约束进行拟合。我们只需定义约束,然后在 constraints()选项中包含约束编号。例如,我们希望拟合模型:

$$\text{mpg}=\beta_0+\beta_1\text{price}+\beta_2\text{weight}+\beta_3\text{displ}+\beta_4\text{gear\_atio}+\beta_5\text{ foreign}+\beta_6\text{length}+u$$

模型参数约束条件为:

$$\beta_1=\beta_2=\beta_3=\beta_6$$
$$\beta_4=-\beta_5=\beta_0/20$$

一般地,对于计量模型,可以设 $\boldsymbol{\beta b}'=\boldsymbol{r}$ 为 $\boldsymbol{\beta}$ 的约束,为 $c\times p$ 维的约束矩阵,即对 p 个参数施加 c 个约束;$\boldsymbol{b}$ 是 $1\times p$ 维的参数向量;$\boldsymbol{r}$ 为 $c\times 1$ 维的约束值向量。

我们希望构造一个 $p\times k$ 维矩阵 T,它将 $\boldsymbol{b}$ 转化为降秩形式,其中 $k=p-c$。显然有很多 T 矩阵可以做到这一点,我们选择一个具有如下属性的矩阵:

$$\boldsymbol{b}_c=\boldsymbol{b}_0T$$
$$\boldsymbol{b}=\boldsymbol{b}_c\boldsymbol{T}'+\boldsymbol{a}$$

其中,$\boldsymbol{b}_c$ 是任何解 $\boldsymbol{b}_0$ 的约化形式投影,也就是说,$\boldsymbol{b}_c$ 是一个维数较小的向量($1\times k$ 维,而不是 $1\times p$ 维),可以将其视为无约束向量。第二个等式表示,$\boldsymbol{b}_c$ 可以映射回更高维度、适当约束的 $\boldsymbol{b}$;$1\times p$ 维向量 $\boldsymbol{a}$ 是一个仅依赖于 $\boldsymbol{\beta}$ 和 $\boldsymbol{r}$ 的常数。

设 n 为观察数，p 为参数总数(在限制之前，包括常数)，c 为约束条件数，则受约束的多元线性回归模型的系数计算公式为：

$$\boldsymbol{b}' = \boldsymbol{T}\{(\boldsymbol{T}'\boldsymbol{X}'\boldsymbol{W}\boldsymbol{X}\boldsymbol{T})^{-1}(\boldsymbol{T}'\boldsymbol{X}'\boldsymbol{W}\boldsymbol{y} - \boldsymbol{T}'\boldsymbol{X}'\boldsymbol{W}\boldsymbol{X}\boldsymbol{a}')\} + \boldsymbol{a}' \tag{1.89}$$

其中，$\boldsymbol{T}$ 为以简化形式纳入约束方程变量参数的 $p \times k$ 维矩阵；$\boldsymbol{a}$ 为约束方程中的 $1 \times p$ 维常数矩阵。如果未指定权重，则默认 $\boldsymbol{W}=\boldsymbol{I}$。如果指定了权重，则令 $\boldsymbol{v}:1 \times n$ 为指定的权重。如果指定了频率权重 fweight，则 $\boldsymbol{W}=\mathrm{diag}(\boldsymbol{v})$。如果指定了分析权重，则 $\boldsymbol{W}=\mathrm{diag}[\boldsymbol{v}/(1'\boldsymbol{v})(\boldsymbol{1}'\boldsymbol{1})]$，这意味着将权重归一化为观察次数的总和。

均方误差为 $s^2=(\boldsymbol{y}'\boldsymbol{W}\boldsymbol{y}-2\boldsymbol{b}'\boldsymbol{X}'\boldsymbol{W}\boldsymbol{y}+\boldsymbol{b}'\boldsymbol{X}'\boldsymbol{W}\boldsymbol{X}\boldsymbol{b})/(n-p+c)$。方差—协方差矩阵为 $s^2\boldsymbol{T}(\boldsymbol{T}'\boldsymbol{X}'\boldsymbol{W}\boldsymbol{X}\boldsymbol{T})^{-1}\boldsymbol{T}'$。

约束回归的命令为 cnsreg。cnsreg 适合受限的线性回归模型。其语法格式为：

cnsreg depvar indepvars [if] [in] [weight], constraints(constraints) [options]

菜单操作路径为：

Statistics>Linear models and related>Constrained linear regression

例 1.21 约束线性回归

* 加载数据

```
. sysuse auto
```

* 限制价格和权重的系数，使之相等

```
. constraint 1 price = weight
```

* 拟合受限的线性回归

```
. cnsreg mpg price weight, constraints(1)
```

运行结果如图 1.110 所示。

```
Constrained linear regression                   Number of obs =         74
                                                F(1, 72)      =      37.59
                                                Prob > F      =     0.0000
                                                Root MSE      =     4.7220

 ( 1)  price - weight = 0
```

mpg	Coefficient	Std. err.	t	P>|t|	[95% conf.	interval]
price	-.0009875	.0001611	-6.13	0.000	-.0013086	-.0006664
weight	-.0009875	.0001611	-6.13	0.000	-.0013086	-.0006664
_cons	30.36718	1.577958	19.24	0.000	27.22158	33.51278

图 1.110

* 定义更多的限制因素

```
. constraint 2 displ = weight
. constraint 3 gear_ratio = - foreign
```

* 拟合受限线性回归，应用所有三个约束条件

```
. cnsreg mpg price weight displ gear_ratio foreign length, c(1-3)
```

运行结果如图 1.111 所示。

```
Constrained linear regression                    Number of obs =      74
                                                 F(3, 70)      =   46.63
                                                 Prob > F      =  0.0000
                                                 Root MSE      =  3.4119

 ( 1)  price - weight = 0
 ( 2)  - weight + displacement = 0
 ( 3)  gear_ratio + foreign = 0
```

mpg	Coefficient	Std. err.	t	P>|t|	[95% conf.	interval]
price	-.0001949	.0001601	-1.22	0.227	-.0005142	.0001243
weight	-.0001949	.0001601	-1.22	0.227	-.0005142	.0001243
displacement	-.0001949	.0001601	-1.22	0.227	-.0005142	.0001243
gear_ratio	1.988421	1.29214	1.54	0.128	-.588671	4.565514
foreign	-1.988421	1.29214	-1.54	0.128	-4.565514	.588671
length	-.1835659	.0226529	-8.10	0.000	-.2287457	-.1383861
_cons	52.22059	5.028111	10.39	0.000	42.19234	62.24884

图 1.111

＊将常数限制为零

. constraint 99 _cons = 0

＊拟合受限线性回归，应用所有四个约束条件

. cnsreg mpg price weight displ gear_ratio foreign length, c(1－3,99)

运行结果如图 1.112 所示。

```
Constrained linear regression                    Number of obs =      74
                                                 F(3, 71)      =  387.91
                                                 Prob > F      =  0.0000
                                                 Root MSE      =  5.4002

 ( 1)  price - weight = 0
 ( 2)  - weight + displacement = 0
 ( 3)  gear_ratio + foreign = 0
 ( 4)  _cons = 0
```

mpg	Coefficient	Std. err.	t	P>|t|	[95% conf.	interval]
price	-.0000143	.0002518	-0.06	0.955	-.0005164	.0004879
weight	-.0000143	.0002518	-0.06	0.955	-.0005164	.0004879
displacement	-.0000143	.0002518	-0.06	0.955	-.0005164	.0004879
gear_ratio	11.3821	1.460552	7.79	0.000	8.469845	14.29436
foreign	-11.3821	1.460552	-7.79	0.000	-14.29436	-8.469845
length	-.0522824	.0297527	-1.76	0.083	-.1116075	.0070428
_cons	0	(omitted)				

图 1.112

第 2 章 线性回归拓展

2.1 最大似然估计法

如果回归模型为非线性，OLS 估计将是不一致的估计，需要使用最大似然估计（MLE）或非线性最小二乘（NLS）方法进行估计。

假设随机向量 y 的概率密度函数为 $f(y;\boldsymbol{\theta})$，其中，$\boldsymbol{\theta}$ 为 k 维未知参数向量。通过抽取随机样本 $\{y_1, y_2, \cdots, y_n\}$ 估计 $\boldsymbol{\theta}$。假设 $\{y_1, y_2, \cdots, y_n\}$ 为 i. i. d，则样本数据的联合密度函数为 $f(y_1;\boldsymbol{\theta})f(y_2;\boldsymbol{\theta})\cdots f(y_n;\boldsymbol{\theta})$。似然函数为：

$$L(\boldsymbol{\theta}; y_1, \cdots, y_n) = \prod_{i=1}^{n} f(y_i;\boldsymbol{\theta})$$

两边取对数，得到对数似然函数：

$$\ln L(\boldsymbol{\theta}; y_1, \cdots, y_n) = \sum_{i=1}^{n} \ln f(y_i;\boldsymbol{\theta}) \tag{2.1}$$

MLE 的基本思想是，给定样本取值后，该样本来自参数为 $\hat{\boldsymbol{\theta}}$ 的概率最大。于是最大化对数似然函数：

$$\max_{\theta \in \Theta} \ln L(\boldsymbol{\theta}; y) \tag{2.2}$$

利用高斯—牛顿迭代法进行数值求解，可得最大似然估计值：

$$\hat{\boldsymbol{\theta}}_{ML} \equiv \operatorname{argmax} \ln L(\boldsymbol{\theta}; y) \tag{2.3}$$

最大似然估计值的主要优点是，大样本性质良好，具有一致性、渐进有效性（即最小渐进方差）和渐进正态。

使用不正确的似然函数得到的最大似然估计，称为准最大似然估计（QMLE）。

MLE 的 Stata 命令为 ml。多数需要使用最大似然估计的情形，Stata 都已经给出了专门命令，无需自行定义似然函数，编程估计模型参数。

正态分布假设检验的命令汇总如表 2.1 所示。

表 2.1 正态分布假设检验的命令

序号	检验名称	Stata 命令	含义
1	LR 检验	lrtest	估计后似然比检验
2	画直方图	hist	正态性检验

（续表）

序号	检验名称	Stata 命令	含义
3	画核密度图	kdensity	正态性检验
4	画 QQ 图	qnorm	正态性检验
5	JB 检验	jb6	正态性检验
6	D'Agostino 检验	sktest	正态性检验
7	Shapiro-Wilk 检验	swilk	正态性检验

2.2 非线性最小二乘估计

2.2.1 可转换的非线性回归模型

在实际经济活动中，经济变量的关系是复杂的，直接表现为线性关系的情况并不多见。如著名的恩格尔曲线(Engle curve)表现为幂函数曲线形式，宏观经济学中的菲利普斯曲线(Phillips curve)表现为双曲线形式等。

在非线性回归模型中，有一些模型经过适当的变量变换或函数变换就可以转化成线性回归模型，从而将非线性回归模型的参数估计问题转化成线性回归模型的参数估计问题，这类模型为可线性化模型。在计量经济分析中经常使用的可线性化模型有对数模型、半对数模型、倒数模型、多项式模型等。

1. 对数模型

对数模型的形式为：

$$\ln y = \beta_0 + \beta_1 \ln x + u \tag{2.4}$$

其中，$\ln y$ 对参数 β_0 和 β_1 是线性的，而且变量的对数形式也是线性的。

令 $y^* = \ln y, x^* = \ln x$，将其代入模型，将模型转化为线性回归模型：

$$y^* = \beta_0 + \beta_1 x^* + u \tag{2.5}$$

变换后的模型不仅参数是线性的，而且变量间也是线性的。该模型的特点为斜率 β_1 度量了 y 关于 x 的弹性。

$$\beta_1 = \frac{d(\ln y)}{d(\ln x)} = \frac{dy/y}{dx/x} \tag{2.6}$$

该模型的适用对象为对观测值取对数，将取对数后的观测值($\ln x, \ln y$)描成散点图，如果近似为一条直线，则适用于对数—线性模型，用来描述 x 与 y 的变量关系。它容易推广到模型中存在多个解释变量的情形，如柯布—道格拉斯生产函数。

2. 半对数模型

在实际的经济问题中，为了探寻经济变量的变动规律，测定其增长率或衰减率是一个重要的方面。在回归分析中，我们可以用半对数模型来测度这些增长率或衰减率。

线性模型与对数模型的混合就是半对数模型。半对数模型包含两种形式，分别为：

对数—线性模型：

$$y=\beta_0+\beta_1\ln x+u \tag{2.7}$$

线性—对数模型：

$$\ln y=\beta_0+\beta_1 x+u \tag{2.8}$$

对数—线性模型中，

$$\beta_1=\frac{\mathrm{d}y}{\mathrm{d}(\ln x)}=\frac{\mathrm{d}y}{\mathrm{d}x/x} \tag{2.9}$$

表示 x 每变动 1%时 y 将变动的绝对量，即变动 β_1 个单位。

线性—对数模型中，

$$\beta_1=\frac{\mathrm{d}(\ln y)}{\mathrm{d}x}=\frac{\mathrm{d}y/y}{\mathrm{d}x} \tag{2.10}$$

表示 x 每变动 1 个单位时 y 将变动的绝对量。特别地，若 x 为时间变量（年份），则系数 β_1 衡量了 y 的年均增长速度。

3. 倒数模型

我们把形如

$$y=\beta_0+\beta_1\frac{1}{x}+u \quad 或 \quad \frac{1}{y}=\beta_0+\beta_1\frac{1}{x}+u \tag{2.11}$$

的模型称为倒数（双曲线函数）模型。

这是一个变量之间是非线性的模型，因为 x 是以倒数形式进入模型的。但这个模型却是参数线性模型，因为模型中参数之间是线性的。这个模型的显著特征是随着 x 无限增大，$\frac{1}{x}$接近于零。

设 $x^*=\frac{1}{x}$，$y^*=\frac{1}{y}$，即进行变量的倒数变换，就可以将其转换成线性回归模型。

4. 多项式模型

多项式回归模型在生产与成本函数领域被广泛地使用。其模型形式为：

$$y=\beta_0+\beta_1 x+\beta_2 x^2+\cdots+\beta_k x^k+u \tag{2.12}$$

设 $x_t=x^t\,(t=1,2,\cdots,k)$，则

$$y=\beta_0+\beta_1 x_1+\beta_2 x_2+\cdots+\beta_k x_k+u \tag{2.13}$$

这样，模型就转换成多元线性回归模型。

上述模型转换方法可以统称为直接变量代换法。对于幂函数模型、指数函数模型，则可以在模型两边取对数，转换为多项式模型，再作变换，将其转换为线性模型。对于较为复杂的函数模型，则可以利用泰勒级数展开法进行转换。

2.2.2 不可转换的非线性回归模型

无论通过什么变换都不可能实现线性化，这样的模型称为非线性化模型。对于非线性化模型，一般采用高斯－牛顿迭代法进行估计，即将其展开成泰勒级数之后，再利用迭代估计方法进行估计。

假设回归方程为：

$$y_t = f(\boldsymbol{x}_t, \boldsymbol{\beta}) + u_t \tag{2.14}$$

其中，f 是解释变量和参数 $\boldsymbol{\beta}$ 的函数。NLS 法就是要选择参数 $\boldsymbol{\beta}$ 的估计值 b 使残差平方和最小。

$$S(b) = \sum_t (y_t - f(\boldsymbol{x}_t, b))^2 = (y - f(\boldsymbol{X}, b))'(y - f(\boldsymbol{X}, b)) \tag{2.15}$$

利用数值求解法，可以计算得到使残差平方和最小化的参数估计值 $\hat{b}_{\mathrm{NLS}}$。$\hat{b}_{\mathrm{NLS}}$ 是真实参数的一致估计量，且服从渐进正态分布。如果满足同方差与无自相关假设，则是渐进有效的。

如果 f 关于参数的导数不依赖于参数 $\boldsymbol{\beta}$，则我们称模型为参数线性的；反之，则称为参数非线性的。例如，

$$\log(y_t) = \beta_1 + \beta_2 \log L_t + \beta_3 \log K_t + u_t$$

是参数线性的，f 关于参数的导数与参数 $\boldsymbol{\beta}$ 无关。而对于

$$y_t = \beta_1 L_t^{\beta_2} K_t^{\beta_3} + u_t$$

因函数的导数仍依赖于参数 $\boldsymbol{\beta}$，所以它是参数非线性的。对于这个模型，没有办法使用 OLS 估计来最小化残差平方和，必须使用 NLS 方法来估计模型参数。

NLS 法根据最小化残差平方和选择参数 $\boldsymbol{\beta}$ 的最优估计值 b。最小化的一阶条件是：

$$\frac{\partial S(b)}{\partial b} = -2\sum_i (y_t - f(\boldsymbol{x}_t, b)) \frac{\partial f(\boldsymbol{x}_t, b)}{\partial b} = 0 \tag{2.16}$$

设 $G(b) = \dfrac{\partial f(\boldsymbol{x}_t, b)}{\partial b}$，则有

$$(G(b))'(y - f(\boldsymbol{X}, b)) = 0$$

其中，$G(b)$ 是 $f(\boldsymbol{X}, b)$ 关于 b 的导数。

估计协方差矩阵为：

$$\hat{\Sigma}_{\mathrm{NLLS}} = s^2 (G(b_{\mathrm{NLLS}})' G(b_{\mathrm{NLLS}}))^{-1} \tag{2.17}$$

对于非线性模型，无法直接求解最小化的一阶条件式。非线性方程有几种近似迭代方法可以完成参数估计。但是利用 Stata 软件估计非线性最小二乘模型很简单。对于任何系数非线性的方程，Stata 会自动应用 NLS 方法，使用迭代算法估计模型。

Stata 软件应用 NLS 方法的命令为 nl，具体分为以下几种情况：

(1) 交互式版本：

```
nl (depvar = <sexp>) [if] [in] [weight] [, options]
```

(2) 可编程替换表达式版本：

```
nl sexp_prog: depvar [varlist] [if] [in] [weight] [, options]
```

(3) 函数计算器程序版本：

```
nl func_prog @ depvar [varlist] [if] [in] [weight], {parameters(namelist)|nparameters(#)} [options]
```

这里，depvar 为因变量；<sexp>和 sexp_prog 是可替代的表达程序；func_prog

是一个函数求值程序。

例 2.1 非线性回归

下面以拟合 CES 生产函数为例，说明 Stata 软件的 nl 命令的实现。CES 生产函数表达式为：

$$\ln Q_i = \beta_0 - \frac{1}{\rho}\ln\{\delta K_i^{-\rho} + (1-\delta)L_i^{-\rho}\} + \varepsilon_i \tag{2.18}$$

其中，$\ln Q_i$ 是公司 i 的产出对数值；K_i 和 L_i 分别是公司 i 的资本和劳动力投入；ε_i 是一个回归误差项。设 $\rho=1,\delta=0.5$。

```
.webuse production
.nl (lnoutput = {b0} - 1/{rho = 1} * ln({delta = 0.5} * capital^( - 1 * {rho}) + (1 - {delta}) * labor^( - 1 * {rho})))
```

运行结果如图 2.1 所示。

Source	SS	df	MS
Model	91.144992	2	45.5724962
Residual	29.365806	97	.302740263
Total	120.5108	99	1.21728079

Number of obs =	100
R-squared =	0.7563
Adj R-squared =	0.7513
Root MSE =	.5502184
Res. dev. =	161.2538

lnoutput	Coefficient	Std. err.	t	P>|t|	[95% conf.	interval]
/b0	3.792158	.099682	38.04	0.000	3.594316	3.989999
/rho	1.386993	.472584	2.93	0.004	.4490443	2.324941
/delta	.4823616	.0519791	9.28	0.000	.3791975	.5855258

Note: Parameter b0 is used as a constant term during estimation.

图 2.1

2.3 删失回归

2.3.1 Tobit 回归

受限被解释变量的删失回归，主要处理取值数据存在删失的被解释变量的回归。被解释变量删失，就是指当潜在取值大于或小于某一临界值时，被解释变量取值都归并为临界值。

由于存在非线性项，使用 OLS 估计时，非线性项纳入扰动项中，导致扰动项与解释变量相关，使得受限被解释变量的删失回归无法得到一致的 OLS 参数估计值。因此，删失回归一般使用 MLE 法估计参数值，即 Tobit 回归。

对于模型 $y_i^* = \boldsymbol{x}_i'\boldsymbol{\beta} + \varepsilon_i, \varepsilon_i \mid \boldsymbol{x}_i \sim N(0,\sigma^2)$，假设删失（即归并）点为 $c=0$，可以

观测到 $y_i=\begin{cases}y_i^*, & 若\ y_i^*>0,\\ 0, & 若\ y_i^*\leqslant 0\end{cases}$,则该删失被解释变量混合分布的概率密度函数为:

$$f(y_i \mid \boldsymbol{x})=[1-\Phi(\boldsymbol{x}_i'\boldsymbol{\beta}/\sigma)]^{1(y_i=0)}\left[\frac{1}{\sigma}\phi((y_i-\boldsymbol{x}_i'\boldsymbol{\beta})/\sigma)\right]^{I(y_i>0)} \quad (2.19)$$

由此写出总体样本的似然函数,然后使用MLE法估计参数值。

Tobit 回归的语法格式为:

tobit depvar [indepvars] [if] [in] [weight] [, options]

其中,选项 options 的设定如表 2.2 所示。

表 2.2 选项 options 设定

符号	含义	备注
ll(#)	左归并	#为归并临界值,不定义则默认为最小值
ul(#)	右归并	#为归并临界值,不定义则默认为最大值
ll(#)ul(#)	双边归并	

MLE法使得Tobit模型对分布依赖性较强,其正态性检验法主要是条件矩检验法,并使用参数自助法,获得校正临界值。Stata实现命令为非官方命令tobcm,该命令仅适用于左归并且归并点为0的情形。具体操作如下:

```
* 下载安装命令 tobcm
.net install tobcm.pkg
* 对正态性分布假设进行条件矩检验
.tobcm,pbs
```

同方差假设的检验,通过构建辅助回归LM统计量检验。

如果模型扰动项不服从正态分布或存在异方差,就要使用更稳健的"归并最小绝对离差法"(CLAD法)估计参数。其他估计方法可以使用样本选择模型或两部分模型。

在扰动项为i.i.d时,CLAD法使离差绝对值之和最小化,得到一致估计。设模型为:

$$y_i=\max(0,\boldsymbol{x}_i'\boldsymbol{\beta}+\varepsilon_i) \quad (2.20)$$

则使用CLAD法的目标函数为:

$$\min_{\beta}\sum_{i=1}^{n}\mid y_i-\max(0,\boldsymbol{x}_i'\boldsymbol{\beta})\mid \quad (2.21)$$

优化求解即可得到CLAD法的参数估计值 $\hat{\beta}_{\text{CLAD}}$。

CLAD法的Stata命令为clad。具体操作如下:

```
* 下载安装命令 clad
.net install sg153.pkg
* CLAD 估计
.clad y x1 x2 x3, ll(#) ul(#)
```

例 2.2　Tobit 回归

下面以 Stata 自带数据集 auto 为例，说明删失回归 Tobit 模型参数估计的实现。

* 下载数据，缩小量纲，生成新变量 wgt

```
. sysuse auto
. generate wgt = weight/1000
```

* 画直方图，观察被解释变量的数据特征

```
. hist mpg
```

运行结果如图 2.2 所示。

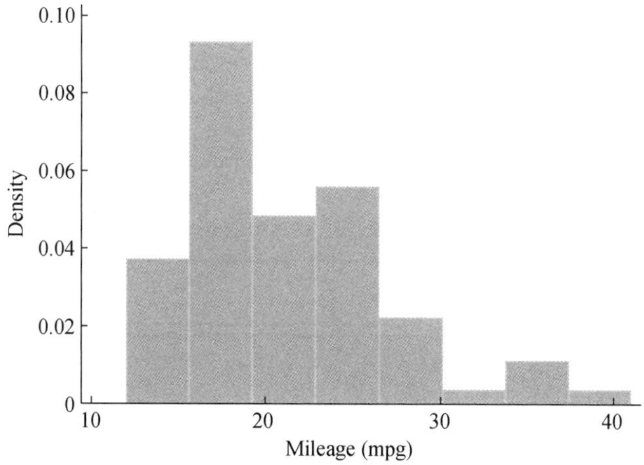

图　2.2

* 左截断的 Tobit 模型估计

```
. tobit mpg wgt, ll(17)
```

运行结果如图 2.3 所示。

```
Tobit regression                                    Number of obs     =     74
                                                           Uncensored =     56
Limits: Lower =    17                                   Left-censored =     18
        Upper = +inf                                   Right-censored =      0

                                                    LR chi2(1)        =  72.85
                                                    Prob > chi2       = 0.0000
Log likelihood = -164.25438                         Pseudo R2         = 0.1815
```

mpg	Coefficient	Std. err.	t	P>|t|	[95% conf.	interval]
wgt	-6.87305	.700257	-9.82	0.000	-8.268661	-5.47744
_cons	41.49856	2.058384	20.16	0.000	37.3962	45.60091
var(e.mpg)	14.78942	2.817609			10.11698	21.61977

图　2.3

* 右截断回归估计

```
.tobit mpg wgt, ul(24)
```

运行结果如图 2.4 所示。

```
Tobit regression                                    Number of obs     =     74
                                                        Uncensored    =     51
Limits: Lower = -inf                                    Left-censored =      0
        Upper =   24                                   Right-censored =     23

                                                    LR chi2(1)        =  90.72
                                                    Prob > chi2       = 0.0000
Log likelihood = -129.8279                          Pseudo R2         = 0.2589

------------------------------------------------------------------------------
         mpg | Coefficient  Std. err.      t    P>|t|     [95% conf. interval]
-------------+----------------------------------------------------------------
         wgt |  -.5080645   .0434931   -11.68   0.000    -.5947461   -.4213829
       _cons |   36.08037   1.432059    25.19   0.000     33.22628    38.93446
-------------+----------------------------------------------------------------
  var(e.mpg)|   5.689926   1.166256                      3.781783    8.560846
------------------------------------------------------------------------------
```

图 2.4

* 上下限双边截断回归估计

```
.tobit mpg wgt, ll(17) ul(24)
```

运行结果如图 2.5 所示。

```
Tobit regression                                    Number of obs     =     74
                                                        Uncensored    =     33
Limits: Lower = 17                                      Left-censored =     18
        Upper = 24                                     Right-censored =     23

                                                    LR chi2(1)        =  77.60
                                                    Prob > chi2       = 0.0000
Log likelihood = -104.25976                         Pseudo R2         = 0.2712

------------------------------------------------------------------------------
         mpg | Coefficient  Std. err.      t    P>|t|     [95% conf. interval]
-------------+----------------------------------------------------------------
         wgt |  -.5764448   .0724542    -7.96   0.000    -.7208457   -.4320438
       _cons |   38.07468   2.255918    16.88   0.000     33.57865    42.57072
-------------+----------------------------------------------------------------
  var(e.mpg)|   8.330942   2.281444                      4.826833    14.37891
------------------------------------------------------------------------------
```

图 2.5

* 清理内存,重新下载数据

```
.webuse gpa, clear
```

* 以变量 gpa2 的最小值为临界值估计参数

.tobit gpa2 hsgpa pincome program, ll

运行结果如图 2.6 所示。

```
Tobit regression                                   Number of obs     =   4,000
                                                       Uncensored    =   2,794
Limits: Lower =    2                                  Left-censored  =   1,206
        Upper = +inf                                 Right-censored  =       0

                                                   LR chi2(3)        = 4712.61
                                                   Prob > chi2       =  0.0000
Log likelihood = -2015.1258                        Pseudo R2         =  0.5390

------------------------------------------------------------------------------
        gpa2 | Coefficient  Std. err.      t    P>|t|     [95% conf. interval]
-------------+----------------------------------------------------------------
       hsgpa |   .6586311   .0128699    51.18   0.000      .633399    .6838632
     pincome |   .3159297   .0074568    42.37   0.000     .3013103    .3305491
     program |   .5554416   .0147468    37.67   0.000     .5265297    .5843535
       _cons |  -.8902578   .0478484   -18.61   0.000    -.9840673   -.7964482
-------------+----------------------------------------------------------------
  var(e.gpa2)|    .161703   .0044004                      .1533019    .1705645
------------------------------------------------------------------------------
```

图 2.6

* 重新下载数据,以 0 为取值上限做删失回归估计

.webuse mroz87

.tobit whrs75 nwinc wedyrs wexper c.wexper#c.wexper wifeage kl6 k618, ll(0)

运行结果如图 2.7 所示。

```
Tobit regression                                   Number of obs     =     753
                                                       Uncensored    =     428
Limits: Lower =    0                                  Left-censored  =     325
        Upper = +inf                                 Right-censored  =       0

                                                   LR chi2(7)        =  271.59
                                                   Prob > chi2       =  0.0000
Log likelihood = -3819.0946                        Pseudo R2         =  0.0343

------------------------------------------------------------------------------
             whrs75 | Coefficient  Std. err.      t    P>|t|     [95% conf. interval]
--------------------+---------------------------------------------------------
              nwinc |  -8.814227   4.459089    -1.98   0.048    -17.56808   -.0603708
             wedyrs |   80.64541   21.58318     3.74   0.000     38.27441    123.0164
             wexper |    131.564   17.27935     7.61   0.000     97.64211     165.486
                    |
c.wexper#c.wexper   |  -1.864153   .5376606    -3.47   0.001    -2.919661   -.8086455
                    |
            wifeage |  -54.40491   7.418483    -7.33   0.000     -68.9685   -39.84133
                kl6 |  -894.0202   111.8777    -7.99   0.000    -1113.653   -674.3875
               k618 |  -16.21805    38.6413    -0.42   0.675    -92.07668    59.64057
              _cons |   965.3068   446.4351     2.16   0.031     88.88827    1841.725
--------------------+---------------------------------------------------------
     var(e.whrs75)  |    1258927   93304.48                      1088458     1456093
------------------------------------------------------------------------------
```

图 2.7

＊总体边际效应分析、预测分析

```
.margins, dydx(wedyrs) predict(ystar(0,.))
```

运行结果如图 2.8 所示。

```
Average marginal effects                          Number of obs = 753
Model VCE: OIM

Expression: E(whrs75*|whrs75>0), predict(ystar(0,.))
dy/dx wrt:  wedyrs
```

	dy/dx	Delta-method std. err.	z	P>|z|	[95% conf.	interval]
wedyrs	47.47306	12.6214	3.76	0.000	22.73558	72.21054

图 2.8

＊需要获得特定备选方案的边际效应时，在边际效应分析命令中加上 at()选项

```
.margins, dydx(wedyrs) predict(ystar(0,.)) at(wedyrs=(8(1)17))
```

运行结果如图 2.9 所示。

	dy/dx	Delta-method std. err.	z	P>|z|	[95% conf.	interval]
wedyrs						
_at						
1	39.58775	8.432006	4.69	0.000	23.06132	56.11418
2	41.4497	9.421414	4.40	0.000	22.98407	59.91533
3	43.30531	10.41233	4.16	0.000	22.89752	63.71309
4	45.14859	11.39804	3.96	0.000	22.80885	67.48833
5	46.97371	12.37208	3.80	0.000	22.72489	71.22254
6	48.77504	13.32825	3.66	0.000	22.65216	74.89793
7	50.54717	14.26071	3.54	0.000	22.5967	78.49765
8	52.28499	15.16403	3.45	0.001	22.56403	82.00594
9	53.98369	16.03324	3.37	0.001	22.55912	85.40827
10	55.63887	16.8639	3.30	0.001	22.58624	88.6915

图 2.9

2.3.2 区间回归

区间回归用一个线性模型拟合一个可能被精确观察到或未被观察到但已知落在某个时间间隔内的被解释变量取值。例如，可以观察结果变量的值（点数据），未被观察到但已知落在具有固定端点的区间内（区间删失数据），未被观察到但已知落在具有

固定上端点的区间内(左删失数据),或未被观察到但已知落在具有固定下限的区间内(右截尾数据),这种经过审查的数据在许多情况下都会自然出现,如工资数据,通常只知道一个人的工资在 3 万美元到 4 万美元之间。

区间回归的 Stata 拟合命令为 intreg。该拟合的区间回归模型是 Tobit 拟合模型的推广,因为它将审查扩展到左删失数据或右删失数据之外。其语法格式为:

intreg depvar1 depvar2 [indepvars] [if] [in] [weight] [, options]

其中,depvar1 和 depvar2 形式如表 2.3 所示。

表 2.3 depvar1 和 depvar2 形式

数据类型	取值区间	depvar1	depvar2
点数据	a=[a,a]	a	a
区间数据	[a,b]	a	b
左截断数据	(−inf,b]	—	b
右截断数据	[a,+inf)	a	—
缺失数据	—	—	—

例 2.3 区间回归

womenwage2. dta 为区间形式的职业妇女年工资。这里调查妇女年度就业收入区间,类别为少于 $5000, $5001—10000, …, $25001—30000, $30001—40000, $40001—50000,以及超过 $50000。

```
.clear all
.use https://www.stata-press.com/data/r17/womenwage2
*列出 wage1 和 wage2 中前 10 项观察结果。
.list wage1 wage2 in 1/10
```

运行结果如图 2.10 所示。

	wage1	wage2
1.	.	5
2.	5	10
3.	5	10
4.	10	15
5.	15	20
6.	20	25
7.	25	30
8.	30	40
9.	40	50
10.	50	.

图 2.10

∗做区间回归估计

```
. intreg wage1 wage2 age c.age#c.age i.nev_mar i.rural school tenure
```

运行结果如图 2.11 所示。

```
Interval regression                              Number of obs     =       488
                                                        Uncensored =         0
                                                     Left-censored =        14
                                                    Right-censored =         6
                                                    Interval-cens. =       468

                                                 LR chi2(6)        =    221.61
Log likelihood = -856.33293                      Prob > chi2       =    0.0000

-------------------------------------------------------------------------------
              | Coefficient  Std. err.      z    P>|z|     [95% conf. interval]
--------------+----------------------------------------------------------------
          age |   .7914438   .4433604     1.79   0.074    -.0775265    1.660414
              |
  c.age#c.age |  -.0132624   .0073028    -1.82   0.069    -.0275757    .0010509
              |
    1.nev_mar |  -.2075022   .8119581    -0.26   0.798    -1.798911    1.383906
      1.rural |  -3.043044   .7757324    -3.92   0.000    -4.563452   -1.522637
       school |   1.334721   .1357873     9.83   0.000     1.068583    1.600859
       tenure |   .8000664   .1045077     7.66   0.000     .5952351    1.004898
        _cons |  -12.70238   6.367117    -1.99   0.046     -25.1817   -.2230583
--------------+----------------------------------------------------------------
     /lnsigma |   1.987823   .0346543    57.36   0.000     1.919902    2.055744
--------------+----------------------------------------------------------------
        sigma |   7.299626   .2529634                       6.82029     7.81265
-------------------------------------------------------------------------------
```

图 2.11

2.4 截尾回归

对于线性模型：

$$y_i = \boldsymbol{x}_i' \boldsymbol{\beta} + \varepsilon_i (i = 1, 2, \cdots, n) \tag{2.22}$$

由于某种原因，只有 $y_i \geqslant c$（c 为常数）时，才能观测到样本数据，而其他区域没有任何相关$\{y_i, \boldsymbol{x}_i\}$数据，这就是左截尾回归。与删失回归一样，截尾回归也有左截断、右截断和双边截断三种情况。

进一步假设 $\varepsilon_i | \boldsymbol{x}_i \sim N(0, \sigma^2)$，则有 $y_i | \boldsymbol{x}_i \sim N(\boldsymbol{x}_i' \boldsymbol{\beta}, \sigma^2)$，可得

$$\mathrm{E}(y_i \mid y_i > c) = \boldsymbol{x}_i' \boldsymbol{\beta} + \sigma \cdot \lambda[(c - \boldsymbol{x}_i' \boldsymbol{\beta}) / \sigma] \tag{2.23}$$

由此可知，如果使用 OLS 估计模型(2.22)，则会遗漏非线性项（即第二项），被纳入扰动项，扰动项与解释变量相关，导致截尾回归的 OLS 估计不是一致性估计，于是需要选用 MLE 法做一致性估计。

左截尾随机变量分布的条件密度函数为：

$$f(y \mid y > c) = \begin{cases} \dfrac{f(y)}{P(y > c)}, & 若\ y > c \\ 0, & 若\ y \leqslant c \end{cases}$$

截尾后被解释变量分布的条件密度函数为：

$$f(y_i \mid y_i > c, \boldsymbol{x}_i) = \frac{\frac{1}{\sigma}\phi[(y_i - \boldsymbol{x}_i'\boldsymbol{\beta})/\sigma]}{1 - \Phi[(c - \boldsymbol{x}_i'\boldsymbol{\beta})/\sigma]} \tag{2.24}$$

由此可以写出整个样本的似然函数,然后使用 MLE 法估计参数。

截尾回归的语法格式为：

truncreg depvar [indepvars] [if] [in] [weight] [, options]

其中的选项设定同删失回归。

菜单操作路径为：

Statistics>Linear models and related>Truncated regression

例 2.4　截尾回归

下面以 Stata 自带数据集为例说明截尾回归的软件实现。

* 下载数据集

.webuse laborsub

* 观察数据分布

.tab lfp

运行结果如图 2.12 所示。

1 if woman worked in 1975	Freq.	Percent	Cum.
0	100	40.00	40.00
1	150	60.00	100.00
Total	250	100.00	

图　2.12

* 做局部样本回归

.regress whrs kl6 k618 wa we if whrs>0

运行结果如图 2.13 所示。

Source	SS	df	MS			
Model	7326995.15	4	1831748.79	Number of obs	=	150
Residual	94793104.2	145	653745.546	F(4, 145)	=	2.80
				Prob > F	=	0.0281
				R-squared	=	0.0717
				Adj R-squared	=	0.0461
Total	102120099	149	685369.794	Root MSE	=	808.55

whrs	Coefficient	Std. err.	t	P>|t|	[95% conf.	interval]
kl6	-421.4822	167.9734	-2.51	0.013	-753.4748	-89.48953
k618	-104.4571	54.18616	-1.93	0.056	-211.5538	2.639668
wa	-4.784917	9.690502	-0.49	0.622	-23.9378	14.36797
we	9.353195	31.23793	0.30	0.765	-52.38731	71.0937
_cons	1629.817	615.1301	2.65	0.009	414.0371	2845.597

图　2.13

* 做左截断回归

```
.truncreg whrs kl6 k618 wa we, ll(0)
```

运行结果如图 2.14 所示。

```
Truncated regression
Limit: Lower =      0                      Number of obs     =        150
       Upper = +inf                        Wald chi2(4)      =      10.05
Log likelihood = -1200.9157                Prob > chi2       =     0.0395
```

whrs	Coefficient	Std. err.	z	P>|z|	[95% conf.	interval]
kl6	-803.0042	321.3614	-2.50	0.012	-1432.861	-173.1474
k618	-172.875	88.72898	-1.95	0.051	-346.7806	1.030579
wa	-8.821123	14.36848	-0.61	0.539	-36.98283	19.34059
we	16.52873	46.50375	0.36	0.722	-74.61695	107.6744
_cons	1586.26	912.355	1.74	0.082	-201.9233	3374.442
/sigma	983.7262	94.44303	10.42	0.000	798.6213	1168.831

图 2.14

* 下载数据集

```
.sysuse auto
.generate lowmpg = 20 if foreign = = 0
.replace lowmpg = 25 if foreign = = 1
```

* 观察数据分布特征

```
.tab lowmpg
```

运行结果如图 2.15 所示。

lowmpg	Freq.	Percent	Cum.
20	52	70.27	70.27
25	22	29.73	100.00
Total	74	100.00	

图 2.15

* 做左截断回归

```
.truncreg mpg price length displacement, ll(lowmpg)
```

运行结果如图 2.16 所示。

```
Truncated regression
Limit: Lower = lowmpg                       Number of obs     =         26
       Upper =   +inf                       Wald chi2(3)      =       6.90
Log likelihood = -65.008966                 Prob > chi2       =     0.0752

         mpg | Coefficient  Std. err.      z    P>|z|     [95% conf. interval]
-------------+----------------------------------------------------------------
       price |   .0002803   .0012821     0.22   0.827    -.0022327    .0027932
      length |  -.3135494   .1625314    -1.93   0.054    -.6321052    .0050063
displacement |  -.0271346   .0377411    -0.72   0.472    -.1011058    .0468366
       _cons |   79.09294   23.70292     3.34   0.001     32.63607    125.5498
-------------+----------------------------------------------------------------
      /sigma |   5.453352   1.498572     3.64   0.000     2.516204      8.3905
```

图 2.16

2.5 异方差线性回归

当误差项的方差不是常数时，回归中会出现异方差性。

具有乘法异方差的线性回归模型为：

$$y_i = \boldsymbol{x}_i \boldsymbol{\beta} + \varepsilon_i ; \quad \sigma_i^2 = \exp(\boldsymbol{z}_i \boldsymbol{\alpha}) \tag{2.25}$$

该模型估计的 Stata 命令为 hetregress，hetregress 通过使用最大似然（ML，默认值）或 Harvey 的两步广义最小二乘（GLS）方法，将方差建模为指定变量的指数函数，从而拟合乘法异方差线性回归。

其对数似然函数为：

$$\ln L = \sum_{i=1}^{n} \frac{w_i}{2} \left\{ \frac{(y_i - \boldsymbol{x}_i \boldsymbol{\beta})^2}{\exp(\boldsymbol{z}_i \boldsymbol{\alpha})} - \ln(2\pi) - \boldsymbol{z}_i \boldsymbol{\alpha} \right\} \tag{2.26}$$

式中，$y_i(i=1,2,\cdots,n)$是因变量；$\boldsymbol{x}_i=(x_{1i},x_{2i},\cdots,x_{ki})$是建模均值函数的 k 个自变量；$\boldsymbol{z}_i=(z_{1i},z_{2i},\cdots,z_{mi})$是建模方差函数的 m 个变量；w_i 是权重；$\boldsymbol{\beta}$ 是均值函数中未知参数的列向量；$\boldsymbol{\alpha}$ 是方差函数中未知参数的列向量。

当指定了 twostep 选项时，hetregress 使用两步 GLS 估计。GLS 估计值 $\hat{\beta}_{\mathrm{GLS}}$ 和 $\hat{\alpha}_{\mathrm{GLS}}$ 用 ML 估计值作初始值。主要步骤为：

（1）使用 OLS 估计回归系数 $\boldsymbol{\beta}$，并计算残差 $e_i(i=1,\cdots,n)$；

（2）使用 OLS 对对数平方残差 $\ln(e_i^2)$做 $\boldsymbol{z}$ 回归估计，并估计 $\boldsymbol{\alpha}$；

（3）对 OLS 估计值 $\boldsymbol{\alpha}$ 进行校正，以获得$\hat{\boldsymbol{\alpha}}_c$ 及其协方差矩阵。

（4）计算 $\hat{\boldsymbol{\sigma}}_i^2=\exp(\boldsymbol{z}_i\hat{\boldsymbol{\alpha}}_c)(i=1,\cdots,n)$；

（5）使用 $\hat{\boldsymbol{\alpha}}_i^2$ 作为权重，重新拟合原始回归模型，以获得 GLS 估计值 $\hat{\beta}_{\mathrm{GLS}}$ 和 $\hat{\alpha}_{\mathrm{GLS}}$。

异方差线性回归的语法格式为：

（1）MLE 法

```
hetregress depvar [indepvars] [if] [in] [weight] [, ml_options]
```

(2) Harvey 的两步 GLS 法

hetregress depvar [indepvars] [if] [in], twostep het(varlist) [ts_options]

当误差项的方差是一个或多个变量的乘法函数时就是乘法异方差。当 het()选项中未指定变量时,hetregress 适用于同构线性回归模型。

菜单操作路径为:

Statistics>Linear models and related>Heteroskedastic linear regression

例 2.5　异方差线性回归

下面以 Stata 自带数据集为例说明异方差线性回归的软件实现。

* 下载数据集

```
.clear
.sysuse auto
```

* 回归,观察方差数据特征

```
.regress price length i.foreign
```

运行结果如图 2.17 所示。

Source	SS	df	MS		
				Number of obs =	74
				F(2, 71) =	16.35
Model	200288930	2	100144465	Prob > F =	0.0000
Residual	434776467	71	6123612.21	R-squared =	0.3154
				Adj R-squared =	0.2961
Total	635065396	73	8699525.97	Root MSE =	2474.6

price	Coefficient	Std. err.	t	P>|t|	[95% conf.	interval]
length	90.21239	15.83368	5.70	0.000	58.64092	121.7839
foreign						
Foreign	2801.143	766.117	3.66	0.000	1273.549	4328.737
_cons	-11621.35	3124.436	-3.72	0.000	-17851.3	-5391.401

图　2.17

* 画图观察 length 残差项的方差特征

```
.rvpplot length,yline(0)
```

运行结果如图 2.18 所示。

* 拟合乘法异方差回归模型,并使用长度对方差进行建模

```
.hetregress price length i.foreign, het(length)
```

运行结果如图 2.19 所示。

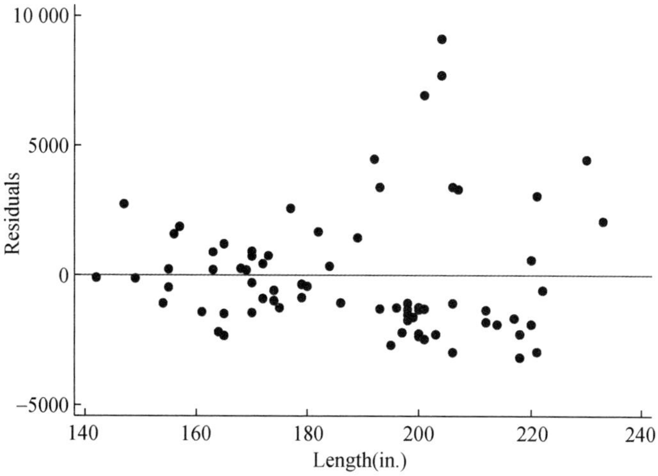

图 2.18

```
Heteroskedastic linear regression                 Number of obs     =         74
ML estimation
                                                   Wald chi2(2)      =      29.58
Log likelihood = -668.9945                         Prob > chi2       =     0.0000

------------------------------------------------------------------------------
       price | Coefficient  Std. err.      z    P>|z|     [95% conf. interval]
-------------+----------------------------------------------------------------
price        |
      length |   64.39123   11.95866     5.38   0.000     40.95269    87.82977
             |
     foreign |
    Foreign  |   1478.235   437.3862     3.38   0.001     620.9738    2335.496
       _cons |  -6490.817   2134.813    -3.04   0.002    -10674.97   -2306.661
-------------+----------------------------------------------------------------
lnsigma2     |
      length |    .049792   .0092888     5.36   0.000     .0315863    .0679976
       _cons |   5.885528   1.753384     3.36   0.001     2.448959    9.322096
------------------------------------------------------------------------------
LR test of lnsigma2=0: chi2(1) = 25.40                 Prob > chi2 = 0.0000
```

图 2.19

* 对均值函数执行 LR 测试，而不是 Wald 测试

```
.hetregress price length i.foreign, het(length) lrmodel
```

运行结果如图 2.20 所示。

* 用 Harvey 两步 GLS 法拟合异方差回归模型

```
.hetregress price length i.foreign, het(length) twostep
```

运行结果如图 2.21 所示。

```
Heteroskedastic linear regression                Number of obs    =        74
ML estimation
                                                 LR chi2(2)       =     28.76
Log likelihood = -668.9945                       Prob > chi2      =    0.0000

------------------------------------------------------------------------------
       price | Coefficient  Std. err.      z    P>|z|     [95% conf. interval]
-------------+----------------------------------------------------------------
price        |
      length |   64.39123   11.95866     5.38   0.000     40.95269    87.82977
             |
     foreign |
    Foreign  |   1478.235   437.3862     3.38   0.001     620.9738    2335.496
       _cons |  -6490.817   2134.813    -3.04   0.002    -10674.97   -2306.661
-------------+----------------------------------------------------------------
lnsigma2     |
      length |    .049792   .0092888     5.36   0.000     .0315863    .0679976
       _cons |   5.885528   1.753384     3.36   0.001     2.448959    9.322096
------------------------------------------------------------------------------
LR test of lnsigma2=0: chi2(1) = 25.40                 Prob > chi2 = 0.0000
```

图 2.20

```
Heteroskedastic linear regression                Number of obs    =        74
Two-step GLS estimation
                                                 Wald chi2(2)     =     34.39
                                                 Prob > chi2      =    0.0000

------------------------------------------------------------------------------
       price | Coefficient  Std. err.      z    P>|z|     [95% conf. interval]
-------------+----------------------------------------------------------------
price        |
      length |   66.70549   11.67666     5.71   0.000     43.81966    89.59132
             |
     foreign |
    Foreign  |   1580.511   428.8698     3.69   0.000     739.9416     2421.08
       _cons |  -6934.137   2085.765    -3.32   0.001    -11022.16   -2846.113
-------------+----------------------------------------------------------------
lnsigma2     |
      length |   .0448232   .0116768     3.84   0.000     .0219371    .0677094
       _cons |   7.122623   2.209595     3.22   0.001     2.791897    11.45335
------------------------------------------------------------------------------
Wald test of lnsigma2=0: chi2(1) = 14.74               Prob > chi2 = 0.0001
```

图 2.21

2.6 Box-Cox 变换模型

Box-Cox 变换模型为：

$$y^{(\lambda)}=\frac{y^{\lambda}-1}{\lambda} \tag{2.27}$$

该模型已广泛应用于数据分析。Box 和 Cox(1964)①发展了该转换，并认为这种转换可以使残差更接近正态，而不是异方差。Cook 和 Weisberg(1982)②也对这种转换进行了分析。因为转换嵌入了几个作为一种主流函数形式的方法，它已经受到了一些关注。

$$y^{(\lambda)}=\begin{cases} y-1 & \text{if } \lambda=1 \\ \ln(y) & \text{if } \lambda=0 \\ 1-1/y & \text{if } \lambda=-1 \end{cases}$$

Box-Cox 变换模型可以获得四种不同模型参数的最大似然估计，最普遍使用的模型是 Theta 模型：

$$y_j^{(\theta)}=\beta_0+\beta_1 x_{1j}^{(\lambda)}+\beta_2 x_{2j}^{(\lambda)}+\cdots+\beta_k x_{kj}^{(\lambda)}+\gamma_1 z_{1j}+\gamma_2 z_{2j}+\cdots+\gamma_l z_{lj}+\varepsilon_j \tag{2.28}$$

式中，$\varepsilon \sim N(0,\sigma^2)$。因变量 y 受参数为 θ 的 Box-Cox 变换的影响；每个解释变量 x_1，x_2，…，x_k 都经过了参数为 λ 的 Box-Cox 变换；在 notrans()选项中指定的 z_1，z_2，…，z_k 是不作转换的独立变量。

Box-Cox 变换的语法格式为：

boxcox depvar [indepvars] [if] [in] [weight] [, options]

boxcox 找到了 Box-Cox 变换参数、自变量系数和正态分布误差标准差的最大似然估计。任何要转换的 depvar 或 indepvars 都必须严格为正。选项可用于控制哪些变量保持未转换状态。

菜单操作路径为：

Statistics>Linear models and related>Box-Cox regression

例 2.6 变换

下面以 Stata 自带数据为例说明 Box-Cox 变换的软件实现。

```
* 下载数据集
.clear
.sysuse auto
* 将 Box-Cox 变换应用于 mpg
.boxcox mpg weight price
```

---

① Box, G. E. P., and D. R. Cox. An Analysis of Transformations. *Journal of the Royal Statistical Society: Series B*, 1964, 26.

② Cook, R. D., and S. Weisberg. *Residuals and Influence in Regression*. New York: Chapman & Hall/CRC, 1982.

运行结果如图 2.22 所示。

```
                                                Number of obs     =        7
                                                LR chi2(2)        =    100.4
Log likelihood = -178.06886                     Prob > chi2       =     0.00

         mpg  Coefficient  Std. err.      z    P>|z|     [95% conf. interval

      /theta   -.7568509   .2902995    -2.61   0.009    -1.325828   -.187874

Estimates of scale-variant parameters

              Coefficient

Notrans
      weight   -.0000263
       price   -1.34e-06
       _cons    1.272474

      /sigma    .0132169


   Test         Restricted      LR statistic
    H0:       log likelihood        chi2       Prob > chi2

theta = -1      -178.41823          0.70          0.403
theta =  0      -181.43399          6.73          0.009
theta =  1      -195.21698         34.30          0.000
```

图 2.22

* 同上，但将 foreign 变量作为未转换的自变量包括在内

. boxcox mpg weight price, notrans(foreign) lrtest

运行结果如图 2.23 所示。

```
                                                Number of obs     =       74
                                                LR chi2(3)        =   105.04
Log likelihood = -175.74705                     Prob > chi2       =    0.000

         mpg  Coefficient  Std. err.      z    P>|z|     [95% conf. interval]

      /theta   -.7826999    .281954    -2.78   0.006     -1.33532   -.2300802

Estimates of scale-variant parameters

              Coefficient  chi2(df)  P>chi2(df)   df of chi2

Notrans
     foreign   -.0097564     4.644     0.031           1
      weight   -.0000294    58.056     0.000           1
       price   -4.66e-07     0.469     0.493           1
       _cons    1.249845

      /sigma    .0118454


   Test         Restricted      LR statistic
    H0:       log likelihood        chi2       Prob > chi2

theta = -1      -176.04312          0.59          0.442
theta =  0      -179.54104          7.59          0.006
theta =  1      -194.13727         36.78          0.000
```

图 2.23

* 将 Box-Cox 变换应用于 weight 和 price

.boxcox mpg weight price, model(rhsonly) lrtest

运行结果如图 2.24 所示。

```
                                                Number of obs   =        74
                                                LR chi2(3)      =     86.73
Log likelihood = -191.02712                     Prob > chi2     =     0.000

         mpg   Coefficient  Std. err.      z    P>|z|     [95% conf. interval]

     /lambda     -1.023598   .6644489   -1.54   0.123    -2.325894    .2786975

Estimates of scale-variant parameters

               Coefficient chi2(df)  P>chi2(df)   df of chi2

Notrans
       _cons      70530.96

Trans
      weight     -53789.02    65.899   0.000            1
       price     -18403.25     3.833   0.050            1

      /sigma      3.197947


   Test          Restricted      LR statistic
    H0:        log likelihood        chi2       Prob > chi2

lambda = -1      -191.02775          0.00          0.972
lambda =  0      -192.18628          2.32          0.128
lambda =  1      -195.21698          8.38          0.004
```

图 2.24

* 使用相同的参数转换 mpg、weight price

.boxcox mpg weight price, model(lambda) lrtest

运行结果如图 2.25 所示。

```
                                                Number of obs   =        74
                                                LR chi2(2)      =    100.28
Log likelihood = -178.12667                     Prob > chi2     =     0.000

         mpg   Coefficient  Std. err.      z    P>|z|     [95% conf. interval]

     /lambda     -.3799989   .2218921   -1.71   0.087    -.8148994    .0549016

Estimates of scale-variant parameters

               Coefficient chi2(df)  P>chi2(df)   df of chi2

Notrans
       _cons      16.61507

Trans
      weight     -4.644448    70.786   0.000            1
       price     -1.260506     8.106   0.004            1

      /sigma      .0413502


   Test          Restricted      LR statistic
    H0:        log likelihood        chi2       Prob > chi2

lambda = -1      -181.86867          7.48          0.006
lambda =  0      -179.58214          2.91          0.088
lambda =  1      -195.21698         34.18          0.000
```

图 2.25

```
* 使用不同于用于转换 weight price 的参数来转换 mpg
. boxcox mpg weight price, model(theta) lrtest
```

运行结果如图 2.26 所示。

```
                                                Number of obs   =         74
                                                LR chi2(3)      =     101.36
Log likelihood = -177.58739                     Prob > chi2     =      0.000

------------------------------------------------------------------------------
         mpg | Coefficient  Std. err.      z    P>|z|     [95% conf. interval]
-------------+----------------------------------------------------------------
     /lambda |   .2908776   .6982748     0.42   0.677    -1.077716    1.659471
      /theta |  -.6103159   .3183125    -1.92   0.055    -1.234197    .0135651
------------------------------------------------------------------------------

Estimates of scale-variant parameters
----------------------------------------------------------
             | Coefficient chi2(df)  P>chi2(df)  df of chi2
-------------+--------------------------------------------
Notrans      |
       _cons |   1.797514
-------------+--------------------------------------------
Trans        |
      weight |   -.011437    71.556   0.000          1
       price |  -.0014915     5.081   0.024          1
-------------+--------------------------------------------
      /sigma |   .0204542
----------------------------------------------------------

---------------------------------------------------------
   Test          Restricted
   H0:         log likelihood      chi2      Prob > chi2
---------------------------------------------------------
theta=lambda = -1   -181.86867      8.56         0.003
theta=lambda =  0   -179.58214      3.99         0.046
theta=lambda =  1   -195.21698     35.26         0.000
---------------------------------------------------------
```

图 2.26

2.7 分位数回归

假设条件分布 $y|\boldsymbol{x}$ 的总体分位数 $y_q(\boldsymbol{x})$是 $\boldsymbol{x}$ 的线性函数，即

$$y_q(\boldsymbol{x}_i)=\boldsymbol{x}_i'\boldsymbol{\beta}_q \tag{2.29}$$

式中，$\boldsymbol{\beta}_q$ 为 q 分位数回归参数，其估计值由加权平均绝对离差最小化得到：

$$\min_{\boldsymbol{\beta}_q}\left[\sum_{i:y_i\geqslant x_i\beta_q}^{n} q\,|\,y_i-\boldsymbol{x}_i'\boldsymbol{\beta}_q\,|+\sum_{i:y_i<x_i\beta_q}^{n}(1-q)\,|\,y_i-\boldsymbol{x}_i'\boldsymbol{\beta}_q\,|\right] \tag{2.30}$$

该目标函数通常使用线性规划法求解计算参数估计值。

定义 τ 为估计的分位数，中位数为 $\tau=0.5$，对每一个观测值 i，设 ε_i 为残差。

$$\varepsilon_i=y_i-\boldsymbol{x}_i'\hat{\boldsymbol{\beta}}_\tau \tag{2.31}$$

最小化目标函数为：

$$\begin{aligned}c_\tau(\varepsilon_i)&=(\tau\mathbf{1}\{\varepsilon_i\geqslant 0\}+(1-\tau)\mathbf{1}\{\varepsilon_i<0\})\,|\,\varepsilon_i\,|\\&=(\tau\mathbf{1}\{\varepsilon_i\geqslant 0\}-(1-\tau)\mathbf{1}\{\varepsilon_i<0\})\varepsilon_i\\&=(\tau-\mathbf{1}\{\varepsilon_i<0)\}\varepsilon_i\end{aligned} \tag{2.32}$$

式中,$\mathbf{1}\{\cdot\}$为标示函数,括号内条件成立时取值为1,不成立时取值为0;选取使$c_\tau(\varepsilon_i)$最小化的$\hat{\boldsymbol{\beta}}_\tau$的问题等价于寻找使$\boldsymbol{x}\hat{\boldsymbol{\beta}}_\tau$最优拟合在$x$的条件下的$y$分布的分位数。用线性规划建立该最小化问题,则为:

$$\min_{\boldsymbol{\beta}_\tau,\boldsymbol{u},\boldsymbol{v}}\{\tau\mathbf{1}_n'\boldsymbol{u}+(1-\tau)\mathbf{1}_n'\boldsymbol{v}\mid \boldsymbol{y}-\boldsymbol{X}\boldsymbol{\beta}_\tau=\boldsymbol{u}-\boldsymbol{v}\} \tag{2.33}$$

分位数回归可使用准R^2测度拟合优度:

$$\tilde{R}^2=1-\frac{\text{分位数估计值的加权偏差和}}{\text{原始分位数的加权偏差和}}$$

该式利用双指数分布$e^{v_i|\varepsilon_i|}$计算的似然值计算。其中,$v_i=\begin{cases}\tau & \varepsilon_i>0\\1-\tau & \varepsilon_i\leqslant 0\end{cases}$。

最小化目标函数就是最小化加权绝对离差和$\sum_i|\varepsilon_i|v_i$。

设第q水平上分位数回归模型为:

$$Q_q(y)=a_q+b_{q,1}x_1+b_{q,2}x_2$$

则75%和25%分位数回归模型为:

$$Q_{0.75}(y)=a_{0.75}+b_{0.75,1}x_1+b_{0.75,2}x_2$$

$$Q_{0.25}(y)=a_{0.25}+b_{0.25,1}x_1+b_{0.25,2}x_2$$

以75%和25%分位数回归说明分位数差分回归(interquantile quantile regression)和联立分位数回归(simultaneous quantile regression),则分位数差分回归模型为:

$$Q_{0.75}(y)-Q_{0.25}(y)=(a_{0.75}-a_{0.25})+(b_{0.75,1}-b_{0.25,1})x_1+(b_{0.75,2}-b_{0.25,2})x_2$$

qreg命令用来分别拟合分位数回归模型$Q_{0.75}(y)$和$Q_{0.25}(y)$等。iqreg命令用来拟合分位数差分模型,如$Q_{0.75}(y)-Q_{0.25}(y)$。iqreg命令报告的系数是两个qreg模型的系数之差,iqreg也报告通过自抽样(bootstrapping)获得的相应标准偏差。

sqreg类似于qreg,同时联立估计多个分位数的方程式:

$$\begin{cases}Q_{0.75}(y)=a_{0.75}+b_{0.75,1}x_1+b_{0.75,2}x_2\\Q_{0.25}(y)=a_{0.25}+b_{0.25,1}x_1+b_{0.25,2}x_2\end{cases}$$

在各分位数方程残差相互独立时,sqreg得到的系数与使用qreg分别估计每个方程得到的系数相同。sqreg与qreg的不同之处在于,sqreg同时估计方程,并通过自举获得方差—协方差分量估计(VCE)。因此,可以对方程内和方程间的系数进行假设检验。

分位数回归的语法格式为:

(1) 只做一个分位数回归

qreg depvar [indepvars] [if] [in] [weight] [, qreg_options]

(2) 分位数范围回归

iqreg depvar [indepvars] [if] [in] [, iqreg_options]

(3) 同时(做多个)分位数回归

sqreg depvar [indepvars] [if] [in] [, sqreg_options]

(4) 自助分位数回归(bootstrapped quantile regression)

bsqreg depvar [indepvars] [if] [in] [, bsqreg_options]

菜单操作路径为:

(1) qreg:Statistics>Nonparametric analysis>Quantile regression

(2) iqreg:Statistics>Nonparametric analysis>Interquantile regression

(3) sqreg:Statistics>Nonparametric analysis>Simultaneous-quantile regression

(4) bsqreg:Statistics>Nonparametric analysis>Bootstrapped quantile regression

qreg 拟合的分位数(包括中位数)回归模型,也称为最小绝对值、最小绝对偏差或最小 L_1 范数值的回归模型,将条件分布的分位数表示为自变量的线性函数。

iqreg 估计分位数范围内的回归、分位数差异的回归。

sqreg 估计同时分位数回归,为每个分位数产生与 qreg 相同的系数,报告的标准误差与 qreg 类似,但 sqreg 通过引导获得 VCE 值。VCE 值包括在分位数块之间,因此可以通过比较描述不同分位数的系数来测试和构造置信区间。

bsqreg 相当于带有一个分位数的 sqreg。

分位数回归模型的基本操作步骤如下:

(1) 绘制散点图,判断数据分布(对称/非对称)是否适合于用分位数回归模型;

(2) 建模估计 qreg、sqreg、bsqreg、qreg2(聚类稳健标准误);

(3) 进行系数之间差异性的 Wald 检验;

(4) 绘制分位数回归曲线图(grqreg)。

例 2.7 分位数回归

下面使用分位数(包括中位数)回归模型,根据每辆车的重量和长度以及是否为外国制造对其价格进行回归。

```
* 清空内存,下载数据集 auto
.clear
.sysuse auto
* 中位数回归
.qreg price weight length foreign
```

运行结果如图 2.27 所示。

Median regression						
Raw sum of deviations 71102.5 (about 4934)				Number of obs =		74
Min sum of deviations 54411.29				Pseudo R2 =		0.2347
price	Coefficient	Std. err.	t	P>|t|	[95% conf.	interval]
weight	3.933588	1.328718	2.96	0.004	1.283543	6.583632
length	-41.25191	45.46469	-0.91	0.367	-131.9284	49.42456
foreign	3377.771	885.4198	3.81	0.000	1611.857	5143.685
_cons	344.6489	5182.394	0.07	0.947	-9991.31	10680.61

图 2.27

* 使用 Bofinger 带宽方法估计 0.25 分位数

.qreg price weight length foreign, quantile(.25) vce(iid, bofinger)

运行结果如图 2.28 所示。

.25 Quantile regression						
Raw sum of deviations 41912.75 (about 4187)				Number of obs =		74
Min sum of deviations 34801.78				Pseudo R2 =		0.1697
price	Coefficient	Std. err.	t	P>|t|	[95% conf.	interval]
weight	1.831789	.5945476	3.08	0.003	.646001	3.017577
length	2.84556	20.34361	0.14	0.889	-37.7285	43.41962
foreign	2209.925	396.1896	5.58	0.000	1419.75	3000.101
_cons	-1879.775	2318.912	-0.81	0.420	-6504.699	2745.149

图 2.28

* 使用 Parzen 核密度估计器和张伯伦带宽方法估计 0.75 分位数

.qreg price weight length foreign, quantile(.75) vce(iid, kernel(parzen) chamberlain)

运行结果如图 2.29 所示。

.75 Quantile regression						
Raw sum of deviations 79860.75 (about 6342)				Number of obs =		74
Min sum of deviations 49197.97				Pseudo R2 =		0.3840
price	Coefficient	Std. err.	t	P>|t|	[95% conf.	interval]
weight	9.22291	1.212015	7.61	0.000	6.805622	11.6402
length	-220.7833	41.47148	-5.32	0.000	-303.4955	-138.071
foreign	3595.133	807.6524	4.45	0.000	1984.321	5205.945
_cons	20242.9	4727.218	4.28	0.000	10814.76	29671.04

图 2.29

```
* 估计分位数的范围[0.25,0.75],执行 100 次引导复制
. iqreg price weight length foreign, quantile(.25 .75) reps(100)
```

运行结果如图 2.30 所示。

```
.75-.25 Interquantile regression                    Number of obs =         74
  bootstrap(100) SEs                                .75 Pseudo R2 =     0.3840
                                                    .25 Pseudo R2 =     0.1697

------------------------------------------------------------------------------
             |              Bootstrap
       price | Coefficient  std. err.      t    P>|t|     [95% conf. interval]
-------------+----------------------------------------------------------------
      weight |   7.391121   2.054408     3.60   0.001     3.293734    11.48851
      length |  -223.6288   67.67791    -3.30   0.002    -358.6082   -88.64951
     foreign |   1385.208   1178.761     1.18   0.244    -965.7575    3736.173
       _cons |   22122.68   7525.147     2.94   0.004     7114.246    37131.11
------------------------------------------------------------------------------
```

图 2.30

```
* 同上
. iqreg price weight length foreign, reps(100)
* 同时估计 0.25、0.5 和 0.75 分位数,执行 100 次引导复制
```

运行结果如图 2.31 所示。

```
Simultaneous quantile regression                    Number of obs =         74
  bootstrap(100) SEs                                .25 Pseudo R2 =     0.1697
                                                    .50 Pseudo R2 =     0.2347
                                                    .75 Pseudo R2 =     0.3840

------------------------------------------------------------------------------
             |              Bootstrap
       price | Coefficient  std. err.      t    P>|t|     [95% conf. interval]
-------------+----------------------------------------------------------------
q25          |
      weight |   1.831789   1.553803     1.18   0.242    -1.267173    4.930751
      length |    2.84556   33.97618     0.08   0.933     -64.9178    70.60892
     foreign |   2209.925   1157.349     1.91   0.060    -98.33356    4518.184
       _cons |  -1879.775   3415.129    -0.55   0.584    -8691.034    4931.485
-------------+----------------------------------------------------------------
q50          |
      weight |   3.933588   2.588685     1.52   0.133    -1.229381    9.096557
      length |  -41.25191   70.45052    -0.59   0.560     -181.761    99.25722
     foreign |   3377.771   1018.267     3.32   0.001     1346.901    5408.641
       _cons |   344.6489   6370.738     0.05   0.957    -12361.39    13050.69
-------------+----------------------------------------------------------------
q75          |
      weight |    9.22291   2.438802     3.78   0.000     4.358872    14.08695
      length |  -220.7833   84.57043    -2.61   0.011    -389.4537   -52.11288
     foreign |   3595.133   1145.662     3.14   0.002     1310.183    5880.084
       _cons |    20242.9   9000.777     2.25   0.028     2291.421    38194.39
------------------------------------------------------------------------------
```

图 2.31

* 带 bootstrap 标准误差的中值回归

运行结果如图 2.32 所示。

```
Median regression, bootstrap(20) SEs                Number of obs =        74
  Raw sum of deviations  71102.5 (about 4934)
  Min sum of deviations 54411.29                    Pseudo R2     =    0.2347
```

price	Coefficient	Std. err.	t	P>|t|	[95% conf.	interval]
weight	3.933588	2.381285	1.65	0.103	-.8157349	8.68291
length	-41.25191	59.85554	-0.69	0.493	-160.63	78.12621
foreign	3377.771	1289.715	2.62	0.011	805.516	5950.026
_cons	344.6489	5706.123	0.06	0.952	-11035.85	11725.15

图 2.32

* 用 bootstrap 标准误差估计 0.75 分位数

运行结果如图 2.33 所示。

```
.75 Quantile regression, bootstrap(20) SEs          Number of obs =        74
  Raw sum of deviations 79860.75 (about 6342)
  Min sum of deviations 49197.97                    Pseudo R2     =    0.3840
```

price	Coefficient	Std. err.	t	P>|t|	[95% conf.	interval]
weight	9.22291	2.508862	3.68	0.000	4.219143	14.22668
length	-220.7833	82.34022	-2.68	0.009	-385.0057	-56.56088
foreign	3595.133	1152.843	3.12	0.003	1295.86	5894.406
_cons	20242.9	8971.656	2.26	0.027	2349.501	38136.31

图 2.33

2.8 分数多项式回归

分数多项式增加了传统多项式模型所不具备的灵活性。虽然多项式在数据分析中很流行，但线性和二次函数的曲线形状范围有限，而三次和高阶函数的曲线通常会产生不需要的边缘效果和波浪等曲线瑕疵。分数多项式与正则多项式的不同之处在于：一是允许对数存在；二是允许非整数幂存在；三是允许幂重复。

我们将用 x 写出一个分数多项式：$x^{(p_1,p_2,\cdots,p_m)'}\boldsymbol{\beta}$。我们将 $x(p)$ 写为正则幂，$x(0)$ 被解释为 $\ln(x)$，而不是 $x(0)=1$。

如果 $(p_1,p_2,\cdots,p_m)$ 中没有重复的幂，即

$$x^{(p_1,p_2,\cdots,p_m)'}\boldsymbol{\beta}=\beta_0+\beta_1 x^{(p_1)}+\beta_2 x^{(p_2)}+\cdots+\beta_m x^{(p_m)}$$

在分数多项式中允许幂重复，每次一个幂重复，它就会乘以另一个 $\ln(x)$。作为一个极端情况，考虑具有所有重复幂次的分数多项式，例如，其中的 m，有

$$x^{(p,p,\cdots,p)'}\boldsymbol{\beta}=\beta_0+\beta_1 x^{(p)}+\beta_2 x^{(p)}\ln(x)+\cdots+\beta_m x^{(p)}\{\ln(x)\}^{m-1}$$

例如：

$$\begin{aligned}x^{(0,0,2)'}\boldsymbol{\beta}&=\beta_0+\beta_1 x^{(0)}+\beta_2 x^{(0)}\ln(x)+\beta_3 x^{(2)}\\&=\beta_0+\beta_1\ln(x)+\beta_2\{\ln(x)\}^2+\beta_3 x^2\end{aligned}$$

有了这个定义，我们可以得到比正则多项式更宽的形状范围。

以 c 为中心的项的分数多项式是：

$$(\mathrm{term}^{(p_1,\cdots,p_m)}-c^{(p_1,\cdots,p_m)})'\boldsymbol{\beta}$$

中心分数多项式的截距可以解释为所有协变量的零效应。当我们使用 c 将分数多项式项居中时，截距被解释为 $\mathrm{term}=c$ 的影响，其他协变量的值为零。

假设我们将 x 的分数多项式的幂(0,0,2)置于 $x=c$ 的中心，即

$$\begin{aligned}&(x^{(0,0,2)}-c^{(0,0,2)})'\boldsymbol{\beta}\\&=\beta_0+\beta_1(x^{(0)}-c^{(0)})+\beta_2\{x^{(0)}\ln(x)-c^{(0)}\ln(c)\}+\beta_3(x^{(2)}-c^{(2)})\\&=\beta_0+\beta_1\{\ln(x)-\ln(c)\}+\beta_2[\{\ln(x)\}^2-\{\ln(c)\}^2]+\beta_3(x^2-c^2)\end{aligned}$$

分数多项式的一般定义，包括可能的重复幂，可以用 $x>0$ 的函数 $H_1(x),\cdots,H_m(x)$写为：

$$\beta_0+\sum_{j=1}^{m}\beta_j H_j(x)$$

式中，$H_1(x)=x^{(p_1)}$，且对 $j=2,\cdots,m$，有

$$H_j(x)=\begin{cases}x^{(p_j)} & \text{if } p_j\neq p_{j-1}\\ H_{j-1}(x)\ln(x) & \text{if } p_j=p_{j-1}\end{cases}$$

分数多项式可以中心化，以便更容易解释截距。当 x 的分数多项式以 c 为中心时，我们从 $x^{(p_1,p_2,\cdots,p_m)}$ 中减去 $c^{(p_1,p_2,\cdots,p_m)}$，其中 $c^{(p_1,p_2,\cdots,p_m)}=[H(x)',0]'$，这时，中心化分数多项式为：

$$(x^{(p_1,\cdots,p_m)}-c^{(p_1,\cdots,p_m)})'\boldsymbol{\beta}$$

模型偏差 D 定义为最大对数似然值的 -2 倍。对于正态误差模型，我们使用以下公式：

$$D=n\left(1-\bar{l}+\ln\frac{2\pi\mathrm{RSS}}{n}\right)$$

其中，n 是样本量，$\bar{l}$ 是对数标准化权重的平均值(如果权重都相等，则 $\bar{l}=0$)，RSS 是

回归拟合的平方和残差。

对于正态误差模型,fp 报告的 p 值的计算方法与其他模型不同。设 D_k 和 D_m 分别为自由度是 k 和 m 模型的偏差。对于正态误差模型,方差比 F 计算如下:

$$F=\frac{d_2}{d_1}\left\{\exp\left(\frac{D_k-D_m}{n}\right)-1\right\}$$

其中,d_1 是分子自由度 df 数,是自由度为 m 的模型相对于自由度为 k 的模型估计的附加参数数量。d_2 是分母自由度,等于自由度为 m 的模型的剩余自由度减去估计的幂数 m。p 值利用 df 上的 F 分布 $F(d_1,d_2)$。

分数多项式回归的语法格式为:

(1) 估计

fp <term> [, est_options]: est_cmd

(2) 指定在估计期间计算 varname 的分数幂

fp <term>(varname) [, est_options]: est_cmd

(3) 重现估计结果

fp [, replay_options]

(4) 创建指定的分数多项式幂变量

fp generate [type] [newvar =] varname^(numlist) [if] [in] [, gen_options]

各选项及含义如下:

(1) est_cmd:可以是任何存储 e(ll)结果的估计命令。

(2) fp:使用此替换执行 est_cmd,在 term 中拟合分数多项式回归。

(3) est_options:可以是:

① powers(# # … #):要搜索的幂,默认值为幂(-2 -1 -0.5 0.5 1 2 3);

② dimension(#):分数多项式的最大次数,默认值为 2;

③ fp(# # … #):使用指定的分数多项式。

菜单操作路径为:

(1) fp

Statistics>Linear models and related>Fractional polynomials>Fractional polynomial regression

(2) fp generate

Statistics>Linear models and related>Fractional polynomials>Create fractional polynomial variables

例 2.8　分数多项式回归

考虑来自 Isaacs 等(1983)[①]的血清免疫球蛋白 G(IgG)数据集,该数据集包括 298

① Isaacs, D., D. G. Altman, C. E. Tidmarsh, H. B. Valman, and A. D. Webster. Serum Immunoglobulin Concentrations in Preschool Children Measured by Laser Nephelometry: Reference Ranges for IgG, IgA, IgM. *Journal of Clinical Pathology*, 1983, 36.

项幼儿独立观察。因变量 sqrtigg 是 IgG 浓度的平方根，自变量年龄是每个孩子的年龄。(初步 Box-Cox 变换分析表明，平方根变换可以消除 IgG 中的偏斜)

我们的目的是找到一个模型，准确预测给定年龄的 sqrtigg 平均值。我们使用 fp 查找最佳的 FP2 模型(默认选项)。每个孩子的年龄都很小，而且都是正值，因此不使用 fp 的缩放选项或自己缩放。

.use https://www.stata-press.com/data/r17/igg, clear

(Immunoglobulin in children)

*分数多项式线性回归

.fp <age>, scale center: regress sqrtigg <age>

(fitting 44 models)

(....10%....20%....30%....40%....50%....60%....70%....80%....90%....100%)

运行结果如图 2.34 所示。

Fractional polynomial comparisons:

age	Test df	Deviance	Residual std. dev.	Deviance diff.	P	Powers
omitted	4	427.539	0.497	108.090	0.000	
linear	3	337.561	0.428	18.113	0.000	1
m = 1	2	327.436	0.421	7.987	0.020	0
m = 2	0	319.448	0.416	0.000	--	-2 2

Note: Test df is degrees of freedom, and P = P > F is sig. level for tests comparing models vs. model with m = 2 based on deviance difference, F(df, 293).

Source	SS	df	MS
Model	22.2846976	2	11.1423488
Residual	50.9676492	295	.172771692
Total	73.2523469	297	.246640898

Number of obs	=	298
F(2, 295)	=	64.49
Prob > F	=	0.0000
R-squared	=	0.3042
Adj R-squared	=	0.2995
Root MSE	=	.41566

sqrtigg	Coefficient	Std. err.	t	P>|t|	[95% conf.	interval]
age_1	-.1562156	.027416	-5.70	0.000	-.2101713	-.10226
age_2	.0148405	.0027767	5.34	0.000	.0093757	.0203052
_cons	2.283145	.0305739	74.68	0.000	2.222974	2.343315

图 2.34

由 fp 创建的新变量包含以 fp 为中心的最佳拟合分数多项式年龄幂。例如，age_1 通过减去年龄的平均值进行−2 次幂运算。

拟合曲线具有不对称的 S 形。最好的模型具有幂(−2.2)和偏差 319.448。我们在 0.05 置信水平上拒绝低阶模型即零、线性和自然对数幂模型。多达 44 个模型被拟合后,寻找最佳模型。现在让我们看看自由度为 4 的模型。允许的最高自由度在 dimension()中指定。我们重新定义先前通过替换生成的分数多项式幂变量。

.fp <age>, dimension(4) center replace: regress sqrtigg <age>

运行结果如图 2.35 所示。

```
(fitting 494 models)
(....10%....20%....30%....40%....50%....60%....70%....80%....90%....100%)

Fractional polynomial comparisons:

-------------------------------------------------------------------------
             |   Test               Residual   Deviance
         age |    df    Deviance    std. dev.      diff.        P   Powers
-------------+-----------------------------------------------------------
     omitted |     8     427.539       0.497     109.795    0.000
      linear |     7     337.561       0.428      19.818    0.007   1
       m = 1 |     6     327.436       0.421       9.692    0.149   0
       m = 2 |     4     319.448       0.416       1.705    0.798   -2 2
       m = 3 |     2     319.275       0.416       1.532    0.476   -2 1 1
       m = 4 |     0     317.744       0.416       0.000       --   0 3 3 3
-------------------------------------------------------------------------
Note: Test df is degrees of freedom, and P = P > F is sig. level for tests
      comparing models vs. model with m = 4 based on deviance difference,
      F(df, 289).

      Source |       SS           df       MS      Number of obs   =       298
-------------+----------------------------------   F(4, 293)       =     32.63
       Model |  22.5754541         4  5.64386353   Prob > F        =    0.0000
    Residual |  50.6768927       293  .172958678   R-squared       =    0.3082
-------------+----------------------------------   Adj R-squared   =    0.2987
       Total |  73.2523469       297  .246640898   Root MSE        =    .41588

------------------------------------------------------------------------------
     sqrtigg | Coefficient  Std. err.      t    P>|t|     [95% conf. interval]
-------------+----------------------------------------------------------------
       age_1 |   .8761824   .1898721     4.61   0.000     .5024962    1.249869
       age_2 |  -.1922029   .0684934    -2.81   0.005    -.3270044   -.0574015
       age_3 |   .2043794    .074947     2.73   0.007     .0568767    .3518821
       age_4 |  -.0560067   .0212969    -2.63   0.009     -.097921   -.0140924
       _cons |   2.238735   .0482705    46.38   0.000     2.143734    2.333736
------------------------------------------------------------------------------
```

图 2.35

FP4 模型似乎与其他分数多项式模型没有显著差异(在 0.05 水平)。

将 $m=2$ 模型的多项式曲线形状与传统四次曲线形状进行比较,其拟合结果明显优于立方体(未显示)。我们使用 fp,以生成所需的年龄幂,即(1;2;3;4)四次方和(−2,2)的二次分数多项式,并对模型进行拟合。fp()选项用于指定幂。我们使用 predict 获得每个回归的拟合值。同时用 fp 拟合两个模型,并用 twoway scatter 绘制结果曲线。

.fp <age>, center fp(1 2 3 4) replace: regress sqrtigg <age>

-> regress sqrtigg age_1 age_2 age_3 age_4

运行结果如图 2.36 所示。

Source	SS	df	MS			
				Number of obs	=	298
				F(4, 293)	=	32.65
Model	22.5835458	4	5.64588646	Prob > F	=	0.0000
Residual	50.668801	293	.172931061	R-squared	=	0.3083
				Adj R-squared	=	0.2989
Total	73.2523469	297	.246640898	Root MSE	=	.41585

sqrtigg	Coefficient	Std. err.	t	P>|t|	[95% conf.	interval]
age_1	2.047831	.4595962	4.46	0.000	1.143302	2.952359
age_2	-1.058902	.2822803	-3.75	0.000	-1.614456	-.5033479
age_3	.2284917	.0667591	3.42	0.001	.0971037	.3598798
age_4	-.0168534	.0053321	-3.16	0.002	-.0273475	-.0063594
_cons	2.240012	.0480157	46.65	0.000	2.145512	2.334511

图 2.36

.predict fit1

(option xb assumed; fitted values)

.label variable fit1 "Quartic"

.fp <age>, center fp(-2 2) replace: regress sqrtigg <age>

-> regress sqrtigg age_1 age_2

运行结果如图 2.37 所示。

Source	SS	df	MS			
				Number of obs	=	298
				F(2, 295)	=	64.49
Model	22.2846976	2	11.1423488	Prob > F	=	0.0000
Residual	50.9676492	295	.172771692	R-squared	=	0.3042
				Adj R-squared	=	0.2995
Total	73.2523469	297	.246640898	Root MSE	=	.41566

sqrtigg	Coefficient	Std. err.	t	P>|t|	[95% conf.	interval]
age_1	-.1562156	.027416	-5.70	0.000	-.2101713	-.10226
age_2	.0148405	.0027767	5.34	0.000	.0093757	.0203052
_cons	2.283145	.0305739	74.68	0.000	2.222974	2.343315

图 2.37

.predict fit2

(option xb assumed; fitted values)

.label variable fit2 "FP 2"

.scatter sqrtigg fit1 fit2 age, c(. l l) m(o i i) msize(small) lpattern(. -_.) ytitle("Square root of IgG") xtitle("Age, years")

运行结果如图 2.38 所示。

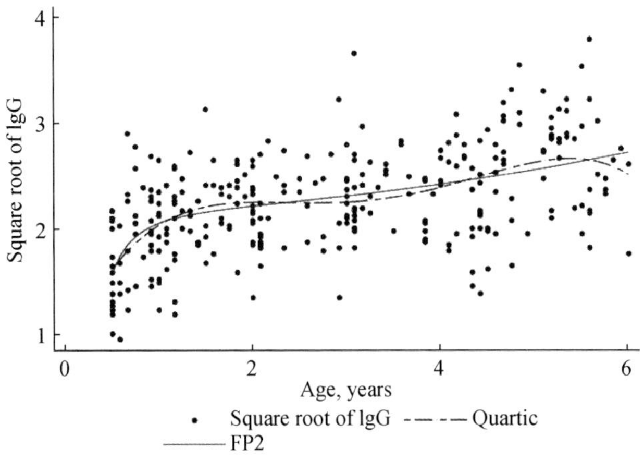

图 2.38

四次曲线具有令人不满意的波浪状外观，这对于已知的 IgG 行为来说是不可信的，IgG 的血清水平在整个生命早期都会增加。分数多项式曲线(FP2)单调增加，因此在生物学上更合理。这两种模型的偏差大致相同。

例 2.9 Cox 回归

Smith 等(1992)①的数据包含了 192 名老年患者两种治疗方法的随机对照临床试验中腿部溃疡完全愈合的时间。有几个协变量可用，其中一个重要的协变量是 mthson，即自记录的溃疡发病以来的月数。这段时间是以整月记录的，而不是一个月的小数，因此，会记录一些零值。

因为响应变量是关注事件的时间，并且一些时间(事实上，大约一半)被删失，所以使用 Cox 回归分析数据是合适的。我们考虑 mthson 中的分数多项式，调整其他四个协变量：年龄、ulcarea(即最初受溃疡影响的组织区域)、deepppg(一个二元变量，指示是否存在深静脉受累)和 treat(表示治疗类型的二进制变量)。

我们用 fp 拟合自由度为 1 和 2 的分数多项式。在 mthson 上指定 scale 执行自动缩放，这使其为正值，并确保其不会太大。在冒号之前指定显示选项 nohr，以便显示回归系数，而不显示危险比。

指定 center 选项以获得自动居中。age 和 ulcarea 也通过使用 summarize 去均值化(demeaned)，然后减去返回结果 r(mean)。

```
.use https://www.stata-press.com/data/r17/legulcer2, clear
(Leg ulcer clinical trial)
.stset ttevent, fail(healed)
```

运行结果如图 2.39 所示。

① Smith, J. M., C. J. Dore, A. Charlett, and J. D. Lewis. A Randomized Trial of Biofilm Dressing for Venous Leg Ulcers. *Phlebology*, 1992, 7.

```
Survival-time data settings

         Failure event: healed!=0 & healed<.
Observed time interval: (0, ttevent]
     Exit on or before: failure

------------------------------------------------------------------------
        192  total observations
          0  exclusions
------------------------------------------------------------------------
        192  observations remaining, representing
         92  failures in single-record/single-failure data
     13,825  total analysis time at risk and under observation
                                                At risk from t =         0
                                     Earliest observed entry t =         0
                                          Last observed exit t =       206
```

图 2.39

. quietly sum age

. replace age = age - r(mean)

variable age was byte now float

(192 real changes made)

. quietly sum ulcarea

. replace ulcarea = ulcarea - r(mean)

variable ulcarea was int now float

(192 real changes made)

. fp <mthson>, center scale nohr: stcox <mthson> age ulcarea deepppg treat

运行结果如图 2.40 所示。

二次最佳拟合分数多项式具有幂(0.5;0.5)和偏差 736.709。然而,该模型的拟合效果并不明显优于 1 次分数多项式(在 0.05 水平),后者具有幂-0.5 和偏差 738.969。我们更喜欢 $m=1$ 的模型。

. fp <mthson>, replace center scale nohr fp(-.5): stcox <mthson> age ulcarea deepppg treat

-> stcox mthson_1 age ulcarea deepppg treat

运行结果如图 2.41 所示。

溃疡新近发作的患者比溃疡已持续数月的患者治愈的风险要高得多。如果想用分数多项式函数对所有预测值建模,对该数据集进行更合适的分析将是使用 mfp。

```
(fitting 44 models)
(....10%....20%....30%....40%....50%....60%....70%....80%....90%....100%)

Fractional polynomial comparisons:
-------------------------------------------------------------------
             |   Test               Deviance
      mthson |    df    Deviance      diff.          P   Powers
-------------+-----------------------------------------------------
     omitted |     4    754.345      17.636      0.001
      linear |     3    751.680      14.971      0.002   1
       m = 1 |     2    738.969       2.260      0.323   -.5
       m = 2 |     0    736.709       0.000         --   .5 .5
-------------------------------------------------------------------
Note: Test df is degrees of freedom, and P = P > chi2 is sig. level
      for tests comparing models vs. model with m = 2 based on
      deviance difference, chi2.

Cox regression with Breslow method for ties

No. of subjects =     192                          Number of obs =     192
No. of failures =      92
Time at risk    = 13,825
                                                   LR chi2(6)    = 108.59
Log likelihood = -368.35446                        Prob > chi2   = 0.0000

------------------------------------------------------------------------------
          _t | Coefficient  Std. err.      z    P>|z|     [95% conf. interval]
-------------+----------------------------------------------------------------
    mthson_1 |   -2.81425   .6996385    -4.02   0.000    -4.185516   -1.442984
    mthson_2 |   1.541451   .4703143     3.28   0.001     .6196521     2.46325
         age |  -.0261111   .0087983    -2.97   0.003    -.0433556   -.0088667
     ulcarea |  -.0017491    .000359    -4.87   0.000    -.0024527   -.0010455
     deepppg |  -.5850499   .2163173    -2.70   0.007    -1.009024   -.1610758
       treat |  -.1624663   .2171048    -0.75   0.454    -.5879838    .2630513
------------------------------------------------------------------------------
```

图 2.40

```
Cox regression with Breslow method for ties

No. of subjects =     192                          Number of obs =     192
No. of failures =      92
Time at risk    = 13,825
                                                   LR chi2(5)    = 106.33
Log likelihood = -369.48426                        Prob > chi2   = 0.0000

------------------------------------------------------------------------------
          _t | Coefficient  Std. err.      z    P>|z|     [95% conf. interval]
-------------+----------------------------------------------------------------
    mthson_1 |   .1985592   .0493922     4.02   0.000     .1017523    .2953662
         age |    -.02691   .0087875    -3.06   0.002    -.0441331   -.0096868
     ulcarea |  -.0017416   .0003482    -5.00   0.000    -.0024241   -.0010591
     deepppg |  -.5740759   .2185134    -2.63   0.009    -1.002354   -.1457975
       treat |  -.1798575   .2175726    -0.83   0.408    -.6062921     .246577
------------------------------------------------------------------------------
```

图 2.41

例 2.10 Logistic 回归

zero 选项允许将分数多项式模型拟合到协变量的正值，将非正值设为零。一个应用就是评估吸烟作为风险因素的影响。Whitehall Ⅰ是一项流行病学研究，Royston 和 Sauerbrei(2008)[①]对 18403 名受雇于伦敦的英国男性公务员进行了调查。我们检查了 Whitehall Ⅰ收集的数据，并使用 Logistic 回归建立了基于吸烟数量分数多项式的死亡概率模型。

非吸烟者可能与吸烟者有质的不同，因此在零支香烟和一支香烟之间，吸烟的影响(被视为一个连续变量)可能不是连续的。为了考虑这种可能性，我们将风险建模为非吸烟者的常数和吸烟者香烟数量的分数多项式函数，根据年龄进行调整。

因变量 all10 是个体是否在研究的 10 年内去世的指标。cigs 是每天消耗的香烟数量。加载数据后，我们把年龄去均值化并创建一个虚拟变量 nonsmoker。然后，我们使用 fp 来拟合模型。

```
.use https://www.stata-press.com/data/r17/smoking, clear
(Smoking and mortality data)
.quietly sum age
.replace age = age - r(mean)
variable age was byte now float
(17,260 real changes made)
.generate byte nonsmoker = cond(cigs = = 0, 1, 0) if cigs <.
*用 fp 拟合
.fp <cigs>, zero: logit all10 <cigs> nonsmoker age
```

运行结果如图 2.42 所示。

省略 zero 选项将导致 fp 停止并显示错误消息，因为除非指定了比例选项，否则非正协变量值(如 cig 值)无效。

一种密切相关的方法涉及 catzero 选项。在这里，我们不再需要在模型中加入非吸烟者，因为 fp 创建了自己的虚拟变量 cigs_0，以指示该个人当天是否不吸烟。

```
*利用 catzero 引入哑变量
.fp <cigs>, catzero replace: logit all10 <cigs> age
```

运行结果如图 2.43 所示。

对比这两种方法，我们可以接受 FP1 模型而不是 FP2 模型。我们用 fp 估计可以接受的模型的参数，即使用 cigs 的自然对数的模型。

```
*利用 fp 估计可接受的模型的参数
.fp <cigs>, catzero replace fp(0): logit all10 <cigs> age
```

运行结果如图 2.44 所示。

---

① Royston, P., and W. Sauerbrei. *Multivariable Model-Building: A Pragmatic Approach to Regression Analysis based on Fractional Polynomials for Modelling Continuous Variables*. Chichester, UK: Wiley, 2008.

```
(fitting 44 models)
(....10%....20%....30%....40%....50%....60%....70%....80%....90%....100%)

Fractional polynomial comparisons:

--------------------------------------------------------------
             |   Test             Deviance
        cigs |    df   Deviance      diff.         P   Powers
-------------+------------------------------------------------
     omitted |     4   9990.804     46.096     0.000
      linear |     3   9958.801     14.093     0.003   1
       m = 1 |     2   9946.603      1.895     0.388   0
       m = 2 |     0   9944.708      0.000        --   -1 -1
--------------------------------------------------------------
Note: Test df is degrees of freedom, and P = P > chi2 is sig. level
      for tests comparing models vs. model with m = 2 based on
      deviance difference, chi2.

Logistic regression                                    Number of obs =  17,260
                                                       LR chi2(4)    = 1029.03
                                                       Prob > chi2   =  0.0000
Log likelihood = -4972.3539                            Pseudo R2     =  0.0938

------------------------------------------------------------------------------
       all10 | Coefficient  Std. err.      z    P>|z|     [95% conf. interval]
-------------+----------------------------------------------------------------
      cigs_1 |  -1.285867   .3358483    -3.83   0.000    -1.944117   -.6276162
      cigs_2 |  -1.982424    .572109    -3.47   0.001    -3.103736   -.8611106
   nonsmoker |  -1.223749   .1119583   -10.93   0.000    -1.443183   -1.004315
         age |   .1194541   .0045818    26.07   0.000     .1104739    .1284343
       _cons |  -1.591489   .1052078   -15.13   0.000    -1.797693   -1.385286
------------------------------------------------------------------------------
```

图 2.42

```
(fitting 44 models)
(....10%....20%....30%....40%....50%....60%....70%....80%....90%....100%)

Fractional polynomial comparisons:

--------------------------------------------------------------
             |   Test             Deviance
        cigs |    df   Deviance      diff.         P   Powers
-------------+------------------------------------------------
     omitted |     5   10175.75    231.047     0.000
      linear |     3    9958.80     14.093     0.003   1
       m = 1 |     2    9946.60      1.895     0.388   0
       m = 2 |     0    9944.71      0.000        --   -1 -1
--------------------------------------------------------------
Note: Test df is degrees of freedom, and P = P > chi2 is sig. level
      for tests comparing models vs. model with m = 2 based on
      deviance difference, chi2.

Logistic regression                                    Number of obs =  17,260
                                                       LR chi2(4)    = 1029.03
                                                       Prob > chi2   =  0.0000
Log likelihood = -4972.3539                            Pseudo R2     =  0.0938

------------------------------------------------------------------------------
       all10 | Coefficient  Std. err.      z    P>|z|     [95% conf. interval]
-------------+----------------------------------------------------------------
      cigs_0 |  -1.223749   .1119583   -10.93   0.000    -1.443183   -1.004315
      cigs_1 |  -1.285867   .3358483    -3.83   0.000    -1.944117   -.6276162
      cigs_2 |  -1.982424    .572109    -3.47   0.001    -3.103736   -.8611106
         age |   .1194541   .0045818    26.07   0.000     .1104739    .1284343
       _cons |  -1.591489   .1052078   -15.13   0.000    -1.797693   -1.385286
------------------------------------------------------------------------------
```

图 2.43

```
-> logit all10 cigs_0 cigs_1 age

Logistic regression                                     Number of obs =  17,260
                                                        LR chi2(3)    = 1027.13
                                                        Prob > chi2   =  0.0000
Log likelihood = -4973.3016                             Pseudo R2     =  0.0936

------------------------------------------------------------------------------
       all10 | Coefficient  Std. err.      z    P>|z|     [95% conf. interval]
-------------+----------------------------------------------------------------
      cigs_0 |   .1883732   .1553093     1.21   0.225    -.1160274    .4927738
      cigs_1 |   .3469842   .0543552     6.38   0.000     .2404499    .4535185
         age |   .1194976   .0045818    26.08   0.000     .1105174    .1284778
       _cons |  -3.003767   .1514909   -19.83   0.000    -3.300683    -2.70685
------------------------------------------------------------------------------
```

图 2.44

输出中 cigs_0 的高 p 值表明，我们不能否认零对非吸烟者没有额外影响。

2.9 多元分数多项式回归

多元分数多项式(multivariable fractional polynomial, mfp)回归模型的语法格式为：

mfp [, options]: regression_cmd [yvar1 [yvar2]] xvarlist [if] [in] [weight] [, regression_cmd_options]

各选项及含义如下：

(1) regression_ cmd：可以是 clogit、glm、intreg、logistic、logit、mlogit、nbreg、ogit、oprobit、poisson、probit、qreg、regression、rreg、stcox、stcrreg、streg 或 xtgee。当 regression_cmd 为 intreg 时，必须同时指定 yvar1 和 yvar2。

(2) yvar1：不允许用于 streg、stcrreg 和 stcox。对于这些命令，必须首先设置数据。

(3) xvarlist：元素类型为 varlist 或(varlist)，或两者兼有。

菜单操作路径为：

Statistics>Linear models and related>Fractional polynomials>Multivariable fractional polynomial models

mfp 命令选择 mfp 模型，该模型可以从 xvarlist 中的右侧变量中最好地预测结果变量。对于 xvarlist 中未括在括号中的元素，mfp 命令把它们命名为 Ixvar_1，Ixvar_2……其中，xvar 表示 xvar1 名称的前四个字母，对于 xvar2、xvar3 等，依此类推。新变量 xvar1，xvar2……包含最佳拟合 FP 的幂。

例 2.11 多元分数多项式回归模型

我们使用数据集 brcancer.dta，其中包含来自德国乳腺癌研究组的淋巴结阳性乳腺癌患者的预后因素数据。响应变量为无复发生存时间(rectime)，截尾变量为 censrec。共有 686 名患者，299 起事件。我们使用 Cox 回归预测预后因素的复发对数风险，其中 5 个是连续的(x1、x3、x5、x6、x7)，3 个是二元的(x2、x4a、x4b)。众所周知，激素疗法(hormon)可以降低复发率，并被强制纳入模型。我们使用 mfp 命令对 8 个预测值的初始集建模，使用返回拟合模型选择算法。对于除 hormon 之外的所有变量，我们将变量和 FP 选择的标准 p 值设置为 0.05,hormon 设置为 1。

.webuse brcancer, clear

(German breast cancer data)

.stset rectime, fail(censrec)

运行结果如图 2.45 所示。

```
Survival-time data settings

         Failure event: censrec!=0 & censrec<.
Observed time interval: (0, rectime]
     Exit on or before: failure

------------------------------------------------------------------------
        686  total observations
          0  exclusions
------------------------------------------------------------------------
        686  observations remaining, representing
        299  failures in single-record/single-failure data
    771,400  total analysis time at risk and under observation
                                                At risk from t =         0
                                     Earliest observed entry t =         0
                                          Last observed exit t =     2,659
```

图 2.45

* 拟合 MFP-Cox 回归;强制 hormon 进入模型,并将其他变量的向后消除阈值设置为 0.05

.mfp, select(0.05, hormon:1): stcox x1 x2 x3 x4a x4b x5 x6 x7 hormon, nohr

运行结果如图 2.46 所示。

```
Final multivariable fractional polynomial model for _t
--------------------------------------------------------------------
    Variable |    -----Initial-----          -----Final-----
             |   df     Select   Alpha     Status    df    Powers
-------------+------------------------------------------------------
          x1 |    4     0.0500   0.0500      in       4    -2 -.5
          x2 |    1     0.0500   0.0500      out      0
          x3 |    4     0.0500   0.0500      out      0
         x4a |    1     0.0500   0.0500      in       1    1
         x4b |    1     0.0500   0.0500      out      0
          x5 |    4     0.0500   0.0500      in       4    -2 -1
          x6 |    4     0.0500   0.0500      in       2    .5
          x7 |    4     0.0500   0.0500      out      0
      hormon |    1     1.0000   0.0500      in       1    1
--------------------------------------------------------------------

Cox regression -- Breslow method for ties
Entry time _t0                                  Number of obs   =        686
                                                LR chi2(7)      =     155.62
                                                Prob > chi2     =     0.0000
Log likelihood = -1710.3619                     Pseudo R2       =     0.0435

------------------------------------------------------------------------------
          _t | Coefficient  Std. err.      z    P>|z|     [95% conf. interval]
-------------+----------------------------------------------------------------
       Ix1__1 |   44.73377   8.256682     5.42   0.000     28.55097    60.91657
       Ix1__2 |  -17.92302   3.909611    -4.58   0.000    -25.58571   -10.26032
         x4a |   .5006982   .2496324     2.01   0.045     .0114276    .9899687
       Ix5__1 |   .0387904   .0076972     5.04   0.000     .0237041    .0538767
       Ix5__2 |  -.5490645   .0864255    -6.35   0.000    -.7184554   -.3796736
       Ix6__1 |  -1.806966   .3506314    -5.15   0.000    -2.494191   -1.119741
      hormon |  -.4024169   .1280843    -3.14   0.002    -.6534575   -.1513763
------------------------------------------------------------------------------
Deviance = 3420.724.
```

图 2.46

.mfp, alpha(.05) select(.05, hormon:1) df(x5e:2) xpowers(x5e:0.5 1 2 3): stcox x1 x2 x3 x4a x4b x5e x6 x7 hormon, nohr

运行结果如图 2.47 所示。

Final multivariable fractional polynomial model for _t

Variable	Initial df	Initial Select	Initial Alpha	Final Status	Final df	Final Powers
x1	4	0.0500	0.0500	in	4	-2 -.5
x2	1	0.0500	0.0500	out	0	
x3	4	0.0500	0.0500	out	0	
x4a	1	0.0500	0.0500	in	1	1
x4b	1	0.0500	0.0500	out	0	
x5e	2	0.0500	0.0500	in	1	1
x6	4	0.0500	0.0500	in	2	.5
x7	4	0.0500	0.0500	out	0	
hormon	1	1.0000	0.0500	in	1	1

Cox regression -- Breslow method for ties
Entry time _t0 　　Number of obs = 686
LR chi2(6) = 153.11
Prob > chi2 = 0.0000
Log likelihood = -1711.6186 　　Pseudo R2 = 0.0428

_t	Coefficient	Std. err.	z	P>|z|	[95% conf.	interval]
Ix1__1	43.55382	8.253433	5.28	0.000	27.37738	59.73025
Ix1__2	-17.48136	3.911882	-4.47	0.000	-25.14851	-9.814212
x4a	.5174351	.2493739	2.07	0.038	.0286713	1.006199
Ix5e__1	-1.981213	.2268903	-8.73	0.000	-2.425909	-1.536516
Ix6__1	-1.84008	.3508432	-5.24	0.000	-2.52772	-1.15244
hormon	-.3944998	.128097	-3.08	0.002	-.6455654	-.1434342

Deviance = 3423.237.

图 2.47

2.10 跨栏回归

churdle 命令拟合线性或指数障碍模型。它将确定因变量边界点的选择模型与确定因变量无界值的结果模型相结合。跨栏模型(hurdle models)将这些边界值视为观察值,而不是截尾值。

跨栏模型可表示为:

$$y_i = s_i h_i^* \tag{2.34}$$

其中,y_i 是因变量的观测值。如果因变量没有界,则选择变量 s_i 为 1,否则为 0。在 Cragg 模型中,约束因变量的下限为 0,因此选择模型为:

$$s_i = \begin{cases} 1 & \text{if } \boldsymbol{z}_i \gamma + \varepsilon_i > 0 \\ 0 & \text{otherwise} \end{cases} \tag{2.35}$$

其中，$\boldsymbol{z}_i$ 是解释变量的向量，γ 是系数的向量，ε_i 是标准正态误差项。churdle 命令允许在 ll()中指定不同的下限，对于线性模型，允许在 ul()中指定上限。如果在 select()中指定了子选项 het()，则允许 ε_i 的条件异方差性。

只有当 $s_i=1$ 时，才能观察到连续潜变量 h_i^*。结果模型可以是线性模型或指数模型，可分别表示为：

$$h_i^* = \boldsymbol{x}_i\boldsymbol{\beta} + \nu_i \quad (\text{linear}) \tag{2.36}$$

$$h_i^* = \exp(\boldsymbol{x}_i\boldsymbol{\beta} + \nu_i) \quad (\text{exponential}) \tag{2.37}$$

其中，x_i 是解释变量的向量，β 是系数的向量，ν_i 是误差项。

对于线性模型，ν_i 具有较低截断点 $-\boldsymbol{x}_i\boldsymbol{\beta}$ 的截断正态分布。对于指数模型，ν_i 具有正态分布。churdle 命令扩展了 Cragg 模型，以在用户指定 het()选项时，允许 ν_i 的条件异方差性。

令 ll 表示下限，ul 表示上限，则其概率分别为：

$$\begin{aligned} \Pr(y_i = ll \mid \boldsymbol{z}_i) &= \Phi(ll - \boldsymbol{z}_i'\gamma_{ll}) \\ \Pr(y_i = ul \mid \boldsymbol{z}_i) &= \Phi(\boldsymbol{z}_i'\gamma_{ul} - ul) \end{aligned} \tag{2.38}$$

其中，$\boldsymbol{z}_i$ 是个体 i 的选择模型的协变量，它可能不同于潜在模型的协变量 $\boldsymbol{x}_i$；Φ 为对应标准正态累积分布函数；γ_{ll} 是下限选择模型的参数向量；γ_{ul} 是上限选择模型的参数向量。

假设 γ_i 具有较低截断点 $ll-\boldsymbol{x}_i'\boldsymbol{\beta}$ 和上截断点 $ul-\boldsymbol{x}_i'\boldsymbol{\beta}$ 的截断正态分布且具有齐次方差，对数似然函数由下式给出：

$$\begin{aligned} \ln\boldsymbol{L} = & \sum_{i=1}^{n}(y_i \leqslant ll)\log\Phi(ll - \boldsymbol{z}_i'\gamma_{ll}) + (y_i \geqslant ul)\log\{1-\Phi(ul - \boldsymbol{z}_i'\gamma_{ul})\} \\ & + (ul > y_i > ll)[\log\{\Phi(ul - \boldsymbol{z}_i'\gamma_{ul}) - \Phi(ll - \boldsymbol{z}_i'\gamma_{ll})\}] \\ & - (ul > y_i > ll)\left[\log\left\{\Phi\left(\frac{ul - \boldsymbol{x}_i'\boldsymbol{\beta}}{\sigma}\right) - \Phi\left(\frac{ll - \boldsymbol{x}_i'\boldsymbol{\beta}}{\sigma}\right)\right\}\right] \\ & + (ul > y_i > ll)\left[\log\left\{\phi\left(\frac{y_i - \boldsymbol{x}_i'\boldsymbol{\beta}}{\sigma}\right)\right\} - \log(\sigma)\right] \end{aligned} \tag{2.39}$$

在没有齐次方差假设的情况下，可以使用 $\sigma^2(\boldsymbol{w}_i)=\exp(2\boldsymbol{w}_i'\boldsymbol{\theta})$ 的形式对异方差进行建模，其中 $\boldsymbol{w}_i$ 是影响 γ_i 的条件方差的变量。通过将 σ 替换为 $\exp(\boldsymbol{w}_i'\boldsymbol{\theta})$ 来获得对数似然函数。

指数模型的对数似然函数为：

$$\begin{aligned} \ln\boldsymbol{L} = & \sum_{i=1}^{n}(y_i \leqslant ll)\log\Phi(ll - \boldsymbol{z}_i'\gamma) + (y_i > ll)[\log\{1-\Phi(ll - \boldsymbol{z}_i'\gamma)\}] \\ & + (y_i > ll)\{\log\{\phi[\log(y_i - ll) - \boldsymbol{x}_i'\boldsymbol{\beta})/\sigma]\} - \log(\sigma) - \log(y_i - ll)\} \end{aligned} \tag{2.40}$$

与线性情况类似，我们可以通过 $\sigma^2(\boldsymbol{w}_i)=\exp(2\boldsymbol{w}_i'\boldsymbol{\theta})$ 来建模异方差。

上述两个似然函数的估计都是通过最大似然法完成的。

Cragg 跨栏回归的语法格式为：

(1) 基本语法

```
churdle linear depvar, select(varlist_s) {ll(...) | ul(...)}
churdle exponential depvar, select(varlist_s) ll(...)
```

(2) churdle linear 的完整语法

```
churdle linear depvar [indepvars] [if] [in] [weight], select(varlist_s
[, noconstant het(varlist_o)]) {ll(#|varname) | ul(#|varname)} [options]
```

(3) churdle 指数的完整语法

```
churdle exponential depvar [indepvars] [if] [in] [weight], select(varlist
_s[, noconstant het(varlist_o)]) ll(#|varname) [options]
```

其中,模型选项及含义为：

(1) select()：为选择模型指定自变量和选项。

(2) +ll(# | varname)：截断下限。

(3) +ul(# | varname)：截断上限。

(4) noconstant：抑制常数项。

(5) constraints(constraints)：应用指定的线性约束。

(6) het(varlist)：指定变量以建模方差。

菜单操作路径为：

Statistics>Linear models and related>Hurdle regression

churdle 命令适用于有界因变量的线性或指数跨栏回归模型。每个模型允许有单独的独立协变量。

例 2.12　Cragg 跨栏回归模型

考虑一个数据集 fitness. dta，其中包含个人每天锻炼的小时数(hours)、年龄(age)、是否单身(single)、每天工作的小时数(whours)、是否吸烟(smoke)、体重(weight)、与最近健身房的距离(distance)，以及平均通勤时间(commute)。

我们将锻炼与否的决定建模为 commute、whours 和 age 的函数。这些变量写在 select()中。一旦决定进行锻炼，个人锻炼的时间将被建模为 age、smoke、distance 和 single 的线性函数。

```
* 下载数据集
.webuse fitness
(Fictional fitness data)
* Cragg 跨栏线性回归
.churdle linear hours age i.smoke distance i.single, select(commute
whours age) ll(0)
```

运行结果如图 2.48 所示。

```
Cragg hurdle regression                         Number of obs =    19,831
                                                LR chi2(4)    =   9059.26
                                                Prob > chi2   =    0.0000
Log likelihood = -23340.044                     Pseudo R2     =    0.1625
```

hours	Coefficient	Std. err.	z	P>|z|	[95% conf.	interval]
hours						
age	.0015116	.000763	1.98	0.048	.0000162	.003007
smoke						
Smoking	-1.06646	.0460578	-23.15	0.000	-1.156731	-.9761879
distance	-.1333868	.0126344	-10.56	0.000	-.1581497	-.1086238
single						
Single	.9940893	.0258775	38.42	0.000	.9433703	1.044808
_cons	.9138855	.0396227	23.06	0.000	.8362264	.9915447
selection_ll						
commute	-.2953345	.0624665	-4.73	0.000	-.4177666	-.1729024
whours	.0022974	.0069306	0.33	0.740	-.0112864	.0158811
age	-.0485347	.0006501	-74.65	0.000	-.049809	-.0472604
_cons	2.649945	.0499795	53.02	0.000	2.551987	2.747903
lnsigma						
_cons	.0083199	.0099648	0.83	0.404	-.0112107	.0278506
/sigma	1.008355	.010048			.9888519	1.028242

图 2.48

* 年龄的平均边际效应

.margins, dydx(age)

运行结果如图 2.49 所示。

```
Average marginal effects                        Number of obs = 19,831
Model VCE: OIM

Expression: Conditional mean estimates of dependent variable, predict()
dy/dx wrt:  age
```

	dy/dx	Delta-method std. err.	z	P>|z|	[95% conf.	interval]
age	-.0216855	.000289	-75.03	0.000	-.022252	-.021119

图 2.49

* 具有方差模型的 Cragg-Bartle 跨栏线性回归

```
.churdle linear hours age i.smoke distance i.single, select(commute whours age, het(age single)) ll(0)
```

运行结果如图 2.50 所示。

```
Cragg hurdle regression                         Number of obs =     19,831
                                                LR chi2(4)    =    9060.30
                                                Prob > chi2   =     0.0000
Log likelihood = -23339.52                      Pseudo R2     =     0.1625
```

hours	Coefficient	Std. err.	z	P>|z|	[95% conf.	interval]
hours						
age	.0015116	.000763	1.98	0.048	.0000162	.003007
smoke						
Smoking	-1.06646	.0460578	-23.15	0.000	-1.156731	-.9761879
distance	-.1333868	.0126344	-10.56	0.000	-.1581497	-.1086238
single						
Single	.9940893	.0258775	38.42	0.000	.9433703	1.044808
_cons	.9138855	.0396227	23.06	0.000	.8362264	.9915447
selection_ll						
commute	-.2959986	.0641594	-4.61	0.000	-.4217488	-.1702484
whours	.0024514	.0069769	0.35	0.725	-.0112231	.0161259
age	-.048886	.0021405	-22.84	0.000	-.0530814	-.0446906
_cons	2.669613	.1139478	23.43	0.000	2.44628	2.892947
lnsigma						
_cons	.0083199	.0099648	0.83	0.404	-.0112107	.0278506
lnsigma_ll						
age	-.0002035	.0008424	-0.24	0.809	-.0018546	.0014475
single	.0268271	.0270133	0.99	0.321	-.0261179	.0797721
/sigma	1.008355	.010048			.9888519	1.028242

图 2.50

* Cragg 跨栏指数回归

```
.churdle exponential hours age i.smoke distance i.single, select(commute whours age) ll(0) nolog
```

运行结果如图 2.51 所示。

* 年龄的平均边际效应

```
.margins, dydx(age)
```

运行结果如图 2.52 所示。

```
Cragg hurdle regression                          Number of obs =    19,831
                                                 LR chi2(4)    =   8663.21
                                                 Prob > chi2   =    0.0000
Log likelihood = -15666.195                      Pseudo R2     =    0.2166
```

hours	Coefficient	Std. err.	z	P>|z|	[95% conf.	interval]
hours						
age	.0008368	.0005341	1.57	0.117	-.00021	.0018836
smoke						
Smoking	-.6431348	.0258509	-24.88	0.000	-.6938016	-.592468
distance	-.0772879	.0079132	-9.77	0.000	-.0927976	-.0617783
single						
Single	.5975111	.016108	37.09	0.000	.5659401	.6290821
_cons	-.0770619	.0254833	-3.02	0.002	-.1270082	-.0271157
selection_ll						
commute	-.2953345	.0624665	-4.73	0.000	-.4177666	-.1729024
whours	.0022974	.0069306	0.33	0.740	-.0112864	.0158811
age	-.0485347	.0006501	-74.65	0.000	-.049809	-.0472604
_cons	2.649945	.0499795	53.02	0.000	2.551987	2.747903
lnsigma						
_cons	-.186917	.0067067	-27.87	0.000	-.200062	-.1737721
/sigma	.8295126	.0055633			.81868	.8404884

图 2.51

```
Average marginal effects                         Number of obs = 19,831
Model VCE: OIM

Expression: Conditional mean estimates of dependent variable, predict()
dy/dx wrt:  age
```

	Delta-method dy/dx	std. err.	z	P>|z|	[95% conf.	interval]
age	-.0245582	.0004805	-51.11	0.000	-.0255	-.0236164

图 2.52

第3章 二元结果

二值选择模型(binary choice model)是离散被解释变量模型的其中一种类型，此时被解释变量只能取两个值。二值选择模型的目的是研究一个群体作某种选择而不作另一种选择的概率，如是否考研、是否参加培训等。

3.1 Logistic 回归

1. 线性概率模型

在生活中，经常会面临两种选择的情况，或者是一个个体只有两种选择的情形，如公司的融资约束情况，可以用 $y=1$(融资约束高)或 $y=0$(融资约束低)来表示，这又取决于企业的大小，是国有企业还是民营企业，以及投资机会等，这些都可以用 $\boldsymbol{x}$ 来表示。

首先，从最简单的线性概率模型(LPM)开始，其回归形式为：

$$y_i=\beta_1 x_{1i}+\beta_2 x_{2i}+\cdots+\beta_k x_{ki}+u_i \quad i=1,2,\cdots,N \tag{3.1}$$

式中，N 是样本量，k 是解释变量个数，x_{ki} 是第 i 个个体特征的取值，u_i 为相互独立且均值为0的随机扰动项。y_i 表示取值为0和1的离散型随机变量。

令 $p_i=P(y_i=1)$，那么 $1-p_i=P(y_i=0)$，则

$$E(y_i)=1\times P(y_i=1)+0\times P(y_i=0)=p_i \tag{3.2}$$

又因为 u_i 均值为0，所以，$E(y_i)=\boldsymbol{x}_i'\boldsymbol{\beta}$，其中，$\boldsymbol{x}_i=(x_{1i},x_{2i},\cdots,x_{ki})'$，$\boldsymbol{\beta}=(\beta_1,\beta_2,\cdots,\beta_k)'$，从而有

$$E(y_i)=P(y_i=1)=p_i=\boldsymbol{x}_i'\boldsymbol{\beta} \tag{3.3}$$

式中，$p_i=\boldsymbol{x}_i'\boldsymbol{\beta}$，因为概率的范围在(0,1)之间，所以，$\boldsymbol{x}_i'\boldsymbol{\beta}$ 的取值也必须在(0,1)之间，但实际应用中，$\boldsymbol{x}_i'\boldsymbol{\beta}$ 的取值并不一定在(0,1)之间，通常可以设定如下线性概率模型：

$$p_i=\begin{cases}\boldsymbol{x}_i'\boldsymbol{\beta}, & 0<\boldsymbol{x}_i'\boldsymbol{\beta}<1\\ 1, & \boldsymbol{x}_i'\boldsymbol{\beta}\geqslant 1\\ 0, & \boldsymbol{x}_i'\boldsymbol{\beta}\leqslant 0\end{cases} \tag{3.4}$$

但式(3.4)的设定过于武断，损失了 $\boldsymbol{x}_i'\boldsymbol{\beta}\geqslant 1$ 和 $\boldsymbol{x}_i'\boldsymbol{\beta}\leqslant 0$ 的相关信息。此外，线性概率模型的另外一个缺点是它存在异方差，即 $\text{var}(\varepsilon)=\boldsymbol{x}_i'\boldsymbol{\beta}(1-\boldsymbol{x}_i'\boldsymbol{\beta})$，这使得参数估

计不再有效。

2. 二值选择模型的设计与估计

在现实中，处理二值选择模型的常用方法是将其与微观效用结合起来。例如，y 是二值选择变量，如果一个人报名了体育项目，则 $y=1$，否则为 0。假设存在一个未被观察到的潜在变量 y_i^*，它能够反映个人报名体育项目的效用，如果效用足够高，那么个人就会选择报名，如果效用不够高，那么个人就不会选择报名。y_i 和 y_i^* 之间存在如下关系：

$$y_i=\begin{cases}1, & y_i^*>0\\0, & y_i^*\leqslant 0\end{cases} \tag{3.5}$$

则线性概率模型可以转换为：

$$y_i^*=\boldsymbol{x}_i'\boldsymbol{\beta}+u_i^* \tag{3.6}$$

则

$$\begin{aligned}&P(y_i=1\mid \boldsymbol{x}_i,\boldsymbol{\beta})=P(y_i^*>0)=P(u_i^*>-\boldsymbol{x}_i'\boldsymbol{\beta})=1-F(-\boldsymbol{x}_i'\boldsymbol{\beta})\\&P(y_i=0\mid \boldsymbol{x}_i,\boldsymbol{\beta})=P(y_i^*\leqslant 0)=P(u_i^*\leqslant-\boldsymbol{x}_i'\boldsymbol{\beta})=F(-\boldsymbol{x}_i'\boldsymbol{\beta})\end{aligned} \tag{3.7}$$

式(3.7)中，如果 F 是对称的，那么 $1-F(\boldsymbol{x}_i'\boldsymbol{\beta})=F(\boldsymbol{x}_i'\boldsymbol{\beta})$，$F$ 是 u_i^* 的分布函数，要求是一个连续函数，且是单调递增的。因此，原回归模型可以看成如下回归模型：

$$y_i=1-F(\boldsymbol{x}_i'\boldsymbol{\beta})+u_i \tag{3.8}$$

分布函数的类型决定了二值选择模型的类型，常用的二值选择模型如表 3.1 所示。

表 3.1 常用的二值选择模型

u_i^* 对应的分布	分布函数 F	相应的二值选择模型
标准正态分布	$\Phi(\boldsymbol{x})$	Probit 模型
逻辑分布	$e^x/(1+e^x)$	Logit 模型
极值分布	$1-\exp(-e^x)$	Extreme 模型

如果将 $F(\cdot)$ 设定为 Logit 分布函数 $\Lambda(\cdot)$，则产生的概率模型为 Logit 模型：

$$\begin{aligned}P(y_i=1\mid \boldsymbol{x}_i,\boldsymbol{\beta})&=1-F(-\boldsymbol{x}_i'\boldsymbol{\beta})=1-\Lambda(-\boldsymbol{x}_i'\boldsymbol{\beta})\\&=1-\frac{\exp(-\boldsymbol{x}_i'\boldsymbol{\beta})}{1+\exp(-\boldsymbol{x}_i'\boldsymbol{\beta})}=\frac{1}{1+\exp(-\boldsymbol{x}_i'\boldsymbol{\beta})}\\&=\frac{\exp(\boldsymbol{x}_i'\boldsymbol{\beta})}{1+\exp(\boldsymbol{x}_i'\boldsymbol{\beta})}=\Lambda(\boldsymbol{x}_i'\boldsymbol{\beta})\end{aligned} \tag{3.9}$$

因为 Logit 模型属于非线性模型，对它进行估计需要选用最大似然估计法。原理如下：

$$\begin{aligned}\mathrm{P}(y_i=1\mid \boldsymbol{x}_i)&=F(\boldsymbol{x}_i'\boldsymbol{\beta})\\\mathrm{P}(y_i=0\mid \boldsymbol{x}_i)&=1-F(\boldsymbol{x}_i'\boldsymbol{\beta})\end{aligned}$$

式(3.8)的似然函数为：

$$L=\prod_{i=1}^{N}(F(\boldsymbol{x}_i'\boldsymbol{\beta}))^{y_i}(1-F(\boldsymbol{x}_i'\boldsymbol{\beta}))^{1-y_i} \tag{3.10}$$

对数似然函数为：

$$\ln L = \sum_{i=1}^{N} (y_i \cdot \ln(\boldsymbol{x}_i' \boldsymbol{\beta}) + (1 - y_i) \cdot \ln(1 - F(\boldsymbol{x}_i' \boldsymbol{\beta})) \tag{3.11}$$

利用对数似然函数对相关参数求偏导，并令其为 0，可得参数估计值。

3. 二值选择模型的检验

二值选择模型的检验包括总体显著性检验与拟合优度检验。由于二值选择模型是非线性的，因此在检验多个系数是否显著时，并不能使用 F 值，可以采用 Wald 统计量、LR(最大似然比)统计量、LM(拉格朗日乘子)统计量等。

以 LR 统计量为例，总体显著性检验的原假设为：$H_0:\beta_1=\beta_2=\cdots=\beta_k=0$，备择假设为：解释变量的系数并不全都为 0。构造一个似然比统计量：

$$\text{LR} = -2[\ln L_0 - \ln L]$$

LR 统计量渐近服从于 $\chi^2(k)$，其中 L_0 为模型满足原假设的似然函数值，L 为无约束模型估计得到的似然函数值。直观上看，如果 LR 较大，表明 L_0 与 L 之间的差较大，倾向于拒绝原假设，而接受模型总体显著的备择假设。

拟合优度检验类似于古典回归中可决系数的度量，二值选择模型也有对模型拟合程度的度量，它就是似然指数，也称为 R^2。

设

$$\ln L_0 = n[P\ln P + (1-P)\ln(1-P)]$$

式中，P 为样本观测值中被解释变量等于 1 的比例，n 为样本量。设 L 为模型估计得到的似然函数值，构造一个统计量：

$$R^2 = 1 - \frac{\ln L}{\ln L_0}$$

显然，如果模型完全不拟合样本观测值，L 等于 L_0，则 $R^2=0$；如果模型完全拟合样本观测值，L 等于 1，则有 $R^2=1$，但较高的可决系数并不能说明回归模型有较强的解释能力。

Logit 模型的 Stata 命令为 logit。logit 命令通过最大似然法拟合二值选择的 Logit 模型，通过建模回归估计给定条件下的正向结果概率。depvar 等于非零且不缺失(通常 depvar 等于 1)时，表示结果为正；depvar 等于零时，表示结果为负。

语法格式为：

```
logit depvar [indepvars] [if] [in] [weight] [, options]
```

菜单操作路径为：

```
Statistics>Binary outcomes>Logistic regression
```

例 3.1 Logit 模型①

以 Stata 软件自带数据集 lbw. dta 为例，估计二值选择模型。该数据集包括：low(出生时体重小于 2500g)，age(母亲年龄)，lwt(产前体重)，i. race(民族)，smoke(怀孕期间是否抽烟)，ptl(预产期劳动次数)，ht(有没有高血压)，ui(身体不适)。拟建立

① 本案例根据 Stata 帮助手册 r. pdf 中的对应例子改编。

以下模型：

$$\ln\left(\frac{P(\text{low}_i=1)}{1-P(\text{low}_i=1)}\right)=\beta_0+\beta_1\text{age}_i+\beta_2\text{lwt}_i+\beta_3\text{race}_i+\beta_4\text{smoke}_i$$
$$+\beta_5\text{ptl}_i+\beta_6\text{ht}_i+\beta_7\text{ui}_i+\varepsilon_i$$

```
.use lbw, clear
.summarize
```

运行结果如图 3.1 所示。

Variable	Obs	Mean	Std. dev.	Min	Max
id	189	121.0794	63.30363	4	226
low	189	.3121693	.4646093	0	1
age	189	23.2381	5.298678	14	45
lwt	189	129.8201	30.57515	80	250
race	189	1.846561	.9183422	1	3
smoke	189	.3915344	.4893898	0	1
ptl	189	.1957672	.4933419	0	3
ht	189	.0634921	.2444936	0	1
ui	189	.1481481	.3561903	0	1
ftv	189	.7936508	1.059286	0	6
bwt	189	2944.286	729.016	709	4990

图 3.1

```
* 作为比较,先使用 OLS 估计线性概率模型
.reg low age lwt i.race smoke ptl ht ui,r
```

运行结果如图 3.2 所示。

Linear regression

Number of obs	=	189
F(8, 180)	=	5.97
Prob > F	=	0.0000
R-squared	=	0.1635
Root MSE	=	.43427

low	Coefficient	Robust std. err.	t	P>|t|	[95% conf.	interval]
age	-0.003	0.006	-0.61	0.545	-0.015	0.008
lwt	-0.003	0.001	-2.32	0.022	-0.005	-0.000
race						
Black	0.221	0.104	2.14	0.034	0.017	0.426
Other	0.144	0.074	1.95	0.053	-0.002	0.289
smoke	0.160	0.070	2.29	0.023	0.022	0.297
ptl	0.115	0.087	1.33	0.186	-0.056	0.287
ht	0.364	0.136	2.67	0.008	0.095	0.632
ui	0.156	0.108	1.45	0.150	-0.057	0.369
_cons	0.507	0.201	2.52	0.012	0.111	0.904

图 3.2

* 使用 logit 命令做 Logit 模型回归

```
.logit low age lwt i.race smoke ptl ht ui,nolog
```

运行结果如图 3.3 所示。

```
Logistic regression                                     Number of obs =    189
                                                        LR chi2(8)    =  33.22
                                                        Prob > chi2   = 0.0001
Log likelihood = -100.724                               Pseudo R2     = 0.1416
```

low	Coefficient	Std. err.	z	P>|z|	[95% conf.	interval]
age	-0.027	0.036	-0.74	0.457	-0.099	0.044
lwt	-0.015	0.007	-2.19	0.029	-0.029	-0.002
race						
Black	1.263	0.526	2.40	0.016	0.231	2.294
Other	0.862	0.439	1.96	0.050	0.001	1.723
smoke	0.923	0.401	2.30	0.021	0.138	1.709
ptl	0.542	0.346	1.56	0.118	-0.137	1.220
ht	1.833	0.692	2.65	0.008	0.477	3.188
ui	0.759	0.459	1.65	0.099	-0.142	1.659
_cons	0.461	1.205	0.38	0.702	-1.900	2.822

图 3.3

两种估计方法的对数似然值相近，无需担心模型设定问题。

* 解释变量的最小变化单位为一单位，为便于解释结果，下面汇报机会比率

```
.logit low age lwt i.race smoke ptl ht ui,or nolog
```

运行结果如图 3.4 所示。

```
Logistic regression                                     Number of obs =    189
                                                        LR chi2(8)    =  33.22
                                                        Prob > chi2   = 0.0001
Log likelihood = -100.724                               Pseudo R2     = 0.1416
```

low	Odds ratio	Std. err.	z	P>|z|	[95% conf.	interval]
age	0.973	0.035	-0.74	0.457	0.906	1.045
lwt	0.985	0.007	-2.19	0.029	0.972	0.998
race						
Black	3.535	1.861	2.40	0.016	1.260	9.918
Other	2.368	1.040	1.96	0.050	1.001	5.600
smoke	2.518	1.009	2.30	0.021	1.148	5.523
ptl	1.719	0.595	1.56	0.118	0.872	3.389
ht	6.250	4.322	2.65	0.008	1.611	24.242
ui	2.135	0.981	1.65	0.099	0.868	5.253
_cons	1.586	1.910	0.38	0.702	0.150	16.813

Note: _cons estimates baseline odds.

图 3.4

结果显示,怀孕期间抽烟会使新生儿体重低的机会比率提高 2.5 倍,其他变量对应的影响可以做类似解释。

* 为与 OLS 估计的回归系数比较,计算平均边际效应

```
.margins,dydx( * )
```

运行结果如图 3.5 所示。

```
Average marginal effects                                 Number of obs = 189
Model VCE: OIM

Expression: Pr(low), predict()
dy/dx wrt:  age lwt 2.race 3.race smoke ptl ht ui
```

	dy/dx	Delta-method std. err.	z	P>|z|	[95% conf.	interval]
age	-0.005	0.006	-0.75	0.456	-0.018	0.008
lwt	-0.003	0.001	-2.28	0.022	-0.005	-0.000
race						
Black	0.233	0.100	2.34	0.019	0.038	0.428
Other	0.151	0.076	1.99	0.047	0.002	0.300
smoke	0.165	0.068	2.41	0.016	0.031	0.298
ptl	0.097	0.060	1.60	0.109	-0.021	0.215
ht	0.327	0.115	2.84	0.004	0.102	0.552
ui	0.135	0.080	1.70	0.090	-0.021	0.291

Note: dy/dx for factor levels is the discrete change from the base level.

图 3.5

通过比较可知,平均边际效应与 OLS 回归系数差别不大。

* 计算样本均值处的边际效应

```
.margins,dydx( * ) atmeans
```

运行结果如图 3.6 所示。

样本均值处的边际效应不同于平均边际效应。

* 利用 margins 命令,计算变量 Sge 在“age=30”处的边际效应

```
.margins,dydx(age) at(age = 30)
```

运行结果如图 3.7 所示。

```
Conditional marginal effects                          Number of obs = 189
Model VCE: OIM

Expression: Pr(low), predict()
dy/dx wrt:  age lwt 2.race 3.race smoke ptl ht ui
At: age     =  23.2381 (mean)
    lwt     = 129.8201 (mean)
    1.race  = .5079365 (mean)
    2.race  = .1375661 (mean)
    3.race  = .3544974 (mean)
    smoke   = .3915344 (mean)
    ptl     = .1957672 (mean)
    ht      = .0634921 (mean)
    ui      = .1481481 (mean)

------------------------------------------------------------------------------
             |            Delta-method
             |      dy/dx   std. err.      z    P>|z|     [95% conf. interval]
-------------+----------------------------------------------------------------
         age |     -0.005      0.007    -0.75   0.455       -0.020      0.009
         lwt |     -0.003      0.001    -2.22   0.026       -0.006     -0.000
             |
        race |
       Black |      0.264      0.117     2.25   0.024        0.035      0.494
       Other |      0.168      0.086     1.94   0.052       -0.001      0.337
             |
       smoke |      0.185      0.079     2.34   0.019        0.030      0.340
         ptl |      0.108      0.070     1.56   0.119       -0.028      0.245
          ht |      0.367      0.138     2.66   0.008        0.096      0.638
          ui |      0.152      0.092     1.65   0.098       -0.028      0.332
------------------------------------------------------------------------------
Note: dy/dx for factor levels is the discrete change from the base level.
```

图 3.6

```
Average marginal effects                              Number of obs = 189
Model VCE: OIM

Expression: Pr(low), predict()
dy/dx wrt:  age
At: age = 30

------------------------------------------------------------------------------
             |            Delta-method
             |      dy/dx   std. err.      z    P>|z|     [95% conf. interval]
-------------+----------------------------------------------------------------
         age |     -0.005      0.006    -0.79   0.427       -0.016      0.007
------------------------------------------------------------------------------
```

图 3.7

*利用 logit 估计后命令 estat classification，计算 Logit 模型分类的混淆矩阵，预测准确比率

.estat classification

运行结果如图 3.8 所示。

```
Logistic model for low

              -------- True --------
Classified |         D            ~D  |      Total
-----------+--------------------------+-----------
     +     |        21            12  |         33
     -     |        38           118  |        156
-----------+--------------------------+-----------
   Total   |        59           130  |        189

Classified + if predicted Pr(D) >= .5
True D defined as low != 0
--------------------------------------------------
Sensitivity                     Pr( +| D)   35.59%
Specificity                     Pr( -|~D)   90.77%
Positive predictive value       Pr( D| +)   63.64%
Negative predictive value       Pr(~D| -)   75.64%
--------------------------------------------------
False + rate for true ~D        Pr( +|~D)    9.23%
False - rate for true D         Pr( -| D)   64.41%
False + rate for classified +   Pr(~D| +)   36.36%
False - rate for classified -   Pr( D| -)   24.36%
--------------------------------------------------
Correctly classified                        73.54%
--------------------------------------------------
```

图 3.8

由计算结果可知，该模型的敏感度等于 35.59%，特质率为 90.77%，总分类准确比率为 73.54%。

*用 age 变量作为聚类变量，用聚类稳健标准误估计 Logit 模型

.logit low age lwt i.race smoke ptl ht ui,nolog vce(cluster age)

运行结果如图 3.9 所示。

*利用估计的 Logit 模型，预测并显示分类

.predict yhat4

.list low yhat4

*利用命令 lroc，绘制 ROC 曲线

.lroc

运行结果如图 3.10 和图 3.11 所示。

```
Logistic regression                               Number of obs =      189
                                                  Wald chi2(8)  =    76.77
                                                  Prob > chi2   =   0.0000
Log pseudolikelihood = -100.724                   Pseudo R2     =   0.1416

                              (Std. err. adjusted for 24 clusters in age)
```

low	Coefficient	Robust std. err.	z	P>|z|	[95% conf.	interval]
age	-0.027	0.030	-0.91	0.364	-0.086	0.031
lwt	-0.015	0.009	-1.77	0.076	-0.032	0.002
race						
Black	1.263	0.405	3.12	0.002	0.469	2.056
Other	0.862	0.449	1.92	0.055	-0.018	1.742
smoke	0.923	0.382	2.42	0.016	0.174	1.673
ptl	0.542	0.311	1.74	0.081	-0.067	1.151
ht	1.833	0.679	2.70	0.007	0.501	3.164
ui	0.759	0.482	1.57	0.116	-0.187	1.704
_cons	0.461	1.268	0.36	0.716	-2.024	2.946

图　3.9

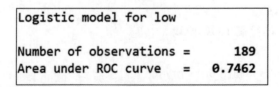

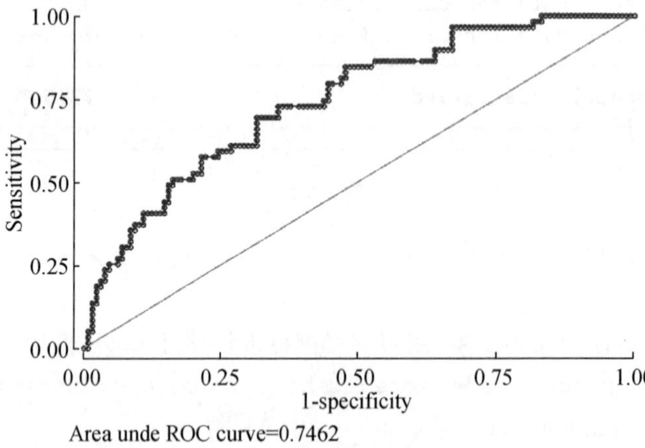

图　3.10

```
Logistic model for low

Number of observations =       189
Area under ROC curve   =    0.7462
```

图　3.11

由计算结果可知，AUROC 等于 0.7462。

```
* 使用命令 estat gof 得出模型拟合优度
.estat gof
```

运行结果如图 3.12 所示。

```
Goodness-of-fit test after logistic model
Variable: low

      Number of observations =     189
Number of covariate patterns =     182
          Pearson chi2(173) =  179.24
                Prob > chi2 =  0.3567
```

图 3.12

3.2 Probit 回归

如果将 $F(\cdot)$设定为标准正态分布函数，即

$$F(-\boldsymbol{x}_i'\boldsymbol{\beta})=\Phi(-\boldsymbol{x}_i'\boldsymbol{\beta})=\int_{-\infty}^{-x_i'\beta}(2\pi)^{-\frac{1}{2}}\exp(-\varepsilon^2/2)\mathrm{d}\varepsilon$$

于是，式(3.8)可以写成：

$$\begin{aligned}P(y_i=1\mid\boldsymbol{x}_i,\boldsymbol{\beta})&=1-\int_{-\infty}^{-x_i'\beta}(2\pi)^{-\frac{1}{2}}\exp(-\varepsilon^2/2)\mathrm{d}\varepsilon\\&=1-\Phi(-\boldsymbol{x}_i'\boldsymbol{\beta})=\Phi(\boldsymbol{x}_i'\boldsymbol{\beta})\end{aligned}\tag{3.12}$$

Probit 模型回归估计的 Stata 命令为 probit。probit 命令适用于二元因变量的 Probit 模型，假设正结果的概率由标准正态累积分布函数给出。probit 可以计算鲁棒性和聚类鲁棒性标准误差，并调整复杂的调查设计结果。

语法格式为：

```
probit depvar [indepvars] [if] [in] [weight] [, options]
```

菜单操作路径为：

Statistics>Binary outcomes>Probit regression

例 3.2 Probit 模型①

下面利用 Stata 软件自带数据集 auto.dta，具体说明 Probit 模型的使用。该数据集包括 make、weight、mileage、foreign 等汽车数据，其中有 22 个外国(foreign)汽车型号，52 个国内(domestic)汽车型号。

```
.use auto, clear
.keep make mpg weight foreign
.describe
```

运行结果如图 3.13 所示。

① 本案例根据 Stata 帮助手册 r.pdf 中的对应例子改编。

```
 Observations:            74              1978 automobile data
    Variables:             4              17 Feb 2022 16:21
                                          (_dta has notes)

Variable      Storage   Display    Value
    name         type    format    label      Variable label

make          str18     %-18s                 Make and model
mpg           int       %8.0g                 Mileage (mpg)
weight        int       %8.0gc                Weight (lbs.)
foreign       byte      %8.0g      origin     Car origin

Sorted by: foreign
     Note: Dataset has changed since last saved.
```

图 3.13

.inspect foreign

运行结果如图 3.14 所示。

```
foreign:  Car origin                         Number of observations
                                     Total      Integers   Nonintegers
 |  #                      Negative      -             -             -
 |  #                      Zero         52            52             -
 |  #                      Positive     22            22             -
 |  #
 |  #   #                  Total        74            74             -
 |  #   #                  Missing       -
+----------------------
0                     1                 74
  (2 unique values)

    foreign is labeled and all values are documented in the label.
```

图 3.14

foreign 变量为二值变量，分别是 0 和 1。0 表示国内汽车，1 表示国外汽车。

拟合的模型为：

$$\Pr(\text{foreign}=1)=\Phi(\beta_0+\beta_1\,\text{weight}+\beta_2\,\text{mpg})$$

其中，Φ 是累积正态分布。

.probit foreign weight mpg

运行结果如图 3.15 所示。

可以看出，重型汽车和燃油节省的汽车，更不可能由国外生产。

* 通过设定 vec(robust)选项，估计稳健标准误下的 Probit 模型

.probit foreign weight mpg, vce(robust) nolog

```
Probit regression                                       Number of obs =     74
                                                        LR chi2(2)    =  36.38
                                                        Prob > chi2   = 0.0000
Log likelihood = -26.844189                             Pseudo R2     = 0.4039
```

foreign	Coefficient	Std. err.	z	P>|z|	[95% conf.	interval]
weight	-0.002	0.001	-4.13	0.000	-0.003	-0.001
mpg	-0.104	0.052	-2.02	0.044	-0.205	-0.003
_cons	8.275	2.554	3.24	0.001	3.269	13.281

图 3.15

运行结果如图 3.16 所示。

```
Probit regression                                       Number of obs =     74
                                                        Wald chi2(2)  =  30.26
                                                        Prob > chi2   = 0.0000
Log pseudolikelihood = -26.844189                       Pseudo R2     = 0.4039
```

foreign	Coefficient	Robust std. err.	z	P>|z|	[95% conf.	interval]
weight	-0.002	0.000	-4.73	0.000	-0.003	-0.001
mpg	-0.104	0.059	-1.75	0.080	-0.220	0.012
_cons	8.275	2.539	3.26	0.001	3.299	13.252

图 3.16

稳健情况下 mpg 的标准误比非稳健情况高 15%。

* 对模型做异方差检验

. hetprob foreign weight, het(mpg)

运行结果如图 3.17 所示。

```
Heteroskedastic probit model                       Number of obs     =     74
                                                   Zero outcomes     =     52
                                                   Nonzero outcomes  =     22

                                                   Wald chi2(1)      =   0.98
Log likelihood = -28.85303                         Prob > chi2       = 0.3221
```

foreign	Coefficient	Std. err.	z	P>|z|	[95% conf.	interval]
foreign						
weight	-0.001	0.001	-0.99	0.322	-0.003	0.001
_cons	2.560	2.739	0.93	0.350	-2.809	7.929
lnsigma						
mpg	-0.016	0.046	-0.34	0.732	-0.106	0.074

```
LR test of lnsigma=0: chi2(1) = 0.11                         Prob > chi2 = 0.7393
```

图 3.17

图 3.17 中上半部分为对原模型的估计结果，下半部分为对方差方程(lnsigma2)的估计结果，同方差假设检验的 p 值为 0.0827，拒绝同方差的原假设，认为模型存在异方差问题。

3.3* 互补重对数回归

在二值选择模型中，随机项使用非对称的极值分布，就可以得到补对数—对数模型即互补重对数模型(complementary log—log model)，该模型可以解决稀有时间偏差问题。其事件发生概率为：

$$p = P(y=1 \mid \boldsymbol{x}) = F(\boldsymbol{x}, \boldsymbol{\beta}) = 1 - \exp\left|- e^{\boldsymbol{x}'\boldsymbol{\beta}}\right| \tag{3.13}$$

互补重对数模型的参数估计使用 MLE 估计法。Stata 软件的估计命令为 cloglog。cloglog 命令适用于二元因变量的互补重对数模型，也可用于拟合 Gompit 模型还可以计算稳健性和集群稳健性标准误差，并调整复杂的调查设计结果。

语法格式为：

cloglog depvar [indepvars] [if] [in] [weight] [, options]

菜单操作路径为：

Statistics>Binary outcomes>Complementary log-log regression

例 3.3 cloglog 命令的应用

继续以之前 auto.dta 数据为例来说明 cloglog 命令的应用。

要拟合的模型为：

$$\Pr(\text{foreign}=1) = F(\beta_0 + \beta_1 \text{weight} + \beta_2 \text{mpg})$$

其中，$F(z) = 1 - \exp\{-\exp(z)\}$。

```
.cloglog foreign weight mpg
```

运行结果如图 3.18 所示。

```
Complementary log-log regression                Number of obs     =        74
                                                Zero outcomes     =        52
                                                Nonzero outcomes  =        22

                                                LR chi2(2)        =     34.58
Log likelihood = -27.742769                     Prob > chi2       =    0.0000
```

foreign	Coefficient	Std. err.	z	P>|z|	[95% conf.	interval]
weight	-0.003	0.001	-4.18	0.000	-0.004	-0.002
mpg	-0.142	0.076	-1.86	0.062	-0.292	0.007
_cons	10.097	3.352	3.01	0.003	3.527	16.666

图 3.18

从估计结果可以看出，较重的汽车不太可能是外国的，而油耗更高的汽车也不太可能是外国的，至少在汽车重量不变的情况下是这样。

3.4 条件 Logistic 回归

条件 Logit 模型(conditional logit model)是由美国经济学家 McFadden 于 1974 年提出的,主要贡献是发展了离散选择的理论和方法。在 McFadden 之前,对于离散变量的研究都缺乏经济理论基础。McFadden 对随机效用作出一些巧妙的分配假设,使得选择各类别的概率(乃至于整个似然函数)都可以用简单的公式表示出来,因此,可以用标准的统计方法将"类别特征"以及"经济个体特征"对类别选择的影响估计出来,他将这种计量模型取名为条件 Logit 模型。

条件 Logit 模型的优势在于,它具有在两个可变换方案(如乘坐地铁和自驾)之间选择相对概率的特殊属性,而对其他交通选择方案的价格和质量不予考虑,这个性质称为非相关选择独立性(简称 IIA),但在有些实际应用中是不现实的。

设 $i=1,2,\cdots,n$ 表示组,$t=1,2,\cdots,T_i$ 表示第 i 组的观测值。被解释变量 y_{it} 表示取值为 0 和 1 的变量。$y_i=(y_{i1},\cdots,y_{iT_i})$ 是第 i 组的结果向量,$\boldsymbol{x}_{it}$ 是协变量行向量。$k_{1i}=\sum_{t=1}^{T_i} y_{it}$ 是第 i 组的被解释变量为 1 的个数。

y_i 以 $\sum_{t=1}^{T_i} y_{it}=k_{1i}$ 为条件的一个可能值的概率为:

$$\Pr\left(y_i \,\middle|\, \sum_{t=1}^{T_i} y_{it}=k_{1i}\right)=\frac{\exp\left(\sum_{t=1}^{T_i} y_{it}\boldsymbol{x}_{it}\boldsymbol{\beta}\right)}{\sum_{\boldsymbol{d}_i\in S_i}\exp\left(\sum_{t=1}^{T_i} d_{it}\boldsymbol{x}_{it}\boldsymbol{\beta}\right)} \tag{3.14}$$

其中,d_{it} 等于 0 或 1,$\sum_{t=1}^{T_i} d_{it}=k_{1i}$,$S_i$ 为 k_{1i} 为 1 和 k_{2i} 为 0 的所有可能集合。

条件 Logit 模型的估计命令为 clogit,主要用于匹配处理控制数据,因此该模型也称为面板固定效应 Logit 模型。

语法格式为:

```
clogit depvar [indepvars] [if] [in] [weight], group(varname) [options]
```

菜单操作路径为:

Statistics>Binary outcomes>Conditional logistic regression

设有一组数据,id 变量包含每组的唯一识别值,结果变量 y 包括 0 和 1。

条件 Logit 模型估计的另一个命令为 cmclogit,该命令拟合 McFadden 选择模型,该模型是条件 Logit 模型的一个具体特例。这个命令要求每个案例具有多个观测值(为一个个体或一个决策者),每个观测值表示一个可能被选择的选项。cmclogit 命令可以使用两类解释变量:一类是与具体选项相关的变量,随着案例和选项而变动;另一类是与案例相关的变量,只随案例而变动,而不随选项变化。

语法格式为:

```
cmclogit depvar [indepvars] [if] [in] [weight] [,options]
```

菜单操作路径为：

Statistics>Choice models>Conditional logit (McFadden's choice) model

例 3.4　条件 Logit 模型的应用[①]

下面利用 Stata 软件自带数据集 carchoice. dta 来说明条件 Logit 模型的应用。该数据集包括的是汽车消费选择数据，共 885 位消费者，每个消费者在美国车、日本车、欧洲车和韩国车中进行选择(即变量 car)，我们想要研究汽车消费选择与消费者性别(即变量 gender)、收入(即变量 income)以及每个国家汽车经销商在消费者社区的数量(即变量 dealers)之间的关系。变量 dealers 是与选项有关的变量，gender 和 income 是与案例有关的变量。每个消费者的选择由变量 purchase 表示。

```
. use carchoice, clear
. list consumerid car purchase dealers gender income
> if consumerid < = 4, sepby(consumerid) abbr(10)
```

运行结果如图 3.19 所示。

	consumerid	car	purchase	dealers	gender	income
1.	1	American	1	9	Male	46.7
2.	1	Japanese	0	11	Male	46.7
3.	1	European	0	5	Male	46.7
4.	1	Korean	0	1	Male	46.7
5.	2	American	1	10	Male	26.1
6.	2	Japanese	0	7	Male	26.1
7.	2	European	0	2	Male	26.1
8.	2	Korean	0	1	Male	26.1
9.	3	American	0	8	Male	32.7
10.	3	Japanese	1	6	Male	32.7
11.	3	European	0	2	Male	32.7
12.	4	American	1	5	Female	49.2
13.	4	Japanese	0	4	Female	49.2
14.	4	European	0	3	Female	49.2

图　3.19

第一位消费者为男性，年收入 46700 美元，选择购买美国车。第三位消费者购买日本车。第三位和第四位消费者没有选择韩国车作为备选项，因为他们所在的地区没有韩国车经销商。

＊执行 cm 类命令

① 本案例根据 Stata 帮助手册 cm. pdf 中的对应例子改编。

```
.cmset consumerid car
.cmchoiceset
```

运行结果如图 3.20 所示。

Tabulation of choice-set possibilities

Choice set	Freq.	Percent	Cum.
1 2 3	380	42.94	42.94
1 2 3 4	505	57.06	100.00
Total	885	100.00	

Note: Total is number of cases.

图 3.20

给 car 变量添加数值标签，1＝American，2＝Japanese，3＝European，4＝Korean。43.93％的消费者所在区域没有韩国车经销商，因而，对他们而言，选择项 4＝Korean 不可获取。对于所有消费者而言，其所在区域均有美国车、日本车和欧洲车经销商，所以，这三种车型是他们的备选项。

```
.cmclogit purchase dealers, casevars(i.gender income)
```

运行结果如图 3.21 所示。

```
Conditional logit choice model                  Number of obs      =      3,075
Case ID variable: consumerid                    Number of cases    =        862

Alternatives variable: car                      Alts per case: min =          3
                                                               avg =        3.6
                                                               max =          4

                                                   Wald chi2(7)    =      51.03
Log likelihood = -948.12096                        Prob > chi2     =     0.0000
```

purchase	Coefficient	Std. err.	z	P>|z|	[95% conf.	interval]
car						
dealers	0.045	0.026	1.70	0.088	-0.007	0.096
American	(base alternative)					
Japanese						
gender						
Male	-0.379	0.171	-2.22	0.027	-0.715	-0.044
income	0.015	0.007	2.38	0.017	0.003	0.028
_cons	-0.479	0.331	-1.44	0.149	-1.128	0.171
European						
gender						
Male	0.653	0.265	2.47	0.014	0.134	1.172
income	0.034	0.008	4.28	0.000	0.019	0.050
_cons	-2.840	0.462	-6.15	0.000	-3.744	-1.935
Korean						
gender						
Male	0.068	0.446	0.15	0.879	-0.807	0.943
income	-0.038	0.016	-2.38	0.017	-0.069	-0.007
_cons	0.051	0.803	0.06	0.949	-1.523	1.626

图 3.21

使用 or 比率，便于对回归结果进行分析。

运行结果如图 3.22 所示。

purchase	Odds ratio	Std. err.	z	P>|z|	[95% conf. interval]	
car						
dealers	1.046	0.027	1.70	0.088	0.993	1.101
American	(base alternative)					
Japanese						
gender						
Male	0.684	0.117	-2.22	0.027	0.489	0.957
income	1.016	0.007	2.38	0.017	1.003	1.029
_cons	0.620	0.205	-1.44	0.149	0.324	1.186
European						
gender						
Male	1.922	0.509	2.47	0.014	1.144	3.229
income	1.035	0.008	4.28	0.000	1.019	1.051
_cons	0.058	0.027	-6.15	0.000	0.024	0.144
Korean						
gender						
Male	1.070	0.478	0.15	0.879	0.446	2.568
income	0.963	0.015	-2.38	0.017	0.933	0.993
_cons	1.053	0.845	0.06	0.949	0.218	5.082

图 3.22

结果显示，与女性相比，男性选择日本车的概率低于选择美国车（相对风险概率为 0.684），但男性选择欧洲车的概率高于选择美国车（相对风险概率为 1.922）。较高收入的消费者，相比购买美国车，更倾向于购买日本车或欧洲车，而更不倾向于购买韩国车。

增加每一国汽车的经销商数量如何影响更多人购买该汽车的可能性？在 cmclogit 估计后，使用 margins 命令来回答这一问题。

```
.margins, at(dealers = generate(dealers)) at(dealers = generate(dealers
+1))
> contrast(atcontrast(r)) alternative(European)
```

运行结果如图 3.23 所示。

增加一个欧洲汽车经销商，使消费者购买欧洲车的概率增加 0.06，这种增加是以其他国家车辆销售下降为代价的，对美国车的影响稍高于对日本车的影响。增加一个欧洲汽车经销商，消费者购买美国车的概率下降 0.003，购买日本车的概率下降 0.002，韩国车受到的影响非常有限。

通过增加 base alternative()来改变基础选项。

运行结果如图 3.24 所示。

在默认的基准比较中，难以对选择欧洲车、韩国车与日本车的概率之间的差异进行比较，现在改变了基准组，比较起来就非常容易了。

通过 altwise 命令可以对缺失值进行处理。在默认情况下，缺失值是以案例为单位的，意味着构成案例的任何观测值的任何缺失，都会导致该案例从估计样本中去掉。如果只是想去掉缺失值的观测值而不是整个案例，可以通过 altwise 命令进行设置。

```
Contrasts of predictive margins                    Number of obs = 3,075
Model VCE: OIM

Expression:  Pr(car|1 selected), predict()
Alternative: European

1._at: dealers =   dealers

2._at: dealers = dealers+1

                          df        chi2     P>chi2

         _at@_outcome
(2 vs 1) American          1        2.81     0.0937
(2 vs 1) Japanese          1        2.80     0.0940
(2 vs 1) European          1        2.82     0.0934
  (2 vs 1) Korean          1        2.52     0.1121
            Joint          3        2.84     0.4177


                                   Delta-method
                       Contrast   std. err.     [95% conf. interval]

         _at@_outcome
(2 vs 1) American        -0.003      0.002       -0.006       0.000
(2 vs 1) Japanese        -0.002      0.001       -0.005       0.000
(2 vs 1) European         0.006      0.003       -0.001       0.012
  (2 vs 1) Korean        -0.000      0.000       -0.001       0.000
```

图 3.23

```
Conditional logit choice model              Number of obs      =      3,075
Case ID variable: consumerid                Number of cases    =        862

Alternatives variable: car                  Alts per case: min =          3
                                                           avg =        3.6
                                                           max =          4

                                               Wald chi2(7)    =      51.03
Log likelihood = -948.12096                    Prob > chi2     =     0.0000

    purchase   Odds ratio   Std. err.      z    P>|z|     [95% conf. interval]

car
     dealers        1.046       0.027    1.70   0.088        0.993       1.101

American
      gender
        Male        1.461       0.250    2.22   0.027        1.045       2.044
      income        0.985       0.006   -2.38   0.017        0.972       0.997
       _cons        1.614       0.535    1.44   0.149        0.843       3.090

Japanese      (base alternative)

European
      gender
        Male        2.809       0.740    3.92   0.000        1.675       4.709
      income        1.019       0.008    2.30   0.021        1.003       1.036
       _cons        0.094       0.043   -5.18   0.000        0.039       0.230

Korean
      gender
        Male        1.564       0.699    1.00   0.317        0.651       3.755
      income        0.948       0.015   -3.32   0.001        0.919       0.978
       _cons        1.699       1.365    0.66   0.510        0.352       8.205
```

图 3.24

```
.cmclogit purchase dealers, casevars(i.gender income) altwise or
> basealternative(American)
```

运行结果如图 3.25 所示。

```
Conditional logit choice model                  Number of obs      =     3,137
Case ID variable: consumerid                    Number of cases    =       885

Alternatives variable: car                      Alts per case: min =         2
                                                               avg =       3.5
                                                               max =         4

                                                   Wald chi2(7)    =     54.18
Log likelihood = -965.0164                         Prob > chi2     =    0.0000
```

purchase	Odds ratio	Std. err.	z	P>|z|	[95% conf.	interval]
car						
dealers	1.051	0.027	1.92	0.055	0.999	1.106
American	(base alternative)					
Japanese						
gender						
Male	0.687	0.117	-2.21	0.027	0.492	0.958
income	1.016	0.007	2.38	0.018	1.003	1.028
_cons	0.629	0.207	-1.41	0.159	0.330	1.199
European						
gender						
Male	1.997	0.527	2.62	0.009	1.191	3.349
income	1.036	0.008	4.44	0.000	1.020	1.052
_cons	0.056	0.026	-6.30	0.000	0.023	0.137
Korean						
gender						
Male	1.067	0.476	0.14	0.885	0.445	2.559
income	0.963	0.015	-2.38	0.017	0.933	0.993
_cons	1.054	0.849	0.07	0.948	0.217	5.112

图 3.25

为了查看在估计中使用样本的变化，可以使用 cmchoiceset 命令进行检验。

```
.cmchoiceset if e(sample) = =1
```

运行结果如图 3.26 所示。

Choice set	Freq.	Percent	Cum.
1 2	2	0.23	0.23
1 2 3	378	42.71	42.94
1 2 3 4	489	55.25	98.19
1 2 4	4	0.45	98.64
1 3	2	0.23	98.87
1 3 4	2	0.23	99.10
2 3	3	0.34	99.44
2 3 4	5	0.56	100.00
Total	885	100.00	

Note: Total is number of cases.

图 3.26

当缺失值处理以案例为单位时，仅有两个不同的选择集：{1,2,3}和{1,2,3,4}。采用不同的缺失值处理方式时，共有六种不同的新的选择集，尽管这些选择集的样本量比较小。

cmclogit 估计后,可以使用后验命令进行系数比较以及概率预测等。继续以 carchoice.dta 数据集为例进行说明。

```
.cmclogit purchase dealers, casevars(i.gender income)
```

以美国车选择为基准,为检验日本车选择和韩国车选择的 1.gender 的系数是否相等,可执行以下命令:

```
.test [Japanese]:1.gender = [Korean]:1.gender
```

运行结果如图 3.27 所示。

```
.   test [Japanese]:1.gender = [Korean]:1.gender

 ( 1)  [Japanese]1.gender - [Korean]1.gender = 0

           chi2(  1) =    1.00
         Prob > chi2 =    0.3169
```

图 3.27

```
.test [Japanese = European = Korean]:1.gender
```

运行结果如图 3.28 所示。

```
.   test [Japanese = European = Korean]:1.gender

 ( 1)  [Japanese]1.gender - [European]1.gender = 0
 ( 2)  [Japanese]1.gender - [Korean]1.gender = 0

           chi2(  2) =   15.62
         Prob > chi2 =    0.0004
```

图 3.28

对于每个案例存在多个选择的情况,以上述汽车选择数据为例,使其包括购买第二辆汽车选择。

```
.list consumerid carnumber car purchase
> if inlist(consumerid, 6, 7), sepby(consumerid carnumber) abbr(10)
```

运行结果如图 3.29 所示。

从数据中可以看到,consumerid=7 有两辆汽车,第一辆为欧洲汽车,第二辆为韩国汽车。consummerid=6 只有一辆美国汽车。

```
.cmset consumerid carnumber car
.cmclogit purchase dealers, casevars(i.gender income) or
> basealternative(American)
```

运行结果如图 3.30 所示。

	consumerid	carnumber	car	purchase
18.	6	1	American	1
19.	6	1	Japanese	0
20.	6	1	European	0
21.	7	1	American	0
22.	7	1	Japanese	0
23.	7	1	European	1
24.	7	1	Korean	0
25.	7	2	American	0
26.	7	2	Japanese	0
27.	7	2	European	0
28.	7	2	Korean	1

图 3.29

```
Conditional logit choice model                Number of obs     =     3,728
Case ID variable: _caseid                     Number of cases   =      1045

Alternatives variable: car                    Alts per case: min =        3
                                                             avg =      3.6
                                                             max =        4

                                                 Wald chi2(7)   =     42.76
Log pseudolikelihood = -1220.8604                Prob > chi2    =    0.0000

                               (Std. err. adjusted for 862 clusters in consumerid)
```

purchase	Odds ratio	Robust std. err.	z	P>|z|	[95% conf.	interval]
car						
dealers	1.021	0.024	0.89	0.373	0.976	1.068
American	(base alternative)					
Japanese						
gender						
Male	0.675	0.110	-2.40	0.016	0.490	0.930
income	1.015	0.006	2.42	0.015	1.003	1.027
_cons	0.518	0.161	-2.12	0.034	0.282	0.952
European						
gender						
Male	1.591	0.341	2.16	0.030	1.045	2.422
income	1.033	0.007	4.45	0.000	1.018	1.048
_cons	0.074	0.031	-6.30	0.000	0.033	0.166
Korean						
gender						
Male	1.134	0.302	0.47	0.638	0.672	1.912
income	0.994	0.010	-0.61	0.541	0.974	1.014
_cons	0.568	0.300	-1.07	0.284	0.201	1.601

图 3.30

3.5 精确 Logistic 回归

精确 Logistic 模型主要用于流行病等研究领域，经常存在小样本、资料结构不平衡以及高度分层的情况，最大似然估计结果不可靠甚至不存在。Cox 和 Snell (1989)[1]首先提出条件最大似然估计法(CMLEs)，该方法在小样本情况下具有良好的统计性质。对分层数据而言，精确 Logistic 模型是条件 Logit 模型的小样本替代。

设 Y_i 是一个伯努利随机变量，观测到的结果为 $Y_i = y_i, i=1,\cdots,n$。相应的协变量为 $1\times p$ 阶的 $\boldsymbol{x}_i$。设 $\pi_i = \Pr(Y_i \mid \boldsymbol{x}_i)$，使用 Logit 模型来表示 Y_i 和 $\boldsymbol{x}_i$ 之间的关系。

$$\log\left(\frac{\pi_i}{1-\pi_i}\right) = \theta + \boldsymbol{x}_i\boldsymbol{\beta}$$

其中，常数项 θ 和 $1\times p$ 阶的 $\boldsymbol{\beta}$ 为待估参数。观测值 $Y_i = y_i$ 的概率为

$$\Pr(\boldsymbol{Y} = y) = \prod_{i=1}^{n} \pi_i^{y_i}(1-\pi_i)^{1-y_i}$$

其中，$\boldsymbol{Y} = (Y_1,\cdots,Y_N)$，$y=(y_1,\cdots,y_n)$。最大化这个函数的对数值即可得到 θ 和 $\boldsymbol{\beta}$ 的最大似然估计。

θ 和 $\beta_j(j=1,\cdots,p)$ 的充分统计量分别为 $M = \sum_{i=1}^{n} Y_i$ 和 $T_j = \sum_{i=1}^{n} Y_i \boldsymbol{x}_{ij}$，并观测到 $M=m, T_j = t_j$。默认情况下，exlogistic 命令将会在给定 $M=m$ 下，拟合 $T=(T_1,\cdots,T_p)$ 的条件分布。条件分布的数量大小为 $\binom{n}{m}$。将其中一个向量表示为 $T^{(k)} = (t_1^{(k)},\cdots,t_p^{(k)})$，$k=1,\cdots,N$，响应的组合系数为 c_k，$\sum_{k=1}^{N} c_k = \binom{n}{m}$。对于每个解释变量 $\boldsymbol{x}_j, j=1,\cdots,p$，通过对其他所有观测到的充分统计量 $T_l = t_l, l\neq j$ 进行条件设置，进一步简化条件分布。$T_j = t_j$ 的条件分布为：

$$\Pr(T_j = t_j \mid T_l = t_l, l\neq j, M=m) = \frac{c e^{t_j\beta_j}}{\sum_k c_k e^{t_j^{(k)}\beta_j}}$$

其中，求和是基于 T 向量的子集使得 $T_1^{(k)} = t_1,\cdots,T_j^{(k)} = t_j,\cdots,T_p^{(k)} = t_p$，$c$ 是与观测到的 t 相关的组合系数。β_j 的条件最大似然估计通过最大化这个函数的对数值得到。

精确 Logistic 模型的估计命令为 exlogisitc，主要用于小样本、资料结构不平衡以及高度分层的数据。

语法格式为：

```
exlogistic depvar [indepvars] [if] [in] [weight] [,options]
```

菜单操作路径为：

Statistics>Exact statistics>Exact logistic regression

[1] Cox, D. R., and E. J. Snell. *Analysis of Binary Data* (2nd ed.). London: Chapman & Hall, 1989.

例 3.5 精准 Logit 模型①

以下利用 Stata 软件自带数据集 hiv1.dta 来说明 exlogistic 命令的应用。该数据集主要包括关于孕期感染 1 型 HIV 病例的数据，通过测度新生儿 6 个月时糖蛋白 CD4 和 CD8 的血清水平预测 HIV 感染的发展。血清水平通过 0，1 和 2 的序数值进行编码。

```
.use hiv1, clear
.list in 1/5
```

运行结果如图 3.31 所示。

	hiv	cd4	cd8
1.	1	0	0
2.	0	0	0
3.	1	0	2
4.	1	1	0
5.	0	1	0

图 3.31

使用 logistic 命令进行估计，以便与精确 Logistic 模型进行比较。

```
.logistic hiv cd4 cd8, coef
```

运行结果如图 3.32 所示。

Logistic regression　　Number of obs = 47

LR chi2(2) = 15.75

Prob > chi2 = 0.0004

Log likelihood = -20.751687　　Pseudo R2 = 0.2751

hiv	Coefficient	Std. err.	z	P>|z|	[95% conf.	interval]
cd4	-2.542	0.839	-3.03	0.002	-4.187	-0.897
cd8	1.659	0.821	2.02	0.043	0.049	3.268
_cons	0.513	0.681	0.75	0.451	-0.821	1.848

图 3.32

```
.exlogistic hiv cd4 cd8, coef
```

运行结果如图 3.33 所示。

由 exlogistic 计算的 p 值来自给定其他参数的充分统计量的每个参数的条件分布。默认情况下，exlogistic 报告回归参数的充分统计量，并给出观察到更极端值的概率。单一参数检验的假设为 $H_0:\beta_{cd4}=0$ 和 $H_0:\beta_{cd8}=0$，条件得分检验则是检验上述两个原假设同时成立。可以发现由 exlogistic 计算的 p 值与 Logistic 模型的 Wald 统计量的 p 值非常接近。

① 本案例根据 Stata 帮助手册 r.pdf 中的对应例子改编。

Exact logistic regression			Number of obs =		47
			Model score =		13.34655
			Pr >= score =		0.0006
hiv	Coefficient	Suff.	2*Pr(Suff.)	[95% conf. interval]	
cd4	-2.387632	10	0.0004	-4.699633	-.8221807
cd8	1.592366	12	0.0528	-.0137905	3.907876

图 3.33

3.6 偏斜 logistic 回归

偏斜 Logistic 模型又称 Scobit 模型，该模型是一种有偏的二值 Logit 模型。① 在传统的二值 Logit 模型中，存在一种默认的假设，即在概率 0.5 处因变量对于自变量的变化最为敏感，其斜率最大，而在现实世界中并非如此。下面对 Scobit 模型进行具体说明。

与二值 Logit 模型类似，假设存在两个选项，分别是选项 0 和选项 1，那么，也可以得出选择选项 0 的概率 p_{n0} 和选择选项 1 的概率 p_{n1} 分别为：

$$p_{n0}=1-F(-(v_{n0}-v_{n1})) \tag{3.15}$$

$$p_{n1}=F(-(v_{n0}-v_{n1})) \tag{3.16}$$

其中，假设 ε_n 服从二重指数分布，模型就转换为标准的二值 Logit 模型。实际上，Scobit 模型是在传统的二值 Logit 模型的概率计算公式中增加一个大于 0 的指数参数 α（斜率系数，也称为 skewness 参数），此时，ε_n 服从 Burr－10 分布，该分布满足在累积概率为 0.5 的情况下，其概率密度函数并非达到最大值，即其累积概率曲线的斜率并非最大。这个增加的斜率系数可以控制累积概率函数接近 0 或者 1 的速度，且在（$-\infty$，$+\infty$）上有意义。Scobit 模型的概率公式可以表示为：

$$p_{n0}=1-F(-(v_{n0}-v_{n1}))=1-\frac{1}{(1+\exp(v_{n0}-v_{n1}))^{\alpha}} \tag{3.17}$$

$$p_{n1}=F(-(v_{n0}-v_{n1}))=\frac{1}{(1+\exp(v_{n0}-v_{n1}))^{\alpha}} \tag{3.18}$$

当 $\alpha=1$ 时，Scobit 模型转化为二值 Logit 模型，因此，Scobit 模型包含了二值 Logit 模型。

偏斜 Logistic 模型的估计命令为 scobit，该命令通过最大似然估计法对偏斜 Logistic 模型进行拟合，估计参数。

语法格式为：

```
scobit depvar [indepvars] [if] [in] [weight] [,options]
```

① Nagler J. Scobit: An Alternative Estimator to Logit and Probit[J]. *American Journal of Political Science*, 1994, 38(1).

菜单操作路径为：

Statistics>Binary outcomes>Skewed logistic regression

例 3.6　偏斜 Logistic 模型①

下面利用 Stata 软件自带数据集 auto.dta 为例来说明偏斜 Logistic 模型的应用。希望通过估计偏斜 Logistic 模型，根据其行驶里程来解释一辆汽车是否为外国生产。

```
. use auto.dta, clear
. keep make mpg weight foreign
. describe
```

运行结果如图 3.34 所示。

```
Contains data from D:\D盘\研究生计量\data\chapter3\auto.dta
 Observations:            74                  1978 automobile data
    Variables:             4                  17 Feb 2022 16:21
                                              (_dta has notes)

Variable      Storage   Display    Value
    name         type    format    label      Variable label

make          str18     %-18s                 Make and model
mpg           int       %8.0g                 Mileage (mpg)
weight        int       %8.0gc                Weight (lbs.)
foreign       byte      %8.0g      origin     Car origin

Sorted by: foreign
     Note: Dataset has changed since last saved.
```

图　3.34

```
. inspect foreign
```

运行结果如图 3.35 所示。

```
foreign:  Car origin                        Number of observations
                                       Total     Integers   Nonintegers
|  #                     Negative          -            -             -
|  #                     Zero             52           52             -
|  #                     Positive         22           22             -
|  #
|  #   #                 Total            74           74             -
|  #   #                 Missing           -
+----------------------
0              1                          74
  (2 unique values)

   foreign is labeled and all values are documented in the label.
```

图　3.35

① 本案例根据 Stata 帮助手册 r.pdf 中的对应例子改编。

可以看出，foreign 取值为 0 和 1，0 表示国内汽车，1 表示国外汽车。目的是估计如下模型：

$$\Pr(\text{foreign}=1)=F(\beta_0+\beta_1\text{mpg})$$

其中，$F(z)=1-1/\{1+\exp(z)\}^{\alpha}$。

```
.scobit foreign mpg
```

运行结果如图 3.36 所示。

Skewed logistic regression　　Number of obs = 74　Zero outcomes = 52　Nonzero outcomes = 22

Log likelihood = **-39.2842**

foreign	Coefficient	Std. err.	z	P>|z|	[95% conf.	interval]
mpg	**0.181**	**0.241**	**0.75**	**0.451**	**-0.290**	**0.653**
_cons	**-4.275**	**1.399**	**-3.06**	**0.002**	**-7.017**	**-1.532**
/lnalpha	**-0.445**	**3.880**	**-0.11**	**0.909**	**-8.049**	**7.159**
alpha	**0.641**	**2.486**			**0.000**	**1286.133**

LR test of alpha=1: chi2(**1**) = **0.01**　　Prob > chi2 = **0.9249**

Note: Likelihood-ratio tests are recommended for inference with scobit models.

图 3.36

可以看出，更高汽油消耗的车更不可能来自国外。似然比检验显示该模型与 Logit 模型不存在显著差异，因此，应该使用更为简约的模型，即 Logit 模型。

```
.scobit foreign mpg, vce(robust) nolog
```

运行结果如图 3.37 所示。

Skewed logistic regression　　Number of obs = 74　Zero outcomes = 52　Nonzero outcomes = 22

Log pseudolikelihood = **-39.2842**

foreign	Coefficient	Robust std. err.	z	P>|z|	[95% conf.	interval]
mpg	**0.181**	**0.303**	**0.60**	**0.549**	**-0.412**	**0.775**
_cons	**-4.275**	**1.336**	**-3.20**	**0.001**	**-6.892**	**-1.657**
/lnalpha	**-0.445**	**4.716**	**-0.09**	**0.925**	**-9.687**	**8.797**
alpha	**0.641**	**3.022**			**0.000**	**6616.919**

图 3.37

稳健标准误情况下，mpg 系数的标准误增长率大约为 25%。

3.7* 含内生协变量的 Probit 回归

含内生解释变量的 Probit 模型(probit model with continuous endogenous covariates)的表达式为：

$$\begin{aligned} y_{2t} &= \boldsymbol{x}_t'\gamma_1 + \boldsymbol{z}_t'\gamma_2 + v_i \\ y_{1t}^* &= \boldsymbol{x}_t'\boldsymbol{\alpha} + \boldsymbol{\beta} y_{2t} + u_i \\ y_{1t} &= \boldsymbol{I}(y_{1t}^* > 0) \end{aligned} \tag{3.19}$$

式中，y_{1t} 为可观测的虚拟变量；y_{1t}^* 为不可观测的潜在变量；y_{2t} 为模型中唯一的内生解释变量(向量)。第一个方程为第一阶段方程或简化式方程，不含内生变量，第二个方程为结构方程，包含内生变量。假设扰动项(u_i，v_i)服从期望值为 0 的二维正态分布，即

$$\begin{pmatrix} u_i \\ v_i \end{pmatrix} \sim N\left[\begin{pmatrix} 0 \\ 0 \end{pmatrix}, \begin{pmatrix} 1 & \rho\sigma_v \\ \rho\sigma_v & 1 \end{pmatrix}\right]$$

含连续内生解释变量的 Probit 模型使用 MLE 估计法，存在不收敛或多个内生解释变量的情形下，则使用两步估计法(又称控制函数法)。其估计命令为 ivprobit。

语法格式为：

最大似然估计法：

ivprobit depvar [varlist1] (varlist2 = varlist_iv) [if] [in] [weight] [, mle_options]

两步估计法：

ivprobit depvar [varlist1] (varlist2 = varlist_iv) [if] [in] [weight], twostep [tse_options]

其中，varlist1 是外部变量的列表。varlist2 是内生变量的列表。varlist_iv 是与 varlist1 一起用作 varlist2 工具的外生变量列表。

菜单操作路径为：

Statistics>Endogenous covariates>Probit model with endogenous covariates

例 3.7 含内生协变量的 ivProbit 模型①

以下利用 Stata 软件自带数据集 laborsup.dta 来说明 ivprobit 命令的应用。该数据集包含 500 个双亲家庭的假设数据，目的是对母亲是否工作进行建模，fem_work 是一个二值变量，1 表示工作，0 表示其他情况。她做出是否工作的决定是家庭孩子数量(kids)、男性在校教育年限(fem_educ)、家庭其他收入(other_inc)的函数。假设影响女性就业决定的不可观察的冲击也会影响家庭的其他收入，因而，other_inc 是内生变量。选择男性在校教育年限(male_educ)作为工具变量。

```
. use laborsup, clear
```

① 本案例根据 Stata 帮助手册 r.pdf 中的对应例子改编。

. ivprobit fem_work fem_educ kids (other_inc = male_educ)

运行结果如图 3.38 所示。

Probit model with endogenous regressors　　Number of obs = 500

Wald chi2(3) = 163.88

Log likelihood = -2368.2062　　Prob > chi2 = 0.0000

	Coefficient	Std. err.	z	P>|z|	[95% conf.	interval]
other_inc	-0.054	0.006	-8.92	0.000	-0.066	-0.042
fem_educ	0.211	0.027	7.86	0.000	0.158	0.264
kids	-0.182	0.048	-3.81	0.000	-0.276	-0.088
_cons	0.367	0.448	0.82	0.412	-0.511	1.245
corr(e.other_inc,e.fem_work)	0.372	0.130			0.095	0.596
sd(e.other_inc)	16.666	0.527			15.665	17.732

Wald test of exogeneity (corr = 0): chi2(1) = 6.70　　Prob > chi2 = 0.0096

Instrumented: other_inc

Instruments: fem_educ kids male_educ

图 3.38

ivprobit 命令使用默认的最大似然估计量。图 3.36 的上面部分给出了样本量，检验所有斜率系数均为 0 的 Wald 统计量及对应 p 值。图 3.36 的下面部分是内生变量外生性的 Wald 检验，拒绝不存在内生性的零假设。

使用两步估计法对模型进行估计。

. ivprobit fem_work fem_educ kids (other_inc = male_educ), twostep

运行结果如图 3.39 所示。

Two-step probit with endogenous regressors　　Number of obs = 500

Wald chi2(3) = 93.97

Prob > chi2 = 0.0000

	Coefficient	Std. err.	z	P>|z|	[95% conf.	interval]
other_inc	-0.058	0.009	-6.26	0.000	-0.077	-0.040
fem_educ	0.227	0.028	8.08	0.000	0.172	0.283
kids	-0.196	0.050	-3.95	0.000	-0.293	-0.099
_cons	0.396	0.498	0.79	0.427	-0.581	1.372

Wald test of exogeneity: chi2(1) = 6.50　　Prob > chi2 = 0.0108

Instrumented: other_inc

Instruments: fem_educ kids male_educ

图 3.39

3.8* 含样本选择的 Probit 回归

含样本选择的 Probit 回归（Van de Ven and Van Pragg，1981）[1]假设存在如下关系：

$$y_j^* = \boldsymbol{x}_j \boldsymbol{\beta} + u_{1j} \quad \text{潜方程} \tag{3.20}$$

使得我们仅能观测到二元结果：

$$y_j^{\text{probit}} = (y_j^* > 0) \quad \text{Probit 方程} \tag{3.21}$$

然而，因变量并不是总能观测到的。关于 j 的因变量，只有在满足如下关系的情况下，才能被观测到：

$$y_j^{\text{select}} = (\boldsymbol{z}_j \gamma + u_{2j} > 0) \quad \text{选择方程} \tag{3.22}$$

其中，$u_1 \sim N(0,1)$，$u_2 \sim N(0,1)$，$\text{corr}(u_1, u_2) = \rho$。当 $\rho \neq 0$ 时，标准的 Probit 回归应用于第一个方程会产生有偏结果。Heckprobit 方法给出了一致、近似有效的估计。

为了使得模型能够被较好识别，选择方程中至少有一个变量没有被包含在 Probit 方程中。否则，这个模型仅是通过函数形式被识别的，系数没有具体的结构性解释。其估计命令为 heckprobit。

语法格式为：

```
heckprobit depvar indepvars [if][in] [weight],
select([depvars = ] varlists [, noconstant offset(varnameo)]) [options]
```

菜单操作路径为：

Statistics>Sample-selection models>Probit model with sample selection

例 3.8 含样本选择的 Probit 模型[2]

下面以 Stata 软件自带数据集 school. dta 来进行说明。在这个数据集中，变量是孩子是否参加私立学校（private）、家庭在现在居住地的年限（years）、财产税的对数（logptax）、收入的对数（loginc），以及一个人是否为提升财产税的提议投票（vote）。

在本例中，我们观察到只有家长为提升财产税投票的家庭，其孩子是否选择私立学校的数据。假设投票受居住在本地区的年限、当前财产税的支付和家庭收入的影响。接下来，对孩子是否参加私立学校与居住在本地区的年限和当前支付的财产税进行建模。

```
. use school.dta, clear
. heckprobit private years logptax, select(vote = years loginc logptax)
```

运行结果如图 3.40 所示。

最终显示几次对数迭代的结果。第一次对数迭代对应于运行的 Probit 模型，对应于这些观测值，已有结果。第二次对数迭代对应于运行选择的 Probit 模型，这是我们所感兴趣的结果。如果 $\rho = 0$，这两个对数似然值的和将等于具有样本选择的 Probit 模型的对数似然值。第三次对数迭代给出迭代的初始值。

---

① Van de Ven, W. P. M. M., and B. M. S. Van Pragg. The Demand for Deductibles in Private Health Insurance: A Probit Model with Sample Selection. *Journal of Econometrics*, 1981, 17.

② 本案例根据 Stata 帮助手册 r. pdf 中的对应例子改编。

Probit model with sample selection Number of obs = **95**
Selected = **59**
Nonselected = **36**

Wald chi2(2) = **1.04**
Log likelihood = **-74.24497** Prob > chi2 = **0.5935**

	Coefficient	Std. err.	z	P>|z|	[95% conf.	interval]
private						
years	-0.114	0.146	-0.78	0.434	-0.401	0.172
logptax	0.352	1.016	0.35	0.729	-1.641	2.344
_cons	-2.781	6.906	-0.40	0.687	-16.316	10.755
vote						
years	-0.017	0.015	-1.13	0.257	-0.046	0.012
loginc	0.992	0.443	2.24	0.025	0.124	1.861
logptax	-1.279	0.572	-2.24	0.025	-2.399	-0.158
_cons	-0.546	4.070	-0.13	0.893	-8.524	7.432
/athrho	-0.866	1.450	-0.60	0.550	-3.708	1.976
rho	-0.699	0.741			-0.999	0.962

LR test of indep. eqns. (rho = 0): chi2(1) = **0.27** Prob > chi2 = **0.6020**

图 3.40

最后的对数迭代拟合具有样本选择的完整模型。这个模型与对比模型的对数似然检验比较在输出结果的最后部分给出。如果设定 vec(robust)选项,则给出的是 Wald 检验,而不是 LR 检验。

. heckprobit private years logptax, sel(vote = years loginc logptax) vce(robust)
  >nolog

运行结果如图 3.41 所示。

Probit model with sample selection Number of obs = **95**
Selected = **59**
Nonselected = **36**

Wald chi2(2) = **2.55**
Log pseudolikelihood = **-74.24497** Prob > chi2 = **0.2798**

	Coefficient	Robust std. err.	z	P>|z|	[95% conf.	interval]
private						
years	-0.114	0.111	-1.03	0.305	-0.333	0.104
logptax	0.352	0.736	0.48	0.633	-1.091	1.794
_cons	-2.781	4.787	-0.58	0.561	-12.162	6.601
vote						
years	-0.017	0.017	-0.97	0.334	-0.051	0.017
loginc	0.992	0.423	2.35	0.019	0.164	1.821
logptax	-1.279	0.510	-2.51	0.012	-2.277	-0.280
_cons	-0.546	4.544	-0.12	0.904	-9.452	8.360
/athrho	-0.866	1.631	-0.53	0.595	-4.062	2.330
rho	-0.699	0.833			-0.999	0.981

Wald test of indep. eqns. (rho = 0): chi2(1) = **0.28** Prob > chi2 = **0.5952**

图 3.41

从估计中可以看出，无论是否设定 vce(robust)选项，结果与分别拟合 Probit 模型和选择模型并无显著区别。

3.9* 异方差 Probit 回归

异方差 Probit 模型是 Probit 模型的一般化形式，该模型的解释变量随着观测值的变化而变化。hetprobit 命令利用最大似然方法来拟合异方差 Probit 模型。

设 $y_j, j=1,\cdots,N$ 是一个二元结果变量，取值为 0(失败)或 1(成功)。在 Probit 模型中，y_j 取 1，对 k 个解释变量 $\boldsymbol{x}_j=(x_{1j},x_{2j},\cdots,x_{kj})$ 线性组合的非线性函数进行建模。

$$\Pr(y_j=1)=\Phi(\Pr(y_j=1)=\Phi\{\boldsymbol{x}_j\boldsymbol{b}/\exp(\boldsymbol{z}_j\gamma)\}\sigma_j^2=\{\exp(\boldsymbol{z}_j\gamma)\}^2) \quad (3.23)$$

其中，$\Phi()$是标准正态分布随机变量的累积分布函数(CDF)。解释变量的线性组合 $\boldsymbol{x}_j\boldsymbol{b}$ 称为索引函数(index)。异方差 Probit 模型将 $\Phi()$扩展到一个正态 CDF，其方差不再固定为 1，而是作为解释变量的函数而变动。hetprobit 命令将方差作为 m 个变量 $\boldsymbol{z}_j=(z_{1j},z_{2j},\cdots z_{mj})$ 的乘积函数来进行建模，即采取如下形式：

$$\sigma_j^2=\{\exp(\boldsymbol{z}_j\gamma)\}^2 \quad (3.24)$$

因而，成功的概率作为所有解释变量的函数，可以表述为：

$$\Pr(y_j=1)=\Phi\{\boldsymbol{x}_j\boldsymbol{b}/\exp(\boldsymbol{z}_j\gamma)\} \quad (3.25)$$

从这个表达式可以看出，不同于索引函数 $\boldsymbol{x}_j\boldsymbol{b}$，如果要对模型进行识别，则 $\boldsymbol{z}_j\gamma$ 中不包括常数项。

假定二元结果变量 y_j 由一个不可观测变量 w_j 的门限值产生，它服从均值为 $\boldsymbol{x}_j\boldsymbol{b}$ 和方差为 1 的正态分布，使得

$$y_j=\begin{cases}1 & \text{if } w_j>0\\ 0 & \text{if } w_j\leqslant 0\end{cases} \quad (3.26)$$

这个过程给出 Probit 模型：

$$\Pr(y_j=1)=\Pr(w_j>0)=\Phi(\boldsymbol{x}_j\boldsymbol{b}) \quad (3.27)$$

现在，假设不可观测变量 w_j 是异方差变量且

$$\sigma_j^2=\{\exp(\boldsymbol{z}_j\gamma)\}^2 \quad (3.28)$$

按照这种方式放松 Probit 模型的同方差假设，得到乘法类型的异方差 Probit 模型：

$$\Pr(y_j=1)=\Phi\{\boldsymbol{x}_j\boldsymbol{b}/\exp(\boldsymbol{z}_j\gamma)\} \quad (3.29)$$

异方差 Probit 模型的对数似然函数为：

$$\ln L=\sum_{j\in S}w_j\ln\Phi\{\boldsymbol{x}_j\boldsymbol{\beta}/\exp(\boldsymbol{z}_j\gamma)\}+\sum_{j\notin S}w_j\ln[1-\Phi\{\boldsymbol{x}_j\boldsymbol{\beta}/\exp(\boldsymbol{z}_j\gamma)\}] \quad (3.30)$$

其中，S 表示所有 $y_j\neq 0$ 的观测值 j 的集合，w_j 是最优权重。其估计命令为 hetprobit。

语法格式为：

```
hetprobit depvar [indepvars] [if] [in] [weight],
```

het(varlist[,offset($varname_o$)]) [options]

菜单操作路径为：

Statistics>Binary outcomes>Heteroskedastic probit regression

例 3.9 异方差 Probit 回归

本部分通过生成模拟数据，说明异方差 Probit 模型的应用。

```
. set obs 1000
. set seed 1234567
. generate x = 1 - 2 * runiform()
. generate xhet = runiform()
. generate sigma = exp(1.5 * xhet)
. generate p = normal((0.3 + 2 * x)/sigma)
. generate y = cond(runiform()< = p,1,0)
. hetprobit y x, het(xhet)
```

运行结果如图 3.42 所示。

```
Heteroskedastic probit model                     Number of obs     =      1,000
                                                 Zero outcomes     =        451
                                                 Nonzero outcomes  =        549

                                                 Wald chi2(1)      =      54.20
Log likelihood = -600.0152                       Prob > chi2       =     0.0000
```

y	Coefficient	Std. err.	z	P>|z|	[95% conf.	interval]
y						
x	1.782	0.242	7.36	0.000	1.308	2.257
_cons	0.314	0.087	3.61	0.000	0.143	0.485
lnsigma						
xhet	1.312	0.301	4.35	0.000	0.721	1.902

LR test of lnsigma=0: chi2(1) = 20.69　　　　Prob > chi2 = 0.0000

图 3.42

首先，模拟出两个变量 x 和 $xhet$，然后模拟模型

$$\Pr(y=1)=F\{(\beta_0+\beta_1 x)/\exp(\gamma_1 \boldsymbol{xhet})\} \tag{3.31}$$

其中，$\beta_0=0.3$，$\beta_1=2$，$\gamma_1=1.5$。根据 hetprobit 的估计结果，所有系数都是显著的。Wald 检验用来检验是异方差模型还是同方差模型，在本例中，异方差模型的索引函数为 $\beta_0+\beta_1\boldsymbol{x}$，同方差的索引函数为 β_0，服从于 $\chi^2(1)=54$，是显著的。类似地，LR 检验用来检验是异方差的完整模型还是同方差的 Probit 模型，也是显著的，其中 $\chi^2(1)=21$。

异方差 Probit 模型同样可以在考虑稳健标准误的情况下进行估计。

```
.hetprobit y x, het(xhet) vce(robust) nolog
```

运行结果如图 3.43 所示。

```
Heteroskedastic probit model                    Number of obs     =      1,000
                                                Zero outcomes     =        451
                                                Nonzero outcomes  =        549

                                                Wald chi2(1)      =      50.49
Log pseudolikelihood = -600.0152                Prob > chi2       =     0.0000
```

y	Coefficient	Robust std. err.	z	P>|z|	[95% conf.	interval]
y						
x	1.782	0.251	7.11	0.000	1.291	2.274
_cons	0.314	0.087	3.60	0.000	0.143	0.485
lnsigma						
xhet	1.312	0.306	4.29	0.000	0.712	1.911

```
Wald test of lnsigma=0: chi2(1) = 18.38                 Prob > chi2 = 0.0000
```

图 3.43

3.10* 含内生变量、样本选择和处理的 Probit 回归[①]

3.10.1 引入

结果变量 y_i 关于协变量 $\boldsymbol{x}_i$ 的 Probit 回归模型可以写为：

$$y_i = 1(\boldsymbol{x}_i\boldsymbol{\beta} + \varepsilon_i > 0) \tag{3.32}$$

其中，误差项 ε_i 服从标准正态分布。对数似然函数可以写成：

$$\ln L = \sum_{i=1}^{N} w_i \{ y_i \ln\Phi(\boldsymbol{x}_i\boldsymbol{\beta}) + (1 - y_i)\ln\Phi(-\boldsymbol{x}_i\boldsymbol{\beta}) \} \tag{3.33}$$

其中，w_i 为权重矩阵。成功的条件概率为：

$$E(y_i \mid \boldsymbol{x}_i) = \Pr(y_i = 1 \mid \boldsymbol{x}_i) = \Phi(\boldsymbol{x}_i\boldsymbol{\beta}) \tag{3.34}$$

标准正态累积分布函数 Φ()是一个单边概率，使得随机变量小于某个点。在后面的模型中，可能会利用双边概率。对于双边概率，定义 Φ_d^* 包含三个输入变量，前两个输入变量是 d 维行向量 **1** 和 $\boldsymbol{u}$，其取值范围为 $\mathrm{IR}\cup\{-\infty, +\infty\}$，最后一个输入变量为 $d\times d$ 维的实值且为正定矩阵 $\boldsymbol{\Sigma}$。

$$\Phi_d^*(\boldsymbol{l}, \boldsymbol{u}, \boldsymbol{\Sigma}) = \int_{l_1}^{u_1} \cdots \int_{l_d}^{u_d} \phi_d(\varepsilon, \boldsymbol{\Sigma}) \mathrm{d}\varepsilon_1 \cdots \mathrm{d}\varepsilon_d \tag{3.35}$$

其中，ϕ_d 为均值为 0，多元正态随机变量的密度函数。概率的计算通过数值积分的方法得到。

---

① 本节内容主要参考了 Stata 帮助手册中的理论和例子。

基于可观测值 y_i 和 $\boldsymbol{x}_i$，不可观测的 ε_i 的下限 l_{1i} 和上限 u_{1i} 可以定义为：

$$l_{1i}=\begin{cases}-\infty & y_i=0\\ -\boldsymbol{x}_i\boldsymbol{\beta} & y_i=1\end{cases}\qquad u_{1i}=\begin{cases}-\boldsymbol{x}_i\boldsymbol{\beta} & y_i=0\\ \infty & y_i=1\end{cases}\tag{3.36}$$

可以把对数似然函数简写为：

$$\ln L=\sum_{i=1}^{N}w_i\ln\Phi_1^*(l_{1i},u_{1i},1)\tag{3.37}$$

成功的条件概率，可以类似地写成：

$$\Pr(y_i=1\mid \boldsymbol{x}_i)=\Phi_1^*(-\boldsymbol{x}_i\boldsymbol{\beta},\infty,1)\tag{3.38}$$

3.10.2 内生协变量

（1）连续内生协变量

y_i 关于外生协变量 $\boldsymbol{x}_i$ 和连续内生协变量 $\boldsymbol{w}_{ci}$ 的 Probit 模型，具有如下形式：

$$\begin{aligned}&y_i=1(\boldsymbol{x}_i\boldsymbol{\beta}+\boldsymbol{w}_{ci}\boldsymbol{\beta}_c+\varepsilon_i>0)\\&\boldsymbol{w}_{ci}=\boldsymbol{z}_{ci}\boldsymbol{A}_c+\boldsymbol{\varepsilon}_{ci}\end{aligned}\tag{3.39}$$

影响 $\boldsymbol{w}_{ci}$ 的向量 $\boldsymbol{z}_{ci}$ 包含外生协变量 $\boldsymbol{x}_i$ 和其他协变量。不可观测到的误差项 ε_i 和 ε_{ci} 是多元正态分布，均值为 0，协方差为：

$$\begin{bmatrix}1 & \boldsymbol{\sigma}'_{1c}\\ \boldsymbol{\sigma}_{1c} & \boldsymbol{\Sigma}_c\end{bmatrix}$$

$\boldsymbol{w}_{ci}$ 的条件密度为：

$$f(\boldsymbol{w}_{ci}\mid \boldsymbol{x}_i,\boldsymbol{z}_{ci})=\phi_C(\boldsymbol{w}_{ci}-\boldsymbol{z}_{ci}\boldsymbol{A}_c,\boldsymbol{\Sigma}_c)\tag{3.40}$$

注意到

$$\Pr(y_i=1\mid \boldsymbol{w}_{ci},\boldsymbol{x}_i,\boldsymbol{z}_{ci})=\Pr(\boldsymbol{x}_i\boldsymbol{\beta}+\boldsymbol{w}_{ci}\boldsymbol{\beta}_c+\varepsilon_i>0\mid \boldsymbol{w}_{ci},\boldsymbol{x}_i,\boldsymbol{z}_{ci})\tag{3.41}$$

因此，y_i 的条件密度可以写为 ε_i 的条件概率。因而，ε_i 的条件概率可以用来发现 y_i 的条件密度。ε_i 以内生和外生协变量为条件的均值和方差为：

$$E(\varepsilon_i\mid \boldsymbol{w}_{ci},\boldsymbol{x}_i,\boldsymbol{z}_{ci})=\boldsymbol{\sigma}'_{1c}\boldsymbol{\Sigma}_c^{-1}(\boldsymbol{w}_{ci}-\boldsymbol{z}_{ci}\boldsymbol{A}_c)'$$

$$\mathrm{Var}(\varepsilon_i\mid \boldsymbol{w}_{ci},\boldsymbol{x}_i,\boldsymbol{z}_{ci})=1-\boldsymbol{\sigma}'_{1c}\boldsymbol{\Sigma}_c^{-1}\boldsymbol{\sigma}_{1c}$$

用于 y_i 概率上下限的条件均值分别是：

$$\begin{aligned}&l_{1i}=\begin{cases}-\infty & y_i=0\\ -\boldsymbol{x}_i\boldsymbol{\beta}-\boldsymbol{\sigma}'_{1c}\boldsymbol{\Sigma}_c^{-1}(\boldsymbol{w}_{ci}-\boldsymbol{z}_{ci}\boldsymbol{A}_c)' & y_i=1\end{cases}\\&u_{1i}=\begin{cases}-\boldsymbol{x}_i\boldsymbol{\beta}-\boldsymbol{\sigma}'_{1c}\boldsymbol{\Sigma}_c^{-1}(\boldsymbol{w}_{ci}-\boldsymbol{z}_{ci}\boldsymbol{A}_c)' & y_i=0\\ \infty & y_i=1\end{cases}\end{aligned}\tag{3.42}$$

利用这些上下限、条件方差和 $\boldsymbol{w}_{ci}$ 的条件密度，我们可以得到对数似然函数：

$$\ln L=\sum_{i=1}^{N}w_i\{\ln\Phi_1^*(l_{1i},u_{1i},1-\boldsymbol{\sigma}'_{1c}\boldsymbol{\Sigma}_c^{-1}\boldsymbol{\sigma}_{1c})+\ln\phi_C(\boldsymbol{w}_{ci}-\boldsymbol{z}_{ci}\boldsymbol{A}_c,\boldsymbol{\Sigma}_c)\}\tag{3.43}$$

设

$$\begin{aligned}&l_{1i1}=-\boldsymbol{x}_i\boldsymbol{\beta}-\boldsymbol{\sigma}'_{1c}\boldsymbol{\Sigma}_c^{-1}(\boldsymbol{w}_{ci}-\boldsymbol{z}_{ci}\boldsymbol{A}_c)'\\&u_{1i1}=\infty\end{aligned}\tag{3.44}$$

成功的条件概率为：

$$\Pr(y_i = 1 \mid \boldsymbol{w}_{ci}, \boldsymbol{x}_i, \boldsymbol{z}_{ci}) = \Phi_1^*(l_{1i1}, u_{1i1}, 1 - \boldsymbol{\sigma}_{1c}' \boldsymbol{\Sigma}_c^{-1} \boldsymbol{\sigma}_{1c}) \tag{3.45}$$

（2）二元或有序内生协变量

本部分通过二元结果变量 y_i 对外生协变量 $\boldsymbol{x}_i$ 和二元或有序内生协变量 $\boldsymbol{w}_{bi} = [w_{b1i}, \cdots, w_{bBi}]$进行建模。可以通过将二元或有序内生协变量与其他协变量交乘，处理效应模型。

设 $j = 1, \cdots, B$。下面是二元内生协变量的 Probit 模型：

$$w_{bji} = 1(\boldsymbol{z}_{bji}\boldsymbol{\alpha}_{bj} + \varepsilon_{bji} > 0) \tag{3.46}$$

对于有序内生协变量 w_{bji}，其取值为 $v_{bj1}, \cdots, v_{bjB_j}$，可得到有序 Probit 模型：

$$w_{bji} = v_{bjh} \quad \text{iff} \quad \kappa_{bj(h-1)} < \boldsymbol{z}_{bji}\boldsymbol{\alpha}_{bj} + \varepsilon_{bji} \leqslant \kappa_{bjh} \tag{3.47}$$

$v_{bj1}, \cdots, v_{bjB_j}$ 为实数，对于 $h < m$，满足 $v_{bjh} < v_{bjm}$。κ_{bj0} 被认为是 $-\infty$，κ_{bjB_j} 被认为是 $+\infty$。误差项 $\varepsilon_{b1i}, \cdots, \varepsilon_{bBi}$ 均值为 0，为多元正态分布，协方差矩阵为：

$$\boldsymbol{\Sigma}_b = \begin{bmatrix} 1 & \rho_{b12} & \cdots & \rho_{b1B} \\ \rho_{b12} & 1 & \cdots & \rho_{b2B} \\ \vdots & \vdots & \ddots & \vdots \\ \rho_{b1B} & \rho_{b2B} & \cdots & 1 \end{bmatrix} \tag{3.48}$$

因为，协变量 w_{bji} 是二元或有序，每类变量对结果方程的影响可以利用示性变量进行表示：

$$\textbf{wind}_{bji} = \begin{bmatrix} 1(w_{bji} = v_{bj1}) \\ \vdots \\ 1(w_{bji} = v_{bjB_j}) \end{bmatrix}' \tag{3.49}$$

结果模型可以在 $\boldsymbol{w}_{bi}$ 的每一个水平利用或不利用相关参数进行建模。与水平具体相关的系数参数可以通过设定 pocorrelation 来获取，该设定在 endogenous()的选项中。

如果相关系数参数不是对具体水平而定，可以得到：

$$y_i = 1(\boldsymbol{x}_i\boldsymbol{\beta} + \textbf{wind}_{b1i}\boldsymbol{\beta}_{b1} + \cdots + \textbf{wind}_{bBi}\boldsymbol{\beta}_{bB} + \varepsilon_i > 0) \tag{3.50}$$

其中，误差项 ε_i 和二元或有序内生误差项 $\varepsilon_{b1i}, \cdots, \varepsilon_{bBi}$ 均值为 0，为多元正态分布，协方差矩阵为：

$$\boldsymbol{\Sigma} = \begin{bmatrix} 1 & \rho_{1b}' \\ \rho_{1b} & \boldsymbol{\Sigma}_b \end{bmatrix} \tag{3.51}$$

对 $j = 1, \cdots, B, h = 0, \cdots, B_j$。设

$$c_{bjih} = \begin{cases} -\infty & h = 0 \\ \kappa_{bjh} - \boldsymbol{z}_{bji}\boldsymbol{\alpha}_{bj} & h = 1, \cdots, B_j - 1 \\ \infty & h = B_j \end{cases} \tag{3.52}$$

w_{bji} 概率的下限为：

$$l_{bji} = c_{bji(h-1)} \quad \text{if} \quad w_{bji} = v_{bjh} \tag{3.53}$$

上限为：

$$u_{bji} = c_{bjih} \quad \text{if} \quad w_{bji} = v_{bjh} \tag{3.54}$$

设

$$c_{bi}=-\boldsymbol{x}_i\boldsymbol{\beta}-\mathbf{wind}_{b1i}\boldsymbol{\beta}_{b1}-\cdots-\mathbf{wind}_{bBi}\boldsymbol{\beta}_{bB} \tag{3.55}$$

y_i 概率的下限和上限分别为：

$$l_{1i}=\begin{cases}-\infty & y_i=0\\ c_{bi} & y_i=1\end{cases}\quad u_{1i}=\begin{cases}c_{bi} & y_i=0\\ \infty & y_i=1\end{cases}$$

$$l_i=[l_{1i}\quad l_{b1i}\quad\cdots\quad l_{bBi}]$$

且

$$u_i=[u_{1i}\quad u_{b1i}\quad\cdots\quad u_{bBi}]$$

这个模型的对数似然函数为：

$$\ln L=\sum_{i=1}^{N}w_i\ln\Phi_{B+1}^{*}(l_i,u_i,\Sigma) \tag{3.56}$$

设

$$l_{bi}=[l_{b1i}\quad\cdots\quad l_{bBi}]$$

$$u_{bi}=[u_{b1i}\quad\cdots\quad u_{bBi}]$$

$$l_{i1}=[-\infty\quad l_{bi}]$$

$$u_{i1}=[c_{bi}\quad u_{bi}]$$

成功事件的条件概率为：

$$\Pr(y_i=1\mid\boldsymbol{x}_i,\boldsymbol{z}_{b1i},\cdots,\boldsymbol{z}_{bBi},\boldsymbol{w}_{bi})=\frac{\Phi_{B+1}^{*}(\boldsymbol{l}_{i1},\boldsymbol{u}_{i1},\boldsymbol{\Sigma})}{\Phi_{B}^{*}(\boldsymbol{l}_{bi},\boldsymbol{u}_{bi},\boldsymbol{\Sigma}_b)} \tag{3.57}$$

当内生有序变量是不同处理水平时，保持不同处理水平的相关参数为常数是潜在结果模型的一个约束形式。在无约束的潜在结果模型中，结果和处理之间的相关系数随着每一个处理水平的变化而变化。

在无约束模型中，每种处理效应的每一水平都存在一个不同的潜在结果误差。例如，当内生处理变量 w_1 有三个水平(0,1 和 2)，内生处理变量 w_2 有 4 个水平(0,1,2 和 3)时，无约束模型共有 $3\times4=12$ 个结果误差。因为每个潜在结果和每个内生处理之间存在一个不同的相关系数，则在这个模型中，潜在结果和处理变量之间共有 2×12 个相关参数。

将内生处理变量 $\boldsymbol{w}_{bi}$ 值的不同组合的数量用 M 来表示，每个组合值的向量用 $\boldsymbol{v}_j$ 来表示($j\in\{1,2,\cdots,M\}$)。设 k_{wp} 是内生有序处理变量 $p\in\{1,2,\cdots,B\}$ 的水平数量，则 $M=k_{w1}\times k_{w2}\times\cdots\times k_{wB}$。结果误差为 $\varepsilon_{1i},\cdots,\varepsilon_{Mi}$。可以得到：

$$y_{1i}=1(\boldsymbol{x}_i\boldsymbol{\beta}+\mathbf{wind}_{b1i}\boldsymbol{\beta}_{b1}+\cdots+\mathbf{wind}_{bBi}\boldsymbol{\beta}_{bB}+\varepsilon_{1i}>0)$$

$$\vdots$$

$$y_{Mi}=1(\boldsymbol{x}_i\boldsymbol{\beta}+\mathbf{wind}_{b1i}\boldsymbol{\beta}_{b1}+\cdots+\mathbf{wind}_{bBi}\boldsymbol{\beta}_{bB}+\varepsilon_{Mi}>0)$$

$$y_i=\sum_{j=1}^{M}1(\boldsymbol{w}_{bi}=\boldsymbol{v}_j)y_{ji}$$

对于 $j=1,\cdots,M$，结果误差 ε_{ji} 和内生误差 $\varepsilon_{b1i},\cdots,\varepsilon_{bBi}$ 均值为 0，为多元正态分布，协方差矩阵为：

$$\boldsymbol{\Sigma}_j=\begin{bmatrix}1 & \rho_{j1b}'\\ \rho_{j1b} & \boldsymbol{\Sigma}_b\end{bmatrix} \tag{3.58}$$

设

$$\boldsymbol{\Sigma}_{i,b}=\sum_{j=1}^{M}1(\boldsymbol{w}_{bi}=\boldsymbol{v}_j)\boldsymbol{\Sigma}_j$$

则模型的对数似然函数为：

$$\ln L=\sum_{i=1}^{N}w_i\ln\Phi_{B+1}^{*}(l_i,u_i,\boldsymbol{\Sigma}_{i,b}) \tag{3.59}$$

成功事件的条件概率为：

$$\Pr(y_i=1\mid \boldsymbol{x}_i,\boldsymbol{z}_{b1i},\cdots,\boldsymbol{z}_{bBi},\boldsymbol{w}_{bi})=\frac{\Phi_{B+1}^{*}(l_{i1},u_{i1},\boldsymbol{\Sigma}_{i,b})}{\Phi_{B}^{*}(l_{bi},u_{bi},\boldsymbol{\Sigma}_b)} \tag{3.60}$$

3.10.3 处理

在潜在结果框架中，处理变量 t_i 是一个取 T 个值的离散变量，对应的 T 种潜在结果为 y_i：$y_{1i},\cdots,y_{Ti}$。

当观察到处理变量 T 的不同水平 $v_1,\cdots,v_T$，有

$$y_i=\sum_{j=1}^{T}1(t_i=v_j)y_{ji} \tag{3.61}$$

因此对应每个观测值，我们只能观察到与处理值对应的潜在结果。

对于外生处理，现有方法相当于回归调节的处理效应估计方法。本部分不对处理分配的过程建模。处理效应和潜在结果均值(POM)的公式等价于内生处理变量部分的公式。当结果和处理误差之间的相关性参数设为 0 时，外生处理对变量 $\boldsymbol{x}_i$ 的处理方法与内生处理是一致的。外生处理的平均处理效应(ATEs)和 POM 估计作为预测边际，与内生处理的方式类似。

此时，对于有序处理变量 t_i，协变量为 $\boldsymbol{z}_{ti}$，得到有序 Probit 模型：

$$t_i=v_h \quad \text{iff} \quad \kappa_{h-1}<\boldsymbol{z}_{ti}\boldsymbol{\alpha}_t+\varepsilon_{ti}\leqslant\kappa_h \tag{3.62}$$

处理值 $v_1,\cdots,v_T$ 是实数，且对于 $h<m$，$v_h<v_m$。κ_0 被认为是 $-\infty$，κ_T 被认为是 $+\infty$。处理误差项 ε_{ti} 是标准正态分布。

取值为{0,1}的二值处理变量的 Probit 模型为：

$$t_i=1(\boldsymbol{z}_{ti}\boldsymbol{\alpha}_t+\varepsilon_{ti}>0)$$

本部分通过 y_i 对外生协变量 $\boldsymbol{x}_i$ 和取值为 $v_1,\cdots,v_T$ 的内生协变量 t_i 建立 Probit 模型，形式为：

$$\begin{aligned}
y_{1i}&=1(\boldsymbol{x}_i\boldsymbol{\beta}_1+\varepsilon_{1i}>0)\\
&\vdots\\
y_{Ti}&=1(\boldsymbol{x}_i\boldsymbol{\beta}_T+\varepsilon_{Ti}>0)\\
y_i&=\sum_{j=1}^{T}1(t_i=v_j)y_{ji}
\end{aligned} \tag{3.63}$$

这个模型可以用不同相关参数来建立，也可以不用相关参数来建立。具体参数的潜在结果可以通过设定 entreat()选项中的 pocorrelation 来实现。

如果相关参数不是具体针对潜在结果的，对于 $j=1,\cdots,T$，ε_{ji} 和 ε_{ti} 是二元正态

分布，均值为 0，协方差矩阵为：

$$\boldsymbol{\Sigma}=\begin{bmatrix}1 & \rho_{1t}\\ \rho_{1t} & 1\end{bmatrix} \tag{3.64}$$

如果 $\rho_{1t}=0$，处理变量是外生的。这时没有对潜在结果误差项之间的相关性结构进行设定。因为不需要这些信息来估计 POMs 和处理效应，所有协变量和结果变量都是通过观测值估计得到的。

接下来讨论含有有序内生变量的模型所得结论与二元处理模型类似。因为未观察到的误差项是二元正态分布，可以利用 Φ_2^* 函数来表述对数似然函数。

对于 $j=1,\cdots,T$，设

$$c_{1ij}=-x_i\boldsymbol{\beta}_j \tag{3.65}$$

y_i 概率的下限和上限分别为：

$$l_{1i}=\begin{cases}-\infty & y_i=0\\ c_{1ij} & y_i=1,t_i=v_j\end{cases} \qquad u_{1i}=\begin{cases}c_{1ij} & y_i=0,t_i=v_j\\ \infty & y_i=1\end{cases} \tag{3.66}$$

对于 $j=1,\cdots,T$，定义

$$c_{tij}=\begin{cases}-\infty & j=0\\ \boldsymbol{\kappa}_j-\boldsymbol{z}_{ti}\boldsymbol{\alpha}_t & j=1,\cdots,T-1\\ \infty & j=T\end{cases} \tag{3.67}$$

因而，对于 t_i 概率，得到下限和上限分别为：

$$l_{ti}=c_{ti(j-1)} \quad \text{if} \quad t_i=v_j \tag{3.68}$$

$$u_{ti}=c_{tij} \quad \text{if} \quad t_i=v_j \tag{3.69}$$

模型的对数似然函数为：

$$\ln L=\sum_{i=1}^{N}w_i\ln\Phi_2^*([l_{1i}\quad l_{ti}],[u_{1i}\quad u_{ti}],\boldsymbol{\Sigma})$$

处理水平 v_h 的条件概率为：

$$\Pr(t_i=v_h\mid z_{ti})=\Phi_1^*(c_{ti(h-1)},c_{tih},1)$$

成功事件在处理水平 v_h 的条件概率为：

$$\Pr(y_i=1\mid \boldsymbol{x}_i,\boldsymbol{z}_{ti},t_i=v_j)=\frac{\Phi_2^*([c_{1ij}\quad c_{ti(j-1)}],[\infty\quad c_{tij}],\Sigma)}{\Phi_1^*(c_{ti(j-1)},c_{tij},1)} \tag{3.70}$$

处理组 j 的条件 POM 为：

$$\text{POM}_j(\boldsymbol{x}_i)=E(y_{ji}\mid \boldsymbol{x}_i)=\Phi_1^*(c_{1ij},\infty,1)$$

以协变量 $\boldsymbol{x}_i$ 和 $\boldsymbol{z}_i$，$t_i=v_h$ 为条件，处理组 j 的 POM 为：

$$\begin{aligned}\text{POM}_j(\boldsymbol{x}_i,\boldsymbol{z}_{ti},t_i=v_h)&=E(y_{ji}\mid \boldsymbol{x}_i,\boldsymbol{z}_{ti},t_i=v_h)\\ &=\frac{\Phi_2^*([c_{1ij}\quad c_{ti(h-1)}],[\infty\quad c_{tih}],\boldsymbol{\Sigma})}{\Phi_1^*(c_{ti(h-1)},c_{tih},1)}\end{aligned} \tag{3.71}$$

处理效应 $y_{ji}-y_{1i}$ 表示对于个体 i，其接受到的处理是 $t_i=v_j$，而不是 $t_i=v_1$。

对于处理组 j，以 $\boldsymbol{x}_i$ 为条件的处理效应(TE)为：

$$\text{TE}_j(\boldsymbol{x}_i)=E(y_{ji}-y_{1i}\mid \boldsymbol{x}_i)=\text{POM}_j(\boldsymbol{x}_i)-\text{POM}_1(\boldsymbol{x}_i) \tag{3.72}$$

对于处理组 j，以 $\boldsymbol{x}_i$ 和 $\boldsymbol{z}_{ti}$ 为条件的处理效应(TET)为：

$$\begin{aligned}\mathrm{TET}_j(\boldsymbol{x}_i,\boldsymbol{z}_{ti},t_i=v_h)&=E(y_{ji}-y_{1i}\mid \boldsymbol{x}_i,\boldsymbol{z}_{ti},t_i=v_h)\\&=\mathrm{POM}_j(\boldsymbol{x}_i,\boldsymbol{z}_{ti},t_i=v_h)-\mathrm{POM}_1(\boldsymbol{x}_i,\boldsymbol{z}_{ti},t_i=v_h)\end{aligned} \tag{3.73}$$

可以通过这些条件预测关于协变量的条件期望,从而得到参数的总体均值。一旦模型通过 eprobit 进行估计后,就可以用 margins 命令估计这些预测,作为预测边际。处理组 j 的 POM 为:

$$\mathrm{POM}_j=E(y_{ji})=E\{\mathrm{POM}_j(\boldsymbol{x}_i)\} \tag{3.74}$$

处理组 j 的平均处理效应(ATE)为:

$$\mathrm{ATE}_j=E(y_{ji}-y_{1i})=E\{\mathrm{TE}_j(\boldsymbol{x}_i)\} \tag{3.75}$$

对于处理组 j,在处理组 h 上的平均处理效应(ATET)为:

$$\begin{aligned}\mathrm{ATET}_{jh}&=E(y_{ji}-y_{1i}\mid t_i=v_h)\\&=E\{\mathrm{TET}_j(\boldsymbol{x}_i,\boldsymbol{z}_{ti},t_i=v_h)\mid t_i=v_h\}\end{aligned} \tag{3.76}$$

如果相关参数与具体潜在结果相关,对于 $j=1,\cdots,T$,ε_{jt} 和 ε_{ti} 为二元整体分布,均值为 0,协方差矩阵为:

$$\boldsymbol{\Sigma}_j=\begin{bmatrix}1 & \rho_{j1t}\\ \rho_{j1t} & 1\end{bmatrix} \tag{3.77}$$

现在定义

$$\boldsymbol{\Sigma}_i=\sum_{j=1}^{T}1(t_i=v_j)\boldsymbol{\Sigma}_j$$

潜在结果设定相关性模型的对数似然函数为:

$$\ln L=\sum_{i=1}^{N}w_i\ln\Phi_2^*([l_{1i}\quad l_{ti}],[u_{1i}\quad u_{ti}],\boldsymbol{\Sigma}_i)$$

成功事件在处理水平 v_j 的条件概率为:

$$\Pr(y_i=1\mid \boldsymbol{x}_i,\boldsymbol{z}_{ti},t_i=v_j)=\frac{\Phi_2^*([c_{1ij}\quad c_{ti(j-1)}],[\infty\quad c_{tij}],\boldsymbol{\Sigma}_j)}{\Phi_1^*(c_{ti(j-1)},c_{tij},1)} \tag{3.78}$$

外生协变量 $\boldsymbol{x}_i$ 和处理组 j 的 POM 与单个相关性情况相同。这里也给出以 $t_i=v_h$ 和 $\boldsymbol{z}_{ti}$ 为条件,处理组 j 的 POM:

$$\begin{aligned}\mathrm{POM}_j(\boldsymbol{x}_i,\boldsymbol{z}_{ti},t_i=v_h)&=E(y_{ji}\mid \boldsymbol{x}_i,\boldsymbol{z}_{ti},t_i=v_h)\\&=\frac{\Phi_2^*([c_{1ij}\quad c_{ti(h-1)}],[\infty\quad c_{tih}],\boldsymbol{\Sigma}_j)}{\Phi_1^*(c_{ti(h-1)},c_{tih},1)}\end{aligned} \tag{3.79}$$

处理效应按照单一相关系数进行建模,是利用了 POM 定义,通过对这些协变量取条件期望得到总体平均参数。一旦使用 eprobit 估计模型后,就可以用 estat teffects 或 margins 命令来估计期望,作为预测边际。

3.10.4 内生样本选择

(1) Probit 内生样本选择

带有 Probit 选择变量 s_i 的结果变量 y_i 的 Probit 模型形式如下:

$$\begin{aligned}y_i&=1(\boldsymbol{x}_i\boldsymbol{\beta}+\varepsilon_i>0)\\s_i&=1(\boldsymbol{z}_{si}\boldsymbol{\alpha}_s+\varepsilon_{si}>0)\end{aligned} \tag{3.80}$$

其中，$\boldsymbol{x}_i$ 是影响结果的协方差，$\boldsymbol{z}_{si}$ 是影响选择的协方差。如果 $s_i=1$，则 y_i 是可观测的；如果 $s_i=0$，则 y_i 是不可观测的。不可观测误差 ε_i 和 ε_{si} 均值为 0，为正态分布，协方差矩阵为：

$$\boldsymbol{\Sigma}=\begin{bmatrix}1 & \rho_{1s}\\ \rho_{1s} & 1\end{bmatrix} \tag{3.81}$$

y_i 概率的下限和上限表达式为：

$$l_{si}=\begin{cases}-\infty & s_i=0\\ -\boldsymbol{z}_{si}\boldsymbol{\alpha}_s & s_i=1\end{cases} \quad u_{si}=\begin{cases}-\boldsymbol{z}_{si}\boldsymbol{\alpha}_s & s_i=0\\ \infty & s_i=1\end{cases} \tag{3.82}$$

对数似然函数为：

$$\ln L=\sum_{i\in S}w_i\ln\Phi_2^*([l_{1i} \quad l_{si}],[u_{1i} \quad u_{si}],\boldsymbol{\Sigma})+\sum_{i\notin S}w_i\ln\Phi_1^*(l_{si},u_{si},1) \tag{3.83}$$

其中，S 是 y_i 可以观察到的观测集。

在这个模型中，成功的概率通常取决于协变量 $\boldsymbol{x}_i$，而不是选择状态 s_i。条件概率公式为：

$$\Pr(s_i=1\mid \boldsymbol{z}_{si})=\Phi_1^*(-\boldsymbol{z}_{si}\boldsymbol{\alpha}_s,\infty,1) \tag{3.84}$$

(2) Tobit 内生样本选择

Tobit 内生样本选择不是将选择示性变量限定为二元变量，而是利用一个审查连续样本选择指示变量，并考虑选择变量是左还是右审查变量。

带有 Tobit 选择变量 s_i 的结果变量 y_i 的 Probit 模型形式如下：

$$y_i=1(\boldsymbol{x}_i\boldsymbol{\beta}+\varepsilon_i>0) \tag{3.85}$$

观测指示变量 s_i，显示潜在选择变量 s_i^* 的选择状态。

$$s_i^*=\boldsymbol{z}_{si}\boldsymbol{\alpha}_s+\varepsilon_{si}$$

$$s_i=\begin{cases}l_i & s_i^*\leqslant l_i\\ s_i^* & l_i<s_i^*<u_i\\ u_i & s_i^*\geqslant u_i\end{cases} \tag{3.86}$$

其中，$\boldsymbol{z}_{si}$ 是影响选择的协变量，l_i 和 u_i 是固定下限和上限。

当审查变量 s_i^* 没有被审查时（$l_i<s_i^*<u_i$），结果变量 y_i 被观测到。当审查变量 s_i^* 是左审查（$s_i^*\leqslant l_i$）或右审查（$s_i^*\geqslant u_i$）时，结果变量 y_i 未被观测到。不可观测误差 ε_i 和 ε_{si} 均值为 0，为正态分布，协方差矩阵为：

$$\begin{bmatrix}1 & \rho_{1s}\sigma_s\\ \rho_{1s}\sigma_s & \sigma_s^2\end{bmatrix} \tag{3.87}$$

对于选择变量，可以将 s_i 作为连续内生自变量。事实上，s_i 甚至可以作为 Probit 回归中的自变量（在 tobit select(…main) 中设定）。在非选定的观测值中，将 s_i 看作 Probit 内生样本选择指示变量。

对于非选择的观测值，有

$$\Pr(s_i^*\leqslant l_i\mid \boldsymbol{z}_{si},\boldsymbol{x}_i)=\Pr(\boldsymbol{z}_{si}\boldsymbol{\alpha}_s+\varepsilon_{si}\leqslant l_i)=\Phi\left(\frac{l_i-\boldsymbol{z}_{si}\boldsymbol{\alpha}_s}{\sigma_s}\right) \tag{3.88}$$

和

$$\Pr(s_i^* \geqslant u_i \mid \boldsymbol{z}_{si}, \boldsymbol{x}_i) = \Pr(\boldsymbol{z}_{si}\boldsymbol{\alpha}_s + \varepsilon_{si} \geqslant u_i) = \Phi\left(\frac{\boldsymbol{z}_{si}\boldsymbol{\alpha}_s - u_i}{\sigma_s}\right) \tag{3.89}$$

在 s_i^* 为左审查的情况下,未选择观测值的 s_i 概率的下限和上限分别为:

$$l_{li} = -\infty$$

$$u_{li} = \frac{l_i - \boldsymbol{z}_{si}\boldsymbol{\alpha}_s}{\sigma_s}$$

在 s_i^* 为右审查的情况下,未选择观测值的 s_i 概率的下限和上限分别为:

$$l_{ui} = \frac{u_i - \boldsymbol{z}_{si}\boldsymbol{\alpha}_s}{\sigma_s}$$

$$u_{ui} = \infty$$

现在,考虑选择观测值。对于 $s_i = s_i^* = S_i$,可以给出被解释变量的联合密度:

$$f(y_i, s_i = S_i \mid \boldsymbol{x}_i, \boldsymbol{z}_{si}) = f(y_i \mid s_i = S_i, \boldsymbol{x}_i, \boldsymbol{z}_{si}) f(s_i = S_i \mid \boldsymbol{x}_i, \boldsymbol{z}_{si}) \tag{3.90}$$

$s_i = S_i$ 的边际密度为:

$$f(s_i = S_i \mid \boldsymbol{x}_i, \boldsymbol{z}_{s,i}) = \phi(S_i - \boldsymbol{z}_{si}\boldsymbol{\alpha}_s, \sigma_s^2) \tag{3.91}$$

y_i 的条件密度可以写成 ε_i 的条件概率。因而,ε_i 的条件概率可以用来发现 y_i 的条件密度。以 $s_i = S_i$ 为条件,ε_i 的均值和方差为:

$$E(\varepsilon_i \mid s_i = S_i, \boldsymbol{x}_i, \boldsymbol{z}_{si}) = \rho_{1s}\sigma_s^{-1}(S_i - \boldsymbol{z}_{si}\boldsymbol{\alpha})$$

$$\mathrm{Var}(\varepsilon_i \mid s_i = S_i, \boldsymbol{x}_i, \boldsymbol{z}_{si}) = 1 - \rho_{1s}^2$$

条件均值可用于 y_i 概率的选择观测值的上下限的确定上,即

$$\begin{aligned} l_{1i} &= \begin{cases} -\infty & y_i = 0 \\ -\boldsymbol{x}_i\boldsymbol{\beta} - \rho_{1s}\sigma_s^{-1}(s_i - \boldsymbol{z}_{si}\boldsymbol{\alpha}) & y_i = 1 \end{cases} \\ u_{1i} &= \begin{cases} -\boldsymbol{x}_i\boldsymbol{\beta} - \rho_{1s}\sigma_s^{-1}(s_i - \boldsymbol{z}_{si}\boldsymbol{\alpha}) & y_i = 0 \\ \infty & y_i = 1 \end{cases} \end{aligned} \tag{3.92}$$

对数似然函数为:

$$\begin{aligned} \ln L = &\sum_{i\in S} w_i \{\ln\Phi_1^*(l_{1i}, u_{1i}, 1 - \rho_{1s}^2) + \ln\phi(s_i - \boldsymbol{z}_{si}\boldsymbol{\alpha}_s, \sigma_s^2)\} \\ &+ \sum_{i\in L} w_i \ln\Phi_1^*(l_{li}, u_{li}, 1) + \sum_{i\in U} w_i \ln\Phi_1^*(l_{ui}, u_{ui}, 1) \end{aligned} \tag{3.93}$$

其中,S 是 y_i 可以被观测的观测数据集合。L 是 s_i^* 为左审查时的观测数据集合,U 是 s_i^* 为右审查时的观测数据集合。

3.10.5 随机效应

面板个体 $i = 1, \cdots, N$,观测值 $j = 1, \cdots, N_i$,结果变量 y_{ij} 对协变量 $\boldsymbol{x}_{ij}$ 的 Probit 回归可以写成:

$$y_{ij} = 1(\boldsymbol{x}_{ij}\boldsymbol{\beta} + \varepsilon_{ij} + u_i > 0) \tag{3.94}$$

随机效应 u_i 是均值为 0、方差为 σ_u^2 的正态分布,它独立于观测水平误差项 ε_{ij},服从标准正态分布。

利用 y_{ij} 关于随机效应 u_i 的边际密度得到似然函数,将之相乘,得到联合密度。

设 $l_{ij}(u)=y_{ij}\Phi(\boldsymbol{x}_{ij}\boldsymbol{\beta}+u)+(1-y_{ij})\Phi(-\boldsymbol{x}_{ij}\boldsymbol{\beta}-u)$，则面板 i 的似然函数为：

$$L_i=\int_{-\infty}^{\infty}\phi\left(\frac{u_i}{\sigma_u}\right)\prod_{j=1}^{N_i}l_{ij}(u_i)\mathrm{d}u_i$$

对于 q 点 Gauss-Hermite 积分，设横坐标和权重用(a_{ki},w_{ki})，$k=1,K,q$ 来进行表示。则 Gauss-Hermite 积分近似为：

$$\int_{-\infty}^{\infty}f(x)\exp(-x^2)\mathrm{d}x\approx\sum_{k=1}^{q}w_{ki}f(a_{ki})$$

Xteprobit 默认近似方法是均值方差自适应 Gauss-Hermite 积分法。这种方法为每个截面选择最优横坐标和权重。

利用积分近似，似然函数为：

$$\ln L=\sum_{i=1}^{N}\ln\left\{\sum_{k=1}^{q}w_{ki}\prod_{j=1}^{N_i}l_{ij}(\sigma_u a_{ki})\right\}\tag{3.95}$$

接下来计算成功事件的条件概率。输入 Φ_1^* 的方差是随机项和观测水平误差的方差。

设

$$\xi_{ij}=\varepsilon_{ij}+u_i$$

其中，ξ_{ij} 的均值为零，方差为 $\sigma_\xi^2=1+\sigma_u^2$。

则成功事件的条件概率为：

$$\Pr(y_{ij}=1\mid x_{ij})=\Phi_1^*(-\boldsymbol{x}_{ij}\boldsymbol{\beta},\infty,\sigma_\xi^2)\tag{3.96}$$

3.10.6 组合模型

本部分给出含有连续内生协变量、有序内生协变量、有序内生处理变量和内生样本选择的 Probit 模型的似然函数，组合了 eprobit 命令对标准 Probit 模型的所有扩展。

在这个模型中，处理变量 t_i 取 T 个值，对于主要结果 y_i 分别进行标示 $y_i:y_{1i},\cdots,y_{Ti}$。有序处理变量 t_i. 处理协变量 $\boldsymbol{z}_{ti}$ 和误差项 ε_{ti} 之间的关系由式(3.62)表示。对于 $j=1,\cdots,B$，有序内生协变量 w_{bji}. 外生协变量 $\boldsymbol{z}_{bji}$ 和误差项 ε_{bji} 之间的关系由式(3.47)给出。模型也使用 $\mathbf{wind}_{bji}$ 的定义即式(3.49)。

y_i 关于外生协变量 $\boldsymbol{x}_i$，连续内生协变量 $\boldsymbol{w}_{ci}$，内生处理变量 t_i 和内生样本选择 s_i，具有如下形式：

$$\begin{aligned}
&y_{1i}=1(\boldsymbol{x}_i\boldsymbol{\beta}_1+\boldsymbol{w}_{ci}\boldsymbol{\beta}_{c1}+\mathbf{wind}_{b1i}\boldsymbol{\beta}_{b11}+\cdots+\mathbf{wind}_{bBi}\boldsymbol{\beta}_{bB1}+\varepsilon_{1i}>0)\\
&\vdots\\
&y_{Ti}=1(\boldsymbol{x}_i\boldsymbol{\beta}_T+\boldsymbol{w}_{ci}\boldsymbol{\beta}_{cT}+\mathbf{wind}_{b1i}\boldsymbol{\beta}_{b1T}+\cdots+\mathbf{wind}_{bBi}\boldsymbol{\beta}_{bBT}+\varepsilon_{Ti}>0)\\
&y_i=\sum_{j=1}^{T}1(t_i=v_j)y_{ji}\\
&\boldsymbol{w}_{ci}=\boldsymbol{z}_{ci}\boldsymbol{A}_c+\boldsymbol{\varepsilon}_{ci}\\
&s_i=1(\boldsymbol{z}_{si}\boldsymbol{\alpha}_s+\varepsilon_{si}>0)
\end{aligned}\tag{3.97}$$

其中，$\boldsymbol{z}_{si}$ 是影响选择的协变量，$\boldsymbol{z}_{ci}$ 是影响连续内生协变量的协变量。如果 $s_i=$

1,可以观测到结果 y_i;如果 $s_i=0$,则无法观测到。

对于 $j=1,\cdots,T$,不可观测到的误差项 $\varepsilon_{ji},\varepsilon_{si},\varepsilon_{ti},\varepsilon_{b1i},\cdots,\varepsilon_{bBi},\varepsilon_{ci}$ 均值为0,为多元正态分布,协方差矩阵为:

$$\boldsymbol{\Sigma}=\begin{bmatrix}1 & \rho_{1s} & \rho_{1t} & \rho'_{1b} & \sigma'_{1c}\\ \rho_{1s} & 1 & \rho_{st} & \rho'_{sb} & \sigma'_{sc}\\ \rho_{1t} & \rho_{st} & 1 & \rho'_{tb} & \sigma'_{tc}\\ \rho_{1b} & \rho_{sb} & \rho_{tb} & \boldsymbol{\Sigma}_b & \boldsymbol{\Sigma}'_{bc}\\ \sigma_{1c} & \sigma_{sc} & \sigma_{tc} & \boldsymbol{\Sigma}_{bc} & \boldsymbol{\Sigma}_c\end{bmatrix} \tag{3.98}$$

如同在连续内生变量中,可以将被解释变量的联合密度函数写成乘积形式:

$$\begin{aligned}&f(y_i,s_i,t_i,\boldsymbol{w}_{bi},\boldsymbol{w}_{ci}\mid \boldsymbol{x}_i,\boldsymbol{z}_{si},\boldsymbol{z}_{ti},\boldsymbol{z}_{b1i},\cdots,\boldsymbol{z}_{bBi},\boldsymbol{z}_{ci})\\ &\quad=f(y_i,s_i,t_i,\boldsymbol{w}_{bi}\mid \boldsymbol{w}_{ci},\boldsymbol{x}_i,\boldsymbol{z}_{si},\boldsymbol{z}_{ti},\boldsymbol{z}_{b1i},\cdots,\boldsymbol{z}_{bBi},\boldsymbol{z}_{ci})f(\boldsymbol{w}_{ci}\mid \boldsymbol{z}_{ci})\end{aligned}$$

对于 $j=1,\cdots,T$,以 $\boldsymbol{w}_{ci}$ 和外生协变量为条件,ε_{ji} 均值为:

$$e_{1i}=E(\varepsilon_{ji}\mid \boldsymbol{w}_{ci},\boldsymbol{x}_i,\boldsymbol{z}_{si},\boldsymbol{z}_{ti},\boldsymbol{z}_{b1i},\cdots,\boldsymbol{z}_{bBi},\boldsymbol{z}_{ci})=\sigma'_{1c}\boldsymbol{\Sigma}_c^{-1}(\boldsymbol{w}_{ci}-\boldsymbol{z}_{ci}\boldsymbol{A}_c)'$$

现在,对于 $j=1,\cdots,T$,设

$$c_{1ij}=\begin{cases}-\boldsymbol{x}_i\boldsymbol{\beta}_1-\boldsymbol{w}_{ci}\boldsymbol{\beta}_{c1}-\mathbf{wind}_{b1i}\boldsymbol{\beta}_{b11}-\cdots-\mathbf{wind}_{bBi}\boldsymbol{\beta}_{bB1}-e_{1i}\\ \vdots\\ -\boldsymbol{x}_i\boldsymbol{\beta}_T-\boldsymbol{w}_{ci}\boldsymbol{\beta}_{cT}-\mathbf{wind}_{b1i}\boldsymbol{\beta}_{b1T}-\cdots-\mathbf{wind}_{bBi}\boldsymbol{\beta}_{bBT}-e_{1i} & j=T\end{cases}$$

y_i 概率的下限和上限分别是:

$$l_{1i}=\begin{cases}-\infty & y_i=0\\ c_{1ij} & y_i=1,t_i=v_j\end{cases}\qquad u_{1i}=\begin{cases}c_{1ij} & y_i=0,t_i=v_j\\ \infty & y_i=1\end{cases}$$

不可观测到的误差项 $\varepsilon_{si},\varepsilon_{ti},\varepsilon_{b1i},\cdots,\varepsilon_{bBi}$ 具有类似于 e_{1i} 的形式,将其表示为 e_{si},$e_{ti},e_{b1i},\cdots,e_{bBi}$。$s_i,t_i$ 和有序内生协变量通过其上下限相减得到。

$$\begin{aligned}l_{si}^*&=l_{si}-e_{si}\\ u_{si}^*&=u_{si}-e_{si}\\ l_{ti}^*&=l_{ti}-e_{ti}\\ u_{ti}^*&=u_{ti}-e_{ti}\\ l_{b1i}^*&=l_{b1i}-e_{b1i}\\ u_{b1i}^*&=u_{b1i}-e_{b1i}\\ &\vdots\\ l_{bBi}^*&=l_{bBi}-e_{bBi}\\ u_{bBi}^*&=u_{bBi}-e_{bBi}\end{aligned}$$

在得到上下限之后,为了得到似然函数,需要 $\boldsymbol{w}_{ci}$ 的条件方差和条件密度。对于 $j=1,\cdots,T$,以 $\boldsymbol{w}_{ci}$ 和外生协变量为条件,$\varepsilon_{ji},\varepsilon_{si},\varepsilon_{ti},\varepsilon_{b1i},\cdots,\varepsilon_{bBi}$ 的方差为:

$$\boldsymbol{\Sigma}_{o|c}=\begin{bmatrix}1 & \rho_{1s} & \rho_{1t} & \rho'_{1b}\\ \rho_{1s} & 1 & \rho_{st} & \rho'_{sb}\\ \rho_{1t} & \rho_{st} & 1 & \rho'_{tb}\\ \rho_{1b} & \rho_{sb} & \rho_{tb} & \boldsymbol{\Sigma}_b\end{bmatrix}-\begin{bmatrix}\sigma'_{1c}\\ \sigma'_{sc}\\ \sigma'_{tc}\\ \boldsymbol{\Sigma}'_{bc}\end{bmatrix}\boldsymbol{\Sigma}_c^{-1}\begin{bmatrix}\sigma'_{1c}\\ \sigma'_{sc}\\ \sigma'_{tc}\\ \boldsymbol{\Sigma}'_{bc}\end{bmatrix}'$$

$\boldsymbol{w}_{ci}$ 的条件密度为：

$$f(\boldsymbol{w}_{ci} \mid \boldsymbol{z}_{ci}) = \phi_C(\boldsymbol{w}_{ci} - \boldsymbol{z}_{ci}\boldsymbol{A}_c, \boldsymbol{\Sigma}_c) \tag{3.99}$$

设

$$l_{1i} = [l_{1i} \quad l_{si}^* \quad l_{ti}^* \quad l_{b1i}^* \quad \cdots \quad l_{bBi}^*]$$

$$u_{1i} = [u_{1i} \quad u_{si}^* \quad u_{ti}^* \quad u_{b1i}^* \quad \cdots \quad u_{bBi}^*]$$

$$l_i = [l_{si}^* \quad l_{ti}^* \quad l_{b1i}^* \quad \cdots \quad l_{bBi}^*]$$

$$u_i = [u_{si}^* \quad u_{ti}^* \quad u_{b1i}^* \quad \cdots \quad u_{bBi}^*]$$

似然函数为：

$$\ln L = \sum_{i \in S} w_i \ln \Phi_{3+B}^*(l_{1i}, u_{1i}, \boldsymbol{\Sigma}_{o|c}) + \sum_{i \notin S} w_i \ln \Phi_{2+B}^*(l_i, u_i, \boldsymbol{\Sigma}_{o|c,-1})$$
$$+ \sum_{i=1}^{N} w_i \ln \phi_C(\boldsymbol{w}_{ci} - \boldsymbol{z}_{ci}\boldsymbol{A}_c, \boldsymbol{\Sigma}_c)$$

其中，S 是 y_i 被观测到的观测值集合，$\boldsymbol{\Sigma}_{o|c,-1}$ 是 $\boldsymbol{\Sigma}_{o|c}$ 矩阵去掉第一行和第一列后的矩阵。

利用联合和边际概率来确定条件概率。

对于 $j=1,\cdots,T$ 和 i，使得 $t_i = v_j$，设

$$l_{i11} = [c_{1ij} \quad l_{ti}^* \quad l_{b1i}^* \quad \cdots \quad l_{bBi}^*]$$

$$u_{i11} = [\infty \quad u_{ti}^* \quad u_{b1i}^* \quad \cdots \quad u_{bBi}^*]$$

$$l_{i12} = [l_{ti}^* \quad l_{b1i}^* \quad \cdots \quad l_{bBi}^*]$$

$$u_{i12} = [u_{ti}^* \quad u_{b1i}^* \quad \cdots \quad u_{bBi}^*]$$

设 $\boldsymbol{\Sigma}_{o|c,-s}$ 是 $\boldsymbol{\Sigma}_{o|c}$ 矩阵去掉第二行和第二列后的矩阵，这是不包括内生样本选择方程部分的条件协方差矩阵；$\boldsymbol{\Sigma}_{o|c,-s-1}$ 是 $\boldsymbol{\Sigma}_{o|c,-s}$ 矩阵去掉第一行和第一列后的矩阵。

对于处理水平 $t_i = v_j$ 的成功事件的条件概率为：

$$\Pr(y_i = 1 \mid \boldsymbol{t}_i = v_j, \boldsymbol{w}_{bi}, \boldsymbol{w}_{ci}, \boldsymbol{x}_i, \boldsymbol{z}_{si}, \boldsymbol{z}_{ti}, \boldsymbol{z}_{b1i}, \cdots, \boldsymbol{z}_{bBi}, \boldsymbol{z}_{ci}) = \frac{\Phi_{2+B}^*(l_{i11}, u_{i11}, \boldsymbol{\Sigma}_{o|c,-s})}{\Phi_{1+B}^*(l_{i12}, u_{i12}, \boldsymbol{\Sigma}_{o|c,-s-1})} \tag{3.100}$$

处理、选择和有序内生协变量的条件概率，按照类似的方法得到。

3.10.7 置信区间

估计的方差总是非负的，估计的相关系数位于区间（-1，1）内。利用对数转换获得方差参数的置信区间。设 $\hat{\sigma}^2$ 是方差参数 σ^2 的点估计，$\mathrm{SE}(\hat{\sigma}^2)$ 是其标准差。$\ln(\sigma^2)$ 的 $(1-\alpha)\times 100\%$ 的置信区间为：

$$\ln(\hat{\sigma}^2) \pm z_{\alpha/2} \frac{\mathrm{SE}(\hat{\sigma}^2)}{\hat{\sigma}^2} \tag{3.101}$$

其中，$z_{\alpha/2}$ 是标准正态分布的 $1-\alpha/2$ 的分位数。设 k_u 是区间的上端点，k_l 是下断点。σ^2 的 $(1-\alpha)\times 100\%$ 的置信区间为：

$$(e^{k_l}, e^{k_u})$$

利用反双曲线正切变化得到相关性参数的置信区间。设 $\hat{\rho}$ 为相关性参数 ρ 的点估计，SE($\hat{\rho}$)是其标准差。则 $a\tanh(\hat{\rho})$的$(1-\alpha)\times 100\%$的置信区间为：

$$a\tanh(\hat{\rho}) \pm z_{\alpha/2}\mathrm{SE}(\hat{\rho})\ \frac{1}{1-\hat{\rho}^2}$$

ρ 的$(1-\alpha)\times 100\%$的置信区间为

$$\{\tanh(k_l),\tanh(k_u)\}$$

估计具有内生性协变量的 Probit 模型的命令为 eprobit，其主要语法格式如下：

(1) 包含内生性协变量的基准 Probit 回归

eprobit depvar [indepvars], endogenous($depvars_{en}$ = $varlist_{en}$) [options]

(2) 包含内生性处理变量安排的基准 Probit 回归

eprobit depvar [indepvars], entreat($depavars_{tr}$ = $varlist_{tr}$) [options]

(3) 包含外生性处理变量安排的基准 Probit 回归

eprobit depvar [indepvars], extreat(tvar) [options]

(4) 包含样本选择的基准 Probit 回归

eprobit depvar [indepvars], select($depavars_s$ = $varlist_s$) [options]

(5) Tobit 样本选择的基准 Probit 回归

eprobit depvar [indepvars], tobitselect($depavars_s$ = $varlist_s$) [options]

(6) 具有随机效应的基准 Probit 回归

xteprobit depvar [indepvars] [, options]

(7) Probit 回归，结合内生协变量、处理协变量和选择协变量

eprobit depvar [indepvars] [if] [in] [weight] [, extensions options]

(8) 具有随机效应的 Probit 回归，结合内生协变量、处理协变量和选择协变量

xteprobit depvar [indepvars] [if] [in] [, extensions options]

菜单操作路径为：

Statistics>Endogenous covariates>Models adding selection and treatment >Probit regression

Statistics > Longitudinal/panel data > Endogenous covariates > Models adding selection and treatment>Probit regression (RE)

例 3.10 含内生变量、样本选择和处理的 Probit 回归[①]

下面以 Stata 软件自带数据集 class. dta 来说明 eprobit 命令的应用。该数据集为一份虚构的数据，包含是否大学毕业(graduate)、高中的绩点(GPA)变量。假设高中的 GPA 较高是大学毕业率的内生变量。变量还包括父母收入，学生是否有高中室友也在该大学。利用高中排名(hscomp)作为高中 GPA 的工具变量。

```
.use class10.dta, clear
.eprobit graduate income i.roommate, endogenous(hsgpa = income i.hscomp)
```

① 本案例根据 Stata 帮助手册 erm. pdf 中的对应例子改编。

> vce(robust)

运行结果如图 3.44 所示。

```
Iteration 0:   log pseudolikelihood = -1418.5008
Iteration 1:   log pseudolikelihood = -1418.4414
Iteration 2:   log pseudolikelihood = -1418.4414

Extended probit regression                          Number of obs =  2,500
                                                    Wald chi2(3)  = 326.79
Log pseudolikelihood = -1418.4414                   Prob > chi2   = 0.0000
```

	Coefficient	Robust std. err.	z	P>|z|	[95% conf.	interval]
graduate						
income	0.160	0.016	10.06	0.000	0.129	0.191
roommate						
yes	0.264	0.056	4.68	0.000	0.153	0.374
hsgpa	1.019	0.432	2.36	0.018	0.171	1.866
_cons	-3.647	1.205	-3.03	0.002	-6.008	-1.286
hsgpa						
income	0.048	0.002	29.07	0.000	0.045	0.051
hscomp						
moderate	-0.136	0.011	-11.83	0.000	-0.158	-0.113
high	-0.225	0.020	-11.55	0.000	-0.264	-0.187
_cons	2.795	0.013	218.43	0.000	2.770	2.820
var(e.hsgpa)	0.069	0.002			0.065	0.073
corr(e.hsgpa,e.graduate)	0.369	0.092	4.01	0.000	0.177	0.534

图 3.44

从估计中可以看出，两个方程的残差相关系数为 0.37，并且显著，因而存在内生性。因为相关性为正向，可以得到不可观测到的因素，提高了高中 GPA，也提高了大学毕业率。

主方程的结果解释与 eprobit 命令估计的解释一致。可以从系数得出效应的方向，但是无法得出效应的大学毕业率。例如，家庭收入和高中 GPA 与大学毕业率都为正相关。

如果将每个学生高中的 GPA 提高 1 个点，即从 2.0 提高到 3.0，从 2.5 提高到 3.5，结果会如何呢？当然，如果一个学生的 GPA 已经高于 3.0，则无法提高 1 个点，因此，将感兴趣的总体限制为绩点小于等于 3.0 的学生。如果设定 at(hsgpa＝generate(hsgpa))，则可以利用 margins 命令，得到学生在当前 GPA 情况下的总体平均预期毕业率。

.margins, at(hsgpa = generate(hsgpa)) at(hsgpa = generate(hsgpa + 1))

＞subpop(if hsgpa ＜= 3) vce(unconditional)

运行结果如图 3.45 所示。

Predictive margins　　Number of obs = **2,500**
Subpop. no. obs = **1,430**

Expression: **Average structural function probability, predict()**
1._at: hsgpa = **hsgpa**
2._at: hsgpa = **hsgpa+1**

	Margin	Unconditional std. err.	z	P>|z|	[95% conf.	interval]
_at						
1	**0.432**	**0.013**	**34.37**	**0.000**	**0.407**	**0.456**
2	**0.774**	**0.106**	**7.31**	**0.000**	**0.566**	**0.981**

图　3.45

对于一个高中 GPA 是 3.0 及以下的学生，其预期毕业率为 43%。如果同一个学生，GPA 增加一个点，则大学毕业率可上升到 77%。

通过 contrast(at(r))项，可以估计两种反事实之间的差异，并估计 GPA 增加 1 个点之后的平均效应。

. margins, at(hsgpa = generate(hsgpa)) at(hsgpa = generate(hsgpa + 1))

＞subpop(if hsgpa ＜= 3) contrast(at(r) nowald effects) vce(unconditional)

运行结果如图 3.46 所示。

Contrasts of predictive margins　　Number of obs = **2,500**
Subpop. no. obs = **1,430**

Expression: **Average structural function probability, predict()**
1._at: hsgpa = **hsgpa**
2._at: hsgpa = **hsgpa+1**

	Contrast	Unconditional std. err.	z	P>|z|	[95% conf.	interval]
_at						
(2 vs 1)	**0.342**	**0.107**	**3.20**	**0.001**	**0.132**	**0.552**

图　3.46

给学生的 GPA 加 1 个点，使大学毕业率提高了 34 个百分点，95%的置信区间提高了16—53个百分点。

这个效应在其他协变量中有区别吗？我们的数据集有一个家庭收入分组变量incomegrp，所以估计每个收入分组中的效应，只需将incomegrp添加到之前的margins命令中。

```
margins, at(hsgpa = generate(hsgpa)) at(hsgpa = generate(hsgpa + 1))
>subpop(if hsgpa < = 3) contrast(at(r) nowald effects) noatlegend
>vce(unconditional) over(incomegrp)
```

运行结果如图3.47所示。

Expression: **Average structural function probability, predict()**
Over: **incomegrp**

	Contrast	Unconditional std. err.	z	P>|z|	[95% conf.	interval]
_at@incomegrp						
(2 vs 1) < 20K	**0.369**	**0.137**	**2.70**	**0.007**	**0.101**	**0.637**
(2 vs 1) 20-39K	**0.370**	**0.125**	**2.95**	**0.003**	**0.124**	**0.616**
(2 vs 1) 40-59K	**0.352**	**0.103**	**3.42**	**0.001**	**0.150**	**0.553**
(2 vs 1) 60-79K	**0.309**	**0.080**	**3.87**	**0.000**	**0.153**	**0.466**
(2 vs 1) 80-99K	**0.255**	**0.057**	**4.46**	**0.000**	**0.143**	**0.367**
(2 vs 1) 100-119K	**0.183**	**0.039**	**4.71**	**0.000**	**0.107**	**0.259**
(2 vs 1) 120-139K	**0.124**	**0.034**	**3.59**	**0.000**	**0.056**	**0.191**
(2 vs 1) 140K up	**0.049**	**0.014**	**3.49**	**0.000**	**0.021**	**0.076**

图 3.47

可见，对于低收入群体，效应是最大的，且随着收入上升而下降；对于收入高于140000的群体，效应几乎可以忽略，可以通过图3.48很清晰地看出这种关系。

```
.marginsplot
```

可见，对低收入群体而言，大学毕业率的效应接近0.4，而对收入高于100000的群体而言，效应下降到低于0.2。

接下来看看是否能够观察到同时影响大学毕业率和高中GPA的不可观测因素。集中分析非常低的组和非常高的组；同时，为了避免室友身份可能带来的混淆，只包括那些有室友身份的人。另外，通过修改数据，简化分析。

```
.gen smpl = roommate = = 1&(income<3|income>10)
.gen byte hlincome  = 1 if income < 3
(1,870 missing values generated)
.replace hlincome  = 2 if income>10
(216 real changes made)
.label define hiloinc 1 "income < $30000" 2 "income> $100000"
.label values hlincome liloinc
```

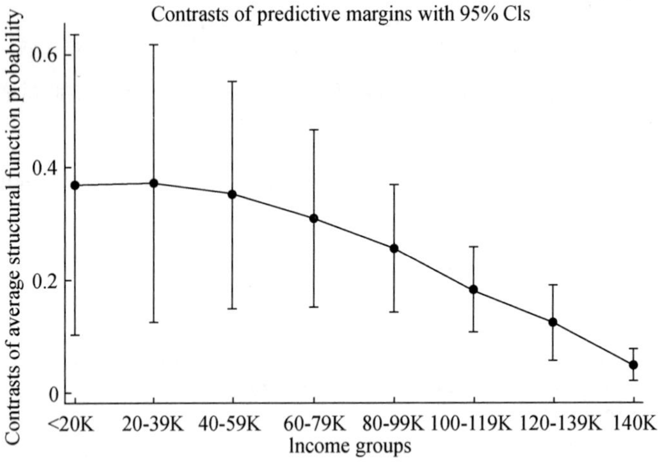

图 3.48

高收入群体的预期毕业率与低收入群体相比，在各个高中 GPA 的阶段，均处于较高水平。

```
.margins, subpop(smpl) over(hsgpagrp hlincome) vce(unconditional)
.marginsplot
```

运行结果如图 3.49 所示。

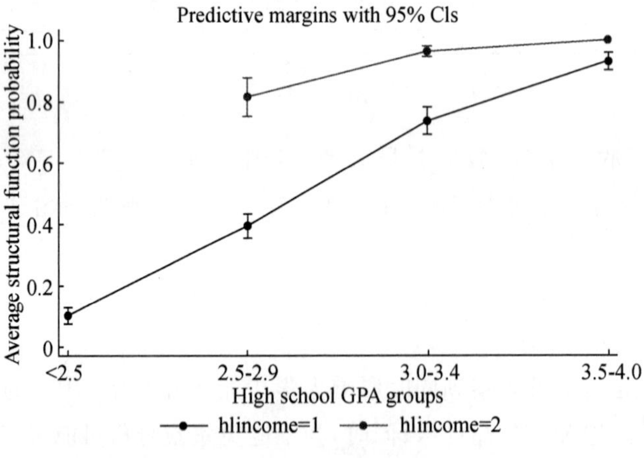

图 3.49

从图 3.49 可以很清楚地看出，高收入群体的预期毕业率更高。

如果创造一个公平的生存环境，给予相同的家庭收入水平，结果会怎么样？给每个人 100000 的收入，这对于低收入群体来说是显著程度的增加，对于高收入群体而言则是某种程度的下降。通过添加 at(income＝10)构建反事实，并通过 margins 命令作图。(见图 3.50)

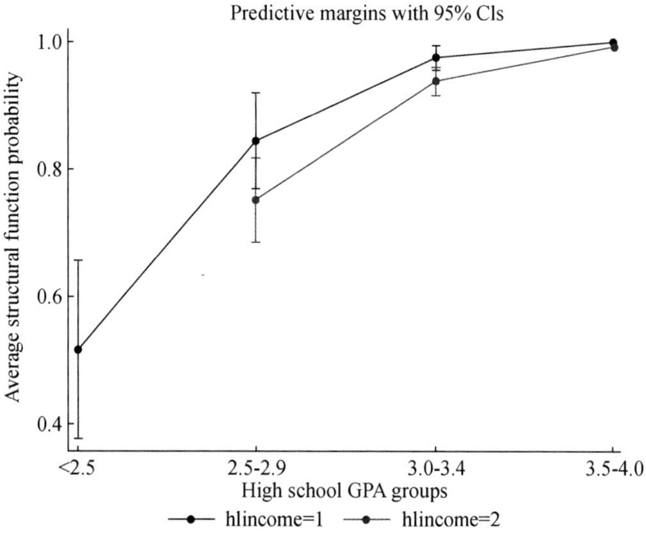

图 3.50

虽然给每个人100000的家庭收入，但每个人仍保持着自己不可观测的特征。图3.50中上面的曲线代表的是初始收入高于100000的人，预期毕业率仍然和之前差不多。收入低于30000的人，预期毕业率远高于过去。

第 4 章 序数结果

4.1 有序 Logistic 回归

多元 Logit 模型不能反映因变量的有序性，而普通回归分析由于将回归量之间的差距看作是等距的，在这里并不适用。

有序 Logit 模型的潜在变量回归模型为：

$$Y^* = X\beta + \mu \tag{4.1}$$

式中，随机项 u 服从逻辑分布。

这里的 Y^* 是无法预测的，于是观察的是 y：

$$\begin{aligned}
&y = 0, \text{如果 } Y^* \leqslant 0\\
&y = 1, \text{如果 } 0 \leqslant Y^* < u_1\\
&y = 2, \text{如果 } u_1 \leqslant Y^* < u_2\\
&\quad\vdots\\
&y = J, \text{如果 } u_{J-1} \leqslant Y^*
\end{aligned}$$

有序 Logit 模型的给定样本 y_j 观测 i 的概率为：

$$\begin{aligned}
p_{ij} &= \Pr(y_j = i) = \Pr(\kappa_{i-1} < \boldsymbol{x}_j \boldsymbol{\beta} + u \leqslant \kappa_i)\\
&= \frac{1}{1 + \exp(-\kappa_i + \boldsymbol{x}_j \boldsymbol{\beta})} - \frac{1}{1 + \exp(-\kappa_{i-1} + \boldsymbol{x}_j \boldsymbol{\beta})}
\end{aligned} \tag{4.2}$$

式中，κ_0 可以定义为$-\infty$，κ_k 可以定义为$+\infty$。

对数似然函数为：

$$\ln L = \sum_{j=1}^{N} w_j \sum_{i=1}^{k} I_i(y_j) \ln p_{ij} \tag{4.3}$$

其中，w_j 是可选权重，$I_i(y_j) = \begin{cases} 1, & \text{如果 } y_j = i \\ 0, & \text{其他} \end{cases}$。

若模型中干扰项服从逻辑斯谛分布（logistic distribution），则可以得到有序 Logit 模型的估计。

有序 logistic 回归的语法格式为：

```
ologit depvar [indepvars] [if] [in] [weight] [, options]
```

菜单操作路径为：

Statistics>Ordinal outcomes>Ordered logistic regression

ologit 在自变量指标上拟合有序变量 depvar 的有序 logit 模型，所采用的因变量与实际值是不相关的，除非假设较大的值对应于“较高”的结果。

例 4.1 有序 Logit 模型

下面以 Statistics with Stata（第 7 版）中的数据来说明有序 Logit 模型的应用。Hamilton 给出了一个引人入胜的例子，表明对于 1986 年 1 月 28 日的挑战者号航天飞机灾难，如果 NASA 官员注意到这些警告信号，就可能会避免。数据涵盖了美国航天飞机的前 25 次飞行。对于每次飞行，测量如表 4-1 所示的变量。

表 4-1 挑战者号航天飞机变量说明

变量名称	变量含义
distress	“热窘迫事件”的次数，其中高温气体损坏了飞行助推火箭的密封接头。密封接头的损坏导致了挑战者号的灾难。它的编码是 1=None，2=1 或 2，3=3 及以上
temp	发射时计算的接头温度。温度在很大程度上取决于天气。较低的温度会导致密封接头的 O 型橡胶圈变得不灵活，因此更容易出现问题
date	日期，以 1960 年 1 月 1 日以来所经过的天数计算（任意起点）。这个变量的基本原理是在航天飞机项目中不受欢迎的变化和老化的硬件可能会导致发射越来越危险

```
.use shuttle2.dta, clear
.ologit distress date temp
```

运行结果如图 4.1 所示。

```
Iteration 0:   log likelihood = -24.955257
Iteration 1:   log likelihood = -18.871284
Iteration 2:   log likelihood =  -18.79755
Iteration 3:   log likelihood =  -18.79706
Iteration 4:   log likelihood =  -18.79706

Ordered logistic regression                      Number of obs =     23
                                                 LR chi2(2)    =  12.32
                                                 Prob > chi2   = 0.0021
Log likelihood = -18.79706                       Pseudo R2     = 0.2468

    distress | Coefficient  Std. err.      z    P>|z|     [95% conf. interval]
-------------+----------------------------------------------------------------
        date |      0.003      0.001    2.60   0.009      0.001       0.006
        temp |     -0.173      0.083   -2.08   0.038     -0.337      -0.010
-------------+----------------------------------------------------------------
       /cut1 |     16.428      9.555                     -2.299      35.155
       /cut2 |     18.122      9.722                     -0.933      37.178
```

图 4.1

模型自由度为 2 的 χ^2 值为 12.32，这是非常显著的，说明日期和/或温度对热损坏事件的数量有显著影响。

McFadden R^2（又称伪 R^2）为：

$$\text{Pseudo } R^2 = \text{LR}/\text{DEV}_0 = 12.32/49.91 = 0.247$$

其中，$\text{DEV}_0 = -2 \times LL_0 = -2 \times (-24.955257) \approx 49.91$。date 的系数为正表示遇险事件的可能性确实随着时间的推移而增加。同样，temp 的系数为负意味着较低的温度的上升使得发生不幸事件的可能性增加。

阈值参数 16.428 和 18.122 说明：Y 有三种可能的值：

$$\begin{cases} Y_i = 1, & \text{如果 } Y_i^* \leqslant 16.428 \\ Y_i = 2, & \text{如果 } 16.428 < Y_i^* \leqslant 18.122 \\ Y_i = 3, & \text{如果 } Y_i^* > 18.122 \end{cases}$$

在解释系数时，可以观察系数的符号和意义，若结合一些假设或真实的数据来进行解释，可以更好地了解系数的意义。

Shuttle filght 13 号发射时的温度是 78，而 date 等于 9044。因此，我们对 filght 13 进行计算：

$$Z_i = (0.00329 \times 9044) - 0.173 \times 78 = 16.195$$

可见，Z_i 值低于最低阈值 16.428。对于 flight 13，可以进一步计算：

$$P(Y=1) = \frac{1}{1+\exp(Z_i - \kappa_1)} = \frac{1}{1+\exp(16.195 - 16.428)} = 0.558$$

$$\begin{aligned} P(Y=2) &= \frac{1}{1+\exp(Z_i - \kappa_2)} - \frac{1}{1+\exp(Z_i - \kappa_1)} \\ &= \frac{1}{1+\exp(16.195 - 18.122)} - \frac{1}{1+\exp(16.195 - 16.428)} \\ &= 0.873 - 0.558 = 0.315 \end{aligned}$$

$$P(Y=3) = 1 - \frac{1}{1+\exp(Z_i - \kappa_2)} = 1 - \frac{1}{1+\exp(16.195 - 18.122)} = 0.127$$

因此，对于在更温暖的条件下比挑战者号早一年多发生的 flight 13 号事件来说，最有可能的结果是密封接头不会受损。事实上，flight 13 号没有任何问题。

也就是说，对 flight 13 号的 Z_i 的估计是 16.195，这是对 Y_i^* 值的"最佳猜测"，这个值将 flight 13 号置于 $Y=1$ 的阈值中。但是，由于存在随机干扰项，Y_i^* 大于 Z_i 至少有一定的可能性，即 flight 13 号的风险比估计表明的更大。如果是这样，则可能会使 flight 13 号进入更高的阈值类别，例如，flight 13 号的 Y_i^* 实际上可能是 17，在这种情况下，Y 将等于 2；Y_i^* 也可以是 18.5，此时 $Y=3$。

考虑到 flight 13 号的 Z_i 的估计非常接近 $Y=1$ 的阈值，发现 $P(Y=1)=0.558$，$P(Y=2)=0.315$，$P(Y=3)=0.127$ 并不奇怪。也就是说，对 flight 13 号来说，$Y=1$ 是最可能的值，但是 $Y=2$ 和 $Y=3$ 也有相当高的概率。如果 Z_i 值非常小，如 2，那么 Y_i^* 实际上不太可能落在更高的阈值范围，这时发现 $P(Y=1)$ 会更高。

对 Shuttle flight 25 号即挑战者号，NASA 官员有可能在发射当天使用这些数据来预测出现问题的可能性。在挑战者号发射时，date 等于 9524，温度是 31(之前最冷的发射温度是 53)。因此，对挑战者号，

$$Z_i=(0.0033\times 9524)-0.1734\times 31=26.0538$$

注意，这个值比 ologit 给出的上限阈值 18.1223 要高得多。使用之前给出的公式和阈值估计，可以计算挑战者号陷入三种不同困境的概率：

$$P(Y=1)=\frac{1}{1+\exp(Z_i-\kappa_1)}=\frac{1}{1+\exp(26.0538-16.4281)}=6.6025\times 10^{-5}$$

$$P(Y=2)=\frac{1}{1+\exp(Z_i-\delta_2)}-\frac{1}{1+\exp(Z_i-\kappa_1)}$$

$$=\frac{1}{1+\exp(26.0538-18.1223)}-\frac{1}{1+\exp(26.0538-16.4281)}$$

$$=0.0004-6.6025\times 10^{-5}=0.0003$$

$$P(Y=3)=1-\frac{1}{1+\exp(Z_i-\kappa_2)}=1-\frac{1}{1+\exp(26.0538-18.1223)}=0.9996$$

因此，根据之前 23 次飞行的经验，挑战者号的密封接头不可能不受损伤。挑战者号肯定会遭遇 3 次或更多次的损坏事故。

综上所述，对挑战者号 Z_i 的估计是 26.0538，远远超过了上限阈值。有可能挑战者号面临的实际风险小于这个值，如 Y^* 值只有 23，但不太可能≤16.4281。对于挑战者号来说，$16.4281\leqslant Y^*\leqslant 18.1223$ 也是有可能的，但事实上并非如此。例如，如果挑战者号的 Z_i 值为 18.5，那么 Y^* 的真实值落入较低阈值范围的可能性就会很大。

顺便说一句，如果用 OLS 回归代替，则挑战者号的 Y^* 预测值是 4.63，而 flight 13 的 Y^* 预测值是 1.65。挑战者号估算的 4.63 当然不是 Y^* 的合理值，但它与当天发射风险非常大的发现是一致的。

Stata 还可以很容易地获得预测的 Z^* 值和三种可能结果的预测概率。在默认情况下，Stata 的 predict 命令通常会计算所有情况的值，而不仅仅是分析中包含的情况。有时候，这很危险，但却为我们提供了挑战者号的预测值。

```
.predict z, xb
.predict none onetwo threeplus, p
.list flight temp date distress z none onetwo threeplus
```

运行结果如图 4.2 所示。

注意，所得到的 flight 13 号和 flight 25 号的值与我们之前计算的值相同。

可以通过几种方法来测试有序 Logit 模型的比例概率假设和平行线假设。这里从布兰特测试(Brant test)开始，它也有助于确切地阐明假设是什么。

如果已经下载并安装了 spost13，可以使用 brant 命令来测试 ologit 平行线假设和比例概率假设。(见图 4.3)

	flight	temp	date	distress	z	none	onetwo	threeplus
1.	STS-1	66	7772	None	14.095978	.91150495	.0709674	.01752765
2.	STS-2	70	7986	1 or 2	14.10568	.91071924	.07158525	.01769551
3.	STS-3	69	8116	None	14.706234	.84837266	.1198293	.03179804
4.	STS-4	80	8213	.	13.117848	.96477981	.02855667	.00666351
5.	STS-5	68	8350	None	15.648532	.68559312	.23668703	.07771985
6.	STS-6	67	8494	1 or 2	16.295091	.53321054	.32821491	.13857456
7.	STS-7	72	8569	None	15.674664	.67993317	.24045308	.07961374
8.	STS-8	73	8642	None	15.741166	.66529086	.25008416	.08462498
9.	STS-9	70	8732	None	16.557031	.46781885	.35928501	.17289614
10.	STS_41-B	57	8799	1 or 2	19.031071	.06894928	.21829605	.71275467
11.	STS_41-C	63	8862	3 plus	18.197837	.14557856	.33553874	.5188827
12.	STS_41-D	70	9008	3 plus	17.463966	.26195403	.39692547	.3411205
13.	STS_41-G	78	9044	None	16.19526	.55795561	.31496261	.12708178
14.	STS_51-A	67	9078	None	18.214111	.143566	.33349002	.52294399
15.	STS_51-C	53	9155	3 plus	20.894386	.01135971	.04749002	.94115026
16.	STS_51-D	67	9233	3 plus	18.72344	.09151201	.26256417	.64592382
17.	STS_51-B	75	9250	3 plus	17.3923	.27604379	.39875503	.32520118
18.	STS_51-G	70	9299	3 plus	18.42019	.12003895	.30602724	.57393381
19.	STS_51-F	81	9341	1 or 2	16.651074	.44449338	.36874582	.1867608
20.	STS_51-I	76	9370	1 or 2	17.613244	.23413368	.39044457	.37542175
21.	STS_51-J	79	9407	None	17.2147	.31290532	.39959744	.28749724
22.	STS_61-A	75	9434	3 plus	17.996923	.17238835	.35890762	.46870404
23.	STS_61-B	76	9461	1 or 2	17.91227	.18480278	.36750541	.44769181
24.	STS_61-C	58	9508	3 plus	21.187466	.00849845	.03606753	.95543403
25.	STS_51-L	31	9524	.	25.921173	.00007537	.00033465	.99958998

图 4.2

Estimated coefficients from binary logits

Variable	y_gt_1	y_gt_2
date	**0.003**	**0.006**
	2.17	**1.80**
temp	**-0.173**	**-0.234**
	-1.48	**-1.86**
_cons	**-13.644**	**-36.845**
	-1.34	**-1.52**

Legend: b/t

Brant test of parallel regression assumption

	chi2	p>chi2	df
All	**0.83**	**0.662**	**2**
date	**0.81**	**0.369**	**1**
temp	**0.22**	**0.643**	**1**

A significant test statistic provides evidence that the parallel regression assumption has been violated.

图 4.3

由图 4.3 可以看出,总体卡方值不显著(在标记为 All 的行中),表明满足了 ologit 的假设。(当然,这个样本很小;在较大的样本中,发现比例概率假设被违背是很正常的)brant 命令也给出了对每个独立变量的检验。

brant 命令的细节选项阐明了为什么有序 Logit 模型有时也被称为平行线或平行回归模型。对二元 Logit 模型,序数变量被二分类。首先是类别 1 与所有更高的类别对比;然后是类别 1 和类别 2 与所有更高的类别对比,等等。如果符合有序 Logit 模型的假设,那么每个逻辑回归的系数(除了常数)都应该是相同的,即回归线将是平行的,只是截距不同。

4.2 有序 Probit 回归

有序 Probit 模型的表达式同有序 Logit 模型,只是随机项分布假设为正态分布。其给定观测为:

$$\begin{aligned} p_{ij} &= \Pr(y_j = i) = \Pr(\kappa_{i-1} < \boldsymbol{x}_j \boldsymbol{\beta} + u \leqslant \kappa_i) \\ &= \Phi(\kappa_i - \boldsymbol{x}_j \boldsymbol{\beta}) - \Phi(\kappa_{i-1} - \boldsymbol{x}_j \boldsymbol{\beta}) \end{aligned} \tag{4.4}$$

式中,Φ()是标准正态累积分布函数,其对数似然函数为式(4.3)。

有序 Probit 回归的语法格式为:

```
oprobit depvar [indepvars] [if] [in] [weight] [, options]
```

菜单操作路径为:

Statistics>Ordinal outcomes>Ordered probit regression

oprobit 在自变量 indepvar 上拟合有序变量 depvar 的有序 Probit 模型,所采用的实际值与因变量是不相关的,除非假设较大的值对应于“较高”的结果。

案例 4.2 有序 Probit 模型

有序 Probit 模型与有序 Logit 模型的主要区别在于随机扰动项的差异。下面利用 Stata 帮助手册 r.pdf 中的系统数据进行说明。

```
.use fullauto, clear
.oprobit rep77 foreign length mpg
```

运行结果如图 4.4 所示。

由图 4.4 可以发现,外国车(foreign)的维修记录更好,大型车(length)和里程评级好(mpg)的车也是如此。

```
.predict p1 p2 p3 p4 p5
.list rep77 p1 p2 p3 p4 p5 in 1/10
```

运行结果如图 4.5 所示。

```
Ordered probit regression                      Number of obs =     66
                                               LR chi2(3)    =  23.75
                                               Prob > chi2   = 0.0000
Log likelihood = -78.020025                    Pseudo R2     = 0.1321
```

rep77	Coefficient	Std. err.	z	P>|z|	[95% conf.	interval]
foreign	1.705	0.425	4.01	0.000	0.873	2.537
length	0.047	0.013	3.71	0.000	0.022	0.072
mpg	0.130	0.038	3.45	0.001	0.056	0.205
/cut1	10.159	3.077			4.129	16.189
/cut2	11.210	3.108			5.119	17.301
/cut3	12.546	3.155			6.361	18.730
/cut4	13.981	3.219			7.672	20.289

图 4.4

	rep77	p1	p2	p3	p4	p5
1.	Fair	.07657592	.27637689	.47807122	.16062498	.00835099
2.	Poor	.43371287	.37799214	.17507805	.01308824	.00012871
3.	.	.27931717	.40016628	.28473088	.03518131	.00060435
4.	Average	.00345249	.04599171	.32705571	.49220652	.13129357
5.	Fair	.004375	.05376928	.34897414	.47781574	.11506583
6.	Good	.00095815	.01913732	.21683823	.52692891	.23613739
7.	Average	.05089363	.22833852	.4942779	.21206165	.01442831
8.	Good	.01381408	.11096973	.44828014	.37423003	.05270602
9.	Good	.00805478	.07960656	.40447305	.42937036	.07849525
10.	.	.11498622	.32567072	.44158651	.11337628	.00438027

图 4.5

4.3 多值排序 Logit 模型

Cmrologit 模型通过最大似然估计拟合有序 Logit 模型(Beggs, Cardell, and Hausman, 1981)①,也称为 Plackett-Luce 模型(Marden, 1995)②。多值排序 Logit 模型可以用于分析决策者如何将方案的属性组合到对这些方案的整体评估中。该模

① Beggs, S., S. Cardell, and J. A. Hausman. Assessing the Potential Demand for Electric Cars. *Journal of Econometrics*, 1981, 17.

② Marden, J. I. *Analyzing and Modeling Rank Data*. London: Chapman & Hall, 1995.

型推广了 McFadden 选择模型的一个版本,其中的替代方案没有确定。它使用关于备选方案比较的信息,即决策者如何对备选方案进行排序,而不仅仅是指定他们最喜欢的方案。

Cmrologit 模型中的数据是类似于 clogit 的长形式,其中每个排序的替代方案形成一个观察,区别在于,前者的 depvar 记录了选项的排名,而后者的 depvar 以不等于零的值表示单个选择的选项。如果数据记录每个案例只有一种首选方案,那么 cmrology 与 clogit 的模型相同。

多值排序 Logit 模型的语法格式为:

```
cmrologit depvar [indepvars] [if] [in] [weight] [, options]
```

菜单操作路径为:

Statistics>Choice models>Rank - ordered logit model

cmrologit 在自变量 indepvar 上拟合有序变量 depvar 的 cmrologit 模型。所采用的实际值与因变量是不相关的,除非假设较大的值对应于"较高"的结果。

例 4.3 多值排序 Logit 模型①

研究雇主对员工性格偏好的常用方法是准实验法即"vignette 方法"。例如,de Wolf (2000)②关于社会科学毕业生的劳动力市场地位的研究。本研究探讨了教育档案(例如,一般技能和特定知识)如何影响短期和长期的劳动力市场机会。

de Wolf 让 22 位人力资源经理(受访者)从 20 个虚构的求职者中选出 6 位最合适的申请人,并让这 6 位申请人为 3 个职位排序,即研究员、管理培训生、政策顾问。申请人的 10 个特征被描述出来,包括年龄、性别、作品集的细节和工作经验等。在本例中,分析数据的一个子集。

数据是长形式的,观察结果对应于备选方案(应用程序),在一个决策任务中提出的备选方案由变量 caseid 确定。图 4.6 列出了 caseid==7 的观察结果,其中受访者考虑了社会科学研究职位的申请人。

这里选出了 6 名申请人,排名存储在变量 pref 中,其中值为 6 代表"申请人中最好的",5 代表"申请人中第二好的",以此类推。排名为 0 的申请人并不是该职位的最佳 6 名申请人之一。申请人没有被要求表达其偏好,但通过诱导程序,它是已知的。

vignette 方法的目的是探索和测试关于员工的哪些属性被雇主重视,这些属性如何根据工作类型(这些数据中描述的可变工作)进行加权,等等。例如,如果价值只取决于申请人的年龄和性别,有

$$value(female_i, age_i) = \beta_1 female_i + \beta_2 age_i + \varepsilon_i$$

这样就可以直接对备选方案的决策(选择)或备选方案的排名进行建模。

在拟合模型之前,我们必须对数据使用命令 cmset。cmset 的参数就是 ID 变量,必须为数字。变量 caseid 用于标识受访者。与其他选择模型不同,该模型的替代方案没有指定,也就是说,在受访者中没有确定具体备选方案的变量。在这个模型中,备选

---

① 本案例根据 Stata 帮助手册 cm.pdf 中的对应案例改编。

② de Wolf, I. *Opleidingsspecialisatie en Arbeidsmarktsucces van Sociale Wetenschappers*. Amsterdam: ThelaThesis, 2000.

pref	female	age	grades	edufit	workexp	boardexp
0	yes	28	A/B	no	none	no
0	no	25	C/D	yes	one year	no
0	no	25	C/D	yes	none	yes
0	yes	25	C/D	no	internship	yes
1	no	25	C/D	yes	one year	yes
2	no	25	A/B	yes	none	no
3	yes	25	A/B	yes	one year	no
4	yes	25	A/B	yes	none	yes
5	no	25	A/B	yes	internship	no
6	yes	28	A/B	yes	one year	yes

图 4.6

方案只是有一些特征。

```
.cmset caseid, noalternatives
```

运行结果如图 4.7 所示。

```
Rank-ordered logit choice model                 Number of obs     =         80
Case ID variable: caseid                        Number of cases   =          8

Ties adjustment: No ties in data                Obs per case:
                                                              min =         10
                                                              avg =      10.00
                                                              max =         10

                                                LR chi2(7)        =      55.01
Log likelihood = -67.90566                      Prob > chi2       =     0.0000
```

pref	Coefficient	Std. err.	z	P>|z|	[95% conf.	interval]
female						
yes	-0.455	0.362	-1.26	0.208	-1.164	0.253
age	-0.085	0.082	-1.03	0.301	-0.246	0.076
grades						
A/B	3.145	0.620	5.07	0.000	1.929	4.360
edufit						
yes	0.764	0.361	2.11	0.035	0.056	1.472
workexp						
internship	1.894	0.630	3.01	0.003	0.660	3.129
one year	2.912	0.620	4.69	0.000	1.696	4.128
boardexp						
yes	0.810	0.397	2.04	0.041	0.032	1.589

图 4.7

只关注其系数在 10%水平上显著的变量(只有 8 名受访者!),选择 1 类工作(研究职位)的申请人的估计价值为:

$$\begin{aligned}\text{value} &= 3.14\times(A/B\ \text{grades})+0.76\times\text{eduf}+t+1.89\times\text{internship}\\&\quad+2.91\times(1-\text{yearworkexp})+0.81\times\text{boardexp}\end{aligned}$$

可见,雇主更喜欢研究职位(job==1)的申请人,他们的教育组合适合该工作,有更好的成绩,有更多相关的工作经验,以及有董事会经验(课外)。

根据雇主对这些评估的估计,考虑每个申请人排名第一的概率,在 ε_i 独立且服从极值Ⅰ型分布的情况下,π_i 的概率,即选择 1 的价值高于选择 2,…,k 的价值,可以写成多元 Logit 模型:

$$\pi_i=\Pr\{\text{value}_1>\max(\text{value}_2,\cdots,\text{value}_m)\}=\frac{\exp(\text{value}_i)}{\sum_{j=1}^{k}\exp(\text{value}_i)}$$

通过 predict 命令,可以方便地计算出备选方案优先排序的概率。

```
.predict p if e(sample)
.sort caseid pref p
.list pref p grades edufit workexp boardexp if caseid = = 7, noobs
```

运行结果如图 4.8 所示。

pref	p	grades	edufit	workexp	boardexp
0	.00219336	C/D	yes	none	yes
0	.00430864	C/D	no	internship	yes
0	.00518238	A/B	no	none	no
0	.01794982	C/D	yes	one year	no
1	.04035975	C/D	yes	one year	yes
2	.02264408	A/B	yes	none	no
3	.26424745	A/B	yes	one year	no
4	.0322894	A/B	yes	none	yes
5	.15056249	A/B	yes	internship	no
6	.46026263	A/B	yes	one year	yes

图 4.8

很明显,备选方案被排在第一位的陈述排名和预测概率之间存在正相关关系,但这种关联并不完全。事实上,不会期望存在一个完全的关联,因为模型指定了一个(非退化的)概率分布在备选方案的可能排名上。这些对 10 个申请人集合的预测也可以用来对备选集合的子集进行预测。例如,假设只有图 4.8 中列出的最后三个申请人是可用的。根据多值排序 Logit 模型的参数估计,这些申请人中的最后一个被选中的概率等于 0.460/(0.032+0.151+0.460)=0.715。

该 Cmrologit 模型假设所有受访者使用相同的估值函数，即应用相同的决策权重，这实际上是假设受访者之间的 β 值为常数。为了探究这一假设，可以测试系数是否在不同的受访者群体之间有所不同。对于受访者的一个度量特征，如 firmsize，可以在估值权重中考虑一个趋势模型：

$$\beta_{ij} = \alpha_{i0} + \alpha_{i1} \text{firmsize}_j$$

可以检验 firmsize 变量的斜率 α_{i1} 为零。

.generate firmsize = employer

.cmrologit pref i.edufit i.grades i.workexp c.firmsize ♯ (1.edufit 1.grades 1.workexp

.2.workexp 1.boardexp) if job = = 1, nolog

运行结果如图 4.9 所示。

```
Rank-ordered logit choice model                  Number of obs      =         80
Case ID variable: caseid                         Number of cases    =          8

Ties adjustment: No ties in data                 Obs per case:
                                                              min =         10
                                                              avg =      10.00
                                                              max =         10

                                                 LR chi2(9)         =      57.84
Log likelihood = -66.49266                       Prob > chi2        =     0.0000
```

pref	Coefficient	Std. err.	z	P>|z|	[95% conf.	interval]
edufit						
yes	1.164	1.134	1.03	0.305	-1.059	3.387
grades						
A/B	6.658	2.402	2.77	0.006	1.951	11.365
workexp						
internship	2.347	1.908	1.23	0.219	-1.393	6.087
one year	2.783	1.794	1.55	0.121	-0.734	6.300
edufit#c.firmsize						
yes	-0.012	0.071	-0.17	0.867	-0.151	0.127
grades#c.firmsize						
A/B	-0.218	0.128	-1.71	0.088	-0.468	0.032
workexp#c.firmsize						
internship	-0.035	0.108	-0.33	0.743	-0.247	0.176
one year	0.008	0.113	0.07	0.945	-0.213	0.228
boardexp#c.firmsize						
yes	0.043	0.024	1.81	0.070	-0.004	0.089

图 4.9

.testparm c.firmsize ♯ (i.edufit i.grades i.workexp i.boardexp)

运行结果如图 4.10 所示。

```
( 1)  1.edufit#c.firmsize = 0
( 2)  1.grades#c.firmsize = 0
( 3)  1.workexp#c.firmsize = 0
( 4)  2.workexp#c.firmsize = 0
( 5)  1.boardexp#c.firmsize = 0

           chi2(  5) =    7.48
         Prob > chi2 =    0.1871
```

图 4.10

相互作用的 firmsize 变量的斜率共同为零的 Wald 检验没有提供会拒绝零假设的证据,也就是说,没有找到证据反对不同规模的公司对属性的恒定估值权重的假设。本例没有将 firmsize 作为预测变量。决策代理的特征在备选方案之间不会发生变化。这些特征对替代方案估值的叠加效应并不影响代理人对替代方案的排名和申请人的选择。因此,firmsize 变量的系数是未识别的。Cmrologit 模型实际上诊断了问题并从分析中去掉了 firmsize 变量。

4.4 多值排序 Probit 模型

cmroprobit 命令用于估计多值排序 Probit 模型。cmroprobit 允许两种类型的自变量:一是选项特定的变量,每个变量的值随选项的不同而不同;二是情况特定的变量,每个变量的值随情况的不同而不同。

对于 J 类选择模型的效用(潜变量)为 $\eta_{ij}=\boldsymbol{x}_{ij}\boldsymbol{\beta}+\boldsymbol{z}_i\boldsymbol{\alpha}_j+\xi_{ij}$,$j=1,\cdots,J$,$i=1,\cdots,n$,且 $\boldsymbol{\xi}_i'=(\xi_{i,1},\cdots,\xi_{i,j})\sim \text{MVN}(\boldsymbol{0},\boldsymbol{\Omega})$。假设第 i 个观察结果是,一个人按照其数字指标的顺序对备选方案进行排序,$y_i=(J,J-1,\cdots 1)$,因而,第一选择是最偏好的,最后一个选择是最不偏好的。这样可以得到效用之差:

$$\begin{aligned} v_{ik} &= \eta_{i,k+1}-\eta_{i,k} \\ &= (\boldsymbol{x}_{i,k+1}-\boldsymbol{x}_{i,k})\boldsymbol{\beta}+\boldsymbol{z}_i(\boldsymbol{\alpha}_{k+1}-\boldsymbol{\alpha}_k)+\xi_{i,k+1}-\xi_{ik} \\ &= \boldsymbol{\delta}_{ik}\boldsymbol{\beta}+\boldsymbol{z}_i\boldsymbol{\gamma}_k+\varepsilon_{ik} \end{aligned} \tag{4.5}$$

式中,$k=1,\cdots,J-1$,$\varepsilon_{ik}=(\varepsilon_{i1},\cdots,\varepsilon_{i,J-1})\sim \text{MVN}(\boldsymbol{0},\boldsymbol{\Sigma}_{(i)})$。记 $\lambda_{ik}=\boldsymbol{\delta}_{ik}\boldsymbol{\beta}+\boldsymbol{z}_j\boldsymbol{\gamma}_k$,则事件 i 的概率为:

$$\begin{aligned} \Pr(y_i) &= \Pr(v_{i1}\leqslant 0,\cdots,v_{i,J-1}\leqslant 0) \\ &= \Pr(\varepsilon_{i1}\leqslant -\lambda_{i1},\cdots,\varepsilon_{i,J-1}\leqslant -\lambda_{i,J-1}) \\ &= (2\pi)^{-(J-1)/2}\left|\boldsymbol{\Sigma}_{(i)}\right|^{-1/2}\int_{-\infty}^{-\lambda_{i1}}\cdots\int_{-\infty}^{-\lambda_{i,J-1}}\exp\left(-\frac{1}{2}\boldsymbol{z}'\Sigma_{(i)}^{-1}\boldsymbol{z}\right)\mathrm{d}z \end{aligned} \tag{4.6}$$

cmroprobit 命令的语法格式为:

cmroprobit depvar [indepvars] [if] [in] [weight] [, options]

菜单操作路径为:

Statistics>Choice models>Rank-ordered probit model

第 5 章 分类结果

5.1 多项 Logistic 回归

多元选择模型问题是最普遍的选择问题，决策者按照效用最大原则在多个可供选择的方案中进行选择。在多元离散选择模型中，应用最多的是 Logit 模型。

一般多元 Logit 选择模型分为两种：一是多项 Logit 选择模型，它研究的是选择某种方案的概率和决策者的特征变量之间的关系；二是条件 Logit 选择模型，它与多项 Logit 选择模型不同的是，它在研究选择某种方案的概率与决策者的特征变量之间的关系上增加了方案的特征变量。

如果只考虑个人特征因素的影响，即研究的是选择某种方案的概率和决策者的特征变量之间的关系，不考虑方案属性对选择结果的影响，可以构建模型为：

$$P_{ij}=P(Y_i=j)=\frac{e^{X_i\beta_j}}{\sum_{j=0}^{J}e^{X_i\beta_j}} \tag{5.1}$$

此模型为多项 Logit 选择模型，在特定的研究问题中，X 中未包含备选方案所具有的属性变量，所以 X 的下标不出现 j。而参数向量 β 对不同的选择方案(即不同的方程)是不同的，所以 β 的下标出现 j。

为了研究方便，进行标准化处理，令 $\boldsymbol{\beta}_0=0$。于是多项 Logit 选择模型变为：

$$P(Y_i=j)=\frac{e^{X_i\beta_j}}{1+\sum_{k=0}^{J}e^{X_i\beta_k}} \quad j=1,2,\cdots,J \tag{5.2}$$

$$P(Y_i=0)=\frac{1}{1+\sum_{k=0}^{J}e^{X_i\beta_k}} \tag{5.3}$$

当 $J=1$ 时，就是二元 Logit 模型。

对于第 i 个决策者，如果选择了第 j 个备选方案，令 $d_{ij}=1$；如果没有选择第 j 个备选方案，令 $d_{ij}=0$。同时，对于第 i 个决策者，在$(J+1)$个备选方案中，只能选择其中一个，即只能存在 1 个 $d_{ij}=1$。记为：

$$d_{ij}=\begin{cases}1 & \text{消费者 } i \text{ 选择 } j\\ 0 & \text{否则}\end{cases}$$

于是，可以写出对数似然函数：

$$\ln L = \sum_{i=1}^{n}\sum_{j=0}^{J} d_{ij} \ln P(Y_i = j) \tag{5.4}$$

其微分形式为：

$$\frac{\partial lnL}{\partial \beta_j} = \sum_i (d_{ij} - P_{ij})\boldsymbol{X}_i \quad j = 0,1,2,\cdots,J$$

$$\frac{\partial^2 lnL}{\partial \beta_j \partial \beta_l'} = -\sum_{i=1}^{n} P_{ij}(\mathbf{1}(j=l) - P_{il})\boldsymbol{X}_i \boldsymbol{X}_i' \tag{5.5}$$

式中，

$$\mathbf{1}(j=l) = \begin{cases} 1 & \text{如果 } j = l \\ 0 & \text{如果 } j \neq l \end{cases}$$

令式(5.5)等于0，即为对数似然函数最大化的一阶条件，利用牛顿迭代方法可以迅速得到方程的解，得到模型的参数估计量。

多项Logit选择模型估计的语法格式为：

mlogit depvar [indepvars] [if] [in] [weight] [, options]

菜单操作路径为：

Statistics>Categorical outcomes>Multinomial logistic regression

例5.1 多项Logit选择模型[①]

进入高中的学生在普通课程、职业课程和学术课程中进行课程选择，他们的选择可能会根据其写作分数和社会经济地位来决定。本例利用的数据集包含200名学生的变量。结果变量是prog，即程序类型。预测变量为社会经济地位(ses)三级分类变量和写作分数(write)连续变量。对相关变量进行描述性统计。

```
.use hsbdemo, clear
.tab prog ses, chi2
```

运行结果如图5.1所示。

type of program	ses low	middle	high	Total
general	16	20	9	45
academic	19	44	42	105
vocation	12	31	7	50
Total	47	95	58	200

Pearson chi2(4) = 16.6044 Pr = 0.002

图 5.1

① 本案例根据 https://data.princeton.edu 上的数据进行改编。

```
.table prog, statistic(mean write) statistic(sd write)
```

运行结果如图 5.2 所示。

	Mean	Standard deviation
type of program		
general	51.33333	9.397775
academic	56.25714	7.943343
vocation	46.76	9.318754
Total	52.775	9.478586

图 5.2

```
.mlogit prog i.ses write, base(2)
```

运行结果如图 5.3 所示。

```
Multinomial logistic regression                     Number of obs =    200
                                                    LR chi2(6)    =  48.23
                                                    Prob > chi2   = 0.0000
Log likelihood = -179.98173                         Pseudo R2     = 0.1182
```

prog	Coefficient	Std. err.	z	P>|z|	[95% conf. interval]	
general						
ses						
middle	-0.533	0.444	-1.20	0.229	-1.403	0.336
high	-1.163	0.514	-2.26	0.024	-2.171	-0.155
write	-0.058	0.021	-2.71	0.007	-0.100	-0.016
_cons	2.852	1.166	2.45	0.014	0.566	5.138
academic	(base outcome)					
vocation						
ses						
middle	0.291	0.476	0.61	0.541	-0.642	1.225
high	-0.983	0.596	-1.65	0.099	-2.150	0.185
write	-0.114	0.022	-5.11	0.000	-0.157	-0.070
_cons	5.218	1.164	4.48	0.000	2.938	7.499

图 5.3

在上面的估计结果输出中，log 似然(－179.98173)可以用于嵌套模型的比较，但这里不会展示一个比较模型的例子。p 值＜0.0001 的似然比卡方 48.23 告诉我们，该模型整体上比空模型(即没有预测因子的模型)拟合得更好。输出有两部分，标记为结果变量 prog 的类别，对应以下两个方程：

$$\ln\left(\frac{P(\text{prog}=\text{general})}{P(\text{prog}=\text{academic})}\right)=b_{10}+b_{11}(\text{ses}=2)+b_{12}(\text{ses}=3)+b_{13}\text{write}$$

$$\ln\left(\frac{P(\text{prog}=\text{vocation})}{P(\text{prog}=\text{academic})}\right)=b_{20}+b_{21}(\text{ses}=2)+b_{22}(\text{ses}=3)+b_{23}\text{write}$$

变量 write 增加一个单位，与学术程序相比，普通程序的相对对数概率减少 0.058。变量 write 的一个单位的增加与职业程序相对于学术程序的相对对数概率下降 0.114 相关。如果从最低水平的 ses（ses=1）到最高水平的 ses（ses=3），一般项目与学术项目的相对对数概率将减少 1.163。

选择一个结果类别的概率与选择基线类别的概率之比通常被称为相对风险(有时也被称为相对风险率)。通过上述线性方程得到的回归系数即为预测变量单位变化的相对风险。可以使用 mlogit 命令中的 rrr 选项来根据相对风险显示回归结果。

.mlogit, rrr

运行结果如图 5.4 所示。

Multinomial logistic regression　　Number of obs = **200**
LR chi2(6) = **48.23**
Prob > chi2 = **0.0000**
Log likelihood = **-179.98173**　　Pseudo R2 = **0.1182**

prog	RRR	Std. err.	z	P>|z|	[95% conf.	interval]
general						
ses						
middle	**0.587**	**0.260**	**-1.20**	**0.229**	**0.246**	**1.400**
high	**0.313**	**0.161**	**-2.26**	**0.024**	**0.114**	**0.856**
write	**0.944**	**0.020**	**-2.71**	**0.007**	**0.905**	**0.984**
_cons	**17.326**	**20.209**	**2.45**	**0.014**	**1.761**	**170.437**
academic	(base outcome)					
vocation						
ses						
middle	**1.338**	**0.638**	**0.61**	**0.541**	**0.526**	**3.404**
high	**0.374**	**0.223**	**-1.65**	**0.099**	**0.116**	**1.203**
write	**0.893**	**0.020**	**-5.11**	**0.000**	**0.855**	**0.932**
_cons	**184.602**	**214.793**	**4.48**	**0.000**	**18.872**	**1805.719**

Note: **_cons** estimates baseline relative risk for each outcome.

图 5.4

在普通程序与学术程序比较中，变量 write 增加一个单位的相对风险是 0.944（exp(−0.0579284)，来自上面第一个 mlogit 命令的输出），从 ses=1 到 ses=3 的相对风险为 0.313。也就是说，社会经济地位高的受试者继续参加普通程序的预期风险较低。

可以使用 test 命令测试 ses 的整体效果。可以看到，ses 的整体影响在统计意义上是显著的。

```
.test 2.ses 3.ses
```

运行结果如图 5.5 所示。

```
( 1)  [general]2.ses = 0
( 2)  [academic]2o.ses = 0
( 3)  [vocation]2.ses = 0
( 4)  [general]3.ses = 0
( 5)  [academic]3o.ses = 0
( 6)  [vocation]3.ses = 0
      Constraint 2 dropped
      Constraint 5 dropped

          chi2(  4) =   10.82
        Prob > chi2 =    0.0287
```

图 5.5

更具体地说，还可以测试 3.ses 的效果。ses 在预测普通程序与学术程序方面的效果等于 3.ses 预测职业程序和学术程序的效果。再次使用 test 命令。测试表明，这些影响在统计意义上彼此没有差异。

```
.test [general]3.ses = [vocation]3.ses
```

运行结果如图 5.6 所示。

```
( 1)  [general]3.ses - [vocation]3.ses = 0

          chi2(  1) =    0.08
        Prob > chi2 =    0.7811
```

图 5.6

还可以使用预测的概率来帮助理解模型。可以使用 margins 命令计算预测的概率。下面，使用 margins 命令计算在 ses 的每个级别上选择每个程序类型的预测概率，以它们的平均值保存模型中的所有其他变量。由于有三种可能的结果，将需要使用 margins 命令三次，每次得到一个结果值。

```
.margins ses, atmeans predict(outcome(1))
```

运行结果如图 5.7 所示。

```
.margins ses, atmeans predict(outcome(2))
```

运行结果如图 5.8 所示。

```
Adjusted predictions                                Number of obs = 200
Model VCE: OIM

Expression: Pr(prog==general), predict(outcome(1))
At: 1.ses =   .235 (mean)
    2.ses =   .475 (mean)
    3.ses =    .29 (mean)
    write = 52.775 (mean)
```

	Margin	Delta-method std. err.	z	P>|z|	[95% conf.	interval]
ses						
low	0.358	0.073	4.93	0.000	0.216	0.501
middle	0.228	0.045	5.06	0.000	0.140	0.317
high	0.178	0.054	3.30	0.001	0.073	0.284

图 5.7

```
Adjusted predictions                                Number of obs = 200
Model VCE: OIM

Expression: Pr(prog==academic), predict(outcome(2))
At: 1.ses =   .235 (mean)
    2.ses =   .475 (mean)
    3.ses =    .29 (mean)
    write = 52.775 (mean)
```

	Margin	Delta-method std. err.	z	P>|z|	[95% conf.	interval]
ses						
low	0.440	0.078	5.64	0.000	0.287	0.593
middle	0.478	0.055	8.65	0.000	0.369	0.586
high	0.701	0.066	10.57	0.000	0.571	0.831

图 5.8

.margins ses, atmeans predict(outcome(3))

运行结果如图 5.9 所示。

可以使用 marginsplot 命令绘制每一类 prog 的 ses 预测概率。由 marginsplot 创建的绘图基于上次运行的 margins 命令。此外，可以使用 graph combine 命令将三个边距图合并到一个图中，以方便进行比较。

.margins ses, atmeans predict(outcome(1))

.marginsplot, name(general)

```
Adjusted predictions                                    Number of obs = 200
Model VCE: OIM

Expression: Pr(prog==vocation), predict(outcome(3))
At: 1.ses =    .235 (mean)
    2.ses =    .475 (mean)
    3.ses =     .29 (mean)
    write = 52.775 (mean)

-------------------------------------------------------------------------------
             |            Delta-method
             |     Margin   std. err.      z    P>|z|     [95% conf. interval]
-------------+-----------------------------------------------------------------
         ses |
         low |      0.202      0.060     3.37   0.001        0.085       0.320
      middle |      0.294      0.050     5.84   0.000        0.195       0.393
        high |      0.121      0.046     2.60   0.009        0.030       0.212
-------------------------------------------------------------------------------
```

图 5.9

```
.margins ses, atmeans predict(outcome(2))
.marginsplot, name(academic)
.margins ses, atmeans predict(outcome(3))
.marginsplot, name(vocational)
.graph combine general academic vocational, ycommon
```

运行结果如图 5.10 所示。

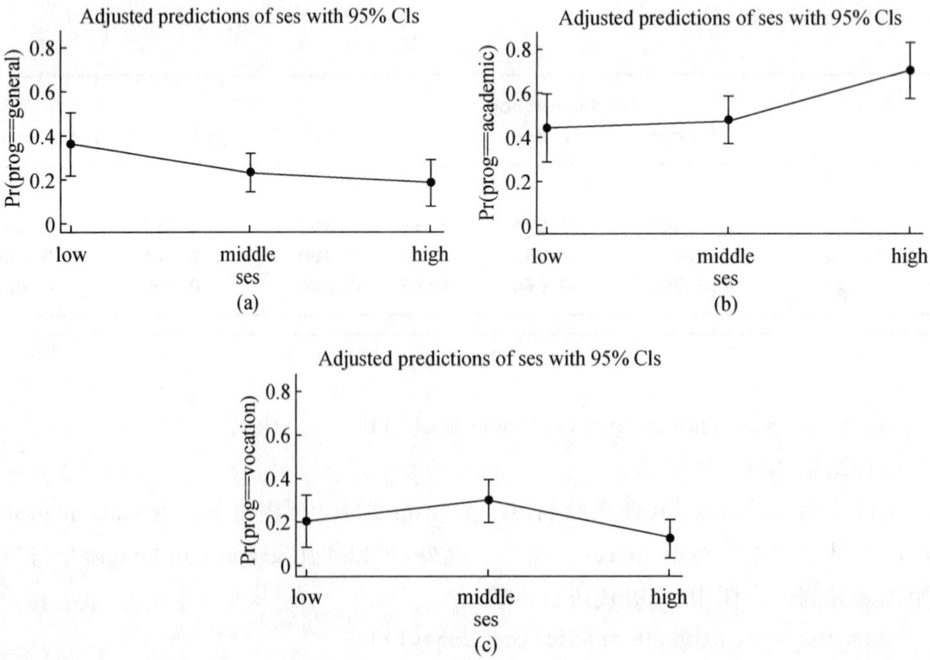

图 5.10

使用预测概率来理解模型的另一种方法是，查看连续预测变量 write 的不同值的平均预测概率，在不同等级的 ses 水平之间取平均值。

```
.margins, at(write = (30(10) 70)) predict(outcome(1)) vsquish
```

运行结果如图 5.11 所示。

```
Predictive margins                                  Number of obs = 200
Model VCE: OIM

Expression: Pr(prog==general), predict(outcome(1))
1._at: write = 30
2._at: write = 40
3._at: write = 50
4._at: write = 60
5._at: write = 70
```

	Margin	Delta-method std. err.	z	P>|z|	[95% conf.	interval]
_at						
1	0.213	0.077	2.75	0.006	0.061	0.365
2	0.257	0.053	4.85	0.000	0.153	0.361
3	0.254	0.034	7.56	0.000	0.188	0.320
4	0.206	0.037	5.54	0.000	0.133	0.279
5	0.142	0.048	2.95	0.003	0.048	0.237

图 5.11

```
.margins, at(write = (30(10) 70)) predict(outcome(2)) vsquish
```

运行结果如图 5.12 所示。

```
Predictive margins                                  Number of obs = 200
Model VCE: OIM

Expression: Pr(prog==academic), predict(outcome(2))
1._at: write = 30
2._at: write = 40
3._at: write = 50
4._at: write = 60
5._at: write = 70
```

	Margin	Delta-method std. err.	z	P>|z|	[95% conf.	interval]
_at						
1	0.135	0.053	2.56	0.010	0.032	0.238
2	0.281	0.055	5.08	0.000	0.172	0.389
3	0.477	0.040	12.01	0.000	0.399	0.555
4	0.668	0.043	15.37	0.000	0.583	0.753
5	0.808	0.055	14.80	0.000	0.701	0.914

图 5.12

```
.margins, at(write = (30(10) 70)) predict(outcome(3)) vsquish
```

运行结果如图 5.13 所示。

```
Predictive margins                                      Number of obs = 200
Model VCE: OIM

Expression: Pr(prog==vocation), predict(outcome(3))
1._at: write = 30
2._at: write = 40
3._at: write = 50
4._at: write = 60
5._at: write = 70

------------------------------------------------------------------------------
             |            Delta-method
             |     Margin   std. err.      z    P>|z|     [95% conf. interval]
-------------+----------------------------------------------------------------
         _at |
          1  |      0.652      0.094    6.91   0.000        0.467       0.837
          2  |      0.462      0.061    7.52   0.000        0.342       0.583
          3  |      0.268      0.034    7.83   0.000        0.201       0.336
          4  |      0.126      0.030    4.18   0.000        0.067       0.185
          5  |      0.050      0.022    2.31   0.021        0.008       0.093
------------------------------------------------------------------------------
```

图 5.13

下面根据结果变量的不同等级的 ses 水平，绘制预测概率与写作分数的关系图。（见图 5.14）

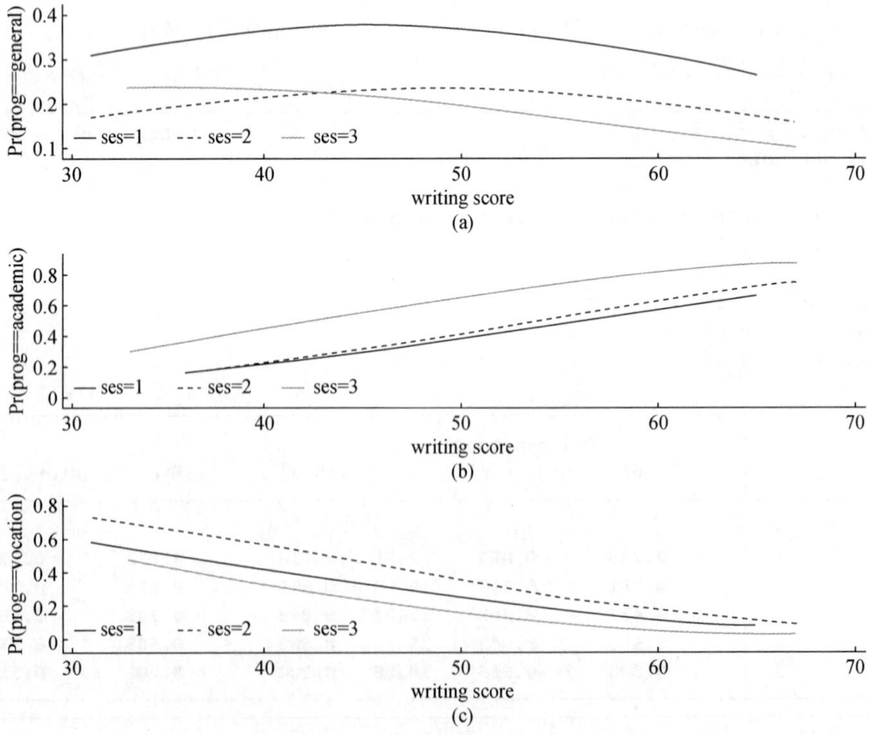

图 5.14

5.2 多项 Probit 回归

多项 Probit(MNP)模型主要是指结果没有自然顺序的分类因变量模型,因变量的实际值是不相关的,误差项假定服从独立、标准正态分布。

多项 Probit 模型通常使用潜变量框架进行表述。对于第 j 个潜在变量的选项, $j=1,\cdots,J$ 。

$$\eta_{ij}=\boldsymbol{z}_i\boldsymbol{\alpha}_j+\xi_{ij} \tag{5.6}$$

其中,$1\times q$ 阶行向量 $\boldsymbol{z}_i$ 包含第 i 个决策者观察到的自变量。与 $\boldsymbol{z}_i$ 对应的是回归系数 $\boldsymbol{\alpha}_j$ 。$\xi_{i1},\cdots,\xi_{iJ}$ 是独立同分布的正态分布随机扰动项。决策者在不同的政策之间进行选择,选择方案 k,使得对于 $m\neq k$,满足 $\eta_{ik}\geqslant\eta_{im}$ 。

假定选择方案 k,则潜变量 η_{ik} 和其余 $J-1$ 个潜变量之间的差分为:

$$\begin{aligned} v_{ijk}&=\eta_{ij}-\eta_{ik}=\boldsymbol{z}_i(\boldsymbol{\alpha}_j-\boldsymbol{\alpha}_k)+\xi_{ij}-\xi_{ik}\\ &=\boldsymbol{z}_i\gamma_{j'}+\varepsilon_{ij'} \end{aligned} \tag{5.7}$$

其中,对于 $j'=1,\cdots,J-1$,如果 $j<k$,有 $j'=j$,如果 $j>k$,有 $j'=j-1$, $\mathrm{Var}(\varepsilon_{ij'})=\mathrm{Var}(\xi_{ij}-\xi_{ik})=2$,对于 $j'\neq l'$,$\mathrm{cov}(\varepsilon_{ij'},\varepsilon_{il'})=1$。方案 k 被选择的概率为:

$$\begin{aligned} \Pr(i\ \text{chooses}\ k)&=\Pr(v_{i1k}\leqslant 0,\cdots,v_{i,J-1,k}\leqslant 0)\\ &=\Pr(\varepsilon_{i1}\leqslant -\boldsymbol{z}_i\gamma_1,\cdots,\varepsilon_{i,J-1}\leqslant -\boldsymbol{z}_i\gamma_{J-1}) \end{aligned} \tag{5.8}$$

多项 Probit 模型估计的语法格式为:

```
mprobit depvar [indepvars] [if] [in] [,options]
```

菜单操作路径为:

Statistics>Categorical outcomes>Multinomial probit regression

例 5.2 多项 Probit 模型[①]

本案例中的数据是关于美国 616 名心理抑郁患者的健康报销类型的数据。病人可能有一个赔偿(按服务收费)计划或一个预付费计划,如 HMO,也可能没有保险。相关个人统计变量包括年龄、性别、种族和地点。赔偿保险(indemnity insurance)是最受欢迎的选择,所以 mprobit 将默认选择它作为基本结果。

```
.use sysdsn1, clear
.mprobit insure age male nonwhite i.site
```

运行结果如图 5.15 所示。

mprobit 的似然函数是在假设所有决策单元都面对同一个选择集的前提下推导出来的,该选择集是数据集中观察到的所有结果的并集。如果模型不是这样,那么另一种选择是使用 cmmprobit 命令,该命令不需要这种假设。

① 本案例根据 Stata 帮助手册 r.pdf 中的对应案例改编。

```
Multinomial probit regression                   Number of obs =     615
                                                Wald chi2(10) =   40.18
Log likelihood = -534.52833                     Prob > chi2   =  0.0000
```

insure	Coefficient	Std. err.	z	P>|z|	[95% conf.	interval]
Indemnity	(base outcome)					
Prepaid						
age	-0.010	0.005	-1.87	0.061	-0.020	0.000
male	0.477	0.172	2.78	0.005	0.141	0.814
nonwhite	0.825	0.198	4.17	0.000	0.437	1.212
site						
2	0.097	0.179	0.54	0.587	-0.254	0.449
3	-0.496	0.190	-2.60	0.009	-0.869	-0.123
_cons	0.223	0.279	0.80	0.424	-0.324	0.770
Uninsure						
age	-0.005	0.008	-0.67	0.500	-0.020	0.010
male	0.333	0.243	1.37	0.171	-0.144	0.810
nonwhite	0.249	0.277	0.90	0.369	-0.294	0.791
site						
2	-0.690	0.280	-2.46	0.014	-1.240	-0.140
3	-0.179	0.248	-0.72	0.471	-0.665	0.307
_cons	-0.986	0.389	-2.53	0.011	-1.748	-0.223

图 5.15

5.3 多项 Probit 选择模型

cmmprobit 命令同样可以用来拟合多项 Probit 选择模型，但与 mprobit 命令不同的是，cmmprobit 能够在多元正态分布的情况下估计随机扰动项，既可以是异方差的，也可以是在不同方案之间存在相关性。

在多项 Probit 模型中，有一组 J 个备选无序方案，决策者选择其中 1 个方案。通过对与方案相关的和与个案相关的协变量建立回归模型，对这些结果变量建模。

$$\eta_{ij} = \boldsymbol{x}_{ij}\boldsymbol{\beta} + \boldsymbol{z}_i\boldsymbol{\alpha}_j + \xi_{ij} \tag{5.9}$$

其中，i 表示个案，j 表示选项，$\boldsymbol{x}_{ij}$ 是 $1\times p$ 阶与方案选择相关的变量，$\boldsymbol{\beta}$ 是 $p\times 1$ 阶参数向量，$\boldsymbol{z}_i$ 是 $1\times q$ 阶与个案相关的变量，$\boldsymbol{\alpha}_j$ 是 $q\times 1$ 阶与第 j 个方案相关的参数，$\xi_{ij}=(\xi_{i1},\cdots,\xi_{iJ})$ 是多元正态分布，其均值为 0，方差—协方差矩阵为 $\boldsymbol{\Omega}$。

第 i 个决策者选择对其来说 η_{ij} 最高的方案。

因为 cmmprobit 可以估计 ξ_{ij} 为更为一般的结构，允许选择一个选项而不是另一个选项的概率取决于剩余的选项。例如，考虑在两个城市之间交通方式的选择，包括航空、火车、长途汽车或自驾汽车，并将其作为旅行方式成本、旅行时间（可选特定变量）和个人收入的函数。选择乘飞机而不是坐长途汽车的概率可能与选择坐火车有关，因为长途汽车和火车都是地面公共交通工具。也就是说，选择乘飞机出行的概率为$\Pr(\eta_{飞机}>\eta_{火车},\eta_{飞机}>\eta_{长途汽车},\eta_{飞机}>\eta_{自驾})$，而且两个事件 $\eta_{飞机}>\eta_{长途汽车}$ 和 $\eta_{飞机}>\eta_{火车}$ 可能是相关的。

并不是所有的回归系数 $\boldsymbol{\alpha}_j$ 的 J 的集合都可识别，方差—协方差矩阵 $\boldsymbol{\Omega}$ 的所有 $J(J+1)/2$ 个元素也不是同时可以识别的。模型需要标准化，因为位置（级别）和效用的尺度是不相关的。为了标准化位置参数，选择一个备选方案 k，并对 k 方案和其余 $J-1$ 个方案进行差分，得到：

$$\begin{aligned} v_{ijk} &= \eta_{ij} - \eta_{ik} = (\boldsymbol{x}_{ij} - \boldsymbol{x}_{ik})\boldsymbol{\beta} + \boldsymbol{z}_i(\boldsymbol{\alpha}_j - \boldsymbol{\alpha}_k) + \xi_{ij} - \xi_{ik} \\ &= \boldsymbol{\delta}_{ij'}\boldsymbol{\beta} + \boldsymbol{z}_i\boldsymbol{\gamma}_{j'} + \varepsilon_{ij'} = \lambda_{ij'} + \varepsilon_{ij'} \end{aligned} \tag{5.10}$$

现在可以得到 $\boldsymbol{\varepsilon}_i'=(\varepsilon_{i1},\cdots,\varepsilon_{i,J-1})$ 的 $(J-1)\times(J-1)$ 维协方差矩阵 $\boldsymbol{\Sigma}_{(k)}$。第 k 个方案是利用 cmmprobit 中的 basealternative()。则决策者 i 选择方案 k 的概率为：

$$\begin{aligned} \Pr(i \text{ chooses } k) &= \Pr(v_{i1k} \leqslant 0,\cdots,v_{i,J-1,k} \leqslant 0) \\ &= \Pr(\varepsilon_{i1} \leqslant -\lambda_{i1},\cdots,\varepsilon_{i,J-1} \leqslant -\lambda_{i,J-1}) \end{aligned} \tag{5.11}$$

为了标准化尺度参数，$\boldsymbol{\Sigma}_{(k)}$ 的其中一个对角矩阵必须固定为常数。在 cmmprobit 命令中，这是由 scalealternative() 确定的备选方案的误差方差。因而，最多只有 $J(J-1)/2-1$ 个可识别的方差—协方差参数。

多项 Probit 选择模型估计的语法格式为：

```
cmmprobit depvar [indepvars] [if] [in] [weight] [,options]
```

菜单操作路径为：

Statistics>Choice models>Multinomial probit model

例 5.3 多项 Probit 选择模型①

Greene(2018)②利用交通方式选择的数据来说明悉尼和墨尔本之间各种离散选择模型的估计参数。数据包含 210 个个人选择的出行方式信息。航空、火车、长途汽车、自驾汽车这 4 种选择的指数分别为 1、2、3、4。

一个可选的特定变量是 travelcost，它是一种广义旅行成本的衡量方法，等于车辆成本和类似工资的衡量方法乘以旅行时间的总和。第二个可选的特定变量是 termtime，对于自驾汽车来说，它是零。还有一个可选的特定变量是 income，它是一个个案相关的变量。

```
.use travel, clear
.list id mode choice travelcost termtime income in 1/12, sepby(id)
```

运行结果如图 5.16 所示。

① 本例数据来自于格林(2018)。

② Greene, W. H. *Econometric Analysis*(8th ed.). New York: Pearson, 2018.

	id	mode	choice	travel~t	termtime	income
1.	1	Air	0	70	69	35
2.	1	Train	0	71	34	35
3.	1	Bus	0	70	35	35
4.	1	Car	1	30	0	35
5.	2	Air	0	68	64	30
6.	2	Train	0	84	44	30
7.	2	Bus	0	85	53	30
8.	2	Car	1	50	0	30
9.	3	Air	0	129	69	40
10.	3	Train	0	195	34	40
11.	3	Bus	0	149	35	40
12.	3	Car	1	101	0	40

图 5.16

然后利用 cmset 命令设定数据类型。

```
.cmset id mode
.cmtab, choice(choice)
```

运行结果如图 5.17 所示。

Tabulation of chosen alternatives (choice = 1)

Travel mode alternatives	Freq.	Percent	Cum.
Air	58	27.62	27.62
Train	63	30.00	57.62
Bus	30	14.29	71.90
Car	59	28.10	100.00
Total	210	100.00	

图 5.17

交通方式选择的模型为：

$$\eta_{ij}=\beta_1 \text{travelcost}_{ij}+\beta_2 \text{termtime}_{ij}+\alpha_{1j}\text{income}_i+\alpha_{0j}+\xi_{ij}$$

备选方案可分为空中旅行和地面旅行两类。考虑到这一点，同时因为 air 和 train 是 mode 变量中的第一个和第二个备选项，所以它们分别是 basealternative() 和 scale-alternative() 的默认值。

运行结果如图 5.18 所示。

```
.cmmprobit choice travelcost termtime, casevars(income)
```

```
Multinomial probit choice model                 Number of obs      =       840
Case ID variable: id                            Number of cases    =       210

Alternatives variable: mode                     Alts per case: min =         4
                                                               avg =       4.0
                                                               max =         4

Integration sequence:      Hammersley
Integration points:               600              Wald chi2(5)    =     32.16
Log simulated-likelihood = -190.09322              Prob > chi2     =    0.0000
```

choice	Coefficient	Std. err.	z	P>|z|	[95% conf.	interval]
mode						
travelcost	-0.010	0.003	-3.51	0.000	-0.015	-0.004
termtime	-0.038	0.009	-4.02	0.000	-0.056	-0.019
Air	(base alternative)					
Train						
income	-0.029	0.009	-3.27	0.001	-0.047	-0.012
_cons	0.562	0.395	1.42	0.154	-0.211	1.335
Bus						
income	-0.013	0.008	-1.61	0.108	-0.028	0.003
_cons	-0.057	0.479	-0.12	0.905	-0.996	0.881
Car						
income	-0.005	0.008	-0.63	0.526	-0.020	0.010
_cons	-1.833	0.817	-2.24	0.025	-3.435	-0.231
/lnl2_2	-0.549	0.389	-1.41	0.158	-1.311	0.213
/lnl3_3	-0.602	0.336	-1.79	0.073	-1.259	0.056
/l2_1	1.133	0.213	5.33	0.000	0.716	1.549
/l3_1	0.972	0.235	4.13	0.000	0.511	1.433
/l3_2	0.520	0.285	1.82	0.068	-0.039	1.079

```
(mode=Air is the alternative normalizing location)
(mode=Train is the alternative normalizing scale)
```

图 5.18

在默认情况下，我们使用了差分协方差参数化，因而模型的协方差矩阵为3×3维。为了使协方差矩阵保持正定，cmmprobit使用了平方根变换，优化了Cholesky因子的方差—协方差。为了使Cholesky估计的对角线元素保持正定，cmmprobit使用了对数变换。

标记为/lnl2_2和/lnl3_3的是Cholesky矩阵的对角元素，标记为/l2_1，/l3_1和/l3_2的是Cholesky矩阵的非主对角元素，分别对应(2,1)(3,1)和(3,2)。

差分协方差参数化变换后的参数难以解释，可以使用estat命令查看未转换的协方差和相关性。

```
.estat covariance
```

运行结果如图5.19所示。

	Train	Bus	Car
Train	2		
Bus	1.601736	1.616288	
Car	1.374374	1.401054	1.515069

Note: Covariances are for alternatives differenced with Air.

图 5.19

进一步给出相关系数矩阵。

```
.estat correlation
```

运行结果如图5.20所示。

	Train	Bus	Car
Train	1.0000		
Bus	0.8909	1.0000	
Car	0.7895	0.8953	1.0000

Note: Correlations are for alternatives differenced with Air.

图 5.20

火车、长途汽车或自驾汽车的选择与航空的选择之间两两相关性都很大。这说明，在控制了travelcost和termtime后，火车、长途汽车和自驾汽车的效用与航空的效用是相似的。为了更仔细地研究火车、长途汽车和自驾汽车在效用方面的相对差异，我们可以把它们依次作为基本选择，并研究这些模型。

可以通过factor(1)选项来降低协方差参数估计的数量。

```
.cmmprobit choice travelcost termtime, casevars(income) factor(1)
```

运行结果如图5.21所示。

```
Multinomial probit choice model                 Number of obs       =        840
Case ID variable: id                            Number of cases     =        210

Alternatives variable: mode                     Alts per case: min =          4
                                                               avg =        4.0
                                                               max =          4

Integration sequence:      Hammersley
Integration points:               600              Wald chi2(5)    =     107.88
Log simulated-likelihood = -196.85472              Prob > chi2     =     0.0000

------------------------------------------------------------------------------
      choice | Coefficient  Std. err.      z    P>|z|     [95% conf. interval]
-------------+----------------------------------------------------------------
mode         |
  travelcost |     -0.009      0.004    -2.58   0.010       -0.016     -0.002
    termtime |     -0.059      0.006    -9.19   0.000       -0.072     -0.047
-------------+----------------------------------------------------------------
Air          |  (base alternative)
-------------+----------------------------------------------------------------
Train        |
      income |     -0.037      0.010    -3.80   0.000       -0.057     -0.018
       _cons |      0.109      0.395     0.28   0.782       -0.665      0.884
-------------+----------------------------------------------------------------
Bus          |
      income |     -0.016      0.011    -1.41   0.157       -0.038      0.006
       _cons |     -1.082      0.468    -2.31   0.021       -1.999     -0.165
-------------+----------------------------------------------------------------
Car          |
      income |      0.004      0.009     0.46   0.645       -0.014      0.022
       _cons |     -3.766      0.554    -6.80   0.000       -4.852     -2.680
-------------+----------------------------------------------------------------
       /c1_2 |      1.183      0.306     3.86   0.000        0.583      1.783
       /c1_3 |      1.228      0.340     3.61   0.000        0.561      1.895
------------------------------------------------------------------------------
(mode=Air is the alternative normalizing location)
(mode=Train is the alternative normalizing scale)
```

图 5.21

标记为/c1_2 和/c1_3 的系数是因子载荷,这些因子载荷生成了不同的协方差矩阵和相关系数。

```
.estat covariance
```

运行结果如图 5.22 所示。

```
.estat correlation
```

运行结果如图 5.23 所示。

	Train	Bus	Car
Train	2		
Bus	1.182696	2.398771	
Car	1.228152	1.452531	2.508358

Note: Covariances are for alternatives differenced with Air.

图 5.22

	Train	Bus	Car
Train	1.0000		
Bus	0.5400	1.0000	
Car	0.5483	0.5922	1.0000

Note: Correlations are for alternatives differenced with Air.

图 5.23

5.4 混合 Logit 选择模型

混合 Logit 选择模型最常用来对一个个体从几个无序备选方案中选择的概率进行建模，也被称为混合多项 Logit 选择模型、随机参数 Logit 选择模型等。

混合 Logit 选择模型属于离散选择模型，体现决策者如何在有限的选项中进行选择。混合 Logit 选择模型可以用来合并不同个体的属性，称为个案相关的变量，如收入、教育程度和年龄。

该模型还可以纳入被观察到的属性，这些属性因选项可变，或因选项和个体而异，称为特定方案变量。渔场的湖的大小是特定方案协变量的一个例子，它只随备选方案而变化。到任何给定渔场的旅行距离是随备选方案和个体而变化的特定方案协变量的一个例子。

在混合 Logit 选择模型中，特定方案变量的系数可以被视为固定的或随机的。指定随机系数可以为方案之间的相关性建模，从而放松多项 Logit 选择模型强加的 IIA 属性。在这个意义上，cmmixlogit 拟合的混合 Logit 选择模型比 mlogit、clogit 和 cm-clogit 拟合的模型更灵活。

对于一个混合 Logit 选择模型，个体 i 可选择不同备选方案 a，$a=1,2,\cdots,A$，该模型可以表示为：

$$U_{ia}=\boldsymbol{x}_{ia}\boldsymbol{\beta}_i+\boldsymbol{w}_{ia}\boldsymbol{\alpha}+\boldsymbol{z}_i\boldsymbol{\delta}_a+\varepsilon_{ia} \tag{5.12}$$

$\boldsymbol{\beta}_i$ 是随个体变化而变化的随机系数，$\boldsymbol{x}_{ia}$ 是由特定方案变量组成的向量。$\boldsymbol{\alpha}$ 是 $\boldsymbol{w}_{ia}$

的系数，是与备选方案相关的变量。$\boldsymbol{\delta}_a$ 是 z_i 的系数，是与具体个案相关的变量。ε_{ia} 是服从 I 类极值分布的随机误差项。

混合 Logit 选择模型估计的语法格式为：

```
>cmmprobit depvar [indepvars] [if] [in] [weight] [,options]
```

菜单操作路径为：

Statistics>Choice models>Mixed logit model

例 5.4　固定和随机系数的混合 Logit 选择模型①

下面以 Stata 软件自带数据集 Inschoice.dta 为例，该数据集记录了 250 个保险计划及其选择，每个个体从 5 个备选方案中选择一个保险计划，记录在 insurance 变量中。二元变量 choice 记录了选择的方案，choice 为 1 表示选择的选项，否则为 0。

```
.use inschoice, clear
.list in 1/10, sepby(id) abbreviate(10)
```

运行结果如图 5.24 所示。

	id	premium	deductible	income	insurance	choice
1.	1	2.87	1.70	5.74	Health	1
2.	1	3.13	2.14	5.74	HCorp	0
3.	1	2.03	2.26	5.74	SickInc	0
4.	1	1.65	2.94	5.74	MGroup	0
5.	1	0.87	3.56	5.74	MoonHealth	0
6.	2	3.52	1.24	2.89	Health	0
7.	2	3.23	1.52	2.89	HCorp	0
8.	2	2.81	2.31	2.89	SickInc	0
9.	2	1.04	2.58	2.89	MGroup	1
10.	2	0.93	3.17	2.89	MoonHealth	0

图　5.24

保险费(premium)和免赔额(deductible)因备选方案而异，因此是备选方案特定的变量。在这个例子中，它们也因个体而异。收入(income)仅因个体而异，因此是具体情况的变量。

希望估计健康保险保费、保险免赔额和个人收入对健康保险计划选择的影响。假设对免赔额的偏好因人而异，但对保费的偏好是恒定的。

```
.cmset id insurance
.cmmixlogit choice premium, random(deductible)
```

运行结果如图 5.25 所示。

① 本案例根据 Stata 帮助手册 cm.pdf 中的相应案例进行改编。

```
Mixed logit choice model                     Number of obs      =      1,250
Case ID variable: id                         Number of cases    =        250

Alternatives variable: insurance             Alts per case: min =          5
                                                            avg =        5.0
                                                            max =          5

Integration sequence:      Hammersley
Integration points:               567           Wald chi2(2)    =      99.32
Log simulated-likelihood = -295.04639           Prob > chi2     =     0.0000

------------------------------------------------------------------------------
      choice | Coefficient  Std. err.      z    P>|z|     [95% conf. interval]
-------------+----------------------------------------------------------------
insurance    |
     premium |     -2.672      0.270    -9.91   0.000       -3.200      -2.144
  deductible |     -1.110      0.337    -3.29   0.001       -1.771      -0.449
-------------+----------------------------------------------------------------
/Normal      |
 sd(deductible)|    0.889      0.364                         0.398       1.984
-------------+----------------------------------------------------------------
Health       |
       _cons |      0.521      0.298     1.75   0.080       -0.063       1.105
-------------+----------------------------------------------------------------
HCorp        |  (base alternative)
-------------+----------------------------------------------------------------
SickInc      |
       _cons |     -0.843      0.291    -2.90   0.004       -1.413      -0.272
-------------+----------------------------------------------------------------
MGroup       |
       _cons |     -2.107      0.444    -4.75   0.000       -2.977      -1.237
-------------+----------------------------------------------------------------
MoonHealth   |
       _cons |     -3.361      0.680    -4.95   0.000       -4.693      -2.029
------------------------------------------------------------------------------
LR test vs. fixed parameters: chibar2(01) =      2.99  Prob >= chibar2 = 0.0420
```

图　5.25

由图 5.25 可见，premium 的估计系数为－2.672，因而，一个保险计划保费的上升降低了其被选择的概率。deductible 正态分布系数的估计均值为－1.110。这些随机系数的估计标准差为 0.889，表明在计划的可扣除额的影响方面，人口中的个体存在异质性。

图 5.25 表格尾部的似然比（LR）检验显示了对一个只有固定系数的模型的检验结果，并表明可以拒绝零假设，即 deductible 的系数是固定的。

cmmixlogit 命令使用蒙特卡洛积分计算似然值。

```
.cmmixlogit choice premium, random(deductible) intpoints(1000)
```

运行结果如图 5.26 所示。

```
Mixed logit choice model                    Number of obs      =      1,250
Case ID variable: id                        Number of cases    =        250

Alternatives variable: insurance            Alts per case: min =          5
                                                           avg =        5.0
                                                           max =          5

Integration sequence:      Hammersley
Integration points:              1000         Wald chi2(2)     =      99.30
Log simulated-likelihood = -295.04713         Prob > chi2      =     0.0000

----------------------------------------------------------------------------
         choice | Coefficient  Std. err.      z    P>|z|     [95% conf. interval]
----------------+-----------------------------------------------------------
insurance       |
        premium |    -2.672      0.270    -9.91   0.000     -3.201     -2.144
     deductible |    -1.110      0.337    -3.29   0.001     -1.771     -0.449
----------------+-----------------------------------------------------------
/Normal         |
 sd(deductible) |     0.889      0.364                       0.398      1.985
----------------+-----------------------------------------------------------
Health          |
          _cons |     0.521      0.298     1.75   0.080     -0.063      1.105
----------------+-----------------------------------------------------------
HCorp           |  (base alternative)
----------------+-----------------------------------------------------------
SickInc         |
          _cons |    -0.843      0.291    -2.90   0.004     -1.413     -0.272
----------------+-----------------------------------------------------------
MGroup          |
          _cons |    -2.107      0.444    -4.75   0.000     -2.977     -1.237
----------------+-----------------------------------------------------------
MoonHealth      |
          _cons |    -3.361      0.680    -4.95   0.000     -4.693     -2.029
----------------------------------------------------------------------------
LR test vs. fixed parameters: chibar2(01) =     2.99  Prob >= chibar2 = 0.0420
```

图 5.26

可以利用 margins 命令估计选择每种保险计划的比率。

.margins

运行结果如图 5.27 所示。

从图 5.27 可以看出，大约有 25.7%的比率会选择 HCorp 保险计划。假设 HCorp 保险计划将保费提高 10%，则人们选择每种保险计划的情况会发生什么变化？

.margins, at(premium = generate(premium * 1.10)) alternative(HCorp)

运行结果如图 5.28 所示。

可以看出，如果 HCorp 保费提升 10%，则选择该保险的比率会下降到 17.5%。

继续上面的例子，并设保费的偏好也是变化的，这时可以估计 premium 和 deductible 的随机系数，同时允许随机系数具有相关性，并服从多元正态分布。

.cmmixlogit choice, random(deductible premium, correlated)

```
Predictive margins                                    Number of obs = 1,250
Model VCE: OIM

Expression: Pr(insurance), predict()
```

	Margin	Delta-method std. err.	z	P>|z|	[95% conf.	interval]
_outcome						
Health	0.204	0.022	9.09	0.000	0.160	0.248
HCorp	0.257	0.024	10.69	0.000	0.210	0.305
SickInc	0.220	0.022	9.83	0.000	0.176	0.263
MGroup	0.187	0.022	8.59	0.000	0.145	0.230
MoonHealth	0.132	0.019	6.85	0.000	0.094	0.169

图　5.27

```
Predictive margins                                    Number of obs = 1,250
Model VCE: OIM

Expression:  Pr(insurance), predict()
Alternative: HCorp
At: premium = premium*1.10
```

	Margin	Delta-method std. err.	z	P>|z|	[95% conf.	interval]
_outcome						
Health	0.229	0.024	9.50	0.000	0.182	0.276
HCorp	0.175	0.019	9.29	0.000	0.138	0.212
SickInc	0.244	0.024	10.24	0.000	0.197	0.291
MGroup	0.207	0.023	8.89	0.000	0.162	0.253
MoonHealth	0.145	0.021	6.99	0.000	0.104	0.185

图　5.28

运行结果如图 5.29 所示。

从图 5.29 可以看出，deductible 和 premium 随机系数的估计均值分别为－1.323 和－3.043，它们对应的标准差和相关系数分别为 1.251、1.067 和 0.549。这些参数的标准差高，说明这些参数没有被精确估计。

```
Mixed logit choice model                          Number of obs      =      1,250
Case ID variable: id                              Number of cases    =        250

Alternatives variable: insurance                  Alts per case: min =          5
                                                                 avg =        5.0
                                                                 max =          5

Integration sequence:      Hammersley
Integration points:               588                Wald chi2(2)    =      43.46
Log simulated-likelihood = -294.03592                Prob > chi2     =     0.0000
```

choice	Coefficient	Std. err.	z	P>|z|	[95% conf.	interval]
insurance						
deductible	-1.323	0.462	-2.86	0.004	-2.229	-0.418
premium	-3.043	0.467	-6.52	0.000	-3.958	-2.129
/Normal						
sd(deductible)	1.251	0.684			0.429	3.651
corr(deductible,premium)	0.549	0.549	1.00	0.317	-0.727	0.974
sd(premium)	1.067	0.612			0.347	3.283
Health						
_cons	0.500	0.325	1.54	0.125	-0.138	1.137
HCorp	(base alternative)					
SickInc						
_cons	-0.889	0.308	-2.88	0.004	-1.493	-0.284
MGroup						
_cons	-2.303	0.507	-4.54	0.000	-3.296	-1.309
MoonHealth						
_cons	-3.693	0.806	-4.58	0.000	-5.273	-2.113

```
LR test vs. fixed parameters: chi2(3) =       5.01        Prob > chi2 = 0.1713

Note: LR test is conservative and provided only for reference.
```

图 5.29

5.5* 面板数据混合 Logit 模型

面板数据混合 Logit 模型主要是指决策者通常在不同的时间段作出重复性的选择。该模型使用随机系数来模拟不同选择之间的相关性。随机系数是关于不同选项的变量(也可能在个人和选择方案上不同),被称为特定方案变量。

对于面板数据混合 Logit 模型,个人 i 在时间 t 从备选方案 a 收到的效用为:

$$U_{iat} = \boldsymbol{x}_{iat}\boldsymbol{\beta}_i + \boldsymbol{w}_{iat}\boldsymbol{\alpha} + z_{it}\delta_a + \varepsilon_{iat} \quad a = 1, 2, \cdots, A \tag{5.13}$$

cmxtmixlogit 通过最大模拟似然(MSL)估计混合 Logit 模型的参数。以随机参数 i 为条件,案例 i 在时间 t 选择备选方案 a 的概率为:

$$P_{iat}(\boldsymbol{\beta})=\frac{e^{x_{iat}}\boldsymbol{\beta}_i+\boldsymbol{w}_{iat}\boldsymbol{\alpha}+\boldsymbol{z}_{it}\boldsymbol{\delta}_a}{\sum_{a=1}^{A}e^{x_{iat}}\boldsymbol{\beta}_i+\boldsymbol{w}_{iat}\boldsymbol{\alpha}+\boldsymbol{z}_{it}\boldsymbol{\delta}_a} \tag{5.14}$$

通过对混合分布 $f(\beta)$积分，我们得到了无条件选择概率 P_{iat}：

$$P_{iat}=\int P_{iat}(\boldsymbol{\beta})f(\boldsymbol{\beta})d\boldsymbol{\beta} \tag{5.15}$$

其中，d 等于随机参数的数量，维数 d 的积分通过模拟近似。第 i 种情况的模拟可能性为：

$$L_i=\prod_{t=1}^{T}\sum_{a=1}^{A}d_{iat}\hat{P}_{iat} \tag{5.16}$$

其中，d_{iat} 是一个指示器，在时间 t 对所选备选方案取值为 1，否则为 0。然后，总体对数模拟可能性为 $\sum_{i=1}^{N}\ln(L_i)$。模拟概率为：

$$\hat{P}_{iat}=\frac{1}{M}\sum_{m=1}^{M}P_{iat}(\boldsymbol{\beta}^m) \tag{5.17}$$

其中，$\boldsymbol{\beta}^m$ 是从 $f(\beta)$中抽取的随机参数，M 是随机抽取的次数。方程可用于近似概率的计算。

面板数据混合 Logit 模型的语法格式为：

```
cmxtmixlogit depvar [indepvars] [if] [in] [weight] [,options]
```

菜单操作路径为：

Statistics>Choice models>Panel - data mixed logit model

例 5.5 面板数据混合 Logit 模型①

下面以 Stata 软件自带数据集 Transport. dta 为例，该数据集虚构了关于交通出行方式选择的数据，记录了 500 个生活在大都市的人到工作地的首选交通出行方式，每个人可以选择的几种不同的交通出行方式，同时包含了每种方式的交通出行成本和旅行时间，以及有关个人年龄和收入等方面的信息，选择变量记录在 alt 中。

二元变量 choice 记录所选的选项，choice 为 1 表示选择的选项，否则为 0。对每个人而言，在每个时间都有一次选择，t 为选择变量，将一个选择集作为一个案例。

```
.use transport, clear
.list in 1/12, sepby(t)
```

运行结果如图 5.30 所示。

从图 5.30 可以看出，这个人在 3 个时间都选择了自驾出行。出行时间(trtime)和出行成本(trcost)是两个与不同选项一个人相关的变量，随着选项、个案和个体的变化而变化，称为 alternative-specific 变量。变量 age、income 和 parttime 是与案例一个体相关的变量，随着每个案例和个体的变化而变化，但是在给定个体和时间的情况下，在所有不同选项中为常数，称为 case-specific 变量。

首先通过 cmset 命令对数据的格式进行设定，然后使用 cmxtmixlogit 命令来估

① 本案例参考 Stata 帮助手册 cm. pdf 中的对应案例改编。

	id	t	alt	choice	trcost	trtime	age	income	parttime
1.	1	1	Car	1	4.14	0.13	3.0	3	Full-time
2.	1	1	Public	0	4.74	0.42	3.0	3	Full-time
3.	1	1	Bicycle	0	2.76	0.36	3.0	3	Full-time
4.	1	1	Walk	0	0.92	0.13	3.0	3	Full-time
5.	1	2	Car	1	8.00	0.14	3.2	5	Full-time
6.	1	2	Public	0	3.14	0.12	3.2	5	Full-time
7.	1	2	Bicycle	0	2.56	0.18	3.2	5	Full-time
8.	1	2	Walk	0	0.64	0.39	3.2	5	Full-time
9.	1	3	Car	1	1.76	0.18	3.4	5	Part-time
10.	1	3	Public	0	2.25	0.50	3.4	5	Part-time
11.	1	3	Bicycle	0	0.92	1.05	3.4	5	Part-time
12.	1	3	Walk	0	0.58	0.59	3.4	5	Part-time

图 5.30

计 trcost、trtime、income 和 age 对交通出行方式的选择。假定所有人对于 trcost 的偏好是一致的，但对于 trtime 的偏好是异质性的，通过关于 trtime 的一个随机系数来对这种异质性进行建模。

.cmset id t alt

运行结果如图 5.31 所示。

```
note: case identifier _caseid generated from id and t.
note: panel by alternatives identifier _panelaltid generated from id and alt.

                    Panel data: Panels id and time t
                Case ID variable: _caseid
           Alternatives variable: alt
Panel by alternatives variable: _panelaltid (strongly balanced)
                   Time variable: t, 1 to 3
                           Delta: 1 unit

Note: Data have been xtset.
```

图 5.31

.cmxtmixlogit choice trcost, random(trtime) casevars(age income)

运行结果如图 5.32 所示。

从图 5.32 可以看出，总共利用了 500 个个体，每个个体在 3 个时间进行选择，所以总共有 1500 个案例；每个案例有 4 个不同选项，所以总共有 6000 个观测值。

trcost 的固定系数为−0.839，随机系数 trtime 的均值估计为−1.509，总共随机系数估计的标准差为 1.946，说明这些系数在群体中的个体之间存在显著的异质性。

每个与案例具体相关的变量，对应于每种选项，系数均不同。这些系数的解释与传统的多项 Logit 选择模型的解释相同。例如，当 car 作为基础选项时，age 对于 pub-

```
Mixed logit choice model                      Number of obs        =      6,000
                                              Number of cases      =      1,500
Panel variable: id                            Number of panels     =        500

Time variable: t                              Cases per panel: min =          3
                                                               avg =        3.0
                                                               max =          3

Alternatives variable: alt                    Alts per case:   min =          4
                                                               avg =        4.0
                                                               max =          4

Integration sequence:      Hammersley
Integration points:               594              Wald chi2(8)    =     432.68
Log simulated-likelihood = -1005.9899              Prob > chi2     =     0.0000
```

choice	Coefficient	Std. err.	z	P>|z|	[95% conf.	interval]
alt						
trcost	-0.839	0.044	-19.13	0.000	-0.925	-0.753
trtime	-1.509	0.264	-5.71	0.000	-2.026	-0.991
/Normal						
sd(trtime)	1.946	0.259			1.498	2.527
Car	(base alternative)					
Public						
age	0.154	0.067	2.29	0.022	0.022	0.286
income	-0.382	0.035	-10.98	0.000	-0.450	-0.313
_cons	-0.576	0.352	-1.64	0.102	-1.265	0.113
Bicycle						
age	0.206	0.085	2.43	0.015	0.040	0.373
income	-0.523	0.046	-11.28	0.000	-0.613	-0.432
_cons	-1.137	0.446	-2.55	0.011	-2.012	-0.263
Walk						
age	0.310	0.107	2.89	0.004	0.100	0.519
income	-0.902	0.069	-13.14	0.000	-1.036	-0.767
_cons	-0.418	0.561	-0.75	0.456	-1.517	0.681

图 5.32

lic 和 bicycle 的影响均为正数，说明随着年龄的增加，选择 public 或 bicycle 出行方式的概率超出自驾出行。与此类似，随着收入的增加，选择 public 和 bicycle 出行方式的概率在下降。

利用 margins 命令来考察一个变量变化情况下，各出行方式选择概率的变化。

```
.margins, at(income = (3 8))
```

运行结果如图 5.33 所示。

```
Predictive margins                                    Number of obs = 6,000
Model VCE: OIM

Expression: Pr(alt), predict()

1._at: income = 3

2._at: income = 8
```

	Margin	Delta-method std. err.	z	P>|z|	[95% conf.	interval]
_outcome#_at						
Car#1	0.333	0.020	16.93	0.000	0.295	0.372
Car#2	0.701	0.011	63.82	0.000	0.679	0.722
Public#1	0.221	0.018	12.00	0.000	0.185	0.257
Public#2	0.180	0.009	19.62	0.000	0.162	0.198
Bicycle#1	0.168	0.018	9.23	0.000	0.132	0.203
Bicycle#2	0.086	0.008	10.68	0.000	0.070	0.102
Walk#1	0.278	0.024	11.41	0.000	0.230	0.326
Walk#2	0.033	0.006	5.54	0.000	0.021	0.044

图 5.33

图 5.33 分别计算了当 income 分别等于 \$30000 和 \$80000 时，每种出行方式被选择的平均概率。如果每个人收入为 \$30000，则选择 car 的概率为 33.3%；如果每个人收入为 \$80000，则选择 car 的概率为 70.1%。而 Walk 出行方式则相反，从低收入的 27.8%下降到高收入的 3.3%，符合预期。

前面的例子估计了两个不同场景在一个时间点上的平均值。基于这一模型，并假设拥有一个随机或具有代表性的样本，可以将这些平均概率的差异解释为 income 为 \$80000 而非 \$30000 的影响。可以使用 contrast()选项来估计这种差异。可通过 over(t)选项分别包含每个时间点。

```
.margins, at(income = (3 8)) contrast(at(r) nowald) over(t)
```

运行结果如图 5.34 所示。

从图 5.34 可以看出，在第一个时间点，如果 income 为 \$80000 而不是 \$30000，则选择 car 的概率增加 36.3%。

```
.marginsplot
```

运行结果如图 5.35 所示。

```
Contrasts of predictive margins                    Number of obs = 6,000
Model VCE: OIM

Expression: Pr(alt), predict()
Over:       t

1._at: 1.t
           income = 3
1._at: 2.t
           income = 3
1._at: 3.t
           income = 3

2._at: 1.t
           income = 8
2._at: 2.t
           income = 8
2._at: 3.t
           income = 8
```

	Contrast	Delta-method std. err.	[95% conf.	interval]
_at@_outcome#t				
(2 vs 1) Car#1	0.363	0.019	0.325	0.401
(2 vs 1) Car#2	0.373	0.020	0.335	0.412
(2 vs 1) Car#3	0.367	0.019	0.329	0.404
(2 vs 1) Public#1	-0.040	0.019	-0.077	-0.003
(2 vs 1) Public#2	-0.047	0.018	-0.083	-0.012
(2 vs 1) Public#3	-0.035	0.018	-0.071	0.000
(2 vs 1) Bicycle#1	-0.084	0.019	-0.122	-0.046
(2 vs 1) Bicycle#2	-0.081	0.018	-0.117	-0.045
(2 vs 1) Bicycle#3	-0.079	0.019	-0.117	-0.040
(2 vs 1) Walk#1	-0.239	0.025	-0.287	-0.191
(2 vs 1) Walk#2	-0.245	0.025	-0.294	-0.196
(2 vs 1) Walk#3	-0.253	0.026	-0.304	-0.202

图 5.34

下面考虑如果与选项相关变量发生变化，那么对于出行结果有什么影响。如 car 相关的成本上升 25%，则出行方式会有什么变化。

```
.margins, alternative(Car) at(trcost = generate(trcost))
.at(trcost = generate(1.25 * trcost)) subpop(if t = = 1)
```

运行结果如图 5.36 所示。

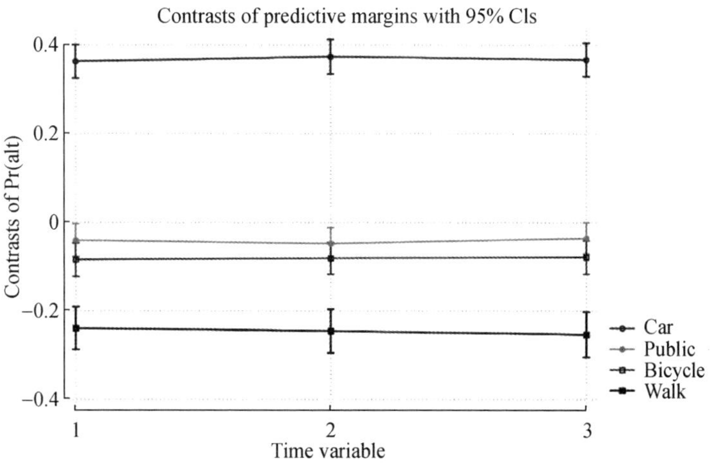

图 5.35

```
Predictive margins                              Number of obs     = 6,000
Model VCE: OIM                                  Subpop. no. obs   = 2,000

Expression:  Pr(alt), predict()
Alternative: Car

1._at: trcost =       trcost

2._at: trcost = 1.25*trcost
```

	Margin	Delta-method std. err.	z	P>|z|	[95% conf.	interval]
_outcome#_at						
Car#1	0.544	0.011	47.71	0.000	0.522	0.566
Car#2	0.441	0.010	43.61	0.000	0.421	0.460
Public#1	0.201	0.010	19.26	0.000	0.181	0.221
Public#2	0.255	0.012	21.60	0.000	0.232	0.278
Bicycle#1	0.126	0.010	13.14	0.000	0.107	0.144
Bicycle#2	0.157	0.011	14.21	0.000	0.135	0.178
Walk#1	0.130	0.010	12.76	0.000	0.110	0.149
Walk#2	0.148	0.011	13.43	0.000	0.126	0.169

图 5.36

从图 5.36 可以看出，当 car 出行成本上升 25%的情况下，选择 car 的概率会从 54.4%下降到 44.1%，选择 public 的概率会从 20.1%上升到 25.5%。

5.6 嵌套 Logit 模型

5.6.1 建模思想

在多项 Logit 选择模型中,两个选项的概率比只与 j 和 k 有关,换一个角度看,当选项集中增加或减少一个选项后,虽然模型的分子和分母的具体概率值都发生了变化,但是比值不会改变,其概率增减变化的比例是相同的,这种性质即 IIA。

实际上,IIA 假设在许多场合是不成立的,一个经典的例子就是 Chipman 和 Debreu 提出的"红蓝巴士悖论"。

IIA 假设在提供便利的同时,限制了模型的适用范围。当选项之间不满足 IIA 假设而存在相关性时,如红蓝巴士,不宜用多项 Logit 选择模型,而嵌套 Logit 模型可以解决被解释变量的各个类别之间存在相关性的问题,建模思想在于把选项集合分割成若干不相关的子集。做法是把存在相关关系的选项引入同一子集,在此基础上,再把有相关关系的子集继续引入同一上层子集,直到子集之间没有相关性,从而成功摆脱 IIA 假设的局限。

在嵌套 Logit 模型中,个体的选择行为可以分为两个阶段:第一阶段,选择最大效用的子集;第二阶段,在选定的子集中选择最大效用。显然,在这两个阶段,各选项之间(子集间或同一子集的选项间)都可以满足 IIA 假设(类似地,子集的设定也可以允许有多个层次,从而构建多层的嵌套 Logit 模型)。由于满足 IIA 假设,在每一个阶段我们都可以利用多项 Logit 选择模型概率计算公式。根据概率的乘法法则,对于具体的一个选项集中的选项,其被选概率等于在这一系列过程中计算所得概率的乘积。

5.6.2 模型设定

嵌套 Logit 模型假设随机误差 ε_n 的联合分布 $F(\varepsilon_n)$ 为广义极值(generalized extreme-value, GEV)分布,即

$$F(\varepsilon_n)=\exp\Big(-\sum_{l=1}^{L}\Big(\sum_{j\in\Omega_l}\exp(-\varepsilon_{n_j/\lambda_l})\Big)^{\lambda_l}\Big) \tag{5.18}$$

GEV 分布是单变量极值分布的广义化,即模型每一选项效用的误差 ε 的边缘分布均为单变量极值分布。GEV 分布下,同一子集 Ω_l 内的误差项之间是相关的,子集之间的误差项是相互独立的。参数 λ_l 是描述第 l 个子集中所有选项的未观察到效用之间相互独立的指标。λ_l 的值越大,说明选项之间相关性越小。λ_l 必须位于 0-1 之间才能保证效用的最大化。如果 $\lambda_l=1$,则说明选项之间完全独立,这就满足了多项 Logit 选择模型对于选项的要求。同时,GEV 分布也就变成了单变量极值分布。因此,多项 Logit 选择模型可以被看成嵌套 Logit 模型的一个特例。

5.6.3 模型估计

如前文所述,在随机误差服从 GEV 假设条件下,在嵌套 Logit 模型中,基于分层的思想,利用多项 Logit 选择模型,估计每一层的概率,再利用乘法法则得到选项的总

概率。

设选项子集以及选项分别用 K、J 作为指标。个体选择的效用可记为：

$$U_{jk}=Y_j\alpha+Z_{jk}\beta_{jk}+\varepsilon_{jk} \qquad j=1,\cdots,J;K=1,\cdots,K \tag{5.19}$$

其中，Z_{jk} 表示影响个体对第一层子集、第二层选项选择的解释变量产生的效用，Y_j 表示影响个体对第一层子集选择的解释变量产生的效用。

1. 第二层概率

根据前面的假设，可以得到选择树干 j 的边缘概率：

$$P_j=\frac{\exp(Y_{ij}\alpha/\lambda_k)}{\sum_{j\in B_k}\exp(Y_{ij}\alpha/\lambda_k)} \tag{5.20}$$

2. 第一层概率

个体选择选项 i 在选择树干 j 的情况下选择树枝 k 的条件概率为：

$$P_{k|j}=\frac{\exp(Z_{ik}\beta_{ik}+\lambda_k I_{ik})}{\sum_{l=1}^{K}\exp(Z_{il}\beta_{ik}+\lambda_l I_{il})} \tag{5.21}$$

其中，$I_{ik}=\ln\sum_{j\in B_k}\exp(Y_{ij}/\lambda_k)$，代表子集内所有选项的平均效用水平。$I_{ik}$ 的系数 λ_k 正是上述描述子集 k 内各选项间独立性的指标。若子集划分正确，λ_k 应介于 0-1 之间。

需要指出的是，第一层各子集之间的 λ 值应为 1，表示对子集的划分到此为止，子集之间再无相关关系。如果 λ 值不等于 1，则需要进一步进行子集的划分，直到其值等于 1，或者划分到最上层子集数目为 2。

3. 总概率

由边缘概率和条件概率的乘积可以得到个体选择某选项的总概率。把式(5.20)和式(5.21)相乘得到：

$$P_{jk}=p_j\times p_{k|j}=\frac{\exp(Y_{ij}\alpha/\lambda_k)}{\sum_{j\in B_k}\exp(Y_{ij}\alpha/\lambda_k)}\times\frac{\exp(Z_{ik}\beta_{ik}+\lambda_k I_{ik})}{\sum_{l=1}^{K}\exp(Z_{il}\beta_{ik}+\lambda_i I_{il})} \tag{5.22}$$

这就是两层决策树的嵌套 Logit 模型的个体 i 选择树干 j 树枝 k 方案的概率计算式，对于两层以上的情形可以仿照上述步骤进行。

根据这个概率计算式，可以写出所有样本的对数似然函数，即可利用对数似然估计法估计模型参数，这就是完全信息最大似然法(FIML)。

与多项 Logit 选择模型不同，由于嵌套 Logit 模型在概率公式中增加了代表子集信息的 λ_k，使得分别位于不同子集 B_m 和 B_n 的两选项的概率比更为复杂，但是，根据公式，概率比仍然可以表达为 $F(\beta,\lambda_m,\lambda_n)$的函数形式，并且函数为增函数。在同一模型中可以根据系数 β 的大小来指示变量对于概率比变化的作用大小。

4. 模型的性质

由于随机项的联合分布函数为 GEV，因此模型有如下特征：同一子集当中的任何两个选项之间的概率比独立于同子集的其他选项的存在和属性，即 IIA 假设在子集内成立；不同子集的两个选项之间的概率比只与这两个子集的选项有关，而与其他子集无关；不同子集中各选项之间的概率比可以不同。

5.6.4 IIA 假设检验

嵌套 Logit 模型的本质在于对不满足 IIA 假设的选项进行适当划分后，在满足 IIA 假设的子集分别建立多项 Logit 模型。因为嵌套 Logit 模型的设定取决于 IIA 假设，所以我们必须对假设进行检验，常用的方法有 Hausman 检验、Small-Hsiao 检验和 IR 检验。

常用的 Hausman 检验法由 Hausman 和 McFadden 于 1984 年提出，基本思想是如果 IIA 假设能够满足，那么，包含全选项的模型和仅包含部分选项的模型的参数估计应该相差不大。

具体的检验步骤分为三步：

(1) 建立包含全选项的模型；

(2) 建立包含去掉了一个或多个选项的限制模型；

(3) 建立如下检验统计量：

$$H=(\hat{\boldsymbol{\beta}}_s-\hat{\boldsymbol{\beta}}_f)'[\hat{\mathbf{V}}_s-\hat{\mathbf{V}}_f]^{-1}(\hat{\boldsymbol{\beta}}_s-\hat{\boldsymbol{\beta}}_f) \tag{5.23}$$

式中，$\hat{\boldsymbol{\beta}}_s$ 和 $\hat{\boldsymbol{\beta}}_f$ 分别表示基于上述两模型的参数向量。$\hat{\mathbf{V}}_s$ 和 $\hat{\mathbf{V}}_f$ 分别是相应的渐进方差矩阵的估计。统计量 H 服从一个受限制的卡方分布。

嵌套 Logit 模型估计的语法格式为：

```
nlogit depvar [indepvars] [if] [in] [weight] [||lev1_equation || lev2_equation...]] ||
>altvar: [byaltvarlist], case(varname) [nlogit_options]
```

菜单操作路径为：

```
>Statistics>Choice models>Nested logit model>Nested logit model
```

例 5.6 嵌套 Logit 模型[①]

下面以 Stata 软件自带数据集 Restaurant.dta 为例，该数据集包括 300 个家庭及其就餐选择数据。Freebirds 和 Mama's Pizza 是快餐店，Café Eccell、Los Norteños 和 Wings'N More 是家庭餐厅，Christopher's 和 Mad Cows 是高档餐厅。要对一个家庭的就餐选择进行建模，影响因素包括家庭收入(income)、家庭孩子的数量(kids)、餐厅评级(rating)、人均餐费(cost)、距离家庭的远近(distance)。

```
.use restaurant, clear
.describe
```

运行结果如图 5.37 所示。

① 本案例利用 Stata 帮助手册 cm.pdf 中的相应例子改编。

```
Observations:          2,100
   Variables:              8                  11 Jun 2022 12:25

Variable      Storage   Display    Value
    name         type    format    label      Variable label

family_id       int     %9.0g                 family ID
restaurant      byte    %12.0g     names      choices of restaurants
income          int     %9.0g                 household income
cost            float   %9.0g                 average meal cost per person
kids            byte    %9.0g                 number of kids in the household
rating          byte    %9.0g                 ratings in local restaurant guide
distance        float   %9.0g                 distance between home and restaurant
chosen          byte    %9.0g                 0 no 1 yes

Sorted by: family_id
```

图 5.37

. list family_id restaurant chosen kids rating distance in 1/21, sepby(fam)
> abbrev(10)

运行结果如图 5.38 所示。

	family_id	restaurant	chosen	kids	rating	distance
1.	1	Freebirds	1	1	0	1.245553
2.	1	MamasPizza	0	1	1	2.82493
3.	1	CafeEccell	0	1	2	4.21293
4.	1	LosNortenos	0	1	3	4.167634
5.	1	WingsNmore	0	1	2	6.330531
6.	1	Christophers	0	1	4	10.19829
7.	1	MadCows	0	1	5	5.601388
8.	2	Freebirds	0	3	0	4.162657
9.	2	MamasPizza	0	3	1	2.865081
10.	2	CafeEccell	0	3	2	5.337799
11.	2	LosNortenos	1	3	3	4.282864
12.	2	WingsNmore	0	3	2	8.133914
13.	2	Christophers	0	3	4	8.664631
14.	2	MadCows	0	3	5	9.119597
15.	3	Freebirds	1	3	0	2.112586
16.	3	MamasPizza	0	3	1	2.215329
17.	3	CafeEccell	0	3	2	6.978715
18.	3	LosNortenos	0	3	3	5.117877
19.	3	WingsNmore	0	3	2	5.312941
20.	3	Christophers	0	3	4	9.551273
21.	3	MadCows	0	3	5	5.539806

图 5.38

利用 nlogitgen 命令对数据的嵌套形式进行展示，尤其是第一层选项的识别。

.nlogitgen type = restaurant(fast: Freebirds| MamasPizza,

> family: CafeEccell| LosNortenos| WingsNmore, fancy: Christophers| MadCows)

运行结果如图 5.39 所示。

```
New variable type is generated with 3 groups
label list lb_type
lb_type:
           1 fast
           2 family
           3 fancy
```

图 5.39

.nlogittree restaurant type, choice(chosen)

运行结果如图 5.40 所示。

```
Tree structure specified for the nested logit model

 type    N       restaurant    N   k
------------------------------------------
 fast   600 -+- Freebirds     300  12
             +- MamasPizza    300  15
 family 900 -+- CafeEccell    300  78
             |- LosNortenos   300  75
             +- WingsNmore    300  69
 fancy  600 -+- Christophers  300  27
             +- MadCows       300  24
------------------------------------------
                     Total   2100 300

k = number of times alternative is chosen
N = number of observations at each level
```

图 5.40

.nlogit chosen cost rating distance || type: income kids, base(family) ||

>restaurant:, noconstant case(family_id)

运行结果如图 5.41 所示。

```
RUM-consistent nested logit regression         Number of obs      =     2,100
Case variable: family_id                       Number of cases    =       300

Alternative variable: restaurant               Alts per case: min =         7
                                                              avg =       7.0
                                                              max =         7

                                                  Wald chi2(7)    =     46.71
Log likelihood = -485.47331                       Prob > chi2     =    0.0000

------------------------------------------------------------------------------
      chosen | Coefficient  Std. err.      z    P>|z|     [95% conf. interval]
-------------+----------------------------------------------------------------
restaurant   |
        cost |    -0.184      0.093    -1.97   0.048       -0.367      -0.001
      rating |     0.464      0.326     1.42   0.156       -0.176       1.104
    distance |    -0.380      0.100    -3.78   0.000       -0.576      -0.183
-------------+----------------------------------------------------------------
type equations
-------------+----------------------------------------------------------------
fast         |
      income |    -0.027      0.012    -2.27   0.023       -0.050      -0.004
        kids |    -0.087      0.139    -0.63   0.529       -0.359       0.184
-------------+----------------------------------------------------------------
family       |
      income |     0.000  (base)
        kids |     0.000  (base)
-------------+----------------------------------------------------------------
fancy        |
      income |     0.046      0.009     5.08   0.000        0.028       0.064
        kids |    -0.396      0.122    -3.24   0.001       -0.635      -0.157
-------------+----------------------------------------------------------------
dissimilarity parameters
-------------+----------------------------------------------------------------
/type        |
    fast_tau |     1.713      1.487                        -1.201       4.627
  family_tau |     2.505      0.965                         0.614       4.396
   fancy_tau |     4.100      2.810                        -1.408       9.608
------------------------------------------------------------------------------
LR test for IIA (tau=1): chi2(3) = 6.87                  Prob > chi2 = 0.0762
```

图 5.41

分隔号“||”可分离不同方程。第一个方程确定了因变量 chosen，三个与方案相关的变量 cost、rating、distance。第二个方程设定 type 变量，识别了第一水平的选项，即餐厅类型，在 type 之后，确定了两个与案例相关的变量，即 income 和 kids。标识底层选项的变量 restaurant 在第二个等式分隔符之后指定。在输出的底部附近是不相似参数，它衡量的是三种类型餐厅中每一种随机冲击的相关程度。

图 5.41 的最底部给出了 IIA 假设的结果，原假设为所有不相似参数等于 1，从结果可以看出，在 10%显著水平下拒绝原假设。

第6章 计数结果

离散计数数据模型的被解释变量观测值表现为非负整数，为计数事件的结果。它的被解释变量是离散计数变量。比如，一段公路上一年内发生事故的次数，那么是哪些原因决定了事故的发生呢？这就要研究事故的影响因素，如天气情况，以及公路上拐弯弧度的大小，经常行驶在公路上的汽车的数量等，这类问题的共同特点是：被解释变量观测值表现为非负整数。

离散计数可以分为以下几种情况：

$$\text{离散计数}=\begin{cases}\text{分散均衡}\Leftrightarrow\text{泊松分布}\Leftrightarrow\text{泊松分布模型}\\ \text{分布不足}\Leftrightarrow\text{二项分布}\Leftrightarrow\text{二项分布模型}\\ \text{分布过度}\Leftrightarrow\text{负二项分布}\Leftrightarrow\text{负二项分布模型}\end{cases}$$

因此，被解释变量观测值具有非负整数特征，而且数据中零元素和绝对值较小的数据比较多，离散特征十分明显，另外，由于模型的异方差特征，决定了不能用经典线性模型进行估计，有必要引进描述非负整数特征的概率分布，从而建立离散计数数据模型。

6.1 泊松回归

有些被解释变量的取值只能是非负整数，即 0,1,2,…，比如，专利个数、风险事件次数、产品销量等，这些就是计数数据。此类取非负整数的变量数据的回归分析，就需要使用泊松回归等方法。泊松回归拟合事件发生次数（计数）的模型，此时泊松分布用于描述各种事件发生次数的概率。

假设每次实验中某事件的发生概率固定为 p，总共进行了 n 次相对独立的随机试验，记该事件发生的次数为 Y，则根据二项分布可知 $Y=y$ 的概率为：

$$P(Y=y)=C_n^y p^y(1-p)^{n-y} \quad (y=0,1,\cdots,n) \tag{6.1}$$

当 $p\to 0$，$n\to\infty$，即事件发生概率很小，事件实验次数很大，且 $np=\lambda>0$ 时，式(6.1)的极限为泊松分布，即

$$\lim_{n\to\infty}P(Y=y)=\lim_{n\to\infty}C_n^y p^y(1-p)^{n-y}=\frac{e^{-\lambda}\lambda^y}{y!} \quad (y=0,1,\cdots,n) \tag{6.2}$$

对于存在计数数据问题的个体 i，设被解释变量为 Y_i，假设 $Y_i=y_i$ 由参数为 λ_i 的

泊松分布决定。

$$P(Y_i = y_i \mid \boldsymbol{x}_i) = \frac{e^{-\lambda_i}\lambda_i^{y_i}}{y_i!} \quad (y_i = 0,1,2,\cdots) \tag{6.3}$$

泊松分布的期望与方差相等，且等于 λ_i，即事件发生的平均次数决定于解释变量 $\boldsymbol{x}_i$。假设被解释变量 Y_i 的条件期望函数为：

$$E(Y_i \mid \boldsymbol{x}_i) = \lambda_i = \exp(\boldsymbol{x}_i' \boldsymbol{\beta}) \tag{6.4}$$

即泊松回归模型为对数线性回归模型：

$$\ln y_i = \boldsymbol{x}_i' \boldsymbol{\beta} + \varepsilon_i \tag{6.5}$$

假设样本独立同分布，则样本的对数似然函数为：

$$\begin{aligned}\ln L(\boldsymbol{\beta}) &= \sum_{i=1}^{n}[-\lambda_i + y_i \ln\lambda_i - \ln(y_i!)] \\ &= \sum_{i=1}^{n}[-\exp(\boldsymbol{x}_i'\boldsymbol{\beta}) + y_i\boldsymbol{x}_i'\boldsymbol{\beta} - \ln(y_i!)]\end{aligned} \tag{6.6}$$

最大化一阶条件为：

$$\sum_{i=1}^{n}[y_i - \exp(\boldsymbol{x}_i'\boldsymbol{\beta})]\boldsymbol{x}_i = \boldsymbol{0} \tag{6.7}$$

通过数值计算可得 $\hat{\boldsymbol{\beta}}_{\mathrm{MLE}}$。根据 MLE 理论，如果似然函数正确，则$\hat{\boldsymbol{\beta}}_{\mathrm{MLE}}$ 为一致估计量。即使似然函数设定有偏误，泊松分布属于线性指数分布，但只要条件期望函数设定正确，则准最大似然估计 $\hat{\boldsymbol{\beta}}_{\mathrm{QMLE}}$ 也是一致的。为稳健估计，必须在准最大似然估计(QMLE)基础上计算稳健标准误。

泊松回归模型参数的经济意义并不是提供边际效应，它为半弹性：$\frac{\partial \ln\lambda_i}{\partial x_k} = \beta_k$。解释变量 $\boldsymbol{x}_i$ 单位变化引发的事件发生率比率的变化为：

$$\frac{\partial y_i}{\partial x_i} = \frac{e^{\ln(E)+\beta_1 x_1+\cdots+\beta_i(x_i+1)+\cdots+\beta_k x_k}}{e^{\ln(E)+\beta_1 x_1+\cdots+\beta_i x_i+\cdots+\beta_k x_k}} = e^{\beta_i} \tag{6.8}$$

泊松回归的语法命令为：

```
poisson depvar [indepvars] [if] [in] [weight] [, options]
```

模型设定选项及含义包括：

(1) noconstant：无常数项；

(2) exposure(varname_e)：在系数约束为 1 的模型中包括 ln(varname_e)；

(3) offset(varname_o)：将 varname_o 包含在系数约束为 1 的模型中；

(4) constraints(constraints)：应用指定的线性约束。

菜单操作路径为：

```
Statistics>Count outcomes>Poisson regression
```

泊松拟合 indepvars 上的 depvar 泊松回归，其中 depvar 是一个非负计数变量。

例 6.1　泊松回归

下面利用一项针对英国男性医生冠状动脉疾病死亡的年龄研究数据，说明泊松回归的实现。

```
*下载数据
.clear all
.webuse dollhill3
*拟合泊松回归
.poisson deaths smokes i.agecat, exposure(pyears)
```

运行结果如图 6.1 所示。

```
Poisson regression                                      Number of obs =     10
                                                        LR chi2(5)    = 922.93
                                                        Prob > chi2   = 0.0000
Log likelihood = -33.600153                             Pseudo R2     = 0.9321

------------------------------------------------------------------------------
      deaths | Coefficient  Std. err.      z    P>|z|     [95% conf. interval]
-------------+----------------------------------------------------------------
      smokes |   .3545356   .1073741     3.30   0.001     .1440862     .564985
             |
      agecat |
      45-54  |   1.484007   .1951034     7.61   0.000     1.101611    1.866403
      55-64  |   2.627505   .1837273    14.30   0.000     2.267406    2.987604
      65-74  |   3.350493   .1847992    18.13   0.000     2.988293    3.712693
      75-84  |   3.700096   .1922195    19.25   0.000     3.323353     4.07684
             |
       _cons |  -7.919326   .1917618   -41.30   0.000    -8.295172   -7.543479
  ln(pyears) |          1  (exposure)
------------------------------------------------------------------------------
```

图 6.1

```
*获取事件发生率比率
.poisson deaths smokes i.agecat, exposure(pyears) irr
```

运行结果如图 6.2 所示。

```
Poisson regression                                      Number of obs =     10
                                                        LR chi2(5)    = 922.93
                                                        Prob > chi2   = 0.0000
Log likelihood = -33.600153                             Pseudo R2     = 0.9321

------------------------------------------------------------------------------
      deaths |        IRR   Std. err.      z    P>|z|     [95% conf. interval]
-------------+----------------------------------------------------------------
      smokes |   1.425519   .1530638     3.30   0.001     1.154984    1.759421
             |
      agecat |
      45-54  |   4.410584   .8605197     7.61   0.000     3.009011    6.464997
      55-64  |    13.8392   2.542638    14.30   0.000     9.654328    19.83809
      65-74  |   28.51678   5.269878    18.13   0.000     19.85177    40.96395
      75-84  |   40.45121   7.775511    19.25   0.000     27.75326    58.95885
             |
       _cons |   .0003636   .0000697   -41.30   0.000     .0002497    .0005296
  ln(pyears) |          1  (exposure)
------------------------------------------------------------------------------
Note: _cons estimates baseline incidence rate.
```

图 6.2

* 在 99 % 的置信水平上显示结果

.poisson, level(99) irr

运行结果如图 6.3 所示。

```
Poisson regression                                      Number of obs =     10
                                                        LR chi2(5)    = 922.93
                                                        Prob > chi2   = 0.0000
Log likelihood = -33.600153                             Pseudo R2     = 0.9321

------------------------------------------------------------------------------
      deaths |        IRR   Std. err.      z    P>|z|     [99% conf. interval]
-------------+----------------------------------------------------------------
      smokes |   1.425519   .1530638     3.30   0.001     1.081078    1.879702
             |
      agecat |
      45-54  |   4.410584   .8605197     7.61   0.000     2.668333    7.290411
      55-64  |    13.8392   2.542638    14.30   0.000     8.621465    22.21472
      65-74  |   28.51678   5.269878    18.13   0.000     17.71624    45.90178
      75-84  |   40.45121   7.775511    19.25   0.000      24.6548     66.3684
             |
       _cons |   .0003636   .0000697   -41.30   0.000     .0002219    .0005959
  ln(pyears) |          1  (exposure)
------------------------------------------------------------------------------
Note: _cons estimates baseline incidence rate.
```

图 6.3

6.2 负二项回归与广义负二项回归

泊松回归的局限在于泊松分布的期望与方差一定要相等，这被称为均等分散。但是这个数据特征经常与实际数据特征不符。对于被解释变量的方差明显大于期望值，即存在过度分散的情况，通常的处理办法是在条件期望函数的对数表达式中加入一项，即

$$\ln\lambda_i = \boldsymbol{x}_i'\boldsymbol{\beta} + \varepsilon_i \tag{6.9}$$

其中，随机变量ε_i 表示条件期望函数当中不可观测的部分或者个体的异质性部分。由式(6.9)可得：

$$\lambda_i = \exp(\boldsymbol{x}_i'\boldsymbol{\beta}) \cdot \exp(\varepsilon_i) \equiv u_i v_i \tag{6.10}$$

式中，$u_i \equiv \exp(\boldsymbol{x}_i'\boldsymbol{\beta})$为$\boldsymbol{x}_i$ 的确定性函数部分，$v_i \equiv \exp(\varepsilon_i) > 0$ 为随机部分。给定 $\boldsymbol{x}_i$ 和 v_i，则 y_i 依然服从泊松分布：

$$\mathrm{P}(Y_i = y_i \mid \boldsymbol{x}_i, v_i) = \frac{\mathrm{e}^{-u_i i_i}(u_i v_i)^{y_i}}{y_i!} \quad (y_i = 0,1,2,\cdots) \tag{6.11}$$

但由于 v_i 不可观测，无法估计该泊松回归。因此，记 v_i 的概率密度函数为 $g(v_i)$，则可以对 v_i 积分，计算 y_i 的边缘分布密度：

$$P(Y_i = y_i \mid \boldsymbol{x}_i) = \int_0^\infty \frac{\mathrm{e}^{-u_i v_i}(u_i v_i)^{y_i}}{y_i!} g(v_i)\mathrm{d}v_i \tag{6.12}$$

由于 $v_i>0$，通常设 $v_i \sim \text{Gamma}(1/\alpha, \alpha)$，其中 $\alpha>0$ 为分散参数，α 越大，过度分散程度越大。泊松（分布）回归假设 $\alpha=0$，负二项（分布）回归假设 $\alpha=\ln\alpha$，广义负二项（分布）回归假设 $\ln\alpha_j=\boldsymbol{z}_j\gamma$，即协变量 $\boldsymbol{z}_j$ 的线性组合。

此时，$E(v_i)=1, Var(v_i)=\alpha$。把 $v_i \sim \text{Gamma}(1/\alpha, \alpha)$ 的概率密度函数代入方程，可得负二项分布的概率密度，由此可推出样本数据的似然函数，做 MLE 估计。这就是负二项（分布）回归，即假设样本来自负二项分布，做计数数据回归。

（1）均值分散模型

均值分散模型假设第 j 个观测值的分数等于 $1+\alpha\exp(\boldsymbol{x}_j\beta+\text{offset}_j)$，则条件期望函数为：

$$y_j \sim \text{Poisson}(\mu_j^*) \tag{6.13}$$

$$\mu_j^* = \exp(\boldsymbol{x}_j\boldsymbol{\beta}+\text{offset}_j+v_j) \tag{6.14}$$

$$e^{v_j} \sim \text{Gamma}(1/\alpha, \alpha) \tag{6.15}$$

$$\mu_j^* \sim \text{Gamma}(1/\alpha, \alpha\mu_j) \tag{6.16}$$

因此有：

$$\begin{aligned}\text{Var}(y_j) &= E\{\text{Var}(y_j \mid \mu_j^*)\} + \text{Var}\{E(y_j \mid \mu_j^*)\} \\ &= E(\mu_j^*) + \text{Var}(\mu_j^*) = \mu_j(1+\alpha\mu_j)\end{aligned} \tag{6.17}$$

对于均值分散模型，负二项分布可以看作泊松随机变量的 Gamma 混合。某事件发生的次数 y_j 服从泊松分布 $P(v_ju_j)$。也就是说，它的条件似然函数是：

$$f(y_j \mid v_j) = \frac{(v_j\mu_j)^{y_j}e^{-v_j\mu_j}}{\Gamma(y_j+1)} \tag{6.18}$$

式中，$\mu_j=\exp(\boldsymbol{x}_j\boldsymbol{\beta}+\text{offset}_j)$，$v_i \sim \text{Gamma}(1/\alpha, \alpha)$ 的概率密度函数为：

$$g(v) = \frac{v^{(1-\alpha)/\alpha}e^{-v/\alpha}}{\alpha^{1/\alpha}\Gamma(1/\alpha)} \tag{6.19}$$

则第 j 个观测值的无条件似然值为：

$$f(y_j) = \int_0^\infty f(y_j \mid v)g(v)dv = \frac{\Gamma(m+y_j)}{\Gamma(y_j+1)\Gamma(m)}p_j^m(1-p_j)^{y_j}$$

式中，$p_j=1/(1+\alpha\mu_j)$，$m=1/\alpha$。

则对数似然函数为：

$$\begin{aligned}\ln L = \sum_{j=1}^n w_j[&\ln\{\Gamma(m+y_j)\} - \ln\{\Gamma(y_j+1)\} \\ &- \ln\{\Gamma(m)\} + m\ln(p_j) + y_j\ln(1-p_j)]\end{aligned} \tag{6.20}$$

式中，$m=1/\alpha$；$p_j=1/(1+\alpha\mu_j)$；$\mu_j=\exp(\boldsymbol{x}_j\boldsymbol{\beta}+\text{offset}_j)$。

对于广义负二项回归（gnbreg），根据参数化 $\ln\alpha_j=\boldsymbol{z}_j\gamma$，$\alpha$ 可以在观测值之间变化。

（2）常数分散模型

常数分散模型假设某事件发生的次数 y_j 服从泊松分布 $P(u_j^*)$，$\mu_j^* \sim \text{Gamma}(\mu_j/\delta, \delta)$，$\delta$ 为分散参数，$\text{Var}(y_j)=\mu_j(1+\delta)$。

均值分散模型假设 $\mu_j^* \sim \text{Gamma}(1/\alpha, \alpha\mu_j)$，由此可得常数分散模型的对数似然函数为：

$$\begin{aligned}\ln L = \sum_{j=1}^{n} w_j [&\ln\{\Gamma(m_j + y_j)\} - \ln\{\Gamma(y_j + 1)\} \\ &- \ln\{\Gamma(m_j)\} + m_j \ln(p) + y_j \ln(1-p)]\end{aligned} \tag{6.21}$$

式中，$m_j = \mu_j/\delta$，$p = 1/(1+\delta)$。

语法格式分别为：

（1）负二项模型

nbreg depvar [indepvars] [if] [in] [weight] [, nbreg_options]

（2）广义负二项模型

gnbreg depvar [indepvars] [if] [in] [weight] [, gnbreg_options]

模型设定选项(options)相比泊松模型增加了：

（1）dispersion(mean)：分数参数化(默认值)；

（2）dispersion(constant)：所有观测值的常数分散。

菜单操作路径为：

（1）nbreg：Statistics>Count outcomes>Negative binomial regression

（2）gnbreg：Statistics>Count outcomes>Generalized negative binomial regression

nbreg 适用于非负计数因变量的负二项回归模型。在该模型中，计数变量被认为由类泊松过程产生，但允许其变化大于真实泊松过程的变化。这种额外的变化被称为过度分散。

gnbreg 适用于负二项平均离散模型的推广。形状参数 alpha 也可以参数化。

例 6.2　负二项回归与广义负二项回归

假设泊松回归模型并观察到缺乏模型拟合的情况并不少见。下面以 Stata 软件自带的 Rodríguez(1993)①数据说明其实现过程。

```
* 下载数据
.clear all
.webuse rod93
.list, sepby(cohort)
```

运行结果如图 6.4 所示。

```
.generate logexp = ln(exposure)
.poisson deaths i.cohort, offset(logexp)
```

运行结果如图 6.5 所示。

① Rodríguez, G. sbe10: An Improvement to Poisson. Stata Technical Bulletin 11: 11-14. Reprinted in Stata Technical Bulletin Reprints. College Station, TX: Stata Press, 1993, 2.

运行结果如图 6.5 所示。

	cohort	age_mos	deaths	exposure
1.	1941-1949	0.5	168	278.4
2.	1941-1949	2.0	48	538.8
3.	1941-1949	4.5	63	794.4
4.	1941-1949	9.0	89	1,550.8
5.	1941-1949	18.0	102	3,006.0
6.	1941-1949	42.0	81	8,743.5
7.	1941-1949	90.0	40	14,270.0
8.	1960-1967	0.5	197	403.2
9.	1960-1967	2.0	48	786.0
10.	1960-1967	4.5	62	1,165.3
11.	1960-1967	9.0	81	2,294.8
12.	1960-1967	18.0	97	4,500.5
13.	1960-1967	42.0	103	13,201.5
14.	1960-1967	90.0	39	19,525.0
15.	1968-1976	0.5	195	495.3
16.	1968-1976	2.0	55	956.7
17.	1968-1976	4.5	58	1,381.4
18.	1968-1976	9.0	85	2,604.5
19.	1968-1976	18.0	87	4,618.5
20.	1968-1976	42.0	70	9,814.5
21.	1968-1976	90.0	10	5,802.5

图 6.4

```
Poisson regression                              Number of obs =     21
                                                LR chi2(2)    =  49.16
                                                Prob > chi2   = 0.0000
Log likelihood = -2159.5159                     Pseudo R2     = 0.0113
```

deaths	Coefficient	Std. err.	z	P>|z|	[95% conf.	interval]
cohort						
1960-1967	-.3020405	.0573319	-5.27	0.000	-.4144089	-.1896721
1968-1976	.0742143	.0589726	1.26	0.208	-.0413698	.1897983
_cons	-3.899488	.0411345	-94.80	0.000	-3.98011	-3.818866
logexp	1	(offset)				

图 6.5

. estat gof

运行结果如图 6.6 所示。

```
Deviance goodness-of-fit  =  4190.689
Prob > chi2(18)           =    0.0000

Pearson goodness-of-fit   =  15387.67
Prob > chi2(18)           =    0.0000
```

图 6.6

拟合优度检验非常显著,表明泊松模型是不合适的,我们应该尝试负二项模型。

* 拟合负二项回归模型

.nbreg deaths i.cohort, exposure(exp)

运行结果如图 6.7 所示。

```
Negative binomial regression                            Number of obs =     21
                                                        LR chi2(2)    =   0.40
Dispersion: mean                                        Prob > chi2   = 0.8171
Log likelihood = -131.3799                              Pseudo R2     = 0.0015

------------------------------------------------------------------------------
      deaths | Coefficient  Std. err.      z    P>|z|     [95% conf. interval]
-------------+----------------------------------------------------------------
      cohort |
   1960-1967 |  -.2676187   .7237203    -0.37   0.712    -1.686085    1.150847
   1968-1976 |  -.4573957   .7236651    -0.63   0.527    -1.875753    .9609618
             |
       _cons |  -2.086731   .5118559    -4.08   0.000     -3.08995   -1.083511
ln(exposure) |          1  (exposure)
-------------+----------------------------------------------------------------
    /lnalpha |   .5939963   .2583615                       .087617    1.100376
-------------+----------------------------------------------------------------
       alpha |   1.811212   .4679475                       1.09157    3.005294
------------------------------------------------------------------------------
LR test of alpha=0: chibar2(01) = 4056.27              Prob >= chibar2 = 0.000
```

图 6.7

* 拟合负二项回归模型

.nbreg deaths i.cohort, offset(logexp)

运行结果如图 6.8 所示。

* 与上述命令相同,但将离散度从平均值更改为常数

.nbreg deaths i.cohort, offset(logexp) dispersion(constant)

运行结果如图 6.9 所示。

```
Negative binomial regression                    Number of obs =       21
                                                LR chi2(2)    =     0.40
Dispersion: mean                                Prob > chi2   =   0.8171
Log likelihood = -131.3799                      Pseudo R2     =   0.0015

------------------------------------------------------------------------------
      deaths | Coefficient  Std. err.      z    P>|z|     [95% conf. interval]
-------------+----------------------------------------------------------------
      cohort |
   1960-1967 |  -.2676187   .7237203    -0.37   0.712    -1.686084    1.150847
   1968-1976 |  -.4573957   .7236651    -0.63   0.527    -1.875753    .9609618
             |
       _cons |  -2.086731    .511856    -4.08   0.000     -3.08995   -1.083511
      logexp |          1  (offset)
-------------+----------------------------------------------------------------
    /lnalpha |   .5939963   .2583615                      .0876171    1.100376
-------------+----------------------------------------------------------------
       alpha |   1.811212   .4679475                       1.09157    3.005295
------------------------------------------------------------------------------
LR test of alpha=0: chibar2(01) = 4056.27              Prob >= chibar2 = 0.000
```

图 6.8

```
Negative binomial regression                    Number of obs =       21
                                                LR chi2(2)    =     1.16
Dispersion: constant                            Prob > chi2   =   0.5598
Log likelihood = -139.66914                     Pseudo R2     =   0.0041

------------------------------------------------------------------------------
      deaths | Coefficient  Std. err.      z    P>|z|     [95% conf. interval]
-------------+----------------------------------------------------------------
      cohort |
   1960-1967 |  -.3180474   .4372491    -0.73   0.467     -1.17504    .5389452
   1968-1976 |   .1368621   .4420315     0.31   0.757    -.7295038    1.003228
             |
       _cons |  -3.914143   .3613023   -10.83   0.000    -4.622282   -3.206003
      logexp |          1  (offset)
-------------+----------------------------------------------------------------
    /lndelta |   4.741895   .3590761                      4.038118    5.445671
-------------+----------------------------------------------------------------
       delta |   114.6512   41.16851                      56.71952    231.7527
------------------------------------------------------------------------------
LR test of delta=0: chibar2(01) = 4039.69              Prob >= chibar2 = 0.000
```

图 6.9

* 拟合广义负二项模型

```
. gnbreg deaths age_mos, lnalpha(i.cohort) offset(logexp)
```

运行结果如图 6.10 所示。

Generalized negative binomial regression					Number of obs =	21
					LR chi2(1) =	28.04
					Prob > chi2 =	0.0000
Log likelihood = -117.56164					Pseudo R2 =	0.1065

deaths	Coefficient	Std. err.	z	P>|z|	[95% conf.	interval]
deaths						
age_mos	-.0516657	.0051747	-9.98	0.000	-.061808	-.0415233
_cons	-1.867225	.2227944	-8.38	0.000	-2.303894	-1.430556
logexp	1	(offset)				
lnalpha						
cohort						
1960-1967	.0939546	.7187748	0.13	0.896	-1.314818	1.502727
1968-1976	.0815279	.7365477	0.11	0.912	-1.362079	1.525135
_cons	-.4759581	.5156502	-0.92	0.356	-1.486614	.5346978

图 6.10

```
.test 2.cohort 3.cohort
```

运行结果如图 6.11 所示。

```
( 1)  [lnalpha]2.cohort = 0
( 2)  [lnalpha]3.cohort = 0

           chi2(  2) =    0.02
         Prob > chi2 =    0.9904
```

图 6.11

6.3 零膨胀泊松回归

如果计数数据中含有大量的"0",就要考虑使用零膨胀泊松(ZIP)回归或零膨胀负二项(ZINB)回归。理论上,决策可以分为两阶段进行,首先,决定取"0(无)"或者取"正整数(有)",这等于一个二元选择。其次,如果决定取"正整数(有)",则进一步确定具体选择哪个"正整数(有)"。

零膨胀泊松模型定义为:

$$\xi_j^{\beta} = \boldsymbol{x}_j \boldsymbol{\beta} + \text{offset}_j^{\beta} \tag{6.22}$$

$$\xi_j^{\gamma} = \boldsymbol{z}_j \gamma + \text{offset}_j^{\gamma} \tag{6.23}$$

$$\lambda_j = \exp(\xi_j^{\beta}) \tag{6.24}$$

$$F_j = F(\xi_j^{\gamma}) \tag{6.25}$$

这里,$F()$为 Logit 函数或 Probit 函数的逆函数。

$$\Pr(Y_j = 0 \mid \boldsymbol{x}_j, \boldsymbol{z}_j) = F_j + (1 - F_j)\exp(-\lambda_j) \tag{6.26}$$

$$\Pr(Y_j = n \mid \boldsymbol{x}_j, \boldsymbol{z}_j) = (1 - F_j)\exp(-\lambda_j)\frac{\lambda_j^n}{n!} \quad (n = 1, 2, \cdots) \tag{6.27}$$

则零膨胀泊松回归的对数似然函数为：

$$\begin{aligned} \ln L = &\sum_{j \in S} w_j \ln\{F_j + (1 - F_j)\exp(-\lambda_j)\} \\ &+ \sum_{j \notin S} w_j \{\ln(1 - F_j) - \lambda_j + \xi_j y_j - \ln(y_j!)\} \end{aligned} \tag{6.28}$$

式中，w_j 为权重，S 为观测值结果为 $y_i = 0$ 的观测集。

零膨胀泊松回归的语法格式为：

zip depvar [indepvars] [if] [in] [weight],inflate(varlist[, offset(varname)]|_cons) [options]

模型设定选项相比负二项模型与广义负二项模型增加了：

(1) inflate()：确定计数是否为零的膨胀方程式；

(2) probit：使用 Probit 模型来描述多余的零，默认为 logit。

菜单操作路径为：

Statistics>Count outcomes>Zero - inflated Poisson regression

zip 适用于零膨胀泊松模型，以对超过零计数的数据进行计数。零膨胀泊松模型假设多余的零计数来自 Logit 或 Probit 模型，剩余计数来自泊松模型。

例 6.3　零膨胀泊松回归

下面利用关于某一天国家公园游客捕获(计数)的鱼类数量的虚构数据进行说明。有些游客不钓鱼，但我们没有一个人是否钓鱼的数据，只有多少鱼被捕获的数据以及几个协变量。

变量计数显示出超过零的观测值(250 个观测值中的 142 个)，超出了泊松模型的预期值。我们怀疑零的数量可能被夸大了，因为许多游客没有钓鱼。也就是说，零观测值可能是一个不幸的游客没有钓到鱼，也可能是因为游客没有钓鱼。标准泊松模型将这两种类型的零观测值视为一个同质组，这通常会导致产生有偏差的统计结果。我们想区分这两种类型并对它们分别进行推断。

zip 命令允许我们对两种类型的零建模。首先，使用所需的选项 explate()，将游客是否钓鱼作为陪同儿童数量以及他或她是否在露营的函数。然后，假设答案变量 count 取决于访客是否使用了活诱饵(livebait)和人员数量，包括来访者及其陪同的任何成年人或儿童。

```
* 下载数据
.clear all
.webuse fish
* 拟合零膨胀泊松回归
.zip count persons livebait, inflate(child camper)
```

运行结果如图 6.12 所示。

Zero-inflated Poisson regression　　Number of obs = 250
Inflation model: logit　　Nonzero obs = 108
Zero obs = 142
LR chi2(2) = 506.48
Log likelihood = -850.7014　　Prob > chi2 = 0.0000

count	Coefficient	Std. err.	z	P>|z|	[95% conf. interval]	
count						
persons	.8068853	.0453288	17.80	0.000	.7180424	.8957281
livebait	1.757289	.2446082	7.18	0.000	1.277866	2.236713
_cons	-2.178472	.2860289	-7.62	0.000	-2.739078	-1.617865
inflate						
child	1.602571	.2797719	5.73	0.000	1.054228	2.150913
camper	-1.015698	.365259	-2.78	0.005	-1.731593	-.2998038
_cons	-.4922872	.3114562	-1.58	0.114	-1.10273	.1181558

图 6.12

* 重现结果,显示发生率比率

.zip, irr

运行结果如图 6.13 所示。

Zero-inflated Poisson regression　　Number of obs = 250
Inflation model: logit　　Nonzero obs = 108
Zero obs = 142
LR chi2(2) = 506.48
Log likelihood = -850.7014　　Prob > chi2 = 0.0000

count	IRR	Std. err.	z	P>|z|	[95% conf. interval]	
count						
persons	2.240917	.1015781	17.80	0.000	2.050415	2.449118
livebait	5.796703	1.417921	7.18	0.000	3.588973	9.362502
_cons	.1132144	.0323826	-7.62	0.000	.0646299	.1983216
inflate						
child	1.602571	.2797719	5.73	0.000	1.054228	2.150913
camper	-1.015698	.365259	-2.78	0.005	-1.731593	-.2998038
_cons	-.4922872	.3114562	-1.58	0.114	-1.10273	.1181558

Note: Estimates are transformed only in the first equation to incidence-rate ratios
Note: _cons estimates baseline incidence rate.

图 6.13

* 存储结果

.estimates store zip

* 拟合泊松回归,存储结果

```
.poisson count persons livebait
```

运行结果如图 6.14 所示。

Poisson regression　　Number of obs = 250
LR chi2(2) = 671.08
Prob > chi2 = 0.0000
Log likelihood = -1312.1779　　Pseudo R2 = 0.2036

count	Coefficient	Std. err.	z	P>|z|	[95% conf.	interval]
persons	.8176556	.0399138	20.49	0.000	.739426	.8958852
livebait	1.894319	.2321191	8.16	0.000	1.439374	2.349264
_cons	-3.026188	.2652824	-11.41	0.000	-3.546132	-2.506244

图 6.14

```
.estimates store pois
* 显示两个模型的 AIC 和 BIC
.estimates stats pois zip
```

运行结果如图 6.15 所示。

Akaike's information criterion and Bayesian information criterion

Model	N	ll(null)	ll(model)	df	AIC	BIC
pois	250	-1647.716	-1312.178	3	2630.356	2640.92
zip	250	-1103.942	-850.7014	6	1713.403	1734.532

Note: BIC uses N = number of observations. See [R] BIC note.

图 6.15

6.4 零膨胀负二项回归

zinb 命令能够最大化一个似然函数，该函数是 Logit 模型(或 Probit 模型)和负二项分布的混合。逻辑分布对产生多余零的未观测过程建模，负二项分布对计数建模。

零膨胀负二项模型定义为：

$$\xi_j^\beta = \boldsymbol{x}_j \boldsymbol{\beta} + \text{offset}_j^\beta \tag{6.29}$$

$$\xi_j^\gamma = \boldsymbol{z}_j \gamma + \text{offset}_j^\gamma \tag{6.30}$$

$$\mu_j = \exp(\xi_j^\beta) \tag{6.31}$$

$$p_j = 1/(1+\alpha\mu_j) \tag{6.32}$$

$$m = 1/\alpha \tag{6.33}$$

这里，向量 $\boldsymbol{x}_j$ 包含在第 j 次观测的 indepvars 中指定的协变量，而 $\boldsymbol{z}_j$ 包含在 inflate()选项中指定的协变量。类似地，在 zinb 系数表的第一个方程中可以找到 $\boldsymbol{\beta}$ 的估计值(在 depvar 之后标记)，在第二个方程中可以找到 γ 的估计值(标记为 inflate)。参数 α 是负二项式过度分散参数，其估计值是系数表中标记为 alpha 的辅助参数。参数 p_j、m 和 u_j 是负二项分布的参数。

零膨胀负二项回归的对数似然函数为：

$$\ln L = \sum_{j \in S} w_j \ln\{F_j + (1 - F_j) p_j^m\} + \sum_{j \notin S} w_j \{\ln(1 - F_j) + \ln\Gamma(m + y_j) - \ln\Gamma(y_j + 1) - \ln\Gamma(m) + m \ln p_j + y_j \ln(1 - p_j)\} \tag{6.34}$$

式中，w_j 为权重；S 为观测值结果为 $y_i=0$ 的观测集；F_j 为逻辑分布函数，即

$$F_j = F(\xi_j^\gamma) = \exp(\xi_j^\gamma)/\{1 + \exp(\xi_j^\gamma)\} \tag{6.35}$$

或者为 probit 选项对应的标准正态分布函数：

$$F_j = F(\xi_j^\gamma) = \Phi(\xi_j^\gamma) \tag{6.36}$$

混合分布的方差为：

$$\mathrm{Var}(y_j \mid \boldsymbol{x}_i, \boldsymbol{z}_i) = \mu_j (1 - F_j)\{1 + \mu_j (F_j + \alpha)\} \tag{6.37}$$

关于模型的选用，Stata 提供了一个"Vuong 统计量"，其渐近分布为标准正态分布，如果 Vuong 统计量为很大的正数，则应该选择零膨胀泊松回归或者零膨胀负二项回归；反之，则应该选择标准的泊松回归或负二项回归。

零膨胀负二项回归的语法格式为：

```
zinb depvar [indepvars] [if] [in] [weight], inflate(varlist[, offset(varname)]|_cons) [options]
```

模型设定选项及含义同零膨胀泊松回归。

菜单操作路径为：

Statistics>Count outcomes>Zero-inflated negative binomial regression

zinb 命令将一个零膨胀负二项模型用于过度分散的计数数据，其中包含过多的零计数。零膨胀负二项模型假设多余的零计数来自 Logit 或 Probit 模型，剩余计数来自负二项模型。

例 6.4 零膨胀负二项回归

本例所用数据同例 6.3。

```
* 下载数据
.clear all
.webuse fish
* 拟合零膨胀负二项回归
.zinb count persons livebait, inflate(child camper)
```

运行结果如图 6.16 所示。

Zero-inflated negative binomial regression
Inflation model: logit

Log likelihood = -401.5478

Number of obs = 250
Nonzero obs = 108
Zero obs = 142
LR chi2(2) = 82.23
Prob > chi2 = 0.0000

count	Coefficient	Std. err.	z	P>|z|	[95% conf.	interval]
count						
persons	.9742984	.1034938	9.41	0.000	.7714543	1.177142
livebait	1.557523	.4124424	3.78	0.000	.7491503	2.365895
_cons	-2.730064	.476953	-5.72	0.000	-3.664874	-1.795253
inflate						
child	3.185999	.7468551	4.27	0.000	1.72219	4.649808
camper	-2.020951	.872054	-2.32	0.020	-3.730146	-.3117567
_cons	-2.695385	.8929071	-3.02	0.003	-4.44545	-.9453189
/lnalpha	.5110429	.1816816	2.81	0.005	.1549535	.8671323
alpha	1.667029	.3028685			1.167604	2.380076

图 6.16

* 重现结果，显示系数、标准误差和小数点后 4 位的 CI

```
.zinb, cformat(%8.4f)
```

运行结果如图 6.17 所示。

Zero-inflated negative binomial regression
Inflation model: logit

Log likelihood = -401.5478

Number of obs = 250
Nonzero obs = 108
Zero obs = 142
LR chi2(2) = 82.23
Prob > chi2 = 0.0000

count	Coefficient	Std. err.	z	P>|z|	[95% conf.	interval]
count						
persons	0.9743	0.1035	9.41	0.000	0.7715	1.1771
livebait	1.5575	0.4124	3.78	0.000	0.7492	2.3659
_cons	-2.7301	0.4770	-5.72	0.000	-3.6649	-1.7953
inflate						
child	3.1860	0.7469	4.27	0.000	1.7222	4.6498
camper	-2.0210	0.8721	-2.32	0.020	-3.7301	-0.3118
_cons	-2.6954	0.8929	-3.02	0.003	-4.4455	-0.9453
/lnalpha	0.5110	0.1817	2.81	0.005	0.1550	0.8671
alpha	1.6670	0.3029			1.1676	2.3801

图 6.17

* 边际效应分析

```
.margins, dydx(child camper) predict(pr)
```

运行结果如图 6.18 所示。

```
Average marginal effects                        Number of obs = 250
Model VCE: OIM

Expression: Pr(count=0), predict(pr)
dy/dx wrt:  child camper
```

	dy/dx	Delta-method std. err.	z	P>|z|	[95% conf.	interval]
child	.257531	.029941	8.60	0.000	.1988477	.3162144
camper	-.1633578	.0503938	-3.24	0.001	-.2621277	-.0645878

图 6.18

6.5 截断泊松回归与截断负二项回归

对于左截断 ll_i 和右截断 ul_i 的非负计数结果 Y，截断泊松回归模型为：

$$f(y_j)=\frac{\exp(-\lambda_j)\lambda_j^{y_j}}{y_j!\ \Pr(ll_j<Y<ul_j\mid\xi_j)}\tag{6.38}$$

式中，$\xi_j=\boldsymbol{x}_j\boldsymbol{\beta}+\text{offset}_j$；$\lambda_j=\exp(\xi_j)$。$\boldsymbol{x}_j$ 是观测协变量向量。$ll_i<y_j<ul_i$ 的条件概率为：

$$\Pr(Y=y_j\mid ll_j<y_j<ul_j,\boldsymbol{x}_j)=\frac{\exp(-\lambda_j)\lambda_j^{y_j}}{y_j!\ \Pr(ll_j<Y<ul_j\mid\boldsymbol{x}_j)}\tag{6.39}$$

则对数似然函数为：

$$\ln L=\sum_{j=1}^{n}w_j[-\lambda_j+\xi_j y_j-\ln(y_j!\ )-\ln\{\Pr(ll_j<Y<ul_j\mid\xi_j)\}]\tag{6.40}$$

式中，没有设定时，权重 $w_j=1$。

截断泊松回归的语法格式为：

tpoisson depvar [indepvars] [if] [in] [weight] [, options]

模型设定选项及含义为：

(1) noconstant：无常数项；

(2) ll(# | varname)：截断下限，如果未指定 ll()或 ul()，则默认值为 ll(0)；

(3) ul(# | varname)：截断上限；

(4) exposure(varname_e)：在系数约束为 1 的模型中包含 ln(varname_e)；

(5) offset(varname_o)：将 varname_o 包含在系数约束为 1 的模型中；

(6) constraints(constraints)：应用指定的线性约束。

菜单操作路径为：

Statistics>Count outcomes>Truncated Poisson regression

当一个事件的发生次数被限制在一个截断点以上、一个截断点以下或两个截断点之间时，tpoisson 符合截断泊松模型。截断泊松模型适用于以下情况：在分布的截断部分，既没有观察到因变量，也没有观察到协变量。默认情况下，tpoisson 假设左截断发生在零处，但可以通过观察在其他固定点或不同的值处指定截断。

例 6.5　截断泊松回归

本例数据来自注册跑步者的跑鞋数据集在线运行日志。跑鞋营销主管想知道购买的跑鞋与哪些因素有关，如性别、婚姻状况、年龄、教育程度、收入、每周典型跑步次数、每周平均跑步距离，以及首选的跑步类型。这些数据自然被截断为零。

```
* 下载数据
.clear all
.webuse runshoes
* 默认截断点为 0 的截断泊松回归
.tpoisson shoes distance i.male age
```

运行结果如图 6.19 所示。

```
Truncated Poisson regression                    Number of obs     =         60
Limits:  lower =          0                     LR chi2(3)        =      15.47
         upper =       +inf                     Prob > chi2       =     0.0015
Log likelihood = -89.894865                     Pseudo R2         =     0.0792
```

shoes	Coefficient	Std. err.	z	P>|z|	[95% conf.	interval]
distance	.7746085	.2108183	3.67	0.000	.3614123	1.187805
1.male	.2363	.2411609	0.98	0.327	-.2363666	.7089667
age	.0096609	.0103858	0.93	0.352	-.0106949	.0300166
_cons	.1222747	.3676623	0.33	0.739	-.5983303	.8428796

图　6.19

```
.replace shoes = . if shoes < 4
* 截断点为 3 且暴露年龄可变的截断泊松回归
.tpoisson shoes distance male, exposure(age) ll(3)
```

运行结果如图 6.20 所示。

与截断泊松回归类似，如果定义截断计数结果 Y 服从负二项分布，就可以进行截断负二项回归(truncated negative binomial reg ression)。

截断负二项回归的语法命令为：

tnbreg depvar [indepvars] [if] [in] [weight] [, options]

模型设定选项及含义为：

(1) noconstant：无常数项；

(2) ll(# | varname)：截断点，默认值为 ll(0)，零截断；

```
Truncated Poisson regression                   Number of obs     =        12
Limits:  lower =          3                    LR chi2(2)        =     15.31
         upper =       +inf                    Prob > chi2       =    0.0005
Log likelihood = -11.356365                    Pseudo R2         =    0.4027

------------------------------------------------------------------------------
       shoes | Coefficient  Std. err.      z    P>|z|     [95% conf. interval]
-------------+----------------------------------------------------------------
    distance |   1.600925    .715772     2.24   0.025     .1980382    3.003813
        male |   16.88439    4341.99     0.00   0.997     -8493.26    8527.028
       _cons |  -20.34098    4341.99    -0.00   0.996    -8530.485    8489.803
     ln(age) |          1  (exposure)
------------------------------------------------------------------------------
```

图 6.20

(3) dispersion(mean):分数参数化(默认值);

(4) dispersion(constant):所有观测值的常数分散;

(5) exposure(varname_e):在系数限制为1的模型中包括ln(varname_e);

(6) offset(varname_o):将varname_o包含在系数约束为1的模型中;

(7) constraints(constraints):应用指定的线性约束。

菜单操作路径为:

Statistics>Count outcomes>Truncated negative binomial regression

tnbreg用最大似然估计截断负二项回归模型的参数。因变量depvar在indepvar上回归,其中depvar是一个正计数变量,其值均高于截断点。

例6.6 截断负二项回归

下面使用1997年的MedPar数据集(Hilbe,1999)[①]说明截断负二项模型的实现。这些数据来自亚利桑那州1495名被分配到诊断相关组(DRG)的有呼吸机的病人患者。因变量逗留时间(los)为正整数,信息技术不能有零值。数据被截断,因为没有观察到在那里待了零天的病人。

本例的目的是确定停留时间是否与二元变量相关,包括died、hmo、type1、type2、type3。

死亡变量被记录为0,否则被记录为1。其他变量也采用了这种编码。如果患者属于健康维护组织(HMO),则hmo取值为1。

type1、type2、type3变量表示患者的入院类型。type1变量表示有紧急情况,type2变量表示紧急承认,type3变量表示选修入院。因为type1、type2、type3相互排斥,三者中只有两个可用于截断负二项回归。

```
* 下载数据
.clear all
.webuse medpar
```

① Hilbe, J. M. sg102: Zero-truncated Poisson and Negative Binomial Regression. Stata Technical Bulletin 47: 37-40. Reprinted in Stata Technical Bulletin Reprints. College Station, TX: Stata Press, 1999, 8.

＊默认截断点为 0 的截断负二项回归

```
.tnbreg los died hmo type2—type3
```

运行结果如图 6.21 所示。

```
Truncated negative binomial regression                  Number of obs =  1,495
Truncation point = 0                                    LR chi2(4)    = 133.95
Dispersion: mean                                        Prob > chi2   = 0.0000
Log likelihood = -4737.535                              Pseudo R2     = 0.0139
```

los	Coefficient	Std. err.	z	P>|z|	[95% conf.	interval]
died	-.2521884	.0447084	-5.64	0.000	-.3398152	-.1645615
hmo	-.0754173	.0582351	-1.30	0.195	-.189556	.0387215
type2	.2685095	.0549962	4.88	0.000	.1607188	.3763001
type3	.7668101	.0830364	9.23	0.000	.6040617	.9295585
_cons	2.224028	.0300223	74.08	0.000	2.165185	2.28287
/lnalpha	-.630108	.0549749			-.7378569	-.5223591
alpha	.5325343	.029276			.4781375	.5931197

```
LR test of alpha=0: chibar2(01) = 4218.24               Prob >= chibar2 = 0.000
```

图 6.21

＊同上，但在 provnum 上集群

```
.tnbreg los died hmo type2—type3, vce(cluster provnum)
```

运行结果如图 6.22 所示。

```
Truncated negative binomial regression                  Number of obs =  1,495
Truncation point = 0                                    Wald chi2(4)  =  36.01
Dispersion: mean                                        Prob > chi2   = 0.0000
Log pseudolikelihood = -4737.535                        Pseudo R2     = 0.0139

                              (Std. err. adjusted for 54 clusters in provnum)
```

los	Coefficient	Robust std. err.	z	P>|z|	[95% conf.	interval]
died	-.2521884	.061533	-4.10	0.000	-.3727908	-.1315859
hmo	-.0754173	.0533132	-1.41	0.157	-.1799091	.0290746
type2	.2685095	.0666474	4.03	0.000	.137883	.3991359
type3	.7668101	.2183505	3.51	0.000	.338851	1.194769
_cons	2.224028	.034727	64.04	0.000	2.155964	2.292091
/lnalpha	-.630108	.0764019			-.779853	-.480363
alpha	.5325343	.0406866			.4584734	.6185588

图 6.22

* 下载数据

```
.clear all
.webuse rod93
```

* 截断点为 9 且离散度为常数的截断负二项回归

```
.tnbreg deaths i.cohort, ll(9) dispersion(constant)
```

运行结果如图 6.23 所示。

Truncated negative binomial regression　　Number of obs = 21
Truncation point = 9　　LR chi2(2) = 0.63
Dispersion: constant　　Prob > chi2 = 0.7300
Log likelihood = -108.13635　　Pseudo R2 = 0.0029

deaths	Coefficient	Std. err.	z	P>|z|	[95% conf.	interval]
cohort						
1960-1967	.0284079	.2786603	0.10	0.919	-.5177562	.574572
1968-1976	-.1886432	.3002085	-0.63	0.530	-.7770411	.3997547
_cons	4.482127	.2023622	22.15	0.000	4.085505	4.87875
/lndelta	3.251467	.3562464			2.553237	3.949697
delta	25.82821	9.201206			12.84863	51.91965

LR test of delta=0: chibar2(01) = 435.33　　Prob >= chibar2 = 0.000

图 6.23

* 同上,但指定暴露变量

```
.tnbreg deaths i.cohort, ll(9) dispersion(constant) exp(exposure)
```

运行结果如图 6.24 所示。

Truncated negative binomial regression　　Number of obs = 21
Truncation point = 9　　LR chi2(2) = 0.02
Dispersion: constant　　Prob > chi2 = 0.9918
Log likelihood = -117.61487　　Pseudo R2 = 0.0001

deaths	Coefficient	Std. err.	z	P>|z|	[95% conf.	interval]
cohort						
1960-1967	-.1343402	2.413037	-0.06	0.956	-4.863806	4.595126
1968-1976	-.5294571	4.929212	-0.11	0.914	-10.19054	9.131622
_cons	-5.181299	1.908899	-2.71	0.007	-8.922673	-1.439926
ln(exposure)	1	(exposure)				
/lndelta	5.256659	.5027054			4.271374	6.241943
delta	191.8395	96.43873			71.62	513.8561

LR test of delta=0: chibar2(01) = 4070.64　　Prob >= chibar2 = 0.000

图 6.24

6.6 删失泊松回归

删失泊松回归(censored poisson regression)是一种分析删失计数数据的方法。删失计数数据最常见的来源之一是top编码,当观察到 x 值或更大时,这些数据只记录 x 值。一个常见原因是观察对象的时间不够长。

对数据的审查可以是右审查、左审查或间隔审查。当我们观察协变量,但只观察到因变量大于或等于上限时,就会发生右审查;当我们观察协变量,但只观察到因变量小于或等于下限时,就是左审查。

假设 y_j 是观测 j 的观测区间删失因变量,y_j^* 是未经审查的潜在因变量。当 y_j 未被审查时,它与 y_j^* 相同。当对 y_j 进行审查时,只观察审查点。设 L_j 表示左删失点(下限),U_j 表示右截取点(上限),即有:

$$y_j=\begin{cases}L_j & \text{if } y_j^* \leqslant L_j \\ y_j^* & \text{if } L_j < y_j^* < U_j \\ U_j & \text{if } y_j^* \geqslant U_j\end{cases}$$

式中,L_j 和 U_j 可能在观察期间有所不同,因此个体可能有不同的左删失点和右删失点。

cpoisson命令可以用于左删失、右删失或两侧删失(称为区间删失)的数据,这里我们给出了区间删失情况下的公式,它适用于所有三种情况。

设 $f(y_j|\boldsymbol{x}_j)$ 表示泊松分布的概率密度函数。定义 $\xi_j=\boldsymbol{x}_j\boldsymbol{\beta}+\text{offset}_j$,即未审查变量的条件均值为 $E(y_j^*|\boldsymbol{x}_j)=\exp(\xi_j)$。第 j 个观测值的似然函数为:

$$l_j=w_j\Bigg[d_j\{-\exp(\xi_j)+y_j\xi_j-\ln(y_j!)\} + (1-d_j)\ln\left\{1-\sum_{k=0}^{U_j-1}f(k|\boldsymbol{x}_j)+\sum_{k=0}^{L_j}f(k|\boldsymbol{x}_j)\right\}\Bigg]$$

这里,$d_j=\begin{cases}0, & y_j^* \leqslant L_j \\ 1, & L_j<y_j^*<U_j \\ 0, & y_j^* \geqslant U_j\end{cases}$。

对数似然函数为:

$$\ln L=\sum_{j=1}^{N}l_j$$

删失泊松回归的语法命令为:

```
cpoisson depvar [indepvars] [if] [in] [weight] [, options]
```

模型设定选项及含义为:

(1) noconstant:压缩常数项;

(2) ll[(varname | #)]:左删失变量或限制;

(3) ul[(varname | #)]:右删失变量或限制;

(4) exposure(varname_e):在系数约束为 1 的模型中包含 ln(varname_e);

(5) offset(varname_o):将 varname_o 包含在系数约束为 1 的模型中;

(6) constraints(constraints):应用指定的线性约束。

菜单操作路径为:

Statistics>Count outcomes>Censored Poisson regression

cpoisson 命令拟合一个计数因变量的泊松模型,该模型具有一些截断值。当因变量被左删失(有下限)、右删失(有上限)或区间删失(有下限和上限)时,可以使用该命令。

例 6.7 删失泊松回归

下面数据为从 ABC 游乐园所在州的随机抽样家庭中收集的关于一个家庭参观 ABC 游乐园多少次的调查数据。受访者被问及去年参观公园的次数(trips)、收入(income),以及家庭中的子女数量(children)。旅行记录中的旅行次数在“三次或三次以上”的排名靠前。我们将右删失旅行建模为收入和子女数量的函数。

```
* 下载数据
.clear all
.webuse trips
* 拟合删失泊松回归
.cpoisson trips income children, ul(3)
```

运行结果如图 6.25 所示。

```
Censored Poisson regression                     Number of obs     =        500
                                                      Uncensored =        278
Limits: Lower = 0                                  Left-censored =          0
        Upper = 3                                 Right-censored =        222

                                                LR chi2(2)        =      49.29
Log likelihood = -600.78415                     Prob > chi2       =     0.0000

------------------------------------------------------------------------------
       trips | Coefficient  Std. err.      z    P>|z|     [95% conf. interval]
-------------+----------------------------------------------------------------
      income |   .0740477   .0137653     5.38   0.000     .0470683    .1010272
    children |   .1346922    .028617     4.71   0.000      .078604    .1907805
       _cons |   .0033918   .1455473     0.02   0.981    -.2818756    .2886592
------------------------------------------------------------------------------
```

图 6.25

第7章 复杂线性回归模型

7.1 分数回归

当研究问题的结果作为分数进行测量时，可能会出现分数响应数据。例如，基尼系数。这些数据也经常被观察到从聚合的二元结果生成比例。例如，对于个别学生是否通过考试的数据，我们可能仅仅有关于比例的数据，以及每个学校通过考试的学生人数数据。

当因变量的值位于区间[0,1]时，分数模型是合适的。如果被解释变量只接受0和1之间的值，Beta回归可能是一个有效的替代方案。Beta回归的因变量平均值分布更灵活，但如果因变量还要等于0或1，则需要用分数模型。

分数模型允许样本误差项存在系列相关或自相关。其一般的模型表达式为：

$$E(y_i \mid \boldsymbol{x}_i) = G(\boldsymbol{x}_i\boldsymbol{\beta}) \tag{7.1}$$

其中，$\{(\boldsymbol{x}_i, y_i): i=1,2,\cdots,N\}$中，$0\leqslant y_i\leqslant 1$。$G(\boldsymbol{x}'_j\boldsymbol{\beta})$函数可以是以下三种形式：

（1）Probit 函数形式：$\Phi(\boldsymbol{x}'_j\boldsymbol{\beta})$

（2）Logit 函数形式：$\exp(\boldsymbol{x}'_j\boldsymbol{\beta})/\{1+\exp(\boldsymbol{x}'_j\boldsymbol{\beta})\}$

（3）Hetprobit 函数形式：$\Phi\{\boldsymbol{x}'_j\boldsymbol{\beta}/\exp(\boldsymbol{z}'_j\gamma)\}$。

其较为一般的 Logit 函数设定是用对数机会比率作为被解释变量的线性函数：

$$E(\log[y/(1-y)] \mid \boldsymbol{x}) = \boldsymbol{x\beta}$$

分数模型的对数似然函数为：

$$\ln L = \sum_{j=1}^{N} w_j y_i \ln\{G(\boldsymbol{x}'_j\boldsymbol{\beta})\} + w_j(1-y_i)\ln\{1-G(\boldsymbol{x}'_j\boldsymbol{\beta})\}$$

其中，y_j为因变量，w_j为可选权重。

分数回归的语法格式为：

（1）分数 Probit 回归的语法格式

```
fracreg probit depvar [indepvars] [if] [in] [weight] [, options]
```

（2）分数 Logistic 回归的语法格式

```
fracreg logit depvar [indepvars] [if] [in] [weight] [, options]
```

（3）异方差 Probit 分数回归的语法格式

fracreg probit depvar [indepvars] [if] [in] [weight], het(varlist[, offset(varname_o)]) [options]

菜单操作路径为：

Statistics>Fractional outcomes>Fractional regression

例 7.1　分数回归

本例中的数据是不同类型公司在401(k)计划中的预期参与率。参与率(prate)是指企业中符合条件的员工参与401(k)计划的比例。

＊下载数据

. use https://www.stata-press.com/data/r17/401k

＊描述统计

. summarize prate

运行结果如图7.1所示。

Variable	Obs	Mean	Std. dev.	Min	Max
prate	4,075	.840607	.1874841	.0036364	1

图　7.1

＊正态分布的分数回归

. fracreg probit prate mrate c.ltotemp# #c.ltotemp c.age# #c.age i.sole

运行结果如图7.2所示。

```
Fractional probit regression                    Number of obs   =   4,075
                                                Wald chi2(6)    =  815.88
                                                Prob > chi2     =  0.0000
Log pseudolikelihood = -1674.6232               Pseudo R2       =  0.0632
```

prate	Coefficient	Robust std. err.	z	P>|z|	[95% conf.	interval]
mrate	.5859715	.0387616	15.12	0.000	.5100002	.6619429
ltotemp	-.6102767	.0615052	-9.92	0.000	-.7308246	-.4897288
c.ltotemp#c.ltotemp	.0313576	.003975	7.89	0.000	.0235667	.0391484
age	.0273266	.0031926	8.56	0.000	.0210691	.033584
c.age#c.age	-.0003159	.0000875	-3.61	0.000	-.0004874	-.0001443
sole						
Only plan	.0683196	.0272091	2.51	0.012	.0149908	.1216484
_cons	3.25991	.2323929	14.03	0.000	2.804429	3.715392

图　7.2

＊逻辑分布的分数回归

. fracreg logit prate mrate c.ltotemp# #c.ltotemp c.age# #c.age i.sole

运行结果如图 7.3 所示。

Fractional logistic regression　　　Number of obs = 4,075
Wald chi2(6) = 817.73
Prob > chi2 = 0.0000
Log pseudolikelihood = -1673.5566　　　Pseudo R2 = 0.0638

prate	Coefficient	Robust std. err.	z	P>|z|	[95% conf.	interval]
mrate	1.143516	.074748	15.30	0.000	.9970125	1.290019
ltotemp	-1.103275	.1130667	-9.76	0.000	-1.324882	-.8816687
c.ltotemp#c.ltotemp	.0565782	.0072883	7.76	0.000	.0422934	.070863
age	.0512643	.0059399	8.63	0.000	.0396223	.0629064
c.age#c.age	-.0005891	.0001645	-3.58	0.000	-.0009114	-.0002667
sole						
Only plan	.1137479	.0507762	2.24	0.025	.0142284	.2132674
_cons	5.747761	.4294386	13.38	0.000	4.906077	6.589445

图　7.3

＊估算机会比率

.fracreg logit prate mrate c. ltotemp ＃ ＃ c. ltotemp c. age ＃ ＃ c. age i. sole, or

运行结果如图 7.4 所示。

Fractional logistic regression　　　Number of obs = 4,075
Wald chi2(6) = 817.73
Prob > chi2 = 0.0000
Log pseudolikelihood = -1673.5566　　　Pseudo R2 = 0.0638

prate	Odds ratio	Robust std. err.	z	P>|z|	[95% conf.	interval]
mrate	3.137781	.2345429	15.30	0.000	2.710173	3.632857
ltotemp	.3317826	.0375136	-9.76	0.000	.2658343	.4140913
c.ltotemp#c.ltotemp	1.058209	.0077125	7.76	0.000	1.043201	1.073434
age	1.052601	.0062524	8.63	0.000	1.040418	1.064927
c.age#c.age	.9994111	.0001644	-3.58	0.000	.999089	.9997333
sole						
Only plan	1.12047	.0568932	2.24	0.025	1.01433	1.237716
_cons	313.4879	134.6238	13.38	0.000	135.1083	727.3771

Note: _cons estimates baseline odds.

图　7.4

7.2 Beta 回 归

因变量(如比率、比例、分数数据)通常大于 0 且小于 1,这就需要 Bata 回归和分数阶 Logistic 回归建模。

Beta 模型是以协变量 $\boldsymbol{x}$ 为条件的因变量 y 的平均值的模型,用 μ_x 表示。因为 y 在(0,1)中,可以使用条件平均值的连接函数,用 $g()$表示,确保 μ_x 也在(0,1)中。Beta 模型的表达式为:

$$g(\mu_x)=\boldsymbol{x\beta} \tag{7.2}$$

或

$$\mu_x=g^{-1}(\boldsymbol{x\beta}) \tag{7.3}$$

连接函数表达式如表 7.1 所示。

表 7.1 连接函数表达式

连接函数	表达式
Logit	$g(\mu_X)=\ln\{\mu_X/(1-\mu_X)\}$
Probit	$g(\mu_x)=\Phi^{-1}(\mu_x)$
Cloglog	$g(\mu_x)=\ln\{-\ln(1-\mu_x)\}$
Loglog	$g(\mu_x)=-\ln\{-\ln(\mu_x)\}$

Logit 连接函数形式的 Beta 回归为:

$$\ln\{\mu_x/(1-\mu_x)\}=\boldsymbol{x\beta} \tag{7.4}$$

$$\mu_x=\exp(\boldsymbol{x\beta})/\{1+\exp(\boldsymbol{x\beta})\} \tag{7.5}$$

Beta 回归用最大似然法估计参数。其对数似然函数为:

$$\sum_{i=1}^{N}\omega_i(\ln\{\Gamma(\psi_{x,i})\}-\ln\{\Gamma(\mu_{x,i}\psi_{x,i})\}-\ln[\Gamma\{(1-\mu_{x,i})\psi_{x,i}\}] \\ +(\mu_{x,i}\psi_{x,i}-1)\ln(y_i)+\{(1-\mu_{x,i})\psi_{x,i}-1\}\ln(1-y_i)) \tag{7.6}$$

Beta 回归的语法格式为:

```
betareg depvar indepvars [if] [in] [weight] [, options]
```

菜单操作路径为:

```
Statistics>Fractional outcomes>Beta regression
```

例 7.2 Beta 回归

假设我们想知道提供暑期教学计划是否能提高学生在学校的学习效率,即学生进行的强制性国家考试的通过率。全校的通过率必须介于 0 和 1 之间,任何学校都不可能没有学生通过或所有学生都通过,因此,我们考虑使用 Beta 回归评估暑期教学计划的效果。数据集 sprogram 包含关于 1000 所学校通过率(prate)的虚构数据。下面示例程序先读取数据并验证 prate 不包含多个 0 或 1。

```
* 下载数据集
.clear
.use https://www.stata-press.com/data/r17/sprogram
* 描述统计
.summarize prate
```

运行结果如图 7.5 所示。

Variable	Obs	Mean	Std. dev.	Min	Max
prate	1,000	.8150803	.1233684	.2986041	.9973584

图 7.5

```
* beta 回归
.betareg prate i.summer freemeals pdonations
```

运行结果如图 7.6 所示。

```
Beta regression                                  Number of obs     =      1,000
                                                 LR chi2(3)        =     164.61
                                                 Prob > chi2       =     0.0000

Link function  :  g(u) = log(u/(1-u))            [Logit]
Slink function :  g(u) = log(u)                  [Log]

Log likelihood =  893.02792
```

prate	Coefficient	Std. err.	z	P>|z|	[95% conf.	interval]
prate						
summer						
Yes	.5560171	.0480307	11.58	0.000	.4618787	.6501555
freemeals	-.4564181	.0834885	-5.47	0.000	-.6200525	-.2927836
pdonations	.0449706	.0097781	4.60	0.000	.025806	.0641353
_cons	1.175013	.0642797	18.28	0.000	1.049027	1.300999
scale						
_cons	2.375433	.0443005	53.62	0.000	2.288606	2.462261

图 7.6

```
* 将比例参数建模为 freemeals 的函数
.betareg prate i.summer freemeals pdonations, scale(freemeals)
```

运行结果如图 7.7 所示。

```
* 模型选择
.quietly betareg prate i.summer freemeals pdonations, scale(freemeals)
```

```
Beta regression                                  Number of obs    =      1,000
                                                 LR chi2(4)       =     169.38
                                                 Prob > chi2      =     0.0000

Link function  :  g(u) = log(u/(1-u))            [Logit]
Slink function :  g(u) = log(u)                  [Log]

Log likelihood =  895.41544

------------------------------------------------------------------------------
       prate | Coefficient  Std. err.      z    P>|z|     [95% conf. interval]
-------------+----------------------------------------------------------------
prate        |
      summer |
         Yes |   .5571133   .0480378    11.60   0.000     .4629609    .6512658
   freemeals |  -.5291892   .0896511    -5.90   0.000    -.7049021   -.3534762
  pdonations |   .0454228   .0097809     4.64   0.000     .0262527    .0645929
       _cons |   1.209179   .0649585    18.61   0.000     1.081863    1.336495
-------------+----------------------------------------------------------------
scale        |
   freemeals |  -.3598137   .1644214    -2.19   0.029    -.6820737   -.0375536
       _cons |   2.547047   .0882327    28.87   0.000     2.374114     2.71998
------------------------------------------------------------------------------
```

图 7.7

. estimates store model1

. quietly betareg prate i. summer freemeals pdonations, scale(freemeals) link(cloglog)

. estimates store model2

. quietly betareg prate i. summer freemeals pdonations, scale(freemeals) slink(root)

. estimates store model3

. quietly betareg prate i. summer freemeals pdonations, scale(freemeals) link(cloglog) slink(root)

. estimates store model4

* 列表展示

. estimates table model1 model2 model3 model4, stats(bic) se

运行结果如图 7.8 所示。

Variable	model1	model2	model3	model4
prate				
summer				
Yes	.55711332	.27762093	.55719742	.27765283
	.04803785	.02460121	.04803698	.02459953
freemeals	-.52918917	-.25685191	-.5300549	-.25729221
	.08965112	.04308385	.08978883	.04314336
pdonations	.04542281	.02162612	.04542462	.02163225
	.00978086	.00444813	.00978099	.00444817
_cons	1.2091789	.37961457	1.2094991	.37977162
	.06495845	.03212448	.06496946	.03212509
scale				
freemeals	-.35981368	-.36808486	-.59912234	-.61295521
	.16442142	.16448631	.27259725	.27273851
_cons	2.5470469	2.5516626	3.5692049	3.5771444
	.0882327	.08821157	.15204032	.15218042
Statistics				
bic	-1749.3843	-1749.9903	-1749.444	-1750.0511

Legend: b/se

图 7.8

7.3 广义线性模型

广义线性模型表达式为：

$$g\{E(y)\}=x\boldsymbol{\beta},\quad y\sim F$$

其中，F 称为分配族。替换不同的 $g()$ 和 F，会产生一系列的线性回归模型。连接函数选项如表 7.2 所示。

表 7.2 连接函数选项

连接函数	glm 选项	连接函数式
Identity	link(identity)	$\eta=g(\mu)=\mu$
Log	link(log)	$\eta=\ln(\mu)$
Logit	link(logit)	$\eta=\ln\{\mu/(1-\mu)\}$
Probit	link(probit)	$\eta=\Phi^{-1}(\mu)$

（续表）

连接函数	glm 选项	连接函数式
Cloglog	link(cloglog)	$\eta=\ln\{-\ln(1-\mu)\}$
Odds power	link(opower #)	$\eta=\{\mu/(1-\mu)\}^n-1 \mid /n$
Power	link(power #)	$\eta=\mu^n$
Negative binomial	link(nbinomial)	$\eta=\ln\{\mu/(\mu+k)\}$
Loglog	link(loglog)	$\eta=-\ln\{-\ln(\mu)\}$
Log-complement	link(logc)	$\eta=\ln(1-\mu)$

分布函数选项如表 7.3 所示。默认连接函数是对于指定的分布族的典型连接(nbinomial 除外)。

表 7.3　分布函数选项

序号	分布类型	glm 选项	默认连接函数
1	Gaussian (normal)	family(gaussian)	link(identity)
2	inverse Gaussian	family(igaussian)	link(power-2)
3	Bernoulli/binomial	family(binomial)	link(logit)
4	Poisson	family(poisson)	link(log)
5	negative binomial	family(nbinomial)	link(log)
6	gamma	family(gamma)	link(power-1)

如果同时指定 family()和 link()，则并非所有组合都有意义，可选组合如表 7.4 所示。

表 7.4　分布函数与连接函数的可选组合

	Identity	Log	Logit	Probit	Cloglog	Power	Opower	Nbinomial	Loglog	Logc
Gaussian (normal)	X	X				X				
inverse Gaussian	X	X				X				
Bernoulli/binomial	X	X	X	X	X	X	X		X	X
Poisson	X	X				X				
negative binomial	X	X				X		X		
gamma	X	X				X				

广义线性模型可以利用迭代加权最小二乘优化法或 MLE 法估计参数。

广义线性模型的语法格式为：

```
glm depvar [indepvars] [if] [in] [weight] [, options]
```

菜单操作路径为：

```
Statistics>Generalized linear models>Generalized linear models (GLM)
```

例 7.3　广义线性回归

我们根据对与低出生体重相关的风险因素进行研究所得的数据拟合了一个模型，可以使用 glm 复制估算。

```
* 下载数据集
. use https://www.stata-press.com/data/r17/lbw
* Logistic 广义线性回归模型
. glm low age lwt i.race smoke ptl ht ui, family(binomial) link(logit)
```

运行结果如图 7.9 所示。

```
Generalized linear models                         Number of obs     =        189
Optimization     : ML                             Residual df       =        180
                                                  Scale parameter   =          1
Deviance         =  201.4479911                   (1/df) Deviance   =   1.119156
Pearson          =  182.0233425                   (1/df) Pearson    =   1.011241

Variance function: V(u) = u*(1-u)                 [Bernoulli]
Link function    : g(u) = ln(u/(1-u))             [Logit]

                                                  AIC               =     1.1611
Log likelihood   = -100.7239956                   BIC               =  -742.0665
```

low	Coefficient	OIM std. err.	z	P>|z|	[95% conf.	interval]
age	-.0271003	.0364504	-0.74	0.457	-.0985418	.0443412
lwt	-.0151508	.0069259	-2.19	0.029	-.0287253	-.0015763
race						
Black	1.262647	.5264101	2.40	0.016	.2309024	2.294392
Other	.8620792	.4391532	1.96	0.050	.0013548	1.722804
smoke	.9233448	.4008266	2.30	0.021	.137739	1.708951
ptl	.5418366	.346249	1.56	0.118	-.136799	1.220472
ht	1.832518	.6916292	2.65	0.008	.4769494	3.188086
ui	.7585135	.4593768	1.65	0.099	-.1418484	1.658875
_cons	.4612239	1.20459	0.38	0.702	-1.899729	2.822176

图 7.9

```
* 报告指数参数
. glm, eform
```

运行结果如图 7.10 所示。

```
* 估计信息准则
. estat ic
```

运行结果如图 7.11 所示。

```
Generalized linear models                          Number of obs     =        189
Optimization     : ML                              Residual df       =        180
                                                   Scale parameter   =          1
Deviance         =  201.4479911                    (1/df) Deviance   =   1.119156
Pearson          =  182.0233425                    (1/df) Pearson    =   1.011241

Variance function: V(u) = u*(1-u)                  [Bernoulli]
Link function    : g(u) = ln(u/(1-u))              [Logit]

                                                   AIC               =     1.1611
Log likelihood   = -100.7239956                    BIC               =  -742.0665

------------------------------------------------------------------------------
             |                 OIM
         low | Odds ratio   std. err.      z    P>|z|     [95% conf. interval]
-------------+----------------------------------------------------------------
         age |   .9732636   .0354759    -0.74   0.457     .9061578    1.045339
         lwt |   .9849634   .0068217    -2.19   0.029     .9716834    .9984249
             |
        race |
      Black  |   3.534767   1.860737     2.40   0.016     1.259736    9.918406
      Other  |   2.368079   1.039949     1.96   0.050     1.001356    5.600207
             |
       smoke |   2.517698    1.00916     2.30   0.021     1.147676    5.523162
         ptl |   1.719161   .5952579     1.56   0.118     .8721455    3.388787
          ht |   6.249602   4.322408     2.65   0.008     1.611152    24.24199
          ui |     2.1351   .9808153     1.65   0.099     .8677528      5.2534
       _cons |   1.586014   1.910496     0.38   0.702     .1496092     16.8134
------------------------------------------------------------------------------
Note: _cons estimates baseline odds.
```

图 7.10

```
-----------------------------------------------------------------------------
       Model |          N   ll(null)  ll(model)      df         AIC        BIC
-------------+---------------------------------------------------------------
           . |        189          .   -100.724       9     219.448   248.6237
-----------------------------------------------------------------------------
Note: BIC uses N = number of observations. See [R] BIC note.
```

图 7.11

```
*清空内存,下载数据集
.clear
.use https://www.stata-press.com/data/r17/ldose
*列表显示数据
```

```
.list, sep(4)
```

运行结果如图 7.12 所示。

	ldose	n	r
1.	1.6907	59	6
2.	1.7242	60	13
3.	1.7552	62	18
4.	1.7842	56	28
5.	1.8113	63	52
6.	1.8369	59	53
7.	1.861	62	61
8.	1.8839	60	60

图 7.12

* Logit 模型

```
.glm r ldose, family(binomial n) link(logit)
```

运行结果如图 7.13 所示。

```
Generalized linear models                         Number of obs     =         8
Optimization     : ML                             Residual df       =         6
                                                  Scale parameter   =         1
Deviance         =  11.23220702                   (1/df) Deviance   =  1.872035
Pearson          =   10.0267936                   (1/df) Pearson    =  1.671132

Variance function: V(u) = u*(1-u/n)               [Binomial]
Link function    : g(u) = ln(u/(n-u))             [Logit]

                                                  AIC               =  5.178781
Log likelihood   = -18.71512262                   BIC               = -1.244442
```

r	Coefficient	OIM std. err.	z	P>|z|	[95% conf. interval]	
ldose	34.27034	2.912141	11.77	0.000	28.56265	39.97803
_cons	-60.71747	5.180713	-11.72	0.000	-70.87149	-50.56346

图 7.13

* Cloglog 模型

```
.glm r ldose, family(binomial n) link(cloglog)
```

运行结果如图 7.14 所示。

```
Generalized linear models                         Number of obs     =          8
Optimization     : ML                             Residual df       =          6
                                                  Scale parameter   =          1
Deviance         =  3.446418004                   (1/df) Deviance   =    .574403
Pearson          =  3.294675153                   (1/df) Pearson    =   .5491125

Variance function: V(u) = u*(1-u/n)               [Binomial]
Link function    : g(u) = ln(-ln(1-u/n))          [Complementary log-log]

                                                  AIC               =   4.205557
Log likelihood   = -14.82222811                   BIC               =  -9.030231

------------------------------------------------------------------------------
             |                 OIM
           r | Coefficient  std. err.      z    P>|z|     [95% conf. interval]
-------------+----------------------------------------------------------------
       ldose |   22.04118   1.793089    12.29   0.000     18.52679    25.55557
       _cons |  -39.57232   3.229047   -12.26   0.000    -45.90114   -33.24351
------------------------------------------------------------------------------
```

图 7.14

7.4 Heckman 选择模型

Heckman(1976)[①]在研究美国已婚妇女是否选择工作这一经济现象时提出了选择性问题。由于能直接观测的是选择工作的已婚妇女的市场工资，而选择不工作的妇女的收入不能观测，显然市场工资只能从选择工作的群体中观测，这样得到的市场工资样本就是所谓的选择性样本。选择性样本不是从已婚妇女这个总体中随机抽取得到的，由此导致使用选择性样本来推断总体特征就有可能产生偏差即所谓的“选择性偏差”，因此模型从设定到估计与检验均须考虑这种选择性数据并基于模型分析其偏差。Heckman 以微观经济理论来解释个体资料的样本选择问题并提出了 Heckman 选择模型。

7.4.1 Heckman 选择模型的形式

在 Heckman 选择框架下，因变量仅对于部分数据可观测得到，本质上是观测值遗失问题。观测值经常由于微观经济主体的“自选择”行为而遗失，观测值遗失原因与未遗失观测值性质之间的关系需要一个精妙的理论结构来解释。Heckman 选择模型有时也被称为 Heckit 模型，是估计存在样本选择偏差的一种方法。令 y 是选择工作

① Heckman, J. J. The Common Structure of Statistical Models of Truncation, Aample Selection and Limited Dependent Variables and a Simple Estimator for Such Models. *Annals of Economic and Social Measurement*, 1976,5.

的已婚妇女的市场工资，x 是 y 的影响因素，由于样本选择问题，它并非总能观测到；z 为二元隐性变量，当 $z_i=1$ 时，已婚妇女选择工作；当 $z_i=0$ 时，已婚妇女不工作，w 是 z 的影响因素。z 的取值决定 y 是否能被观测到，选择不工作的妇女的收入不能被观测到。Heckman 线性选择模型包含两个方程，分别为响应方程（response equation）和选择方程（selection equation），模型的形式为：

响应方程：

$$y_i = x_i\beta + u_i \tag{7.8}$$

选择方程：

$$z_i = w_i'\gamma + \varepsilon_i \tag{7.9}$$

式中，z_i 为一个二元变量，仅当 $z_i=1$ 时，y_i 可被观测到，即

$$z_i = \begin{cases} 1 & y_i \text{ 可被观测到} \\ 0 & y_i \text{ 不可被观测到} \end{cases}$$

u_i 和 ε_i 是服从二元正态分布的误差项：

$$\begin{bmatrix} u_i \\ \varepsilon_i \end{bmatrix} \sim N\begin{bmatrix} \sigma^2 & \rho\sigma \\ \rho\sigma & 1 \end{bmatrix}$$

其中，σ 为尺度参数，ρ 为相关系数，在这个模型中 ε_i 的方差可不识别，不妨设为 1。选择方程用来确定 y_i 是否可被观测到。估计 Heckman 选择模型通常有两种方法：Heckman 两步法和最大似然法。

7.4.2 Heckman 两步法

Heckman 两步法是基于下面的观察：

$$E(y_i \mid z_i=1) = \boldsymbol{x}_i'\boldsymbol{\beta} + \rho\sigma\lambda_i(w_i'\gamma) \tag{7.10}$$

式中，$\lambda(x)=\phi(x)/\Phi(x)$，称为逆米尔斯比率（inverse Mills ratio），$\phi(x)$ 和 $\Phi(x)$ 分别是标准正态密度和累积分布函数。这样我们可以指定一个回归模型：

$$y_i = \boldsymbol{x}_i'\boldsymbol{\beta}_i + \rho\sigma\lambda_1(w_i'\gamma) + v_i \tag{7.11}$$

Heckman 两步法首先估计选择公式得到 $\hat{\gamma}$，并计算

$$\hat{\lambda}_i = \phi(\boldsymbol{w}_i'\hat{\gamma}/\Phi(w_i'\hat{\gamma}) \tag{7.12}$$

然后利用最小二乘法估计方程：

$$y_i = \boldsymbol{x}_i'\boldsymbol{\beta}_i + \rho\sigma\hat{\lambda}_i + v_i \tag{7.13}$$

得到 β 和 $\theta=\rho\sigma$ 的一致估计。标准误偏差的估计量可以从通常的回归标准误差 s 中得到。也可计算得到 ρ 的估计量 $\hat{\rho}=\hat{\theta}/s$。

Heckman 两步法的系数协方差矩阵由下式给出：

$$\hat{\boldsymbol{\Omega}} = \hat{\sigma}^2(\boldsymbol{X}^{*\prime}\boldsymbol{X}^*)^{-1}(\boldsymbol{X}^{*\prime}(I-\hat{\rho}^2\hat{\boldsymbol{\Delta}})\boldsymbol{X}^* + \boldsymbol{Q})(\boldsymbol{X}^{*\prime}\boldsymbol{X}^*)^{1} \tag{7.14}$$

式中，$X_i^*=(\boldsymbol{x}_i',\hat{\lambda}_i)'$，$\hat{\boldsymbol{\Delta}}$ 是对角线元素为 $\hat{\delta}_i=\hat{\lambda}_i(\hat{\lambda}_i-w_i'\hat{\gamma})$ 的对角矩阵，I 是单位矩阵，$\boldsymbol{Q}=\hat{\boldsymbol{\rho}}^2(\boldsymbol{X}^*\hat{\boldsymbol{\Delta}}\boldsymbol{W})\hat{\boldsymbol{V}}(\boldsymbol{X}^*\hat{\boldsymbol{\Delta}}\boldsymbol{W})$，$\hat{\boldsymbol{V}}$ 是从选择公式得到的系数协方差矩阵，$\boldsymbol{W}$ 是选择的

解释变量矩阵。

7.4.3 最大似然法

最大似然法利用给定的对数似然函数估计 Heckman 选择模型：

$$\ln L(\boldsymbol{\beta},\gamma,\rho,\sigma \mid \boldsymbol{X},\boldsymbol{W})=\sum_{i\mid z_i=0}\ln(1-\Phi(\boldsymbol{w}_i'\gamma))+\sum_{i\mid z_i=1}-\ln(\sigma)+\ln\left(\phi\left(\frac{y_i-\boldsymbol{x}_i'\boldsymbol{\beta}}{\sigma}\right)\right)$$

$$+\ln\left(1-\Phi\left(\frac{-\left(w_i'\gamma+\rho\left(\frac{y_i-\boldsymbol{x}_i'\boldsymbol{\beta}}{\sigma}\right)\right)}{\sqrt{1-\rho^2}}\right)\right) \tag{7.15}$$

式中，$\boldsymbol{W}$ 是响应公式的解释变量矩阵，第一个求和项表示 $z_i=0$ 时的观测（即 y_i 不可观测时），第二个求和项是 $z_i=1$ 时的观测（即 y_i 可观测时）。这是一个简单的关于参数 $\boldsymbol{\beta}$、γ、ρ、σ 最大化对数似然函数问题。

使用上面列出的 Heckman 两步法可以得到优化的起始值。与大多数最大似然估计一样，估计参数的协方差矩阵可以通过 $(-H)^{-1}$（H 为 Hessian 矩阵、信息矩阵）或 GG^{-1}（G 是梯度矩阵）计算，或利用 $H^{-1}GG^{-1}H^{-1}$（Huber/White 矩阵）来计算。

7.4.4 Heckman 选择模型的 Stata 实现

Heckman 选择模型的语法格式为：

（1）基本语法格式

heckman depvar [indepvars], select(varlist_s) [twostep]

或者

heckman depvar [indepvars], select(depvar_s = varlist_s) [twostep]

（2）仅用于最大似然估计的完整语法格式

heckman depvar [indepvars] [if] [in] [weight], select([depvar_s =] varlist_s [, noconstant offset(varname_o)]) [heckman_ml_options]

（3）Heckman 两步一致估计的完整语法格式

heckman depvar [indepvars] [if] [in], twostep select([depvar_s =] varlist_s [, noconstant]) [heckman_ts_options]

菜单操作路径为：

Statistics>Sample-selection models>Heckman selection model

例 7.4 Heckman 选择模型

下面以 Stata 自带数据集 womenwk 说明 Heckman 选择模型的实现。该数据集收集了 2000 位妇女的工作工资情况，其中 1343 位有工作。我们假设小时工资是教育和年龄的函数，而工作的可能性（观察工资的可能性）是婚姻状况、在家子女数量和（隐含）工资（也包括年龄和教育情况，我们认为这决定了工资）的函数。

* 加载数据

```
. webuse womenwk
```

* 仅用于最大似然估计

```
. heckman wage educ age, select(married children educ age)
```

运行结果如图 7.15 所示。

```
Iteration 0:   log likelihood = -5178.7009
Iteration 1:   log likelihood = -5178.3049
Iteration 2:   log likelihood = -5178.3045

Heckman selection model                         Number of obs     =      2,000
(regression model with sample selection)              Selected    =      1,343
                                                      Nonselected =        657

                                                Wald chi2(2)      =     508.44
Log likelihood = -5178.304                      Prob > chi2       =     0.0000

------------------------------------------------------------------------------
        wage | Coefficient  Std. err.      z    P>|z|     [95% conf. interval]
-------------+----------------------------------------------------------------
wage         |
   education |   .9899537   .0532565    18.59   0.000     .8855729    1.094334
         age |   .2131294   .0206031    10.34   0.000     .1727481    .2535108
       _cons |   .4857752   1.077037     0.45   0.652    -1.625179     2.59673
-------------+----------------------------------------------------------------
select       |
     married |   .4451721   .0673954     6.61   0.000     .3130794    .5772647
    children |   .4387068   .0277828    15.79   0.000     .3842534    .4931601
   education |   .0557318   .0107349     5.19   0.000     .0346917    .0767718
         age |   .0365098   .0041533     8.79   0.000     .0283694    .0446502
       _cons |  -2.491015   .1893402   -13.16   0.000    -2.862115   -2.119915
-------------+----------------------------------------------------------------
     /athrho |   .8742086   .1014225     8.62   0.000     .6754241    1.072993
    /lnsigma |   1.792559    .027598    64.95   0.000     1.738468     1.84665
-------------+----------------------------------------------------------------
         rho |   .7035061   .0512264                      .5885365    .7905862
       sigma |   6.004797   .1657202                       5.68862    6.338548
      lambda |   4.224412   .3992265                      3.441942    5.006881
------------------------------------------------------------------------------
LR test of indep. eqns. (rho = 0): chi2(1) = 61.20        Prob > chi2 = 0.0000
```

图 7.15

* Heckman 两步一致估计的完整语法

```
. heckman wage educ age, select(married children educ age) twostep
```

运行结果如图 7.16 所示。

```
Heckman selection model -- two-step estimates   Number of obs     =      2,000
(regression model with sample selection)              Selected    =      1,343
                                                      Nonselected =        657

                                                Wald chi2(2)      =     442.54
                                                Prob > chi2       =     0.0000

------------------------------------------------------------------------------
        wage | Coefficient  Std. err.      z    P>|z|     [95% conf. interval]
-------------+----------------------------------------------------------------
wage         |
   education |   .9825259   .0538821    18.23   0.000     .8769189    1.088133
         age |   .2118695   .0220511     9.61   0.000     .1686502    .2550888
       _cons |   .7340391   1.248331     0.59   0.557    -1.712645    3.180723
-------------+----------------------------------------------------------------
select       |
     married |   .4308575    .074208     5.81   0.000     .2854125    .5763025
    children |   .4473249   .0287417    15.56   0.000     .3909922    .5036576
   education |   .0583645   .0109742     5.32   0.000     .0368555    .0798735
         age |   .0347211   .0042293     8.21   0.000     .0264318    .0430105
       _cons |  -2.467365   .1925635   -12.81   0.000    -2.844782   -2.089948
-------------+----------------------------------------------------------------
/mills       |
      lambda |   4.001615   .6065388     6.60   0.000     2.812821     5.19041
-------------+----------------------------------------------------------------
         rho |    0.67284
       sigma |  5.9473529
------------------------------------------------------------------------------
```

图 7.16

```
* 分别定义和使用每个方程式
.global wage_eqn wage educ age
.global seleqn married children age
.heckman $wage_eqn, select($seleqn)
```

运行结果如图 7.17 所示。

```
Iteration 0:   log likelihood = -5192.4816
Iteration 1:   log likelihood = -5192.0225
Iteration 2:   log likelihood = -5192.0216
Iteration 3:   log likelihood = -5192.0216

Heckman selection model                         Number of obs     =      2,000
(regression model with sample selection)              Selected    =      1,343
                                                      Nonselected =        657

                                                Wald chi2(2)      =     535.39
Log likelihood = -5192.022                      Prob > chi2       =     0.0000

------------------------------------------------------------------------------
        wage | Coefficient  Std. err.      z    P>|z|     [95% conf. interval]
-------------+----------------------------------------------------------------
wage         |
   education |   .8828608   .0479762    18.40   0.000     .7888293    .9768924
         age |   .2232676   .0208669    10.70   0.000     .1823692     .264166
       _cons |   1.492342   1.004229     1.49   0.137    -.4759097    3.460594
-------------+----------------------------------------------------------------
select       |
     married |   .5086602    .066093     7.70   0.000     .3791204       .6382
    children |   .4332317   .0275388    15.73   0.000     .3792565    .4872068
         age |   .0396621   .0040985     9.68   0.000     .0316293     .047695
       _cons |  -1.914098   .1512829   -12.65   0.000    -2.210607   -1.617589
-------------+----------------------------------------------------------------
     /athrho |   .8882665   .1012562     8.77   0.000      .689808    1.086725
    /lnsigma |    1.79643   .0277997    64.62   0.000     1.741944    1.850917
-------------+----------------------------------------------------------------
         rho |   .7105365   .0501358                      .5978586    .7956797
       sigma |   6.028091    .167579                       5.70843    6.365653
      lambda |   4.283179   .3964808                       3.50609    5.060267
------------------------------------------------------------------------------
LR test of indep. eqns. (rho = 0): chi2(1) = 62.46        Prob > chi2 = 0.0000
```

图 7.17

* 用一个变量来确定选择

```
. generate wageseen = (wage <. )
. heckman wage educ age, select(wageseen = married children educ age)
```

运行结果如图 7.18 所示。

```
Iteration 0:   log likelihood = -5178.7009
Iteration 1:   log likelihood = -5178.3049
Iteration 2:   log likelihood = -5178.3045

Heckman selection model                         Number of obs     =      2,000
(regression model with sample selection)              Selected    =      1,343
                                                      Nonselected =        657

                                                Wald chi2(2)      =     508.44
Log likelihood = -5178.304                      Prob > chi2       =     0.0000

------------------------------------------------------------------------------
             | Coefficient  Std. err.      z    P>|z|     [95% conf. interval]
-------------+----------------------------------------------------------------
wage         |
   education |   .9899537   .0532565    18.59   0.000     .8855729    1.094334
         age |   .2131294   .0206031    10.34   0.000     .1727481    .2535108
       _cons |   .4857752   1.077037     0.45   0.652    -1.625179     2.59673
-------------+----------------------------------------------------------------
wageseen     |
     married |   .4451721   .0673954     6.61   0.000     .3130794    .5772647
    children |   .4387068   .0277828    15.79   0.000     .3842534    .4931601
   education |   .0557318   .0107349     5.19   0.000     .0346917    .0767718
         age |   .0365098   .0041533     8.79   0.000     .0283694    .0446502
       _cons |  -2.491015   .1893402   -13.16   0.000    -2.862115   -2.119915
-------------+----------------------------------------------------------------
     /athrho |   .8742086   .1014225     8.62   0.000     .6754241    1.072993
    /lnsigma |   1.792559    .027598    64.95   0.000     1.738468     1.84665
-------------+----------------------------------------------------------------
         rho |   .7035061   .0512264                      .5885365    .7905862
       sigma |   6.004797   .1657202                       5.68862    6.338548
      lambda |   4.224412   .3992265                      3.441942    5.006881
------------------------------------------------------------------------------
LR test of indep. eqns. (rho = 0): chi2(1) = 61.20        Prob > chi2 = 0.0000
```

图 7.18

* 指定稳健的方差

. heckman wage educ age, select(married children educ age) vce(robust)

运行结果如图 7.19 所示。

```
Iteration 0:   log pseudolikelihood = -5178.7009
Iteration 1:   log pseudolikelihood = -5178.3049
Iteration 2:   log pseudolikelihood = -5178.3045

Heckman selection model                         Number of obs     =      2,000
(regression model with sample selection)              Selected    =      1,343
                                                      Nonselected =        657

                                                Wald chi2(2)      =     497.82
Log pseudolikelihood = -5178.304                Prob > chi2       =     0.0000

------------------------------------------------------------------------------
             |               Robust
        wage | Coefficient  std. err.      z    P>|z|     [95% conf. interval]
-------------+----------------------------------------------------------------
wage         |
   education |   .9899537   .0534141    18.53   0.000     .8852641    1.094643
         age |   .2131294   .0211095    10.10   0.000     .1717555    .2545034
       _cons |   .4857752   1.099121     0.44   0.659    -1.668462    2.640013
-------------+----------------------------------------------------------------
select       |
     married |   .4451721   .0668243     6.66   0.000     .3141988    .5761453
    children |   .4387068   .0272779    16.08   0.000      .385243    .4921705
   education |   .0557318   .0108899     5.12   0.000      .034388    .0770755
         age |   .0365098   .0042243     8.64   0.000     .0282303    .0447893
       _cons |  -2.491015   .1884227   -13.22   0.000    -2.860317   -2.121713
-------------+----------------------------------------------------------------
     /athrho |   .8742086   .1051331     8.32   0.000     .6681514    1.080266
    /lnsigma |   1.792559   .0288316    62.17   0.000      1.73605    1.849068
-------------+----------------------------------------------------------------
         rho |   .7035061   .0531006                      .5837626    .7932976
       sigma |   6.004797   .1731281                      5.674882    6.353893
      lambda |   4.224412   .4172197                      3.406676    5.042147
------------------------------------------------------------------------------
Wald test of indep. eqns. (rho = 0): chi2(1) = 69.14      Prob > chi2 = 0.0000
```

图 7.19

```
* 指定以 county 为单位进行聚类
. heckman $wage_eqn, select($seleqn) vce(cluster county)
```

运行结果如图 7.20 所示。

```
Iteration 0:   log pseudolikelihood = -5192.4816
Iteration 1:   log pseudolikelihood = -5192.0225
Iteration 2:   log pseudolikelihood = -5192.0216
Iteration 3:   log pseudolikelihood = -5192.0216

Heckman selection model                         Number of obs     =      2,000
(regression model with sample selection)              Selected    =      1,343
                                                      Nonselected =        657

                                                Wald chi2(2)      =     357.97
Log pseudolikelihood = -5192.022                Prob > chi2       =     0.0000

                                   (Std. err. adjusted for 10 clusters in county)
------------------------------------------------------------------------------
             |               Robust
        wage | Coefficient  std. err.      z    P>|z|     [95% conf. interval]
-------------+----------------------------------------------------------------
wage         |
   education |   .8828608   .0588469    15.00   0.000     .7675231    .9981985
         age |   .2232676   .0203559    10.97   0.000     .1833709    .2631644
       _cons |   1.492342   1.240457     1.20   0.229    -.9389079    3.923592
-------------+----------------------------------------------------------------
select       |
     married |   .5086602   .0843269     6.03   0.000     .3433826    .6739379
    children |   .4332317   .0298662    14.51   0.000      .374695    .4917683
         age |   .0396621   .0039086    10.15   0.000     .0320014    .0473229
       _cons |  -1.914098   .1075827   -17.79   0.000    -2.124956   -1.703239
-------------+----------------------------------------------------------------
     /athrho |   .8882665   .1389807     6.39   0.000     .6158694    1.160664
    /lnsigma |    1.79643   .0260575    68.94   0.000     1.745359    1.847502
-------------+----------------------------------------------------------------
         rho |   .7105365   .0688146                      .5482455    .8212561
       sigma |   6.028091   .1570771                      5.727955    6.343954
      lambda |   4.283179   .5105152                      3.282587     5.28377
------------------------------------------------------------------------------
Wald test of indep. eqns. (rho = 0): chi2(1) = 40.85       Prob > chi2 = 0.0000
```

图 7.20

* 报告第一步的 Probit 估计

. heckman wage educ age, select(married children educ age) first

运行结果如图 7.21、图 7.22 所示。

```
Iteration 0:   log likelihood = -1266.2225
Iteration 1:   log likelihood = -1040.0608
Iteration 2:   log likelihood = -1027.2398
Iteration 3:   log likelihood = -1027.0616
Iteration 4:   log likelihood = -1027.0616

Probit regression                                       Number of obs =  2,000
                                                        LR chi2(4)    = 478.32
                                                        Prob > chi2   = 0.0000
Log likelihood = -1027.0616                             Pseudo R2     = 0.1889

------------------------------------------------------------------------------
      select | Coefficient  Std. err.      z    P>|z|     [95% conf. interval]
-------------+----------------------------------------------------------------
     married |   .4308575    .074208     5.81   0.000     .2854125    .5763025
    children |   .4473249   .0287417    15.56   0.000     .3909922    .5036576
   education |   .0583645   .0109742     5.32   0.000     .0368555    .0798735
         age |   .0347211   .0042293     8.21   0.000     .0264318    .0430105
       _cons |  -2.467365   .1925635   -12.81   0.000    -2.844782   -2.089948
------------------------------------------------------------------------------
```

图 7.21

```
Iteration 0:   log likelihood = -5178.7009
Iteration 1:   log likelihood = -5178.3049
Iteration 2:   log likelihood = -5178.3045

Heckman selection model                         Number of obs     =      2,000
(regression model with sample selection)              Selected    =      1,343
                                                      Nonselected =        657

                                                Wald chi2(2)      =     508.44
Log likelihood = -5178.304                      Prob > chi2       =     0.0000

------------------------------------------------------------------------------
        wage | Coefficient  Std. err.      z    P>|z|     [95% conf. interval]
-------------+----------------------------------------------------------------
wage         |
   education |   .9899537   .0532565    18.59   0.000     .8855729    1.094334
         age |   .2131294   .0206031    10.34   0.000     .1727481    .2535108
       _cons |   .4857752   1.077037     0.45   0.652    -1.625179     2.59673
-------------+----------------------------------------------------------------
select       |
     married |   .4451721   .0673954     6.61   0.000     .3130794    .5772647
    children |   .4387068   .0277828    15.79   0.000     .3842534    .4931601
   education |   .0557318   .0107349     5.19   0.000     .0346917    .0767718
         age |   .0365098   .0041533     8.79   0.000     .0283694    .0446502
       _cons |  -2.491015   .1893402   -13.16   0.000    -2.862115   -2.119915
-------------+----------------------------------------------------------------
     /athrho |   .8742086   .1014225     8.62   0.000     .6754241    1.072993
    /lnsigma |   1.792559    .027598    64.95   0.000     1.738468     1.84665
-------------+----------------------------------------------------------------
         rho |   .7035061   .0512264                      .5885365    .7905862
       sigma |   6.004797   .1657202                       5.68862    6.338548
      lambda |   4.224412   .3992265                      3.441942    5.006881
------------------------------------------------------------------------------
LR test of indep. eqns. (rho = 0): chi2(1) = 61.20        Prob > chi2 = 0.0000
```

图 7.22

* 创建包含非选择危险的 mymills

. heckman $ wage_eqn, select($ seleqn) mills(mymills)

运行结果如图 7.23 所示。

```
Iteration 0:   log likelihood = -5192.4816
Iteration 1:   log likelihood = -5192.0225
Iteration 2:   log likelihood = -5192.0216
Iteration 3:   log likelihood = -5192.0216

Heckman selection model                         Number of obs     =      2,000
(regression model with sample selection)              Selected    =      1,343
                                                      Nonselected =        657

                                                Wald chi2(2)      =     535.39
Log likelihood = -5192.022                      Prob > chi2       =     0.0000

------------------------------------------------------------------------------
        wage | Coefficient  Std. err.      z    P>|z|     [95% conf. interval]
-------------+----------------------------------------------------------------
wage         |
   education |   .8828608   .0479762    18.40   0.000     .7888293    .9768924
         age |   .2232676   .0208669    10.70   0.000     .1823692     .264166
       _cons |   1.492342   1.004229     1.49   0.137    -.4759097    3.460594
-------------+----------------------------------------------------------------
select       |
     married |   .5086602    .066093     7.70   0.000     .3791204       .6382
    children |   .4332317   .0275388    15.73   0.000     .3792565    .4872068
         age |   .0396621   .0040985     9.68   0.000     .0316293     .047695
       _cons |  -1.914098   .1512829   -12.65   0.000    -2.210607   -1.617589
-------------+----------------------------------------------------------------
     /athrho |   .8882665   .1012562     8.77   0.000      .689808    1.086725
    /lnsigma |    1.79643   .0277997    64.62   0.000     1.741944    1.850917
-------------+----------------------------------------------------------------
         rho |   .7105365   .0501358                      .5978586    .7956797
       sigma |   6.028091    .167579                       5.70843    6.365653
      lambda |   4.283179   .3964808                       3.50609    5.060267
------------------------------------------------------------------------------
LR test of indep. eqns. (rho = 0): chi2(1) = 62.46        Prob > chi2 = 0.0000
```

图 7.23

* 模型中不包含常数项

. heckman wage educ age, noconstant select(married children educ age)

运行结果如图 7.24 所示。

```
Iteration 0:   log likelihood = -5178.8448
Iteration 1:   log likelihood = -5178.4063
Iteration 2:   log likelihood = -5178.4061

Heckman selection model                         Number of obs     =      2,000
(regression model with sample selection)              Selected    =      1,343
                                                      Nonselected =        657

                                                Wald chi2(2)      =   10835.39
Log likelihood = -5178.406                      Prob > chi2       =     0.0000

------------------------------------------------------------------------------
        wage | Coefficient  Std. err.      z    P>|z|     [95% conf. interval]
-------------+----------------------------------------------------------------
wage         |
   education |   1.004534   .0425004    23.64   0.000     .9212344    1.087833
         age |   .2195003   .0150617    14.57   0.000     .1899799    .2490208
-------------+----------------------------------------------------------------
select       |
     married |   .4439903   .0670568     6.62   0.000     .3125614    .5754192
    children |    .436248   .0271893    16.04   0.000      .382958    .4895381
   education |    .056493   .0105706     5.34   0.000      .035775    .0772111
         age |   .0369106   .0040494     9.12   0.000      .028974    .0448472
       _cons |  -2.512111   .1827862   -13.74   0.000    -2.870365   -2.153857
-------------+----------------------------------------------------------------
     /athrho |   .8969637   .0868199    10.33   0.000     .7267998    1.067128
    /lnsigma |   1.797936   .0248575    72.33   0.000     1.749216    1.846656
-------------+----------------------------------------------------------------
         rho |   .7148162   .0424582                      .6211036    .7883766
       sigma |   6.037172   .1500692                      5.750092    6.338585
      lambda |   4.315468   .3348349                      3.659204    4.971733
------------------------------------------------------------------------------
LR test of indep. eqns. (rho = 0): chi2(1) = 107.08       Prob > chi2 = 0.0000
```

图 7.24

* 选择方程中不包含常数项

. heckman wage educ age, select(married children educ age, noconstant)

运行结果如图 7.25 所示。

```
Iteration 0:   log likelihood = -5271.4478
Iteration 1:   log likelihood = -5271.1983
Iteration 2:   log likelihood = -5271.1981

Heckman selection model                         Number of obs     =      2,000
(regression model with sample selection)              Selected    =      1,343
                                                      Nonselected =        657

                                                Wald chi2(2)      =     407.12
Log likelihood = -5271.198                      Prob > chi2       =     0.0000

------------------------------------------------------------------------------
        wage | Coefficient  Std. err.      z    P>|z|     [95% conf. interval]
-------------+----------------------------------------------------------------
wage         |
   education |   .8256035   .0521069    15.84   0.000     .7234759     .927731
         age |   .1532225   .0193746     7.91   0.000      .115249     .191196
       _cons |   4.843314   .8828602     5.49   0.000      3.11294    6.573689
-------------+----------------------------------------------------------------
select       |
     married |    .492558   .0652284     7.55   0.000     .3647126    .6204034
    children |   .3426915    .024255    14.13   0.000     .2951526    .3902303
   education |  -.0295773   .0082984    -3.56   0.000    -.0458418   -.0133129
         age |   .0021273   .0031298     0.68   0.497    -.0040069    .0082615
-------------+----------------------------------------------------------------
     /athrho |   .9049301   .1086783     8.33   0.000     .6919247    1.117936
    /lnsigma |   1.811933   .0301923    60.01   0.000     1.752757    1.871108
-------------+----------------------------------------------------------------
         rho |     .71869   .0525443                       .599217    .8068497
       sigma |   6.122268   .1848453                      5.770489    6.495492
      lambda |   4.400013   .4319568                      3.553393    5.246633
------------------------------------------------------------------------------
LR test of indep. eqns. (rho = 0): chi2(1) = 52.47        Prob > chi2 = 0.0000
```

图 7.25

7.5 含样本选择的泊松回归

含样本选择的泊松模型由一个计数结果 y 和一个二元选择指示符 s 的方程组成。指示符 s 始终处于观察状态，取值为 0 或 1。但结果 y 只有在 $s=1$ 时才能被观察到，即得到协变量和选择状态的完整信息。然而，感兴趣的主要结果 y 的价值有时是未知的。

假设计数结果 y 服从泊松分布，其条件均值为泊松回归方程：

$$E(y_j \mid \boldsymbol{x}_j, \varepsilon_{1j}) = \exp(\boldsymbol{x}_j \boldsymbol{\beta} + \varepsilon_{1j}) \tag{7.16}$$

计数结果 y 的条件概率为：

$$\Pr(Y = y_j \mid \boldsymbol{x}_j, \varepsilon_{1j}) = \frac{\mu_j^{y_j} e^{-\mu_j}}{y_j!} \tag{7.17}$$

然而，对于第 j 个观测，只有 $s_j=1$ 时，才能观测到 y：

$$s_j=\begin{cases}1, & \text{if } \boldsymbol{w}_j\gamma+\varepsilon_{2j}>0\\0, & \text{otherwise}\end{cases} \tag{7.18}$$

这里，$\varepsilon_1\sim N(0,\sigma)$；$\varepsilon_2\sim N(0,1)$；$\text{corr}(\varepsilon_1,\varepsilon_2)=\rho$。

当 $\rho\neq 0$ 时，基于观察到的 y 的标准泊松回归会产生有偏估计。而 heckpoisson 命令为此类模型中的参数提供了一致、渐近有效的估计。与标准泊松回归不同，带有样本选择的泊松模型允许欠分散和过度分散。

这些模型参数可视为发生率比率，也就是说，模型中所有其他的 $\boldsymbol{x}$ 不变，只有 $\boldsymbol{x}_i$ 发生一单位变化引发被解释变量发生的变化，公式为：

$$\text{IRR}(\boldsymbol{x}_i)=\frac{e^{\ln(E)+\beta_1x_1+\cdots+\beta_i(x_i+1)+\cdots+\beta_kx_k+e_1}}{e^{\ln(E)+\beta_1x_1+\cdots+\beta_ix_i+\cdots+\beta_kx_k+e_1}}=e^{\beta_i} \tag{7.19}$$

假设误差项 ε_1 和 ε_2 是均值为零和协方差矩阵为 $\begin{bmatrix}\sigma^2 & \sigma\rho\\ \sigma\rho & 1\end{bmatrix}$ 的二元正态分布，其中 σ 和 ρ 对二元正态分布有其通常的解释。非零 ρ 意味着所选样本不能代表整个群体，因此推断基于标准泊松回归，使用观察样本是不正确的。

在最大似然估计中，估计的是 $\ln\sigma$ 和 $\text{atanh}\rho$，而不是直接估计的 σ 和 ρ。

$$\text{atanh}\rho=\frac{1}{2}\ln\left(\frac{1+\rho}{1-\rho}\right) \tag{7.20}$$

联合对数似然函数为：

$$\begin{aligned}\ln L(\boldsymbol{\theta})=\sum_{i=1}^{N}[s_j\times\ln\{\Pr(y_j,s_j=1)\mid \boldsymbol{x}_j,\boldsymbol{w}_j,\boldsymbol{\theta}\}\\+(1-s_j)\times\ln\{\Pr(s_j=0\mid \boldsymbol{w}_j,\boldsymbol{\theta})\}]\end{aligned} \tag{7.21}$$

式中，为简化表述，θ 表示($\boldsymbol{\beta},\gamma,\rho,\sigma$)。

联合概率为：

$$\begin{aligned}&\Pr(y_j,s_j=1\mid \boldsymbol{x}_j,\boldsymbol{w}_j,\boldsymbol{\theta})\\&=\int_{-\infty}^{\infty}\Pr(y_j\mid \boldsymbol{x}_j,\varepsilon_1)\Phi\left(\frac{\boldsymbol{w}_j\gamma+\rho/\sigma\varepsilon_1}{\sqrt{1-\rho^2}}\right)\phi(\varepsilon_1/\sigma)\mathrm{d}\varepsilon_1\end{aligned} \tag{7.22}$$

式中，$\phi()$为标准正态密度函数，$\Phi()$为标准正态累积分布函数。

$$\Pr(s_j=0\mid \boldsymbol{w}_j,\boldsymbol{\theta})=\int_{-\infty}^{\infty}\Phi\left(-\frac{\boldsymbol{w}_j\gamma+\rho/\sigma\varepsilon_1}{\sqrt{1-\rho^2}}\right)\phi(\varepsilon_1/\sigma)\mathrm{d}\varepsilon_1 \tag{7.23}$$

式(7.22)和式(7.23)中的积分没有闭合形式解析解，必须使用高斯—埃尔米特求积(Gauss-Hermite quadrature)近似。

含样本选择的泊松回归的语法格式为：

heckpoisson depvar indepvars [if] [in] [weight], select([depvar_s =] indepvars_s [, noconstant offset(varname_os)]) [options]

模型设定选项及含义为：

(1) select()：指定选择方程，包括因变量和自变量，是否有常数项和偏移变量；

(2) noconstant：无常数项；

(3) exposure(varname_e) :在系数约束为1的模型中包括ln(varname_e);

(4) offset(varname_o) :将 varname_o 包含在系数约束为1的模型中;

(5) constraints(constraints) :应用指定的线性约束。

菜单操作路径如下:

Statistics>Sample-selection models>Poisson model with sample selection

heckpoisson 命令拟合具有内生样本选择的泊松模型。这种情况有时被称为选择的不可忽略性、随机缺失或选择偏差。与标准泊松模型不同,含样本选择的泊松模型不存在等离散度假设。

例 7.5 含样本选择的泊松回归

假设我们想知道研发(R&D)支出对一家公司在过去两年中获得的专利数量的影响。本例中的专利数据集包含关于不同行业10000家公司的专利数量的虚构数据。读入数据后,我们将 npatents 的频率与一家公司是否申请专利(已申请)的指标进行对比。

```
* 下载数据
.clear all
.webuse patent
.tabulate npatents applied, missing
```

运行结果如图7.26所示。

Number of patents (last 2 yrs)	Applied for patent Not apply	Apply	Total
0	0	1,127	1,127
1	0	1,455	1,455
2	0	1,131	1,131
3	0	710	710
4	0	479	479
5	0	266	266
6	0	126	126
7	0	98	98
8	0	66	66
9	0	42	42
10	0	19	19
11	0	24	24
12	0	5	5
13	0	7	7
14	0	5	5
15	0	10	10
17	0	1	1
18	0	1	1
19	0	2	2
22	0	1	1
.	4,425	0	4,425
Total	4,425	5,575	10,000

图 7.26

＊用内生样本选择拟合泊松模型

```
.heckpoisson npatents expenditure i.tech, select(applied = expenditure size i.tech)
```

运行结果如图 7.27 所示。

```
Poisson regression with endogenous selection      Number of obs     =     10,000
(25 quadrature points)                                  Selected    =      5,575
                                                        Nonselected =      4,425

                                                  Wald chi2(2)      =     443.90
Log likelihood = -17440.44                        Prob > chi2       =     0.0000

------------------------------------------------------------------------------
    npatents | Coefficient  Std. err.      z    P>|z|     [95% conf. interval]
-------------+----------------------------------------------------------------
npatents     |
 expenditure |    .497821   .0507866     9.80   0.000      .398281     .597361
             |
        tech |
  IT sector  |   .5833501   .0300366    19.42   0.000     .5244795    .6422207
       _cons |  -1.855143    .208204    -8.91   0.000    -2.263216   -1.447071
-------------+----------------------------------------------------------------
applied      |
 expenditure |   .1369954   .0447339     3.06   0.002     .0493185    .2246723
        size |   .2774201   .0469132     5.91   0.000     .1854718    .3693683
             |
        tech |
  IT sector  |   .2750208   .0277032     9.93   0.000     .2207236     .329318
       _cons |  -1.660778   .2631227    -6.31   0.000    -2.176489   -1.145066
-------------+----------------------------------------------------------------
     /athrho |   1.161677   .2847896     4.08   0.000     .6034999    1.719855
    /lnsigma |  -.3029685   .0499674    -6.06   0.000    -.4009028   -.2050342
-------------+----------------------------------------------------------------
         rho |   .8215857   .0925557                      .5395353    .9378455
       sigma |   .7386224    .036907                      .6697151    .8146195
------------------------------------------------------------------------------
Wald test of indep. eqns. (rho = 0): chi2(1) =    16.64   Prob > chi2 = 0.0000
```

图 7.27

＊重现结果，但显示系数图例，而不是系数的统计信息

```
.heckpoisson, coeflegend
```

运行结果如图 7.28 所示。

```
Poisson regression with endogenous selection        Number of obs     =     10,000
(25 quadrature points)                                    Selected    =      5,575
                                                          Nonselected =      4,425

                                                    Wald chi2(2)      =     443.90
Log likelihood = -17440.44                          Prob > chi2       =     0.0000

-----------------------------------------------------------------------------------
     npatents | Coefficient  Legend
--------------+--------------------------------------------------------------------
npatents      |
  expenditure |    .497821  _b[npatents:expenditure]
              |
         tech |
    IT sector |   .5833501  _b[npatents:1.tech]
        _cons |  -1.855143  _b[npatents:_cons]
--------------+--------------------------------------------------------------------
applied       |
  expenditure |   .1369954  _b[applied:expenditure]
         size |   .2774201  _b[applied:size]
              |
         tech |
    IT sector |   .2750208  _b[applied:1.tech]
        _cons |  -1.660778  _b[applied:_cons]
--------------+--------------------------------------------------------------------
      /athrho |   1.161677  _b[/athrho]
     /lnsigma |  -.3029685  _b[/lnsigma]
--------------+--------------------------------------------------------------------
          rho |   .8215857
        sigma |   .7386224
-----------------------------------------------------------------------------------
Wald test of indep. eqns. (rho = 0): chi2(1) =    16.64   Prob > chi2 = 0.0000
```

图 7.28

* 估算 IRR

```
.heckpoisson, irr
```

运行结果如图 7.29 所示。

```
Poisson regression with endogenous selection        Number of obs     =     10,000
(25 quadrature points)                                    Selected    =      5,575
                                                          Nonselected =      4,425

                                                    Wald chi2(2)      =     443.90
Log likelihood = -17440.44                          Prob > chi2       =     0.0000

--------------------------------------------------------------------------------
    npatents |      IRR   Std. err.      z    P>|z|     [95% conf. interval]
-------------+------------------------------------------------------------------
npatents     |
 expenditure |  1.645133   .0835508     9.80   0.000     1.489262    1.817316
             |
        tech |
  IT sector  |  1.792032   .0538265    19.42   0.000     1.689579    1.900697
       _cons |  .1564305   .0325695    -8.91   0.000     .1040154    .2352583
-------------+------------------------------------------------------------------
applied      |
 expenditure |  .1369954   .0447339     3.06   0.002     .0493185    .2246723
        size |  .2774201   .0469132     5.91   0.000     .1854718    .3693683
             |
        tech |
  IT sector  |  .2750208   .0277032     9.93   0.000     .2207236     .329318
       _cons | -1.660778   .2631227    -6.31   0.000    -2.176489   -1.145066
-------------+------------------------------------------------------------------
     /athrho |  1.161677   .2847896     4.08   0.000     .6034999    1.719855
    /lnsigma | -.3029685   .0499674    -6.06   0.000    -.4009028   -.2050342
-------------+------------------------------------------------------------------
         rho |  .8215857   .0925557                      .5395353    .9378455
       sigma |  .7386224    .036907                      .6697151    .8146195
--------------------------------------------------------------------------------
Note: Estimates are transformed only in the first equation to incidence-rate ratios.
Note: _cons estimates baseline incidence rate.
Wald test of indep. eqns. (rho = 0): chi2(1) =    16.64   Prob > chi2 = 0.0000
```

图 7.29

第 8 章 单变量时间序列

时间序列数据是按照时间维度在不同时点上连续观察样本特征变量所收集到的时间样本数据。时间序列数据的主要特征是具有较高的序列相关性。对时间序列数据建模需要作出一些关键假设，在这些关键假设下才会得到一致有效估计。一个重要的假设就是对统计均衡关系作某种形式的假设，即平稳性假设，该假设认为一个平稳时间序列能够有效地用其均值、方差和自相关函数加以描述。

8.1 序列自相关与偏自相关

8.1.1 自相关

时间序列的自协方差函数 $x_1, x_2, \cdots, x_n$ 被定义为 $|v|<n$，如

$$\hat{R}(v)=\frac{1}{n}\sum_{i=1}^{n-|v|}(x_i-\bar{x})(x_{i+v}-\bar{x}) \tag{8.1}$$

其中，$\bar{x}$ 是样本均值。然后将自相关函数定义为：

$$\hat{\rho}_v=\frac{\hat{R}(v)}{\hat{R}(0)} \tag{8.2}$$

$\hat{\rho}_v$ 的方差由 MA(q) 过程公式给出：

$$\operatorname{Var}(\hat{\rho}_v)=\begin{cases}1/n & v=1\\ \dfrac{1}{n}\left\{1+2\sum_{i=1}^{v-1}\hat{\rho}^2(i)\right\} & v>1\end{cases} \tag{8.3}$$

8.1.2 偏自相关

间隔为 v 的偏自相关系数意味着移除 $x_{t+1}, \cdots, x_{t+v-1}$ 的影响效应之后 x_t 和 x_{t+v} 之间的相关关系。我们基于 $x_{t-1}, \cdots, x_{t-v}$ 和一个常数项对 x_t 进行 OLS 回归：

$$x_t=\alpha_0+\alpha_1 x_{t-1}+\cdots+\alpha_{k-1}x_{t-(v-1)}+\phi_{v,v}x_{t-v}+\varepsilon_t$$

其中，x_{t-v} 的估计系数源自对第 v 个偏自相关的估计。残差方差是该回归的估计方差，然后通过除以方差 $\hat{R}(0)$ 对其进行标准化。

我们使用 Yule-Walker 方程来估计偏自相关。设 ϕ_{vv} 表示第 v 个偏自相关系数。

然后有

$$\hat{\phi}_{11} = \hat{\rho}_1 \tag{8.4}$$

对于 $v>1$，有

$$\hat{\phi}_{vv} = \frac{\hat{\rho}_v - \sum_{j=1}^{v-1} \hat{\phi}_{v-1,j}\hat{\rho}_{v-j}}{1 - \sum_{j=1}^{v-1} \hat{\phi}_{v-1,j}\hat{\rho}_j} \tag{8.5}$$

得

$$\hat{\phi}_{vj} = \hat{\phi}_{v-1,j} - \hat{\phi}_{vv}\hat{\phi}_{v-1,v-j}, \quad j=1,2,\cdots,v-1 \tag{8.6}$$

与基于回归的方法不同，基于 Yule-Walker 方程的方法确保第一个样本的偏自相关系数等于第一个样本的自相关系数。

8.1.3 自相关和偏自相关的 Stata 实现

序列相关分析的语法格式为：

(1) 自相关、偏自相关和 portmanteau(Q)统计

corrgram varname if [] in [], corrgram options[]

(2) 带置信区间的自相关图

ac varname [if] [in] [, ac_options]

(3) 带置信区间的偏自相关图

pac varname [if] [in] [, pac_options]

菜单操作路径为：

(1) corrgram

Statistics>Time series>Graphs>Autocorrelations & partial autocorrelations

(2) ac

Statistics>Time series>Graphs>Correlogram (ac)

(3) pac

Statistics>Time series>Graphs>Partial correlogram (pac)

corrgram 命令生成一个自相关、偏自相关和 portmanteau(Q)统计表，同时还显示自相关和偏自相关图。portmanteau(Q)检验原理见 8.2.5 节。

ac 命令根据 Bartlett 的 MA(q)过程公式生成自相关图。

pac 命令生成一个偏自相关图，置信区间使用 1/sqrt(n)的标准误差计算。每个滞后的剩余方差可选择性地包括在图上。

例 8.1　时序数据的相关性检验

这里使用国际航空公司乘客数据集(Box *et al.*, 2016)[1]。此数据集包括从 1949 年至 1960 年国际航空公司乘客数量的月度数据，共有 144 个观察值。我们可以使用

[1] Box, G. E. P., G. M. Jenkins, G. C. Reinsel, and G. M. Ljung. *Time Series Analysis: Forecasting and Control* (5th ed.). Hoboken, NJ: Wiley, 2016.

corrgram 命令列出自相关和偏自相关系数。

```
.use https://www.stata-press.com/data/r17/air2
(TIMESLAB: Airline passengers)
.corrgram air, lags(20)
```

运行结果如图 8.1 所示。

LAG	AC	PAC	Q	Prob>Q
1	0.9480	0.9589	132.14	0.0000
2	0.8756	-0.3298	245.65	0.0000
3	0.8067	0.2018	342.67	0.0000
4	0.7526	0.1450	427.74	0.0000
5	0.7138	0.2585	504.8	0.0000
6	0.6817	-0.0269	575.6	0.0000
7	0.6629	0.2043	643.04	0.0000
8	0.6556	0.1561	709.48	0.0000
9	0.6709	0.5686	779.59	0.0000
10	0.7027	0.2926	857.07	0.0000
11	0.7432	0.8402	944.39	0.0000
12	0.7604	0.6127	1036.5	0.0000
13	0.7127	-0.6660	1118	0.0000
14	0.6463	-0.3846	1185.6	0.0000
15	0.5859	0.0787	1241.5	0.0000
16	0.5380	-0.0266	1289	0.0000
17	0.4997	-0.0581	1330.4	0.0000
18	0.4687	-0.0435	1367	0.0000
19	0.4499	0.2773	1401.1	0.0000
20	0.4416	-0.0405	1434.1	0.0000

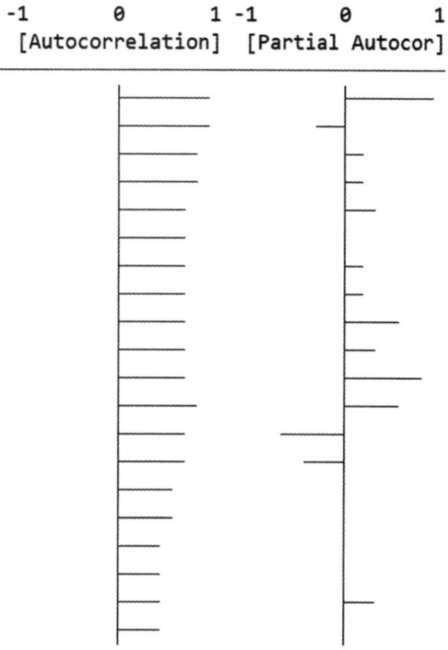

图 8.1

我们可以使用 ac 生成自相关图。(见图 8.2)

```
.ac air, lags(20)
```

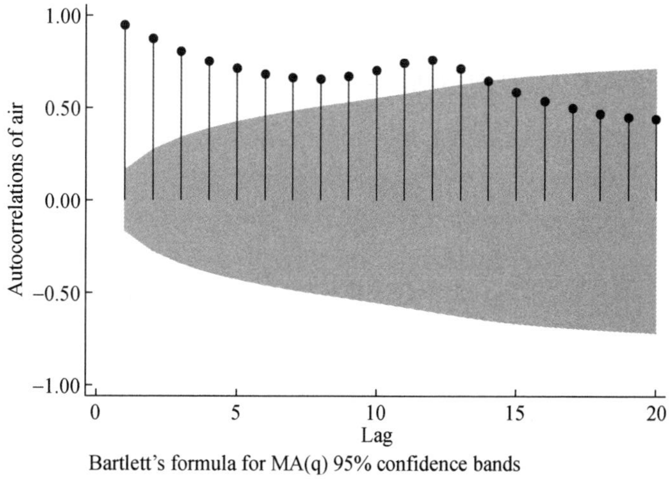

图 8.2

数据可能具有趋势成分和季节性成分。一阶差分将减轻趋势的影响，而季节性差分将有助于控制季节性。为了实现这个目标，我们可以使用 Stata 的时间序列运算符。在这里，我们绘制了控制趋势和季节性后的偏自相关图。（见图 8.3）我们还可以使用 srv 命令来包含标准化残差方差。

```
.pac DS12.air, lags(20) srv
```

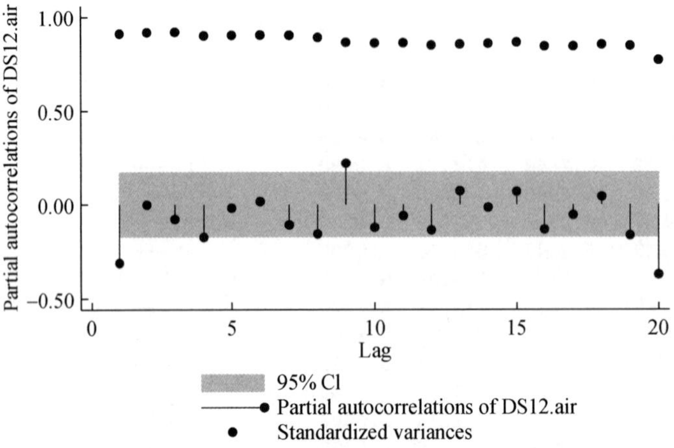

图 8.3

8.2 序列平稳性及其检验

如果时间序列数据 $x_t=\{\cdots,x_{-1},x_0,x_1,x_2,\cdots,x_T,x_{T+1},\cdots\}$ 的均值、方差和自协方差都不取决于 t，即对所有的 t，$E(x_t)=\mu$，$\text{var}(x_t)=\sigma^2$，同时对所有的 t 和 s，$\text{cov}(x_t,x_{t-s})=E(x_t-\mu)(x_{t-s}-\mu)=\gamma_s$，则称 $\{x_t\}$ 是协方差平稳的或弱平稳的。

8.2.1 DF 检验

如果 $\{\varepsilon_t\}$ 独立同分布，且期望值为 0，方差有限，则称 $\{\varepsilon_t\}$ 为独立白噪声。考虑 AR(1)模型：

$$y_t=\beta_0+\beta_1 y_{t-1}+\gamma t+\varepsilon_t \tag{8.7}$$

其中，γt 为时间趋势，ε_t 为独立白噪声。对该模型做单边检验：

$$H_0:\beta_1=1 \quad vs \quad H_1:\beta_1<1 \tag{8.8}$$

其中，备择假设为 $H_1:\beta_1<1$。如果 H_0 成立，则 y_t 为带漂移项 β_0 的随机游走。在方程两边同时减去 y_{t-1}，可得：

$$\Delta y_t=\beta_0+\delta y_{t-1}+\gamma t+\varepsilon_t \tag{8.9}$$

其中，$\delta=\beta_1-1$。因此原假设也可以改为：

$$H_0:\delta=0 \quad vs \quad H_1:\delta<0 \tag{8.10}$$

对模型做 OLS 回归，可得估计值 $\hat{\delta}$ 及其 t 检验统计量。此时的 t 检验统计量，就是 DF(Dickey-Fuuer)检验统计量 $Z(t)$。$Z(t)$不服从渐进正态分布，其临界值需要通过蒙特卡洛模拟获得。$Z(t)$越小,则越倾向于拒绝原假设。由原假设可知,DF 检验为左侧检验,拒绝域只在分布的最左侧。

8.2.2 ADF 检验

考虑 y_t 存在 p 阶序列相关,用 p 阶自回归过程来修正。

$$y_t = a + \phi_1 y_{t-1} + \phi_2 y_{t-2} + \cdots + \phi_p y_{t-p} + u_t \tag{8.11}$$

在式(8.7)两端减去 y_{t-1},通过添项和减项的方法,可得

$$\Delta y_t = a + \eta y_{t-1} + \sum_{i=1}^{p-1} \beta_i \Delta y_{t-i} + u_t \tag{8.12}$$

式中,

$$\eta = \sum_{i=1}^{p} \phi_i - 1, \quad \beta_i = -\sum_{j=i+1}^{p} \phi_j \tag{8.13}$$

ADF 检验(augmented Dickey-Fuller test)方法通过在回归方程右边加入因变量 y_t 的滞后差分项来控制高阶序列相关。

$$\Delta y_t = \eta y_{t-1} + \sum_{i=1}^{p-1} \beta_i \Delta y_{t-i} + u_t \quad t = 1, 2, \cdots, T \tag{8.14}$$

$$\Delta y_t = \eta y_{t-1} + a + \sum_{i=1}^{p-1} \beta_i \Delta y_{t-i} + u_t \quad t = 1, 2, \cdots, T \tag{8.15}$$

$$\Delta y_t = \eta y_{t-1} + a + \delta t + \sum_{i=1}^{p-1} \beta_i \Delta y_{t-i} + u_t \quad t = 1, 2, \cdots, T \tag{8.16}$$

扩展定义将检验

$$\begin{cases} H_0: \eta = 0 \\ H_1: \eta < 0 \end{cases} \tag{8.17}$$

也就是说,原假设为:序列至少存在一个单位根;备选假设为:序列不存在单位根。序列 y_t 可能还包含常数项和时间趋势项。通过检验 η 的估计值 $\hat{\eta}$ 是否不拒绝原假设,进而判断一个高阶自相关序列 AR(p)过程是否存在单位根。ADF 检验的临界值与 DF 检验的临界值相同。

ADF 检验的语法格式为:

```
wntestb varname if [] in [], options[]
```

菜单操作路径为:

Statistics>Time series>Tests>Augmented Dickey-Fuller unit-root test

例 8.2 ADF 检验

本例利用的数据集同例 8.1。由于数据显示出明显的上升趋势,我们使用 dfuller 的趋势选项在扩展 ADF 回归中包含常数和时间趋势。

```
.use https://www.stata-press.com/data/r17/air2
(TIMESLAB: Airline passengers)
.dfuller air, lags(3) trend regress
```

运行结果如图 8.4 所示。

```
Augmented Dickey-Fuller test for unit root          Number of obs   =       140

                               ———— Interpolated Dickey-Fuller ————
                  Test         1% Critical       5% Critical      10% Critical
               Statistic           Value             Value             Value
------------------------------------------------------------------------------
 Z(t)             -6.936            -4.027            -3.445            -3.145
------------------------------------------------------------------------------
MacKinnon approximate p-value for Z(t) = 0.0000

------------------------------------------------------------------------------
D.air        |      Coef.   Std. Err.      t    P>|t|     [95% Conf. Interval]
-------------+----------------------------------------------------------------
         air |
         L1. |  -.5217089   .0752195    -6.94   0.000      -.67048   -.3729379
         LD. |   .5572871   .0799894     6.97   0.000      .399082    .7154923
        L2D. |    .095912   .0876692     1.09   0.276    -.0774825    .2693065
        L3D. |     .14511   .0879922     1.65   0.101    -.0289232    .3191433
      _trend |   1.407534   .2098378     6.71   0.000     .9925118    1.822557
       _cons |   44.49164    7.78335     5.72   0.000     29.09753    59.88575
------------------------------------------------------------------------------
```

图 8.4

在这里，我们可以在所有常见显著性水平上拒绝单位根的原假设。回归结果显示，估计的 β 为 -0.522，意味着 $\rho=(1-0.522)=0.478$。

8.2.3 DFGLS 检验

在经验研究中，尽管 DF 检验是应用最广泛的单位根检验，但是它的检验功效偏低，尤其是在小样本条件下，数据的生成过程为高度自相关时，检验的功效非常不理想。另外，DF 检验和 ADF 检验对于含有时间趋势的退势平稳序列的检验是失效的。

为了改进 DF 和 ADF 检验的效能，Elliott、Rothenberg 和 Stock(1996)[①]提出了基于 GLS 方法的退势 DF 检验，简称为 DFGLS 检验，其基本原理如下：

首先，定义序列 y_t 的拟差分序列如下：

$$d(y_t \mid a)=\begin{cases} y_t & t=1 \\ y_t-ay_{t-1} & t>1 \end{cases} \tag{8.18}$$

并且构造如下回归方程：

$$d(y_t \mid a)=d(x_t' \mid a)\delta(a)+u_t \tag{8.19}$$

令 $\hat{\delta}(a)$ 表示公式(8.15)参数的最小二乘估计量，在实际计算中通常这样定义参数 a：

$$a=\begin{cases} 1-7/T & x_t=(1) \\ 1-13.5/T & x_t=(1,t)' \end{cases} \tag{8.20}$$

式中，$x_t=(1)$ 表示 y_t 中只含有截距项，$x_t=(1,t)'$ 表示 y_t 中含有截距项和趋势项。

利用公式(8.15)的估计参数定义退势后的序列 y_t^d：

$$y_t^d=y_t-x_t'\delta(\bar{a}) \tag{8.21}$$

① Elliott, G. R., T. J. Rothenberg, and J. H. Stock. Efficient Tests for an Autoregressive Unit Root. *Econometrica*, 1996, 64.

然后，对退势后的序列 y_t^d 应用 ADF 检验，即为 DFGLS 检验。检验过程如下：

$$\Delta y_t^d = \eta y_{t-1}^d + \sum_{i=1}^{p-1} \beta_i \Delta y_{t-1}^d + u_t \tag{8.22}$$

原假设和备选假设与 ADF 检验一致，即

$$\begin{cases} H_0: \eta = 0 \\ H_1: \eta < 0 \end{cases} \tag{8.23}$$

Elliott、Rothenberg 和 Stock(1996)①给出了不同置信水平下的临界值，DFGLS 检验与一般的 ADF 检验一样是左侧单边检验。

DFGLS 检验的语法格式为：

```
dfgls varname if [] in[], options []
```

菜单操作路径为：

Statistics>Time series>Tests>DF-GLS test for a unit root

例 8.3 DFGLS 检验

本例使用德国宏观经济数据集检验投资的自然对数是否具有单位根。我们使用 dfgls 命令的默认选项。

```
.use https://www.stata-press.com/data/r17/lutkepohl2
(Quarterly SA West German macro data, Bil DM, from Lutkepohl 1993 Table E.1)
.dfgls ln_inv
```

运行结果如图 8.5 所示。

```
DF-GLS for ln_inv                                        Number of obs =    80
Maxlag = 11 chosen by Schwert criterion

               DF-GLS tau      1% Critical       5% Critical      10% Critical
  [lags]     Test Statistic        Value             Value             Value
------------------------------------------------------------------------------
    11           -2.925           -3.610            -2.763            -2.489
    10           -2.671           -3.610            -2.798            -2.523
    9            -2.766           -3.610            -2.832            -2.555
    8            -3.259           -3.610            -2.865            -2.587
    7            -3.536           -3.610            -2.898            -2.617
    6            -3.115           -3.610            -2.929            -2.646
    5            -3.054           -3.610            -2.958            -2.674
    4            -3.016           -3.610            -2.986            -2.699
    3            -2.071           -3.610            -3.012            -2.723
    2            -1.675           -3.610            -3.035            -2.744
    1            -1.752           -3.610            -3.055            -2.762

Opt Lag (Ng-Perron seq t) =  7 with RMSE  .0388771
Min SC   = -6.169137 at lag  4 with RMSE  .0398949
Min MAIC = -6.136371 at lag  1 with RMSE  .0440319
```

图 8.5

从结果来看，滞后 1—3 期的单位根假设没有被拒绝，滞后 9—10 期的单位根假设

① Elliott, G. R., T. J. Rothenberg, and J. H. Stock. Efficient Tests for an Autoregressive Unit Root. *Econometrica*, 1996, 64.

在 10%水平上被拒绝，滞后 4—8 期和 11 期的单位根假设在 5%水平上被拒绝。为了比较，我们还通过使用具有两种不同滞后期的 dfuller 来检验投资序列中的单位根。我们需要将趋势选项与 dfuller 一起使用，因为默认情况下不包含该选项。运行结果见图 8.6。

```
. dfuller ln_inv, lag(4) trend

Augmented Dickey-Fuller test for unit root          Number of obs   =        87

                               ---------- Interpolated Dickey-Fuller ---------
                  Test         1% Critical       5% Critical      10% Critical
               Statistic           Value             Value             Value
------------------------------------------------------------------------------
 Z(t)             -3.133            -4.069            -3.463            -3.158
------------------------------------------------------------------------------
MacKinnon approximate p-value for Z(t) = 0.0987

. dfuller ln_inv, lag(7) trend

Augmented Dickey-Fuller test for unit root          Number of obs   =        84

                               ---------- Interpolated Dickey-Fuller ---------
                  Test         1% Critical       5% Critical      10% Critical
               Statistic           Value             Value             Value
------------------------------------------------------------------------------
 Z(t)             -3.994            -4.075            -3.466            -3.160
------------------------------------------------------------------------------
MacKinnon approximate p-value for Z(t) = 0.0090
```

图　8.6

MacKinnon 的近似 p 值小于 0.1，4 个滞后期的 dfuller 产生的临界值和检验统计量不拒绝原假设，7 个滞后期的临界值和检验统计量在 5%的水平上拒绝了原假设。由于有趋势的 DFGLS 检验已被证明比标准的 ADF 检验效果更强，因此 dfuller 的效果不如 dfgls 的效果。

8.2.4　PP 检验

类似于 DF 检验的作用，Phillips 和 Perron(1988)①提出一种非参数方法来检验一阶自回归过程 AR(1)的平稳性，对于方程

$$\Delta y_t = \eta y_{t-1} + u_t \qquad t = 1,2,\cdots,T \tag{8.24}$$

$$\Delta y_t = \eta y_{t-1} + a + u_t \qquad t = 1,2,\cdots,T \tag{8.25}$$

$$\Delta y_t = \eta y_{t-1} + a + \delta t + u_t \qquad t = 1,2,\cdots,T \tag{8.26}$$

原假设和备选假设为：

$$\begin{cases} H_0: \eta = 0 \\ H_1: \eta < 0 \end{cases} \tag{8.27}$$

① Phillips, P. C. B., and P. Perron. Testing for a Unit Root in Time Series Regression. *Biometrika*. 1988,75.

接受原假设，意味着存在单位根；反之，接受备选假设，意味着不存在单位根。PP 检验(Phillips-Perrontest)也是通过构造一个具有 t 分布的统计量 $t_{p,p}$ 来检验 $\hat{\eta}$ 的取值情况，只是此时 t 统计量相对于 DF 检验的统计量更为稳健。

统计量 $t_{p,p}$ 的具体构造形式如下：

$$t_{p,p}=t_{\hat{\eta}}\left(\frac{\gamma_0}{f_0}\right)^{\frac{1}{2}}-\frac{T(f_0-\gamma_0)s_{\hat{\eta}}}{2f_0^{\frac{1}{2}}\hat{\sigma}} \tag{8.28}$$

其中，f_0 是频率为零时的残差谱密度估计值，$t_{\hat{\eta}}$ 是 $\hat{\eta}$ 的 t 统计量，$s_{\hat{\eta}}$ 是 $\hat{\eta}$ 的标准差，$\hat{\sigma}$ 是回归残差标准差，γ_0 是回归残差方差的一致估计量，有

$$\gamma_0=\frac{T-k}{T}\hat{\sigma}^2 \tag{8.29}$$

式中，k 是外生变量的个数。同 ADF 检验的 t 统计量一样，通过模拟可以给出 PP 检验的统计量在不同显著性水平下的临界值，使得我们能够很容易地实施检验。PP 检验中滞后阶数的选择可以通过 AIC 准则等方法来确定。

PP 检验的语法格式为：

```
pperron varname if [] in[], options[]
```

菜单操作路径为：

Statistics>Time series>Tests>Phillips-Perron unit-root test

例 8.4 Philips-Perron 检验

本例利用的数据集同例 8.1。因为随着时间的推移，数据呈现出明显的上升趋势，我们将使用趋势选项。

```
.use https://www.stata-press.com/data/r17/air2
(TIMESLAB: Airline passengers)
.pperron air, lags(4) trend regress
```

运行结果如图 8.7 所示。

我们在所有常见显著性水平上拒绝单位根的原假设。Z_t 的插值临界值略有不同，因为样本量不同，在增广的 Dickey-Fuller 回归中，由于包含滞后差异项作为回归量，我们会丢失观测值。

8.2.5 Bartlett 基于周期图的白噪声检验

如果 $x(1),\cdots,x(T)$是方差为 σ^2 的白噪声过程的实现，对于 $\omega\in[0,1]$，频谱分布将由 $F(\omega)=\sigma^2\omega$ 给出，我们期望数据的累积周期图接近点 $S_k=k/q$，其中 $q=[n/2]+1$，$[n/2]$是小于或等于 $n/2$ 的最大整数，$k=1,\cdots,q$。

除 $\omega=0$ 和 $\omega=0.5$ 外，随机变量 $2\hat{f}(\omega_k)/\sigma^2$ 渐近独立且同分布为 χ_2^2。因为 χ_2^2 与均值为 1 的指数分布的随机变量的两倍相同，所以累积周期图与来自均匀(在单位间隔上)分布的有序值具有大致相同的分布。Feller (1948)①指出：

① Feller, W. On the Kolmogorov-Smirnov Limit Theorems for Empirical Distributions. *The Annals of Mathematical Statistics*, 1948, 19.

```
Phillips-Perron test for unit root              Number of obs   =       143
                                                Newey-West lags =         4

                          ——— Interpolated Dickey-Fuller ———
                  Test       1% Critical      5% Critical     10% Critical
               Statistic         Value            Value            Value
─────────────────────────────────────────────────────────────────────────
 Z(rho)          -46.405         -27.687          -20.872          -17.643
 Z(t)             -5.049          -4.026           -3.444           -3.144
─────────────────────────────────────────────────────────────────────────
MacKinnon approximate p-value for Z(t) = 0.0002
```

air	Coef.	Std. Err.	t	P>|t|	[95% Conf.	Interval]
air						
L1.	.7318116	.0578092	12.66	0.000	.6175196	.8461035
_trend	.7107559	.1670563	4.25	0.000	.3804767	1.041035
_cons	25.95168	7.325951	3.54	0.001	11.46788	40.43547

图 8.7

$$\lim_{g\to\infty}\Pr\left(\max_{1\leqslant k\leqslant g\sqrt{q}}\left|U_k-\frac{k}{q}\right|\leqslant a\right)=\sum_{j=-\infty}^{\infty}(-1)^j e^{-2a^2j^2}=G(a) \tag{8.30}$$

其中,U_k 是有序均匀分位数。Bartlett 统计量计算式为:

$$B=\max_{1\leqslant k\leqslant q}\sqrt{\frac{n}{2}}\left|\hat{F}_k-\frac{k}{q}\right| \tag{8.31}$$

其中,$\hat{F}_k$ 是根据样本谱密度 $\hat{f}$ 定义的累积周期图:

$$\hat{F}_k=\frac{\sum_{j=1}^{k}\hat{f}(\omega_j)}{\sum_{j=1}^{q}\hat{f}(\omega_j)} \tag{8.32}$$

利用 Feller(1948)[①]的结果,Bartlett 统计量的置信区间计算为 $1-G(B)$。

Bartlett 基于周期图的白噪声检验的语法格式为:

wntestb varname if [] in [], options []

菜单操作路径为:

Menu Statistics>Time series>Tests>Bartlett's periodogram-based white-noise test

例 8.5　Bartlett 基于周期图的白噪声检验

本例生成了两个时间序列,并展示了可以从这个命令获得的图形和统计检验。第一个时间序列是白噪声过程,第二个时间序列是嵌入确定性余弦曲线的白噪声过程。

① Feller, W. On the Kolmogorov-Smirnov Limit Theorems for Empirical Distributions. *The Annals of Mathematical Statistics*, 1948, 19.

```
.drop _all
.set seed 12393
.set obs 100
Number of observations (_N) was 0, now 100
.generate x1 = rnormal()
.generate x2 = rnormal() + cos(2 * _pi * (_n - 1)/10)
.generate time = _n
.tsset time
Time variable: time, 1 to 100
      Delta: 1 unit
```

然后，我们可以通过输入以下内容将白噪声数据提交给 wntestb 命令：

```
.wntestb x1
```

运行结果如图 8.8 所示。

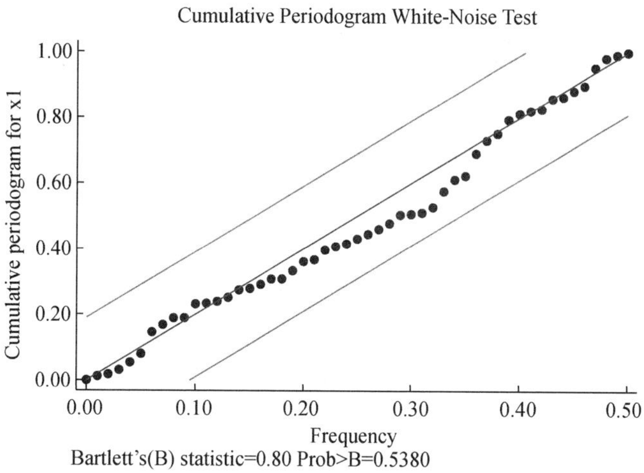

图 8.8

由图 8.8 可以看出，这些值永远不会出现在置信带之外。检验统计量的 p 值为 0.91，因此可以得出结论，该过程与白噪声没有区别。如果只想要统计数据而不用绘图，则可以使用 table 选项。

将注意力转向其他系列 (x_2)，我们输入：

```
.wntestb x2
```

可见，该过程确实出现在置信带之外。事实上，它以 0.1 的频率跳出置信区间。我们还能够通过检验统计量(p 值为 0.001)确认该过程与白噪声显著不同。

8.2.6 Portmanteau Q 白噪声检验

Portmanteau 检验依赖于这样一个事实：$x(1), \cdots, x(n)$是白噪声过程。定义 Q 统计量为：

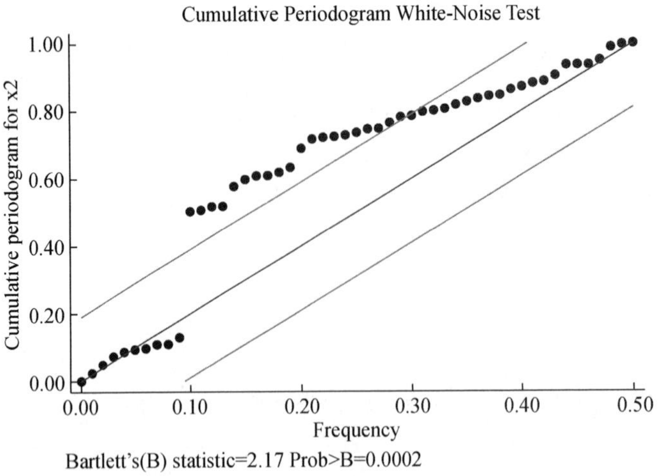

图 8.9

$$Q = n(n+2)\sum_{j=1}^{m}\frac{1}{n-j}\hat{\rho}^2(j) \rightarrow \chi_m^2 \tag{8.33}$$

其中，m 是计算的自相关系数(等于指定的滞后数)，表示分布收敛到具有 m 个自由度的 χ^2 分布，$\hat{\rho}_j$ 是滞后的自相关估计系数。

p 阶滞后的 Q 统计量的原假设是：序列不存在 p 阶自相关；备选假设为：序列存在 p 阶自相关。

如果 Q 统计量在某一滞后阶数显著不为零，则说明序列存在某种程度上的序列相关。在实际检验中，通常会计算出不同滞后阶数的 Q 统计量、自相关系数和偏自相关系数。如果各阶 Q 统计量都没有超过由设定的显著性水平决定的临界值，则不拒绝原假设，即不存在序列相关；并且此时，各阶自相关和偏自相关系数都接近于 0。

反之，如果在某一滞后阶数 p 阶，Q 统计量超过设定的显著性水平的临界值，则拒绝原假设，说明残差序列存在 p 阶自相关。由于 Q 统计量的 p 值要根据自由度 p 来估算，因此，一个较大的样本容量是保证 Q 统计量有效的重要因素。

Portmanteau 语法格式为：

```
wntestq varname
```

菜单操作路径为：

Menu Statistics>Time series>Tests>Portmanteau white-noise test

例 8.6　Portmanteau Q 白噪声检验

在 wntestb 命令的例子中，我们生成了两个时间序列。一个(x_1)是白噪声过程，另一个(x_2)是嵌入确定性余弦曲线的白噪声过程。在这里，我们比较两个检验的输出。

```
.drop _all
.set seed 12393
.set obs 100
```

```
Number of observations (_N) was 0, now 100
.generate x1 = rnormal()
.generate x2 = rnormal() + cos(2 * _pi * (_n - 1)/10)
.generate time = _n
.tsset time
Time variable: time, 1 to 100
      Delta: 1 unit
.wntestb x1, table
```

运行结果如图 8.10 所示。

```
Cumulative periodogram white-noise test
---------------------------------------
 Bartlett's (B) statistic  =     0.8038
 Prob > B                  =     0.5380
```

图 8.10

```
.wntestq x1
```

运行结果如图 8.11 所示。

```
Portmanteau test for white noise
---------------------------------------
 Portmanteau (Q) statistic =    31.0396
 Prob > chi2(40)           =     0.8443
```

图 8.11

```
.wntestb x2, table
```

运行结果如图 8.12 所示。

```
Cumulative periodogram white-noise test
---------------------------------------
 Bartlett's (B) statistic  =     2.1653
 Prob > B                  =     0.0002
```

图 8.12

```
.wntestq x2
```

运行结果如图 8.13 所示。

```
Portmanteau test for white noise
---------------------------------------
 Portmanteau (Q) statistic =   225.6211
 Prob > chi2(40)           =     0.0000
```

图 8.13

这个例子表明两种检验的结果是一致的。对于第一个过程，Bartlett 和 Portmanteau 检验的统计量不显著：wntestb 的 p 值为 0.5380，wntestq 的 p 值为 0.8443。对于第二个过程，每种检验的显著性都低于 0.0005。

8.3 回归后的时间序列设定检验

8.3.1 使用未知突变日期检验结构突变

每个最高检验统计量都是从样本中可能的中断日期范围内的一系列 Wald 或 LR 检验中获得的检验统计量的最大值。令 b 表示样本量 T 的 $[b_1, b_2]$ 范围内的可能中断日期。

用于检验 k 系数没有结构变化的原假设的最高检验统计量由下式给出：

最高形式：

$$S_T = \sup_{b_1 \leqslant b \leqslant b_2} S_T(b) \tag{8.34}$$

其中，$S_T(b)$ 是在潜在中断日期 b 评估的 Wald 或 LR 检验统计量。检验统计量的平均形式和指数形式分别是：

平均形式：

$$S_T = \frac{1}{b_2 - b_1 + 1} \sum_{b=b_1}^{b_2} S_T(b) \tag{8.35}$$

指数形式：

$$S_T = \ln\left[\frac{1}{b_2 - b_1 + 1} \sum_{b=b_1}^{b_2} \exp\left\{\frac{1}{2} S_T(b)\right\}\right] \tag{8.36}$$

检验统计量的极限分布由下式给出：

最高形式：

$$S_T \rightarrow_d \sup_{\lambda \in [\varepsilon_1, \varepsilon_2]} S(\lambda) \tag{8.37}$$

平均形式：

$$S_T \rightarrow_d \frac{1}{\varepsilon_2 - \varepsilon_1} \int_{\varepsilon_1}^{\varepsilon_2} S(\lambda) \mathrm{d}\lambda \tag{8.38}$$

指数形式：

$$S_T \rightarrow_d \ln\left[\frac{1}{\varepsilon_2 - \varepsilon_1} \int_{\varepsilon_1}^{\varepsilon_2} \exp\left\{\frac{1}{2} S(\lambda) d\lambda\right\}\right] \tag{8.39}$$

其中，

$$S(\lambda) = \frac{\{B_k(\lambda) - \lambda B_k(1)\}' \{B_k(\lambda) - \lambda B_k(1)\}}{\lambda(1-\lambda)} \tag{8.40}$$

$B_k(\lambda)$ 是 k 维独立布朗运动的向量，$\varepsilon_1 = b_1/T$，$\varepsilon_2 = b_2/T$，并且 $\lambda = \varepsilon_2(1-\varepsilon_1)/$

$\{\varepsilon_1(1-\varepsilon_2)\}$。非标准极限分布的 p 值在计算上很复杂。对于每个检验，使用 Hansen (1997)①中的方法计算报告的 p 值。

该检验的语法格式为：

estat sbsingle [, options]

例 8.7　回归后的时间序列设定检验

本例检验具有未知突变日期的结构中断。我们使用来自圣路易斯联邦储备银行提供的联邦储备经济数据库（FRED）的 1954 年第 3 季度至 2010 年第 4 季度的联邦基金系列数据。

考虑一个联邦基金利率模型，它是一阶滞后和通货膨胀率的函数。我们想检验系数是否在未知的中断日期发生了变化。下面使用回归拟合模型，并利用 estat sbsingle 执行检验。

```
. use https://www.stata-press.com/data/r17/usmacro
(Federal Reserve Economic Data-St. Louis Fed)
. regress fedfunds L.fedfunds inflation
(output omitted)
. estat sbsingle
```

运行结果如图 8.14 所示。

```
Full sample:                    1955q3 - 2010q4
Trimmed sample:                 1964q1 - 2002q3
Estimated break date:           1980q4
Ho: No structural break

     Test             Statistic          p-value
------------------------------------------------
     swald             14.1966            0.0440
------------------------------------------------
Exogenous variables:          L.fedfunds inflation
Coefficients included in test: L.fedfunds inflation _cons
```

图　8.14

默认情况下，执行最高 Wald 检验。输出表明，在 5%水平上拒绝了没有结构性突破的原假设，并且估计的突破日期是 1980 年第 4 季度。下面展示了最高 Wald、平均 Wald 和平均 LR 检验的结果。

```
. estat sbsingle, swald awald alr
```

运行结果如图 8.15 所示。

① Hansen, B. E. Approximate Asymptotic P Values for Structural-change Tests. *Journal of Business and Economic Statistics*, 1997, 15.

```
Full sample:                  1955q3 - 2010q4
Trimmed sample:               1964q1 - 2002q3
Ho: No structural break

     Test             Statistic          p-value

     swald              14.1966           0.0440
     awald               4.5673           0.1474
       alr               4.6319           0.1411

Exogenous variables:          L.fedfunds inflation
Coefficients included in test: L.fedfunds inflation _cons
```

图 8.15

只有最高 Wald 检验拒绝不中断的原假设。

8.3.2 使用已知突变日期检验结构突变

可以通过使用指示变量拟合线性回归来构建具有已知中断日期的结构中断检验，即

$$y_t = \boldsymbol{x}_t\boldsymbol{\beta} + (b \leqslant t)\boldsymbol{x}_t\boldsymbol{\delta} + \varepsilon_t$$

没有结构断裂的原假设是 $H_0:\boldsymbol{\delta}=\boldsymbol{0}$。这可以通过构建 Wald 统计量或 LR 统计量来检验，两者均以 $\chi^2(k)$ 作为极限分布，其中 k 表示模型中的参数数量。

具有多个中断的回归模型可以表示为：

$$y_t = \boldsymbol{x}_t\boldsymbol{\beta} + \boldsymbol{x}_t\{(b_1 \leqslant t < b_2)\boldsymbol{\delta}_1 + (b_2 \leqslant t < b_3)\boldsymbol{\delta}_2 + \cdots + (b_m \leqslant t)\boldsymbol{\delta}_m\} + \varepsilon_t$$

其中，$b_1,\cdots,b_m$ 是 $m \geqslant 2$ 个休息日期。无结构中断的原假设是由 H_0 给出的联合检验：$H_0:\boldsymbol{\delta}_1=\cdots=\boldsymbol{\delta}_m=\boldsymbol{0}$。

该检验的语法格式为：

estat sbsingle [, options]

例 8.8　检验结构中断

本例检验一个已知日期的中断。本例利用的数据集同例 8.7。我们希望将联邦基金利率建模为一阶滞后的函数，但担心在 1981 年第 2 季度之后可能会出现结构性中断。我们使用回归拟合模型参数，然后使用 estat sbknown 命令来检验结构中断。

```
. use https://www.stata-press.com/data/r17/usmacro
(Federal Reserve Economic Data-St. Louis Fed)
. regress fedfunds L.fedfunds
(output omitted)
```

运行结果如图 8.16 所示。

```
. estat sbknown, break(tq(1981q2))
Wald test for a structural break: Known break date
Sample:   1954q4—2010q4
```

Source	SS	df	MS			
				Number of obs	=	225
				F(1, 223)	=	2847.07
Model	2400.62145	1	2400.62145	Prob > F	=	0.0000
Residual	188.031506	223	.843190608	R-squared	=	0.9274
				Adj R-squared	=	0.9270
Total	2588.65296	224	11.5564864	Root MSE	=	.91825

fedfunds	Coef.	Std. Err.	t	P>|t|	[95% Conf.	Interval]
fedfunds						
L1.	.9645128	.0180763	53.36	0.000	.9288906	1.000135
_cons	.1897176	.1160063	1.64	0.103	-.0388911	.4183264

图 8.16

Break date：1981q2

Ho：No structural break

chi2(2) = 6.4147

Prob>chi2 = 0.0405

Exogenous variables： L.fedfunds

Coefficients included in test：L.fedfunds _cons

可见在 5%水平上拒绝没有结构性中断的原假设。

下面示例检验多个已知的中断。假设我们将数据分为三个子样本，分别为 1954 年第 4 季度至 1970 年第 1 季度、1970 年第 2 季度至 1995 年第 1 季度和 1995 年第 2 季度至 2010 年第 4 季度，同时指定 1970 年第 1 季度和 1995 年第 1 季度的中断日期。我们想检验这些子样本中的系数是否相同，于是在 break()选项中指定多个日期。

```
.estat sbknown, break(tq(1970q1) tq(1995q1))
```

运行结果如图 8.17 所示。

```
Wald test for a structural break: Known break date

                                        Number of obs  =         225
Sample:       1954q4 - 2010q4
Break date:   1970q1 1995q1
Ho: No structural break

              chi2(4)       =     4.6739
              Prob > chi2   =     0.3224

Exogenous variables:            L.fedfunds
Coefficients included in test: L.fedfunds _cons
```

图 8.17

可见未能拒绝在指定日期没有结构中断的原假设。

8.3.3 参数稳定性累积和检验

考虑一个具有 k 个变量的线性回归模型：

$$y_t = \boldsymbol{x}_t'\boldsymbol{\beta}_t + e_t \quad t=1,\cdots,T \tag{8.41}$$

其中，y_t 是因变量，$\boldsymbol{x}_t$ 是可能包含因变量滞后的协变量向量，$\boldsymbol{\beta}_t$ 是时变参数的向量，e_t 是独立且相同分布的误差项。

基于递归残差的 CUSUM 检验是使用提前一步的标准化预测误差构建的，即

$$e_t^{\mathrm{rec}} = \frac{y_t - \boldsymbol{x}_t'\hat{\boldsymbol{\beta}}_{t-1}}{\sqrt{1+\boldsymbol{x}_t'(\boldsymbol{X}_{t-1}'\boldsymbol{X}_{t-1})\boldsymbol{x}_t}} \quad t=k+1,\cdots,T \tag{8.42}$$

其中，$\hat{\boldsymbol{\beta}}_{t-1}$ 是第一个 $t-1$ 个观察和 $\boldsymbol{X}_{t-1}'=(\boldsymbol{x}_1,\cdots,\boldsymbol{x}_{t-1})$ 的 $\boldsymbol{\beta}$ 估计值。参数稳定性检验的零假设为 $H_0:\boldsymbol{\beta}_t=\boldsymbol{\beta}$，这意味着参数不变。在零假设条件下，序列$\{e_t^{\mathrm{rec}}\}$是独立同分布且服从 $N(0,\sigma^2)$。CUSUM 检验的统计量为：

$$C_t^{\mathrm{rec}} = \frac{1}{\hat{\sigma}}\sum_{j=k+1}^{j=t} e_j^{\mathrm{rec}} \tag{8.43}$$

式中，$\hat{\sigma}^2=\{1/(T-k)\}\sum\limits_{t=k+1}^{T}(e_t^{\mathrm{rec}}e_t^{-\mathrm{rec}})^2$。序列$\{C_t^{\mathrm{rec}}\}$的极限分布是在时刻 $t=k+1$ 从 0 开始的一个均值为 0、方差为 $t-k$ 的几何布朗运动。其非线性边界值的线性函数近似值为：$\pm c\{1+2(t-k)/(T-k)\}$。参数 c 可以通过求解等式 $\Phi(3c)+\exp(-4c^2)\{1-\Phi(c)\}=0.5\alpha$ 得到。因此，CUSUM 检验的统计量也可表示为：

$$\max_{k+1\leqslant t\leqslant T} \frac{|C_t^{\mathrm{rec}}|}{1+2\dfrac{t-k}{T-k}} \tag{8.44}$$

例 8.9 参数稳定性的 CUSUM 检验

```
* 下载数据，清理内存
.clear
.webuse wpi1
.regress D.ln_wpi
```

运行结果如图 8.18 所示。

Source	SS	df	MS			
				Number of obs	=	123
				F(0, 122)	=	0.00
Model	0	0	.	Prob > F	=	.
Residual	.02521709	122	.000206697	R-squared	=	0.0000
				Adj R-squared	=	0.0000
Total	.02521709	122	.000206697	Root MSE	=	.01438

D.ln_wpi	Coefficient	Std. err.	t	P>|t|	[95% conf.	interval]
_cons	.0108215	.0012963	8.35	0.000	.0082553	.0133878

图 8.18

* 使用递归残差的累积值检验平均值的稳定性

```
.estat sbcusum
```

运行结果如图 8.19 所示。

```
Cumulative sum test for parameter stability

Sample: 1960q2 thru 1990q4                    Number of obs = 123
H0: No structural break

                  Test       ────── Critical value ──────
      Type     statistic          1%           5%          10%
─────────────────────────────────────────────────────────────────
 Recursive        1.9030      1.1430       0.9479       0.8499
─────────────────────────────────────────────────────────────────
```

图 8.19

运行结果如图 8.20 所示。

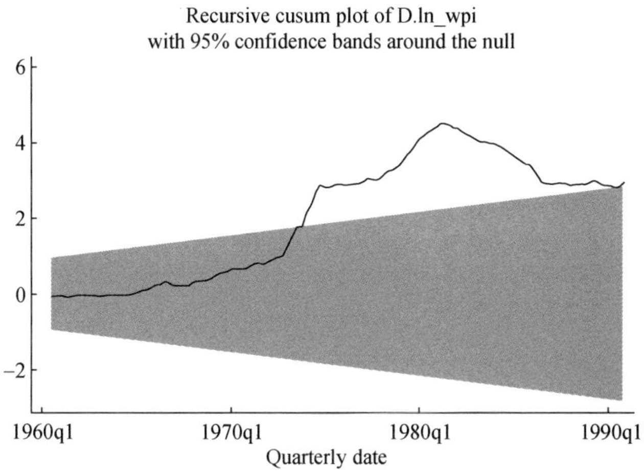

图 8.20

* 使用 OLS 残差的累积值检验稳定性

```
.estat sbcusum, ols
```

运行结果如图 8.21 和图 8.22 所示。

Cumulative sum test for parameter stability

Sample: 1960q2 thru 1990q4　　Number of obs = 123
H0: No structural break

Type	Test statistic	Critical value 1%	5%	10%
OLS	1.9854	1.6276	1.3581	1.2238

图 8.21

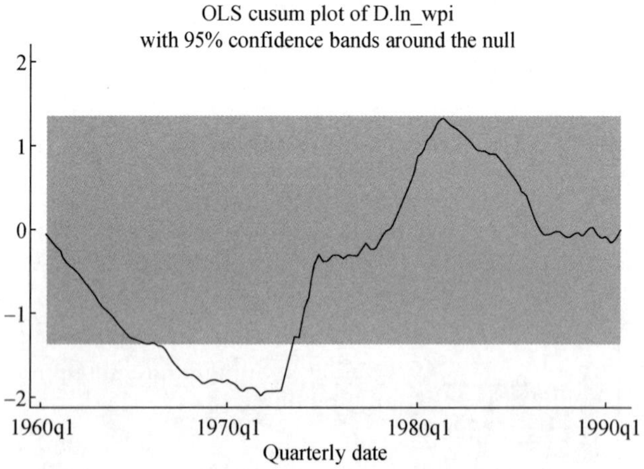

图 8.22

8.3.4 BGLM 检验

与 DW 统计量仅检验扰动项是否存在一阶自相关不同，Breush-Godfrey LM 检验（BGLM 检验）也可应用于检验回归方程的残差序列是否存在高阶自相关，而且在方程中存在滞后因变量的情况下，LM 检验仍然有效。

LM 检验原假设为：直到 p 阶滞后不存在序列相关，p 为预先定义好的整数；备选假设是：存在 p 阶自相关。

BGLM 检验的原假设是不存在 p 阶序列相关，即

$$H_0: \rho_1 = 0, \cdots, \rho_p = 0 \tag{8.45}$$

（1）估计回归方程，并求出残差 e_t。BGLM 检验的辅助回归模型为：

$$e_t = y_t - \hat{\beta}_0 - \hat{\beta}_1 x_{1t} - \hat{\beta}_2 x_{2t} - \cdots - \hat{\beta}_k x_{kt} \tag{8.46}$$

（2）检验统计量可以基于如下回归得到：

$$e_t = X_t\gamma + \alpha_1 e_{t-1} + \cdots + \alpha_p e_{t-p} + v_t \tag{8.47}$$

这是对原始回归因子 X_t 和直到 p 阶的滞后残差的回归。LM 检验通常给出两个统计量：F 统计量和 NR^2 统计量。其中，F 统计量是对所有滞后残差联合显著性的一种检验。对于检验统计量 NR^2，N 是辅助回归模型中的观测值数量，R^2 为辅助回归模型的拟合优度。BGLM 检验统计量服从自由度为 p 的卡方分布 $\chi^2(p)$。对于小样本，则用 $F(p, N-p-k)$ 计算 p 值。在给定的显著性水平下，如果这两个统计量小于设定显著性水平下的临界值，说明序列在设定的显著性水平下不存在序列相关；反之，如果这两个统计量大于设定显著性水平下的临界值，则说明存在序列相关。

estat bgodfrey 对扰动中的高阶序列相关执行 BGLM 检验。该检验不要求所有回归量都是严格外生的。

该检验的语法格式为：

Statistics>Postestimation

菜单操作路径为：

estat bgodfrey [, bgodfrey options]

8.3.5 Durbin 的替代检验

1. DW 检验

Durbin-Watson 检验（DW 检验）的原假设是不存在一阶自相关，用于确定线性回归模型中的误差项是否遵循 AR(1)过程。对于线性模型

$$y_t = \boldsymbol{x}_t\boldsymbol{\beta} + u_t \tag{8.48}$$

AR(1) 过程可以写成：

$$u_t = \rho u_{t-1} + \varepsilon_t \tag{8.49}$$

一般来说，AR(1) 过程只要求 ε_t 是独立同分布。然而，DW 检验要求 ε_t 服从 $N(0,\sigma^2)$。此外，只有当回归量是严格外生的时，才可以应用 DW 检验。如果所有 s 和 t 的 $\mathrm{Corr}(x_s, u_t)=0$，则回归量 $\boldsymbol{x}$ 是严格外生的，这排除了在将因变量的滞后值作为回归量的模型中使用 DW 检验统计量。DW 检验统计量为：

$$\text{D. W.} = \frac{\sum_{t=2}^{T}(\hat{u}_t - \hat{u}_{t-1})^2}{\sum_{t=1}^{T}\hat{u}_t^2} \approx 2(1-\hat{\rho}) \tag{8.50}$$

DW 检验统计量(d)可以取 0 到 4 之间的值。如果序列不相关，d 值在 2 附近。d 值小于 2 表示正自相关($\rho>0$)，d 值大于 2 表示负自相关 ($\rho<0$)。计算统计量的准确分布是困难的，但经验上限和下限已根据样本量和回归量的数量确定。正序列相关最为普遍，根据经验，对于有大于 50 个观测值和较少解释变量的方程，若 d 值小于 1.5，说明残差序列存在强的正一阶序列相关。Savin 和 White (1977)[①]已发布了 d 统

① Savin, N. E., and K. J. White. The Durbin-Watson Test for Serial Correlation with Extreme Sample Sizes or Many Regressors. *Econometrica*, 1977, 45.

计量的扩展表。例如，对一个具有 30 个观测值和 3 个回归量（包括常数项）的模型而言，原假设为无自相关，备择假设为正自相关，d 统计量的下限为 1.284，而在 5%的显著性水平上，上限为 1.567。如果 $d<1.284$，将拒绝 null；如果 $d>1.567$，将无法拒绝。落在（1.284，1.567）范围内的值不会导致关于是否拒绝原假设的结论。

2. Durbin 的替代检验

当回归变量中包含滞后因变量时，误差项的过去值与时间 t 的滞后变量相关，这意味着它们不是严格的外生回归变量。包含非严格外生的协变量会导致 d 统计量偏向接受原假设。Durbin（1970）①建议对具有滞后因变量的模型进行替代检验，并将该检验扩展到更一般的 AR(p) 序列相关过程：

$$u_t=\rho_1 u_{t-1}+\cdots+\rho_p u_{t-p}+\varepsilon_t \tag{8.51}$$

其中，ε_t 是独立同分布。方差为 σ^2，但不假定或要求对检验是正态的。

Durbin 的替代检验和 BGLM 检验的原假设都是不存在 p 阶序列相关，即

$$H_0:\rho_1=0,\cdots,\rho_p=0 \tag{8.52}$$

另一种方法是至少有一个 ρ 是非零的。尽管原假设最初是针对 AR(p)过程推导出来的，但该检验结果证明其对 MA(p)过程也具有效力。因此，该检验的实际零值不存在直到 p 阶的序列相关，因为 MA(p)和 AR(p)模型是零值下的局部等效替代方案。

Durbin 的替代检验实际上是 LM 检验，但它最容易通过 Wald 检验对滞后残差的系数在滞后残差的辅助 OLS 回归和原始回归中的所有协变量进行计算。考虑线性回归模型：

$$y_t=\beta_1 x_{1t}+\cdots+\beta_k x_{kt}+u_t \tag{8.53}$$

其中，协变量 $\boldsymbol{x}_1$ 到 $\boldsymbol{x}_k$ 被假定为严格外生的，u_t 被假定为独立同分布，且具有有限的方差。该过程也被假定为是平稳的。通过 OLS 估计中的参数可获得残差 $\hat{u}_t$。接下来对 $\hat{u}_t$ 执行另一个 OLS 回归，即

$$\hat{u}_t=\gamma_1\hat{u}_{t-1}+\cdots+\gamma_p\hat{u}_{t-p}+\beta_1 x_{1t}+\cdots+\beta_k x_{kt}+\varepsilon_t \tag{8.54}$$

其中，ε_t 代表此辅助 OLS 回归中的随机误差项。然后，通过执行 $\gamma_1,\cdots,\gamma_p$ 联合为零的 Wald 检验来获得 Durbin 的替代检验。在估计（8.47）中的回归时，通过使用稳健的 VCE 估计量，可以使检验对未知形式的异方差具有稳健性。当只有严格的外生回归变量且 $p=1$ 时，此检验渐近等效于 DW 检验。

在拟合中，滞后残差的值在初始期间不存在。正如 Davidson 和 MacKinnon（1993）②所指出的，在这个受限样本中，残差不会与模型中的其他协变量正交，这意味着当滞后残差被排除时，辅助回归的 R^2 不会为零。因此，BGLM 的 NR^2 版本的检验可能会在小样本中过度拒绝。为了纠正这个问题，Davidson 和 MacKinnon（1993）③

① Durbin, J. Testing for Serial Correlation in Least-squares Regressions When Some of the Regressors Are Lagged Dependent Variables. *Econometrica*, 1970, 38.

② Davidson, R., and J. G. MacKinnon. *Estimation and Inference in Econometrics*. New York: Oxford University Press, 1993.

③ Ibid.

建议将滞后残差的缺失值设置为零，并对式(8.40)中使用的完整样本运行式(8.41)中的辅助回归。对于 BGLM 检验和 Durbin 的替代检验，这种小样本校正已经成为惯例，并且它是两个命令的默认值。指定 nomiss0 选项会覆盖此默认行为，并将通过滞后残差回归生成的初始缺失值视为缺失。因此，nomiss0 会导致这些初始观察值从辅助回归的样本中删除。

Durbin 的替代检验和 BGLM 检验最初是针对没有 vce(robust)选项的回归所涵盖的情况得出的。但是，在有 regress、vce(robust)和 newey 选项之后，Durbin 的替代检验仍然有效，如果指定了 robust 和 force 选项就可以调用。

该检验的语法格式为：

```
estat durbinalt, durbinalt options
```

8.3.6 Durbin-Watson *d* 统计量

回归模型如下：

$$y_t = \beta_1 x_{1t} + \cdots + \beta_k x_{kt} + u_t$$

式中，一些协变量并非严格的外生变量。特别是，一些 $\boldsymbol{x}_{it}$ 可以是因变量的滞后。我们感兴趣的是 u_t 是否是序列相关的。

estat dwatson 命令报告的 Durbin-Watson *d* 统计量为：

$$d = \frac{\sum_{t=1}^{n-1}(\hat{u}_{t+1} - \hat{u}_t)^2}{\sum_{t=1}^{n}\hat{u}_t^2} \tag{8.55}$$

式中，$\hat{u}_t$ 是第 t 个观测值的残差。

语法格式为：

```
estat dwatson
```

例 8.10　序列相关性检验

本例使用来自 Klein (1950)①的数据，我们首先使用 OLS 回归模型，拟合政府工资账单对消费的影响：

```
. use https://www.stata-press.com/data/r17/klein
. tsset yr
Time variable: yr, 1920 to 1941
        delta: 1 unit
. regress consump wagegovt
```

运行结果如图 8.23 所示。

如果我们假设 wagegovt 是一个严格的外生变量，我们可以使用 DW 检验来检查误差中的一阶序列相关性。

```
. estat dwatson
```

① Klein, L. R. *Economic Fluctuations in the United States 1921—1941*. New York: Wiley, 1950.

Source	SS	df	MS			
				Number of obs	=	22
				F(1, 20)	=	17.72
Model	532.567711	1	532.567711	Prob > F	=	0.0004
Residual	601.207167	20	30.0603584	R-squared	=	0.4697
				Adj R-squared	=	0.4432
Total	1133.77488	21	53.9892799	Root MSE	=	5.4827

consump	Coef.	Std. Err.	t	P>|t|	[95% Conf.	Interval]
wagegovt	2.50744	.5957173	4.21	0.000	1.264796	3.750085
_cons	40.84699	3.192183	12.80	0.000	34.18821	47.50577

图 8.23

.Durbin-Watson d-statistic(2, 22) = .3217998

Durbin-Watson d 统计量为 0.32,远离其分布的中心($d=2.0$)。给定模型中的 22 个观测值和两个回归量(包括常数项),5%的下限约为 0.997,远大于计算的 d 统计量。假设 wagegovt 变量是严格外生的,我们可以拒绝没有一阶序列相关的原假设。拒绝原假设并不一定意味着符合 AR 过程;其他形式的误差设定也可能导致产生显著的检验统计量。如果我们愿意假设误差项遵循 AR(1)过程,并且 wagegovt 变量是严格外生的,则可以使用 arima 或 prais 选项重新对误差项拟合模型。

如果我们不愿意假设 wagegovt 是严格外生的,可以改为使用 Durbin 的替代检验或 BGLM 检验来检查一阶序列相关性。因为只有 22 个观测值,所以使用 small 选项。

.estat durbinalt, small

运行结果如图 8.24 所示。

Durbin's alternative test for autocorrelation

lags(*p*)	F	df	Prob > F
1	35.035	(1, 19)	0.0000

H0: no serial correlation

图 8.24

.estat bgodfrey, small

运行结果如图 8.25 所示。

这两个检验都强烈拒绝无一阶序列相关的零值,因此我们决定用两个消费滞后作为回归量重新拟合模型,然后重新运行 estat durbinalt 和 estat bgodfrey。由于修正后的模型包括因变量的滞后值,因此不适用 DW 检验。

.regress consump wagegovt L.consump L2.consump

运行结果如图 8.26 所示。

Breusch-Godfrey LM test for autocorrelation			
lags(*p*)	F	df	Prob > F
1	14.264	(1, 19)	0.0013
H0: no serial correlation			

图 8.25

Source	SS	df	MS			
Model	702.660311	3	234.220104	Number of obs	=	20
Residual	85.1596011	16	5.32247507	F(3, 16)	=	44.01
				Prob > F	=	0.0000
Total	787.819912	19	41.4642059	R-squared	=	0.8919
				Adj R-squared	=	0.8716
				Root MSE	=	2.307

consump	Coef.	Std. Err.	t	P>|t|	[95% Conf.	Interval]
wagegovt	.6904282	.3295485	2.10	0.052	-.0081835	1.38904
consump						
L1.	1.420536	.197024	7.21	0.000	1.002864	1.838208
L2.	-.650888	.1933351	-3.37	0.004	-1.06074	-.241036
_cons	9.209073	5.006701	1.84	0.084	-1.404659	19.82281

图 8.26

.estat durbinalt, small lags(1/2)

运行结果如图 8.27 所示。

Durbin's alternative test for autocorrelation			
lags(*p*)	F	df	Prob > F
1	0.080	(1, 15)	0.7805
2	0.260	(2, 14)	0.7750
H0: no serial correlation			

图 8.27

.estat bgodfrey, small lags(1/2)

运行结果如图 8.28 所示。

尽管在 5% 的水平上，wagegovt 和常数项在统计上不再不同于零，但 estat durbinalt 和 estat bgodfrey 的输出表明，包括两个消费滞后已经消除了误差中的任何

Breusch-Godfrey LM test for autocorrelation			
lags(p)	F	df	Prob > F
1	0.107	(1, 15)	0.7484
2	0.358	(2, 14)	0.7056
H0: no serial correlation			

图 8.28

序列相关性。

Engle (1982)①建议使用 LM 检验来检查误差中的自回归条件异方差(ARCH)。p 阶 ARCH 模型可以写成：

$$\sigma_t^2 = E(u_t^2 \mid u_{t-1}, \cdots, u_{t-p}) = \gamma_0 + \gamma_1 u_{t-1}^2 + \cdots + \gamma_p u_{t-p}^2 \tag{8.56}$$

为了检验无自回归条件异方差性的原假设(即 $\gamma_1 = \cdots = \gamma_p = 0$)，我们首先拟合 OLS 回归模型 $y_t = \beta_1 x_{1t} + \cdots + \beta_k x_{kt} + u_t$，获得残差 $\hat{u}_t$，然后对滞后残差运行另一个 OLS 回归，即

$$\hat{u}_t^2 = \gamma_0 + \gamma_1 \hat{u}_{t-1}^2 + \cdots + \gamma_p \hat{u}_{t-p}^2 + \varepsilon \tag{8.57}$$

检验统计量为 NR^2，其中 N 是样本中的观测数，R^2 是回归模型中的 R^2。在原假设下，检验统计量服从 χ_p^2 分布。

8.3.7 信息准则

Akaike (1974)②将信息准则定义为：

$$\text{AIC} = -2\ln L + 2k$$

其中，$\ln L$ 是模型的最大对数似然值，k 是估计的参数数量。一些学者将 AIC 定义为上述表达式除以样本大小。

Schwarz(1978)③的贝叶斯信息标准是另一种拟合度量，定义为：

$$\text{BIC} = -2\ln L + k\ln N$$

其中，N 是样本大小。

语法格式为：

estat ic [, n(#)]

例 8.11 信息准则计算

本例使用关于美国 616 名心理抑郁患者的健康保险类型的数据(Tarlov *et al.*,

---

① Engle, R. Autoregressive Conditional Heteroscedasticity with Estimates of the Variance of United Kingdom Inflation. *Econometrica*, 1982, 50(4).

② Akaike, H. A New Look at the Statistical Model Identification. *IEEE Transactions on Automatic Control*, 1974, 19.

③ Schwarz, G. Estimating the Dimension of a Model. *Annals of Statistics*, 1978, 6.

1989①; Wells *et al.*, 1989②)。保险分为两种:赔偿计划和预付计划,主体也可能没有参加任何保险。我们首先使用 mlogit 拟合了一个模型,该模型根据年龄、性别、种族和学习地点来解释一个人所拥有的保险类型。我们分别在使用和不使用位置虚拟变量的情况下重新拟合模型并进行比较。

```
. use https://www.stata-press.com/data/r17/sysdsn1
(Health insurance data)
. mlogit insure age male nonwhite
(output omitted)
```

运行结果如图 8.29 所示。

```
Multinomial logistic regression                 Number of obs     =        615
                                                LR chi2(6)        =      20.54
                                                Prob > chi2       =     0.0022
Log likelihood = -545.58328                     Pseudo R2         =     0.0185
```

insure	Coef.	Std. Err.	z	P>|z|	[95% Conf.	Interval]
Indemnity	(base outcome)					
Prepaid						
age	-.0111915	.0060915	-1.84	0.066	-.0231305	.0007475
male	.5739825	.2005221	2.86	0.004	.1809665	.9669985
nonwhite	.7312659	.218978	3.34	0.001	.302077	1.160455
_cons	.1567003	.2828509	0.55	0.580	-.3976773	.7110778
Uninsure						
age	-.0058414	.0114114	-0.51	0.609	-.0282073	.0165245
male	.5102237	.3639793	1.40	0.161	-.2031626	1.22361
nonwhite	.4333141	.4106255	1.06	0.291	-.371497	1.238125
_cons	-1.811165	.5348606	-3.39	0.001	-2.859473	-.7628578

图 8.29

```
. estat ic
```

运行结果如图 8.30 所示。

① Tarlov, A. R., J. E. Ware Jr., S. Greenfield, E. C. Nelson, E. Perrin, and M. Zubkoff. The Medical Outcomes Study: An application of Methods for Monitoring the Results of Medical Care. *Journal of the American Medical Association*, 1989, 262.

② Wells, K. B., R. D. Hays, M. A. Burnam, W. H. Rogers, S. Greenfield, and J. E. Ware Jr. Detection of Depressive Disorder for Patients Receiving Prepaid or Fee-for-service Care: Results from the Medical Outcomes Survey. *Journal of the American Medical Association*, 1989, 262.

Akaike's information criterion and Bayesian information criterion

Model	N	ll(null)	ll(model)	df	AIC	BIC
.	615	-555.8545	-545.5833	8	1107.167	1142.54

Note: BIC uses N = number of observations. See [R] BIC note.

图 8.30

```
.mlogit insure age male nonwhite i.site
```

运行结果如图 8.31 所示。

Multinomial logistic regression　　　Number of obs = 615
　　　LR chi2(10) = 42.99
　　　Prob > chi2 = 0.0000
Log likelihood = -534.36165　　　Pseudo R2 = 0.0387

insure	Coef.	Std. Err.	z	P>|z|	[95% Conf.	Interval]
Indemnity	(base outcome)					
Prepaid						
age	-.011745	.0061946	-1.90	0.058	-.0238862	.0003962
male	.5616934	.2027465	2.77	0.006	.1643175	.9590693
nonwhite	.9747768	.2363213	4.12	0.000	.5115955	1.437958
site						
2	.1130359	.2101903	0.54	0.591	-.2989296	.5250013
3	-.5879879	.2279351	-2.58	0.010	-1.034733	-.1412433
_cons	.2697127	.3284422	0.82	0.412	-.3740222	.9134476
Uninsure						
age	-.0077961	.0114418	-0.68	0.496	-.0302217	.0146294
male	.4518496	.3674867	1.23	0.219	-.268411	1.17211
nonwhite	.2170589	.4256361	0.51	0.610	-.6171725	1.05129
site						
2	-1.211563	.4705127	-2.57	0.010	-2.133751	-.2893747
3	-.2078123	.3662926	-0.57	0.570	-.9257327	.510108
_cons	-1.286943	.5923219	-2.17	0.030	-2.447872	-.1260134

图 8.31

```
.estat ic
```

运行结果如图 8.32 所示。

Akaike's information criterion and Bayesian information criterion

Model	N	ll(null)	ll(model)	df	AIC	BIC
.	615	-555.8545	-534.3616	12	1092.723	1145.783

Note: BIC uses N = number of observations. See [R] BIC note.

图 8.32

AIC 表示使用位置虚拟变量的模型更适合，而 BIC 则相反。通常情况下，不同的模型选择标准会导致产生相互矛盾的结论。

8.4 平稳时序建模

8.4.1 AR 模型

时序变量 y_t 的 p 阶自回归模型，即 AR(p)模型为：

$$y_t = \beta_0 + \beta_1 y_{t-1} + \cdots + \beta_p y_{t-p} + \varepsilon_t \tag{8.58}$$

AR(p)模型的参数估计利用条件 MLE 法，即利用在给定$\{y_1, \cdots, y_p\}$的情况下的$\{y_{p+1}, \cdots, y_T\}$的条件分布，建立条件最大似然函数，最大化即可得到参数的一致估计值。

对于 AR(p)模型，其 ACF 函数在 p 阶之后拖尾，即逐渐衰减，而 PACF 函数截尾，即等于 0。如果序列相关性分析结果显示这样的特征，就需要选用 AR(p)模型。

8.4.2 MA 模型

时序变量 y_t 的 q 阶移动平均模型，即 MA(q)模型为：

$$y_t = \mu + \varepsilon_t + \theta_1 \varepsilon_{t-1} + \theta_2 \varepsilon_{t-2} + \cdots + \theta_q \varepsilon_{t-t} \tag{8.59}$$

该模型的参数估计也是利用条件 MLE 法，可以得到参数的一致估计值。

对于 MA(q)模型，其 ACF 函数在 q 阶之后截尾，即等于 0，而其 PACF 函数拖尾，即逐渐衰减。如果序列相关性分析结果显示这样的特征，就需要选用 MA(q)模型。

8.4.3 ARMA 模型

时序数据往往既有序列相关特征，也有随机的白噪声成分，为更好地拟合这类数据特征，需要把 AR(p)模型和 MA(q)模型组合起来，构建自回归移动平均模型，即 ARMA(p,q)模型：

$$y_t = \beta_0 + \beta_1 y_{t-1} + \cdots + \beta_p y_{t-p} + \varepsilon_t + \theta_1 \varepsilon_{t-1} + \cdots + \theta_q \varepsilon_{t-q} \tag{8.60}$$

如果序列相关性分析结果显示，ACF 函数在 p 阶后和 PACF 函数在 q 阶后都拖尾，即逐渐衰减，就需要选用 ARMA(p,q)模型拟合该时序数据。ARMA(p,q)模型的参数估计也是利用条件 MLE 法。

8.5 含 AR(1)随机项的线性回归

Prais-Winsten 回归，即含 AR(1)随机项的线性回归。其实现命令为 prais，该命令使用广义最小二乘法估计线性回归模型中的参数，其中误差是串行相关的。具体而言，假设误差遵循一阶自回归过程。

考虑命令"prais y x z"。第 0 次迭代通过从标准线性回归中估计 a、b 和 c 获得，即

$$y_t = ax_t + bz_t + c + u_t \tag{8.61}$$

然后获得残差中相关性的估计值。默认情况下，prais 使用辅助回归：

$$u_t = \rho u_{t-1} + e_t \tag{8.62}$$

这可以更改为 rhotype()选项中记录的任何计算。

接下来，我们将 Cochrane-Orcutt 变换应用于 $t=2,\cdots,n$ 观测值，得到：

$$y_t - \rho y_{t-1} = a(x_t - \rho x_{t-1}) + b(z_t - \rho z_{t-1}) + c(1-\rho) + v_t \tag{8.63}$$

应用于 $t=1$ 观测值，得到：

$$\sqrt{1-\rho^2}\,y_1 = a(\sqrt{1-\rho^2}\,x_1) + b(\sqrt{1-\rho^2}\,z_1) + c\sqrt{1-\rho^2} + \sqrt{1-\rho^2}\,v_1 \tag{8.64}$$

式(8.63)和式(8.64)用于转换数据，获得 a、b、c 的新估计值。

当指定 twostep 选项时，估计过程在此点停止并报告这些估计。在迭代收敛的默认行为下，重复此过程，直到 ρ 估计值的变化处于指定的公差范围内。

新的估计值用于生成拟合值 $\hat{y}_t = \hat{a}x_t + \hat{b}z_t + \hat{c}$，然后，默认情况下，使用回归 $y_t - \hat{y}_t = \rho(y_{t-1} - \hat{y}_{t-1}) + u_t$，再估计 ρ。接下来，使用 ρ 的新估计重新估计式(8.63)，并继续在式(8.63)和式(8.64)之间迭代，直到 ρ 的估计收敛。

prais 和 estat dwatson 报告的 Durbin-Watson d 统计量为：

$$d = \frac{\sum_{j=1}^{n-1}(u_{j+1} - u_j)^2}{\sum_{j=1}^{n} u_j^2} \tag{8.65}$$

式中，u_j 表示第 j 个观测值的残差。

Prais-Winsten 估计量是一种广义最小二乘估计量。Prais-Winsten 方法源自上述误差项的 AR(1)模型。而 Cochrane-Orcutt 方法使用滞后定义，并通过迭代法，即 Prais-Winsten 方法保留了第一个观察结果。在小样本中，这可能是一个显著的优势。

语法格式为：

prais depvar [indepvars] [if] [in] [, options]

菜单操作路径为：

Statistics>Time series>Prais-Winsten regression

例 8.12　含 AR(1)随机项的线性回归

* 下载数据，清理内存

```
.clear
.webuse idle
.tsset t
Time variable: t, 1 to 30
      Delta: 1 unit
```

* 执行 Prais-Winsten AR(1)回归

```
.prais usr idle
```

运行结果如图 8.33 所示。

```
Prais-Winsten AR(1) regression with iterated estimates

      Source |       SS           df       MS      Number of obs   =        30
-------------+----------------------------------   F(1, 28)        =      7.12
       Model |  43.0076941         1  43.0076941   Prob > F        =    0.0125
    Residual |  169.165739        28  6.04163354   R-squared       =    0.2027
-------------+----------------------------------   Adj R-squared   =    0.1742
       Total |  212.173433        29  7.31632528   Root MSE        =     2.458

------------------------------------------------------------------------------
         usr | Coefficient  Std. err.      t    P>|t|     [95% conf. interval]
-------------+----------------------------------------------------------------
        idle |  -.1356522   .0472195    -2.87   0.008    -.2323769   -.0389275
       _cons |   15.20415   4.160391     3.65   0.001     6.681978    23.72633
-------------+----------------------------------------------------------------
         rho |   .5535476
------------------------------------------------------------------------------
Durbin-Watson statistic (original)    = 1.295766
Durbin-Watson statistic (transformed) = 1.476004
```

图　8.33

* 执行 Cochrane-Orcutt AR(1)回归

```
.prais usr idle, corc
```

运行结果如图 8.34 所示。

* 同上，但要求稳健的标准误差

```
.prais usr idle, corc vce(robust)
```

运行结果如图 8.35 所示。

```
Cochrane-Orcutt AR(1) regression with iterated estimates

      Source |       SS           df       MS      Number of obs   =        29
-------------+----------------------------------   F(1, 27)        =      6.49
       Model |  40.1309584         1  40.1309584   Prob > F        =    0.0168
    Residual |  166.898474        27  6.18142498   R-squared       =    0.1938
-------------+----------------------------------   Adj R-squared   =    0.1640
       Total |  207.029433        28  7.39390831   Root MSE        =    2.4862

------------------------------------------------------------------------------
         usr | Coefficient  Std. err.      t    P>|t|     [95% conf. interval]
-------------+----------------------------------------------------------------
        idle |  -.1254511   .0492356    -2.55   0.017    -.2264742    -.024428
       _cons |   14.54641   4.272299     3.40   0.002      5.78038    23.31245
-------------+----------------------------------------------------------------
         rho |   .5707918
------------------------------------------------------------------------------
Durbin-Watson statistic (original)    = 1.295766
Durbin-Watson statistic (transformed) = 1.466222
```

图 8.34

```
Cochrane-Orcutt AR(1) regression with iterated estimates

Linear regression                               Number of obs     =         29
                                                F(1, 27)          =       3.14
                                                Prob > F          =     0.0878
                                                R-squared         =     0.1938
                                                Root MSE          =     2.4862

------------------------------------------------------------------------------
             |             Semirobust
         usr | Coefficient  std. err.      t    P>|t|     [95% conf. interval]
-------------+----------------------------------------------------------------
        idle |  -.1254511   .0708259    -1.77   0.088    -.2707739    .0198717
       _cons |   14.54641   6.554731     2.22   0.035     1.097217    27.99561
-------------+----------------------------------------------------------------
         rho |   .5707918
------------------------------------------------------------------------------
Durbin-Watson statistic (original)    = 1.295766
Durbin-Watson statistic (transformed) = 1.466222
```

图 8.35

* 下载数据，清理内存

. clear

. webuse qsales

* 执行 Cochrane-Orcutt AR(1)回归并搜索数值，使得 Cochrane-Orcutt 转换后的方程残差之和最小。

. prais csales isales, corc ssesearch

运行结果如图 8.36 所示。

```
Cochrane-Orcutt AR(1) regression with SSE search estimates

      Source |       SS           df       MS      Number of obs   =        19
-------------+----------------------------------   F(1, 17)        =    553.14
       Model |  2.33199178         1  2.33199178   Prob > F        =    0.0000
    Residual |  .071670369        17  .004215904   R-squared       =    0.9702
-------------+----------------------------------   Adj R-squared   =    0.9684
       Total |  2.40366215        18  .133536786   Root MSE        =    .06493

------------------------------------------------------------------------------
      csales | Coefficient  Std. err.      t    P>|t|     [95% conf. interval]
-------------+----------------------------------------------------------------
      isales |   .1605233   .0068253    23.52   0.000     .1461233    .1749234
       _cons |   1.738946   1.432674     1.21   0.241    -1.283732    4.761624
-------------+----------------------------------------------------------------
         rho |   .9588209
------------------------------------------------------------------------------
Durbin-Watson statistic (original)    = 0.734728
Durbin-Watson statistic (transformed) = 1.724419
```

图 8.36

＊以 99%置信区间重现结果

.prais, level(99)

运行结果如图 8.37 所示。

```
Cochrane-Orcutt AR(1) regression with SSE search estimates

      Source |       SS           df       MS      Number of obs   =        19
-------------+----------------------------------   F(1, 17)        =    553.14
       Model |  2.33199178         1  2.33199178   Prob > F        =    0.0000
    Residual |  .071670369        17  .004215904   R-squared       =    0.9702
-------------+----------------------------------   Adj R-squared   =    0.9684
       Total |  2.40366215        18  .133536786   Root MSE        =    .06493

------------------------------------------------------------------------------
      csales | Coefficient  Std. err.      t    P>|t|     [99% conf. interval]
-------------+----------------------------------------------------------------
      isales |   .1605233   .0068253    23.52   0.000     .1407421    .1803045
       _cons |   1.738946   1.432674     1.21   0.241    -2.413274    5.891166
-------------+----------------------------------------------------------------
         rho |   .9588209
------------------------------------------------------------------------------
Durbin-Watson statistic (original)    = 0.734728
Durbin-Watson statistic (transformed) = 1.724419
```

图 8.37

8.6 Newey-West 标准误差回归

Newey-West 标准误差回归的 Stata 实现命令为 newey。该命令为 OLS 回归估计的系数产生 newey-West 标准误差。假设该误差结构是异方差的,并且可能具有某种滞后的自相关。newey 命令计算的参数估计及其方差估计为:

$$\hat{\boldsymbol{\beta}}_{\text{OLS}}=(\boldsymbol{X}'\boldsymbol{X})^{-1}\boldsymbol{X}'\boldsymbol{y} \tag{8.66}$$

$$\text{Var}(\hat{\boldsymbol{\beta}}_{\text{OLS}})=(\boldsymbol{X}'\boldsymbol{X})^{-1}\boldsymbol{X}'\boldsymbol{\Omega}\boldsymbol{X}(\boldsymbol{X}'\boldsymbol{X})^{-1} \tag{8.67}$$

参数估计是最简单的 OLS 线性回归估计值。

没有自相关时,使用 White 公式计算方差估计:

$$\boldsymbol{X}'\boldsymbol{\Omega}\boldsymbol{X}=\boldsymbol{X}'\boldsymbol{\Omega}_0\boldsymbol{X}=\frac{n}{n-k}\sum_i \hat{e}_i^2\boldsymbol{x}_i'\boldsymbol{x}_i$$

式中,$\hat{e}_i=y_i-\boldsymbol{x}_i\hat{\boldsymbol{\beta}}_{\text{OLS}}$,$\boldsymbol{x}_i$ 是矩阵 $\boldsymbol{X}$ 的第 i 行,n 是观测数,k 是模型预测数。

m 阶自相关时,方差估计使用 Newey-West 公式:①

$$\boldsymbol{X}'\boldsymbol{\Omega}\boldsymbol{X}=\boldsymbol{X}'\boldsymbol{\Omega}_0\boldsymbol{X}+\frac{n}{n-k}\sum_{l=1}^{m}\left(1-\frac{l}{m+1}\right)\sum_{t=l+1}^{n}\hat{e}_t\hat{e}_{t-l}(\boldsymbol{x}_t'\boldsymbol{x}_{t-l}+\boldsymbol{x}_{t-l}'\boldsymbol{x}_t)$$

式中,$\boldsymbol{x}_t$ 是 t 时刻观测到的矩阵 $\boldsymbol{X}$ 的行。

语法格式为:

```
newey depvar [indepvars] [if] [in] [weight], lag(#) [options]
```

菜单操作路径为:

Statistics>Time series>Regression with Newey-West std. errors

例 8.13 Newey-West 标准误差回归

```
* 下载数据,清理内存
.clear
.webuse idle2
.tsset time
Time variable: time, 1 to 30
        Delta: 1 unit
* 以 3 为自相关最大滞后阶的 Newey-West 标准误差回归
.newey usr idle, lag(3)
```

运行结果如图 8.38 所示。

```
* 以 99%置信区间重播结果
.newey, level(99)
```

运行结果如图 8.39 所示。

① Newey, W. K., and K. D. West. A Simple, Positive Semi-definite, Heteroskedasticity and Autocorrelation Consistent Covariance Matrix. *Econometrica*, 1987, 55.

Regression with Newey-West standard errors　　Number of obs = 30
Maximum lag = 3　　F(1, 28) = 10.90
Prob > F = 0.0026

usr	Coefficient	Newey-West std. err.	t	P>|t|	[95% conf. interval]	
idle	-.2281501	.0690927	-3.30	0.003	-.3696801	-.08662
_cons	23.13483	6.327031	3.66	0.001	10.17449	36.09516

图 8.38

Regression with Newey-West standard errors　　Number of obs = 30
Maximum lag = 3　　F(1, 28) = 10.90
Prob > F = 0.0026

usr	Coefficient	Newey-West std. err.	t	P>|t|	[99% conf. interval]	
idle	-.2281501	.0690927	-3.30	0.003	-.4190715	-.0372287
_cons	23.13483	6.327031	3.66	0.001	5.65158	40.61808

图 8.39

8.7 ARIMA 模型

时间序列一般包括趋势、周期、季节和随机四个成分。非平稳序列可以先通过差分、季节(或周期)调整、趋势成分分解分离等退势方法,分离出非平稳序列成分,再对其平稳序列成分建模。

有些非平稳时序过程可以利用差分运算,消除确定性趋势成分,得到其平稳性成分,则为差分平稳序列。一般地,如果序列 y_t 通过 d 次差分成为一个平稳序列,而这个序列差分 $d-1$ 次时却不平稳,那么称序列 y_t 为 d 阶单整序列,记为 $y_t \sim I(d)$。特别地,如果序列 y_t 本身是平稳的,则为零阶单整序列,记为 $y_t \sim I(0)$。对于 d 阶单整序列,能够通过 d 次差分将非平稳序列转化为平稳序列。

设 y_t 是 d 阶单整序列,即 $y_t \sim I(d)$,则

$$w_t = \Delta^d y_t = (1-L)^d y_t \tag{8.68}$$

式中,w_t 为平稳序列,即 $w_t \sim I(0)$,于是对 w_t 建立 ARMA(p,q)模型:

$$w_t = c + \phi w_{t-1} + \cdots + \phi_p w_{t-p} + \varepsilon_1 + \theta_1 \varepsilon_{t-1} + \cdots + \theta_q \varepsilon_{t-q} \tag{8.69}$$

定义滞后算子 L 为:$L^0 y_t = y_t$,$L^p y_t = y_{t-p}$,$p=1,2,\cdots,p$。则一次差分运算为:$\Delta y_t = y_t - y_{t-1} = (1-L) y_t$。式中,$\Delta$ 为差分算子。

用滞后算子 L 表示，则为：

$$\Phi(L)w_t = c + \Theta(L)\varepsilon_t \tag{8.70}$$

式中

$$\Phi(L) = 1 - \phi_1 L - \phi_2 L^2 - \cdots - \phi_p L^p \tag{8.71}$$

$$\Theta(L) = 1 + \theta_1 L + \theta_2 L^2 + \cdots + \theta_q L^q \tag{8.72}$$

经过 d 阶差分变换后的 ARMA(p,q)模型称为 ARIMA(p,d,q)模型(autoregressive integrated moving average model)，把式(8.68)代入式(8.70)，就可以得到用滞后算子表示的 ARIMA(p,d,q)模型：

$$\Phi(L)(1-L)^d y_t = c + \Theta(L)\varepsilon_t \tag{8.73}$$

如果均值方程的随机误差项为 ARMA(p,q)模型，即

$$y_t = \boldsymbol{x}_t\boldsymbol{\beta} + \mu_t$$

$$\mu_t = \sum_{i=1}^{p}\rho_i\mu_{t-i} + \sum_{j=1}^{q}\theta_j\varepsilon_{t-j} + \varepsilon_t$$

把随机项方程代入均值方程，可得单一方程：

$$y_t = \boldsymbol{x}_t\boldsymbol{\beta} + \sum_{i=1}^{p}\rho_i(y_{t-i} - x_{t-i}\boldsymbol{\beta}) + \sum_{j=1}^{q}\theta_j\varepsilon_{t-j} + \varepsilon_t$$

其中，一些参数 ρ_i 和 θ_j 可以等于 0。对于乘法季节模型，式中可以为参数的乘积。

估计 ARIMA(p,d,q)模型同估计 ARMA(p,q)模型具体步骤相同，唯一不同的是在估计之前要确定原序列的差分阶数 d，对 y_t 进行 d 阶差分。因此，ARIMA(p,d,q)模型区别于 ARMA(p,q)模型之处就在于前者的自回归部分的特征多项式含有 d 个单位根。因此，对一个序列建模之前，应当首先确定该序列是否具有非平稳性，这就需要对序列的平稳性进行检验，特别是要检验其是否含有单位根及所含有的单位根的个数。

arima 命令既适合在因变量中存在自回归的 ARIMA 模型，也适合带有 ARMA 干扰项的结构模型。考虑一个一阶自回归移动平均过程，然后使用 arima 命令来估计模型中的所有参数。假设 ARMA(1,1)模型的结构方程和干扰项方程的设定如下：

结构方程：

$$y_t = \boldsymbol{x}_t\boldsymbol{\beta} + \mu_t \tag{8.74}$$

干扰项方程：

$$\mu_t = \rho\mu_{t-1} + \theta\varepsilon_{t-1} + \varepsilon_t \tag{8.75}$$

其中，ρ 是一阶自相关参数，θ 是一阶移动平均参数，$\varepsilon_t \sim$ i. i. d. $N(0,\sigma^2)$，意味着 ε_t 是白噪声干扰。

可以结合这两个方程并在扰动过程中写出 ARMA(p, q)模型的一般形式：

$$y_t = \boldsymbol{x}_t\boldsymbol{\beta} + \rho_1(y_{t-1} - \boldsymbol{x}_{t-1}\boldsymbol{\beta}) + \rho_2(y_{t-2} - \boldsymbol{x}_{t-2}\boldsymbol{\beta}) + \cdots + \rho_p(y_{t-p} - \boldsymbol{x}_{t-p}\boldsymbol{\beta}) + \theta_1\varepsilon_{t-1} + \theta_2\varepsilon_{t-2} + \cdots + \theta_q\varepsilon_{t-q} + \varepsilon_t \tag{8.76}$$

可以使用滞后运算符表示法更简洁地写出 ARMA(p,q)模型的一般形式：

$$\boldsymbol{\rho}(L^p)(y_t - \boldsymbol{x}_t\boldsymbol{\beta}) = \boldsymbol{\theta}(L^q)\varepsilon_t \tag{8.77}$$

其中

$$\boldsymbol{\rho}(L^p) = 1 - \rho_1 L - \rho_2 L^2 - \cdots - \rho_p L^p \tag{8.78}$$

$$\boldsymbol{\theta}(L^q) = 1 + \theta_1 L + \theta_2 L^2 + \cdots + \theta_q L^q \tag{8.79}$$

并且 $L^j y_t = y_{t-j}$。

乘法季节性 ARIMA 模型和 ARIMA 模型也可以拟合。对于平稳序列,通过卡尔曼滤波器获得完整或无条件的最大似然估计。对于非平稳序列,如果存在一些先验信息,则可以使用 state0() 和 p0() 指定过滤器的初始值。

例 8.14 ARIMA 模型估计

本例使用 1960 年第 1 季度至 1990 年第 4 季度期间的季度美国批发价格指数(WPI)数据来拟合 ARIMA 模型。(Enders, 2004)①

最简单的 ARIMA 模型是 ARIMA(1,1,1) 模型。

```
.use https://www.stata-press.com/data/r17/wpi1
.arima wpi, arima(1,1,1)
*ARIMA 回归
```

运行结果如图 8.40 所示。

```
Sample:  1960q2 - 1990q4                        Number of obs     =        123
                                                Wald chi2(2)      =     310.64
Log likelihood = -135.3513                      Prob > chi2       =     0.0000

------------------------------------------------------------------------------
             |                 OPG
       D.wpi |      Coef.   Std. Err.      z    P>|z|     [95% Conf. Interval]
-------------+----------------------------------------------------------------
wpi          |
       _cons |   .7498197   .3340968     2.24   0.025     .0950019    1.404637
-------------+----------------------------------------------------------------
ARMA         |
          ar |
         L1. |   .8742288   .0545435    16.03   0.000     .7673256     .981132
             |
          ma |
         L1. |  -.4120458   .1000284    -4.12   0.000    -.6080979   -.2159938
-------------+----------------------------------------------------------------
      /sigma |   .7250436   .0368065    19.70   0.000     .6529042    .7971829
------------------------------------------------------------------------------
Note: The test of the variance against zero is one sided, and the two-sided
      confidence interval is truncated at zero.
```

图 8.40

检查估计结果,可见 AR(1) 系数为 0.874,MA(1) 系数为 −0.412,两者都非常显著。白噪声干扰 ε 的估计标准偏差为 0.725。

该模型也可以通过键入下面的命令来拟合:

```
arima D.wpi, ar(1) ma(1)
```

放置在因变量 wpi 前面的 D. 是用于差分的 Stata 时间序列算子。因此,我们将对 1960 年第 2 季度到 1990 年第 4 季度的 WPI 的一阶差分进行建模。由于差分的操作,第一个观察值丢失了,第二种语法命令允许有更丰富的模型选择。

① Enders, W. *Applied Econometric Time Series*. NJ: Wiley, 2004.

8.8 SARIMA 模型

8.8.1 加法季节效应的 SARIMA 模型

许多时间序列表现出周期性的季节性成分，例如，空调的月度销售数据具有很强的季节性成分，夏季销量高，冬季销量低。

我们先利用加法季节效应的 SARIMA 模型来拟合考虑季度效应：

$$(1-\rho_1 L)\{\Delta\ln(\mathrm{wpi}_t)-\beta_0\}=(1+\theta_1 L+\theta_4 L^4)\varepsilon_t \tag{8.80}$$

例 8.15　加法季节效应的 SARIMA 模型

本例利用的数据集同例 8.14。在检查了 WPI 的一阶差分后，Enders 选择了一个自然对数差分模型来拟合时间序列。原始数据和对数的一阶差分如图 8.41 所示。

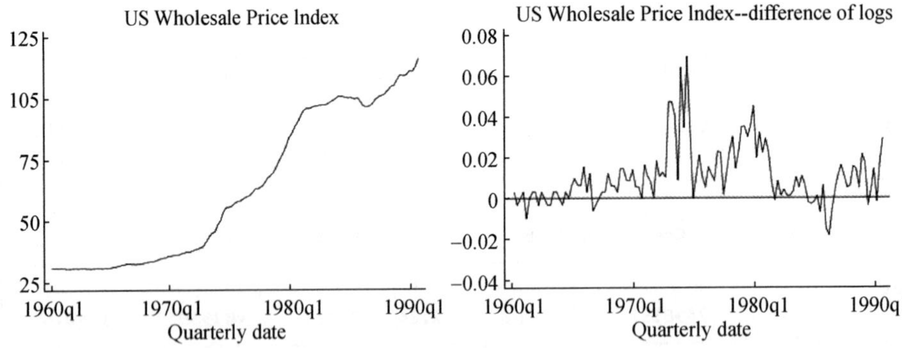

(a)　　(b)

图　8.41

根据自相关、偏自相关(见图 8.42)和初步估计的结果，Enders 在对数差分序列中确定了一个 ARMA 模型。

```
.ac D.ln_wpi, ylabels(-.4(.2).6)
.pac D.ln_wpi, ylabels(-.4(.2).6)
```

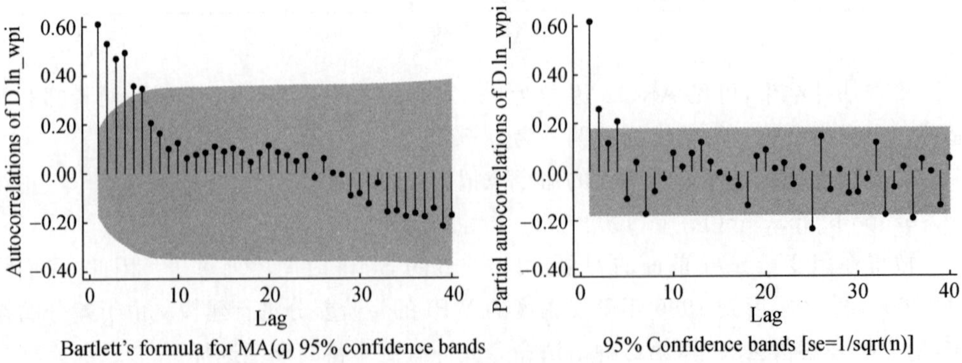

(a)　　(b)

图　8.42

除了自回归项和 MA(1)项外，还包括一个 MA(4)项以说明剩余的季度效应。因此要拟合的模型是：

$$\Delta\ln(\text{wpi}_t) = \beta_0 + \rho_1\{\Delta\ln(\text{wpi}_{t-1}) - \beta_0\} + \theta_1\varepsilon_{t-1} + \theta_4\varepsilon_{t-4} + \varepsilon_t$$

我们可以用 arima 和 Stata 的标准差分算子来拟合这个模型：

```
.arima D.ln_wpi, ar(1) ma(1 4)
```

运行结果如图 8.43 所示。

```
ARIMA regression

Sample:  1960q2 - 1990q4                        Number of obs     =        123
                                                Wald chi2(3)      =     333.60
Log likelihood =  386.0336                      Prob > chi2       =     0.0000

------------------------------------------------------------------------------
             |                 OPG
    D.ln_wpi |      Coef.   Std. Err.      z    P>|z|     [95% Conf. Interval]
-------------+----------------------------------------------------------------
ln_wpi       |
       _cons |   .0110493   .0048349     2.29   0.022     .0015731    .0205255
-------------+----------------------------------------------------------------
ARMA         |
          ar |
         L1. |   .7806991   .0944946     8.26   0.000     .5954931     .965905
             |
          ma |
         L1. |  -.3990039   .1258753    -3.17   0.002    -.6457149   -.1522928
         L4. |   .3090813   .1200945     2.57   0.010     .0737003    .5444622
-------------+----------------------------------------------------------------
      /sigma |   .0104394   .0004702    22.20   0.000     .0095178    .0113609
------------------------------------------------------------------------------
Note: The test of the variance against zero is one sided, and the two-sided
      confidence interval is truncated at zero.
```

图 8.43

在这个最终形式的模型中，对数差分序列仍然高度自相关，处于 0.781 的水平，尽管创新在随后的一个季度(−0.399)产生了负面影响，并在接下来的一年产生了 0.309 的正面季节性影响。

8.8.2 乘法季节性 SARIMA 模型

处理季度效应的另一种方法是拟合乘法季节性 ARIMA 模型。$\ln(\text{wpi}_t)$序列的 $(1,1,1)\times(0,0,1)_4$ 阶乘法季节性 SARIMA 模型是：

$$(1 - \rho_1 L)\{\Delta\ln(\text{wpi}_t) - \beta_0\} = (1 + \theta_1 L)(1 + \theta_{4,1}L^4)\varepsilon_t \tag{8.81}$$

或

$$\Delta\ln(\text{wpi}_t) = \beta_0 + \rho_1\{\Delta\ln(\text{wpi}_{t-1}) - \beta_0\} + \theta_1\varepsilon_{t-1} + \theta_{4,1}\varepsilon_{t-4} + \theta_1\theta_{4,1}\varepsilon_{t-5} + \varepsilon_t \tag{8.82}$$

在符号$(1,1,1)\times(0,0,1)_4$中，$(1,1,1)$表示有一个非季节性自回归项$(1-\rho_1 L)$和一个非季节性移动平均项$(1+\theta_1 L)$，并且时间序列是一阶差分的；$(0,0,1)_4$表示没有滞后 4 的季节性自回归项，有一个滞后 4 的季节性移动平均项$(1+\theta_{4,1}L^4)$，并且该序列的季节性差异为零次。这被称为乘法季节性 SARIMA 模型，因为非季节性和季节性因素以乘法方式起作用：$(1+\theta_1 L)(1+\theta_{4,1}L^4)$。将这些项相乘会对五阶滞后值的参数施加非线性约束；arima 自动施加这些约束。

为了进一步阐明符号，考虑一个$(2,1,1)\times(1,1,2)_4$乘法季节性 SARIMA 模型：

$$(1-\rho_1 L-\rho_2 L^2)(1-\rho_{4,1}L^4)\Delta\Delta_4 z_t=(1+\theta_1 L)(1+\theta_{4,1}L^4+\theta_{4,2}L^8)\varepsilon_t \tag{8.83}$$

其中，Δ表示差分算子，Δ_s表示滞后s阶的季节性差异算子，我们有

$$\begin{aligned}\tilde{z}_t=&\rho_1\tilde{z}_{t-1}+\rho_2\tilde{z}_{t-2}+\rho_{4,1}\tilde{z}_{t-4}-\rho_1\rho_{4,1}\tilde{z}_{t-5}-\rho_2\rho_{4,1}\tilde{z}_{t-6}\\&+\theta_1\varepsilon_{t-1}+\theta_{4,1}\varepsilon_{t-4}+\theta_1\theta_{4,1}\varepsilon_{t-5}+\theta_{4,2}\varepsilon_{t-8}+\theta_1\theta_{4,2}\varepsilon_{t-9}+\varepsilon_t\end{aligned} \tag{8.84}$$

其中，

$$\tilde{z}_t=\Delta\Delta_4 z_t=\Delta(z_t-z_{t-4})=z_t-z_{t-1}-(z_{t-4}-z_{t-5}) \tag{8.85}$$

如果模型中包含回归变量，则$z_t=y_t-\boldsymbol{x}_t\boldsymbol{\beta}$；如果仅包含常数项，则$z_t=y_t-\beta_0$；否则$z_t=y_t$。

更一般地，一个$(p,d,q)\times(P,D,Q)_s$乘法季节性 SARIMA 模型为：

$$\boldsymbol{\rho}(L^p)\boldsymbol{\rho}_s(L^P)\Delta^d\Delta_s^D z_t=\boldsymbol{\theta}(L^q)\boldsymbol{\theta}_s(L^Q)\varepsilon_t \tag{8.86}$$

其中，

$$\boldsymbol{\rho}_s(L^P)=(1-\rho_{s,1}L^s-\rho_{s,2}L^{2s}-\cdots-\rho_{s,P}L^{P_s}) \tag{8.87}$$

$$\boldsymbol{\theta}_s(L^Q)=(1+\theta_{s,1}L^s+\theta_{s,2}L^{2s}+\cdots+\theta_{s,Q}L^{Q_s}) \tag{8.88}$$

$\boldsymbol{\rho}(L^p)$和$\boldsymbol{\theta}(L^q)$是先前定义的，Δ^d表示应用Δ算子d次，同样适用于Δ_s^D。通常，d和D为 0 或 1；p、q、P和Q很少超过 2 或 3。对于季度数据，s通常为 4；对于月度数据，s通常为 12。事实上，该模型可以扩展到包括月度和季度季节性因素。

如果数据图表明季节性效应与序列的平均值成正比，那么季节性效应可能是乘法的，乘法季节性 SARIMA 模型可能是合适的。Box 等(2016)[①]建议从具有显示季节性因素的任何数据的乘法 SARIMA 模型开始，如果乘法模型不能很好地拟合数据，则探索非乘法 SARIMA 模型。Chatfield (2004)[②]建议采用序列的对数使季节效应相加，这适合于加法季节效应的 SARIMA 模型。

语法格式分别为：

(1) 具有 ARMA 干扰的回归模型的基本语法

```
arima depvar [ indepvars ], ar(numlist) ma(numlist)
```

(2) ARIMA(p, d, q) 模型的基本语法

```
arima depvar, arima(#p,#d,#q)
```

① Box, G. E. P., G. M. Jenkins, G. C. Reinsel, and G. M. Ljung. *Time Series Analysis: Forecasting and Control*(5th ed.). NJ: Wiley, 2016.

② Chatfield, C. *The Analysis of Time Series: An Introduction*(6 ed.). Boca Raton: CRC Press, 2004.

(3) 乘法季节性 ARIMA$(p,d,q)\times(P,D,Q)_s$ 模型的基本语法

```
arima depvar, arima(#p,#d,#q) sarima(#P,#D,#Q,#s)
```

(4) 完整语法

```
arima depvar [ indepvars ] [ if ] [ in ] [ weight ] [, options ]
```

例 8.16 乘法季节性 SARIMA 模型

本例利用 Stata 自带数据集 air2.dta 说明具有季节效应的 ARIMA 模型的实现。

最常见的乘法季节性 SARIMA 模型之一是 Box 等(2016)①的$(0,1,1)\times(0,1,1)_{12}$“航空公司”模型。数据集 air2.dta 包含 1949 年 1 月至 1960 年 12 月之间的每月国际航空乘客数据。在对数据进行第一次和季节性差分后,我们不怀疑存在趋势分量,因此使用具有 arima 的非恒定选项。

```
.clear all
.use https://www.stata-press.com/data/r17/air2
(TIMESLAB: Airline passengers)
.describe
```

运行结果如图 8.44 所示。

```
Contains data from https://www.stata-press.com/data/r17/air2.dta
 Observations:           144                  TIMESLAB: Airline passengers
    Variables:             3                  3 Mar 2020 10:01
```

Variable name	Storage type	Display format	Value label	Variable label
air	int	%8.0g		Airline passengers (1949-1960)
time	float	%9.0g		Time (in months)
t	int	%9.0g		Time

Sorted by: t

图 8.44

```
.summarize
```

运行结果如图 8.45 所示。

Variable	Obs	Mean	Std. dev.	Min	Max
air	144	280.2986	119.9663	104	622
time	144	1954.958	3.476109	1949	1960.917
t	144	72.5	41.71331	1	144

图 8.45

① Box, G. E. P., G. M. Jenkins, G. C. Reinsel, and G. M. Ljung. *Time Series Analysis: Forecasting and Control*(5th ed.). NJ: Wiley, 2016.

```
. generate lnair = ln(air)
. arima lnair, arima(0,1,1) sarima(0,1,1,12) noconstant
```

运行结果如图 8.46 所示。

```
ARIMA regression

Sample: 14 thru 144                             Number of obs     =        131
                                                Wald chi2(2)      =      84.53
Log likelihood = 244.6965                       Prob > chi2       =     0.0000
```

DS12.lnair	Coefficient	OPG std. err.	z	P>|z|	[95% conf.	interval]
ARMA						
ma						
L1.	-.4018324	.0730307	-5.50	0.000	-.5449698	-.2586949
ARMA12						
ma						
L1.	-.5569342	.0963129	-5.78	0.000	-.745704	-.3681644
/sigma	.0367167	.0020132	18.24	0.000	.0327708	.0406625

Note: The test of the variance against zero is one sided, and the two-sided confidence interval is truncated at zero.

图 8.46

由估计结果可得乘法季节性 SARIMA 模型：

$$\Delta\,\Delta_{12}\ln \text{air}_t = -0.402\varepsilon_{t-1} - 0.557\varepsilon_{t-12} + 0.224\varepsilon_{t-13} + \varepsilon_t$$

$$\hat{\sigma} = 0.037$$

```
. arima DS12.lnair, ma(1) mma(1, 12) noconstant
```

运行结果如图 8.47 所示。

下面拟合乘法季节性 SARIMA 模型：

$$(1-\rho L)(1-\rho_{4,1}L^4)(1-\rho_{12,1}L^{12})(\Delta\,\Delta_4\Delta_{12}\text{sales}_t - \beta_0)$$
$$= (1+\theta L)(1+\theta_{4,1}L^4)(1+\theta_{12,1}L^{12})\varepsilon_t$$

```
. arima DS4S12.lnair, ar(1) mar(1 2, 4) mar(1, 12) ma(1) mma(1, 4) mma(1 3, 12)
```

运行结果如图 8.48 所示。

```
ARIMA regression

Sample: 18 thru 144                           Number of obs     =        127
                                              Wald chi2(5)      =      80.86
Log likelihood = 226.8638                     Prob > chi2       =     0.0000

------------------------------------------------------------------------------
             |                 OPG
DS4S12.lnair | Coefficient  std. err.      z    P>|z|     [95% conf. interval]
-------------+----------------------------------------------------------------
lnair        |
       _cons |  -.0000628   .0001433    -0.44   0.661    -.0003436     .000218
-------------+----------------------------------------------------------------
ARMA         |
          ar |
         L1. |   .0427245   .2178303     0.20   0.845    -.3842151    .4696641
             |
          ma |
         L1. |    -.44891   .1950166    -2.30   0.021    -.8311355   -.0666846
-------------+----------------------------------------------------------------
ARMA4        |
          ar |
         L1. |  -.0900091   .1056876    -0.85   0.394     -.297153    .1171347
             |
          ma |
         L1. |  -.9999986          .        .       .            .           .
-------------+----------------------------------------------------------------
ARMA12       |
          ar |
         L1. |  -.1267821   .1850384    -0.69   0.493    -.4894508    .2358866
             |
          ma |
         L1. |  -.4588886   .2090942    -2.19   0.028    -.8687058   -.0490714
-------------+----------------------------------------------------------------
      /sigma |   .0368337   .0023888    15.42   0.000     .0321517    .0415157
------------------------------------------------------------------------------
Note: The test of the variance against zero is one sided, and the two-sided
      confidence interval is truncated at zero.
```

图 8.47

```
ARIMA regression

Sample: 18 thru 144                             Number of obs     =        127
                                                Wald chi2(7)      =      93.69
Log likelihood = 227.4433                       Prob > chi2       =     0.0000

------------------------------------------------------------------------------
             |                 OPG
DS4S12.lnair | Coefficient  std. err.      z    P>|z|     [95% conf. interval]
-------------+----------------------------------------------------------------
lnair        |
       _cons |  -.0000551   .0001235    -0.45   0.656     -.000297    .0001869
-------------+----------------------------------------------------------------
ARMA         |
          ar |
         L1. |   .0548235   .2279152     0.24   0.810    -.3918822    .5015291
             |
          ma |
         L1. |  -.4554206   .2021447    -2.25   0.024     -.851617   -.0592242
-------------+----------------------------------------------------------------
ARMA4        |
          ar |
         L1. |  -.1395508   .1115925    -1.25   0.211    -.3582681    .0791665
         L2. |  -.0397748   .1020751    -0.39   0.697    -.2398382    .1602887
             |
          ma |
         L1. |         -1          .        .       .            .           .
-------------+----------------------------------------------------------------
ARMA12       |
          ar |
         L1. |  -.0028724   .1704353    -0.02   0.987    -.3369195    .3311747
             |
          ma |
         L1. |  -.6401628   .1762052    -3.63   0.000    -.9855186    -.294807
         L3. |   .1541695   .1275535     1.21   0.227    -.0958308    .4041699
-------------+----------------------------------------------------------------
      /sigma |   .0362903   .0023626    15.36   0.000     .0316597     .040921
------------------------------------------------------------------------------
Note: The test of the variance against zero is one sided, and the two-sided
      confidence interval is truncated at zero.
```

图 8.48

8.9 ARMAX 族模型

8.9.1 ARMAX 模型

扩展自回归移动平均(autoregressive moving average exogenous，ARMAX)模型是一种典型的描述时间序列变化的时序模型，由 AR 模型、MA 模型和回归项三个部分组合而成。ARMAX(p,r,q)模型表达式为：

$$
\begin{aligned}
&\Theta(L)y(t)=\Phi(L)u(t)+\Omega(L)e(t)\\
&\Theta(L)=1+\theta_1 L+\theta_2 L^2+\cdots+\theta_p L^P\\
&\Phi(L)=\phi_1+\phi_2 L+\phi_3 L^2+\cdots+\phi_r L^{r-1}\\
&\Omega(L)=1+\omega_1 L+\omega_2 L^2+\cdots+\omega_q L^q
\end{aligned}
\tag{8.89}
$$

其中，p,r,q 分别是自回归、差分次数、移动平均即回归项的阶数，$\theta_i(i=1\cdots p)$，$\phi_j(j=1\cdots r)$，$w_k(k=1\cdots q)$是模型的待定系数，e_i 是均值为 0、方差不为 0 的白噪声序列，模型输出变量为平稳时序。ARMAX 模型融合了 AR 模型和 MA 模型的特点，通过对过去的观测值、现在的干扰值以及过去的干扰值线性组合进行预测。与传统的 ARMA 模型相比，通过引入与输出序列相关的另一序列作为回归项，模型的准确性及鲁棒性更高。利用 ARMA 模型解决问题的一般步骤如图 8.49 所示，核心环节是序列平稳化及模型参数的求取。

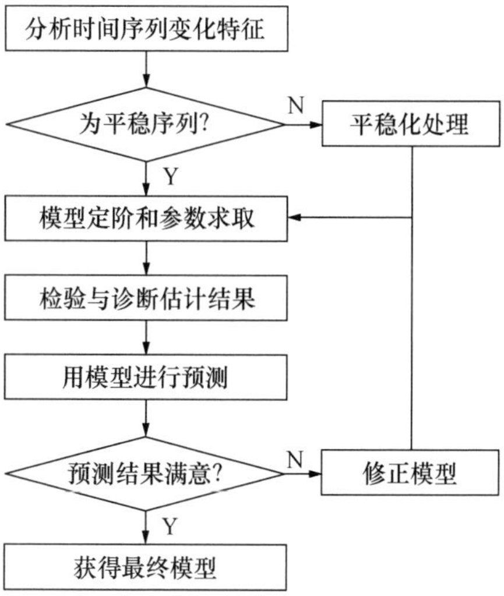

图 8.49

8.9.2 ARIMAX 模型

ARIMAX 模型是指含外生解释变量回归项的 ARIMA 模型，又称扩展的 ARIMA 模型。回归项的引入有利于提高模型的预测效果。引入的回归项一般是与预测对象(即被解释变量)相关程度较高的变量。

ARIMAX 模型构造前必须满足响应变量 y_t 和输入变量 $\boldsymbol{x}_{1t},\boldsymbol{x}_{2t},\cdots,\boldsymbol{x}_{nt}$ 为平稳序列，若不是平稳序列，则需采用差分使时间序列变为平稳序列，然后再构造响应变量与输入变量之间的模型。ARIMAX 模型表达式为：

$$
\begin{cases}
y_t=\mu+\displaystyle\sum_{i=1}^{n}\frac{\Theta_i(L)}{\phi_i(L)}L^{l_i}\boldsymbol{x}_{it}+\varepsilon_t\\
\varepsilon_t=\dfrac{\Theta_i}{\phi_i}a_t
\end{cases}
\tag{8.90}
$$

其中，$\Theta_i(L)$为第 i 个输入变量的自回归系数多项式，$\phi_i(L)$为第 i 个输入变量的移动平均系数多项式，l_i 是第 i 个输入变量的滞后阶数，ε_t 为残差序列，Θ_i 为残差序列的自回归系数多项式，ϕ_i 为残差序列的移动平均回归系数多项式，a_t 为白噪声序列。建模步骤为：①

第一步，对输入变量 $\boldsymbol{x}_{1t}, \boldsymbol{x}_{2t}, \cdots, \boldsymbol{x}_{nt}$ 进行平稳性检验，如不平稳，则进行 d 阶差分使其平稳；

第二步，对 d 阶差分平稳的输入变量 $\boldsymbol{x}_{1t}, \boldsymbol{x}_{2t}, \cdots, \boldsymbol{x}_{nt}$ 构建 ARMA 模型，并检验残差序列 ε_t 是否为白噪声序列；

第三步：利用建立的输入变量 ARMA 模型，拟合 ARIMAX 模型和残差序列 a_t。

8.9.3 SARIMAX 模型

对于序列$\{Z_t\}_{t=1}^T$，设 L 为滞后算子，即 $LZ_t = Z_{t-1}$，则季节性 SARIMA 模型为：

$$\phi_p(L)\Phi_P(L^{12})(1-L)^d(1-L^{12})^D Z_t = \theta_q(L)\Theta_Q(L^{12})a_t \tag{8.91}$$

式中，$\phi_p(L)$和 $\theta_q(L)$是 L 的 p 阶和 q 阶多项式，分别为模型的自回归项和移动平均项，$\Phi_P(L^{12})$和 $\Theta_Q(L^{12})$是 L^{12} 的 P 阶和 Q 阶多项式，代表模型的季节性自回归项和季节性移动平均项；$\phi_p(L)$、$\theta_q(L)$、$\Phi_P(L^{12})$、$\Theta_Q(L^{12})$的根都在单位圆之外。d 表示常规差分的阶数，D 代表季节性差分的阶数，多数情况下，d 与 D 之和不超过 2；$\{a_t\}$是期望为 0、方差为 $\sigma_a^2 > 0$ 的白噪声序列。

在 SARIMA 模型中加入 k 个外生解释变量 H 后得到的模型就是 SARIMAX 模型：②

$$\phi_p(L)\Phi_P(L^{12})(1-L)(1-L^{12})\left(Z_t - \sum_{i=1}^{k}\beta_i H_{it}(\tau_i)\right) = \theta_q(L)\Theta_Q(L^{12})a_t \tag{8.92}$$

例 8.17　ARMAX 模型

对于包含协变量的模型的简单示例，我们可以估计代表货币数量论的 Friedman 和 Meiselman（1963）③方程的更新。他们假设个人消费支出（consump）与以 M2(m2)衡量的货币供应量之间存在直接关系：

$$\text{consump}_t = \beta_0 + \beta_1 \text{m2}_t + \mu_t \tag{8.93}$$

Friedman 和 Meiselman 在截至 1956 年的时期内拟合了该模型，我们将在 1959q1 到 1981q4 期间重新拟合模型。我们将注意力限制在 1982 年之前的时期，因为美联储在 20 世纪 80 年代后期广泛操纵货币供应量以控制通货膨胀，而消费与货币供应量之间的关系变得更加复杂。

---

① 王向前，吴东隆，郑健彤. 货物吞吐量预测的改进 ARIMAX 方法——以天津港为例. 运筹与管理，2022，(3).

② 王振中，陈松蹊，涂云东. 中国居民消费价格指数的动态结构研究及中美量化比较. 数理统计与管理，2022，(3).

③ Friedman, M., and D. Meiselman. The Relative Stability of Monetary Velocity and the Investment Multiplier in the United States: 1897—1958. in Commission on Money and Credit. *Stabilization Policies*. Englewood Cliffs: Prentice Hall, 1963.

为了演示 arima,我们将在模型中包含一个自回归项和一个移动平均项来表示干扰,最初的估计数都不包括在内。因此,我们将结构方程的扰动建模为:

$$\mu_t = \rho\mu_{t-1} + \theta\varepsilon_{t-1} + \varepsilon_t \tag{8.94}$$

这种关系是根据季节性调整的数据估计的,因此无需明确包括季节性影响。获取未经季节性调整的数据并同时对结构和季节性影响进行建模可能更可取。

我们将通过在 if 表达式中使用 tin()函数来限制对所需样本的估计,通过将 tin()的第一个参数留空,我们将包括到第二个日期(1981q4)的所有可用数据。我们通过键入如下命令来拟合模型:

```
.use https://www.stata-press.com/data/r17/friedman2, clear
.arima consump m2 if tin(, 1981q4), ar(1) ma(1)
```

运行结果如图 8.50 所示。

```
ARIMA regression

Sample:  1959q1 - 1981q4                        Number of obs     =         92
                                                Wald chi2(3)      =    4394.80
Log likelihood = -340.5077                      Prob > chi2       =     0.0000
```

consump	Coef.	OPG Std. Err.	z	P>|z|	[95% Conf.	Interval]
consump						
m2	1.122029	.0363563	30.86	0.000	1.050772	1.193286
_cons	-36.09872	56.56703	-0.64	0.523	-146.9681	74.77062
ARMA						
ar L1.	.9348486	.0411323	22.73	0.000	.8542308	1.015467
ma L1.	.3090592	.0885883	3.49	0.000	.1354293	.4826891
/sigma	9.655308	.5635157	17.13	0.000	8.550837	10.75978

Note: The test of the variance against zero is one sided, and the two-sided confidence interval is truncated at zero.

图 8.50

在此期间,尽管消费只是收入速度的一个方面,但相对于消费而言,货币流通速度相对较小(1.122)。此外,干扰项存在较强的一阶自相关,以及统计显著的一阶移动平均。

我们可能会担心模型导致了异方差或非高斯的干扰,这时使用 vce(robust) 选项重新拟合模型。(见图 8.51)

```
ARIMA regression

Sample:  1959q1 - 1981q4                        Number of obs     =         92
                                                Wald chi2(3)      =    1176.26
Log pseudolikelihood = -340.5077                Prob > chi2       =     0.0000
```

consump	Coef.	Semirobust Std. Err.	z	P>|z|	[95% Conf.	Interval]
consump						
m2	1.122029	.0433302	25.89	0.000	1.037103	1.206954
_cons	-36.09872	28.10478	-1.28	0.199	-91.18308	18.98564
ARMA						
ar						
L1.	.9348486	.0493428	18.95	0.000	.8381385	1.031559
ma						
L1.	.3090592	.1605359	1.93	0.054	-.0055854	.6237038
/sigma	9.655308	1.082639	8.92	0.000	7.533375	11.77724

```
Note: The test of the variance against zero is one sided, and the two-sided
      confidence interval is truncated at zero.
```

图 8.51

结果显示，估计的标准误差大幅增加，而曾经非常显著的移动平均项现在只有轻微的显著性。

8.10 ARFIMA 模型

我们对观察到的二阶平稳时间序列 $y_t, t=1,\cdots,T$ 进行建模，使用 p 阶自回归、d 次差分与 q 阶移动平均的自回归分整移动平均(autoregressive fractionally integrated moving average, ARFIMA)模型表达式为：

$$\boldsymbol{\rho}(L^p)(1-L)^d(y_t-\boldsymbol{x}_t\boldsymbol{\beta})=\boldsymbol{\theta}(L^q)\varepsilon_t \tag{8.95}$$

其中，

$$\boldsymbol{\rho}(L^p)=1-\rho_1 L-\rho_2 L^2-\cdots-\rho_p L^p \tag{8.96}$$

$$\boldsymbol{\theta}(L^q)=1+\theta_1 L+\theta_2 L^2+\cdots+\theta_q L^q \tag{8.97}$$

$$(1-L)^d=\sum_{j=0}^{\infty}(-1)^j\frac{\Gamma(j+d)}{\Gamma(j+1)\Gamma(d)}L^j \tag{8.98}$$

滞后算子定义为 $L^j y_t=y_{t-j}, t=1,\cdots,T$ 且 $j=1,\cdots,t-1$；$\varepsilon_t\sim N(0,\sigma^2)$；$\Gamma()$是伽马函数；$-0.5<d<0.5$ 且 $d\neq 0$。在 arfima 语法中行向量 $\boldsymbol{X}_t$ 包含外生变量。

在 $-0.5<d<0.5$ 且 $d\neq 0$ 的情况下，该过程是平稳的、可逆的；AR 多项式的根 $\boldsymbol{\rho}(z)=1-\rho_1 z-\rho_2 z^2-\cdots-\rho_p z^p=0$，以及 MA 多项式的根 $\boldsymbol{\theta}(z)=1+\theta_1 z+\theta_2 z^2+\cdots$

$+\theta_q z^q=0$，位于单位圆之外，没有公共根。当 $0<d<0.5$ 时，该过程具有长记忆，即自变量函数 γ_h 以双曲线速度衰减到0，因此 $\sum_{h=-\infty}^{\infty}|\gamma_h|=\infty$。当 $-0.5<d<0$ 时，该过程也具有长记忆，即自变量函数 γ_h 以双曲线速度衰减到0，因此 $\sum_{h=-\infty}^{\infty}|\gamma_h|<\infty$。

对 ARFIMA 模型参数 ρ,θ,d,β 和 σ^2 的估计采用最大似然法。给定参数估计 $\hat{\eta}=(\hat{\rho}',\hat{\theta}',\hat{d},\hat{\beta}',\hat{\sigma}^2)$ 条件下 y 的对数高斯似然为：

$$l(y\mid\boldsymbol{\eta})=-\frac{1}{2}\{T\log(2\pi)+\log|\mathbf{V}|+(\boldsymbol{y}-\boldsymbol{X\beta})'\mathbf{V}^{-1}(\boldsymbol{y}-\boldsymbol{X\beta})\}$$

其中，协方差矩阵 $\mathbf{V}$ 具有 Toeplitz 结构：

$$\mathbf{V}=\begin{bmatrix}\gamma_0 & \gamma_1 & \gamma_2 & \cdots & \gamma_{T-1}\\ \gamma_1 & \gamma_0 & \gamma_1 & \cdots & \gamma_{T-2}\\ \vdots & \vdots & \vdots & \ddots & \vdots\\ \gamma_{T-1} & \gamma_{T-2} & \gamma_{T-3} & \cdots & \gamma_0\end{bmatrix}$$

式中，$\gamma_0=\mathrm{Var}(y_t)$，$\gamma_h=\mathrm{Cov}(y_t,y_{t-h})$，$h=1,2,\cdots,T-1$ 且 $t=1,\cdots,T$。

ARFIMA(p,d,q)模型的参数估计命令为 arfima。

语法格式为：

```
arfima depvar [indepvars] [if] [in] [, options]
```

菜单操作路径为：

```
Statistics>Time series>ARFIMA models
```

各选项及含义如表 8.1 所示。

表 8.1　选项及含义

	options	描述
Model	noconstant	抑制常数项
	ar(numlist)	自回归项
	ma(numlist)	移动平均数项
	smemory	估计没有分数积分的短记忆模型
	mle	最大似然估计
	mpl	最大修正概率估计
	constraints(numlist)	应用指定的线性约束
	collinear	不丢弃相邻的变量
SE/Robust	vce(vcetype)	vcetype 可以是 oim 或 robust

例 8.18　ARFIMA 模型

本例利用坎皮托山的树木年轮数据进行说明。Baillie(1996)①对坎皮托山上的鬃毛松年轮数据进行了探讨。这个序列包含了从公元前 3436 年到公元 1969 年在该树上形成的年轮的测量结果。从本质上讲，宽度较大的年份对该树而言是好年份，而宽

① Baillie, R. T. Long Memory Processes and Fractional Integration in Econometrics. *Journal of Econometrics*, 1996, 73.

度较窄的年份是恶劣的年份。

我们首先绘制时间序列图。(见图 8.52)

```
.use https://www.stata-press.com/data/r17/campito
(Campito Mnt. tree ring data from 3435BC to 1969AD)
.tsline width, xlabel(-3435(500)1969) ysize(2)
```

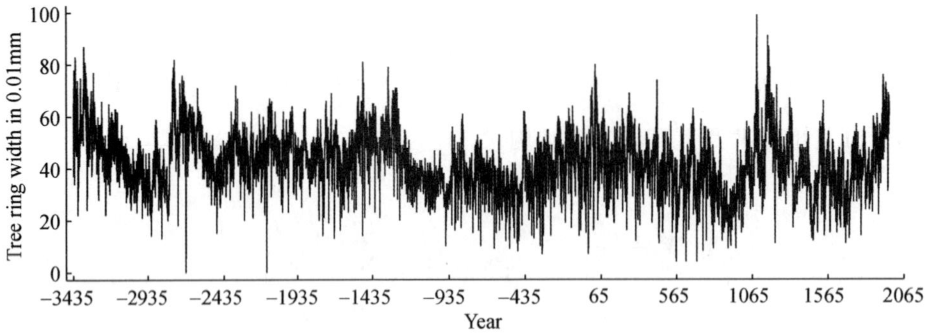

图 8.52

好年头和坏年头似乎都在一起,造成了当地趋势的出现。局部趋势是依赖性的证据,但它们并不像非平稳序列中那样明显。

接下来绘制自相关图。(见图 8.53)

```
.ac width, ysize(2)
```

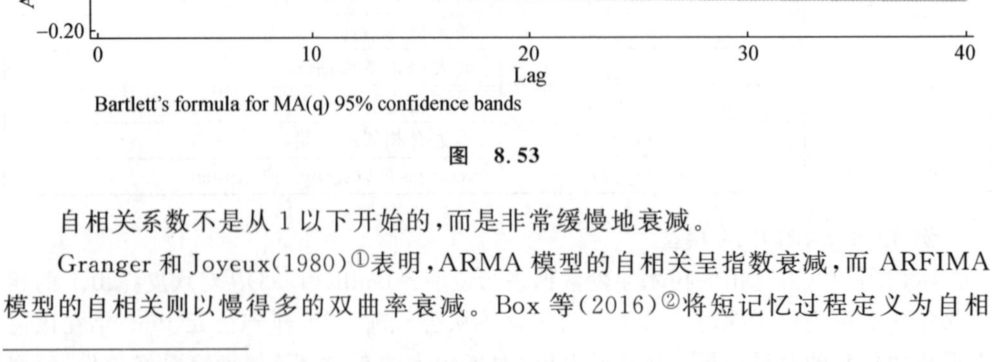

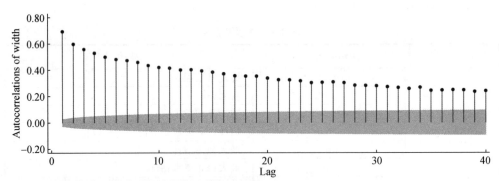

图 8.53

自相关系数不是从 1 以下开始的,而是非常缓慢地衰减。

Granger 和 Joyeux(1980)①表明,ARMA 模型的自相关呈指数衰减,而 ARFIMA 模型的自相关则以慢得多的双曲率衰减。Box 等(2016)②将短记忆过程定义为自相

① Granger, C. W. J., and R. Joyeux. An Introduction to Long-memory Time Series Models and Fractional Differencing. *Journal of Time Series Analysis*, 1980, 1.

② Box, G. E. P., G. M. Jenkins, G. C. Reinsel, and G. M. Ljung. *Time Series Analysis: Forecasting and Control* (5th ed.). Hoboken, NJ: Wiley, 2016.

关性以指数速度衰减的过程,将长记忆过程定义为自相关性以双曲线速度衰减的过程。上面的自相关图更接近于双曲线速度衰减而非指数速度衰减。

综上所述,我们认为这一序列是通过一个漫长的记忆过程产生的。我们看到的证据表明,序列是平稳的,但自相关消失的速度比短记忆过程预测的要慢得多。

鉴于数据是由平稳过程生成的,我们首先将数据拟合到 ARMA 模型。这里使用短记忆模型,因为结果的比较突出了使用 ARFIMA 模型进行长记忆过程的优势。

```
.arima width, ar(1/2) ma(1) technique(bhhh 4 nr)
```

运行结果如图 8.51 所示。

```
ARIMA regression

Sample:  -3435 - 1969                           Number of obs     =       5405
                                                Wald chi2(3)      =  133686.46
Log likelihood = -18913.21                      Prob > chi2       =     0.0000
```

width	Coef.	OIM Std. Err.	z	P>|z|	[95% Conf.	Interval]
width						
_cons	42.45055	1.02142	41.56	0.000	40.44861	44.4525
ARMA						
ar						
L1.	1.264367	.0253199	49.94	0.000	1.214741	1.313994
L2.	-.2848827	.0227534	-12.52	0.000	-.3294785	-.2402869
ma						
L1.	-.8066007	.0189699	-42.52	0.000	-.8437811	-.7694204
/sigma	8.005814	.0770004	103.97	0.000	7.854896	8.156732

Note: The test of the variance against zero is one sided, and the two-sided confidence interval is truncated at zero.

图 8.54

上述方法估计的系数似乎很高,我们使用 estat aroots 命令进行进一步检验。

```
.estat aroots
```

运行结果如图 8.55 和 8.56 所示。

Eigenvalue stability condition

Eigenvalue	Modulus
.9709661	.970966
.2934013	.293401

All the eigenvalues lie inside the unit circle.
AR parameters satisfy stability condition.

图 8.55

Eigenvalue stability condition

Eigenvalue	Modulus
.8066007	.806601

All the eigenvalues lie inside the unit circle.
MA parameters satisfy invertibility condition.

图 8.56

AR 多项式的根是 0.971 和 0.293,MA 多项式的根是 0.807,这些根都小于 1,表明该序列是静止的、可逆的,但具有高度的持久性。

下面我们估计一个 ARFIMA 模型的参数,它的参数只有分数差分参数和一个常数。

```
.arfima width
```

运行结果如图 8.57 所示。

ARFIMA regression

Sample: -3435 - 1969   Number of obs = 5,405
Wald chi2(1) = 1864.43
Log likelihood = -18907.279   Prob > chi2 = 0.0000

width	Coef.	OIM Std. Err.	z	P>|z|	[95% Conf.	Interval]
width						
_cons	44.01432	9.174317	4.80	0.000	26.03299	61.99565
ARFIMA						
d	.4468888	.0103497	43.18	0.000	.4266038	.4671737
/sigma2	63.92927	1.229754	51.99	0.000	61.519	66.33955

Note: The test of the variance against zero is one sided, and the two-sided confidence interval is truncated at zero.

图 8.57

d 的估计值很大,而且具有统计学意义。ARFIMA 模型的相对解析力表现在:5 个参数的 ARMA 模型和 3 个参数的 ARFIMA 模型的特异性误差的标准差估计值是相同的。

让我们为上述 ARFIMA 模型添加一个 AR 参数。

```
.arfima width, ar(1)
```

运行结果如图 8.58 所示。

```
ARFIMA regression

Sample: -3435 - 1969                            Number of obs     =      5,405
                                                Wald chi2(2)      =    1875.36
Log likelihood = -18907.233                     Prob > chi2       =     0.0000
```

width	Coef.	OIM Std. Err.	z	P>|z|	[95% Conf.	Interval]
width						
_cons	43.98774	8.685075	5.06	0.000	26.9653	61.01017
ARFIMA						
ar						
L1.	.0063326	.0204669	0.31	0.757	-.0337817	.0464469
d	.4432469	.0156627	28.30	0.000	.4125487	.4739452
/sigma2	63.92915	1.229754	51.99	0.000	61.51888	66.33942

Note: The test of the variance against zero is one sided, and the two-sided confidence interval is truncated at zero.

图 8.58

估计的 AR 项很小，而且在统计学意义上不显著，这表明 d 参数已经解释了该序列中的所有依赖性。

如上所述，从某种意义上说，ARFIMA 模型相较 ARMA 模型在长记忆过程中的主要优势是，ARFIMA 参数化相对简洁且能够将长期效应与短期效应分开。如果真正的过程是由 ARFIMA 模型产生的，那么有很多项的 ARMA 模型可以接近这个过程，但这些项使估计变得困难，而且缺乏独立的长期和短期参数，使解释变得复杂。

8.11 时间序列预测

8.11.1 ARIMA 模型预测

例 8.19 ARIMA 模型预测与脉冲响应分析

本例说明使用 ARIMA 命令拟合 ARIMA、ARMAX 和其他动态模型后预测的一些特征。拟合模型为：

$$\Delta \ln(\mathrm{wpi}_t) = \beta_0 + \rho_1\{\Delta \ln(\mathrm{wpi}_{t-1}) - \beta_0\} + \theta_1 \varepsilon_{t-1} + \theta_4 \varepsilon_{t-4} + \varepsilon_t$$

```
* 下载数据，清理内存
.clear
.webuse wpi1
* 具有加法季节效应的 ARIMA 模型拟合
.arima D.ln_wpi, ar(1) ma(1 4)
```

运行结果如图 8.59 所示。

```
Sample: 1960q2 thru 1990q4                      Number of obs     =        123
                                                Wald chi2(3)      =     333.60
Log likelihood = 386.0336                       Prob > chi2       =     0.0000
```

D.ln_wpi	Coefficient	OPG std. err.	z	P>|z|	[95% conf.	interval]
ln_wpi						
_cons	.0110493	.0048349	2.29	0.022	.0015731	.0205255
ARMA						
ar						
L1.	.7806991	.0944946	8.26	0.000	.5954931	.965905
ma						
L1.	-.3990039	.1258753	-3.17	0.002	-.6457149	-.1522928
L4.	.3090813	.1200945	2.57	0.010	.0737003	.5444622
/sigma	.0104394	.0004702	22.20	0.000	.0095178	.0113609

```
Note: The test of the variance against zero is one sided, and the two-sided
      confidence interval is truncated at zero.
```

图 8.59

* 计算 D. ln\u wpi 的预测

.predict xb

(option xb assumed; predicted values)

xb_t 计算式为：

$$xb_t = \hat{\beta}_0 + \hat{\rho}_1\{\Delta\ln(\text{wpi}_{t-1}) - \hat{\beta}_0\} + \hat{\theta}_1\hat{\varepsilon}_{t-1} + \hat{\theta}_4\hat{\varepsilon}_{t-4}$$

式中，$\hat{\varepsilon}_{t-j} = \begin{cases} \Delta\ln(\text{wpi}_{t-j}) - xb_{t-j} & t-j>0 \\ 0 & \text{otherwise} \end{cases}$。

* 在进行预测时，只考虑结构成分，忽略 ARMA 项

.predict xbs, structural

(option xb assumed; predicted values)

估计式为：$xbs_t = \hat{\beta}_0$。

* 计算 ln_wpi 的预测，反转估计中应用的任何时间序列运算符

.predict y, y

(1 missing value generated)

计算式为：

$y_t = xb_t + \ln(\text{wpi}_{t-1})$。

* 计算 ln_wpi 的预测，使用 1970q1 后预测的滞后预测值，而不是滞后实际值

.predict yd, y dynamic(tq(1970q1))

```
(1 missing value generated)
```

* 绘制时间序列折线图

```
.tsline y yd
```

运行结果如图 8.60 所示。

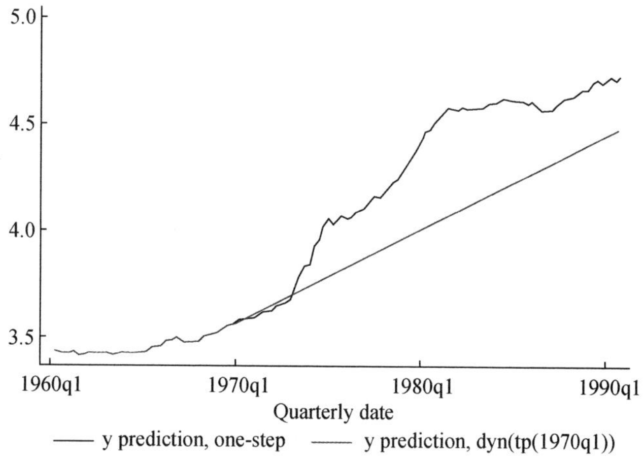

图 8.60

下面进行 ARIMA 模型的脉冲响应分析。

考虑 Enders(2004)①的一个关于美国货币供应量(M1)的季度数据模型。Enders(2004)②讨论了为什么季节性购物模式会对 M1 产生季节性影响。变量 lnm1 包含货币供应量自然对数的数据。我们拟合季节性和非季节性 ARIMA 模型,并比较两个模型计算的 IRF。

我们拟合以下非季节性 ARIMA 模型:

$$\Delta\Delta_4 \text{lnm1}_t = \rho_1(\Delta\Delta_4 \text{lnm1}_{t-1}) + \rho_4(\Delta\Delta_4 \text{lnm1}_{t-4}) + \varepsilon_t$$

季节性 ARIMA 模型为:

$$(1-\rho_1 L)(1-\rho_{4,1} L^4)\Delta\Delta_4 \text{lnm1}_t = \varepsilon_t$$

```
.use https://www.stata-press.com/data/r17/m1nsa, clear
(U.S. money supply (M1) from Enders (2004), 95—99.)
```

* 拟合非季节性 ARIMA 模型

```
.arima DS4.lnm1, ar(1 4) noconstant nolog
```

运行结果如图 8.61 所示。

```
.irf create nonseasonal, set(myirf) step(30)
(file myirf.irf now active)
(file myirf.irf updated)
```

* 拟合季节性 ARIMA 模型

① Enders, W. *Applied Econometric Time Series*. NJ: Wiley, 2004.

② Ibid.

```
ARIMA regression

Sample: 1961q2 thru 2008q2                      Number of obs     =        189
                                                Wald chi2(2)      =      78.34
Log likelihood = 579.3036                       Prob > chi2       =     0.0000

------------------------------------------------------------------------------
             |                 OPG
    DS4.lnm1 | Coefficient  std. err.      z    P>|z|     [95% conf. interval]
-------------+----------------------------------------------------------------
ARMA         |
          ar |
         L1. |   .3551862   .0503011     7.06   0.000     .2565979    .4537745
         L4. |  -.3275808   .0594953    -5.51   0.000    -.4441895    -.210972
-------------+----------------------------------------------------------------
      /sigma |   .0112678   .0004882    23.08   0.000     .0103109    .0122246
------------------------------------------------------------------------------
Note: The test of the variance against zero is one sided, and the two-sided
      confidence interval is truncated at zero.
```

图 8.61

```
. arima DS4.lnm1, ar(1) mar(1,4) noconstant nolog
```

运行结果如图8.62所示。

```
ARIMA regression

Sample: 1961q2 thru 2008q2                      Number of obs     =        189
                                                Wald chi2(2)      =     119.78
Log likelihood = 588.6689                       Prob > chi2       =     0.0000

------------------------------------------------------------------------------
             |                 OPG
    DS4.lnm1 | Coefficient  std. err.      z    P>|z|     [95% conf. interval]
-------------+----------------------------------------------------------------
ARMA         |
          ar |
         L1. |    .489277   .0538033     9.09   0.000     .3838245    .5947296
-------------+----------------------------------------------------------------
ARMA4        |
          ar |
         L1. |  -.4688653   .0601248    -7.80   0.000    -.5867076   -.3510229
-------------+----------------------------------------------------------------
      /sigma |   .0107075   .0004747    22.56   0.000     .0097771    .0116379
------------------------------------------------------------------------------
Note: The test of the variance against zero is one sided, and the two-sided
      confidence interval is truncated at zero.
```

图 8.62

```
. irf create seasonal, step(30)
(file myirf.irf updated)
. irf graph irf
```

运行结果如图 8.63 所示。

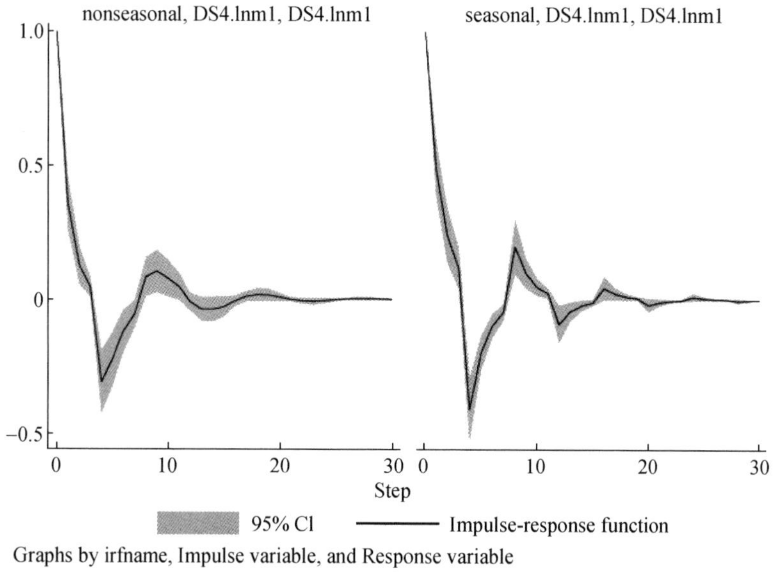

图 8.63

IRF 函数的轨迹是相似的。每个图都显示,对 lnm1 的冲击会导致 lnm1 中的暂时振荡,该振荡在大约 15 个时间段后消失。这种行为是短内存进程的特征。

8.11.2 ARFIMA 模型预测

记 $\gamma_h, h=1,\cdots,t$ 是时间间隔为 h 的两个观测值 y_t 和 y_{t-h} 的 ARFIMA(p,d,q) 过程的自协方差函数。长度 T 过程的协方差矩阵 $\mathbf{V}$ 的 Toeplitz 结构为:

$$\mathbf{V}=\begin{bmatrix}\gamma_0 & \gamma_1 & \gamma_2 & \cdots & \gamma_{T-1}\\ \gamma_1 & \gamma_0 & \gamma_1 & \cdots & \gamma_{T-2}\\ \vdots & \vdots & \vdots & \ddots & \vdots\\ \gamma_{T-1} & \gamma_{T-2} & \gamma_{T-3} & \cdots & \gamma_0\end{bmatrix}$$

其中,过程方差为 $\gamma_0=\mathrm{Var}(y_t)$。对 $\mathbf{V}$ 进行矩阵分解,$\boldsymbol{V}=\boldsymbol{LDL}'$,其中 $\boldsymbol{L}$ 为下三角形,$\boldsymbol{D}=\mathrm{Diag}(v_t)$。$\boldsymbol{L}$ 的逆矩阵为:

$$\boldsymbol{L}^{-1}=\begin{bmatrix}1 & 0 & 0 & \cdots & 0 & 0\\ -\tau_{1,1} & 1 & 0 & \cdots & 0 & 0\\ -\tau_{2,2} & -\tau_{2,1} & 1 & \cdots & 0 & 0\\ \vdots & \vdots & \vdots & \ddots & \vdots & \vdots\\ -\tau_{T-1,T-1} & -\tau_{T-1,T-2} & -\tau_{T-1,T-2} & \cdots & -\tau_{T-1,1} & 1\end{bmatrix}$$

式中,$\tau_t=\boldsymbol{V}_t^{-1}\gamma_t$,则有

$$y=\boldsymbol{L}^{-1}(y-\boldsymbol{X\beta})+\boldsymbol{X\beta} \tag{8.99}$$

例 8.20　ARFIMA 模型预测与脉冲响应分析

本例利用 import fred 命令从联邦储备银行(FRED)数据库导入一年期国债二级市场利率的月度数据。下面将 ARFIMA 模型与数据拟合,该模型包含两个自回归项和一个移动平均项。

```
* 下载数据,清理内存
.clear
.webuse tb1yr
* 基于1年期国库券数据拟合 ARFIMA(2,d,1)模型
.arfima tb1yr, ar(1/2) ma(1)
```

运行结果如图 8.64 所示。

```
ARFIMA regression

Sample: 1959m7 thru 2001m8                    Number of obs     =        506
                                              Wald chi2(4)      =    1864.16
Log likelihood = -235.11868                   Prob > chi2       =     0.0000
```

tb1yr	Coefficient	Std. err.	z	P>|z|	[95% conf.	interval]
tb1yr						
_cons	5.496707	2.920395	1.88	0.060	-.2271618	11.22058
ARFIMA						
ar						
L1.	.2326096	.1136622	2.05	0.041	.0098357	.4553834
L2.	.3885209	.0835643	4.65	0.000	.2247378	.552304
ma						
L1.	.775585	.0669554	11.58	0.000	.6443548	.9068151
d	.4606498	.0646499	7.13	0.000	.3339383	.5873614
/sigma2	.1466495	.009232	15.88	0.000	.1285551	.1647438

Note: The test of the variance against zero is one sided, and the two-sided confidence interval is truncated at zero.

图　8.64

```
* tb1yr 的一步预测
.predict ptb
* 过滤 wpi,应用分数差
.predict fdtb, fdifference
* 绘制时间序列、预测和过滤估计
.twoway tsline tb1yr ptb fdtb
```

运行结果如图 8.65 所示。

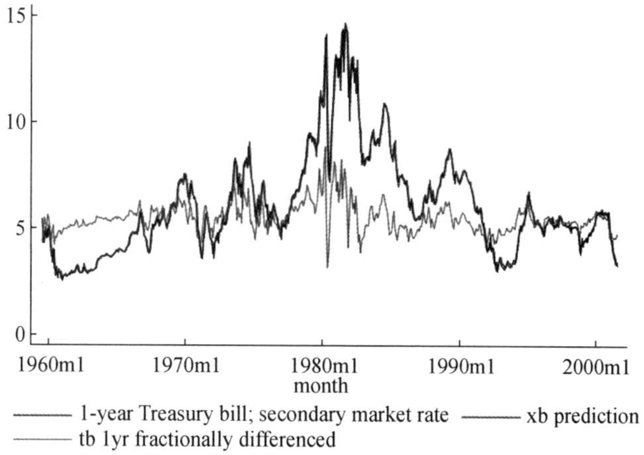

图 8.65

```
*将数据延长1年
.tsappend, add(12)
*计算1991年dwpi预测及其RMSE
.predict ftb, xb dynamic(tm(2001m9)) rmse(rtb)
```

现在,我们计算动态预测的90%置信区间,并绘制原始序列、样本内预测、动态预测和动态预测的置信区间图。

```
*计算大约90%的预测间隔
.scalar z = invnormal(0.95)
.generate lb = ftb-z*rtb if month>=tm(2001m9)
(506 missing values generated)
.generate ub = ftb + z*rtb if month>=tm(2001m9)
(506 missing values generated)
*绘制时间序列折线图
.twoway tsline tb1yr ftb if month>tm(1998m12)|| tsrline lb ub if month>=tm(2001m9), legend(cols(1) label(3 "80% prediction interval"))
```

运行结果如图8.66所示。

```
*脉冲响应分析
.irf create arfima, step(50) set(myirf)
(file myirf.irf created)
(file myirf.irf now active)
(file myirf.irf updated)
.irf graph irf
```

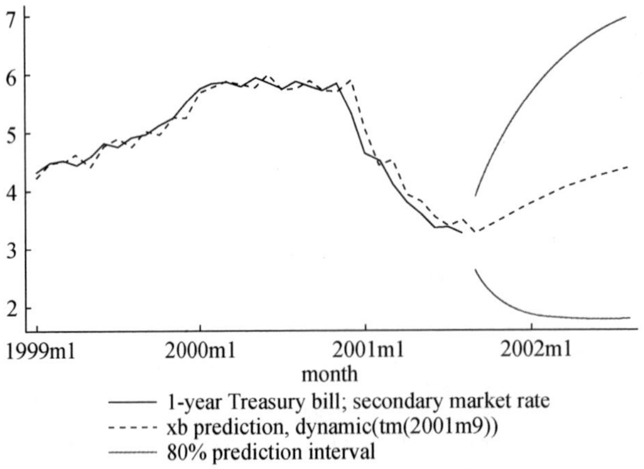

图 8.66

运行结果如图 8.67 所示。

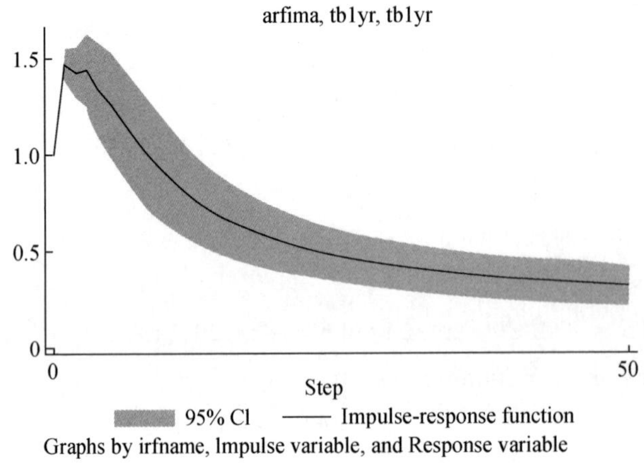

图 8.67

第 9 章 GARCH 模型

9.1 ARCH 模型

时间序列数据一般都具有时变序列方差，而且波动具有集聚性和不对称性。自回归条件件异方差(autoregressive conditional heteroskedasticity, ARCH)模型把未来波动作为前期波动的函数，用于拟合时变序列方差。Stata 的 arch 命令使用条件最大似然值估计 ARCH 模型。

ARCH 模型包括条件均值方程和条件方差方程。其中，均值方程为：

$$y_t = \boldsymbol{x}_t\boldsymbol{\beta} + \varepsilon_t \tag{9.1}$$

$$\sigma_t^2 = \gamma_0 + \gamma_1\varepsilon_{t-1}^2 + \gamma_2\varepsilon_{t-2}^2 + \cdots + \gamma_m\varepsilon_{t-m}^2 \tag{9.2}$$

式中，ε_t^2 为方差，γ_i 为 ARCH 项参数。

对于 ARCH 模型的参数估计，一般把前 p 个观测值$\{\varepsilon_1, \varepsilon_2, \cdots, \varepsilon_p\}$视为给定，然后使用条件 MLE 法估计，即可得到参数的一致估计值，即 ARCH 的似然函数有一个特别简单的形式。给定 ε_t、ε_t^2 和 σ_t^2 的初始(或条件)值，针对每个 ε_t(预测误差)，上述均值方程都可以递归求解。同样，通过使用方差方程，可以递归计算每个观测值的条件方差。

使用这些预测误差及其相关方差，如果假设 $\varepsilon_t \sim N(0, \sigma_t^2)$，则第 t 个观测值的对数似然函数为：

$$\ln L_t = -\frac{1}{2}\left\{\ln(2\pi\sigma_t^2) + \frac{\varepsilon_t^2}{\sigma_t^2}\right\} \tag{9.3}$$

如果假设 $\varepsilon_t \sim t(\mathrm{d}f)$，则第 t 个观测值的对数似然函数为：

$$\begin{aligned}\ln L_t = {} & \ln\Gamma\left(\frac{\mathrm{d}f+1}{2}\right) - \ln\Gamma\left(\frac{\mathrm{d}f}{2}\right) \\ & - \frac{1}{2}\left[\ln\{(\mathrm{d}f-2)\pi\sigma_t^2\} + (\mathrm{d}f+1)\ln\left\{1 + \frac{\varepsilon_t^2}{(\mathrm{d}f-2)\sigma_t^2}\right\}\right]\end{aligned} \tag{9.4}$$

如果假设 $\varepsilon_t \sim \mathrm{GED}(s)$，则 t 个观测值的对数似然函数为：

$$\ln L_t = \ln s - \ln\lambda - \frac{s+1}{s}\ln 2 - \ln\Gamma(s^{-1}) - \frac{1}{2}\left|\frac{\varepsilon_t}{\lambda\sigma_t}\right|^s \tag{9.5}$$

式中，$\lambda = \left\{\frac{\Gamma(s^{-1})}{2^{2/s}\Gamma(3s^{-1})}\right\}^{1/2}$。为施加约束 $s>0$，估计 $r=\ln s$。

9.2 残差的 ARCH 效应 LM 检验

残差的 ARCH 效应是指扰动项的条件方差依赖于其以前各期残差的取值，即残差有序列相关性。Engle(1982)①建议使用 LM 检验来检查误差中的自回归条件异方差(ARCH)。ARCH 模型表达式为：

$$\sigma_t^2 = E(u_t^2 \mid u_{t-1}, \cdots, u_{t-p}) = \gamma_0 + \gamma_1 u_{t-1}^2 + \cdots + \gamma_p u_{t-p}^2$$

为了检验无自回归条件异方差的零假设(即 $\gamma_1 = \gamma_2 = \cdots = \gamma_p = 0$)，我们首先拟合 OLS 模型 $y_t = \beta_1 x_{1t} + \cdots + \beta_k x_{kt} + u_t$，获得残差 $\hat{u}_t$，然后对滞后残差进行另一次 OLS 回归，即得到 ARCH 效应 LM 检验的辅助拟合回归模型：

$$\hat{u}_t^2 = \gamma_0 + \gamma_1 \hat{u}_{t-1}^2 + \cdots + \gamma_p \hat{u}_{t-p}^2 + \varepsilon \tag{9.6}$$

检验统计量为 nR^2，渐进服从自由度为 p 的 χ_p^2 分布。

语法格式为：

estat archlm [, archlm options]

菜单操作路径为：

Statistics>Postestimation

例 9.1　残差的 ARCH 效应 LM 检验

我们重新拟合不包括两个消费滞后的原始模型，然后使用 estat archlm 命令查看是否有证据表明误差是自回归条件异方差。

```
* 清理内存,下载数据
.clear
.webuse klein
* 定义时序数据 yr
.tsset yr
* 回归分析
.regress consump wagegovt
```

运行结果如图 9.1 所示。

Source	SS	df	MS		
Model	532.567711	1	532.567711	Number of obs =	22
Residual	601.207167	20	30.0603584	F(1, 20) =	17.72
				Prob > F =	0.0004
				R-squared =	0.4697
				Adj R-squared =	0.4432
Total	1133.77488	21	53.9892799	Root MSE =	5.4827

consump	Coef.	Std. Err.	t	P>|t|	[95% Conf.	Interval]
wagegovt	2.50744	.5957173	4.21	0.000	1.264796	3.750085
_cons	40.84699	3.192183	12.80	0.000	34.18821	47.50577

图 9.1

① Engle, R. Autoregressive Conditional Heteroscedasticity with Estimates of the Variance of United Kingdom Inflation. *Econometrica*, 1982, 50(4).

```
* archlm 检验
. estat archlm, lags(1 2 3)
```

运行结果如图 9.2 所示。

LM test for autoregressive conditional heteroskedasticity (ARCH)

lags(p)	chi2	df	Prob > chi2
1	5.543	1	0.0186
2	9.431	2	0.0090
3	9.039	3	0.0288

H0: no ARCH effects   vs.   H1: ARCH(p) disturbance

图 9.2

利用 estat archlm 命令分别显示了 ARCH(1)、ARCH(2)和 ARCH(3)效应的检验结果。在 5%的显著性水平上,所有检验都拒绝误差不是自回归条件异方差的原假设。

9.2 GARCH 模型

为减少待估计参数,通常在方差方程中引入条件方差的滞后项,把高阶 ARCH 模型简化为经典的一般化 ARCH 模型(GARCH 模型),可以说 GARCH(1,1)模型等价于无穷阶 ARCH 模型。GARCH 模型表达式为:

$$y_t = \boldsymbol{x}_t\boldsymbol{\beta} + \varepsilon_t \tag{9.7}$$

$$\sigma_t^2 = \gamma_0 + \gamma_1\varepsilon_{t-1}^2 + \gamma_2\varepsilon_{t-2}^2 + \cdots + \gamma_m\varepsilon_{t-m}^2 + \delta_1\sigma_{t-1}^2 + \delta_2\sigma_{t-2}^2 + \cdots + \delta_k\sigma_{t-k}^2 \tag{9.8}$$

式中,δ_i 为 GARCH 项的参数。

对 GARCH 模型及其扩展模型的扰动项的分布,一般会有 3 个假设:正态(高斯)分布、t-分布和广义误差分布(GED)。给定一个分布假设,GARCH 模型常常使用最大似然估计法进行估计。

9.3 基本 GARCH 模型的扩展

9.3.1 一般 GARCH 族模型

为较好拟合时序数据特征,在原始 GARCH 模型框架中发展出系列特色的 GARCH 模型。这些 GARCH 族模型的一般均值方程可以选择性地包括 ARCH 均值和 ARMA 项:

$$y_t = \boldsymbol{x}_t\boldsymbol{\beta} + \sum_{i=1}^{p}\psi_i g(\sigma_{t-i}^2) + \sum_{j=1}^{p}\rho_j\left\{y_{t-j} - x_{t-j}\boldsymbol{\beta} - \sum_{i=1}^{p}\psi_i g(\sigma_{t-j-i}^2)\right\} + \sum_{k=1}^{q}\theta_k\varepsilon_{t-k} + \varepsilon_t \tag{9.9}$$

式中，$\boldsymbol{\beta}$ 为回归参数，ψ 为均值方程中的 ARCH 项参数，ρ 为自回归参数，θ 为移动平均参数，$g()$为一般函数。条件平均值的完整规范中的任何参数都可能为零。例如，模型不需要具有移动平均参数($\theta=0$)或 ARCH 平均参数($\psi=0$)。

一般均值 y_t 方程可以利用 ARMA 模型表示为：

$$y_t = \boldsymbol{x}_t\boldsymbol{\beta} + \sum_i \psi_i g(\sigma_{t-i}^2) + \text{ARMA}(p,q) + \varepsilon_t \tag{9.10}$$

GARCH 族模型的一般方差方程可以是下面三个公式之一：

$$\text{Var}(\varepsilon_t) = \sigma_t^2 = \gamma_0 + A(\boldsymbol{\sigma},\boldsymbol{\varepsilon}) + B(\boldsymbol{\sigma},\boldsymbol{\varepsilon})^2 \tag{9.11}$$

$$\ln\sigma_t^2 = \gamma_0 + C(\ln\boldsymbol{\sigma},z) + A(\boldsymbol{\sigma},\boldsymbol{\varepsilon}) + B(\boldsymbol{\sigma},\boldsymbol{\varepsilon})^2 \tag{9.12}$$

$$\sigma_t^{\varphi} = \gamma_0 + D(\boldsymbol{\sigma},\boldsymbol{\varepsilon}) + A(\boldsymbol{\sigma},\boldsymbol{\varepsilon}) + B(\boldsymbol{\sigma},\boldsymbol{\varepsilon})^2 \tag{9.13}$$

式中，$A(\boldsymbol{\sigma},\boldsymbol{\varepsilon})$，$B(\boldsymbol{\sigma},\boldsymbol{\varepsilon})$，$C(\ln\boldsymbol{\sigma},z)$和 $\text{D}(\boldsymbol{\sigma},\boldsymbol{\varepsilon})$是相关 ARCH 项的线性和；如果模型中没有 EGARCH 项或幂 ARCH 项，则使用等式(9.11)；如果包含 EGARCH 项，则使用等式(9.12)；如果包含任何幂 ARCH 项，则使用等式(9.13)。该一般方差方程中也可以引入解释变量。

根据数据特征和研究需要，可以在 GARCH 族模型的一般均值方程(9.10)和一般方差方程(9.11)、(9.12)、(9.13)及均值方程的随机项分布(即正态分布、t 分布和广义误差分布)三个要素中，选用不同的选项组合，这样就可以扩展得到相应的 GARCH 模型。如门限 ARCH 模型、GJR 形式的门限 ARCH 模型、简单不对称 ARCH 模型、幂 ARCH 模型、非线性 ARCH 模型、含一个移位的非线性 ARCH 模型、非对称幂 ARCH 模型和非线性幂 ARCH 模型。

GARCH 族模型的一般方差方程中如果未指定任何选项，则 $A()=B()=0$，模型为线性回归。

如果将表 9.1 中的选项添加到 $A(\boldsymbol{\sigma},\boldsymbol{\varepsilon})$($\alpha,\gamma,\kappa$ 表示要估计的参数)，则得到相应的方差方程。

表 9.1 各选项添加到 $A(\boldsymbol{\sigma},\boldsymbol{\varepsilon})$得到的方差方程

Option	Terms added to A()
arch()	$A()=A()+\alpha_{1,1}\varepsilon_{t-1}^2+\alpha_{1,2}\varepsilon_{t-2}^2+\cdots$
garch()	$A()=A()+\alpha_{2,1}\sigma_{t-1}^2+\alpha_{2,2}\sigma_{t-2}^2+\cdots$
saarch()	$A()=A()+\alpha_{3,1}\varepsilon_{t-1}+\alpha_{3,2}\varepsilon_{t-2}+\cdots$
tarch()	$A()=A()+\alpha_{4,1}\varepsilon_{t-1}^2(\varepsilon_{t-1}>0)+\alpha_{4,2}\varepsilon_{t-2}^2(\varepsilon_{t-2}>0)+\cdots$
aarch()	$A()=A()+\alpha_{5,1}(\lvert\varepsilon_{t-1}\rvert+\gamma_{5,1}\varepsilon_{t-1})^2+\alpha_{5,2}(\lvert\varepsilon_{t-2}\rvert+\gamma_{5,2}\varepsilon_{t-2})^2+\cdots$
narch()	$A()=A()+\alpha_{6,1}(\varepsilon_{t-1}-\kappa_{6,1})^2+\alpha_{6,2}(\varepsilon_{t-2}-\kappa_{6,2})^2+\cdots$
narchk()	$A()=A()+\alpha_{7,1}(\varepsilon_{t-1}-\kappa_7)^2+\alpha_{7,2}(\varepsilon_{t-2}-\kappa_7)^2+\cdots$

如果将表 9.2 中的选项添加到 $B(\boldsymbol{\sigma},\boldsymbol{\varepsilon})$，也得到相应的方差方程。

表 9.2 各选项添加到 $B(\boldsymbol{\sigma},\boldsymbol{\varepsilon})$ 得到的方差方程

Option	Terms added to B()
abarch()	$B()=B()+\alpha_{8,1}\lvert\varepsilon_{t-1}\rvert+\alpha_{8,2}\lvert\varepsilon_{t-2}\rvert+\cdots$
atarch()	$B()=B()+\alpha_{9,1}\lvert\varepsilon_{t-1}\rvert(\varepsilon_{t-1}>0)+\alpha_{9,2}\lvert\varepsilon_{t-2}\rvert(\varepsilon_{t-2}>0)+\cdots$
sdgarch()	$B()=B()+\alpha_{10,1}\sigma_{t-1}+\alpha_{10,2}\sigma_{t-2}+\cdots$

每个选项的括号中都需要一个数字列表(numlist),该数字列表确定滞后时间项,numlist 中间有空格或逗号。有许多速记约定可以减少必要的键入量。如“1 2 3”为三个数字:1,2,3;“3/1”表示逆序的三个数:3,2,1;“1 2 to 5”或者“1 2:5”表示五个数字:1,2,3,4,5;等等。

比如,选项 arch 表示 $\alpha_{1,1}\varepsilon_{t-1}^2$,arch(2)表示 $\alpha_{1,2}\varepsilon_{t-2}^2$,arch(1,2)表示 $\alpha_{1,1}\varepsilon_{t-1}^2+\alpha_{1,2}\varepsilon_{t-2}^2$,arch(1/3)表示 $\alpha_{1,1}\varepsilon_{t-1}^2+\alpha_{1,2}\varepsilon_{t-2}^2+\alpha_{1,3}\varepsilon_{t-3}^2$,等等。

9.3.2 ARCH-M 模型

ARCH 均值模型即 ARCH-M 模型允许序列的条件方差影响条件均值。这使得对于金融系列中的风险—回报关系建模特别方便。在其他条件相同的情况下,一项投资的风险越高,其预期回报越低。ARCH-M 模型表达式为:

$$y_t=\boldsymbol{x}_t\boldsymbol{\beta}+\psi\sigma_t^2+\varepsilon_t \tag{9.14}$$

ARCH-M 模型的另一种不同形式是将条件方差换成条件标准差,或取对数。

虽然当前条件方差中,这种线性形式在文献中占主导地位,但 arch 命令允许条件方差通过非线性变换 $g()$进入均值方程,并允许同时或滞后地包含该变换项。

$$y_t=\boldsymbol{x}_t\boldsymbol{\beta}+\psi_0 g(\sigma_t^2)+\psi_1 g(\sigma_{t-1}^2)+\psi_2 g(\sigma_{t-2}^2)+\cdots+\varepsilon_t \tag{9.15}$$

平方根是最常用的 $g()$变换,因为研究人员希望在条件标准偏差中包含一个线性项,但任何变换 $g()$都是允许的。

9.3.3 EARCH/EGARCH 模型

如果 earch()或者 egarch()选项被指定,则一般 GARCH 模型变为指数形式的 GARCH 模型即 EGARCH 模型,表达式为:

$$y_t=\boldsymbol{x}_t\boldsymbol{\beta}+\sum_i\psi_i g(\sigma_{t-i}^2)+\text{ARMA}(p,q)+\varepsilon_t$$

$$\ln\text{Var}(\varepsilon_t)=\ln\sigma_t^2=\gamma_0+C(\ln\boldsymbol{\sigma},\boldsymbol{z})+A(\boldsymbol{\sigma},\boldsymbol{\varepsilon})+B(\boldsymbol{\sigma},\boldsymbol{\varepsilon})^2 \tag{9.16}$$

$z_t=\varepsilon_t/\sigma_t$,$A()$和 $B()$见上文,但 $A()$和 $B()$现在加到 $\ln\sigma_t^2$ 而不是 σ_t^2 上(这里的 $A()$和 $B()$很少指定)。各选项添加到 $C(\ln\sigma,z)$得到的方差方程如表 9.3 所示。

表 9.3 各选项添加到 $C(\ln\boldsymbol{\sigma},z)$ 得到的方差方程

Option	Terms added to C()
earch()	$C()=C()+\alpha_{11,1}z_{t-1}+\gamma_{11,1}(\lvert z_{t-1}\rvert-\sqrt{2/\pi})+\alpha_{11,2}z_{t-2}+\gamma_{11,2}(\lvert z_{t-2}\rvert-\sqrt{2/\pi})+\cdots$
egarch()	$C()=C()+\alpha_{12,1}\ln\sigma_{t-1}^2+\alpha_{12,2}\ln\sigma_{t-2}^2+\cdots$

EGARCH模型的条件方差方程为：

$$\ln\sigma_t^2=\alpha_0+\alpha_1\underbrace{(\varepsilon_{t-1}/\sigma_{t-1})}_{\text{EARCH}}+\lambda_1\underbrace{|\varepsilon_{t-1}/\sigma_{t-1}|}_{\text{EARCH\_a}}+\beta_1\underbrace{\ln\sigma_{t-1}^2}_{\text{EGARCH}} \tag{9.17}$$

其中，$(\varepsilon_{t-1}/\sigma_{t-1})$为$\varepsilon_{t-1}$减去其均值(0)除以自己的标准差后的标准化分数，为EARCH项；如果$\alpha_1\neq 0$，则说明具备不对称效应；$|\varepsilon_{t-1}/\sigma_{t-1}|$表示对称效应，为EARCH_a项；$\ln\sigma_{t-1}^2$为EGARCH项。

9.3.4 PARCH族模型

如果指定parch()、tparch()、aparch()、nparch()、nparchk()或者pgarch()，则一般GARCH模型变为：

$$y_t=\boldsymbol{x}_t\boldsymbol{\beta}+\sum_i\psi_i g(\sigma_{t-i}^2)+\text{ARMA}(p,q)+\varepsilon_t$$

$$\{\text{Var}(\varepsilon_t)\}^{\varphi/2}=\sigma_t^{\varphi}=\gamma_0+D(\boldsymbol{\sigma},\boldsymbol{\varepsilon})+A(\boldsymbol{\sigma},\boldsymbol{\varepsilon})+B(\boldsymbol{\sigma},\boldsymbol{\varepsilon})^2 \tag{9.18}$$

式中，φ是一个带估计的参数，$A()$和$B()$见上文，但$A()$和$B()$加到σ_t^{φ}上(这里的$A()$和$B()$很少指定)。各选项添加到$D(\sigma,\varepsilon)$得到的方差方程如表9.4所示。

表9.4 各选项添加到$D(\boldsymbol{\sigma},\boldsymbol{\varepsilon})$得到的方差方程

Option	Terms added to D()
parch()	$D()=D()+\alpha_{13,1}\varepsilon_{t-1}^{\varphi}+\alpha_{13,2}\varepsilon_{t-2}^{\varphi}+\cdots$
tparch()	$D()=D()+\alpha_{14,1}\varepsilon_{t-1}^{\varphi}I(\varepsilon_{t-1}>0)+\alpha_{14,2}\varepsilon_{t-2}^{\varphi}I(\varepsilon_{t-2}>0)+\cdots$
aparch()	$D()=D()+\alpha_{15,1}(\|\varepsilon_{t-1}\|+\gamma_{15,1}\varepsilon_{t-1})^{\varphi}+\alpha_{15,2}(\|\varepsilon_{t-2}\|+\gamma_{15,2}\varepsilon_{t-2})^{\varphi}+\cdots$
nparch()	$D()=D()+\alpha_{16,1}\|\varepsilon_{t-1}-\kappa_{16,1}\|^{\varphi}+\alpha_{16,2}\|\varepsilon_{t-2}-\kappa_{16,2}\|^{\varphi}+\cdots$
nparchk()	$D()=D()+\alpha_{17,1}\|\varepsilon_{t-1}-\kappa_{17}\|^{\varphi}+\alpha_{17,2}\|\varepsilon_{t-2}-\kappa_{17}\|^{\varphi}+\cdots$
pgarch()	$D()=D()+\alpha_{18,1}\sigma_{t-1}^{\varphi}+\alpha_{18,2}\sigma_{t-2}^{\varphi}+\cdots$

PARCH(power ARCH)模型指定的条件方差方程为：

$$\sigma_t^{\delta}=\omega+\sum_{j=1}^{q}\beta_j\sigma_{t-j}^{\delta}+\sum_{i=1}^{p}\alpha_i(|u_{t-i}|-\gamma_i u_{t-i})^{\delta} \tag{9.19}$$

其中，$\delta>0$。当$i=1,2,\cdots,r$时，$|\gamma_i|\leqslant 1$；当$i>r$时，$i=0$，$r\leqslant p$。

在PARCH模型中，标准差的幂参数δ是估计的，而不是指定的，用来评价冲击对条件方差的影响幅度；而γ是捕捉直到r阶的非对称效应的参数。在对称的PARCH模型中，对于所有的i，$\gamma_i=0$。需要注意，如果对于所有的i，$\delta=2$且$\gamma_i=0$，PARCH模型就退化为一个标准的GARCH模型。和前面介绍的非对称模型一样，只要$\gamma_i\neq 0$，非对称效应就会出现。

9.3.5 TGARCH模型

"坏消息"对资产价格波动的影响往往大于"好消息"。非对称的门限GARCH模型即TGARCH模型可以拟合这种非对称的杠杆效应。该模型的条件方差方程为：

$$\sigma_t^2=\alpha_0+\alpha_1\varepsilon_{t-1}^2+\lambda_1\underbrace{\varepsilon_{t-1}^2\cdot\mathbf{1}(\varepsilon_{t-1}<0)}_{\text{TGARCH}}+\beta_1\sigma_{t-1}^2 \tag{9.20}$$

式中，$\mathbf{1}()$为示性函数，即当 $\varepsilon_{t-1}<0$ 时，取值为 1；反之，则为 0。$\varepsilon_{t-1}^2 \cdot \mathbf{1}(\varepsilon_{t-1}<0)$为 TGARCH 项。在这个模型中，好消息($u_t>0$)和坏消息($u_t<0$)对条件方差有不同的影响：好消息有一个对 α_1 的冲击；坏消息有一个对 $\alpha_1+\lambda_1$ 的冲击。如果 $\lambda_1\neq 0$，则信息是非对称的；如果 $\lambda_1>0$，则存在杠杆效应，非对称效应的主要效果是使得波动加大；如果 $\lambda_1<0$，则非对称效应的作用是使得波动减小。

9.3.6 带约束的 GARCH 模型

在估计一个 GARCH 模型时，有两种方式可以对 GARCH 模型的参数进行约束。一种方式是单整 GARCH 模型(intergrated GARCH model，IGARCH 模型)方法，它将模型的方差方程中的所有参数之和限定为 1，并且去掉常数项，即

$$\sigma_t^2=\sum_{j=1}^{q}\beta_j\sigma_{t-j}^2+\sum_{i=1}^{p}\alpha_i u_{t-i}^2 \tag{9.21}$$

其中，$\sum_{j=1}^{q}\beta_j+\sum_{i=1}^{p}\alpha_i=1$。

另一种是方差目标(variance target)方法，它把方差方程中的常数项设定为 GARCH 模型的参数和无条件方差的方程，即

$$\omega=\hat{\sigma}^2\left(1-\sum_{j=1}^{q}\beta_j-\sum_{i=1}^{p}\alpha_i\right) \tag{9.22}$$

式中，$\hat{\sigma}^2$ 为残差的无条件方差。

9.4 GARCH 族模型及其预测的实现

ARCH 族模型的估计命令为 arch。arch 拟合回归模型，其中序列的波动性随时间而变化。ARCH 模型把未来波动率作为先前波动率的函数进行估计。为此，arch 使用条件最大似然法拟合 ARCH 模型。除 ARCH 项外，模型还可能包括多种类型的异方差。模型支持高斯分布、t 分布和广义误差分布。

语法格式如下：

```
arch depvar [indepvars] [if] [in] [weight] [, options]
```

关于回归方程本身，模型也可能包含均值 ARCH 和 ARMA 项。常用模型拟合时的选项设定如表 9.5 所示。

表 9.5 选项设定

模型	选项设定
ARCH	arch()
GARCH	arch(),garch()
ARCH-in-mean	Archm,arch(),[garch()]
GARCH with ARMA terms	arch(),garch(),ar(),ma()
EGARCH	earch(),egarch()

（续表）

模型	选项设定
TARCH, threshold ARCH	abarch(), atarch(), sdgarch()
GJR, form of threshold ARCH	arch(), arch(), [garch()]
SAARCH, simple asymmetric ARCH	arch(), saarch(), [garch()]
PARCH, power ARCH	parch(), [pgarch()]
NARCH, nonlinear ARCH	narch(), [garch()]
NARCHK, NARCH with one shift	narchk(), [garch()]
A-PARCH, asymmetric power ARCH	aparch(), [pgarch()]
NPARCH, nonlinear power ARCH	nparch(), [pgarch()]
多元状态空间模型	sspace
动态因子模型	dfactor

菜单操作路径为：

(1) ARCH/GARCH

Statistics>Time series>ARCH/GARCH>ARCH and GARCH models

(2) EARCH/EGARCH

Statistics>Time series>ARCH/GARCH>Nelson's EGARCH model

(3) ABARCH/ATARCH/SDGARCH

Statistics>Time series>ARCH/GARCH>Threshold ARCH model

(4) ARCH/TARCH/GARCH

Statistics>Time series>ARCH/GARCH>GJR form of threshold ARCH model

(5) ARCH/SAARCH/GARCH

Statistics>Time series>ARCH/GARCH>Simple asymmetric ARCH model

(6) PARCH/PGARCH

Statistics>Time series>ARCH/GARCH>Power ARCH model

(7) NARCH/GARCH

Statistics>Time series>ARCH/GARCH>Nonlinear ARCH model

(8) NARCHK/GARCH

Statistics>Time series>ARCH/GARCH>Nonlinear ARCH model with one shift

(9) APARCH/PGARCH

Statistics>Time series>ARCH/GARCH>Asymmetric power ARCH model

(10) NPARCH/PGARCH

Statistics>Time series>ARCH/GARCH>Nonlinear power ARCH model

例 9.2　ARCH/GARCH 模型

本例利用的数据集同例 8.14。

我们利用 arima 命令拟合了 WPI 中持续复合变化率的模型：$\ln(WPI_t)-\ln(WPI_{t-1})$。

同时，我们用 OLS 回归拟合了一个只有常数的模型，并用 Engle 的 Lagrange 乘数检验(estat archlm)检查了 ARCH 效应。

```
.use https://www.stata-press.com/data/r17/wpi1
.regress D.ln_wpi
```

运行结果如图 9.3 所示。

Source	SS	df	MS			
				Number of obs	=	123
				F(0, 122)	=	0.00
Model	0	0	.	Prob > F	=	.
Residual	.02521709	122	.000206697	R-squared	=	0.0000
				Adj R-squared	=	0.0000
Total	.02521709	122	.000206697	Root MSE	=	.01438

D.ln_wpi	Coef.	Std. Err.	t	P>|t|	[95% Conf.	Interval]
_cons	.0108215	.0012963	8.35	0.000	.0082553	.0133878

图 9.3

```
.estat archlm, lags(1)
```

运行结果如图 9.4 所示。

LM test for autoregressive conditional heteroskedasticity (ARCH)

lags(*p*)	chi2	df	Prob > chi2
1	8.366	1	0.0038

H0: no ARCH effects vs. H1: ARCH(*p*) disturbance

图 9.4

由于 LM 检验显示 p 值为 0.0038，远低于 0.05，拒绝了无 ARCH(1)效应的原假设，因此可以通过指定 ARCH(1)来进一步估计 ARCH(1)参数。

我们可以通过输入如下命令来估计对数差分序列的 GARCH(1,1)过程：

```
.arch D.ln_wpi, arch(1) garch(1)
```

运行结果如图 9.5 所示。

可见，估计 ARCH(1)参数为 0.436，GARCH(1)参数为 0.454，因此拟合的 GARCH(1,1)模型是：

$$y_t = 0.0061 + \varepsilon_t$$

$$\sigma_t^2 = 0.436\varepsilon_{t-1}^2 + 0.454\sigma_{t-1}^2$$

其中，$y_t = \ln(\text{wpi}_t) - \ln(\text{wpi}_{t-1})$

模型 Wald 检验和概率均报告为缺失，按照惯例，Stata 会报告均值方程的模型检

```
ARCH family regression

Sample: 1960q2 - 1990q4                         Number of obs    =       123
Distribution: Gaussian                          Wald chi2(.)     =         .
Log likelihood =   373.234                      Prob > chi2      =         .

------------------------------------------------------------------------------
             |                 OPG
    D.ln_wpi |      Coef.   Std. Err.      z    P>|z|     [95% Conf. Interval]
-------------+----------------------------------------------------------------
ln_wpi       |
       _cons |   .0061167   .0010616     5.76   0.000     .0040361    .0081974
-------------+----------------------------------------------------------------
ARCH         |
        arch |
         L1. |   .4364123   .2437428     1.79   0.073    -.0413147    .9141394
             |
       garch |
         L1. |   .4544606   .1866606     2.43   0.015     .0886127    .8203086
             |
       _cons |   .0000269   .0000122     2.20   0.028     2.97e-06    .0000508
------------------------------------------------------------------------------
```

图 9.5

验。在这里，对于 ARCH 模型，均值方程很常见，只包含一个常数，没有什么要检验的。

例 9.3　ARMA 过程的 ARCH 模型

我们可以保留条件方差的 GARCH(1,1)形式，并将均值建模为带有 AR(1)和 MA(1)项以及第 4 个滞后 MA 项的 ARMA 过程，以通过键入如下命令来控制季度季节效应：

```
.arch D.ln_wpi, ar(1) ma(1 4) arch(1) garch(1)
```

运行结果如图 9.6 所示。

我们可以将模型写成：

$$y_t = 0.007 + 0.792(y_{t-1} - 0.007) - 0.342\varepsilon_{t-1} + 0.245\varepsilon_{t-4} + \varepsilon_t$$

$$\sigma_t^2 = 0.204\varepsilon_{t-1}^2 + 0.695\sigma_{t-1}^2$$

其中，$y_t = \ln(wpi_t) - \ln(wpi_{t-1})$

ARCH(1)系数 0.204 与 0 没有显著差异，但 ARCH(1)和 GARCH(1)系数共同显著。我们可以通过进一步的 test 命令进行检查。

```
.test [ARCH] L1.arch [ARCH] L1.garch
(1) [ARCH]L.arch = 0
(2) [ARCH]L.garch = 0
          chi2(2) = 84.92
        Prob>chi2 = 0.0000
```

```
ARCH family regression -- ARMA disturbances

Sample: 1960q2 - 1990q4                         Number of obs     =        123
Distribution: Gaussian                          Wald chi2(3)      =     153.56
Log likelihood =  399.5144                      Prob > chi2       =     0.0000

------------------------------------------------------------------------------
             |                 OPG
    D.ln_wpi |      Coef.   Std. Err.      z    P>|z|     [95% Conf. Interval]
-------------+----------------------------------------------------------------
ln_wpi       |
       _cons |   .0069541   .0039517     1.76   0.078     -.000791    .0146992
-------------+----------------------------------------------------------------
ARMA         |
          ar |
         L1. |   .7922674   .1072225     7.39   0.000     .5821153     1.00242
             |
          ma |
         L1. |   -.341774   .1499943    -2.28   0.023    -.6357575   -.0477905
         L4. |   .2451724   .1251131     1.96   0.050    -.0000447    .4903896
-------------+----------------------------------------------------------------
ARCH         |
        arch |
         L1. |   .2040449   .1244991     1.64   0.101    -.0399688    .4480587
             |
       garch |
         L1. |   .6949687   .1892176     3.67   0.000     .3241091    1.065828
             |
       _cons |   .0000119   .0000104     1.14   0.253    -8.52e-06    .0000324
------------------------------------------------------------------------------
```

图 9.6

例 9.4 EGARCH 模型

本例利用的数据集同例 8.14。进一步研究 WPI 数据,我们可能会担心整个经济会作出反应,该反应与批发价格意外上涨不同,也与意外下跌不同。也许意外上涨会导致现金流问题,影响库存,并导致更多的损失波动。我们可以通过指定一个 ARCH 模型来确定数据是否支持这一假设,其中最受欢迎的模型是 EGARCH 模型。Nelson (1991)[1]可以指定 WPI 的完整一阶 EGARCH 模型。

```
.use https://www.stata-press.com/data/r17/wpi1, clear
.arch D.ln_wpi, ar(1) ma(1 4) earch(1) egarch(1)
```

运行结果如图 9.7 所示。

① Nelson, D. B. Conditional Heteroskedasticity in Asset Returns: A New Approach. *Econometrica*. 1991,59.

```
ARCH family regression -- ARMA disturbances

Sample: 1960q2 - 1990q4                         Number of obs     =        123
Distribution: Gaussian                          Wald chi2(3)      =     156.02
Log likelihood =  405.3145                      Prob > chi2       =     0.0000

------------------------------------------------------------------------------
             |                 OPG
    D.ln_wpi |      Coef.   Std. Err.      z    P>|z|     [95% Conf. Interval]
-------------+----------------------------------------------------------------
ln_wpi       |
       _cons |   .0087342   .0034004     2.57   0.010     .0020695    .0153989
-------------+----------------------------------------------------------------
ARMA         |
          ar |
         L1. |   .7692141   .0968393     7.94   0.000     .5794126    .9590156
             |
          ma |
         L1. |  -.3554624   .1265721    -2.81   0.005    -.6035392   -.1073856
         L4. |   .2414626   .0863834     2.80   0.005     .0721542    .4107709
-------------+----------------------------------------------------------------
ARCH         |
       earch |
         L1. |   .4063935   .1163501     3.49   0.000     .1783515    .6344355
             |
     earch_a |
         L1. |   .2467328   .1233357     2.00   0.045     .0049993    .4884664
             |
      egarch |
         L1. |   .8417335   .0704073    11.96   0.000     .7037377    .9797294
             |
       _cons |  -1.488363   .6604352    -2.25   0.024    -2.782792   -.1939333
------------------------------------------------------------------------------
```

图 9.7

方差结果是：

$$\ln(\sigma_t^2) = -1.49 + 0.406z_{t-1} + 0.247(|z_{t-1}| - \sqrt{2/\pi}) + 0.842\ln(\sigma_{t-1}^2)$$

其中，$z_t = \varepsilon_t/\sigma_t$，服从标准正态分布。

这是杠杆效应的有力证据。正 L1. earch 系数意味着积极信息(意料之外的价格上涨)比消极信息更具破坏性。这种效应似乎很强(0.406)，并且远大于对称效应(0.247)。事实上，这两个系数的相对大小暗示了正杠杆完全主导了对称效应。

例 9.5 A-PARCH 模型

本例采用道琼斯工业平均指数每日收盘数据。为了避免 20 世纪上半个世纪纽约证券交易所周六开放交易，仅使用 1953 年 1 月 1 日之后的数据。该序列的复合收益率为因变量，如图 9.8 所示。

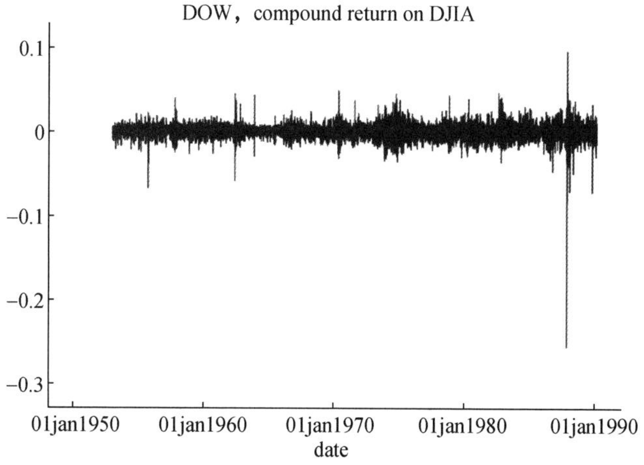

图 9.8

这个时间序列是日度数据，每一个观测值代表当天的道琼斯指数。对该序列进行对数差分处理，并且把周五到下个周一的时间跨度设定为一天。为了实现这个操作，我们建立了一个新变量，按照顺序对观测值进行编号，并且通过 tsset 命令获得了想要的差分序列。

```
.generate t = _n
.tsset t
.use https://www.stata-press.com/data/r17/dow1, clear
.generate dayofwk = dow(date)
.list date dayofwk t ln_dow D.ln_dow in 1/8
```

运行结果如图 9.9 所示。

	date	dayofwk	t	ln_dow	D. ln_dow
1.	02jan1953	5	1	5.677096	.
2.	05jan1953	1	2	5.682899	.0058026
3.	06jan1953	2	3	5.677439	-.0054603
4.	07jan1953	3	4	5.672636	-.0048032
5.	08jan1953	4	5	5.671259	-.0013762
6.	09jan1953	5	6	5.661223	-.0100365
7.	12jan1953	1	7	5.653191	-.0080323
8.	13jan1953	2	8	5.659134	.0059433

图 9.9

```
.list date dayofwk t ln_dow D.ln_dow in -8/l
```

运行结果如图 9.10 所示。

	date	dayofwk	t	ln_dow	D. ln_dow
9334.	08feb1990	4	9334	7.880188	.0016198
9335.	09feb1990	5	9335	7.881635	.0014472
9336.	12feb1990	1	9336	7.870601	-.011034
9337.	13feb1990	2	9337	7.872665	.0020638
9338.	14feb1990	3	9338	7.872577	-.0000877
9339.	15feb1990	4	9339	7.88213	.009553
9340.	16feb1990	5	9340	7.876863	-.0052676
9341.	20feb1990	2	9341	7.862054	-.0148082

图 9.10

差分运算符 D 跨越周末,因为指定的时间变量 t 不是真实日期,并且所有观测值的差为 1。我们必须在估算过程中保留这个人为的时间变量,否则 arch 估计会有偏差。

Ding、Granger 和 Engle (1993)①拟合了 1928 年 1 月 3 日至 1991 年 8 月 30 日标准普尔 500 指数(S&P 500)的日收益率 A-PARCH 模型。我们将对上述道琼斯指数数据采用相同的模型,该模型包括 AR(1)项和条件方差的 A-PARCH 形式。

```
.arch D.ln_dow, ar(1) aparch(1) pgarch(1)
```

运行结果如图 9.11 所示。

在迭代日志中,最终迭代报告消息“已备份”。对于大多数估计器来说,以“备份”消息结尾会引起很大的关注,但对于 arch 或 arima,只要不指定 gtolerance()选项,就不会引起很大的关注。默认情况下,arch 和 arima 只在梯度足够小的情况下监控梯度并宣布收敛。

拟合模型显示出很大的不对称性,具有较大的负 L1. aparch_e 系数,表明市场对收益意外下降(坏消息)的反应比对收益意外增加(好消息)的反应更具波动性。

例 9.6 EGARCH 模型预测

```
.clear
.webuse wpi1
*拟合 EGARCH 模型
.arch D.ln_wpi, ar(1) ma(1,4) earch(1) egarch(1)
```

运行结果略。

```
*创建范围约为-4 到 4 的变量
.generate et = (_n-64)/15
```

① Ding, Z., C. W. J. Granger, and R. F. Engle. A Long Memory Property of Stock Market Returns and a New Model. *Journal of Empirical Finance*, 1993, 1.

```
ARCH family regression -- AR disturbances

Sample: 2 - 9341                              Number of obs   =      9,340
Distribution: Gaussian                        Wald chi2(1)    =     175.46
Log likelihood =  32273.56                    Prob > chi2     =     0.0000
```

D.ln_dow	Coef.	OPG Std. Err.	z	P>|z|	[95% Conf.	Interval]
ln_dow						
_cons	.0001786	.0000875	2.04	0.041	7.15e-06	.00035
ARMA						
ar						
L1.	.1410944	.0106519	13.25	0.000	.1202171	.1619716
ARCH						
aparch						
L1.	.0626323	.0034307	18.26	0.000	.0559082	.0693564
aparch_e						
L1.	-.3645093	.0378485	-9.63	0.000	-.4386909	-.2903277
pgarch						
L1.	.9299015	.0030998	299.99	0.000	.923826	.935977
_cons	7.19e-06	2.53e-06	2.84	0.004	2.23e-06	.0000121
POWER						
power	1.585187	.0629186	25.19	0.000	1.461869	1.708505

图 9.11

* 条件方差的静态预测,假设滞后方差是 e_t 值在 −4 到 4 之间的方差

.predict sigma2, variance at(et 1)

.line sigma2 et in 2/l, m(i) c(l) title(News response function)

运行结果如图 9.12 所示。

例 9.7 门限 ARCH(TARCH)模型

本例利用 Stata 自带数据集说明 TARCH 模型的实现。

* 清理内存,调用数据

.clear

.webuse dow1

* 拟合门限 ARCH 模型(TARCH)

.arch D.ln_dow, tarch(1)

运行结果如图 9.13 所示。

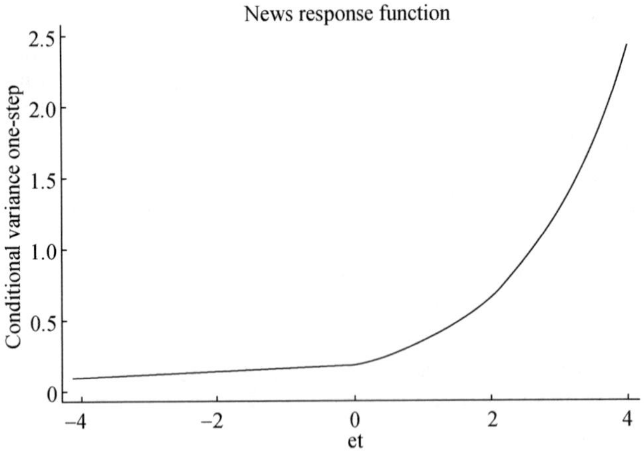

图 9.12

Sample: 2 thru 9341　　　　Number of obs = 9340
　　　　　　　　　　　　　　Wald chi2(.) = .
Log likelihood = 30882.94　　Prob > chi2 = .

D.ln_dow	Coefficient	OPG std. err.	z	P>|z|	[95% conf.	interval]
ln_dow						
_cons	.0002104	.0000968	2.17	0.030	.0000206	.0004002
ARCH						
tarch						
L1.	.0727015	.0059465	12.23	0.000	.0610466	.0843564
_cons	.0000763	1.81e-07	422.16	0.000	.000076	.0000767

图 9.13

例 9.8　带约束的 GARCH 模型的预测

```
.clear
.webuse wpi1, clear
* 施加递减滞后结构
.constraint 1 (3/4) * [ARCH]l1.arch = [ARCH]l2.arch
.constraint 2 (2/4) * [ARCH]l1.arch = [ARCH]l3.arch
.constraint 3 (1/4) * [ARCH]l1.arch = [ARCH]l4.arch
* 使用约束拟合 ARCH 模型
.arch D.ln_wpi, ar(1) ma(1 4) arch(1/4) constraints(1 2 3)
```

运行结果略。

```
* 估计条件方差模型的 α 参数
.lincom [ARCH]l1.arch/.4
```

运行结果如图 9.14 所示。

```
( 1)  2.5*[ARCH]L.arch = 0
```

D.ln_wpi	Coefficient	Std. err.	z	P>|z|	[95% conf. interval]	
(1)	.5450344	.1844468	2.95	0.003	.1835253	.9065436

图 9.14

第10章 时间序列成分分解及预测

10.1 不可观测成分模型

不可观测成分模型(unobserved components model, UCM)的一般形式可以表示为:

$$y_t = \tau_t + \gamma_t + \psi_t + \boldsymbol{x}_t \boldsymbol{\beta} + \varepsilon_t \tag{10.1}$$

其中,τ_t 是趋势,γ_t 是季节性成分,ψ_t 是周期,$\boldsymbol{\beta}$ 是 $\boldsymbol{x}_t$ 的回归系数,ε_t 是方差为 σ_ε^2 的特异性误差。

我们可以将该趋势分解为:

$$\tau_t = \mu_t \tag{10.2}$$

$$\mu_t = \mu_{t-1} + \alpha_{t-1} + \eta_t \tag{10.3}$$

$$\alpha_t = \alpha_{t-1} + \xi_t \tag{10.4}$$

其中,μ_t 是局部截距,α_t 是局部斜率,η_t 和 ξ_t 是均值为 0、方差分别为 σ_η^2 和 σ_ξ^2 的正态误差。

接下来考虑季节性成分 γ_t,周期为 s 个时间单位。忽略季节性干扰项,季节性影响的总和将为零,即 $\sum_{j=0}^{s-1}\gamma_{t-j} = 0$。加入一个正常误差项 ω_t,其均值为 0,方差为 σ_ω^2,我们将季节性成分表示为:

$$\gamma_t = -\sum_{j=1}^{s-1}\gamma_{t-j} + \omega_t \tag{10.5}$$

最后,周期分量 ψ_t 是频率 λ 的函数,单位是弧度,还有一个无单位的缩放变量 ρ,称为阻尼效应,$0<\rho<1$。我们需要用两个方程来表达周期:

$$\psi_t = \psi_{t-1}\rho\cos\lambda + \widetilde{\psi}_{t-1}\rho\sin\lambda + \kappa_t \tag{10.6}$$

$$\widetilde{\psi}_t = -\psi_{t-1}\rho\sin\lambda + \widetilde{\psi}_{t-1}\rho\cos\lambda + \widetilde{\kappa}_t \tag{10.7}$$

其中,κ_t 和 $\widetilde{\kappa}_t$ 干扰为正态分布,均值为 0,方差为 σ_κ^2。

扰动项 ε_t,η_t,ξ_t,ω_t,κ_t 和 $\widetilde{\kappa}_t$ 是独立的。

随机周期模型由以下公式给出:

$$\psi_t = \rho(\psi_{t-1}\cos\lambda_c + \psi_{t-1}^*\sin\lambda_c) + \kappa_{t,1} \tag{10.8}$$

$$\psi_t^* = \rho(-\psi_{t-1}\sin\lambda_c + \psi_{t-1}^*\cos\lambda_c) + \kappa_{t,2} \tag{10.9}$$

其中，$\kappa_{t,j} \sim$ i. i. d. $N(0,\sigma_\kappa^2)$，并且 $0<\rho<1$ 是一个阻尼效应。周期是方差稳定的，当 $\rho<1$ 时，因为 $\mathrm{Var}(\psi_t)=\sigma_\kappa^2/(1-\rho)$，我们将把趋势中加入周期性成分的 UCM 表示为：

$$y_t = \mu_t + \psi_t + \varepsilon_t \tag{10.10}$$

其中，μ_t 可以是前面讨论的任何一种趋势的参数化。

高阶循环，$k=2$ 或 $k=3$，被定义为：

$$\psi_{t,j} = \rho(\psi_{t-1,j}\cos\lambda_c + \psi_{t-1,j}^*\sin\lambda_c) + \psi_{t-1,j+1} \tag{10.11}$$

$$\psi_{t,j}^* = \rho(-\psi_{t-1,j}\sin\lambda_c + \psi_{t-1,j}^*\cos\lambda_c) + \psi_{t-1,j+1}^* \tag{10.12}$$

当 $j<k$ 时，

$$\psi_{t,k} = \rho(\psi_{t-1,k}\cos\lambda_c + \psi_{t-1,k}^*\sin\lambda_c) + \kappa_{t,1} \tag{10.13}$$

$$\psi_{t,k}^* = \rho(-\psi_{t-1,k}\sin\lambda_c + \psi_{t-1,k}^*\cos\lambda_c) + \kappa_{t,2} \tag{10.14}$$

Harvey 和 Trimbur(2003)①讨论了该模型及其状态空间公式的性质。

语法格式为：

ucm depvar [indepvars] [if] [in] [, options]

菜单操作路径为：

Statistics>Time series>Unobserved-components model

各选项及含义如表 10.1 和表 10.2 所示。

表 10.1 选项(options)及含义

	options	含义
Model	model(model)	指定趋势和特异性成分，详见下表
	seasonal(#)	包括一个季节性成分，周期为#个时间单位
	cycle(# [,frequency()]	包括一个阶数为#的周期成分，并可选择将初始频率设置为$\#_f$，$0<\#_f<\pi$；cycle()最多可以被指定三次
	constraints(constraints)	应用指定的线性约束
SE/Robust	vce(vcetype)	vcetype 可以是 oim 或 robust
Reporting	level(#)	设置置信度；默认为 level(95)
	nocnsreport	不显示约束条件
	display_options	控制列和列的格式，行间距，显示省略的变量和基数及空单元格，以及因子变量的标签
Maximization	maximize options	控制最大化过程
	collinear	保留相邻的变量
	coeflegend	显示图例而不是统计数据

① Harvey, A. C., and T. M. Trimbur. General Model-based Filters for Extracting Cycles and Trends in Economic Time Series. *Review of Economics and Statistics*, 2003, 85.

表 10.2 选项(model)及含义

model	含义
rwalk	随机游走模型,默认
none	无趋势或特异性成分
ntrend	无趋势成分,但包括特异性成分
dconstant	带有特异性成分的确定性常数
llevel	局部水平模型
dtrend	带有特异性成分的确定趋势模型
lldtrend	具有确定趋势的局部模型
rwdrift	带漂移的随机行走模型
lltrend	局部线性趋势模型
strend	平滑趋势模型
rtrend	随机趋势模型

例 10.1 随机游走模型

我们下载绘制了美国平民失业率的月度数据。

```
.use https://www.stata-press.com/data/r17/unrate
.tsline unrate, name(unrate)
```

运行结果如图 10.1 所示。

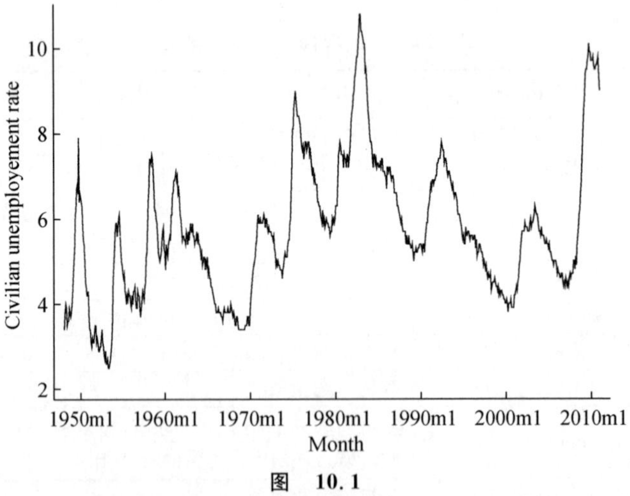

图 10.1

这一序列看起来很像是一个随机游走模型。形式上,随机游动模型由以下公式给出:

$$y_t = \mu_t$$

$$\mu_t = \mu_{t-1} + \eta_t$$

随机游走模型的应用非常广泛,至少作为一个初始模型,它是 ucm 的默认模型。

在下面的输出命令中，我们将随机游走模型拟合到失业数据中。

```
. ucm unrate
```

运行结果如图 10.2 所示。

```
Unobserved-components model
Components: random walk

Sample: 1948m1 - 2011m1                         Number of obs     =        757
Log likelihood =  84.401307
```

unrate	Coef.	OIM Std. Err.	z	P>|z|	[95% Conf.	Interval]
var(level)	.0467196	.002403	19.44	0.000	.0420098	.0514294

```
Note: Model is not stationary.
Note: Tests of variances against zero are one sided, and the two-sided
      confidence intervals are truncated at zero.
```

图 10.2

输出结果表明，该模型是非平稳的，所有随机游走模型都是如此。我们在下一个例子中考虑一个更丰富的模型。

例 10.2 平稳周期分量的随机周期模型

我们认为，应该存在一个平稳的周期性成分，围绕随机游走趋势产生连续相关的冲击。Harvey(1989)①推导出这些平稳周期分量的随机周期模型。

随机周期模型有三个参数：随机分量居中的频率、用于参数化随机分量在中心频率周围分散的阻尼因子，以及作为比例因子的随机循环过程的方差。然后将这一模型与失业数据相匹配。

```
. ucm unrate, cycle(1)
```

运行结果如图 10.3 所示。

周期分量估计的中心频率很小，这意味着周期分量集中在低频分量上。高阻尼系数表明，所有周期分量都接近估计的中心频率。随机周期过程的估计方差很小，但显著。

接下来，使用 estat period 命令将中心频率的估计值转换为估计的中心周期。

```
. estat period
```

运行结果如图 10.4 所示。

① Harvey, A. C. *Forecasting, Structural Time Series Models and the Kalman Filter*. Cambridge: Cambridge University Press, 1989.

```
Unobserved-components model
Components: random walk, order 1 cycle

Sample: 1948m1 - 2011m1                      Number of obs     =        757
                                             Wald chi2(2)      =   26650.81
Log likelihood =  118.88421                  Prob > chi2       =     0.0000
```

unrate	Coef.	OIM Std. Err.	z	P>|z|	[95% Conf.	Interval]
frequency	.0933466	.0103609	9.01	0.000	.0730397	.1136535
damping	.9820003	.0061121	160.66	0.000	.9700207	.9939798
var(level)	.0143786	.0051392	2.80	0.003	.004306	.0244511
var(cycle1)	.0270339	.0054343	4.97	0.000	.0163829	.0376848

```
Note: Model is not stationary.
Note: Tests of variances against zero are one sided, and the two-sided
      confidence intervals are truncated at zero.
```

图 10.3

```
. estat period
```

cycle1	Coef.	Std. Err.	[95% Conf.	Interval]
period	67.31029	7.471004	52.6674	81.95319
frequency	.0933466	.0103609	.0730397	.1136535
damping	.9820003	.0061121	.9700207	.9939798

```
Note: Cycle time unit is monthly.
```

图 10.4

因为我们有月度数据，估计的中心周期为 67.31，这意味着周期性成分由随机成分组成，这些随机成分发生在大约 5.61 年的中心周期附近。这一估计值符合 Burns 和 Mitchell(1946)①对 1.5 年到 8 年之间发生的商业周期冲击的传统定义。

根据 Harvey(1989)②，我们可以将周期分量的估计参数转换为周期分量的估计谱密度。周期分量的谱密度描述了不同频率下随机分量的相对重要性。

① Burns, A. F, and W. C. Mitchell. Measuring Business Cycles. *National Bureau of Economic Research*, 1946.

② Harvey, A. C. *Forecasting, Structural Time Series Models and the Kalman Filter*. Cambridge: Cambridge University Press, 1989.

```
.psdensity sdensity omega
.line sdensity omega
```

运行结果如图 10.5 所示。

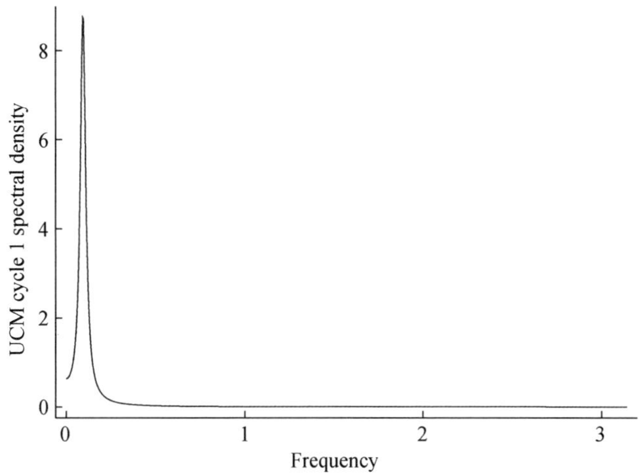

图 10.5

周期分量估计谱密度表明,循环成分由在低频峰值处紧密分布的随机成分组成。

例 10.3 有两个周期性成分的 UCM

现在先回顾一下例 10.2,尽管我们的模型确定了平稳周期性成分,但我们认为可能存在高频周期性成分。用两个或更多的随机周期模型来估计 UCM 的参数是很困难的。提供中心频率的起始值对优化程序有很大帮助。下面估计一个有两个周期性成分的 UCM,一个模型会采集低频成分,另一个会采集高频成分。我们使用 frequency()子选项来提供中心频率的起始值,指定低频模型的阶数为 2,以使其在任何给定的阻尼系数下都不会出现峰值。

```
.ucm unrate, cycle(1, frequency(2.9)) cycle(2, frequency(.09))
```

运行结果如图 10.6 所示。

输出结果表明,存在第二个高频周期。高频分量的中心值为 2.88,而低频分量的中心值为 0.067。高频周期的估计阻尼系数为 0.700,而低频周期的估计阻尼系数为 0.907,这表明高频分量在 2.88 处的分布比低频分量在 0.067 处的分布更为分散。

我们可以通过以下命令来获得估计谱密度:

```
.psdensity sdensity2a omega2a
.psdensity sdensity2b omega2b, cycle(2)
.line sdensity2a sdensity2b omega2a, legend(col(1))
```

运行结果如图 10.7 所示。

```
Unobserved-components model
Components: random walk, 2 cycles of order 1 2

Sample: 1948m1 - 2011m1                         Number of obs     =        757
                                                Wald chi2(4)      =    7681.33
Log likelihood =  146.28326                     Prob > chi2       =     0.0000

------------------------------------------------------------------------------
             |                 OIM
      unrate |      Coef.   Std. Err.      z    P>|z|     [95% Conf. Interval]
-------------+----------------------------------------------------------------
cycle1       |
   frequency |   2.882382   .0668017    43.15   0.000     2.751453    3.013311
     damping |   .7004295   .1251571     5.60   0.000     .4551262    .9457328
-------------+----------------------------------------------------------------
cycle2       |
   frequency |   .0667929   .0206849     3.23   0.001     .0262513    .1073345
     damping |   .9074708   .0142273    63.78   0.000     .8795858    .9353559
-------------+----------------------------------------------------------------
  var(level) |   .0207704   .0039669     5.24   0.000     .0129953    .0285454
 var(cycle1) |   .0027886   .0014363     1.94   0.026            0    .0056037
 var(cycle2) |    .002714    .001028     2.64   0.004     .0006991    .0047289
------------------------------------------------------------------------------
Note: Model is not stationary.
Note: Tests of variances against zero are one sided, and the two-sided
      confidence intervals are truncated at zero.
```

图 10.6

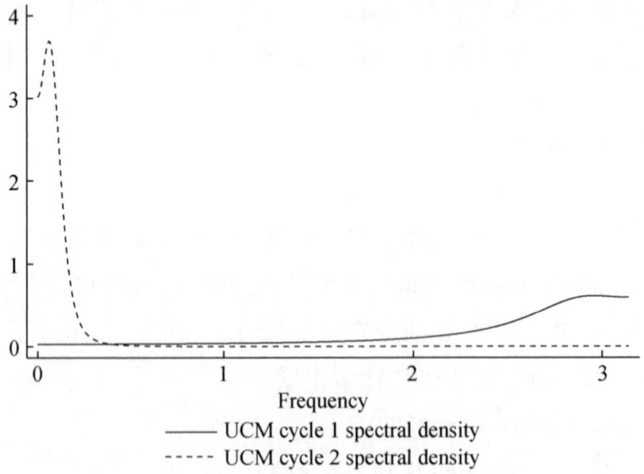

图 10.7

估计谱密度表明，我们发现了两种不同的周期性成分。

10.2 平滑法/单变量预测

10.2.1 单指数平滑

单指数平滑方法适用于序列值在一个常数均值上下随机波动、无趋势及季节要素的情况。时间序列 y_t 的平滑序列 $\hat{y}_t$ 计算公式如下：

$$\hat{y}_t = \alpha y_t + (1-\alpha)\hat{y}_{t-1} \quad 0 \leqslant \alpha \leqslant 1,\ t=2,3,\cdots,T \tag{10.15}$$

式中，α 为平滑因子，α 越小，$\hat{y}_t$ 越平缓。重复迭代，可得到：

$$\hat{y}_t = \alpha \sum_{s=0}^{t-1} (1-\alpha)^s y_{t-s} \tag{10.16}$$

预测值 $\hat{y}_t$ 是 y_t 过去值的加权平均，而权数被定义为以时间为指数的形式。单指数平滑的预测对所有未来的观测值而言都是常数，这个常数为 $\hat{y}_{T+k}=\hat{y}_T$（对所有的 $k>0$），T 是时间序列的最终点。

语法格式为：

```
tssmooth exponential type[] newvar = exp if[] in[], options[]
```

菜单操作路径为：

Menu Statistics>Time series>Smoothers/univariate forecasters>Single-exponential smoothing

例 10.4 使用确定参数平滑序列

我们预测了三个时期的销售数据，平滑参数为 0.4。

```
.use https://www.stata-press.com/data/r17/sales1
.tssmooth exponential sm1 = sales, parms(.4) forecast(3)
exponential coefficient    =    0.4000
sum-of-squared residuals   =    8345
root mean squared error    =    12.919
```

为了将我们的预测与实际数据进行比较，绘制序列图并预测序列随时间的变化。

```
.line sm1 sales t, title("Single exponential forecast") ytitle(Sales) xtitle(Time)
```

运行结果如图 10.8 所示。

图 10.8 表明，我们预测的序列可能无法快速调整以适应实际序列的变化。可以通过平滑参数 α 控制预测调整的速度，α 值越小，预测调整的速度就越慢。因此，我们有理由认为选择的 0.4 太小，需要作出调整以使预测误差的平方和最小。

```
.tssmooth exponential sm2 = sales, forecast(3)
computing optimal exponential coefficient (0,1)
optimal exponential coefficient =    0.7815
sum-of-squared residuals        =    6727.7056
root mean squared error         =    11.599746
```

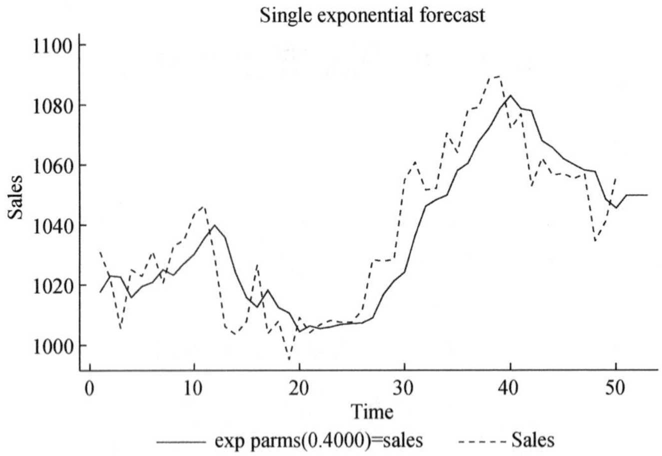

图 10.8

输出表明，0.4 太小，调整后，如图 10.9 所示，新的预测比之前的预测更接近实际值。

```
.line sm2 sales t, title("Single exponential forecast with optimal alpha")
ytitle(Sales) xtitle(Time)
```

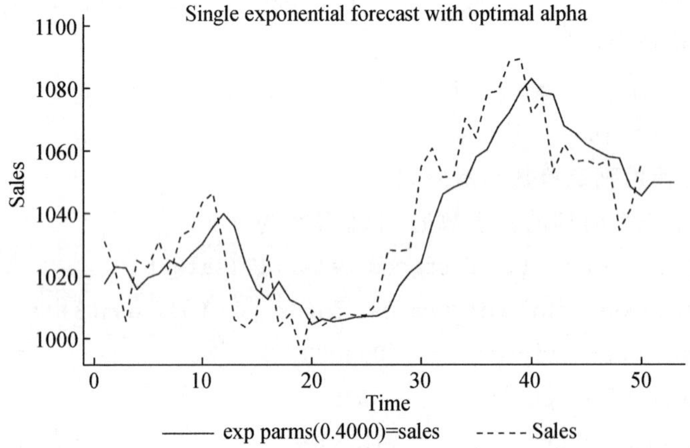

图 10.9

单指数预测对 ARIMA(0,1,1)模型来说是最佳的。Chatfield (2001)[①]给出了有用的推导，将 ARIMA(0,1,1)模型中的 MA 系数与单指数平滑中的平滑参数联系起来。ARIMA(0,1,1)模型的表达式为：

$$x_t - x_{t-1} = \varepsilon_t + \theta\varepsilon_{t-1}$$

其中，ε_t 是一个独立同分布的白噪声误差项，给定 $\hat{\theta}$ 为 θ 的估计，$\hat{x}_{t+1}$ 的最优一步预测是 $\hat{x}_{t+1} = x_t + \hat{\theta}\varepsilon_t$。因为 ε_t 是不可观测的，所以它可以被替换为：

$$\hat{\varepsilon}_t = x_t - \hat{x}_{t-1}$$

$$\hat{x}_{t+1} = x_t + \hat{\theta}(x_t - \hat{x}_{t-1})$$

令 $\hat{\alpha} = 1 + \hat{\theta}$，则有

① Chatfield, C. *Time-Series Forecasting*. London: Chapman & Hall/CRC, 2001.

$$\hat{x}_{t+1}=(1+\hat{\theta})x_t-\hat{\theta}\hat{x}_{t-1}$$
$$\hat{x}_{t+1}=\hat{\alpha}x_t-(1-\hat{\alpha})\hat{x}_{t-1}$$

10.2.2 双指数平滑

这种方法进行两次单指数平滑(使用相同的参数),适用于有线性趋势序列。时间序列 y_t 的双指数平滑以递归形式定义为:

$$S_t=ay_t+(1-a)S_{t-1} \tag{10.17}$$
$$D_t=aS_t+(1-a)D_{t-1} \tag{10.18}$$

式中,$0\leqslant a\leqslant 1$, S_t 是单指数平滑后的序列,D_t 是对 S_t 序列又进行一次单指数平滑,即对原序列进行双指数平滑得到的序列。双指数平滑的预测如下:

$$\hat{y}_{T+k}=\left(2+\frac{ak}{1-a}\right)S_T-\left(1+\frac{ak}{1-a}\right)D_T=2S_T-D_T+\frac{a}{1-a}(S_T-D_T)k \tag{10.19}$$

式中,$k>0$。式(10.19)表明,双指数平滑的预测具有截距为 $2S_T-D_T$,斜率为 $\frac{a}{1-a}(S_T-D_T)$的线性趋势。

语法格式为:

```
tssmooth dexponential type[] newvar = exp if[] in[], options[]
```

菜单操作路径为:

Statistics>Time series>Smoothers/univariate forecasters>Double-exponential smoothing

例 10.5　指数平滑

假设有一本书的月销售数据,我们想要平滑这些数据。下面的例子说明了双指数平滑就是平滑平滑序列。因为起始值被视为时间零值,当平滑平滑序列时,我们实际上失去了 2 个观测值。

首先,打开数据集,画 t 与 sales 的相关图。(见图 10.10)

```
.use https://www.stata-press.com/data/r17/sales2.dta
.line sales t
```

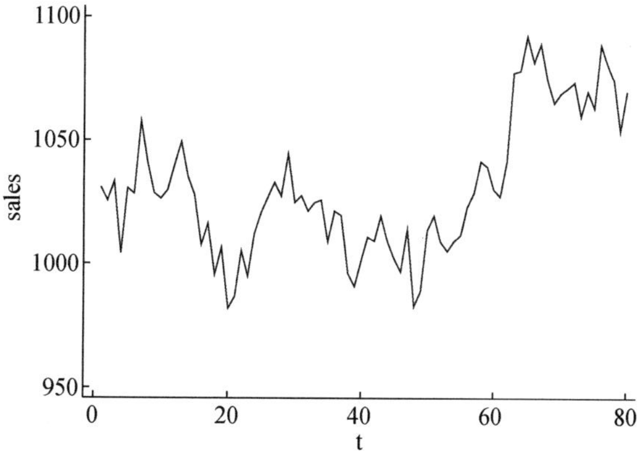

图　10.10

图 10.10 说明这些数据随时间呈局部趋势，因此我们不能使用单指数平滑。

然后，平滑序列。

```
. tssmooth exponential double sm1 = sales, p(.7) s0(1031)
exponential coefficient     =     0.7000
sum-of-squared residuals    =     13923
root mean squared error     =     13.192
. tssmooth exponential double sm2 = sm1, p(.7) s0(1031)
exponential coefficient     =     0.7000
sum-of-squared residuals    =     7698.6
root mean squared error     =     9.8098
```

接着，平滑平滑序列，出现了 2 个缺失值。

```
. tssmooth dexponential double sm2b = sales, p(.7) s0(1031 1031)
double-exponential coefficient =     0.7000
sum-of-squared residuals       =     3724.4
root mean squared error        =     6.8231
. generate double sm2c  =  f2.sm2
(2 missing values generated)
```

最后，列出 sm2b 和 sm2c 的表。（见图 10.11）

```
. list sm2b sm2c in 1/10
```

	sm2b	sm2c
1.	1031	1031
2.	1028.3834	1028.3834
3.	1030.6306	1030.6306
4.	1017.8182	1017.8182
5.	1022.938	1022.938
6.	1026.0752	1026.0752
7.	1041.8587	1041.8587
8.	1042.8341	1042.8341
9.	1035.9571	1035.9571
10.	1030.6651	1030.6651

图　10.11

双指数平滑法也可以被看作一种预测机制。预测值 $\hat{x}_t$ 是在 $t=t_1,\cdots,T+$forecast ()的情况下得到的。这些预测是作为平滑序列和双平滑序列的函数得到的。对于 $t\in[t_0,T]$，有

$$\hat{x}_t=\left(2+\frac{\alpha}{1-\alpha}\right)S_t-\left(1+\frac{\alpha}{1-\alpha}\right)S_t^{[2]}$$

其中，S_t 和 $S_t^{[2]}$ 已给出。样本外预测是作为常数项、在样本中最后一次观测时的平滑级数的非常数项和时间的函数得到的。常数项为 $a_T=2S_T-S_T^{[2]}$，非常数项为 $b_T=$

$\frac{\alpha}{1-\alpha}(S_T-S_T^{[2]})$，第 t 步领先的样本外预测为 $\hat{x}_t=a_t+\tau b_T$。

例 10.6 计算双指数预测

指定预测选项会将双指数预测放到新变量中，下面给出的代码使用前面生成的平滑序列 sm1 和 sm2 来说明它是如何计算双指数预测的：

```
.tssmooth dexponential double f1 = sales, p(.7) s0(1031 1031) forecast(4)
double-exponential coefficient  =    0.7000
sum-of-squared residuals        =    20737
root mean squared error         =    16.1
.generate double xhat = (2 +.7/.3) * sm1 - (1 +.7/.3) * f.sm2
(5 missing values generated)
.list xhat f1 in 1/10
```

运行结果如图 10.12 所示。

	xhat	f1
1.	1031	1031
2.	1031	1031
3.	1023.524	1023.524
4.	1034.8039	1034.8039
5.	994.0237	994.0237
6.	1032.4463	1032.4463
7.	1031.9015	1031.9015
8.	1071.1709	1071.1709
9.	1044.6454	1044.6454
10.	1023.1855	1023.1855

图 10.12

例 10.7 选择一个最优参数进行预测

一般来说，当我们进行预测时，并不知道平滑参数。双指数平滑法计算一个序列的双指数预测，并通过寻找使样本内预测误差之和最小的平滑参数来获得最佳平滑参数。

```
.tssmooth dexponential f2 = sales, forecast(4)
computing optimal double-exponential coefficient (0,1)
optimal double-exponential coefficient  =   0.3631
sum-of-squared residuals                =   16075.805
root mean squared error                 =   14.175598
```

图 10.13 描述了将双指数预测方法应用于销售数据所得到的拟合结果。在单指数的情况下，样本外的动态预测不是恒定的。

```
.line f2 sales t, title("Double exponential forecast with optimal alpha")
ytitle(Sale> s) xtitle(time)
```

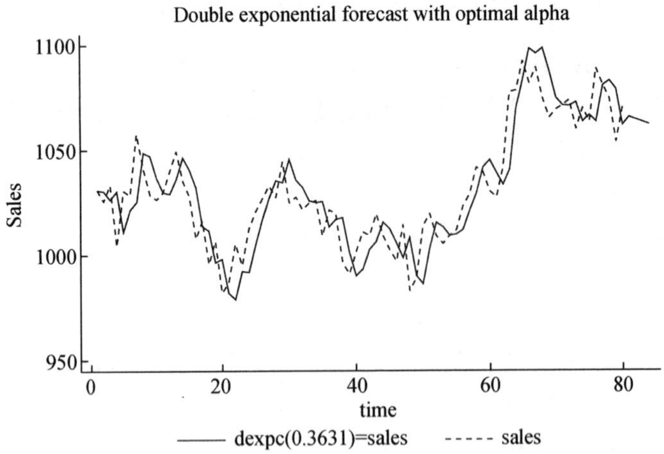

图　10.13

双指数平滑法会自动从 tsset 数据集提供的信息中检测面板数据。每个序列的起始值都是单独选择的，如果平滑参数被选择为最小化平方预测误差之和，那么优化将在每个面板上单独进行，存储的结果包含最后一个面板的结果。样本开始时的缺失值将从样本中排除，在找到至少一个值之后，缺失的值会用上一期的一步预测值填入。

10.2.3　Holt-Winters 无季节性模型

这种方法适用于具有线性时间趋势但无季节变化的序列。与双指数平滑法一样，这种方法以线性趋势进行预测，但不同的是，双指数平滑法只用一个参数，而这种方法用两个参数。y_t 平滑后的序列 $\hat{y}_t$ 由下式给出：

$$\hat{y}_{t+k} = a_t + b_t k \tag{10.20}$$

式中，$k>0$。a_t 表示截距，b_t 表示斜率，这两个参数由如下递归式定义：

$$a_t = a y_t + (1-a)(a_{t-1} + b_{t-1}) \tag{10.21}$$

$$b_t = \beta(a_t - a_{t-1}) + (1-\beta) b_{t-1}$$

式中，a、β、γ 在 0～1 之间，为阻尼因子。预测值由下式计算：

$$\hat{y}_{T+k} = a_T + b_T k \tag{10.22}$$

语法格式为：

```
tssmooth hwinters type[] newvar = exp if[] in[], options[]
```

菜单操作路径为：

Statistics>Time series>Smoothers/univariate forecasters>Holt-Winters nonseasonal smoothing

例 10.8　无季节性模型

本例展示了在特定的平滑参数情况下如何使用无季节性模型，表明 Holt-Winters 方法可以较好地拟合。假设有一本书的月销售数据，我们想用 Holt-Winters 方法来预测这个序列。

```
. use https://www.stata-press.com/data/r17/bsales.dta
```

```
.tssmooth hwinters hw1 = sales, parms(.7.3) forecast(3)
Specified weights:
          alpha  =  0.7000
          beta  =  0.3000
sum-of-squared residuals  =  2301.046
root mean squared error  =  6.192799
.line sales hw1 t, title("Holt-Winters Forecast with alpha = .7 and beta =
.3") ytitle(> Sales) xtitle(Time)
```

运行结果如图 10.14 所示。

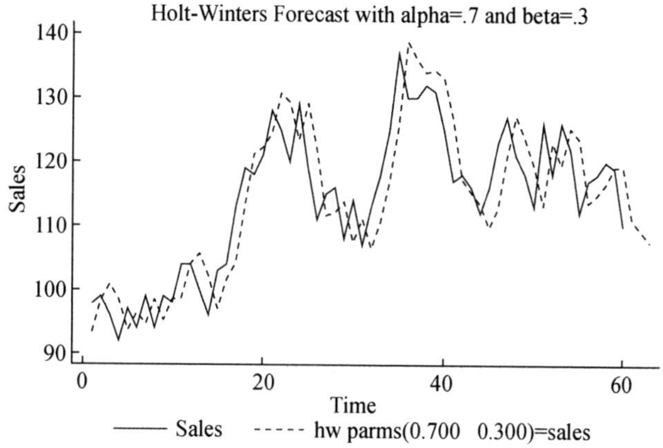

图 10.14

图 10.14 显示,该预测显示的销售额呈线性下降趋势,给定 a_T 和 b_T,样本外预测是时间的线性函数,在这个例子中,坡度似乎太陡了,可能是因为我们选择了 α 和 β。

例 10.9 优化选择初始值

图 10.14 说明线性序列和常数序列的起始值会影响预测序列对前几个观测值的样本内拟合。前面示例使用默认的方法来获取递归的初始值。下面的输出结果说明有差异性的初始值为前几个观测值提供了更好的样本内拟合。然而,基于差分的初始值并不总是优于基于回归的初始值。此外,输出结果显示,对于一系列合理的长度,所产生的预测几乎是相同的。

```
.tssmooth hwinters hw2 = sales, parms(.7.3) forecast(3) diff
Specified weights:
                    alpha  =  0.7000
                    beta  =  0.3000
sum-of-squared residuals  =  2261.173
root mean squared error  =  6.13891
.list hw1 hw2 if _n<6 | _n>57
```

运行结果如图 10.15 所示。

	hw1	hw2
1.	93.31973	97.80807
2.	98.40002	98.11447
3.	100.8845	99.2267
4.	98.50404	96.78276
5.	93.62408	92.2452
58.	116.5771	116.5771
59.	119.2146	119.2146
60.	119.2608	119.2608
61.	111.0299	111.0299
62.	109.2815	109.2815
63.	107.5331	107.5331

图 10.15

当选择平滑参数来最小化样本内预测误差的平方和时，改变初始值会影响最优 α 和 β 的选择。当改变初始值导致 α 和 β 的最优值不同时，预测结果也会有所不同。

当 Holt-Winters 方法能够很好地拟合数据时，通常能找到最优平滑参数。当模型拟合较差时，很难找到最小化样本内预测误差平方和的 α 和 β。

例 10.10　使用最优参数进行预测

本例使用最小化样本内预测误差平方和的 α 和 β 来预测图书销售数据。

```
. tssmooth hwinters hw3 = sales, forecast(3)
Optimal weights:
                          alpha = 0.8209
                           beta = 0.0067
penalized sum-of-squared residuals = 1975.904
          sum-of-squared residuals = 1975.904
           root mean squared error = 5.738617
```

图 10.16 显示出使用最优 α 和 β 进行的预测，将此图与图 10.14 进行比较，说明 α 和 β 的不同选择会导致不同的预测结果。新的预测不是销售额的线性下降，而是销售额的线性增长。

```
. line sales hw3 t, title("Holt-Winters Forecast with optimal alpha and beta") ytitle(> Sales) xtitle(Time)
```

10.2.4　Holt-Winters 加法模型

该方法适用于具有线性趋势和加法季节变化的序列。y_t 平滑后的序列 $\hat{y}_t$ 由下式给出：

$$\hat{y}_{t+k} = a_t + b_t k + S_{t+k} \quad t = s+1, s+2, \cdots, T \tag{10.23}$$

式中，a_t 表示截距，b_t 表示斜率，$a_t + b_t k$ 表示趋势，$k>0$，S_{t+k} 为乘法模型的季节因子，s 表示季节周期长度，月度数据 $s=12$，季度数据 $s=4$。需要用简单的方法给出季

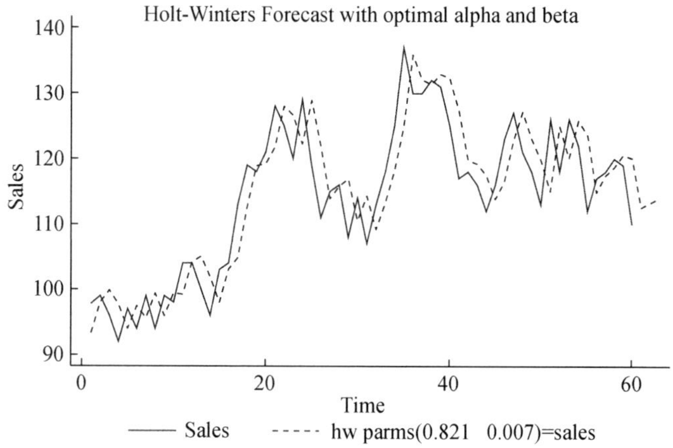

图 10.16

节因子第一年的初值,以及截距和斜率的初值。这三个系数由下面的递归式定义:

$$\begin{aligned} a_t &= a(y_t + S_{t-s}) + (1+a)(a_{t-1} + b_{t-1}) \\ b_t &= \beta(a_t - a_{t-1}) + (1-\beta)b_{t-1} \\ S_t &= \gamma(y_t - a_t) + (1-\gamma)S_{t-s} \end{aligned} \tag{10.24}$$

式中,a、β、γ 在 0~1 之间,为阻尼因子。预测值由下式计算:

$$\hat{y}_{T+k} = a_T + b_T k + S_{T+k-s} \tag{10.25}$$

式中,S_{T+k-s} 为样本数据最后一年的季节因子。

10.2.5 Holt-Winters 乘法模型

这种方法适用于具有线性趋势和乘法季节变化的序列。y_t 的平滑序列 $\hat{y}_t$ 由下式给出:

$$\hat{y}_{t+k} = (a_t + b_t k)S_{t+k} \quad t = s+1, s+2, \cdots, T \tag{10.26}$$

各参数含义同式(10.23)。需要用简单的方法给出季节因子第一年的初值,以及截距和斜率的初值。这三个系数定义如下:

$$\begin{aligned} a_t &= a\frac{y_t}{s_{t-s}} + (1-a)(a_{t-1} + b_{t-1}) \\ b_t &= \beta(a_t - a_{t-1}) + (1-\beta)b_{t-1} \\ S_t &= \gamma\frac{y_t}{a_t} + (1-\gamma)S_{t-s} \end{aligned} \tag{10.27}$$

式中,a、β、γ 在 0~1 之间,为阻尼因子。预测值由下式计算:

$$\hat{y}_{T+k} = (a_T + b_T k)S_{T+k-s} \tag{10.28}$$

式中,S_{T+k-s} 为样本数据最后一年的季节因子。

语法格式为:

```
tssmooth shwinters type [] newvar = exp if[] in[], options[]
```

菜单操作路径为:

Statistics>Time series>Smoothers/univariate forecasters>Holt-Winters seasonal smoothing

例 10.11 Holt-Winters 乘法模型预测

本例使用的是上世纪 90 年代一家新生产商火鸡销售的季度数据，这些数据具有很强的季节性成分和上升趋势，我们使用 Holt-Winters 乘法模型来预测 2000 年的销售额。因为我们已经将数据设置为季度格式，所以不需要指定 period()选项。

```
. use https://www.stata-press.com/data/r17/turksales
. tssmooth shwinters shw1 = sales, forecast(4)
Optimal weights:
                          alpha = 0.1310
                           beta = 0.1428
                          gamma = 0.2999
penalized sum-of-squared residuals = 106.1409
          sum-of-squared residuals = 106.1409
          root mean squared error  = 1.628964
```

图 10.17 描述了拟合和预测的结果。

```
. line sales shw1 t, title("Multiplicative Holt-Winters forecast") xtitle
(Time) ytit
> le(Sales)
```

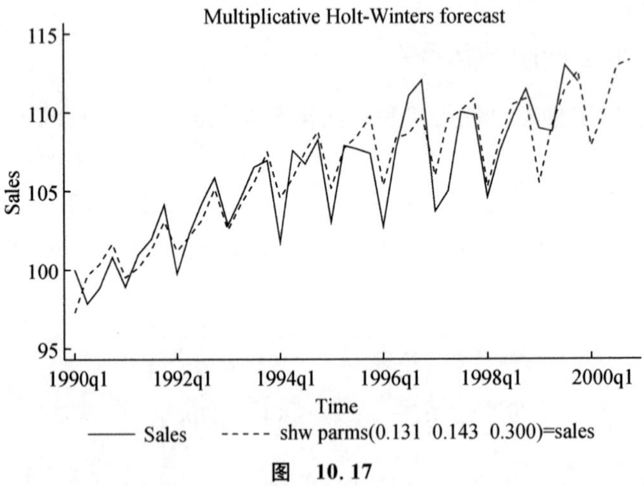

图 10.17

例 10.12 加法模型预测

本例将例 10.11 中的数据拟合到加法模型中，以预测下一年的销售额，我们使用 snt_v()选项来保存前一年在新的变量 seas 中的季节项。

```
. tssmooth shwinters shwa = sales, forecast(4) snt_v(seas) normalize ad-
ditive
Optimal weights:
```

```
                     alpha  =  0.1219
                      beta  =  0.1580
                     gamma  =  0.3340
penalized sum-of-squared residuals  =  107.6644
          sum-of-squared residuals  =  107.6644
           root mean squared error  =  1.640613
```

输出结果表明,乘法模型具有较好的样本内拟合性,图 10.18 显示,乘法模型的预测值高于加法模型。

```
. line shw1 shwa t if t>= tq(2000q1), title("Multiplicative and additive""
Holt-Winters forecasts") xtitle("Time") ytitle("Sales") legend(cols(1))
```

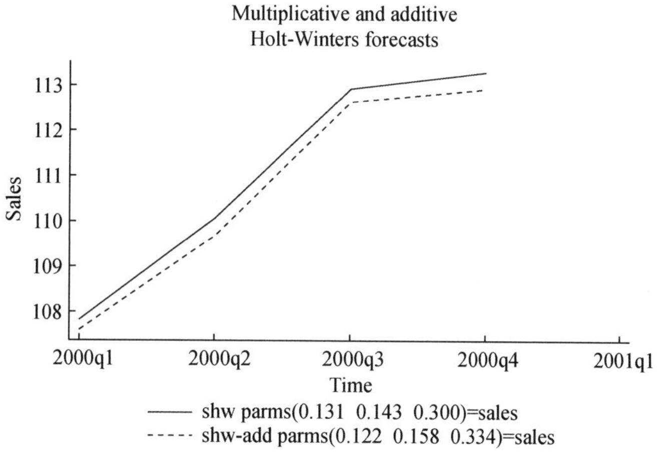

图 10.18

为了检查估计的季节性成分是否直观合理,我们列出了去年的季节性成分。

```
. list t seas if seas <.
```

运行结果如图 10.19 所示。

	t	seas
37.	1999q1	-2.7533393
38.	1999q2	-.91752573
39.	1999q3	1.8082417
40.	1999q4	1.8626233

图 10.19

输出结果表明,估计的季节项的符号与我们的判断一致。

10.3 周期成分滤波

当每个面板上有许多观测数据时,所有的过滤器都可以同时使用时间序列数据和面板数据。当使用面板数据时，计算在每个面板中分别进行。如果 y_t 是一个时间序列，那么循环因子是：

$$c_t = B(L)y_t = \sum_{j=-\infty}^{\infty} b_j y_{t-j} \tag{10.29}$$

其中，b_j 为理想滤波器的脉冲响应序列的系数，脉冲响应序列是方波还是阶跃函数的傅里叶反变换，取决于滤波器是带通滤波器还是高通滤波器，在有限序列中，需要用有限脉冲响应序列来近似计算 $\hat{b}_j$：

$$\hat{c}_t = \hat{B}_t(L)y_t = \sum_{j=-n_1}^{n_2} \hat{b}_j y_{t-j} \tag{10.30}$$

在该滤波器中实现的滤波器的无限阶脉冲响应序列是对称的和不随时间变化的，在频域内，真实循环因子与其有限估计之间的关系分别为：

$$c(\omega) = B(\omega)y(\omega) \tag{10.31}$$

$$\hat{C}(\omega) = \hat{B}(\omega)y(\omega) \tag{10.32}$$

其中，$B(\omega)$和 $\hat{B}(\omega)$为滤波器 B 和 $\hat{B}$ 的频率传递函数。公式为：

$$B(\omega) = |B(\omega)| \exp\{i\theta(\omega)\} \tag{10.33}$$

其中，$|B(\omega)|$是滤波器的增益函数，$\theta(\omega)$是滤波器的相位函数。增益函数决定了随机周期的振幅在一个特定的频率下是增加还是减少。相位函数决定了一个特定频率的周期如何在时间上向前或向后移动。在这种形式下，可以证明循环因子的谱密度函数 $f_c(\omega)$与 y_t 序列的谱密度函数 $f_y(w)$通过平方增益相关。

$$f_c(\omega) = |B(\omega)|^2 f_y(\omega) \tag{10.34}$$

ts 滤波器中的四个滤波器都有一个选项返回增益函数及其相关的比例频率 $a = \omega/\pi$，其中 $0 \leqslant \omega \leqslant \pi$。这些是$|B(\omega)|$的一致估计，来自理想线性滤波器的增益。

带通滤波器，包括 *Baxter-King*（*BK*）和 *Christiano-Fitzgerald*（*CF*）滤波器，使用方波作为理想的传递函数：

$$B(\omega) = \begin{cases} 1 & \text{if} \quad |\omega| \in [\omega_l, \omega_h] \\ 0 & \text{if} \quad |\omega| \notin [\omega_l, \omega_h] \end{cases} \tag{10.35}$$

高通滤波器，包括 *Hodrick-Prescott*（*HP*）和 *Butterworth* 滤波器，使用一个阶跃函数作为理想的传递函数：

$$B(\omega) = \begin{cases} 1 & \text{if} \quad |\omega| \geqslant \omega_h \\ 0 & \text{if} \quad |\omega| < \omega_h \end{cases} \tag{10.36}$$

与许多时间序列分析一样，基本结果是处理协方差平稳过程，附加结果是处理一些非平稳情况。我们给出协变膨胀过程的一些有用的结果，并讨论如何处理非平稳时序数据。

对自协方差，$j \in \{0, 1, \cdots$ 协方差平稳过程，$\infty\}$，指定它的方差和依赖结构。在时间序列分析的频域方法中，y_t 和自协方差是根据发生在频率 $\omega \in [-\pi, \pi]$上的独立随机周期指定的。谱密度函数 $f_y(\omega)$指定了在每个频率 ω 上的随机周期相对于 y_t 的方差的贡献，用 σ_y^2 表示，方差和自协方差可以表示为谱密度函数的积分：

$$\gamma_j = \int_{-\pi}^{\pi} e^{i\omega j} f_y(\omega) d\omega \tag{10.37}$$

其中，i 是虚数，$i=\sqrt{-1}$。

上式用来显示 y_t 的方差的多少比例可归因于特定频率范围内的随机循环。如果 $f_y(\omega=0)$，且 $\omega \in [\omega_1, \omega_2]$，那么在这些频率下的随机循环对 y_t 的方差和自协方差的贡献为零。

时间序列滤波器的目标是将原始序列转换为一个新的序列 y_t^*，其中滤波后的序列的谱密度函数 $f_{y^*}(\omega)$ 对于不需要的频率为零，对于期望的频率等于 $f_y(\omega)$。y_t 的线性滤波器可以写成：

$$y_t^* = \sum_{j=-\infty}^{\infty} \alpha_j y_{t-j} = \alpha(L) y_t \tag{10.38}$$

令 y_t 是一个无穷级数，为了查看滤波器在每个频率 ω 上对 y_t 分量的影响，我们需要一个关于 $f_{y^*}(\omega)$ 和滤波器权重 α_j 的 $f_y(\omega)$ 的表达式。Wei(2006)[①]表明，对于每个 ω，都有

$$f_{y^*}(\omega) = |\alpha(e^{i\omega})|^2 f_y(\omega) \tag{10.39}$$

其中，$|\alpha(e^{i\omega})|$ 称为滤波器的增益函数。该方程也明确表明了平方增益函数 $|\alpha(e^{i\omega})|^2$ 将原始级数的谱密度函数 $f_y(\omega)$ 转换为滤波级数的谱密度函数 $f_{y^*}(\omega)$。特别地，对于每个频率 ω，滤波序列的谱密度函数都是滤波器的增益函数与原始序列的谱密度函数的乘积。

在实际应用中，我们不能精确地找到这样一个理想的滤波器，因为对于只有有限数量的观测值的时间序列，一个理想的滤波器对滤波器系数的约束不能被满足。

理想情况下，滤波器通过增益 1 或 0 以指定频率通过或阻塞随机循环。带通滤波器，如 BK 和 CF 滤波器，在指定频率通过随机循环，并阻塞所有其他随机循环。高通滤波器，如 HP 和 Butterworth 滤波器，只允许在指定频率或超过指定频率通过随机循环并阻塞较低频率的随机循环。对于带通滤波器，设 $[\omega_0, \omega_1]$ 是期望频率的集合，所有其他频率都属于不期望频率。对于高通滤波器，设 ω_0 为仅需要 $\omega \geqslant \omega_0$ 的频率的截止频率。

语法格式为：

(1) 单变量滤波

```
tsfilter filter type[] newvar = varname if[] in[], options[]
```

(2) 多变量滤波，唯一名称

```
tsfilter filter type[] newvarlist = varlist if[] in[], options[]
```

(3) 多变量滤波，通用名称

```
tsfilter filter type[] stub* = varlist if[] in[], options[]
```

例 10.13　趋势时间序列

```
.use https://www.stata-press.com/data/r17/ipq.dta
(Federal Reserve Economic Data, St. Louis Fed)
```

---

① Wei, W. W. S. *Time Series Analysis: Univariate and Multivariate Methods* (2nd ed.). Boston: Pearson, 2006.

```
.tsline ip_ln
```

运行结果如图 10.20 所示。

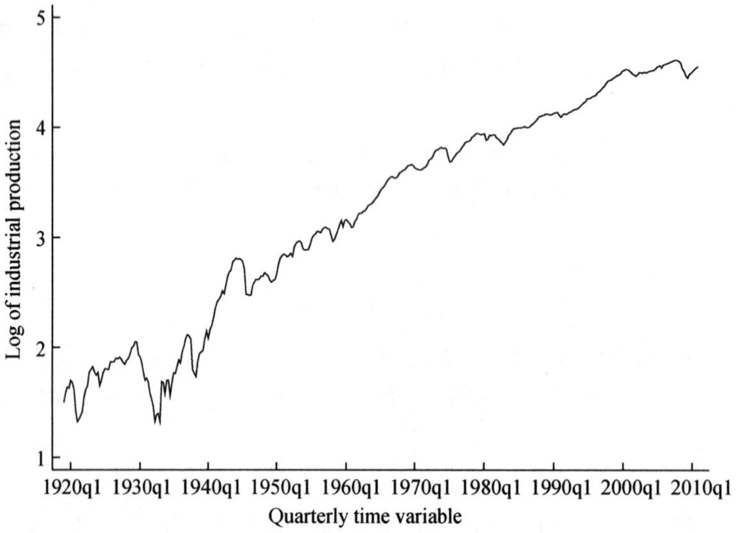

图 10.20

图 10.20 显示，ip_ln 包含一个趋势变量，时间序列可能包含确定性趋势或随机趋势，时间的多项式函数是最常见的确定性趋势，综合过程是最常见的随机趋势，综合过程是一个随机变量，必须相差一次或多次才能静止。在 tsfilter 中实现的不同滤波允许不同顺序的确定性趋势或集成过程。

现在说明 tsfilter 中实现不同滤波的四种方法，每种方法都能够消除趋势并估计业务周期成分。Burns 和 Mitchell(1946)[1]将商业数据中周期在 1.5 年到 8 年之间的振荡定义为商业周期波动。

例 10.14　消除趋势的 SMA 滤波器

我们使用滤波器过滤 ip_ln：

$$-0.2ip\_ln_{t-2}-0.2ip\_ln_{t-1}+0.8ip\_ln_{t}-0.2ip\_ln_{t+1}-0.2ip\_ln_{t+2}$$

并绘制过滤后的序列，我们甚至不需要使用 ts 滤波器来实现这个二阶 SMA 滤波，而是使用如下命令：

```
.generate ip_sma = -.2*L2.ip_ln-.2*L.ip_ln+.8*ip_ln-.2*F.ip_
ln-.2*F2.ip_ln
(4 missing values generated)
.tsline ip_sma
```

运行结果如图 10.21 所示。

该滤波已消除了趋势，因此我们没有充分的理由选择特定的 SMA 滤波。Baxter

① Burns, A. F., and W. C. Mitchell. Measuring Business Cycles. National Bureau of Economic Research, 1946.

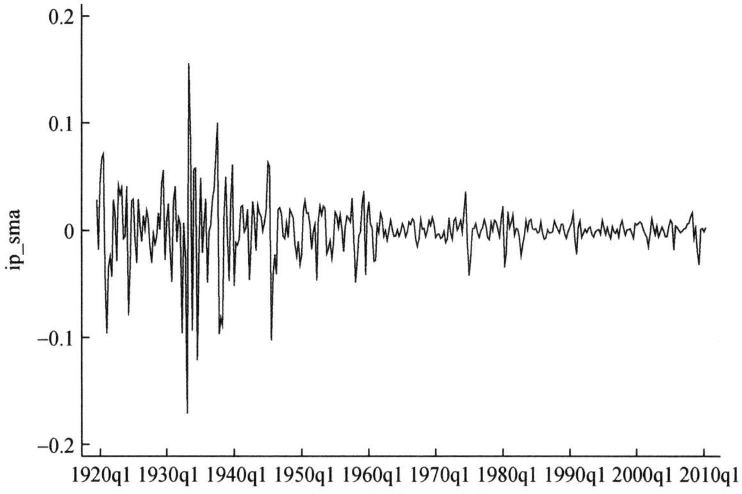

图 10.21

和 King(1999)[①]导出了一类 SMA 滤波，其系数之和为零，并尽可能接近于只保持指定的循环分量。

例 10.15 商业周期成分的 BK 估计

我们使用增加了 BK 滤波的 tsfilter bk 来估计由 6 个到 32 个周期之间的随机周期组成的业务周期成分，然后绘制出图形。

```
.tsfilter bk ip_bk = ip_ln, minperiod(6) maxperiod(32)
.tsline ip_bk
```

运行结果如图 10.22 所示。

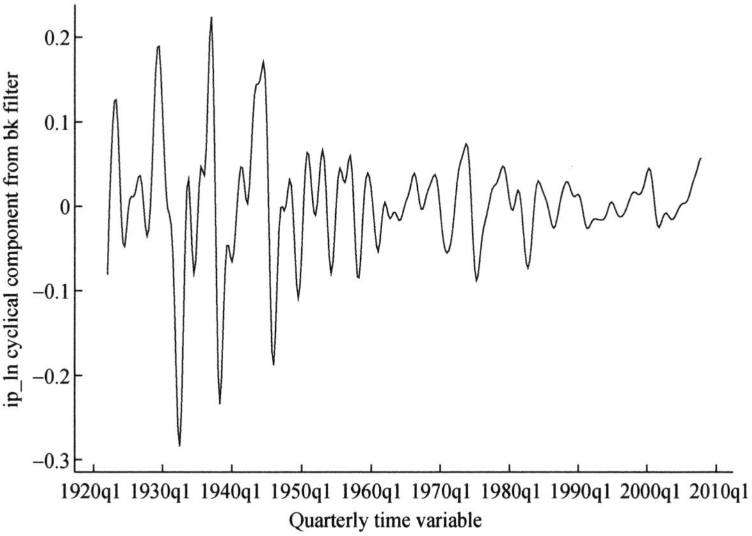

图 10.22

① Baxter, M., and R. G. King. Measuring Business Cycles: Approximate Band-pass Filters for Economic Time Series. *Review of Economics and Statistics*, 1999, 81.

我们绘制了业务周期组件的 BK 滤波估计值的周期图(见图 10.23),以自然频率显示结果,自然频率是标准频率除以 2π。我们使用 xline()选项在较低的固有频率截止处(1/32=0.03125)和较高的固有频率截止处(1/6≈0.16667)绘制垂直线。

```
.pergram ip_bk, xline(0.03125 0.16667)
```

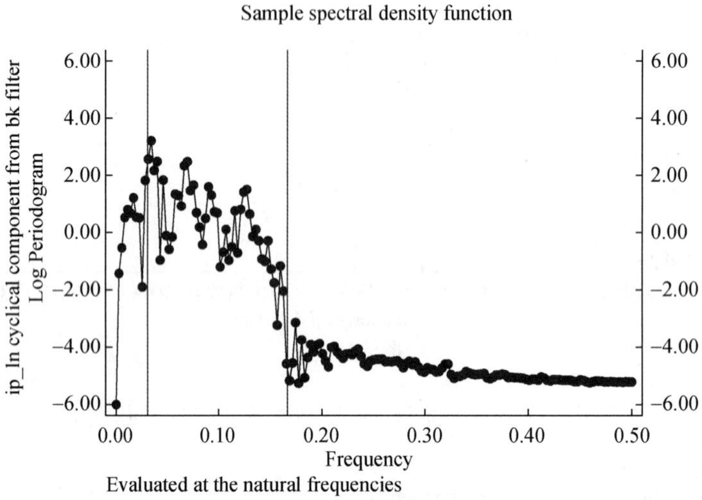

图 10.23

如果滤波器完全消除与不需要的频率相对应的随机周期,周期图将是一条最小值为−6 的垂线。周期图在指定范围外的值大于−6,这表明 BK 滤波器不能在指定频率只通过随机周期。我们还可以通过绘制 BK 滤波器的增益函数和一个理想滤波器的增益函数来评估 BK 滤波器。下面我们重新进行估计,以存储指定参数的 BK 滤波器的增益(BK 滤波器的系数和增益完全由指定的最小周期、最大周期和 SMA 滤波器的顺序决定)。

```
.drop ip_bk
.tsfilter bk ip_bk = ip_ln, minperiod(6) maxperiod(32) gain(bkgain abk)
.label variable bkgain "BK filter"
```

我们生成了理想的滤波器增益函数,并绘制出理想滤波器的增益和 BK 滤波器的增益图。(见图 10.24)

```
.generate f = _pi*(_n-1)/_N
.generate ideal = cond(f<_pi/16, 0, cond(f<_pi/3, 1,0))
.label variable ideal "Ideal filter"
.twoway line ideal f || line bkgain abk
```

图 10.24 显示,BK 滤波器的增益明显偏离理想滤波器的方波增益。通过 smaorder()选项增加对称移动平均线将导致 BK 滤波器的增益更接近于理想滤波器的增益,但代价是过滤序列中的观测值会丢失。

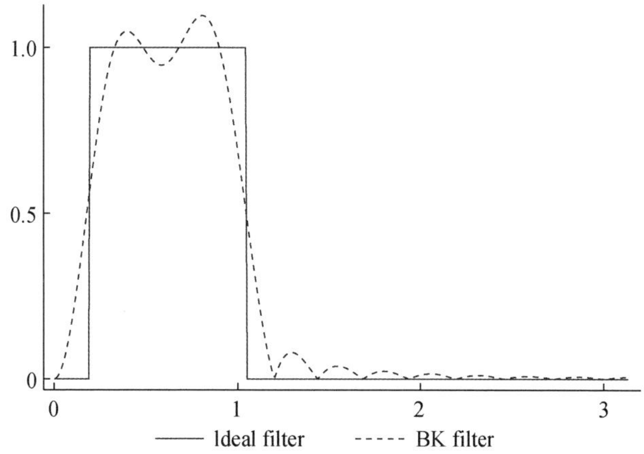

图 10.24

10.4 预 测

forecast 是一套通过求解模型来获得预测的命令，这些模型是共同确定一个或多个变量结果的方程集合。方程可以是使用 regress、ivregress、var、orreg3 等估计命令拟合的随机关系；也可以是非随机关系，称为恒等式，将一个变量表示为其他变量的确定性函数。预测模型还可能包括外生变量。forecast 命令还可用于获得单方程模型中的动态预测。

forecast 命令通过使用添加因子和类似的结构将外部信息纳入预测之中，可以指定一些模型变量的未来路径，并获得以该路径为条件的其他变量的预测结果。

forecast 命令同时适用于时间序列和面板序列，时间序列可能不包含任何间隙，而面板序列必须是强平衡的。

语法格式为：

forecast subcommand …, [, options]

各子命令及含义如表 10.3 所示。

表 10.3 子命令及含义

子命令	描述
Create	创建新模型
Estimates	将估计结果添加到当前模型中
Identity	指定一个特征(非随机方程)
Coefvector	通过一个系数向量指定一个方程
Exogenous	声明外生变量
Solve	获得单步超前或动态预测
Adjust	通过添加因式分解、替换等方式调整变量
Describe	描述一个模型

（续表）

子命令	描述
List	列出构成当前模型的所有预测命令
Clear	从内存中清除当前模型
Drop	去除预测变量
Query	检查预测模型是否已启动

例 10.16　Klein 模型预测

在介绍三阶段最小二乘法时，我们尝试使用 reg3 命令来拟合 Klein(1950)①的美国经济模型。这里我们关注的是一旦参数被估计出来，如何通过该模型进行预测。在克莱因模型(Klein 模型)中，用 7 个方程描述了 7 个内生变量。其中三个方程是随机关系，其余的都是恒等式。

$$c_t = \beta_0 + \beta_1 p_t + \beta_2 p_{t-1} + \beta_3 w_t + \varepsilon_{1t}$$
$$i_t = \beta_4 + \beta_5 p_t + \beta_6 p_{t-1} + \beta_7 k_{t-1} + \varepsilon_{2t}$$
$$wp_t = \beta_8 + \beta_9 y_t + \beta_{10} y_{t-1} + \beta_{11} yr_t + \varepsilon_{3t}$$
$$y_t = c_t + i_t + g_t$$
$$p_t = y_t - t_t - wp_t$$
$$k_t = k_{t-1} + i_t$$
$$w_t = wg_t + wp_t$$

本模型中的变量定义如表 10.4 所示。

表 10.4　变量定义

变量名称	描述	类型
c	消费	内生变量
p	企业利润	内生变量
wp	企业工资	内生变量
wg	政府部门工资	外生变量
w	总工资	内生变量
i	投资	内生变量
k	股本	内生变量
y	国民收入	内生变量
g	政府支出	外生变量
t	间接营业税＋净出口	外生变量
yr	时间趋势＝年份－1931	外生变量

我们的模型有 4 个外生变量：政府部门工资(wg)、政府支出(g)、时间趋势(yr)以及间接营业税和净出口(t)。为了作出样本外的预测，我们必须在求解模型之前，在整个预测范围内填充这些变量。

① Klein, L. R. *Economic Fluctuations in the United States 1921—1941*. New York: Wiley, 1950.

我们将说明拟合模型和预测模型的整个过程。在建立模型之前，我们首先通过加载数据集并调用 reg3 来估计随机方程的参数。

```
. use https://www.stata-press.com/data/r17/klein2.dta
. reg3 (c p L.p w) (i p L.p L.k) (wp y L.y yr), endog(w p y) exog(t wg g)
Three-stage least-squares regression
```

运行结果如图 10.25 所示。

Equation	Obs	Parms	RMSE	"R-sq"	chi2	P
c	21	3	.9443305	0.9801	864.59	0.0000
i	21	3	1.446736	0.8258	162.98	0.0000
wp	21	3	.7211282	0.9863	1594.75	0.0000

	Coef.	Std. Err.	z	P>|z|	[95% Conf.	Interval]
c						
p						
--.	.1248904	.1081291	1.16	0.248	-.0870387	.3368194
L1.	.1631439	.1004382	1.62	0.104	-.0337113	.3599992
w	.790081	.0379379	20.83	0.000	.715724	.8644379
_cons	16.44079	1.304549	12.60	0.000	13.88392	18.99766
i						
p						
--.	-.0130791	.1618962	-0.08	0.936	-.3303898	.3042316
L1.	.7557238	.1529331	4.94	0.000	.4559805	1.055467
k						
L1.	-.1948482	.0325307	-5.99	0.000	-.2586072	-.1310893
_cons	28.17785	6.793768	4.15	0.000	14.86231	41.49339
wp						
y						
--.	.4004919	.0318134	12.59	0.000	.3381388	.462845
L1.	.181291	.0341588	5.31	0.000	.1143411	.2482409
yr	.149674	.0279352	5.36	0.000	.094922	.2044261
_cons	1.797216	1.115854	1.61	0.107	-.3898181	3.984251

Endogenous variables: c i wp w p y
Exogenous variables: L.p L.k L.y yr t wg g

图 10.25

reg3 的输出表明，总共有 6 个内生变量，尽管模型中实际上有 7 个。这种差异源于 Klein 模型的第 6 个公式。股本(k)是内生变量投资的函数，因此本身是内生变量，但却没有出现在模型的随机方程中，所以我们没有在 reg3 的 endog()选项中设定。从纯粹估计的角度来看，资本存量变量的同期值与模型无关，尽管它确实在解决模型问题方面发挥了作用。接下来，我们使用 estimates store 保存估计结果：

```
.estimates store klein
```

现在使用预测命令来定义模型，我们首先建立 Stata 初始化的一个新模型，将其命名为 kleinmodel：

```
.forecast create kleinmodel
Forecast model kleinmodel started
```

然后将所有方程添加到模型中。为了添加使用 reg3 拟合的三个随机方程，我们使用 forecast estimates：

```
.forecast estimates klein
Added estimation results from reg3
Forecast model kleinmodel now contains 3 endogenous variables
```

该命令告诉 Stata 找到存储为 klein 的估计值，并将它们添加到模型中。

forecast estimates 使用这些估计结果来确定有 3 个内生变量(c、i 和 wp)，它将保存估计参数和其他信息，解决预测问题需要获得对这些变量的预测。预测估计证实了我们的请求，报告表明增加的估计结果来自规则 3。

预测模型有 3 个内生变量，因为 reg3 命令包含 3 个左侧变量，我们在 reg3 的内生变量 endog()选项中指定 3 个额外的内生变量，因此 reg3 总共报告了 6 个内生变量，这与预测无关，最重要的是模型中左侧变量的数量。

还需要指定 4 个恒等式，即 Klein 模型的后四个方程，以确定模型中的其他 4 个内生变量，为此使用 forecast identity 命令：

```
.forecast identity y = c + i + g
Forecast model kleinmodel now contains 4 endogenous variables.
.forecast identity p = y - t - wp
Forecast model kleinmodel now contains 5 endogenous variables.
.forecast identity k = L.k + i
Forecast model kleinmodel now contains 6 endogenous variables.
.forecast identity w = wg + wp
Forecast model kleinmodel now contains 7 endogenous variables.
```

最后告诉 Stata 关于这 4 个外生变量的情况，对此可用预测的外部命令来实现：

```
.forecast exogenous wg
Forecast model kleinmodel now contains 1 declared exogenous variable.
.forecast exogenous g
Forecast model kleinmodel now contains 2 declared exogenous variables.
.forecast exogenous t
```

```
Forecast model kleinmodel now contains 3 declared exogenous variables.
.forecast exogenous yr
Forecast model kleinmodel now contains 4 declared exogenous variables.
.forecast exogenous wg g t yr
Forecast model kleinmodel now contains 4 declared exogenous variables.
```

为了获得这些向前一步预测，我们键入如下命令：

```
.forecast solve, prefix(s_) begin(1921) static

Computing static forecasts for model kleinmodel.
---------------------------------------------------------

Starting period: 1921
Ending period: 1941
Forecast prefix: s_
Forecast 7 variables spanning 21 periods.
---------------------------------------------------------
```

我们指定要求进行预测的第一年是1921年。我们的模型包括滞后一个时期的变量，因为数据始于1920年，1921年是可以评估模型的所有方程的第一年。如果我们不指定 begin(1921)选项，将在1941年开始预测。默认情况下，预测求解会寻找任何内生变量包含缺失值的最早时间段，并在该时间段内开始预测。

10.5 参数谱密度估计

如果 y_t 是一个具有绝对可加自变量的协方差静止过程，其谱密度函数为：

$$g_y(\omega)=\frac{1}{2\pi}\gamma_0+\frac{1}{\pi}\sum_{k=1}^{\infty}\gamma_k\cos(\omega k) \tag{10.40}$$

其中，$g_y(\omega)$是频率为 ω 时的 y_t 的谱密度函数，而 γ_k 是 y_t 的第 k 个自协方差。对该方程的每一边进行傅里叶反变换，得到相应的结果：

$$\gamma_k=\int_{-\pi}^{\pi}g_y(\omega)\mathrm{e}^{\mathrm{i}\omega k}\mathrm{d}\omega \tag{10.41}$$

其中，i 是虚数，$\mathrm{i}=\sqrt{-1}$。

当 $k=0$ 时可得：

$$\gamma_0=\int_{-\pi}^{\pi}g_y(\omega)\mathrm{d}\omega \tag{10.42}$$

这意味着 y_t 的方差可以根据 $g_y(\omega)$来分解。$g_y(\omega)\mathrm{d}\omega$ 是 y_t 的方差中归因于区间$(\omega,\omega+\mathrm{d}\omega)$的随机成分部分。谱密度取决于测量 y_t 的单位，因为它依赖于 γ_0。

将式(10.40)两侧除以 γ_0，得到 y_t 的无标度谱密度：

$$f_y(\omega)=\frac{1}{2\pi}+\frac{1}{\pi}\sum_{k=1}^{\infty}\rho_k\cos(\omega k) \tag{10.43}$$

同时有：

$$\int_{-\pi}^{\pi} f_y(\omega)\mathrm{d}\omega = 1 \tag{10.44}$$

所以，$f_y(\omega)\mathrm{d}\omega$ 也是 y_t 的方差中归因于区间$(\omega, \omega+\mathrm{d}\omega)$的随机成分部分。

语法格式为：

Psdensity type[] newvarsd newvarf if[] in[], options[]

菜单操作路径为：

Statistics>Time series>Postestimation>Parametric spectral density

例 10.17　参数谱密度

本例考虑美国制造业员工数量的变化。

```
.use https://www.stata-press.com/data/r17/manemp2.dta
(FRED data: Number of manufacturing employees in U.S.)
.tsline D.manemp, yline(-0.206)
```

运行结果如图 10.26 所示。

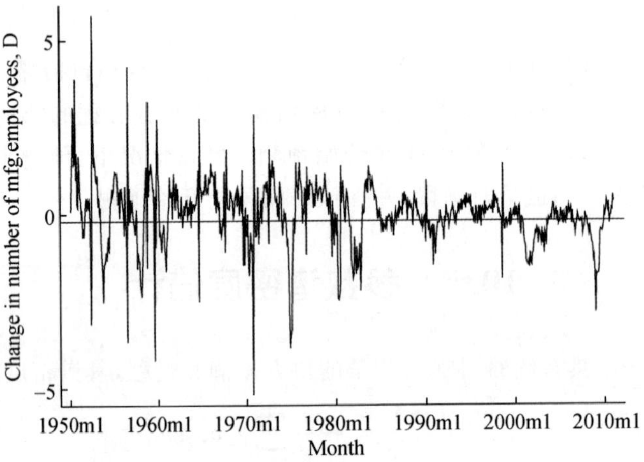

图　10.26

我们在−0.206 的样本平均值处添加一条水平线，以强调独立同分布过程生成的数据在平均值上下的运行比我们预期的要多。

使用 arima 估计一个一阶自回归(AR(1))模型的参数。在形式上，AR(1)模型公式如下：

$$y_t = \alpha y_{t-1} + \varepsilon_t$$

其中，y_t 为因变量，α 为自回归系数，t 为独立同分布误差项。

```
.arima D.manemp, ar(1) noconstant
ARIMA regression
Sample: 1950m2—2011m2                         Number of obs  =  733
                                              Wald chi2(1)   =  730.51
Log likelihood = -870.6479                    Prob>chi2      =  0.0000
```

运行结果如图 10.27 所示。

D.manemp	Coef.	OPG Std. Err.	z	P>|z|	[95% Conf. Interval]	
ARMA						
ar						
L1.	.5179561	.0191638	27.03	0.000	.4803959	.5555164
/sigma	.7934554	.0080636	98.40	0.000	.777651	.8092598

图 10.27

Note: The test of the variance against zero is one sided, and the two-sided confidence interval is truncated at zero

自回归系数为 0.518,表明在该序列中存在显著的正自相关。协方差平稳过程的谱密度在 0 左右是对称的。按照惯例,可通过 psdensity 估计区间[0,π)的谱密度。

```
.psdensity psden1 omega
.line psden1 omega
```

运行结果如图 10.28 所示。

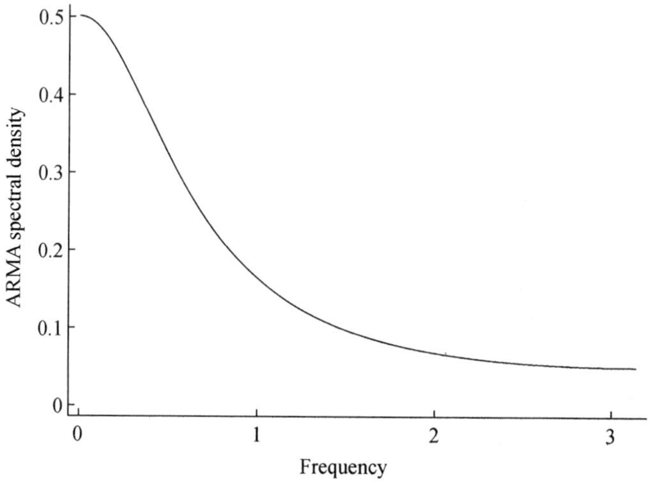

图 10.28

图 10.28 是一个具有正系数的 AR(1)过程的谱密度的典型图像。曲线在频率为 0 时最高,并向零或正渐近线逐渐变小。估计的谱密度告诉我们,低频随机成分是具有正自回归系数的 AR(1)过程中最重要的随机成分。α 越接近于 1,低频成分相对于高频成分就越重要。为了说明这一点,我们绘制了 $\alpha=0.1$ 和 $\alpha=0.9$ 的 AR(1)模型所暗示的谱密度图。(见图 10.29)

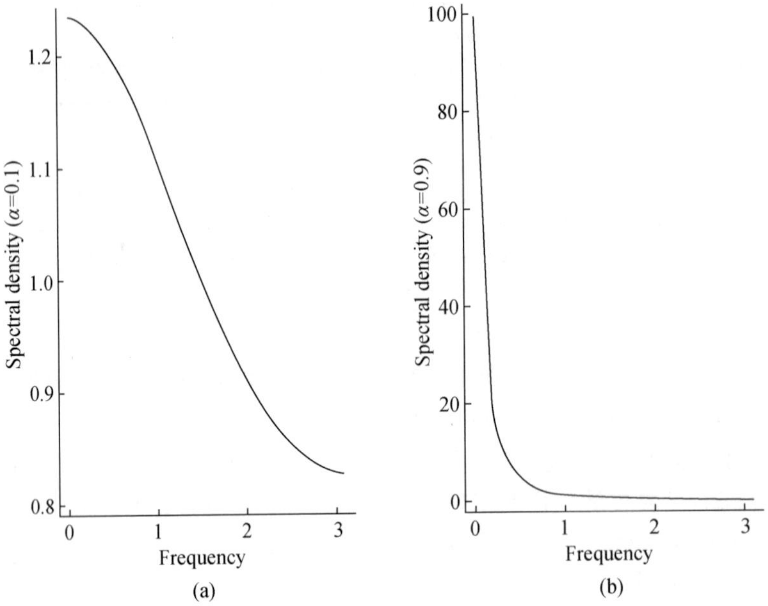

图　10.29

当 α 越来越接近于 1 时,谱密度图越来越接近于频率为 0 时的峰值,这意味着只有最低频率的因素是重要的。

10.6　滚动窗口和递归估计

rolling 命令可在一系列观察窗口中的每一个窗口上执行命令并存储结果。它可以执行通常称为滚动回归、递归回归和反向递归回归的操作。然而,rolling 不仅仅限于线性回归分析,任何将结果存储在 e()或 r()中的命令都可以与 rolling 一起使用。

语法格式为:

(1) 使用 tsset 数据,用 20 期滚动窗口为 y 拟合一个 AR(1)模型

```
rolling, window(20): arima y, ar(1)
```

(2) 具有固定起始期的递归滚动窗口估计

```
rolling, window(20) recursive: arima y, ar(1)
```

(3) 具体说明此估计起止时间为 1990 年到 2011 年

```
rolling, window(20) recursive start(1990) end(2011): arima y, ar(1)
```

(4) 固定最后一个周期的反向递归滚动窗口估计

```
rolling, window(20) rrecursive start(1990) end(2011): arima y, ar(1)
```

(5) 将来自 20 期的滚动窗口估计的结果保存到新的数据集 mydata.dta

```
rolling, window(20) saving(mydata): arima y, ar(1)
```

注意:任何接受滚动命令的前缀都可以被替换为 arima。

菜单操作路径为:

Statistics>Time series>Rolling-window and recursive estimation

例 10.18　递归估计

本例以 IBM 股票(ibm)、标准普尔 500 指数(spx)和短期利率(irx)的每日回报的数据为样本,希望通过使用每个日期的前 200 个交易日来创建一个包含 IBM 测试版的序列数据。

```
.use https://www.stata-press.com/data/r17/ibm.dta
(Source: Yahoo! Finance)
.tsset t
    time variable: t, 1 to 494
            delta: 1 unit
.generate ibmadj = ibm - irx
(1 missing value generated)
.generate spxadj = spx - irx
(1 missing value generated)
.rolling _b _se, window(200) saving(betas, replace) keep(date): regress ibmadj spxadj
file betas.dta saved
```

数据集既有一个连续运行的时间变量 *t*,也有一个测量日历日期的日期变量 *date*,因此在周末和假期有间隙。如果使用日期变量作为时间变量,rolling 命令将使用包含 200 个自然日而不是 200 个交易日的窗口,每个窗口将不会有 200 个观察结果。我们使用 keep(date)选项,这样就可以在处理结果数据集时引用 *date* 变量。

可以列出通过 rolling 创建的数据集的一部分。

```
.use betas, clear
(rolling: regress)
.sort date
.list in 1/3, abbreviate(10) table
```

运行结果如图 10.30 所示。

	start	end	date	_b_spxadj	_b_cons	_se_spxadj	_se_cons
1.	1	200	16oct2003	1.043422	-.0181504	.0658531	.0748295
2.	2	201	17oct2003	1.039024	-.0126876	.0656893	.074609
3.	3	202	20oct2003	1.038371	-.0235616	.0654591	.0743851

图　10.30

变量的 start 和 end 表示每次滚动调用回归时使用的第一次和最后一次观察,并且 *date* 变量包含与 end 所表示的周期对应的日历日期。其余变量是回归后的估计系数和标准误差。_b_spxadj 包含估计的 beta,_b_cons 包含估计的 alpha,_se_spxadj 和_se_cons 有相应的标准误差。

最后，计算 beta 的置信区间，并检查它们是如何随时间变化的。

```
. generate lower = _b_spxadj - 1.96 * _se_spxadj
. generate upper = _b_spxadj + 1.96 * _se_spxadj
. twoway (line _b_spxadj date) (rline lower upper date) if date >= td
(1oct2003),ytitle("Beta")
```

运行结果如图 10.31 所示。

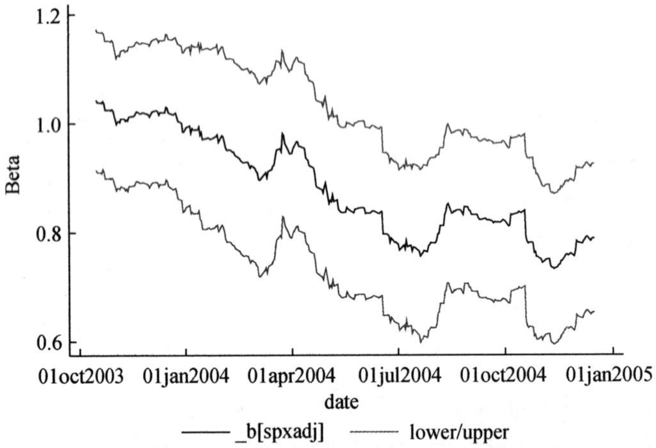

图 10.31

2004 年以后，IBM 的股票回报受到整体市场回报的影响较小。从 2004 年 6 月开始，IBM 的 beta 在 95%置信水平上有显著不同。除了滚动窗口分析之外，还可以执行递归分析，再次假设我们在连续 100 个时间点收集了数据，现在键入如下命令：

```
. rolling _b, window(20) recursive clear: regress depvar indepvar
```

Stata 将首先使用观测值 1—20 对 depvar 进行回归，然后使用观测值 1—21、观测值 1—22 等进行回归，以此类推，最后使用所有 100 个观测值进行回归。在这种情况下，起点是固定的，并依次增加观测值的数量。而在滚动回归中，观测值的数量是固定的，但起点和终点是移动的。

第 11 章 时序结构转换分析

11.1 马尔可夫转换模型

马尔可夫转换模型用于在有限的一组数据上未被观察到的状态转换的序列,允许过程在每个状态中以不同的方式演化。这种转换符合马尔可夫链(Markov chains)过程,即从一种状态过渡到另一种状态的时间和持续时间是随机的。这类模型可用于理解经济增长在扩张和衰退之间过渡的时间,以及每个周期的持续时间。

马尔可夫链过程如下:时序过程 s_t 是一个不可减、非周期的马尔可夫链,$\pi=(\pi_1,\cdots,\pi_k)$,从其遍历分布开始;s_t 等于 $j\in(1,\cdots,k)$的概率仅取决于最近的状态 s_{t-1},即

$$\Pr(s_t=j \mid s_{t-1}=i)=p_{ij} \tag{11.1}$$

从一种状态到另一种状态的所有可能转换都可以收集在 $k\times k$ 转换矩阵中,即

$$\boldsymbol{P}=\begin{bmatrix} p_{11} & \cdots & p_{k1} \\ p_{12} & \cdots & p_{k2} \\ \vdots & \ddots & \vdots \\ p_{1k} & \cdots & p_{kk} \end{bmatrix} \tag{11.2}$$

由 $\sum_{j=1}^{k} p_{ij}=1$ 可知:

$$p_{ij}=\frac{\exp(-q_{ij})}{1+\exp(-q_{i1})+\exp(-q_{i2})+\cdots+\exp(-q_{i(k-1)})},\quad j\in\{1,2,\cdots,k-1\} \tag{11.3}$$

规范化可得:

$$p_{ij}=\frac{1}{1+\exp(-q_{i1})+\exp(-q_{i2})+\cdots+\exp(-q_{i(k-1)})} \tag{11.4}$$

常用的马尔可夫转换模型有马尔可夫转换动态回归(Markovs witching dynamic regression,MSDR)模型和马尔可夫转换自回归(Markovs witching AR,MSAR)模型。

MSDR 模型允许在过程状态改变后进行快速调整。这类模型通常用于对月度和更高频率的数据建模。当时序在时间 t 处于状态 s 时,MSDR 模型表达式为:

$$y_t=\mu_{s_t}+\boldsymbol{x}_t\boldsymbol{\alpha}+\boldsymbol{z}_t\boldsymbol{\beta}_{s_t}+\boldsymbol{\varepsilon}_s \tag{11.5}$$

其中，y_t 是因变量；μ_{s_t} 是状态相关的截距；$\boldsymbol{x}_t$ 是外生解释变量的向量，是不随状态变化系数 $\boldsymbol{\alpha}$ 的解释变量；$\boldsymbol{z}_t$ 是具有状态依赖性系数 $\boldsymbol{\beta}_{s_t}$ 的外生变量向量；$\boldsymbol{\varepsilon}_s$ 是平均值为 0 和状态相关方差为 σ_s^2 的独立同分布正态误差；$\boldsymbol{x}_t$ 和 $\boldsymbol{z}_t$ 可以包含 y_t 的滞后项。MS-DR 模型允许状态根据马尔可夫链过程进行切换。

MSAR 模型的表达式为：

$$y_t = \mu_{s_t} + \boldsymbol{x}_t\boldsymbol{\alpha} + \boldsymbol{z}_t\boldsymbol{\beta}_{s_t} + \sum_{i=1}^{p}\phi_{i,s_t}(y_{t-i} - \mu_{s_{t-i}} - \boldsymbol{x}_{t-i}\boldsymbol{\alpha} - \boldsymbol{z}_{t-i}\boldsymbol{\beta}_{s_{t-i}}) + \varepsilon_{s_t} \quad (11.6)$$

式中，ϕ_{i,s_t} 是状态 s_t 的第 i 个 AR 项；其他符号含义同 MSDR 模型。

马尔可夫转换模型利用最大似然估计法估计参数。

设被解释变量 y_t 的条件密度为 $f(y_t \mid s_t=i, y_{t-1}; \boldsymbol{\theta})$，$y_t$ 的边缘密度是通过将条件密度按其各自的概率加权得到的：

$$f(y_t \mid \boldsymbol{\theta}) = \sum_{i=1}^{k} f(y_t \mid s_t = i, y_{t-1}; \boldsymbol{\theta})\Pr(s_t = i; \boldsymbol{\theta})$$

则似然函数为：

$$L(\boldsymbol{\theta}) = \sum_{t=1}^{T}\log f(y_t \mid y_{t-1}; \boldsymbol{\theta}) \quad (11.7)$$

式中，$f(y_t \mid y_{t-1}; \boldsymbol{\theta}) = \mathbf{1}'(\xi_{t\mid t-1} \odot \boldsymbol{\eta}_t)$

1. 平滑概率

设 $\xi_{t|T}$，$t<T$，表示条件概率 $\Pr(s_t = i \mid y_T; \boldsymbol{\theta})$ 的 $k\times1$ 向量，代表时间 T 内的可用观测值得到 $s_t = i$ 的概率。平滑概率为：

$$\xi_{t\mid T} = \xi_{t\mid t} \odot \{\boldsymbol{P}'(\xi_{t+1\mid T}(\div)\xi_{t+1\mid t})\} \quad (11.8)$$

式中的(÷)表示元素乘法。利用迭代法可以得到平滑概率序列。

2. 无条件状态概率

对数似然函数具有从无条件状态开始的递归结构概率 $\xi_{1|0}$。这些无条件状态概率是未知的，默认情况下，可通过选项 p_0(转换)，根据模型的条件转移概率和马尔可夫结构估计得到。具体来说，无条件状态概率向量的计算公式为：

$$\pi = (\boldsymbol{A}'\boldsymbol{A})^{-1}\boldsymbol{A}'\boldsymbol{e}_{k+1} \quad (11.9)$$

$$\boldsymbol{A} = \begin{bmatrix} \boldsymbol{I}_k - \boldsymbol{P} \\ \mathbf{1}' \end{bmatrix} \quad (11.10)$$

式中，$\boldsymbol{I}_k$ 表示 $k \times k$ 单位矩阵，e_k 表示 $\boldsymbol{I}_k$ 的第 k 列。

语法格式如下：

(1) MSDR 模型估计

mswitch dr depvar [nonswitch_varlist] [if] [in] [, options]

(2) MSAR 模型估计

mswitch ar depvar [nonswitch_varlist], ar(numlist) [msar_options options]

mswitch 命令的参数及选项描述如表 11.1 所示。

表 11.1 mswitch 参数及选项描述

参数及选项	类型	功能描述
mswitch	Stata 命令	估计马尔可夫转换模型
dr	必要项	回归方式定义为动态回归(dr)
depvar	必要项	变量名称
nonswitch_varlist	选用项	具有状态不变系数的变量列表
if	选用项	定义建模分析的样本数据条件
in	选用项	定义建模分析的样本数据范围
ar	必要项	回归方式定义为自回归(ar)
options	Main	指定状态数;默认值为 2 个状态
		指定具有切换系数的变量;默认情况下,常数项依赖于状态,除非指定了(,noconstant)转换
		允许一个状态不变的常数项;可以使用(,noconstant)转换指定
		指定依赖于状态的方差参数;默认情况下,方差参数在所有状态下都是常数
		指定初始无条件概率,类型包括过渡、固定或平滑;默认值为 p_0(转换)
		应用指定的线性约束
	SE/Robust	vetype 可以是 oim 或 robust
	Reporting	设定置信水平;默认为级别(95)
		不显示约束条件
		控制列和列格式、行间距、线宽、省略变量的显示以及空单元格和因子变量标记
	EM options	指定期望最大化(EM)迭代次数;默认值为 emitrate(10)
		显示 EM 迭代日志
		将 EM 迭代显示为点
	Maximization	控制最大化过程
		显示图例而不是统计信息
msar_options	Model	指定自相关 AR 的阶数
		指定状态相关 AR 的系数

(3) 估计后预测

predict [type] {stub* | newvarlist} [if] [in] [, statistic options]

菜单操作路径为:

Statistics>Postestimation

(4) 估计后估计

列表显示转移概率:

estat transition [, level(#)]

列表显示正态预期持续期:

estat duration [, level(#)]

菜单操作路径为:

Statistics>Time series>Markov-switching model

例 11.1　马尔可夫转换模型

假设要为联邦基金利率建模：$r_t = \mu_{s_t} + \varepsilon_t$，其中，$r_t$ 为联邦基金利率，s_t 为状态，μ_{s_t} 为每个状态的均值。在数据集 usmacro 中，我们从美联储经济数据库中获得了 1954 年第三季度至 2010 年第四季度的系列数据，该数据库是一个由圣路易斯联邦储备银行提供的宏观经济数据库。

```
* 清空内存，下载数据
.clear
.use https://www.stata-press.com/data/r17/usmacro
* 转换截距的马尔可夫转换动态回归
.mswitch dr fedfunds
```

运行结果如图 11.1 所示。

Markov-switching dynamic regression

Sample: 1954q3 thru 2010q4	Number of obs = 226
Number of states = 2	AIC = 4.5455
Unconditional probabilities: transition	HQIC = 4.5760
	SBIC = 4.6211
Log likelihood = -508.63592	

fedfunds	Coefficient	Std. err.	z	P>|z|	[95% conf.	interval]
State1						
_cons	3.70877	.1767083	20.99	0.000	3.362428	4.055112
State2						
_cons	9.556793	.2999889	31.86	0.000	8.968826	10.14476
sigma	2.107562	.1008692			1.918851	2.314831
p11	.9820939	.0104002			.9450805	.9943119
p21	.0503587	.0268434			.0173432	.1374344

图 11.1

```
* 转换截距和参数的 MSDR 模型
.mswitch dr fedfunds, switch(L.fedfunds)
```

运行结果如图 11.2 所示。

```
Markov-switching dynamic regression

Sample: 1954q4 thru 2010q4                          Number of obs =     225
Number of states = 2                                AIC           =  2.4152
Unconditional probabilities: transition             HQIC          =  2.4581
                                                    SBIC          =  2.5215
Log likelihood = -264.71069
```

fedfunds	Coefficient	Std. err.	z	P>|z|	[95% conf.	interval]
State1						
fedfunds						
L1.	.7631424	.0337234	22.63	0.000	.6970457	.8292392
_cons	.724457	.2886657	2.51	0.012	.1586826	1.290231
State2						
fedfunds						
L1.	1.061174	.0185031	57.35	0.000	1.024908	1.097439
_cons	-.0988764	.1183837	-0.84	0.404	-.3309043	.1331515
sigma	.6915759	.0358644			.6247373	.7655653
p11	.6378175	.1202616			.3883032	.830089
p21	.1306295	.0495924			.0600137	.2612432

图 11.2

* 两个状态的 MSDR 模型拟合泰勒规则模型

```
.mswitch dr fedfunds, switch(L.fedfunds ogap inflation)
```

运行结果如图 11.3 所示。

```
Markov-switching dynamic regression

Sample: 1955q3 thru 2010q4                    Number of obs =    222
Number of states = 2                          AIC           = 2.1645
Unconditional probabilities: transition       HQIC          = 2.2325
                                              SBIC          = 2.3331
Log likelihood = -229.25614
```

fedfunds	Coefficient	Std. err.	z	P>|z|	[95% conf.	interval]
State1						
fedfunds						
L1.	.8314458	.0333236	24.95	0.000	.7661328	.8967587
ogap	.1355425	.0294113	4.61	0.000	.0778975	.1931875
inflation	-.0273928	.0408057	-0.67	0.502	-.1073704	.0525849
_cons	.6554954	.1373889	4.77	0.000	.386218	.9247727
State2						
fedfunds						
L1.	.9292574	.0270852	34.31	0.000	.8761713	.9823435
ogap	.0343072	.0240138	1.43	0.153	-.0127589	.0813733
inflation	.2125275	.0297351	7.15	0.000	.1542477	.2708072
_cons	-.0944924	.1279231	-0.74	0.460	-.3452171	.1562324
sigma	.5764495	.0302562			.5200968	.638908
p11	.7279288	.0929915			.5159594	.8703909
p21	.2114578	.0641179			.1120643	.3629704

图 11.3

* 三个状态的 MSDR 模型拟合泰勒规则模型

```
. mswitch dr fedfunds, switch(L.fedfunds ogap inflation) states(3)
```

运行结果如图 11.4 所示。

```
Markov-switching dynamic regression

Sample: 1955q3 thru 2010q4                       Number of obs =     222
Number of states = 3                             AIC           = 1.8819
Unconditional probabilities: transition          HQIC          = 1.9995
                                                 SBIC          = 2.1732
Log likelihood = -189.89493
```

fedfunds	Coefficient	Std. err.	z	P>|z|	[95% conf.	interval]
State1						
fedfunds						
L1.	.846454	.033352	25.38	0.000	.7810853	.9118228
ogap	.1201955	.0232714	5.16	0.000	.0745843	.1658067
inflation	-.0425594	.0354264	-1.20	0.230	-.1119939	.026875
_cons	.5261294	.1266917	4.15	0.000	.2778183	.7744405
State2						
fedfunds						
L1.	.9690068	.0264821	36.59	0.000	.9171028	1.020911
ogap	.0464138	.0200191	2.32	0.020	.007177	.0856505
inflation	.1298916	.0246792	5.26	0.000	.0815212	.178262
_cons	-.0034049	.1073025	-0.03	0.975	-.2137139	.2069041
State3						
fedfunds						
L1.	.41787	.0809388	5.16	0.000	.2592328	.5765072
ogap	.1075425	.1131628	0.95	0.342	-.1142525	.3293376
inflation	.9099208	.0732995	12.41	0.000	.7662564	1.053585
_cons	.601772	.8893754	0.68	0.499	-1.141372	2.344916
sigma	.4383762	.0247955			.3923749	.4897706
p11	.7253661	.0807813			.5440001	.8539618
p12	.2564083	.0784302			.1334304	.4357374
p21	.1641277	.0548573			.0822961	.3006697
p22	.799429	.0578692			.6627017	.8899373
p31	.6178137	.348164			.0824337	.966763
p32	.3821863	.3481641			.033237	.9175664

图 11.4

```
* 清空内存,下载数据集
.clear
```

```
. use https://www.stata-press.com/data/r17/snp500
```

*转换方差

```
. mswitch dr areturns, switch(L.areturns) varswitch
```

运行结果如图 11.5 所示。

Markov-switching dynamic regression

Sample: 2004w19 thru 2014w18　　Number of obs = 520
Number of states = 2　　AIC = 2.8992
Unconditional probabilities: transition　　HQIC = 2.9249
SBIC = 2.9647

Log likelihood = -745.7977

areturns	Coefficient	Std. err.	z	P>|z|	[95% conf.	interval]
State1						
areturns						
L1.	.0790744	.0301862	2.62	0.009	.0199105	.1382384
_cons	.7641424	.0782852	9.76	0.000	.6107063	.9175784
State2						
areturns						
L1.	.527953	.0857841	6.15	0.000	.3598193	.6960867
_cons	1.972771	.2784204	7.09	0.000	1.427077	2.518465
sigma1	.5895792	.0517753			.4963544	.7003134
sigma2	1.605333	.1262679			1.375985	1.872908
p11	.7530865	.0634386			.6097999	.856167
p21	.6825357	.0662574			.5414358	.7965346

图　11.5

*清空内存，下载数据集

```
. clear
. use https://www.stata-press.com/data/r17/rgnp
```

*转换截距的 MSAR 模型

```
. mswitch ar rgnp, ar(1/4)
```

运行结果如图 11.6 所示。

```
Markov-switching autoregression

Sample: 1952q2 thru 1984q4                    Number of obs =     131
Number of states = 2                          AIC           =  2.9048
Unconditional probabilities: transition       HQIC          =  2.9851
                                              SBIC          =  3.1023
Log likelihood = -181.26339
```

rgnp	Coefficient	Std. err.	z	P>|z|	[95% conf.	interval]
rgnp						
ar						
L1.	.0134871	.1199941	0.11	0.911	-.2216971	.2486713
L2.	-.0575212	.137663	-0.42	0.676	-.3273357	.2122933
L3.	-.2469833	.1069103	-2.31	0.021	-.4565235	-.037443
L4.	-.2129214	.1105311	-1.93	0.054	-.4295583	.0037155
State1						
_cons	-.3588127	.2645396	-1.36	0.175	-.8773007	.1596753
State2						
_cons	1.163517	.0745187	15.61	0.000	1.017463	1.309571
sigma	.7690048	.0667396			.6487179	.9115957
p11	.754671	.0965189			.5254555	.8952432
p21	.0959153	.0377362			.0432569	.1993221

图 11.6

* 转换 AR 参数

.mswitch ar rgnp, ar(1/2) arswitch

运行结果如图 11.7 所示。

```
Markov-switching autoregression

Sample: 1951q4 thru 1984q4                      Number of obs =      133
Number of states = 2                            AIC           =   2.8319
Unconditional probabilities: transition         HQIC          =   2.9114
                                                SBIC          =   3.0275

Log likelihood = -179.32354
```

rgnp	Coefficient	Std. err.	z	P>|z|	[95% conf.	interval]
State1						
ar						
L1.	.3710719	.1754383	2.12	0.034	.0272191	.7149246
L2.	.7002937	.187409	3.74	0.000	.3329787	1.067609
_cons	-.0055216	.2057086	-0.03	0.979	-.408703	.3976599
State2						
ar						
L1.	.4621503	.1652473	2.80	0.005	.1382715	.7860291
L2.	-.3206652	.1295937	-2.47	0.013	-.5746642	-.0666662
_cons	1.195482	.1225987	9.75	0.000	.9551925	1.435771
sigma	.6677098	.0719638			.5405648	.8247604
p11	.3812383	.1424841			.1586724	.6680876
p21	.3564492	.0994742			.1914324	.5644178

图 11.7

* 有约束的马尔可夫转换模型

```
.constraint 1 [p11]_cons = -1.0986123
.mswitch ar rgnp, ar(1/4) constraints(1)
```

运行结果如图 11.8 所示。

```
Markov-switching autoregression

Sample: 1952q2 thru 1984q4                    Number of obs =      131
Number of states = 2                          AIC           =   2.8895
Unconditional probabilities: transition       HQIC          =   2.9609
                                              SBIC          =   3.0651
Log likelihood = -181.26456

 ( 1)  [p11]_cons = -1.098612
```

rgnp	Coefficient	Std. err.	z	P>|z|	[95% conf.	interval]
rgnp						
ar						
L1.	.0133924	.1196067	0.11	0.911	-.2210324	.2478172
L2.	-.0591073	.133834	-0.44	0.659	-.3214172	.2032025
L3.	-.247326	.1067244	-2.32	0.020	-.456502	-.0381499
L4.	-.2130605	.1106088	-1.93	0.054	-.4298498	.0037288
State1						
_cons	-.3648129	.23039	-1.58	0.113	-.8163689	.0867432
State2						
_cons	1.163125	.0738402	15.75	0.000	1.018401	1.307849
sigma	.7682327	.0644585			.6517376	.9055508
p11	.75	(constrained)				
p21	.0962226	.037246			.0439668	.1977399

图 11.8

11.2 门限转换回归模型

假设样本数据为$\{y_i, \boldsymbol{x}_i, q_i\}_{i=1}^{n}$，其中，$q_i$ 为划分样本的门限变量，可以是外生解释变量 $\boldsymbol{x}_i$ 的一部分，则单一门限变量的单门限值的单门限模型的分段函数表达式为：

$$\begin{cases} y_i = \boldsymbol{\beta}_1' \boldsymbol{x}_i + \varepsilon_i & \text{if} \quad q_i \leqslant \gamma \\ y_i = \boldsymbol{\beta}_2' \boldsymbol{x}_i + \varepsilon_i & \text{if} \quad q_i > \gamma \end{cases} \tag{11.11}$$

其中，γ 为待估计的门限值，外生解释变量 $\boldsymbol{x}_i$ 与扰动项 ε_i 相关。

两区制的单门限模型也可以按照参数是否随区制变换，把解释变量分为不变换的变量和变换的变量，设定为：

$$\begin{aligned} y_t &= \boldsymbol{x}_t \boldsymbol{\beta} + \boldsymbol{z}_t \boldsymbol{\delta}_1 + \varepsilon_t \quad \text{if} \quad -\infty < q_t \leqslant \gamma \\ y_t &= \boldsymbol{x}_t \boldsymbol{\beta} + \boldsymbol{z}_t \boldsymbol{\delta}_2 + \varepsilon_t \quad \text{if} \quad \gamma < q_t < \infty \end{aligned} \tag{11.12}$$

单一门限变量的单门限模型的分段函数表达式可以合并为：

$$y_i = \underbrace{\boldsymbol{\beta}_1' \boldsymbol{x}_i \cdot \mathbf{1}(q_i \leqslant \gamma)}_{=z_{i1}} + \underbrace{\boldsymbol{\beta}_2' \boldsymbol{x}_i \cdot \mathbf{1}(q_i > \gamma)}_{=z_{i2}} + \varepsilon_i \tag{11.13}$$

其中，$\mathbf{1}(\cdot)$为示性函数，即如果括号中的表达式成立，则取值为 1，反之取值为 0。由单门限模型的合并表达式可以知道，该模型是一个非线性回归模型。因此，可以用非线性最小二乘法(NLS)直接估计，也可以用两步法估计。如果 γ 的取值已知，就可以通过定义 $z_{i1} = \boldsymbol{x}_i \mathbf{1}(q_i \leqslant \gamma)$ 和 $z_{i2} = \boldsymbol{x}_i \mathbf{1}(q_i > \gamma)$，把单门限模型的合并表达式转化为参数为 $\boldsymbol{\beta}_1'$、$\boldsymbol{\beta}_2'$ 的线性回归模型：

$$y_i = \boldsymbol{\beta}_1' z_{i1} + \boldsymbol{\beta}_2' z_{i2} + \varepsilon_i \tag{11.14}$$

两步法估计，就是首先确定 γ 的取值，使用 OLS 估计参数，计算残差平方和，然后最小化残差平方和，得到参数估计值。

同理，可以设定多门限值的门限回归。如两个门限值 $\gamma_1 < \gamma_2$，则单一门限变量的两个门限值的回归模型为：

$$y_i = \boldsymbol{\beta}_1' \boldsymbol{x}_i \cdot \mathbf{1}(q_i \leqslant \gamma_1) + \boldsymbol{\beta}_2' \boldsymbol{x}_i \cdot \mathbf{1}(\gamma_1 < q_i \leqslant \gamma_2) + \boldsymbol{\beta}_3' \boldsymbol{x}_i \cdot \mathbf{1}(q_i > \gamma_2) + \varepsilon_i \tag{11.15}$$

门限转换模型估计的语法格式为：

threshold depvar [indepvars] [if] [in], threshvar(varname) [options]

其中，indepvars 是不随时序变换参数的解释变量；threshvar(varname)是门限变量。

菜单操作路径为：

Statistics>Time series>Threshold regression model

例 11.2　门限转换模型

下面下载数据集说明模型的实现。

$fedfunds_t = \delta_{10} + \delta_{11}$l. fedfunds $+ \delta_{12}$inflation $+ \delta_{13}$ogap $+ \varepsilon_t$ 　if 　$-\infty <$ l. fedfunds $\leqslant \gamma$

$fedfunds_t = \delta_{20} + \delta_{21}$l. fedfunds $+ \delta_{22}$inflation $+ \delta_{23}$ogap $+ \varepsilon_t$ 　if 　$\gamma <$ l. fedfunds $< \infty$

```
* 下载数据集
.clear
.use https://www.stata-press.com/data/r17/usmacro
* 门限回归模型
.threshold fedfunds, regionvars(l.fedfunds inflation ogap) threshvar(l.fedfunds)
```

运行结果如图 11.9 所示。

```
Threshold regression
                                            Number of obs =        222
Full sample: 1955q3 thru 2010q4             AIC           =  -63.1438
Number of thresholds = 1                    BIC           =  -35.9224
Threshold variable: L.fedfunds              HQIC          =  -52.1535
```

Order	Threshold	SSR
1	9.3500	155.4266

fedfunds	Coefficient	Std. err.	z	P>|z|	[95% conf.	interval]
Region1						
fedfunds						
L1.	.9268958	.0356283	26.02	0.000	.8570656	.996726
inflation	.0602282	.0401287	1.50	0.133	-.0184227	.1388791
ogap	.0990296	.0234809	4.22	0.000	.0530079	.1450513
_cons	.1966223	.1447802	1.36	0.174	-.0871416	.4803863
Region2						
fedfunds						
L1.	.6974113	.0783207	8.90	0.000	.5439056	.850917
inflation	.1676449	.0540984	3.10	0.002	.061614	.2736757
ogap	.0558738	.073411	0.76	0.447	-.088009	.1997567
_cons	2.16261	.8081146	2.68	0.007	.578734	3.746485

图 11.9

* 选取门限变量

```
.estimates store Model1
.threshold fedfunds, regionvars(l.fedfunds inflation ogap) threshvar(l.ogap)
.estimates store Model2
.threshold fedfunds, regionvars(l.fedfunds inflation ogap) threshvar(l2.ogap)
.estimates store Model3
.estimates table Model1 Model2 Model3, stats(ssr aic bic hqic)
```

运行结果如图 11.10 所示。

Variable	Model1	Model2	Model3
Region1			
fedfunds			
L1.	.92689581	.90860624	.8533835
inflation	.0602282	.19755936	.28187753
ogap	.0990296	.29553563	.14449944
_cons	.19662232	1.4172835	.54280799
Region2			
fedfunds			
L1.	.69741126	.90512493	.90879685
inflation	.16764486	.0896271	.08361366
ogap	.05587384	.15549667	.15233276
_cons	2.1626095	.17554381	.15764634
Statistics			
ssr	155.42663	145.96457	142.0608
aic	-63.143795	-77.087586	-83.105746
bic	-35.922376	-49.866167	-55.884327
hqic	-52.153481	-66.097272	-72.115432

图 11.10

* 选取门限数量

```
. threshold fedfunds, regionvars(l.fedfunds inflation ogap) threshvar(l2.ogap) optthresh(5) nodots
```

运行结果如图 11.11 所示。

Threshold regression

Full sample: 1955q3 thru 2010q4
Number of thresholds = 2
Threshold variable: L2.ogap

Number of obs = 222
Max thresholds = 5
BIC = -60.0780

Order	Threshold	SSR
1	-3.1787	142.0608
2	-0.5351	126.4718

fedfunds	Coefficient	Std. err.	z	P>|z|	[95% conf.	interval]
Region1						
fedfunds						
L1.	.8533835	.0435617	19.59	0.000	.7680042	.9387628
inflation	.2818775	.0679414	4.15	0.000	.1487148	.4150403
ogap	.1444994	.072028	2.01	0.045	.0033272	.2856717
_cons	.542808	.4297171	1.26	0.207	-.299422	1.385038
Region2						
fedfunds						
L1.	.9406721	.0338085	27.82	0.000	.8744087	1.006935
inflation	-.0191805	.0462729	-0.41	0.679	-.1098737	.0715128
ogap	.2387934	.0565521	4.22	0.000	.1279534	.3496334
_cons	.638354	.1591717	4.01	0.000	.3263832	.9503249
Region3						
fedfunds						
L1.	.8892742	.0593484	14.98	0.000	.7729535	1.005595
inflation	.1851127	.0532112	3.48	0.001	.0808206	.2894047
ogap	.1984744	.039236	5.06	0.000	.1215733	.2753754
_cons	-.3086232	.2215645	-1.39	0.164	-.7428817	.1256352

图 11.11

11.3 平滑转换模型

一般平滑转换模型的表达式为：

$$y_t = \boldsymbol{x}_t \boldsymbol{\beta} + G(s_t; c, \gamma) \boldsymbol{z}_t \boldsymbol{\alpha} + \varepsilon_t \tag{11.16}$$

式中，$G(s_t;c,\gamma)$是取值在 0 至 1 之间的平滑转换函数，可以选用对数、正态和指数三种平滑转换函数，表达式为：

$$G(s_t;c,\gamma)=\begin{cases}\dfrac{1}{1+\exp[-\gamma(s_t-c)]} & \text{Logistic, or LSTR}\\ 1-\exp[-\gamma(s_t-c)^2] & \text{exponential, or ESTR}\\ \Phi[-\gamma(s_t-c)] & \text{normal CDF}\\ \dfrac{1}{1+\exp[-\gamma(s_t-c_1)(s_t-c_2)]} & \text{2nd order Logistic, or L2STR}\end{cases} \tag{11.17}$$

转换函数中的 $\gamma>0$，反映了转换的速度和平滑程度。当 $\gamma\to+\infty$时，转换函数变为示性函数，对于 LSTR 和 NSTR：

$$G(s_t;c,\gamma)=\begin{cases}1/2 & s_t\geqslant c\\ 0 & s_t<c\end{cases}$$

对于 ESTR：

$$G(s_t;c,\gamma)=\begin{cases}1 & s_t\geqslant c\\ 0 & s_t<c\end{cases}$$

有时，LSTR 会拓展为多区制平滑转换：

$$G(s_t;c,\gamma)=\left\{1+\exp\left[-\gamma\prod_{j=1}^{m}(s_t-c_j)\right]\right\}^{-1} \tag{11.18}$$

在时序分析中，变量如有序列相关性，则需要建立动态自回归平滑转换模型：

$$y_t=\boldsymbol{\beta}_0+\sum_{k=1}^{K}\boldsymbol{\beta}_k y_{t-k}+G(y_{t-d};c,\gamma)\sum_{k=1}^{K}y_{t-k}\boldsymbol{\alpha}_k+\varepsilon_t \tag{11.19}$$

按照转换函数选用情况，平滑转换模型可分为对数平滑转换自回归(logistic smoothing transition auto regressive,LSTAR)模型和指数平滑转换自回归(exponential smoothing transition auto regressive,ESTAR)模型。

平滑转换模型估计的语法格式为：

```
stregress depvar [indepvars] [if] [in], rx(varlist) sx(varname) [ stfunc(weight) const(spec) nolog ]
```

其中，depvar 是因变量，indepvars 是与制度无关的解释变量。

该模型的主要特征包括：

(1) 适用于时间序列、截面数据和面板数据。

(2) 包含 LSTR、ESTR、NSTR、L2STR 多种平滑转换函数。

(3) 包含模型的线性特征检验、模型的充分性检验(残差的线性特征检验)、残差的自相关检验、残差 Q 检验、参数的常数特征检验。

(4) 可以应用标准的 estat、predict 等模型分析和预测的指令。

① estat stplot：绘制平滑函数图；

② estat linearity：模型的线性特征检验；

③ estat reslinearity:残差的线性特征检验;

④ estat pconstant:参数的常数特征检验,是用趋势变量做转移变量的线性特征检验。

例 11.3　平滑转换模型

下面下载数据集说明平滑转换模型的实现。

```
* 打开数据集,描述数据集
.clear all
.use lstar, clear
.describe
* 描述统计变量
.summarize
```

运行结果如图 11.12 所示。

Variable	Obs	Mean	Std. dev.	Min	Max
entry	250	125.5	72.31298	1	250
y	250	.6262886	3.432647	-7.638614	7.646513

图　11.12

```
* 进行回归
.reg y L.y
```

运行结果如图 11.13 所示。

Source	SS	df	MS			
Model	894.711773	1	894.711773	Number of obs	=	249
Residual	2036.99777	247	8.24695453	F(1, 247)	=	108.49
				Prob > F	=	0.0000
Total	2931.70954	248	11.8214094	R-squared	=	0.3052
				Adj R-squared	=	0.3024
				Root MSE	=	2.8718

y	Coefficient	Std. err.	t	P>|t|	[95% conf.	interval]
y L1.	.5524939	.0530436	10.42	0.000	.4480185	.6569693
_cons	.2779957	.1849324	1.50	0.134	-.0862498	.6422413

图　11.13

```
* Ramsey RESET 检验
.estat ovtest
```

运行结果如图 11.14 所示。

```
F(3, 244) =  95.60
 Prob > F = 0.0000
```

图 11.14

＊LSTR 模型

```
. stregress y L.y, lstr(L.y, L.y, 1, 1)
```

运行结果如图 11.15 所示。

Smoothing transition regression (lstr)

log-likelihood	= -343.0403	Number of obs	=	249
AIC	= 696.0806	R-squared	=	0.9218
BIC	= 713.6679	Adj R-squared	=	0.9202
HQIC	= 703.1598	Root MSE	=	0.9712

y	Coefficient	Std. err.	z	P>|z|	[95% conf.	interval]
Linear						
y						
L1.	.9228752	.0202354	45.61	0.000	.8832146	.9625359
_cons	.9415277	.0645322	14.59	0.000	.815047	1.068008
L.y						
y						
L1.	-1.179278	.4822916	-2.45	0.014	-2.124552	-.2340037
_cons	-5.862783	2.852799	-2.06	0.040	-11.45417	-.2713987
threshold1	5.002021	.0161304	310.10	0.000	4.970406	5.033636
lngamma	2.416536	.161012	15.01	0.000	2.100958	2.732113

图 11.15

＊估计后命令

```
. est store lstr
. estat stcoef
```

运行结果如图 11.16 所示。

	Coef	se	z	P>|z|	CILower	CIUpper
L.y						
gamma	11.2070	1.8045	6.21	0.0000	7.6703	14.7436

图 11.16

```
.nlcom exp(_b[L.y:lngamma])
```

运行结果如图 11.17 所示。

y	Coefficient	Std. err.	z	P>|z|	[95% conf.	interval]
_nl_1	11.20697	1.804456	6.21	0.000	7.670299	14.74364

图 11.17

```
.estat stplot
```

运行结果如图 11.18 所示。

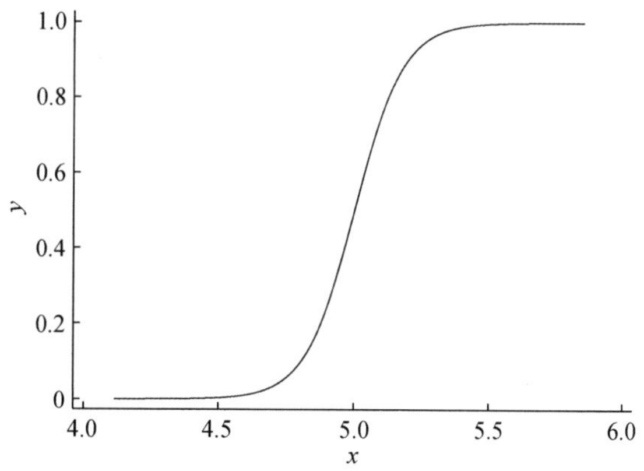

图 11.18

```
.estat linear
```

运行结果如图 11.19 所示。

Linearity (homegeneity) test for all nonlinear parts:

Ho	chi2	df1	df2	prob
b1=0	97.1847	1	246	1.552e-19
b1=b2=0	120.6137	2	245	3.428e-37
b1=b2=b3=0	95.6005	3	244	6.090e-41
b1=b2=b3=b4=0	73.8761	4	243	6.951e-41

Escribano-Jorda linearity test (based on 4th Taylor expansion):

Ho	chi2	df1	df2	prob
b1=b3=0(HoL)	98.1343	2	243	5.747e-32
b2=b4=0(HoE)	69.5963	2	243	1.270e-24

Note: HoL against LSTR, HoE against ESTR

Terasvirta sequential test:

Ho	chi2	df1	df2	prob
b1=0|b2=b3=0	97.1847	1	246	1.552e-19
b2=0|b3=0	103.5352	1	245	1.637e-20
b3=0	23.4600	1	244	2.267e-06

图 11.19

```
* ESTR 模型
. stregress y L.y, estr(L.y, L.y, 1) nolog
```

运行结果如图 11.20 所示。

```
. est store estr
* NSTR 模型
. stregress y L.y, nstr(L.y, L.y, 1) nolog
```

运行结果如图 11.21 所示。

```
Smoothing transition regression (estr)

log-likelihood  =    -407.9327          Number of obs   =       249
AIC             =     825.8655          R-squared       =    0.8683
BIC             =     843.4528          Adj R-squared   =    0.8656
HQIC            =     832.9447          Root MSE        =    1.2604

-------------------------------------------------------------------------------
           y | Coefficient  Std. err.      z    P>|z|     [95% conf. interval]
-------------+-----------------------------------------------------------------
Linear       |
           y |
         L1. |  -9.359187    .654429   -14.30   0.000    -10.64184    -8.07653
             |
       _cons |   44.45418   3.507606    12.67   0.000      37.5794    51.32896
-------------+-----------------------------------------------------------------
L.y          |
           y |
         L1. |     10.261   .6421489    15.98   0.000     9.002414    11.51959
             |
       _cons |  -43.58213   3.548313   -12.28   0.000    -50.53669   -36.62756
  threshold1 |   6.021604   .0695954    86.52   0.000     5.885199    6.158008
     lngamma |  -.9945757   .0820346   -12.12   0.000    -1.155361   -.8337908
-------------------------------------------------------------------------------
```

图 11.20

```
Smoothing transition regression (nstr)

log-likelihood  =    -343.5223          Number of obs   =       249
AIC             =     697.0445          R-squared       =    0.9215
BIC             =     714.6318          Adj R-squared   =    0.9199
HQIC            =     704.1237          Root MSE        =    0.9731

-------------------------------------------------------------------------------
           y | Coefficient  Std. err.      z    P>|z|     [95% conf. interval]
-------------+-----------------------------------------------------------------
Linear       |
           y |
         L1. |   .9208112    .020173    45.65   0.000     .8812729    .9603496
             |
       _cons |   .9370218    .064502    14.53   0.000     .8106002    1.063443
-------------+-----------------------------------------------------------------
L.y          |
           y |
         L1. |  -1.247186   .4870774    -2.56   0.010     -2.20184   -.2925315
             |
       _cons |   -5.38349   2.880605    -1.87   0.062    -11.02937    .2623912
  threshold1 |   5.000119   .0162844   307.05   0.000     4.968202    5.032036
     lngamma |   1.914159   .1678509    11.40   0.000     1.585177    2.243141
-------------------------------------------------------------------------------
```

图 11.21

```
. est store nstr
* 比较三个平滑方式
. est table lstr estr nstr, stat(r2 aic bic hqic) star(.1.05.01)
```

运行结果如图 11.22 所示。

Variable	lstr	estr	nstr
Linear			
y			
L1.	.92287523***	-9.3591874***	.92081123***
_cons	.94152772***	44.454179***	.9370218***
L.y			
y			
L1.	-1.1792779**	10.261003***	-1.2471857**
_cons	-5.8627827**	-43.582126***	-5.38349*
threshold1	5.002021***	6.0216035***	5.0001189***
lngamma	2.4165357***	-.99457568***	1.914159***
Statistics			
r2	.92181804	.86833468	.9215148
aic	698.08063	827.86549	699.04454
bic	719.18535	848.97021	720.14926
hqic	703.1598	832.94465	704.12371

Legend: * p<.1; ** p<.05; *** p<.01

图 11.22

附录A Stata计量应用基础

A.1 Stata软件简介

Stata软件具有强大的数据分析和处理功能，是当今较为流行的统计质量分析软件。与其他软件相比，Stata软件的优势较为突出。

1. 操作简单便利

Stata软件为每项操作都同时提供了一一对应的菜单操作和程序操作两种方式，对每项功能的实现，可以通过点击菜单设置选项完成，也可以通过输入代码编程运行完成。命令语句简洁明快，逻辑清晰。

2. 能够跟踪学科发展前沿及时更新

Stata软件是一个开放性的软件系统，可以通过多种途径及时下载实现更新，保障用户将最新的理论成果应用于问题的统计计量分析。其开放性主要体现在：第一，用户可以到Stata官方网站(http://www.stata.com)下载相关模块更新，也可以直接在命令窗口中输入【update】，在联网的情况下实现更新。第二，使用【findit】命令，找到所需要的功能模块，下载安装即可运行。第三，通过菜单选项help→SJ and Use-written Programs，下载由其他用户编写的Stata模块，安装运行。用户也可以自己编写程序，从而实现所需要的功能。

3. 具有强大的数据分析功能

Stata软件的微观计量分析功能系统完善，基本可以实现所有的统计与计量分析。在统计方面，可以实现数据的描述分析、方差分析、假设检验、主成分分析，聚类分析等；在计量分析方面，可以实现多种计量模型的应用，如单方程回归、联立方程回归、离散解释变量模型、受限因变量模型、时间序列模型、面板数据模型、分位数回归模型等。Stata软件通过有机结合统计与质量分析功能，使用户可以完成复杂性高、综合性强的分析研究。

4. 具有强大的图形制作功能

目前图形制作分析仍然是各种数据分析的必要内容。Stata软件具有强大的图形制作功能。利用Stata软件可以完成散点图、直方图、折线图、条形图、回归诊断图、时间序列图、ROC图、面板数据图和生存分析图等图形的制作。另外，用户也可以根据自身的需要编辑修改图形，也可以直接利用图形处理软件和文字处理软件调用这些图形，这些功能使 Stata 软件的画图功能便利高效。

A.2 窗口及帮助系统

A.2.1 窗口说明

Stata 软件安装完成后，运行 Stata，就会打开 Stata 操作界面，如图 A.1 所示。

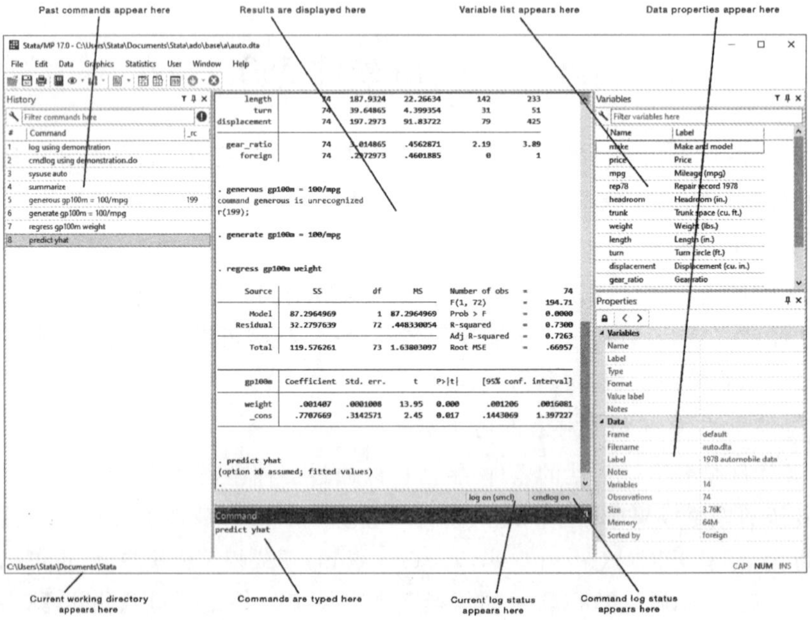

图 A.1

操作界面主要由菜单栏、工具栏和 5 个窗口组成。

由左往右，菜单栏主要包括文件、编辑、数据、图形、统计、用户、窗口和帮助 8 个下拉子菜单。

工具栏包含的按钮可以快速访问 Stata 更常用的功能，如图 A.2 所示。如果忘记了按钮的功能，请将鼠标指针放在按钮上片刻，然后显示工具提示将显示该按钮的说明。

图 A.2

工具栏常用的工具由左往右依次为：打开（文件或数据集）、保存（至当前路径）、打印、日志文件(Log)、视图（打开）、图形窗口（移至前端）、do 文件编辑器、数据编辑器

(编辑)、数据编辑器(浏览)、变量管理器、显示更多结果和暂停。

窗口一般为三列排列组合方式。由左往右,第一列窗口是历史(命令回顾)窗口;第二列窗口中,上面为结果窗口,下面为命令(输入)窗口;第三列窗口中,上面为变量窗口,下面为属性窗口。

A.2.2 帮助系统

帮助系统主要由系统帮助、搜索帮助、命令帮助和搜索、用户指导和操作手册、视频、Stata 期刊等部分组成。

常用的帮助是利用 Stata 的自带帮助下拉菜单。一种方法是从帮助下拉菜单中选择“搜索”或“stata 命令”,然后输入查询的命令,回车即可显示查询结果;另一种方法是使用 help 命令,语法格式为:

```
help [所要查询的命令]
```

网络帮助系统也非常丰富。用户可以在网上查找 Stata 还没有内置化的命令,实现自行安装。命令有两个:

```
findit [所要查询的命令],net
search [所要查询的命令],net
```

显示查询结果后,就可以按照提示命令,下载安装运行。

网站资源主要有:

(1) http://www.stata.com

(2) http://www.stata-press.com

(3) http://www.stata-journal.com

A.3 数据导入与处理

A.3.1 数据的录入和导入

(1) 用菜单方式从键盘输入数据

单击工具栏中的【数据编辑器(编辑)】工具,就会弹出数据编辑器表格,在【数据录入】框中输入相应数据;再给变量命名;在所有数据输入之后,双击【var1】;在【变量名】中输入变量的名称;在【变量标签】中输入标签的内容,单击【OK】就完成一项数据录入操作。

(2) 使用命令读取数据

数据输入的基本命令为:

```
input [varlist] [, automatic label]
```

input 将数据直接输入内存中的数据集。

(3) 数据文件的下载打开

Stata 默认的数据格式是“. dta”。这种格式的文件可以直接用命令 use 打开应用。

① 加载 Stata 格式数据集(文件扩展名为".dta")的语法格式为:

```
use filename [, clear nolabel]
```

② 加载 Stata 格式数据集的子集的语法格式为:

```
use [varlist] [if] [in] using filename [, clear nolabel]
```

如果电脑连接了网络,use 命令也可以从互联网上读入数据。

③ 使用与 Stata 一起安装的示例数据集的语法格式为:

```
sysuse ["]filename["] [, clear]
```

④ 列出与 Stata 一起安装的 Stata 数据集示例的语法格式为:

```
sysuse dir [, all]
```

Stata 格式数据集也可以用【文件打开】工具打开。

⑤ 使用 Stata 网站上的数据集的语法格式具体如下:

通过 web 加载数据集:

```
webuse ["]filename["] [, clear]
```

从中获取数据集的报告 URL:

```
webuse query
```

指定从中获取数据集的 URL:

```
webuse set [https://]url[/]
webuse set [http://]url[/]
```

将 URL 重置为默认值:

```
webuse set
```

菜单操作路径为:

```
File>Example datasets...
```

webuse filename 加载指定的数据集,并通过 web 获取该数据集。默认情况下,数据源为 https://www.stata-press.com/data/r17/.。如果指定的文件名没有后缀,则假设为 dta。

webuse query 报告将从中获取数据集的 URL。

webuse set 允许用户指定要用作数据集源的 URL。不带参数的 webuse set 将源重置为 https://www.stata-press.com/data/r17/.。

(4) 数据导入

其他格式数据集数据的导入,可以用【文件】下拉菜单中的【导入】菜单,导入 excel、SPSS、SAS、文本数据等,即 File>Import>Excel spreadsheet (*.xls; *.xlsx)。

也可以使用命令 import 导入 excel 数据文件,语法格式为:

```
import excel [using] filename [, import_excel_options]
```

从 Excel 文件加载变量子集的语法格式为:

```
import excel extvarlist using filename [, import_excel_options]
```

描述 Excel 文件的内容的语法格式为:

```
import excel [using] filename, describe
```

(5) 数据集描述

描述内存中的数据的语法格式为：

describe [varlist] [, memory_options]

描述文件中的数据的语法格式为：

describe [varlist] using filename [, file_options]

菜单操作路径为：

Data>Describe data>Describe data in memory or in a file

describe 生成内存中的数据集或存储在 Stata 格式数据集中的数据的摘要。

(6) 数据列表显示

数据列表显示的语法格式为：

list [varlist] [if] [in] [, options]

list 命令显示变量的值。如果未指定 varlist，则显示所有变量的值。另请参见[D]编辑中的浏览。

(7) 创建或更改变量

创建新变量的语法格式为：

generate [type] newvar[:lblname] = exp [if] [in] [, before(varname) | after(varname)]

菜单操作路径为：

Data>Create or change data>Create new variable

generate 创建一个新变量。变量的值由=exp 指定。

替换现有变量的内容的语法格式为：

replace oldvar =exp [if] [in] [, nopromote]

菜单操作路径为：

Data>Create or change data>Change contents of variable

replace 更改现有变量的内容。因为 replace 会改变数据，所以该命令不能缩写。

(8) 清除内存数据

清除内存中的数据和任何相关的数据标签的命令为 clear；清除内存中的所有内容的命令为 clear all。

A.3.2 数据描述统计与制表

数据描述统计的语法格式为：

summarize [varlist] [if] [in] [weight] [, options]

菜单操作路径为：

Statistics>Summaries, tables, and tests>Summary and descriptive statistics>Summary statistics

summarize 计算并显示各种单变量摘要统计信息，如观测值、均值、标准差、最小值、最大值、分位数、方差、偏度和峰度等。如果未指定 varlist，则会计算数据集中所有变量的汇总统计信息。

频率汇总表制作的语法格式为：

table (rowspec) (colspec) [(tabspec)] [if] [in] [weight] [, options]

菜单操作路径为：

Statistics>Summaries, tables, and tests>Tables of frequencies, summaries, and command results

table 是一个灵活的命令，用于创建多种类型的表，包括汇总统计表、回归结果表等。这种表可以计算要显示在表中的摘要统计信息，还可以包括来自其他 Stata 命令的结果。

A.3.3 数据计算

显示标量表达式的字符串和值的语法格式为：

display [display_directive [display_directive [...]]]

菜单操作路径为：

Data>Other utilities>Hand calculator

作为手动计算器的命令为：

```
.display 2 + 2
```

在 do 文件和程序中可能会用到以下命令：

```
.sysuse auto
.summarize mpg
.display as text "mean of mpg =" as result r(mean)
```

A.4 Stata 命令

A.4.1 基本命令

所有的 Stata 命令分为 e-类命令和 r-类命令。e-类命令为“估计命令”，如“regress”；所有其他命令为 r-类命令，如“summarize”。e-类命令的运行结果都存储在“e()”中，可以通过输入命令“ereturn list”显示。r-类命令的运行结果都存储在“r()”中，可以通过输入命令“return list”显示。可以调用这些结果作进一步的计算。

可以把命令或命令的一部分缩写成最简短的字符串，一般只有两个或三个字符，例如，将 summarize 命令缩写为 su。

命令的基本语法格式为：

[by varlist:] command [varlist] [= exp] [if exp] [in range] [weight] [,options]

其中，[]中的内容表示可以省略的部分；by varlist 表示对分类变量中的不同类别分别进行操作；varlist 表示多个变量，变量之间用空格隔开；command 为执行的命令；=exp 是赋值语句；if exp 为条件表达式；in range 为命令执行的样本观测值范围；weight 为观测值权重；options 为命令选项。

在 Stata 说明文件中，命令前一般用圆点“.”，圆点后面为 Stata 命令。在 do 文件和 ado 文件中，如需注释命令的功能或者解释程序的原理，则用星号“*”注明。

如需全面掌握 Stata 命令，可以查询 Stata 命令的帮助文件，其内容比较全面，一般包括命令的语法(Syntax)、菜单操作路径(Menu)、描述说明(Description)、说明文件 PDF 连接(Links to PDF documentation)、选项解释(Options)、示例(Examples)、视频示例(Video examples)、结果储存(Stored results)和参考文献(References)。其中，语法中都有【估计后命令】(postestimation)连接，可以进一步了解模型方法估计后的检验、预测、画图等相关命令。

A.4.2 算子

Stata 中的算术算子分别是＋(加)、－(减)、*(乘)、/(除)、^(求幂)和前缀－(负号)。例如，计算和显示 $-2\times 9/(8+2-7)^2$，则输入

.display -2 * 9/(8 + 2 - 7)^2

关系算子分别是＞(大于)、＜(小于)、＞＝(大于等于)、＜＝(小于等于)、！＝(不等于)。

逻辑算子分别是 &(且)、|(或)、！(非)。

字符串算子为＋(合并字符串)。

所有算子的计算顺序为：！(或者～)，^，－(负号)，/，*，－(减号)，＋，！＝(或者～＝)，＞，＜，＜＝，＞＝，＝＝，& 和|。

A.4.3 命令更新

Stata 命令更新的语法格式为：

.update all

Stata 非官方命令的主要下载平台为“统计软件成分”(Statistical Software Components，SSC)。其下载安装命令为：

.ssc install newcommand * 自动下载安装 SSC 提供的所有非官方命令“newcommand”

.search keyword * 搜索帮助文件

.findit keyword * 搜索“keyword”的相关命令内容及网络资源

对于不是 SSC 的命令，需要自行安装，把所有相关文件下载到指定的 Stata 文件夹中(一般为 ado\plus\)。如果文件复制下载安装路径，可以先输入系统路径查询命令：

.sysdir

然后把下载的新命令文件复制到 plus 指示的文件夹中即可。

从软件包中安装 ado 文件和帮助文件的语法格式为：

net install pkgname [, all replace force from(directory_or_url)]

例如：

.net install superscatter.pkg, replace

A.5 画图命令

完整的图形主要包括标题、副标题、坐标轴刻度与标题、图例说明和注释语句等。常用操作流程是用命令画出图形主体，用菜单修改细节。Stata软件的画图操作都可以在图形(G)下拉菜单中点击实现。常用的画图命令汇总如表A.1所示。

表A.1 常用的绘制图形的命令及其语法与功能

图形	命令语法与功能
二维图	[graph] twoway plot [if] [in] [, twoway_options] Twoway绘制数字变量 y 和 x 的一系列曲线图。plot的语法格式为： [(] plottype varlist ..., options [)] [||]
二维线性图	[twoway] line varlist [if] [in] [, options] 这里，varlist是y_1 [y_2 [...]] x
直方图	histogram varname [if] [in] [weight] [, [continuous_opts | discrete_opts] options] histogram绘制varname的直方图，除非指定了离散选项，否则假定varname为连续变量的名称
条形图	(1) graph bar yvars [if] [in] [weight] [, options] graph bar绘制垂直条形图。在垂直条形图中，y轴是数字轴，x轴是分类轴 (2) graph hbar yvars [if] [in] [weight] [, options] graph hbar绘制水平条形图。在水平条形图中，数字轴仍然称为y轴，分类轴仍然称为x轴，但y水平显示，x垂直显示
饼图	(1) graph pie varlist [if] [in] [weight] [, options] 切片作为每个变量的总数或百分比 (2) graph pie varname [if] [in] [weight], over(varname) [options] 在over()类别中以总计或百分比的形式显示切片 (3) graph pie [if] [in] [weight], over(varname) [options] 在over()类别中作为频率进行切片
箱线图	(1) graph box yvars [if] [in] [weight] [, options] graph box绘制垂直方框图。在垂直方框图中，y轴是数字轴，x轴是分类轴 (2) graph hbox yvars [if] [in] [weight] [, options] graph hbox绘制水平方框图。在水平方框图中，数字轴仍然称为y轴，分类轴仍然称为x轴，但y水平显示，x垂直显示
分布诊断图	(1) symplot varname [if] [in] [, options1] symplot绘制varname的对称图 (2) quantile varname [if] [in] [, options1] quantile根据均匀分布的分位数绘制varname的有序值 (3) qqplot varname1 varname2 [if] [in] [, options1] qqplot绘制varname1的分位数与varname2的分位数图(Q-Q图) (4) qnorm varname [if] [in] [, options2] qnorm根据正态分布的分位数图(Q-Q图)绘制varname的分位数 (5) pnorm varname [if] [in] [, options2] pnorm图是标准正态概率图(P-P图)

（续表）

图形	命令语法与功能
分布诊断图	(6) qchi varname [if] [in] [, options3] qchi 根据卡方分布的分位数绘制 varname 的分位数图(Q-Q 图) (7) pchi varname [if] [in] [, options3] pchi 绘制卡方概率图(P-P 图)
ROC 曲线	roctab refvar classvar [if] [in] [weight] [, options] roctab 利用评级和离散分类数据进行 ROC(receiver operating characteristic)分析
面板数据折线图	(1) xtline varlist [if] [in] [, panel_options] (2) xtline varname [if] [in], overlay [overlaid_options] xtline 为面板数据绘制线图

A.6 结果输出

A.6.1 Stata 软件结果输出为日志文件

如需每次储存运行结果，可以利用 Stata 软件的日志(log)功能。可以利用下拉菜单【文件】下的【日志】，也可以点击工具栏中的按钮，进行日志相关操作。

在打开 Stata 软件的运行界面之后，日志功能的选项即在左上角菜单区域，其中包括几个子功能：begin(创建日志)，close(保存和关闭日志)，suspend(暂停日志记录)，resume(恢复日志记录)，viewsnapshot(当前日志内容快照)。日志功能支持两种形式的日志文件：*.log 纯文本日志文件和 *.smcl 通过 SMCL 标记格式的日志文件。

将日志或 ASCII 文件转换为各种输出格式的命令为：

logout, [options: command]

logout 提供了一种快速简便的方法，可以将日志或 ASCII 文件转换为与 Word、Excel、LaTex 或 Stata 数据文件兼容的各种输出格式，可以用作前缀，也可以在创建日志文件后单独使用。

A.6.2 Stata 软件直接输出结果到 word 文件

Stata 软件直接把结果输出到 Word 文件的命令为【asdoc】，该命令为外部命令。需要在 Stata 中输入代码“ssc install asdoc, replace”，或者在 help 中搜索“asdoc”命令并安装，已经安装的用户可以跳过这个步骤。

该命令的语法格式为：

[bysort varname:] asdoc Stata_Commands, [Stata_command_options asdoc_options]

asdoc 命令将 Stata 输出发送为 Word/RTF 格式。asdoc 通过各种 Stata 命令创建高质量的、可供发布的表格。asdoc 的使用非常简单，只需要将 asdoc 作为前缀添加到 Stata 命令中。asdoc 有几个内置例程，用于专门计算和制作格式良好的表格。

例如，计算所有数值变量之间的相关性。

```
.sysuse auto, clear
.asdoc cor
*制作简单回归结果的列表，给表加标题
.asdoc reg price mpg rep78 headroom, title(Table 1: Regression results)
save(Table_1.doc) append
*制作一个包含四个回归的嵌套表格
.asdoc reg price mpg rep78, nest replace
*使用 add(Foreign,yes)选项添加文本图例，并从表中删除 Foreign 的系数
.asdoc reg price mpg rep78 weight foreign, nest append text(Foreign dummy,
yes) drop(foreign)
```

运行命令后，软件会自动生成一个 myfile.doc(Word)文件。只需要点击这个文件，打开之后就可以看到数据分析的结果。

根据存储的估计值制作回归表的语法格式为：

estout [what] [using filename] [, options]

estout 输出一个或多个之前由 estimates store 或 eststo 拟合和存储的模型汇编的系数、显著性、汇总统计、标准误差、t 或 z 统计、p 值、置信区间和其他统计数据表。然后，它会在 Stata 的"结果"窗口中显示该表，或将其写入使用文件名指定的文本文件中。默认情况下，使用 SMCL 格式标记和水平线来构造表。但是，如果指定了 using，则会生成一个以制表符分隔的表(不带行)。

显示格式化的回归表的命令为：

esttab [namelist] [using filename] [, options]

esttab 是 estout 的包装器。它从存储的估计值中生成一个有吸引力的出版物样式回归表，无需太多输入。编译后的表格将显示在 Stata Results 窗口中，或者写入使用文件名指定的文本文件中。如果指定的文件名没有后缀，则会根据指定的文档格式添加默认后缀(.smcl 代表 smcl，.txt 代表 fixed and tab，.csv 代表 csv and scsv，.rtf 代表 rft，.html 代表 html，.tex 代表 tex and booktabs)。

eststo 是 Stata 估计存储的包装器，首先拟合和存储一些模型，然后将 esttab 应用于这些存储的估计：

```
. eststo clear
. sysuse auto
(1978 Automobile Data)
. eststo: quietly regress price weight mpg
  (est1 stored)
. eststo: quietly regress price weight mpg foreign
  (est2 stored)
. esttab, ar2
```

运行结果如图 A.3 所示。

	(1)	(2)
	price	price
weight	1.747**	3.465***
	(2.72)	(5.49)
mpg	-49.51	21.85
	(-0.57)	(0.29)
foreign		3673.1***
		(5.37)
_cons	1946.1	-5853.7
	(0.54)	(-1.73)
N	74	74
adj. R-sq	0.273	0.478

t statistics in parentheses

* p<0.05, ** p<0.01, *** p<0.001

图 A.3

putdocx 是一套命令，用于将段落、图像和表格写入 Office Open XML(.docx)文件，允许用户创建包含 Stata 结果和图形的 Word 文档。putdocx 生成与 Microsoft Word 2007 及更高版本兼容的文件。

(1) 创建、保存和添加.docx 文件

putdocx begin：创建用于导出的 docx 文件；

putdocx：描述活动内容的.docx 文件；

putdocx save：保存并关闭.docx 文件；

putdocx clear：关闭.docx 文件，不保存更改；

putdocx append：追加多个内容的.docx 文件。

(2) 在文档中插入分页符.docx 文件

putdocx pagebreak：将分页符添加到文档中；

putdocx sectionbreak：向文档添加新节。

(3) 添加带有文本和图像的段落

putdocx paragraph：向活动文档添加新段落；

putdocx text：将文本添加到活动段落；

putdocx textblock：将文本块添加到活动段落或新段落；

putdocx textfile：使用预定义的样式向新段落添加一块预格式化文本；

putdocx image：将图像附加到活动段落；

putdocx pagenumber：向页眉或页脚中的段落添加页码。

(4) 将表添加到.docx 文件

putdocx table：在中创建一个新表，包含估计结果、摘要统计信息或内存中的数据的.docx 文件。

(5) 将集合中的表添加到. docx 文件

putdocx collect:将 collect 或 table 创建的自定义表添加到. docx 文件。

A.6.3 Stata 软件直接导出结果到 excel 文件

Stata 软件将返回结果导出到 Excel 文件的命令为:

`putexcel ul_cell = returnset [, colwise overwritefmt]`

其中,ul_cell 是使用标准 Excel 符号指定的有效 Excel 左上角单元格

将上一个估算命令中的系数表添加到 Excel 文件中的命令为:

`putexcel ul_cell = etable[(#1 #2 ... #n)]`

将 Stata 矩阵导出到 Excel 的命令为:

`putexcel ul_cell = matrix(matname) [, matrix_options format_options]`

putexcel 可将 Stata 表达式、矩阵、表格、图像和返回的结果写入 Excel 文件,还可以格式化工作表中的单元格,允许用户自动导出和格式化数据,如 Stata estimation 结果支持 Excel 1997/2003(. xls)文件和 Excel 2007/2010 及更新的(. xlsx)文件。

putexcel set 用来设置要在后续 putexcel 命令中创建、修改或替换 Excel 文件。在使用任何其他 Excel 命令之前,必须设置目标文件。putexcel save 用于关闭使用命令"putexcel set…"打开的文件,打开并将文件保存至磁盘。putexcel clear 用于清除 putexcel 集合设置的文件信息。putexcel describe 按 putexcel 集合显示文件信息集合。

菜单操作路径为:

`File>Export>Results to Excel spreadsheet (*.xls; *.xlsx)`

将内存中的数据保存到 Excel 文件中的命令为:

`export excel [using] filename [if] [in] [, export_excel_options]`

若采用窗口操作,相应的命令为:

`File>Export>Data to Excel spreadsheet (*.xls; *.xlsx)`

将回归、总结和制表整理成一个说明性表格的命令为:

`outreg2 [varlist] [estlist] using filename [, options] [: command]`

回归后,使用 Word/Excel 自动生成 Word/Excel 文件的命令为:

```
reg price mpg rep78 headroom trunk weight
outreg2 using myfile, word excel replace
```

其他相关内容可查阅 Stata 官网上公开发表的 *Stata Reporting Reference Manual*。